The HEALTH PSYCHOLOGY HANDBOOK

To my earliest teachers, Roz and Gertrude, and to my family,
Michelle, Fred, Hazel, Alan, Lucy, and Penny.
L. M. C.

To the cornerstones of my life.
Thank you Jodi, Paul, Diane, and Stephanie.
D. E. M.

To Robin and Erin.
Thank you for sharing me with my work and sharing your life with me.
F. L. C.

The HEALTH PSYCHOLOGY HANDBOOK

Practical Issues for
the Behavioral
Medicine Specialist

Editors

Lee M. Cohen
Texas Tech University

Dennis E. McChargue
University of Illinois, Chicago

Frank L. Collins, Jr.
Oklahoma State University

SAGE Publications
International Educational and Professional Publisher
Thousand Oaks ▪ London ▪ New Delhi

For information:

Sage Publications, Inc.
2455 Teller Road
Thousand Oaks, California 91320
E-mail: order@sagepub.com

Sage Publications Ltd.
6 Bonhill Street
London EC2A 4PU
United Kingdom

Sage Publications India Pvt. Ltd.
B-42, Panchsheel Enclave
Post Box 4109
New Delhi 110 017 India

Printed in the United States of America

Library of Congress Cataloging-in-Publication data

The health psychology handbook : practical issues for the behavioral
medicine specialist / editors, Lee M. Cohen, Dennis E. McChargue,
Frank L. Collins, Jr.
    p. cm.
Includes bibliographical references and index.
ISBN 0-7619-2614-3 (cloth)
   1. Clinical health psychology—Handbooks, manuals, etc. I. Cohen, Lee M.
II. McChargue, Dennis E. III. Collins, Frank L., Jr.
R726.7.H43357 2003
613′.01′9—dc21

                          2003007165

03   04   05   06   07   9   8   7   6   5   4   3   2   1

Acquiring Editor:	Jim Brace-Thompson
Editorial Assistant:	Karen Ehrmann
Production Editor:	Sanford Robinson
Typesetter:	C&M Digitals (P) Ltd.
Copy Editor:	D. J. Peck
Indexer:	David Luljak
Cover Designer:	Michelle Lee

Contents

Part IV.   Special Issues   441

Foreword

Writing a foreword for *The Health Psychology Handbook* has stimulated me to look both backward and forward. Although research and practice in health and behavior has a long history, the year 2003 marks the 25th anniversary of the formalization of health psychology in the United States. It was in 1978 that a number of us obtained sufficient support to establish the Division of Health Psychology within the American Psychological Association. During that same year, we met in Chicago to establish the Society of Behavioral Medicine with the purpose of bringing together scientists and practitioners from multiple disciplines to advance knowledge of behavior and health. Shortly thereafter, the Institute of Medicine (1982) published *Health and Behavior: Frontiers of Research in the Biobehavioral Sciences*, a landmark study that promoted a surge of federal funding for health and behavior research. Research programs expanded, journals grew, and education and training flourished. Recently, within 20 years of that initial report, the Institute of Medicine (2001) published *Health and Behavior: The Interplay of Biological, Behavioral, and Societal Influences*. This report is also a landmark; it not only updates research on health and behavior but also identifies effective applications of behavioral interventions and promotes their implementation in our health care delivery system. Although there is much more to do, there is little doubt that health psychology has now become mainstream.

What has often been missing from the literature in health psychology are those works that provide the kinds of nuts-and-bolts information that facilitates the translation of psychological science to practice. In 1985, while writing the first primer for practitioners in clinical health psychology (Belar & Deardorff, 1995, is a revised edition), my postdoctoral fellows and I focused on what I had been teaching at the University of Florida and Kaiser Permanente Health Care Program about working in tertiary care settings. There was a dearth of practical advice available at that time. When I began my career during the early 1970s, I had had excellent role models in training (e.g., Doyle Gentry, Joe Matarazzo), but there were few written resources; we learned by watching and doing. As I was reading the chapters for this current handbook, I found myself wishing that it had been a resource available to me then; there was nothing of the kind.

EDITORS' NOTE: These views are those of the author and not those of the American Psychological Association.

What this handbook does is facilitate the progression of the learner from the classroom to the clinical setting by focusing on the translation of science to practice using practical examples. It does so by reviewing literature on behaviors that compromise overall health status (e.g., smoking, nonadherence) and behavioral aspects of selected medical problems (e.g., cancer, pain, coronary heart disease). The nature of the health problems is described, related psychological concepts are defined, measurement issues are addressed, and relevant treatments are detailed. There are analyses of evidence-based clinical assessments and interventions that identify what is known as well as current gaps in knowledge. However, in addition, experienced authors discuss the application of those interventions in the real world, noting pitfalls and providing the kind of practical advice never found in scholarly journals. For each problem, a case study is presented that facilitates understanding of the implementation process; the reader can learn what an experienced clinician has actually "said" to a patient and the rationale behind decisions made regarding treatment. It is sure to be an invaluable resource to scientist-practitioners during the education and training process as well as to those continuing their professional development—which includes all of us.

In addition to addressing specific health problems, this handbook contains a wealth of information related to professional issues such as working with a multidisciplinary staff, conducting research in a medical setting, and evaluating clinical outcomes. The chapter on public health approaches contextualizes clinical health psychology in our health system, highlighting that it involves more than those services provided in medical settings and by traditional health care providers. The public health emphasis represents a major thrust in health care policy that is likely to receive increasing support during the 21st century given the importance of population-based approaches to health, the increased awareness of behavioral components in chronic disease, and the need for attention to issues of diversity in our health care system.

I have always believed that our students should surpass us in knowledge and skills related to our areas of teaching, research, and practice. Looking backward, it is apparent that those beginning their careers today are at a much different starting point than when we entered the field. This is good. Looking forward, I continue to see great opportunities for the development of health psychology, which these students have an opportunity to maximize given this different starting point. If I have an opportunity to write a foreword to a revised *Health Psychology Handbook* 20 years from now, I anticipate that it will contain many chapters on issues such as technology, prevention, genetic counseling, and health informatics. For example, there are numerous technologies that have been developed during recent years for which we do not have long-term follow-up data to inform our clinical work (e.g., assisted reproductive technologies). Other developments have presented challenges in coping and care for which we are still designing and testing appropriate behavioral interventions (e.g., genetic testing for diabetes, breast cancer) or assessing the impact of medical interventions (e.g., prophylactic mastectomy). In other cases, interventions that look promising now will have been sufficiently tested through widespread randomized controlled studies (e.g., telehealth delivery of behavioral interventions). Given the explosion in knowledge and information delivery systems, there will also be increased focus on how to access and evaluate information as well as how to facilitate clinical decision making. But in the meantime, with this current handbook, we have a great resource to facilitate what is ready for translation from research to practice *now*. Our patients can benefit from these services *now*, and we need a well-trained health care workforce to meet these needs.

—Cynthia D. Belar, Ph.D., A.B.P.P.

REFERENCES

Belar, C. D., & Deardorff, W. W. (1995). *Clinical health psychology in medical settings: A practitioner's guidebook*. Washington, DC: American Psychological Association.

Institute of Medicine. (1982). *Health and behavior: Frontiers of research in the biobehavioral sciences*. Washington, DC: National Academy Press.

Institute of Medicine. (2001). *Health and behavior: The interplay of biological, behavioral, and societal influences*. Washington, DC: National Academy Press.

Part I

PRACTICAL ISSUES FOR THE BEHAVIORAL MEDICINE SPECIALIST

Introduction to Part I

The first five chapters of this handbook provide an overview and frame of reference for the clinical health psychologist. These chapters attempt to build on the broad and general training common to all professional psychology training programs and provide an overview of some of the unique skills critical for becoming a behavioral medicine specialist.

In Chapter 1, Seime, Clark, and Whiteside provide the reader with a broad overview of the unique roles played by psychologists working in medical settings. Role identification is critical because many of the experiences of psychologists in medical settings are in stark contrast to experiences in traditional psychology clinics. The authors emphasize the unique contributions in the areas of assessment, treatment, and research that psychology brings to medical settings as well as the unique experiences that come from working in a system dominated by the medical model.

In Chapter 2, Franzen builds on the framework presented in Chapter 1 by providing detailed examples of the similarities and unique aspects of psychological assessment in medical settings as compared with traditional psychology clinics. Attention is given to cognitive, intellectual, and psychiatric screenings, pointing out the unique role of psychology in medical settings. The chapter concludes with specific recommendations for assessment and training needed to work as a clinical health psychologist in a medical setting.

In Chapter 3, Winefield and Chur-Hansen provide a detailed discussion of the challenges and rewards of working in a multidisciplinary setting. This is perhaps the aspect of clinical health psychology that most differentiates it from other professional psychology settings. Medical settings are by their nature multidisciplinary, and psychologists are often not trained to function in this professional arena. The authors provide both a historical perspective and detailed information about the specific skills that will facilitate integration into medical settings.

In Chapter 4, Leffingwell describes the importance of motivational enhancement interventions for use in medical settings. The chapter reviews the historical basis of these procedures and provides a great deal of detail for how these interventions can and should be used for helping clients to change health-related behaviors. The author provides specific examples of dialogue between the therapist and the client to illustrate the conceptual and practical aspects of these interventions.

Finally, in Chapter 5, Wiebe, Bloor, and Smith present a review of other brief interventions and group methods used in the practice of clinical health psychology. The chapter illustrates how these interventions fit within a biopsychosocial model, with an emphasis on the unique goals for intervention with health-related problems. The authors provide reviews of the use of psychoeducational, cognitive-behavioral, and interpersonal approaches for reducing the risk of disease, improving disease outcomes, and improving quality of life. As with the other chapters in this section, a major focus is the unique training necessary to serve as a clinical health psychologist.

CHAPTER 1

Health Psychology Practice in Medical Settings

RICHARD J. SEIME, MATTHEW M. CLARK, AND STEPHEN P. WHITESIDE

There has been tremendous growth in the number of psychologists with a primary interest in practicing in medical settings. In this chapter, we cannot provide an exhaustive review of the literature but instead present a perspective that will help put the subsequent chapters into a professional context. The goal of this chapter is to briefly review the roles of clinical health psychologists, address some issues of practice in a medical setting, and focus on specific strategies and recommendations on "how to" function as a clinical health psychologist in an academic health science center. The authors of this chapter represent different levels of training and background; therefore, they provide the perspectives of a psychologist in training (Stephen Whiteside), a health psychology researcher/clinician/educator (Matthew Clark), and a senior clinician/educator/administrator (Richard Seime).

BACKGROUND

The health issues facing Americans have changed greatly over the past century. People live longer, and they experience different challenges to their health. Previously, many died from infectious diseases such as tuberculosis and influenza. The death rate from life-threatening infectious diseases declined during the mid-20th century due to advances in preventive measures and medical care. While the AIDS epidemic has created complex and important new challenges, most Americans will experience health problems related to cardiovascular disease, cancer, cerebrovascular disease, unintentional injuries, and chronic obstructive pulmonary disease (Kaplan, Sallis, & Patterson, 1993). Americans are becoming more obese, are being less physically active, and are consuming more dietary fat (Kottke et al., 2000). It has been estimated that lifestyle behaviors account for more than 50% of the mortality from these diseases (McGinness & Foege, 1993). Smoking, physical activity level, and nutrition all are lifestyle factors, but so are mood, social support, and personality. Thus, clinical health psychology has an opportunity to contribute to the health and wellness of our population. Two case examples may help to highlight these issues.

Case 1: Mr. Smith is a 55-year-old business executive who recently completed his annual physical. His father died at 58 years of age from a myocardial infarction, or heart attack, and Mr. Smith worries frequently about his health. However, he is 40 pounds overweight, has not been a consistent exerciser since college, smokes one pack of cigarettes per day, and has three alcoholic drinks after work to "unwind." He is on antihypertensive and lipid-lowering medications. His physician is recommending numerous lifestyle changes, and Mr. Smith was referred to you, a clinical health psychologist, for consultation.

Case 2: Ms. Jones is a 65-year-old, recently widowed female who has coronary artery disease and had coronary artery bypass surgery. Her cardiologist referred her to a 12-week cardiac rehabilitation program, but Ms. Jones does not attend on a regular basis. When present, she appears lethargic, does not follow instructions, and reports that she is frequently feeling alone and isolated. Her cardiologist wants your assistance in evaluating her mood and providing assistance in her care.

These cases highlight different aspects of clinical health psychology. The first case may benefit from cognitive-behavioral therapy for lifestyle changes. Record keeping, stimulus control, enhancing social support, stress management techniques, and/or goal-setting strategies could be beneficial. The second case portrays how psychiatric comorbidity may affect adherence to recommendations for health behavior changes. Depression in cardiac patients, for example, increases the risk of reoccurrence (Frasure-Smith, Lesperance, & Talajic, 1995) and lowers medication adherence (Carney, Freedland, Eisen, Rich, & Jaffe, 1995). Thus, assessment and treatment of comorbid depression would be important for the second case example.

UNIQUE CONTRIBUTIONS OF PSYCHOLOGISTS

Increasingly over the past 25 years, the field of medicine has been recognizing the benefits of the biopsychosocial model. This philosophy adds an understanding and incorporation of psychosocial variables to the traditional biomedical approach (Engel, 1977). As experts in measuring and altering behavior, psychologists have a unique set of skills to combine with the practice of our medical colleagues in an effort to apply the biopsychosocial model to patient care. In an environment consisting of multiple health and mental health professions, psychology's most important contributions are its study of complex behavior and its commitment to critical evaluation of treatment strategies and outcomes (cf. Schofield, 1969).

As a subspecialty of psychology, clinical health psychology applies assessment and learning theories to a unified view of physical and psychological health. Through this integration, health psychology can evaluate and treat many areas that frequently have not been addressed by the more traditional practices of clinical psychology and psychiatry. For instance, Belar and Deardorff (1995) identified three areas of consultation that clinical health psychologists address more directly than do other mental health practitioners: (a) treatment involving psychophysiological self-regulation or learning theory to medical problems, (b) predictions of response to medical-surgical treatments, and (c) reduction of health risk behaviors. The distinct ability of clinical health psychology to address these types of questions stems from differences with other mental health fields in four general areas: training, assessment, treatment, and research.

Training

Professional training influences the manner in which health care professionals think about clinical issues and influences the tools with which they evaluate and subsequently treat patients. The training of clinical health psychologists is complementary to the medical training of physicians due to its focus on the empirical investigation of cognition, behavior, emotions, and interpersonal relationships. Specifically, psychologists are trained in research, program evaluation, and measurement of behavior, areas in which psychiatrists and other mental health practitioners are not as thoroughly trained (Belar & Deardorff, 1995). The focus on health behavior change and prevention in training for the clinical health psychology subspecialty equips practitioners with a perspective that has advantages over both traditional clinical psychology and psychiatry training models. Namely, the former two disciplines are often viewed as being overly focused on psychopathology (Belar & Deardorff, 1995), thereby limiting services primarily to individuals with diagnosable mental disorders. This focus on psychopathology excludes patients without psychiatric disorders who, nonetheless, are exhibiting maladaptive cognitive or behavioral patterns that affect their health status and quality of life. Training in clinical health psychology, in contrast, incorporates the study of behaviors that promote good physical and emotional health, such as smoking cessation, weight management, development of adaptive coping mechanisms, and adjustment to chronic illness, in addition to traditional mental health training. Health psychologists are thereby able to assess these areas and intervene to promote healthy behaviors with or without a DSM-IV (*Diagnostic and Statistical Manual of Mental Disorders*, fourth edition) diagnosis (American Psychiatric Association, 1994).

Assessment

The foundation of clinical health psychology is in standardized assessment, a practice that continues to be a hallmark of the discipline. Consultations often incorporate psychometric assessment, which may be one of clinical health psychology's most unique contributions to patient care (Belar & Deardorff, 1995). Use of standardized measures, such as self-report questionnaires, reduces the chance of interviewer bias in assessment and adds an objective piece of information that can be used to standardize the assessment and monitor the success of the treatment interventions. No other mental health field has this foundation and expertise in psychometrics.

Another strength of the discipline is the type of information collected by clinical health psychologists. Some disciplines focus primarily on deriving a diagnostic label; in contrast, clinical health psychologists frequently conduct a functional analysis. A functional analysis of the symptoms incorporates the antecedents and consequences of each symptom or behavior. The singular use of psychiatric diagnoses has a number of pitfalls and liabilities. First, DSM-IV diagnoses (American Psychiatric Association, 1994) are not etiology based but rather descriptive in nature. Thus, psychiatric diagnoses do not adequately address or describe the factors that may have precipitated and/or maintained a patient's symptoms and therefore do not provide sufficient information to determine which treatment interventions are likely to be successful for a given patient (Beutler, Wakefield, & Williams, 1994). Second, diagnostic labels, such as hypochondriasis and borderline personality disorder, can have pejorative or moral connotations that lead to negative effects (Van Egeren & Striepe, 1998). For example, these diagnoses can influence health care professionals to inaccurately attribute patients' physical complaints to symptoms of psychopathology (Belar & Geisser, 1995) or can increase patients' fear that their symptoms will not be taken seriously (Van Egeren & Striepe, 1998). Finally, diagnostic labeling can contribute to mind-body dichotomous thinking. For example, although the DSM-IV diagnosis of "psychological factors affecting a medical condition" is an improvement over the previous nomenclature of "psychogenic pain," this new diagnosis still maintains a unidirectional causal link rather than acknowledging the interaction between patients' physical symptoms and their behavior and emotional functioning (Van Egeren & Striepe, 1998).

A functional analysis has the strengths of objectively quantifying the frequency and intensity of a target symptom and locating where within the environmental context it occurs. This approach acknowledges that behavioral symptoms interact with emotional, cognitive, social, and physical processes within the patient. The patient is seen as not merely acting on his or her environment but rather as responding and reacting to behaviors from health professionals and the demands of being in the hospital. Moreover, the patient's environment extends beyond health care factors, so a thorough "assessment requires awareness of life circumstances and an appreciation of expectancies placed on patients by themselves and others" (Rozensky, Sweet, & Tovian, 1997, p. 63). Completing a functional analysis to understand the environment in which a target behavior occurs, including the precipitating stimuli and reinforcing consequences, logically suggests a treatment plan to alter the expression of the symptom. Ultimately, providing information that clearly leads to a treatment is the goal of any clinical health psychology consultation.

More so than any other discipline, psychology has developed a body of knowledge regarding behavioral assessment (through interview and direct observation) that can be applied to understanding maladaptive behaviors not only by the patient but also by caregivers, both familial and professional. This approach stands in stark contrast to a purely biological explanation that locates pathology primarily within the patient. The contribution of clinical health psychology lies in emphasizing the role that learning and reinforcement play in maladaptive behaviors while also acknowledging biologically based personality and psychopathology factors.

Treatment

As in assessment, one of the strengths of psychologists in a medical center is that they can add a unique set of skills and options to the treatment plan. Although many physicians request that complicated psychopharmacological management be managed by their psychiatric colleagues, an attending physician will frequently employ a first-line antidepressant or anxiolytic before requesting a psychiatry consult. However, many physicians understandably lack the training expertise or comfort level to address many of the issues routinely treated by psychologists such as application of motivational interviewing to health behavior change (Bellg, 1998). Thus, consultation to a clinical health psychologist can add a novel treatment approach to a complex and challenging medical patient.

Many of the strengths of the treatments offered by clinical health psychologists emerge directly from their training and assessment. For example, because clinical health psychologists have expanded from a narrow focus on psychopathology, they can offer treatment options for patients who are not described by DSM-IV diagnoses (American Psychiatric Association, 1994). Clinical health psychologists can work with psychologically well-functioning individuals who are faced with challenging health problems. This is an important quality because it is not necessary to suffer from psychopathology to have difficulties in the hospital setting, in coping with illness, or in adhering to medical recommendations. To illustrate, adherence rates in pediatric populations can be as low as 5%, and thus many patients will benefit from assistance with adherence strategies (Dickey, Mattar, & Chudzik, 1975). Clearly, a singular focus on psychopathology, defined in part as a deviation from "normal" functioning, would not address a problem that occurs in the majority of individuals faced with a given medical situation. As a result of this expanded focus, clinical health psychology interventions with nonpsychiatric patients have facilitated health-promoting behavior changes and can have direct effects on biological factors that influence the onset and progression of disease (Bellg, 1998).

An additional strength of the interventions enlisted by clinical health psychologists is that they are theory driven, with an understanding of the mechanism of action. This is particularly true for interventions based on learning and behavioral principles. The opportunities for clinical health psychologists to apply these skills in medical centers are numerous, including stimulus control strategies to help patients with cardiovascular disease manage their environments, treatment of adjustment to medical illness, behavior problems and adherence in chronic health problems, cognitive distortions exacerbating symptoms of anxiety in patients with medical disease, and family problems exacerbating and resulting from health problems faced by the patient (cf. Camic & Knight, 1998).

Research

The fourth general area of unique contributions by clinical health psychology to medical center consultation is the application of research to patient care. Training in research design, implementation, and interpretation is emphasized in doctoral training in psychology to a greater degree than in medical training. These research skills can be applied at the individual patient level or at the treatment team level (Malec, 1991). For example, clinical

health psychologists can systematically study the effectiveness of a particular treatment within a single patient or can compare separate treatments within an individual patient. This could be accomplished by obtaining structured behavioral observations of target symptoms before and after interventions from health care providers. Psychologists can also apply their research training to the evaluation of new treatment protocols. To date, among numerous other accomplishments, psychology has demonstrated the effectiveness of psychological interventions in reducing hospitalization rates in asthmatic and diabetic children (Christie-Seely & Crouch, 1987) and in managing chronic pain (Hardin, 1998).

Summary

Clearly, because of the nature of their training, clinical health psychologists have a multitude of unique skills and techniques that can be applied to the assessment and treatment of patients in medical centers. The contribution of a psychological consultation is being able to assess the biopsychosocial factors that affect a patient and then provide a cogent explanation to the patient for why he or she is experiencing difficulties. This empirically based explanation focuses on the patient as an individual with a history of experiences interpreted through the patient's specific cognitive and emotional processing and logically suggests potential interventions. However, communicating and applying these skills effectively in the medical center, an environment that can feel alien to the inexperienced psychologist, can be challenging.

IMPORTANT ISSUES IN MEDICAL SETTINGS THAT AFFECT PSYCHOLOGICAL PRACTICE

The Medical Model

Clinical health psychologists have clinical and research training and skills that are transportable from the doctoral training arena to the medical setting (cf. Belar, 1980). However, psychologists frequently confront a setting that is steeped in the medical model. The medical model is the cornerstone of clinical practice in health science centers. The medical model assumes that a practitioner will diagnose a problem, identify etiological factors, and ultimately correct the underlying issues that result in the overt dysfunction or problem. This is often seen initially by psychologists and psychologists in training who are unfamiliar with practice in a medical setting as antithetical to behavioral or psychological formulation. As Shows (1976) pointed out, doctoral students often emerge from their doctoral training with negative attitudes about the medical model. Mistakenly, psychologists' initial reaction to the medical model is that physicians may be trying to find a disease where none exists. In fact, historically some of the tension between psychologists and psychiatrists in the medical setting is around the medicalization or pathologizing of behavioral issues or emotional distress. At its worst, the medical model can "portray the patient as sick and dependent and the professional as imperialistic and heroic" (Belar & Deardorff, 1995, p. 30). So, psychologists must come to terms with the medical model.

Psychologists often malign the medical model, but it is a "fact of life" in medical settings. Therefore, it is important to address one's attitude about the medical model so that one can effectively communicate, collaborate, and intervene in the medical setting. It may be helpful to reframe this model as representing an empirical approach to diagnosis and treatment. A common value held by both clinical health psychologists and our medical colleagues is an emphasis on empiricism. Likewise, it is important to get to know colleagues and to ascertain their attitudes toward psychology and psychologists. With the increased representation of psychologists in medical settings, medical colleagues have become aware of the unique skills that psychologists bring to the medical setting. It has been our experience that these colleagues appreciate the clinical health psychologist who is able to help both the patient and the physician to understand problematic emotions and behavior and to intervene effectively.

Concerns Related to the Medical Model

Diagnosis by Exclusion. It is essential that clinical health psychologists avoid making a diagnosis by exclusion. Often patients are referred when there are no positive physical findings but there is dysfunction, and referring colleagues may erroneously conclude that this equates with the assumption that "there must be something psychologically wrong." In such a circumstance, we as psychologists must still identify positive findings to conclude that psychological or behavioral factors can account for a problem. Here is where our skills in functional analysis, use of data gathering, and psychometric assessment all can play a role in determining what might account for dysfunction in the absence of physical findings. It is important to have a working knowledge of the pathophysiology, behavioral, and psychological issues common with medical disorders that we are called on to evaluate as a consultant. Keep in mind also that some diseases, such as multiple sclerosis, have elusive or equivocal findings. In most cases, it is far too simpleminded to dismiss as psychological or functional a patient's presenting problems if no definitive physical signs or findings are obtained. In cases such as this, it behooves us to recognize that we play an important role in ensuring that the patient continues to feel that we will encourage an ongoing consultation with the referring physician as we also work to help the patient get well. Somatizing patients in particular can represent a real challenge, but even patients with somatization disorders have legitimate needs for ongoing medical evaluation and care. What we have to offer these difficult patients is a different model for addressing their dysfunction that looks at behavioral, social, and psychological factors as they interact with biological factors to account for their difficulties and dysfunction.

Ignoring Psychological Factors. This is the converse in a sense of diagnosis by exclusion. In this pitfall, a physician may have recently diagnosed a physical or biological problem after having not been able to do so for some time. Perhaps a patient has been suffering from distress or depression, engaging in maladaptive behaviors, or reinforced for sick role behavior. Now the patient has received a medical diagnosis, and this new "organic" finding is seen as accounting for all of his or her difficulties and symptoms. This error in thinking can lead to poor patient management in some cases. For example, assume that an individual has been having severe anxiety and panic attacks that have led to agoraphobic behaviors. A recent physical now reveals abnormally high thyroid hormone levels. Does the fact that this individual may be more prone to anxiety as a result now account for the behavioral dysfunction? The basic principle is simply that in the process of serial diagnosis of problems, it is not necessarily the case that a particular physical finding accounts for all of the subsequent or preceding problems. From a biopsychosocial perspective, many factors are at work simultaneously. What we are best at doing as psychologists is assessing what is happening in the dimensions of behavior, cognition, and emotion as well as in the social milieu of the patient that provides some avenue for understanding the current dysfunction and how to ameliorate the dysfunction.

Medical Background Versus Psychology Background

There are obvious differences between psychologists and physicians in the nature of their training. From the time a physician graduates from medical school, he or she is expected to be caring for patients, making decisions, being on the "front line," and quickly diagnosing and treating medical issues. However, physicians frequently have limited confidence in their ability to counsel patients or deal with psychological and behavioral issues due to a lack of training. Thus, it is important to realize that physicians often feel quite inadequate in addressing the behavioral and emotional factors that are present in so many of the patients they evaluate and treat (e.g., Kroenke & Mangelsdorff, 1989; Philbrick, Connelly, & Wofford, 1996).

The psychology trainee who is new to the medical setting, or the psychologist who has little experience in the medical setting, can find the medical environment quite intimidating. Besides often feeling as though his or her medical knowledge is lacking, the psychologist can be intimidated by the pace, the presumed expectation of certainty about psychological formulations and interventions, and the expectation of "answers." To manage these feelings and assumed expectations, remember that although physicians have had a different "track" in their training compared with other health professionals, this does not in any way invalidate the unique knowledge, clinical assessment, and intervention skills that clinical health psychologists bring to the health care arena. In terms of training, Belar and Deardorff (1995) stated that didactic experiences alone are not sufficient for the practice of health psychology. They emphasized the importance of appropriate role models, supervisors, and mentors. This is consistent with our experience in having trained and supervised practicum students, predoctoral interns, and postdoctoral fellows. Those trainees and psychologists who have had mentors working in medical settings, who have had physician collaborators and mentors, and who have had the opportunity to train side by side with physician trainees have an appreciation for physician knowledge without being intimidated.

Working Within the Organizational and Political Structure of a Medical Setting

The clinical health psychologist with a solid training background in assessment, intervention, and professional skills enters a challenging environment in the medical setting. It is an environment governed by formalized rules (e.g., hospital bylaws, staff privileging) and informal "rules," many of which are not familiar to psychology graduate students. Therefore, we emphasize the importance of receiving training in a medical setting from mentors who are familiar with the medical setting. It has been our experience that physicians and other allied health professionals are welcoming of psychologists—but pitfalls abound. Belar and Deardorff (1995) discussed the implicit and explicit power hierarchy that affects a psychologist's role function in a medical setting. Psychologists, especially those who are new to the field or who are still in training, need to be especially sensitive to the role of the referring physician—the provider who is in charge of ordering consultations and who ultimately is responsible for the patient in a hospital setting. A clinical health psychologist is invited to see a patient by the physician who orders a consultation. Although it is important to have excellent relationships with an entire treatment team, ultimately it is the attending physicians who have the final say as to who sees their patients and what is offered to the patients. This process can be confusing to the clinical health psychology trainee or psychologist more familiar with outpatient practice, where several consultants may be working with the same patient. In our experience, a psychologist needs to consider both the formal aspects (i.e., rules and regulation governing practice) of how to function as a psychologist in a consultative role and the

informal aspects of how best to be effective in a consultative role. The informal aspects of effectiveness include the quality of the collaborative relations with other disciplines (Sweet & Rozensky, 1991) and the psychologist's personal style. For example, Belar and Deardorff (1995) suggested that the most effective clinical health psychologists in a hospital setting are those who are "active, open, direct, assertive, and energetic" (p. 33) and who have a higher tolerance for frustration. We would add that the most effective psychologists are those who have the background, knowledge, interest, clinical training, and interpersonal skills needed to deal with both complex patient care issues and a complex, multilayered health care delivery environment.

At a minimum, the clinical health psychologist who intends to work effectively in a medical setting needs to understand the formal governance aspects of psychological practice in a medical setting. This topic is addressed only briefly here, and the reader is referred to expanded yet succinct coverage of these issues by others (e.g., Belar & Deardorff, 1995; Rozensky et al., 1997). The medical staff/hospital bylaws, rules, and regulations govern how psychologists are formally recognized in the hospital setting. What a psychologist is able to do professionally in a hospital or medical center is governed by staff privileges (i.e., what a psychologist is permitted to do once granted a formal status with the hospital). Whether a psychologist participates in formally determining rules and in setting standards for practice in the hospital organization is determined by the category of staff membership (e.g., active staff, consulting staff, courtesy staff, allied heath staff). Only voting staff membership (i.e., active staff) permits a formal voice in medical staff/hospital staff affairs.

A clinical health psychologist also needs to be well aware of the administrative structure of psychology in the medical setting where he or she works. The psychologist needs to know the organized "unit," whether it be a section or division within other clinical departments or an independent department of psychology. An organized psychology unit facilitates the individual psychologist's professional role function in the medical setting. Frank (1997) and Seime (1998) reviewed some of the issues associated with the organizational structures within health science settings. Connecting with the administrative structure for psychology is required in most institutions. The medical setting provides such an enticing wealth of professional opportunities that novice psychologists can make serious mistakes, without intending to do so, that may jeopardize their future practice. Thus, as Rozensky (1991) pointed out, it is important to both understand and master a specific hospital's "political milieu." Fortunately, we are now at a stage in the development of clinical health psychology throughout many medical settings and academic health science centers where seasoned clinicians/mentors are readily available to assist the junior psychologist in how to be effective in medical settings.

Consulting and Liaison Opportunities

The role of a consultant in a medical setting can take many forms, and serving as such is the most common role for clinical health psychologists. Typically, a consultation involves an evaluation whereby the patient is provided with a formulation and treatment recommendations. Often, the patient is referred for further services that may require additional medical consultation, mental health services, and/or other health care services (e.g., occupational or physical therapy, nutritional counseling). This consultation model fits well with a traditional outpatient practice. There also has been a recent surge of interest in psychologists affiliating with primary care clinics or departments of family practice where ongoing consultation is provided to both patients and health care professionals. In this capacity, the psychologist serves the dual role of a consultant and a liaison psychologist (e.g., being involved with a program, regularly interacting about psychological and behavioral adjustment of patients, consulting with staff, treating patients). As the clinical health psychologist gets involved in a liaison role, he or she begins to move away from a more traditional mental health practice and toward a clinical health psychology practice. Liaison roles provide a rich opportunity for both research and clinical collaboration. The physician or other health care professional is not directly referring patients "to the psychologist," but the psychologist becomes a regular part of the program's evaluation and service delivery. A liaison role also provides an excellent opportunity for the psychologist to intervene with the treatment team, to educate, and to affect program development.

Typically, consulting roles involve fee-for-service. The psychologist interviews the patient and assesses for behavioral, cognitive, social, and/or mental health difficulties. There may be difficulties in billing for these services, particularly for patients who do not have a mental health diagnosis under the DSM-IV criteria. However, as of January 2002, there are now "current procedural codes" (American Medical Association, 2001) that include health and behavior assessment and intervention codes for patients whose primary diagnosis is physical. This is a major breakthrough to permit appropriate reimbursement for the delivery of psychological services to the patient with significant physical problems requiring psychological intervention but without a DSM-IV mental health diagnosis.

Liaison roles for psychologists are satisfying, but practical fiscal issues can limit the psychologist's time in such activities. It is important to negotiate with a program to compensate for the psychologist's time that does not involve direct billable services. In our experience, it is not uncommon for programs to greet the involvement of a clinical health psychologist in the liaison role but to not be able to pay for the intensive time involved in such efforts. In academic health science settings, one strategy is for psychologists to pair the ongoing liaison role with a research endeavor funded by a grant that serves to both purchase time and fulfill research interests and goals.

Training Background and Skills

Belar and colleagues (2001) noted that graduate students now have a multitude of opportunities to obtain appropriate preparatory supervised experiences as graduate students, predoctoral interns, or postdoctoral fellows. Graduate school training serves as the foundation by providing training in the biological, cognitive, affective, social, and psychological bases of behavior. Such training could be integrated with graduate training, but it has been our experience that this training more typically is obtained during the predoctoral internship year or as a postdoctoral fellow.

Although postdoctoral fellowship programs have existed for a number of years, only recently has there been an emphasis on having organized, structured, and accredited postdoctoral fellowship training. Recently the Committee on Accreditation of the American Psychological Association (APA) has recognized specialty postdoctoral fellowship programs in clinical health psychology. There are a few postdoctoral programs that have received APA accreditation, with others soon to be added. Training at the predoctoral internship level in an APA-accredited program within a medical setting will ensure supervised experience in the medical environment. The opportunity to practice under supervision, to consult regularly with other health professionals, and to evaluate and treat medically referred patients is an invaluable training experience. The opportunity to then obtain further depth and breadth of experience and expertise is provided by postdoctoral fellowship training. Postdoctoral fellowship training will also go a long way

toward assisting the psychologist in becoming board certified in clinical health psychology. The American Board of Professional Psychology has recognized clinical health psychology as a specialty since 1990 (Belar & Jeffrey, 1995).

As we advance in our careers, we all will need to constantly further our knowledge and develop new skills. For a practicing psychologist, whether early or late in his or her career, there are suggested principles that can guide self-directed learning to remain competent and to develop new areas of competency as a psychologist providing services to medical-surgical patients. Belar and colleagues (2001) developed a template for self-assessment for the practicing clinical health psychologist. The template is presented in Table 1.1.

Translating Psychology Practice and Skills Into a Medical Setting

As noted previously, graduate education may provide doctoral students with training that will facilitate their functioning as clinical health psychologists. These educational experiences include course work and clinical training in epidemiology, health psychology, psychological testing, behavior therapy, family therapy, geriatrics, and psychopharmacology. Unfortunately, it has been our experience that some needed skills are not taught and that some psychology practices do not translate well into medical centers.

Pitfalls. There are many skills that are critical for the successful practice of clinical health psychology but that are overlooked during graduate training. Some skills are unique to health settings (e.g., managing on-call schedules, learning ICD-10 [*International Classification of Diseases,* 10th edition] codes), whereas other skills are general practice skills often overlooked in graduate education (e.g., billing procedures, documentation requirements and modalities). Many clinical

Table 1.1   Template for Self-Assessment of Readiness for Delivery of Services to Patient With Medical-Surgical Problems

1. Do I have the knowledge of the biological bases of health and disease as related to this problem? How is this related to the biological bases of behavior?
2. Do I have knowledge of the cognitive-affective bases of health and disease as related to this problem? How is this related to the cognitive-affective bases of behavior?
3. Do I have the knowledge of the social bases of health and disease as related to this problem? How is this related to the social bases of behavior?
4. Do I have the knowledge of the developmental and individual bases of health and disease as related to this problem? How is this related to the developmental and individual bases of behavior?
5. Do I have the knowledge of the interactions among biological, affective, cognitive, social, and developmental components (e.g., psychophysiological aspects)? Do I understand the relationships between this problem and the patient and his or her environment (including family, health care system, and sociocultural environment)?
6. Do I have the knowledge and skills in the empirically supported clinical assessment methods for patients with this problem and how assessment might be affected by information in areas described by Questions 1 to 5?
7. Do I have knowledge of, and skill in implementing, the empirically supported interventions relevant to patients with this problem? Do I have knowledge of how the proposed psychological interventions affect physiological processes and vice versa?
8. Do I have knowledge of the roles and functions of other health care professionals relevant to this patient's problem? Do I have skills to communicate and collaborate with them?
9. Do I understand the sociopolitical features of the health care delivery system that can affect this problem?
10. Do I understand health policy issues relevant to this problem?
11. Am I aware of distinctive ethical issues related to practice with this problem?
12. Am I aware of the distinctive legal issues related to practice with this problem?
13. Am I aware of special professional issues associated with practice with this problem?

SOURCE: Copyright © 2001 by the American Psychological Association. Adapted with permission.

health psychology trainees are not initially prepared for the unique challenges posed by medical centers. It is not uncommon for trainees to be asked to make a diagnosis after conducting a brief bedside consultation (e.g., 15 minutes) with a client in a medical setting, whereas mental health clinics would frequently set aside at least 1 full hour for an initial intake interview. Likewise, trainees are often taught to write extensive evaluation reports primarily intended for other psychologists, whereas clinical health psychology reports are expected to be brief and to use language easily understood by a number of different health care professionals. In a mental health care setting, psychologists are providing most (if not all) of the treatment, whereas in a health care setting, psychologists are only part of the treatment team where psychological interventions must be coordinated with medical treatments. This transition is not always easy for individuals who have little or no experience with interdisciplinary teams.

In spite of the challenges and pitfalls, it has been our experience that the transition to a medical center is a rewarding yet challenging experience that can be facilitated through adequate preparation. A template for effective practice is described in the next section.

Strategies for Effective Practice

First, the psychologist should select an area of high interest. The patient population needs to be one for which the provider has a "passion." Much time, energy, and devotion will be needed to develop expertise, so being passionate about one's work is important. The psychologist should also pursue additional training through seminars, workshops, readings, and supervised clinical experience as suggested in the self-assessment template presented in Table 1.1. Once the psychologist has the expertise, forming an alliance with physicians will ensure continuity of medical care and will facilitate referrals. Completing comprehensive evaluations with clear recommendations will enhance satisfaction from referring physicians. Ongoing communication with health care providers is essential for patient care and will promote future referrals (Jowsey, Taylor, Schneekloth, & Clark, 2001). Maintaining contact with applied psychologists and other mental health providers will enhance the psychologist's effectiveness with his or her medical colleagues. For example, "No, I'm not able to assist your patient with couples counseling, but I can offer an excellent referral" is a more useful response than "Sorry, I don't provide couples counseling." We do not expect physicians to treat all problems, but we do expect them to refer as needed.

Finally, developing research projects focusing on program evaluation will assist in solidifying a clinical practice and will allow for documentation of effectiveness of services. As noted earlier, one of the distinctive skills that psychology brings to the medical setting is psychologists' extensive training in research. Psychologists are in the unique position of continuing to contribute to scholarly endeavors as part of their professional practice.

Psychologists have professional ethical guidelines and standards of practice to follow that may differ from those of other professions. It has been our experience that direct clear communication can prevent many dilemmas and will be well received by one's medical colleagues. For example, the importance of limiting and preventing dual relationships can be explained in a manner that is well received. In addition, discussions about how psychological test data and reports are different from lab work, and thus have different needs for confidentiality, have been well received by our medical institutions.

Trainees can be wonderful bridge builders. Having psychology trainees mentored, educated, or supervised by physicians has built many bonds for us. Similarly, mentoring, educating, or supervising medical students, residents, and fellows builds relationships with potential future colleagues and builds relationships with the medical training faculty. Our predoctoral interns and postdoctoral fellows have established numerous collaborative clinical and research projects with our medical staff. Collaborative research not only improves the quality and comprehensiveness of the research but also fosters collaborative clinical projects. Struggling through a grant application, preparation for a presentation, or a chart review can be a wonderful team-building experience (Bock et al., 1997).

THE FUTURE IS BRIGHT

Although psychologists have been an integral part of medical settings for a long time, the past quarter century has been a time of rapid growth. Many professional societies have emerged as a result of the new and exciting opportunities for psychologists in medical settings. These organizations include the Society of Behavioral Medicine and the Association for the Behavioral Sciences and Medical Education. In addition, divisions of APA, such as Division 38 (Health Psychology), Division 40 (Clinical Neuropsychology), Division 54 (Society of Pediatric Psychology), and Division

12 (Society of Clinical Psychology), have grown and developed around the interests of those working in medical settings. There are a host of APA-accredited internships in medical settings and a growing number of postdoctoral fellowship programs focusing on clinical health psychology. Likewise, journals that have clinically relevant research specifically related to medical settings have emerged (e.g., *Annals of Behavioral Medicine, Health Psychology, Journal of Behavioral Medicine, Journal of Clinical Psychology in Medical Settings*). The growth of information technology offers incredible opportunities for psychologists to be informed and to practice in an evidence-based fashion. Journal articles are available online, and literature searches are readily accessible through resources such as PsycINFO, MEDLINE, and EBM (Evidence-Based Medicine)–Cochrane Database of Systematic Reviews. Information relevant to psychological practice now is at our fingertips.

Psychologists will continue to play a significant role in medical settings through the delivery of clinical services, teaching, research, and health service administration. Perhaps the next frontier will be the involvement of clinical health psychologists in the genomic revolution as advances in the understanding and use of genetic data affect how diseases are treated, prevented, and understood (Patenaude, Guttmacher, & Collins, 2002).

REFERENCES

American Medical Association. (2001). *Physicians' current procedural terminology 2002*. Chicago: Author.

American Psychiatric Association. (1994). *Diagnostic and statistical manual of mental disorders* (4th ed.). Washington, DC: Author.

Belar, C. D. (1980). Training the clinical psychology student in behavioral medicine. *Professional Psychology, 11,* 620–627.

Belar, C. D., Brown, R. A., Hersch, L. E., Hornyak, L. M., Rozensky, R. H., Sheridan, E. P., Brown, R. T., & Reed, G. E. (2001). Self-assessment in clinical health psychology: A model for ethical expansion of practice. *Professional Psychology: Research and Practice, 32,* 135–141.

Belar, C. D., & Deardorff, W. W. (1995). *Clinical health psychology in medical settings: A practitioner's guidebook* (rev. ed.). Washington, DC: American Psychological Association.

Belar, C. D., & Geisser, M. (1995). Roles of the clinical health psychologist in the management of chronic illness. In P. Nicassio & T. Smith (Eds.), *Managing chronic illness: A biopsychological perspective* (pp. 33–58). Washington, DC: American Psychological Association.

Belar, C. D., & Jeffrey, T. (1995). Board certification in health psychology. *Journal of Clinical Psychology in Medical Settings, 2,* 129–132.

Bellg, A. J. (1998). Clinical cardiac psychology. In P. M. Camic & S. J. Knight (Eds.), *Clinical handbook of health psychology: A practical guide to effective interventions* (pp. 53–98). Seattle, WA: Hogrefe & Huber.

Beutler, L., Wakefield, P., & Williams, R. (1994). Use of psychological tests/instruments for treatment planning. In M. Maruish (Ed.), *The use of psychological tests for treatment planning and outcome assessment* (pp. 55–74). Hillsdale, NJ: Lawrence Erlbaum.

Bock, B., Albrecht, A., Traficante, R., Clark, M., Pinto, B., Tilkemeier, P., & Marcus, B. (1997). Predictors of exercise adherence following participation in a cardiac rehabilitation program. *International Journal of Behavioral Medicine, 4*(1), 60–75.

Camic, P. M., & Knight, S. J. (Eds.). (1998). *Clinical handbook of health psychology: A practical guide to effective interventions*. Seattle, WA: Hogrefe & Huber.

Carney, R., Freedland, K., Eisen, S., Rich, M., & Jaffe, A. (1995). Major depression and medication adherence in elderly patients with coronary artery disease. *Health Psychology, 14,* 88–90.

Christie-Seely, J., & Crouch, M. (1987). The history of the family in medicine. In M. Crouch & L. Roberts (Eds.), *The family in medical practice* (pp. 1–29). Berlin: Springer-Verlag.

Dickey, F., Mattar, M., & Chudzik, G. (1975). Pharmacist counseling increases drug regimen compliance. *Hospitals, 49,* 85–86.

Engel, G. L. (1977). The need for a new medical model: A challenge for biomedicine. *Science, 196,* 129–136.

Frank, R. G. (1997). Marketing psychology at academic health science centers. *Journal of Clinical Psychology in Medical Settings, 4,* 41–50.

Frasure-Smith, N., Lesperance, F., & Talajic, M. (1995). The impact of negative emotions on prognosis following myocardial infarction: Is it more than depression? *Health Psychology, 14,* 388–398.

Hardin, K. N. (1998). Chronic pain management. In P. M. Camic & S. J. Knight (Eds.), *Clinical handbook of health psychology: A practical guide to effective interventions* (pp. 123–165). Seattle, WA: Hogrefe & Huber.

Jowsey, S., Taylor, M., Schneekloth, T., & Clark, M. (2001). Psychosocial challenge in transplantation. *Journal of Psychiatric Practice, 7,* 404–414.

Kaplan, R., Sallis, J., Jr., & Patterson, T. (1993). *Health and human behavior.* New York: McGraw-Hill.

Kottke, T., Brekke, M., Brekke, L., Dale, L., Brandel, C., DeBoer, S., Hayes, S., Hoffman, R., Menzel, P., Nguyen, T., & Thomas, R. (2000). The CardioVision 2020 baseline community report card. *Mayo Clinic Proceedings, 75,* 1153–1159.

Kroenke, K., & Mangelsdorff, A. D. (1989). Common symptoms in ambulatory care: Incidence, evaluation, therapy, and outcome. *American Journal of Medicine, 86,* 262–266.

Malec, J. (1991). Research in the medical setting: Implementing the scientist-practitioner model. In J. Sweet, R. Rozensky, & S. Tovian (Eds.), *Handbook of clinical psychology in medical settings* (pp. 269–284). New York: Plenum.

McGinness, J., & Foege, W. (1993). Actual causes of death in the United States. *Journal of the American Medical Association, 270,* 2207–2212.

Patenaude, A. F., Guttmacher, A. E., & Collins, F. S. (2002). Genetic testing and psychology: New roles, new responsibilities. *American Psychologist, 57,* 271–282.

Philbrick, J. T., Connelly, J. E., & Wofford, A. B. (1996). The prevalence of mental disorders in rural office practice. *Journal of General Internal Medicine, 11,* 9–15.

Rozensky, R. H. (1991). Psychologists, politics, and hospitals. In J. Sweet, R. Rozensky, & S. M. Tovian (Eds.), *Handbook of clinical psychology in medical settings* (pp. 59–79). New York: Plenum.

Rozensky, R. H., Sweet, J. J., & Tovian, S. M. (1997). *Psychological assessment in medical settings.* New York: Plenum.

Schofield, W. (1969). The role of psychology in the delivery of health services. *American Psychologist, 24,* 565–584.

Seime, R. J. (1998). The section of psychology: Psychology in an academic health sciences center's department of behavioral medicine and psychiatry. *Journal of Clinical Psychology in Medical Settings, 5,* 215–232.

Shows, W. D. (1976). Problem of training interns in medical schools: A case of trying to change the leopard's spots. *Professional Psychology, 7,* 393–395.

Sweet, J. J., & Rozensky, R. H. (1991). Professional relations. In M. Hersen, A. Kazdin, & A. Bellack (Eds.), *The clinical psychology handbook* (2nd ed.). Elmsford, NY: Pergamon.

Van Egeren, L., & Striepe, M. I. (1998). Assessment approaches in health psychology: Issues and practical considerations. In P. M. Camic & S. J. Knight (Eds.), *Clinical handbook of health psychology: A practical guide to effective interventions* (pp. 16–50). Seattle, WA: Hogrefe & Huber.

CHAPTER 2

Psychological Assessment Screening in Medical Settings

MICHAEL D. FRANZEN

The presence of a psychologist in specialty medical settings has been common since the late 1960s and 1970s. During that era, there was increasing attention paid to the use of psychological principles to understand or enhance the treatment of cancer patients, cardiac patients, and chronic pain patients. Recently, more attention has been given to the potential role of psychologists in general medical or family practice and pediatric clinics. These health care providers, namely pediatricians, primary practice physicians (sometime known as primary care physicians [PCPs]), and family practice doctors, are the frontline care providers, even in those situations where it might be necessary to involve specialists. For example, most of the antidepressant prescriptions in the United States are written by general practitioners. In addition, even if a diagnosis requires specialized care, the first person to come into contact with the patient is most likely to be the person's PCP.

Psychological interventions begin with a psychological assessment. Psychological assessment has various forms, from behavioral functional analysis to personality assessment and psychological/psychiatric diagnosis. Because psychological interventions in medical settings focus more on enhancing the provision of medical care than on in-depth psychotherapy, assessment must be tailored to the needs of the setting. The psychologist might be called on to develop a plan to help manage chronic pain from a psychological perspective or to help manage anxiety related to upcoming surgery. In all of these cases, the assessment is aimed at elucidating psychological and environmental factors that could be useful in the provision of adequate medical care. In addition to formulating interventions, the psychologist might be called on to assess the patient for the presence of psychological or cognitive factors that would negatively affect the provision of medical care. These interfering factors may include cognitive impairment, psychological distress, or substance abuse behaviors.

Screening assessment is one type of psychological assessment frequently used in the medical setting. The purpose of screening is to identify important areas that may require more detailed assessment and evaluation. Therefore, the screening target is partially a function of the setting, the base rate of potential problem areas, and the population being seen. For example, the base rate of active psychosis in a family practice is fairly low, and it would make little sense to screen for symptoms of schizophrenia on a regular basis. Alternatively, there is a fairly high comorbidity between depression and certain medical conditions, and it would be eminently sensible to screen for depression in an endocrinology outpatient clinic.

PSYCHOLOGY IN THE CLINIC VERSUS PSYCHOLOGY IN THE MEDICAL SETTING

The practice of psychology in a medical setting has characteristics that differentiate it from the general practice of psychology. For example, the issue of assessment in a medical setting is complicated by the other variables in addition to environmental influences that may impinge on the patient's behavior. In behavioral assessment, it is assumed that the medical and physiological factors have been ruled out. In personality or traditional psychological assessment, it is assumed that the medical factors are already accounted for. In neuropsychological assessment, it is assumed that environmental variables have been minimized. In screening and evaluating the medical patient in a behavioral framework, none of these assumptions can be reasonably made. In fact, a more accurate assumption would be that all of these variables are playing a role in the current clinical presentation. Therefore, it would be important for the behavioral medicine clinician to consider medical, cognitive, and psychological features. Screening assessment seeks to identify the possibility of an issue such as cognitive impairment. Psychological assessment seeks to identify the construct at issue and provide an estimate of the precise level of that construct.

There are some features of screening that distinguish it from general psychological assessment. First and most obvious, screening is conducted in a more restricted time frame than is general assessment. This is true both for the administration of procedures and for the interpretations and recommendations made on the basis of the assessment results. In general psychological assessment, an appointment may be made for the following week and the typed report may be ready a week after that. In screening, whether for an inpatient setting or an outpatient setting, the person must be screened in the same appointment as the identification of the problem is raised and the interpretation must frequently be provided to the referral source outside the consultation room. A second feature that distinguishes screening from general assessment is the length of the procedures and the sensitivity and completeness with which the target constructs are evaluated.

The three areas of most concern in general medical settings are the possibilities of neurologically based cognitive impairment, of psychological or psychiatric disorders, and of substance abuse. Even if a specific psychiatric diagnosis is not appropriate, it may be helpful to screen for the presence of anxiety or depression, either of which can significantly affect medical outcome. The two reasons for screening for these variables are that their presence can negatively affect the medical treatment and that their presence may indicate the need for referral for further evaluation or specialized treatment.

PSYCHOMETRIC CONSIDERATIONS IN SCREENING

Even though psychological screening might not necessarily entail the full range of psychometric complexity that comprehensive or diagnostic assessment might, it is still important to pay attention to the relevant psychometric considerations. The several issues of validity and accuracy that need to be addressed in assessment are simplified somewhat in screening. The most relevant aspect of the psychometric properties of the screening instrument is related to its accuracy in identifying the presence of a pathological state and its utility in the decision-making process leading to a referral for comprehensive assessment. The construct underlying the instrument, whether it be memory or attention, is less important in screening than whether a score above a certain level is indicative of some form of cognitive problem with an organic basis.

In choosing a screening instrument and in setting a cutoff score, it is important to ask what the likelihood is that a certain score would be associated with a correct decision to pursue further evaluation. Similarly, it is important to ask what the likelihood is that a certain score would be associated with a correct decision to not pursue further evaluation. The first question is an issue of sensitivity. The second question is an issue of specificity. Sensitivity is the extent to which the assessment instrument identifies the presence of the target construct. Specificity is the extent to which positive assessment findings do not occur in the absence of the target construct. Positive predictive power is the accuracy with which a positive score predicts the target. Negative predictive power is the accuracy with which a negative score predicts the absence of the construct. In screening, it may be more important in some cases that an instrument be sensitive even when it might not be specific. For example, in high-risk situations where the incorrect decision to not pursue further evaluation could result in missing the presence of a growing brain tumor, the fact that many cases of no tumor are found with high scores (poor specificity) is less important than the fact that cases of tumor are found with high scores (good sensitivity).

THE USE OF THE INTERVIEW

The most potent weapon in the armamentarium of the clinician is the interview and history. There are two sources of clinical information derived from the interview. The first is the content information such as whether certain symptoms have been noticed or brought to the attention of the patient. Other content information includes the time course of the symptoms and whether there are any consistent changes in the level of symptoms. A second important source of information comes from the clinical observations made by the clinician. The clinician can note the quality of the verbalizations of the patient. Is the articulation understandable? Is the diction accurate? Is there any word-finding difficulty, paraphasic error, or paucity of speech? Are the station and gait normal? What is the appearance of the person? Is the grooming and hygiene adequate (inadequate hygiene may reflect either depression or cognitive impairment)? These factors were addressed in greater depth in Berg, Franzen, and Wedding (1994).

In addition to using the observations to generate hypotheses regarding which areas to consider for screening purposes, the clinician can use the historical information for that purpose as well. Any changes in usual functions can be a "red flag" that cognitive screening might be useful. A history of recent minor automobile accidents might be an indication to screen for attention or for visual-spatial skills. The clinician may want to also screen for any alcohol or substance abuse. If the patient has had to change jobs or was forced into early retirement, cognitive screening may be in order. A history of multiple sex partners or of high-risk sexual behavior may also indicate the need for screening. Occupational history also gives useful information. If the patient worked in an industrial setting with exposure to solvents, heavy metals, or insecticides, cognitive screening may be indicated.

COGNITIVE SCREENING

Cognitive screening is not as simple as it may seem. Although discussion of screening frequently involves only a single instrument, there is no adequate single instrument for screening all populations in all settings. There is a range of decisions that need to be made in the choice of an appropriate instrument, and because of the nature of screening itself, interpretations and conclusions are limited. One of the first decisions is also one of the most difficult ones to make. The clinician needs to decide just which aspects of cognition are suspected of being impaired. Although there is usually considerable correlation among different cognitive skills, this correlation tends to be disrupted under conditions of impairment. It is quite possible for conversational speech to be intact while short-term memory is severely impaired and vice versa. Choosing a screening instrument that is sensitive to memory skills when the person is suspected of having a cerebral vascular accident with expressive language impairment will not be a useful endeavor.

Broad-based screening requires that a range of impairments be considered. There are a few instruments that are sensitive to a broad range of types of impairment. Their sensitivity is derived from the fact that several cognitive skills are required for adequate performance. An example is the Digit Symbol subtest of the Wechsler Adult Intelligence Scale-III (WAIS-III). The Digit Symbol test requires eye-hand coordination, visual scanning, symbolic translation, and motor speed as well as learning skill. Impairment in any one of these areas may result in poor performance on the Digit Symbol test. Other examples of such instruments include Part B of the Trail Making test and the Category test of the Halstead-Reitan Neuropsychological Battery. These instruments tend to be sensitive to psychiatric disturbance and also have significant age-related effects. Interpretation of the results of such an instrument is problematic because poor performance can be the result of any number of impairments. However, this seeming drawback is also the instrument's strength because when the area of impairment is unknown, it is useful to have a single instrument that can detect impairment in any one of the suspected areas. The lack of specificity is not a tremendous shortcoming in

the context of screening because a positive result would be followed by more extensive evaluation in which the nature and extent of the impairment could be delineated more extensively.

To guide the psychologist in the screening procedure, there is little available in terms of training at the graduate level where the emphasis is on either specialized assessment methods (e.g., neuropsychological, marital, career) or traditional intellectual and personality methods. The psychologist who wishes to learn how to screen needs to seek out supervised experience in a medical setting such as might be available at the internship level and through continuing education opportunities. In addition, there is some published material. Two excellent book resources are *Clinical Neuropsychology: A Pocket Handbook* (Snyder & Nussbaum, 1998) and *Screening for Brain Impairment* (Berg et al., 1994).

Screening for Dementia

Dementia is broadly defined as any acquired cognitive impairment sufficient to disrupt occupational, social, or adaptive functioning. There can be many causes and different manifestations. However, the most frequent cognitive difficulty evidenced by dementia patients is memory impairment. Therefore, a brief memory screening procedure can be helpful in uncovering dementia. The Digit Span procedure is relatively useless in this situation and has limited utility in screening in general. The maximum span forward in the digit procedure is relatively impervious to acquired impairment until either the late stages of a progressive condition or the severe range of an injury. Suggested procedures for memory screening include the Hopkins Verbal Learning Test (Brandt, 1991), the Rey Auditory Verbal Learning Test (Schmidt, 2000), the Brief Visual Spatial Memory Test (Benedict, 1997), and the Benton Visual Retention Test (Sivan, 1992).

Folstein Mini Mental State Exam (MMSE)

The Folstein Mini Mental State Exam (MMSE) (Folstein, Folstein, & McHugh, 1975) is perhaps the most widely used (and some say the most widely abused) instrument for the quick assessment of cognitive status. The MMSE is nearly ubiquitous among physicians, especially those working in neurological or psychiatric settings. The MMSE screens for different cognitive functions, frequently using only one item for each construct (e.g., one item taps visual-spatial construction by asking the individual to copy a drawing of two overlapping pentagons). The MMSE is heavily weighted toward orientation questions, with 10 of a possible 30 points being directed at orientation to time, place, and date.

The MMSE has been criticized for producing too many false negatives, but part of the problem may exist in the use of suboptimal cut points. The degree of accuracy depends on the eventual diagnosis of the individual (Harper, Chacko, Kotik-Harper, & Kirby, 1992), something that is not usually known at the time of the screening. The MMSE, the Mattis Dementia Rating Scale, and the Neurobehavioral Cognitive Status Exam were found to be roughly equivalent in discriminating patients with Alzheimer's or vascular dementia from healthy elderly when optimal cut points were used rather than the cut points suggested in the literature. Because the MMSE takes less time to administer, it has an advantage over the other two tests. To increase the clinical utility of the MMSE, it would be helpful to use more extensive norms as well as norms that are sensitive to the differences associated with age and education. Grigoletto (1999) presented norms on 908 healthy Italian elderly persons. More data like this are needed.

Barbarotto, Cerri, Acerbi, Molinari, and Capatani (2000) reported data from a study of 27 patients with a variety of cognitive disorders. These authors concluded that the MMSE was less useful and less reliable when the total scores dip below 10 to 12 points. This is an important consideration in the overall use of the MMSE, but it might not be a substantial problem in a general medical setting where cognitive impairment is likely to be more subtle and total scores of 10 to 12 may be infrequent. Bidzan and Bidzan (2002) reported on a 5-year follow-up study involving 204 individuals over the age of 55 years. Eventually, 19 of these individuals were diagnosed with Alzheimer's dementia. The Folstein MMSE, the Cognitive subscale of the Alzheimer's Dementia Assessment Scale, the Instrumental Activity of Daily Living Scale, and the Physical Maintenance Scale were found to contribute to predicting eventual dementia, although a comparison among the instruments was not conclusive. There have been reported demographic effects on total scores of the MMSE, making it obvious that good normative information is necessary. Jones and colleagues (2002) presented normative data regarding the performance of community-dwelling elderly persons. Such data are very helpful in interpreting the scores of older persons.

Clock Drawing Test

The Clock Drawing Test (Freedman et al., 1994) is, as its name suggests, a test in which individuals are asked to draw a clock face with the hands set to "10 after 11." After the clock is drawn from command, a line-drawing model is provided for the same task. Adunsky, Flessig, Levenkrohn, Arad, and Noy (2002) reported that the Clock Drawing Test is roughly equivalent to the MMSE in identifying impairment. However, the greater variety of items in the MMSE may provide for a broad-based evaluation. The Clock Drawing Test has its greatest utility with the elderly.

Other Cognitive Screening Tests

There are several additional screening tests available for the psychologist. Some were designed specifically for screening, whereas others are part of larger test procedures or shortened from the original versions. The Trail Making test (especially Part B) of the Halstead-Reitan Neuropsychological Battery is very sensitive to any cognitive impairment. It is easy to administer and takes less than 10 minutes to complete. The disadvantages are that it is not very specific and that psychiatric conditions such as depression can affect it. The Digit Symbol subtest of the Wechsler Adult Intelligence Scale–Revised is the most sensitive of all the Wechsler subtests. The corresponding research on the WAIS-III has not yet been conducted, but the modification introduced by the WAIS-III will probably make it more specific as well as more sensitive. Somewhat longer alternatives include the Neurobehavioral Cognitive Status Exam (Northern California Neurobehavioral Group, 1988). This test includes subtests of attention, memory, construction, language skills, and practical problem solving, but the meaning of the various subtest profiles is unclear, and it is best to stick with the total score as an indicator of cognitive impairment.

INTELLECTUAL SCREENING

The utility of intelligence quotient (IQ) scores is largely related to academic planning and the suitability of the person for certain services available from the state. In certain cases, a physician may question the intelligence level of a patient where the documentation of mental retardation may make the patient eligible for government-reimbursed support services. In other instances, there may be questions about the capacity of the person to follow a complicated medical regimen or about the competency of the person to make decisions related to medical care. Screening assessment is insufficient to answer these questions. However, screening for intellectual capacity may guide the clinician in deciding whether to refer the person for a more complete evaluation. Although short forms of the Wechsler Adult Intelligence Scale are available (Kulas & Axelrod, 2002), and there is even a short form available from the publisher (Axelrod, 2002), it appears that a seven-subtest short form is as abbreviated as one can go and still expect reasonable reliability (Axelrod, Ryan, & Ward, 2001). Other options include the use of short tests and procedures that have been shown to correlate acceptably (but not optimally) with longer, more comprehensive intellectual exams such as the WAIS-III and the Stanford-Binet-IV. These short tests include the Slosson Intelligence Test, the Beta-III, and the Test of Nonverbal Intelligence-2.

The Slosson Intelligence Test is a short test based on the Stanford-Binet. Although short and easy to administer, it may have significant limitations in estimating IQ in the lower ranges (Kunen, Overall, & Salles, 1996). The Beta-III (Kellogg & Morton, 2001) is a set of five nonverbal procedures that can be administered in less than 15 minutes and give a reasonably culture-fair estimate of intelligence. The Test of Nonverbal Intelligence-2 (Brown, Sherbenou, & Johnsen, 1990) also provides a reasonable estimate of culture-fair intelligence by assessing visual abstraction skills. It does not have as many different types of tasks as the Beta-III, and it is somewhat shorter in administration time.

PSYCHIATRIC SCREENING

Affective problems are typically brought to the attention of primary care providers (PCPs) first. This is not sufficient unless the PCPs can accurately recognize emotional disorders. Wittchen and colleagues (2002) reported that in a study of more than 20,000 patients,

PCPs were able to reasonably well identify the presence of serious psychiatric disorders but were not as accurate in determining the actual diagnoses. The role of psychologists here is to act as a resource to whom PCPs can turn when emotional disorder is suspected to provide correct diagnoses and recommend appropriate treatments.

Derogatis and Dellapietra (1994) discussed screening for psychiatric disorders but did so largely from a perspective of the outpatient psychiatric clinic. They reviewed a variety of screening instruments, including the Symptom Checklist-90 Revised, the brief Psychiatric Rating Scale, the Center for Epidemiological Studies–Depression Scale (CES-D), the Self-Rating Depression Scale, and the Hamilton Anxiety and Depression scales.

The Beck Scales

The Beck Depression Inventory (BDI) (Beck & Steer, 1987) is one of the most widely used self-report instruments for the assessment of depression. Although its authors recommend the BDI as an instrument suitable for evaluating the level of depression as well as sensitive to changes in level, the BDI has great utility as a screening instrument. It is brief, consisting of 21 items that are endorsed at one of four levels. There is an even shorter form that consists of 13 items. There is considerable agreement between these two instruments (Reynolds & Gould, 1981), and the short form might be preferable when there are time constraints.

Beck and his associates developed other self-report instruments that have utility in a screening setting. The Beck Hopelessness Scale (Beck & Steer, 1988) taps the feelings of negative expectations about the future and global cognitions of despair. Although it has been found to be helpful in identifying suicidal risk in clinical populations, at least one study has questioned the utility of the instrument in a more general setting (Steed, 2001).

The Beck Anxiety Inventory (Beck & Steer, 1990) has 21 items that are endorsed on a scale from 1 to 3. It correlates well with other instruments to measure anxiety and is fairly accurate in identifying DSM-III (*Diagnostic and Statistical Manual of Mental Disorders,* third edition) (American Psychiatric Association, 1988) anxiety diagnoses. The Beck Scale for Suicide Ideation (Beck & Steer, 1991) has 19 items that can be helpful in quickly obtaining information regarding the possibility of suicide-related thoughts but that is not particularly accurate in predicting actual suicide attempts.

An even shorter assessment instrument is the Center for Epidemiological Studies–Depression Scale, with only 10 items. The CES-D has been used in multiple settings, including Puerto Rican primary care patients (Robison, Gruman, Gaztambide, & Blank, 2002). It has generally been found to have adequate sensitivity and specificity.

Often, the decision to screen is made after some suspicion regarding a general probability that a disorder might be present. For example, in cases where individuals complain of cardiac symptoms and describe histories of going to emergency rooms because of fear that myocardial infarcts were occurring, the clinicians might suspect a panic disorder, and screening efforts would be directed at this construct using an instrument such as the Autonomic Nervous System Questionnaire, a self-report instrument that contains only five items but has been found to have good sensitivity but low specificity (Stein et al., 1999).

PSYCHOLOGICAL ADAPTATION TO ILLNESS

Yet another feature of psychological screening is particular to the medical setting. The construct of interest here can be broadly defined as psychological reaction to the medical condition. For example, individuals may vary in the degree to which they develop maladaptive behaviors in response to the medical condition. The Illness Behaviour Questionnaire is an example of an instrument that can evaluate these responses, defined as the inappropriate experience of the state of health (Pilowsky, 1994). Unfortunately, attempts to shorten the test (cf. Chaturvedi, Bhandari, Beena, & Rao, 1996) have not been successful (Bond & Clark, 2002). Another example of an instrument that is somewhat shorter is the Health Anxiety Questionnaire (Lucock & Morley, 1996).

The Illness Behaviour Questionnaire has also been used in patients with chronic pain (Pilowsky & Katsikitis, 1994). But there are also instruments that are more directly focused on pain behaviors and cognitions, including the Pain Anxiety Symptoms Scale, the Fear Avoidance Beliefs Questionnaire, and the Fear of Pain Questionnaire (McCracken, Gross, Aikens, & Carnike, 1996).

SCREENING FOR SUBSTANCE ABUSE BEHAVIORS

Individuals who abuse alcohol and/or other substances are overrepresented in psychiatric settings and in general medical settings. A large number of health problems can arise from alcohol abuse, including disorders of the pancreas, stomach, liver, and intestines as well as hypertension. Obviously, a psychologist working in a medical setting will be exposed to alcoholism continuously. There is a need to screen for substance abuse behaviors on a regular basis.

One of the simplest measures that is useful in screening for alcohol abuse is known as the "CAGE" (cut, annoy, guilty, eye) questions. These questions are as follows:

- Have you ever tried to cut down on your alcohol consumption?
- Does it make you annoyed when people discuss your alcohol use?
- Have you ever felt guilty about your alcohol use?
- Did you ever need a drink as an eye opener?

As simple as this assessment method is, it is also fairly effective at identifying people who are likely to have been abusing alcohol (Bradley, Boyd-Wickizer, Powell, & Burman, 1998; Ewing, Bradley, & Burman, 1998; Nadeau, Guyon, & Bourgault, 1998). It has all the prerequisites of a screening procedure; it is short, simple, and easy to use and score. In addition, it is not generally intrusive and is acceptable to patients. It also possesses the shortcoming common to screening procedures, namely fairly high false positives.

Other procedures for screening for substance abuse behaviors include the Maryland Addiction Questionnaire (O'Donnell, DeSoto, & DeSoto, 1997) and the Michigan Alcoholism Screening Test (MAST) (Seltzer, 1971).

REPORT WRITING

Report writing for psychological consultation in a medical setting follows the same format of the consult notes written by medical practitioners. These reports are brief, concise, and pointed toward answering the referral question. Unfortunately, sometimes the referral question is not well articulated or thought out. In those instances, it would be helpful to have a brief conversation with the referral source to clarify the information needed. This conversation can serve to elucidate the current concerns as well as to educate the referral source as to future consultation requests. Psychologists sometimes have a tendency to "show and tell" all that went into an assessment. This is good and well when the recipient of the report is the patient's psychotherapist or when the psychologist's assessment skills are being assessed, but in a medical setting it is the bottom line that is most important. That is not to say that fine points or subtlety should be ignored. However, the concise report is the report that gets read and used.

Specialized Training and Skills Needed

The psychologist who desires to work in a medical setting should first receive supervised clinical training in that setting. Any good clinical psychology graduate training program will provide training in psychological assessment, but much of graduate training in assessment is conducted in an environment very different from the typical medical setting. Graduate psychology training in assessment typically takes place in the university clinic, where entire days might be spent administering psychological tests. Reports are written over the course of several weeks and are lengthy treatises.

In contrast, psychological assessment and screening in a general health care setting takes place at the bedside in a hospital or in an examining room in the outpatient clinic of the medical service. The psychologist is not on his or her home turf and must be prepared to conduct the assessment with whatever materials have been brought to the appointment. The report may include a dictated note that can be up to one page long, but an initial note should be on the chart or given to the referral agent immediately on finishing the administration of assessment instruments. For these reasons, traditional graduate training in assessment is necessary but insufficient. There must also be training in the context of a general health care setting. Interpretation needs

to be quick, and the psychologist is often called on to think on his or her feet.

The psychologist clinician should have familiarity with a range of medical disorders and know their basic pathophysiology, etiology, and treatment. For example, it would be important for the psychologist to know that hypertension can be associated with mildly impaired attention and memory and that some antihypertensive medications can cause side effects that mimic depression. In particular, the psychologist should be familiar with the types of patients and disorders seen in that clinic. Cultural sensitivity is a must. If the psychologist is not totally familiar with the particulars of that clinic, he or she should seek out learning experiences. The physician is a good resource for medical information regarding the disorders, and the nursing and support staff are good sources of information regarding the patients and their subculture.

OPTIMAL CHARACTERISTICS OF A SCREENING PROCEDURE

It would be useful to briefly reiterate the characteristics of a good screening test. It should be accurate. It should be sensitive to the construct under consideration. It should possess at least moderate specificity. It should have moderate positive predictive power and high negative predictive power. It could be administered by paraprofessional staff or self-administered, thereby meeting the final characteristic of using a minimal amount of professional time.

REFERENCES

Adunsky, A., Flessig, Y., Levenkrohn, S., Arad, M., & Noy, S. (2002). A comparative study of Mini-Mental test, Clock Drawing, and Cognitive FIM in evaluating functional outcome of elderly hip fracture patients. *Clinical Rehabilitation, 16,* 414–419.

American Psychiatric Association. (1988). *Diagnostic and statistical manual of mental disorders* (3rd ed.). Washington, DC: Author.

Axelrod, B. N. (2002). Validity of the Wechsler Abbreviated Scale of Intelligence and other very short forms of estimating intellectual functioning. *Assessment, 9,* 17–23.

Axelrod, B. N., Ryan, J. J., & Ward, C. L. (2001). Evaluation of seven-subtest short forms of the Wechsler Adult Intelligence Scale-III in a referred sample. *Archives of Clinical Neuropsychology, 16,* 1–8.

Barbarotto, R., Cerri, M., Acerbi, A., Molinari, S., & Capatani, E. (2000). Is the SIB or BNP better than MMSE in discriminating the cognitive performance of severely impaired elderly patients? *Archives of Clinical Neuropsychology, 15,* 21–29.

Beck, A. T., & Steer, R. A. (1987). *Manual for the Revised Beck Depression Inventory.* San Antonio, TX: Psychological Corporation.

Beck, A. T., & Steer, R. A. (1988). *Manual for the Beck Hopelessness Scale.* San Antonio, TX: Psychological Corporation.

Beck, A. T., & Steer, R. A. (1990). *Beck Scale Anxiety Inventory manual.* San Antonio, TX: Psychological Corporation.

Beck, A. T., & Steer, R. A. (1991). *Beck Scale for Suicidal Ideation: Manual.* San Antonio, TX: Psychological Corporation.

Benedict, R. H. B. (1997). *Brief Visuospatial Memory Test–Revised.* Odessa, FL: Psychological Assessment Resources.

Berg, R. A., Franzen, M. D., & Wedding, D. (1994). *Screening for brain impairment.* New York: Springer.

Bidzan, L., & Bidzan, M. (2002). The predictive values of MMSE, ADAS-cog, IADL, and PSMS as instruments for the diagnosis of pre-clinical phase of dementia of Alzheimer's type. *Archives of Psychiatry and Psychotherapy, 4,* 27–33.

Bond, M. J., & Clark, M. S. (2002). A comparison of alternative indices of abnormal illness behavior derived from the Illness Behaviour Questionnaire. *Psychology, Health, and Medicine, 7,* 203–213.

Bradley, K. A., Boyd-Wickizer, J., Powell, S. H., & Burman, M. L. (1998). Alcohol screening questionnaires in women: A critical review. *Journal of the American Medical Association, 280,* 166–171.

Brandt, J. (1991). The Hopkins Verbal Learning Test: Development of new memory test with six alternate forms. *The Clinical Neuropsychologist, 5,* 125–142.

Brown, L., Sherbenou, R. J., & Johnsen, S. K. (1990). *Test of Nonverbal Intelligence–2nd edition.* Austin, TX: Pro-Ed.

Chaturvedi, S. K., Bhandari, S., Beena, M. B., & Rao, S. (1996). Screening for abnormal illness behaviour. *Psychopathology, 29,* 325–330.

Derogatis, L. R., & Dellapietra, L. (1994). Psychological tests in screening for psychiatric disorder. In M. E. Maruish (Ed.), *The use of psychological testing in screening for psychiatric disorder* (pp. 22–54). Hillsdale, NJ: Lawrence Erlbaum.

Ewing, J. A., Bradley, K. A., & Burman, M. L. (1998). Screening for alcoholism using CAGE. *Journal of the American Medical Association, 280,* 1904.

Folstein, M. E., Folstein, S. E., & McHugh, P. R. (1975). "Mini Mental State": A practical method for grading the cognitive state of patients for the clinician. *Journal of Psychiatric Research, 12,* 189–198.

Freedman, M., Leach, L., Kaplan, E., Winocur, G., Shulman, K., & Delis, D. (1994). *Clock drawing: A neuropsychological analysis.* New York: Oxford University Press.

Grigoletto, F. (1999). Norms for the Mini-Mental State Examination in a healthy population. *Neurology, 53,* 315–320.

Harper, R. G., Chacko, R. C., Kotik-Harper, D., & Kirby, H. B. (1992). Comparison of two cognitive screening measures for efficacy in differentiating dementia from depression in a geriatric inpatient population. *Journal of Neuropsychiatry and Clinical Neurosciences, 4,* 179–184.

Jones, T. G., Schinka, J. A., Vanderploeg, R. D., Small, B. J., Graves, A. B., & Mortimer, J. A. (2002). 3MS normative information for the elderly. *Archives of Clinical Neuropsychology, 17,* 171–177.

Kellogg, C. E., & Morton, N. W. (2001). *Beta III manual.* San Antonio, TX: Psychological Corporation.

Kulas, J. F., & Axelrod, B. N. (2002). Comparison of seven-subtest and Satz-Mogel short forms of the WAIS-III. *Journal of Clinical Psychology, 58,* 773–782.

Kunen, S., Overall, S., & Salles, C. (1996). Concurrent validity study of the Slosson Intelligence–Revised in mental retardation testing. *Mental Retardation, 34,* 380–386.

Lucock, M. P., & Morley, S. (1996). The Health Anxiety Questionnaire. *British Journal of Health Psychology, 1,* 137–150.

McCracken, L. M., Gross, R. T., Aikens, J., & Carnike, C. L. M., Jr. (1996). The assessment of fear and anxiety in persons with chronic pain: A comparison of instruments. *Behaviour Research and Therapy, 34,* 927–933.

Nadeau, L., Guyon, L., & Bourgault, C. (1998). Heavy drinkers in the general population: Comparison of two measures. *Addiction Research, 6,* 165–187.

Northern California Neurobehavioral Group. (1988). *Manual for the Neurobehavioral Cognitive Status Examination.* Fairfax, CA: Author.

O'Donnell, W. E., DeSoto, C. B., & DeSoto, J. L. (1997). *Maryland Addictions Questionnaire.* Los Angeles: Western Psychological Services.

Pilowsky, I. (1994). Abnormal illness behaviour: A 25th anniversary review. *Australian and New Zealand Journal of Psychiatry, 28,* 566–573.

Pilowsky, I., & Katsikitis, M. (1994). A classification of illness behaviour in pain clinic patients. *Pain, 57,* 91–94.

Reynolds, W. M., & Gould, J. W. (1981). A psychometric investigation of the standard and short forms of the Beck Depression Inventory. *Journal of Consulting and Clinical Psychology, 49,* 306–307.

Robison, J., Gruman, C., Gaztambide, S., & Blank, K. (2002). Screening for depression in middle-aged and older Puerto Rican primary care patients. *Journal of Gerontology: Biological Sciences and Medical Science, 57,* M308–M314.

Schmidt, M. (2000). *The Rey Auditory Verbal Learning Test manual.* Odessa, FL: Psychological Asssessment Resources.

Seltzer, M. L. (1971). The Michigan Alcoholism Screening Test: The quest for a new diagnostic instrument. *American Journal of Psychiatry, 127,* 117–126.

Sivan, A. B. (1992). *The Benton Visual Retention Test–Revised* (5th ed.). New York: Psychological Corporation.

Snyder, P. J., & Nussbaum, P. D. (1998). *Clinical neuropsychology: A pocket handbook.* Washington, DC: American Psychological Association.

Steed, L. (2001). Further validity and reliability evidence for Beck Hopelessness Scale. *Educational and Psychological Measurement, 61,* 303–316.

Stein, M. B., Roy-Byrne, P. P., McQuaid, J. R., Laffaye, C., Russo, J., McCahill, M. E., Katon, W., Craske, M., Bystritsky, A., & Sherbourne, C. D. (1999). Development of a brief diagnostic screen for panic disorder in primary care. *Psychosomatic Medicine, 61,* 359–364.

Wittchen, H-U., Kessler, R. C., Beesdo, K., Krouse, P., Hoefler, M., & Hoyer, J. (2002). Generalized anxiety and depression in primary care: Prevalence, recognition, and management. *Journal of Clinical Psychiatry, 63,* 24–34.

CHAPTER 3

Working With a Multidisciplinary Staff

Helen R. Winefield and Anna Chur-Hansen

There are unique problems for clinical health psychologists in multidisciplinary settings compared with those faced by psychologists working in more traditional settings such as mental health clinics and private practice. These include professional isolation and the difficulties of communication with other professionals trained with different vocabularies and conceptual frameworks, status conflicts, and the risks of role ambiguity among the treatment team members as well as public confusion over roles affecting the expectations of patients/clients. Jones and Salmon (2001) consider "multidisciplinary" as two or more professional groups with parallel but independent goals, whereas "interprofessional" is the preferred term for situations where professionals from different backgrounds work together to achieve collaboration. In this chapter, however, these two terms are not strictly separated.

A number of authors have identified education at undergraduate and postgraduate levels as the linchpin for successful interprofessional practice. The United States, the United Kingdom, and Scandinavia all have in place a formalized system of policies that promote interprofessional agendas (Jones & Salmon, 2001), but this is not the case in Australia, even though public sector mental health services are most often provided by multidisciplinary teams, including psychologists (Australian Department of Health and Aged Care, 2000; Herrman, Trauer, Warnock, & Professional Liaison Committee [Australia] Project Team, 2002).

It is somewhat ironic that many of the interpretations and analyses of teamwork, decision making, and interprofessional relations are based on models from social and cognitive psychology, yet psychology as a profession is often not represented. In terms of a scientist-practitioner model, it appears that the science of psychology is used in an interdisciplinary way more often than are the practitioner aspects of the discipline. Because of this dearth of specific information, this chapter generalizes principles from studies involving a range of health care professions.

The traditional sociological wisdom that professions are self-interested groups divided by different identities, statuses, and autonomies was rejected by Hudson (2002) as pessimistic and problematic. He argued that members of one profession may have more in common with members of a different profession than with members of their own profession and that the promotion of professional values of trust and service to users can form the basis of interprofessional partnership. He further proposed that socialization to an immediate work group can override professional or hierarchical differences among staff, that professionals and bureaucracies can join forces in a collective effort to achieve their goals, and that effective interprofessional working can lead to more effective service delivery and user outcomes. Hudson's vision is an enticing one, but to consider strategies to move toward his ideal, we first need to consider the benefits and obstacles of multidisciplinary health care. Advantages that have been identified include continuity of care for the patient, a wider range of skills and talents, greater choice for the patients in choosing a practitioner from the preferred gender, cultural/language background or sexual orientation (Balon, 1999), a more holistic approach to management, and (for the coworkers) more emotional and professional support as well as a more satisfying work environment and ethic (Cook, Gerrish, & Clarke, 2001).

We need to specify relevant outcomes to assess the success of multidisciplinary staff teams as opposed to other sorts of staff teams. The following seem the most important: (a) job satisfaction and consequent physical and psychological well-being for the clinical health psychologists and the other health professionals who work together as well as better staff morale, retention, and productivity (Barnes, Carpenter, & Bailey, 2000); (b) improved cost-effectiveness of service delivery such as better use of the skills and knowledge of professionals with diverse backgrounds, higher quality work performance, and fewer mistakes and errors in diagnosis and treatment; and (c) greater satisfaction with services for the clients as well as improved mental and physical health, including quality of life and functional capabilities.

HISTORICAL ISSUES

The various health disciplines likely to be working together with psychologists in health care settings include physicians, psychiatrists, and other medical specialists; nurses; social workers; occupational therapists; physiotherapists; and other allied health professionals such as podiatrists, audiologists, speech pathologists, and nutritionists. The collaboration between psychologists and medical practitioners is reported more fully in the psychological literature than is the collaboration between psychologists and other health care professionals. Whatever the reason for that, the sparse literature about nurse-psychologist collaboration or social worker-psychologist collaboration deserves augmentation through careful research investigations. The collaboration among the other disciplinary groups, excluding psychology, must be left for books about integrated care of those sorts (e.g., medicine with nursing, social work with physiotherapy). Other allied health professions may have a less ambiguous relationship with medicine than does psychology because they are more clearly identified as providers of auxiliary services. In contrast, psychology defines itself as a science as well as a health care profession.

Much of what follows focuses primarily on effective collaboration between psychologists and medical professionals, whether specialists (principally psychiatrists) or those providing primary care. But several authors have drawn attention to the need for psychologists to learn to collaborate with other nonmedical health professions, pointing out, for example, the key role of nurses, especially in hospital care. It is clear that psychologists may need to develop effective models for working with mental health-trained nurses also in primary care. There are many more nurses than psychologists and will be for the foreseeable future, and nurses seem likely to have important functions to provide basic supportive community care.

Consultation-liaison psychiatry is based on the psychosomatic idea of health and disease arising from an interaction of biological, psychological, and social factors. Lipowski (1967) defined consultation-liaison psychiatry as the subspecialty of psychiatry concerned with clinical service, teaching, and research in nonpsychiatric health care settings. The parallel development in psychology has been that of the subspecialty of clinical health psychology (Belar & Deardorff, 1995). As explained by Horne,

> The clinical psychologist is an expert in the application of clinical assessment and treatment skills to change an individual's maladaptive behavior, thoughts, and emotions. Health psychology provides an expanding knowledge base regarding psychological factors in health and illness within a biological and sociological context. The clinical health psychologist draws on expertise from both clinical and health psychology to work as a practitioner in a medical/health care setting. (Strain & Horne, 2001, p. 111)

Horne then outlined the key issues particularly well managed by psychologists, including (a) clinician-patient communication, (b) factors in adherence to treatment, (c) dealing with medical anxieties and phobias in patients and clinicians, and (d) preparing patients for invasive and surgical procedures (Strain & Horne, 2001).

Disadvantages of interprofessional practice between psychologists and psychiatrists have been identified, including factors such as the following:

- Perceptions by some members of the medical profession that shared care is unethical
- An unwillingness by some psychiatrists and psychologists to let go of ideological prejudices

- A concern that psychologists might not have sufficient expertise to deal with serious mental health problems
- Differences in training between psychiatrists and psychologists, in particular the biological bent of the former against the behavioral bent of the latter (Goldsmith, Paris, & Riba, 1999)
- A lack of knowledge about each other's roles and capabilities (Neal & Calarco, 1999)
- Dilution of psychologists' responsibility for patients
- The potential for personality clashes, compounded by professional differences
- The complexity of coordinating and arranging teamwork (Cook et al., 2001)

In a report on the roles and relationships of psychiatrists and other service providers, Herrman and colleagues (2002) identified five main obstacles to effective teamwork: (a) ambiguity or conflict over roles, with a common assumption in practice and in the literature that the psychiatrist or medical professional is the team leader who allocates roles and duties, with the other professionals viewed as "physician extenders" (Schuster, Kern, Kane, & Nettleman, 1994); (b) conflict and confusion over leadership, whereby the psychiatrist usually assumes leadership on the basis of superior knowledge and training; (c) differing understandings of responsibility and accountability, with psychiatrists sometimes hesitating to work in teams because they are concerned that they may be held responsible for other professionals' errors (which in fact is not the case); (d) interprofessional misperceptions related to differences in skills and training, values, culture, socialization, and cognitive style; and (e) differing rewards among professions, with power, status, and income all playing a role. Gilbert and colleagues (2000) noted that these differences in rewards across professions may also become confounded with gender disparities across professions.

Nicholas and Wright (2001), in discussing collaborative work by psychologists and psychiatrists in pain clinics, commented that mostly the question of who provides which service should be decided on the grounds of who can do it best, not a priori on the grounds of discipline. However, as they noted, the biomedical background of psychiatrists makes them better able to use psychotropic medications and to assess how these may interact with other medical aspects of the patient's condition, whereas psychologists are usually better able to use cognitive and behavioral interventions for individuals and groups and have more expertise in the development and use of psychometric measures. This situation is not static. Recently, some U.S. psychologists have gained the right to prescribe psychotropic drugs despite intense resistance to this innovation by psychiatrists—and some psychologists (Goode, 2002).

There are historical influences on the expectations of each profession regarding its roles in patient care, and in different amounts of emphasis on the scientific evidence base and how to evaluate the scientific literature and whether one is expected to contribute to it. Each profession probably has a different view of where it stands on various "skills pyramid" conceptualizations. The Australian Psychological Society (2000), for example, developed a model of the levels of expertise in mental health care that has specialized clinical psychologists at the top level, dealing with complex cases, innovations to treatment, and evaluations of effectiveness. At the bottom level are generic counselors who, after being trained by psychologists, offer first-line help to those in need and can recognize the need to refer upward as appropriate. The middle level of skill is characterized by the delivery of interventions (after some training) such as assertive therapy, couples therapy, and manualized cognitive-behavioral therapy. The middle level might be where medical practitioners with appropriate extra training would best fit, although in normal circumstances many of them will not have the time or interest to

undergo the necessary extra training, thereby bolstering the argument for more public access to psychologists.

Other historical (and some continuing) influences include the reimbursement schedules via government and other third-party payers, insurers, and managed care organizations. In Australia, the universal public health insurance does not include payment for psychologist services; it includes payment only for medically qualified practitioners (including, of course, psychiatrists). Accordingly, private practitioner psychologists are very limited in what proportion of the population can afford their services. A recent governmental policy innovation, the Better Outcomes for Mental Health initiative, implies more extensive possible roles for psychologists in two ways, although their involvement is not stated explicitly. One is that primary care physicians, or general practitioners, will need training in mental health care to qualify for higher rebates for the longer consultations that this form of treatment requires. The other is that general practitioners may gain discretionary government funding to pay for specialist mental health care for their patients, and if they hire psychologists to provide this care, they will overcome the financial burden for patients that seeing a psychologist currently imposes.

In Britain, all clinical psychologists are employed by the publicly funded National Health Service and work alongside doctors and other health professionals, again at the discretion of the general practitioners who direct the spending of government funds for health care. The fact that psychologists are salaried rather than private practitioners, of course, increases their accessibility to the public enormously.

In the United States, the managed care movement has created much consternation for mental health workers who were not accustomed to concepts of accountability and cost-effectiveness (Todd, 1994). However, its focus on brief, evidence-based, problem-focused treatments sits well with the usual mode of psychological intervention in medical settings. Conversely, psychologists' familiarity with empirically supported treatments is entirely compatible with medicine's current emphasis on evidence-based practice.

SPECIALIZED SKILLS NEEDED FOR MULTIDISCIPLINARY WORK IN HEALTH SETTINGS

Although medical patients are likely to show high rates of anxiety, depression, and other affective and cognitive pathologies, psychologists and other clinicians working in medical settings need a thorough understanding of normal psychosocial development, stress and coping, and behavioral health issues. In our society that retains dualistic mind-body concepts, the effort to bridge health and mental health may always be challenging. As Belar, Paoletti, and Jordan (2001) pointed out, psychologists and psychiatrists in medical settings act as bridges between their core disciplines and the rest of health care, being mainstream in neither. They have to accept a consultative role, and they also need to become comfortable in working with patients who are sick, disabled, disfigured, injured, or even dying. This is despite the possibility that a desire to avoid contact with illness and death might have been a motivating factor for some health professionals to be drawn to psychology or psychiatry.

Beyond patient care, there are large areas of interprofessional collaboration where the specific training of the psychology graduate may enhance the professional effectiveness and job satisfaction of health coworkers. The scientist-practitioner model equips psychologists to understand empirical evidence and interpret the literature critically; this skill is not emphasized in the training of many other health professionals. The model may assist members of a health care team to monitor their own practice and its outcomes in a scientific way, to keep useful records of the process and results of care, to design controlled studies of innovative treatments, and to communicate with others through the professional literature. One recent step in this direction has been the acknowledgment that the effort to be scientific about practice need not be abandoned if the "gold standard" multisite randomized control trial is impractical to undertake. Psychology has a history of deriving valid and reliable conclusions from the small-sample research study (Morgan & Morgan, 2001; Radley & Chamberlain, 2001). This methodological expertise is newly valued, particularly when managed care demands maximum accountability and the identification and use of the most cost-effective treatment plan.

Another contribution that psychologists may be able to offer their professional colleagues is their understanding of systemic factors in the workplace that may facilitate or impede effective delivery of care. Specifically, jobs in health care are often high in the demands they make on workers (e.g., workload, responsibility, complexity). Therefore, organizational theories such as the demand–control–support model (Johnson & Hall, 1988) predict that the levels of control and autonomy that workers have, and the supportiveness of coworkers and supervisors, will have a major impact on worker satisfaction, retention, and even quality of work performance (Dollard, Winefield, Winefield, & De Yonge, 2000; Judge, Thoresen, Bono, & Patton, 2001; Winefield, 2003). Although risk management in health care is a huge and specialized field that must take account of the multiple pathways through which mistakes and adverse events may occur, psychologists' educational background may uniquely fit them to see the management and job design issues behind these and other work stressors and to suggest sustainable remedies (Barach & Small, 2000; Griffiths, Randall, Santos, & Cox, 2003; Jones et al., 1988).

Skills Needed for Hospital Settings

Milgrom, Burrows, and Schwartz (2001) provided a checklist for new psychologists adapting to work in medical settings. Items include being brief and clear in communication, respecting the organizational culture and unwritten rules of conduct, becoming familiar with medical procedures and drugs as well as their side effects, being prepared to admit ignorance and ask for advice, and adopting a long-term approach to educate colleagues over time. For example, it will be necessary to attend and participate in team meetings, however time-consuming this seems, in the interest of increasing familiarity and confidence among team members.

Nicholas and Wright (2001) described the gradual replacement of "multidisciplinary" health care teams (headed by physicians) with "interdisciplinary" teams (led by individuals who can coordinate the collaboratively agreed-on treatment plan and manage the team dynamics). These are bound to be tense occasionally as people with different conceptual frameworks try to deal effectively with highly distressed and complex patients. It is essential, according to Nicholas and Wright, that team members agree on the treatment model they are using and that mechanisms exist for them to cope with disagreements and continue supporting each other.

Milgrom and colleagues (2001) noted that nurses often have a unique role to observe patients, their responses to treatment, and their family interactions on a daily basis, making nurses key members of multidisciplinary teams. Doctors may seem pressed for time but should not be excluded from consideration of the psychosocial aspects of patient care. Such teams have a complex and largely unspoken hierarchy of status roles and expectations that are bound to cause some conflict. Psychologists and psychiatrists, with their training in interpersonal relations, should be in a good position to keep the systemic perspective in mind and to facilitate the resolution of these conflicts. Mutual respect and understanding among team members is vital for the team to function effectively. Dual relationships increase the risk of exploiting the power differences between therapists and patients, confidentiality can raise difficulties, and all practitioners have a responsibility to continually update their own professional learning. Team approaches increase the possibility that responsibility for patient care may become diffused (Belar et al., 2001), so it becomes very important to maintain alertness to follow-up and to appropriate documentation of cases.

At the more preventive health promotional level, Michie (1998) wrote about consultancy or targeted research undertaken at the request of another health professional. The examples she cited came from requests from surgeons, physiotherapists, nurses, occupational health officers, medical educators, and primary health care visitors and nurses. She commented on the empathy and tact, in addition to the communication skills and research design expertise, needed by consultant psychologists. She also advocated that psychologists in this role act collectively and strive to avoid "the trap of the individualism that has sometimes been associated with psychologists" (p. 167). Members of the College of Health Psychologists of the Australian Psychological Society are also trained in public health psychology and health promotion. Very few physicians, with the possible exception of epidemiologists and public health specialists (who rarely work directly with patients in delivery of care settings), have this perspective, and neither do nurses or other allied health professionals.

Skills Needed for Primary Health Care

All of this is relevant to psychologists working in multidisciplinary primary care settings, although these settings have their own special characteristics as well and in fact represent one of the most exciting new directions for applied health psychology at the current time. With the unresolved difficulties of providing mental health care through a separate system that is often parallel but inferior in resources to the "physical" health system, countries such as Britain and Australia are actively exploring the value to consumers of making treatment for psychological difficulties and dysfunctions available where the public is—in primary health care.

In Australia, 82% of the population is likely to visit a primary health care physician (general practitioner) each year. Although about one of five adults will experience a psychological problem sufficient to interfere significantly with daily life and function (Andrews, Hall, Teesson, & Henderson, 1999), only a minority of those receive any mental health treatment, and when they do it is unlikely to be from a mental health specialist. However, general practitioners are poor at both detecting and treating high-prevalence psychological disorders such as anxiety, depression, and substance abuse.

Untreated anxiety disorders are associated with substantial health care costs, including unnecessary ambulance trips, hospital emergency department presentations, diagnostic procedures such as ECGs (electrocardiograms), and frequent use of primary health services. Greenberg and colleagues (1999) estimated the annual cost of anxiety disorders, adjusted for demographic factors and comorbid psychiatric conditions, to be U.S. $1,542 per sufferer in 1990, with 54% of the total costs being for nonpsychiatric medical care. The human and social costs of anxiety disorders are also substantial (Mendlowicz & Stein, 2000). Psychological interventions have been demonstrated to be successful treatments for a range of conditions, including anxiety and depression (Chambless & Hollon, 1998; Chambless & Ollendick, 2001). In addition, psychological interventions have been shown to increase the well-being and decrease the health care use of a group of patients generally regarded as problematic and frustrating in primary care, namely those individuals with undiagnosable physical symptoms and high rates of consultation, sometimes referred to as somatizers. Many of these patients are likely to be suffering from anxiety or depression (cf. McLeod, Budd, & McClelland, 1997).

Bray and Rogers (1997) provided some valuable examples of the differences in professional culture and practices between clinical psychology (focused on understanding and questioning) and primary health care (focused on fixing problems). The number of patients seen per day, speed of access to referral sources, and expectations about the confidentiality of patient records all vary greatly, as do reimbursement opportunities. Practical tips about how a doctor can manage referrals to a therapist center on demonstrating the collaborative nature of the care, making it clear that the therapist will provide specialist help while the doctor continues to provide other medical care, with a shared first consultation in the doctor's office for resistant patients. Physical proximity of the providers and regular settings for contact seem crucial to the maintenance of the collaboration between practitioners, just as physical sharing of training experiences is crucial to their initial entry into the collaboration. Openness to the emotional impact of the work (especially in difficult cases) and the chance to discuss such issues within the team may help the professionals to prevent burnout and secondary trauma. Being able to give each other feedback and support creates a cohesive team that is greater than the sum of its parts (McDaniel & Campbell, 1997).

Stulp deGroot, Price, and Leslie (1998) reported their experiences in developing a collaborative primary health care service for more than 10,000 patients using primary care physicians (PCPs) and mental health clinicians (MHCs). They carefully documented this process and were able to derive the following conclusions about how to make the project successful. First, the MHCs had to learn to listen and ask questions in a way that helped the PCPs to sort things out for themselves rather than to give them answers to their questions. Second, collaboration involves the whole system—including office staff, family members, case managers, and so on—and not just the PCPs and MHCs. Third, frequent and timely communication is essential in the various forms of face-to-face hallway conversations, written chart notes, voice messages, e-mails, and responses to pages. Fourth, roles should stay flexible and include attention to the mental health needs of the staff. Fifth, collaboration can work best when the process is informal. Sixth, not everyone engages in the collaborative process at the same rate.

TRAINING TO WORK IN MULTIDISCIPLINARY HEALTH CARE SETTINGS

In what follows, it is assumed that the specifically health psychology content of the health psychologist's training and education has been thoroughly mastered. It must contain, as we have seen, a comprehensive review of the knowledge base in psychology as applied to health and illness, measurement, research design, and an understanding of health service delivery systems. Hopefully but less predictably, the other health professionals with whom the psychologist will end up working conjointly will also have received at least basic training in the principles of human behavior and how to study it scientifically (cf. Winefield, 1998). This section focuses specifically on methods to facilitate effective collaborative work shared by health professionals with multidisciplinary backgrounds.

McDaniel and Campbell (1997) described in detail the training experiences that facilitate collaborative care by psychologists and physicians. First and foremost, members of each

discipline must experience shared training. Here they learn about each other's knowledge bases, conceptual frameworks, and expectations of both patients and how the health system operates. The frequently negative stereotypes that physical and psychological health professionals have of each other need to be discussed and set in the context of the different professional cultures and working styles.

In the United States, interprofessional collaboration is facilitated by the Interdisciplinary Professional Education Collaborative, a body that stresses the need to incorporate interprofessional expectations and skills into education (Gelmon, White, Carlson, & Norman, 2000). The collaborative has identified some of the obstacles to achieving integration of professions at the training level. Historically, there has been reluctance by staff from the different health science disciplines to interact with one another in teaching as well as in the professional sense (Gilbert et al., 2000). Although psychologists are often employed within medical schools, their role within the teaching of medicine and medical students tends to be in the role of scientists rather than practitioners. Psychology students do not, as a rule, train next to medical students in the clinical components of their courses as fellow apprentices.

A further difficulty is the method of teaching that is commonly employed at universities. Didactic teaching through lectures, where students sit passively in the classroom, will not result in better collaboration between professionals (Gelmon et al., 2000). Hilton and Morris (2001) argued that the ideal learning environment for developing skills for collaborative practice is the clinical setting, where learning is experiential and in context. They stressed that in addition to students being on placements, successful implementation requires collaboration between clinicians and academics, with the former sharing their practice philosophies and the latter promoting appropriate teaching and learning principles. Because most clinicians are trained not as educators but rather as supervisors, academics have an essential support role. The responsibility of students is also stressed; during clinical placements, more senior students should be responsible for the coordination of an aspect of patient care within the team. Some educators have attempted to use simulated placements (Fallsberg & Hammar, 2000) or 2-day workshops (Gilbert et al., 2000) instead of real clinical placements using an existing authentic team due to the number of difficulties involved in arranging such placements. To date, we have no empirical studies to provide us with information about the relative merits and weaknesses of particular teaching approaches. However, Hilton and Morris (2001) are convinced that encouraging students to collaborate with other professionals in a real setting with experiential learning is educationally beneficial in terms of outcome. Such student experiences are likely to result in graduates who are able to function as team members, with more positive attitudes, abilities in collaborative problem solving, and better professional development.

In situations where didactic lectures are the most appropriate, students from across different disciplines could be taught together, where the same base knowledge is required. Problem-based learning curricula in medicine work on the premise that there are no departmental or discipline boundaries (Harden, Davis, & Crosby, 1997). Therefore, the problem-based philosophy lends itself easily to the incorporation of interprofessional collaboration in training. Rather than groups of eight medical students, groups composed of students across a range of health professions would be possible. This ambitious suggestion would require a major shift in university structures. Indeed, the Interdisciplinary Professional Education Collaborative (Gilbert et al., 2000) suggested that higher education institutions offer many barriers to implementation of change that would foster interprofessionalism. It listed as major challenges a lack of

institutional reward structures for faculty engaged in curriculum improvement, traditions of inflexibility and fear of the innovative, and a resistance to community-based and project learning. Few interprofessional courses have been incorporated into curricula, with time, expense, funding, cooperation, and coordination difficulties hampering implementation (Gilbert et al., 2000).

Multidisciplinary work is highly politicized and complex, so students of professions where teamwork will be required need "policy acumen" (Jones & Salmon, 2001, p. 67), which should be included as part of their education. Psychologists, like all health care professionals, need an understanding of the social, political, and economic frameworks around which policies that affect their work are structured, and curricula need to address this. Such knowledge will encourage proactive responses to social policy so as to benefit both the individual practitioner and the wider professional body. Without such knowledge, there may be a tendency to focus on profession-centered arguments and perceptions that are antithetical to interprofessionalism.

McDaniel, Hargrove, Belar, Schroeder, and Freeman (in press) prepared a detailed curriculum for the education of psychologists to practice and research in primary health care settings. For example, in the "professional issues" module, they suggested the following student exercises that neatly demonstrate some of the necessary skills:

1. Construct a strategy for seeking reimbursement in your community for psychoeducational groups and collaborative sessions (i.e., sessions for which there is more than one clinician present).

2. Write a justification to an insurance company for a child to be treated by a psychologist for attention deficit hyperactivity disorder.

3. Write a one-page advocacy statement for inclusion of psychological services in

primary care for submission to your state legislature.

This training needs to be carried out jointly by members of the disciplines concerned who model a respectful partnership, shared care, and shared inquiry.

Students need to learn which sorts of problems need which kind of professional expertise. In their article on teaching health care professionals to collaborate, McDaniel and Campbell (1997) urged primary care doctors to use counseling skills for simple and mild problems and to use collaboration with a therapist for more complex problems such as nonadherence, somatization, significant anxiety or depression, and coping with terminal illness. In addition, these authors distinguished "red flag" problems that demand collaboration and referral, including psychosis, physical or sexual abuse, previous treatment failure, and nonresponse to three or four counseling sessions with the primary care physician.

In the literature about training health professionals to enhance their capacity for later multidisciplinary work, it is noteworthy that although authors are quite often able to report on long experiences with large numbers of students and practitioners, there are very few reports of controlled studies. Yet especially to psychologists with their awareness of methodological issues in discovering new knowledge, it is a concern that the powerful nonspecific effects of having enthusiastic, highly committed faculty offering innovative programs with determination to seek student feedback could engender a corresponding student enthusiasm for the training method that was independent of other outcomes. It is only by random allocation of students to treatment and control groups (including placebo control groups) that the highest standards of scientific evidence could be attained. Such standards are probably unreachable in most educational settings.

There is a body of interesting qualitative literature emerging into the efficacy of teamwork and interprofessionalism, but there is a lack of hard evidence to demonstrate the effectiveness of interprofessional training across the board and there is a need for quantitative, large-scale, longitudinal evaluation studies (Jones & Salmon, 2001). Hammick, Barr, Freeth, Koppel, and Reeves (2002) have conducted a substantial systematic review of evaluations of interprofessional education seeking evidence linking professional education to a change in either professional practice or patient care, but their work has not yet been published. In educating students about interprofessionalism, the users of services are also stakeholders, so their views must be solicited and taken into account in any evaluation.

A major methodological consideration of any evaluation of interprofessional training or practice is that studies conducted in one location might not necessarily be meaningfully compared cross-culturally because cultural factors can affect the strategies used. For example, Skjørshammer (2001), in his study on interprofessional negotiations in a Norwegian hospital, suggested that the high incidence of avoidance to allay conflict may reflect a cultural norm of evasion rather than a generalizable finding. Jones and Salmon (2001) also pointed out that different issues are pertinent, depending on the setting, even within the same culture. The results of research into interprofessional training and practice will be difficult to generalize across different situations and teams due to the considerable variations encountered in educational institutions and team composition as well as to cross-cultural differences.

There are even greater difficulties of demonstrating better quality of health care work in multidisciplinary settings compared with the other models such as that of parallel work by different professions. The problems hinge mostly on the unsolved task of measuring quality of health care work. Beyond patient satisfaction, other measures might be the job satisfaction of the health care providers and the numbers of patients cured or returned to work or normal activities. But to demonstrate the cost-effectiveness in economic terms that are meaningful to accountants and shareholders is more challenging. Certainly, one requirement would be a way in which to capture the entire health system utilization costs for patients treated with the two models of professional care (multidisciplinary and parallel).

SUMMARY

This chapter has reviewed some of the potential hazards and advantages for clinical health psychologists of working with colleagues who have multidisciplinary backgrounds. This challenge is not unique to medical settings, but in these highly responsible and complex workplaces and in caring for very vulnerable patients, the need to develop high-quality work practices is acute and unarguable. Further careful research is still required to establish the details of the most effective models for health care shared among providers from diverse professions, but this chapter focused on how psychologists may extract the maximum benefit from this arrangement for their clients, their coworkers, and themselves.

The history of interprofessional relationships in health care has included suspicion, stereotyping, and jealousy. Nonetheless, there seems to be agreement among experienced practitioners that these negatives can be overcome by mutual respect and a focus on the common goal of improved patient well-being. This chapter suggested that psychologists' particular contributions to multidisciplinary teams, beyond their specific expertise in understanding patient behaviors, can lie in reducing conflict within mixed groups, translating scientific evidence for colleagues, and monitoring the stressfulness of the work environment.

To gain acceptance in multidisciplinary hospital and primary care settings, psychologists need to learn about these settings' prevailing cultures and acquire the skills needed to negotiate them effectively. There is now a growing literature about how to do this, although it is a descriptive literature rather than an experimental one. A fundamental recommendation about shared training opportunities to teach such skills has often proved to be too difficult to test in practice. There are likely to be many opportunities for psychologists to add to the current scientific literature and to use this chapter's findings constructively to improve the contribution of psychologist practitioners within multidisciplinary health care teams as well as to enhance the functioning of such teams.

REFERENCES

Andrews, G., Hall, W., Teesson, M., & Henderson, S. (1999). *The mental health of Australians.* Canberra, Australia: Commonwealth Department of Health and Aged Care, Mental Health Branch.

Australian Department of Health and Aged Care. (2000). *Toward a national approach to information sharing in mental health crisis situations* (Expert Advisory Committee on Information Sharing in Mental Health Crisis Situations report). Canberra, Australia: Author.

Australian Psychological Society. (2000). *The role of psychological treatments in managing high prevalence mental health disorders.* Information statement. (Available on request from natloff@psychsociety.com.au)

Balon, R. (1999). Positive aspects of collaborative treatment. In M. B. Riba & R. Balon (Eds.), *Psychopharmacology and psychotherapy: A collaborative approach* (pp. 1–31). Washington, DC: American Psychiatric Press.

Barach, P., & Small, S. D. (2000). Reporting and preventing medical mishaps: Lessons from non-medical near miss reporting systems. *British Medical Journal, 320,* 759–763.

Barnes, D., Carpenter, J., & Bailey, D. (2000). Partnerships with service users in interprofessional education for community mental health: A case study. *Journal of Interprofessional Care, 14,* 189–200.

Belar, C. D., & Deardorff, W. W. (1995). *Clinical health psychology in medical settings: A practitioner's guidebook* (rev. ed.). Washington, DC: American Psychological Association.

Belar, C. D., Paoletti, N., & Jordan, C. (2001). Assessment and intervention in a medical environment. In J. Milgrom & G. D. Burrows (Eds.), *Psychology and psychiatry: Integrating medical practice* (pp. 65–92). Chichester, UK: Wiley.

Bray, J. H., & Rogers, J. C. (1997). The Linkages Project: Training behavioral health professionals for collaborative practice with primary care physicians. *Families, Systems, and Health, 15,* 55–63.

Chambless, D. L., & Hollon, S. D. (1998). Defining empirically supported therapies. *Journal of Consulting and Clinical Psychology, 66,* 7–18.

Chambless, D. L., & Ollendick, T. H. (2001). Empirically supported psychological interventions: Controversies and evidence. *Annual Review of Psychology, 52,* 685–716.

Cook, G., Gerrish, K., & Clarke, C. (2001). Decision-making in teams: Issues arising from two U.K. evaluations. *Journal of Interprofessional Care, 15,* 141–151.

Dollard, M., Winefield, H. R., Winefield, A. H., & De Yonge, J. (2000). Psychosocial job strain and productivity in human service workers: A test of the demand–control–support model. *Journal of Occupational and Organizational Psychology, 73,* 501–510.

Fallsberg, M. B., & Hammar, M. (2000). Strategies and focus at an integrated, interprofessional training ward. *Journal of Interprofessional Care, 14,* 337–350.

Gelmon, S. B., White, A. W., Carlson, L., & Norman, L. (2000). Making organizational change to achieve improvement and interprofessional learning: Perspectives from health profession educators. *Journal of Interprofessional Care, 14,* 131–146.

Gilbert, J. H. V., Camp, R. D., Cole, C. D., Bruce, C., Fielding, D. W., & Stanton, S. J. (2000). Preparing students for interprofessional teamwork in health care. *Journal of Interprofessional Care, 14,* 223–235.

Goldsmith, R. J., Paris, M., & Riba, M. B. (1999). Negative aspects of collaborative treatment. In M. B. Riba & R. Balon (Eds.), *Psychopharmacology and psychotherapy: A collaborative approach* (pp. 33–63). Washington, DC: American Psychiatric Press.

Goode, E. (2002, March 26). Psychologists get prescription pads and furor erupts. *The New York Times.*

Greenberg, P. E., Sisitsky, T., Kessler, R. C., Finkelstein, S. N., Berndt, E. R., Davidson, J. R., Ballenger, J. C., & Fyer, A. J. (1999). The economic burden of anxiety disorders in the 1990s. *Journal of Clinical Psychiatry, 60,* 427–435.

Griffiths, A., Randall, R., Santos, A., & Cox, T. (2003). Senior nurses: Interventions to reduce work stress. In M. F. Dollard, A. H. Winefield, & H. R. Winefield (Eds.), *Occupational stress in the human services professions* (pp. 165–185). London: Taylor & Francis.

Hammick, M., Barr, H., Freeth, D., Koppel, I., & Reeves, S. (2002). Systematic reviews of evaluations of interprofessional education: Results and work in progress. *Journal of Interprofessional Care, 16,* 80–84.

Harden, R. M., Davis, M. H., & Crosby, J. R. (1997). The new Dundee medical curriculum: A whole that is greater than the sum of the parts. *Medical Education, 31,* 264–271.

Herrman, H., Trauer, T., Warnock, J., & Professional Liaison Committee (Australia) Project Team. (2002). The roles and relationships of psychiatrists and other service providers in mental health services. *Australian and New Zealand Journal of Psychiatry, 36,* 75–80.

Hilton, R., & Morris, J. (2001). Student placements: Is there evidence supporting team skill development in clinical practice settings? *Journal of Interprofessional Care, 15,* 171–183.

Hudson, B. (2002). Interprofessionality in health and social care: The Achilles' heel of partnership? *Journal of Interprofessional Care, 16,* 7–17.

Johnson, J. V., & Hall, E. M. (1988). Job strain, workplace social support, and cardiovascular disease: A cross-sectional study of a random sample of Swedish working population. *American Journal of Public Health, 78,* 1336–1342.

Jones, J. W., Barge, B. N., Steffy, B. D., Fay, L. M., Kunz, L. K., & Wuebker, L. J. (1988). Stress and medical malpractice: Organizational risk assessment and intervention. *Journal of Applied Psychology, 73,* 727–735.

Jones, M., & Salmon, D. (2001). The practitioner as policy analyst: A study of student reflections of an interprofessional course in higher education. *Journal of Interprofessional Care, 15,* 67–77.

Judge, T. A., Thoresen, C. J., Bono, J. E., & Patton, G. K. (2001). The job satisfaction–job performance relationship: A qualitative and quantitative review. *Psychological Bulletin, 127,* 376–407.

Lipowski, Z. J. (1967). Review of consultation psychiatry and psychosomatic medicine: I. General principles. *Psychosomatic Medicine, 29,* 153–171.

McDaniel, S. H., & Campbell, T. L. (1997). Training health professionals to collaborate. *Families, Systems, and Health, 15,* 353–359.

McDaniel, S. H., Hargrove, D. S., Belar, C. D., Schroeder, C., & Freeman, E. L. (in press). Recommendations for education and training in primary care psychology. In R. Frank, S. McDaniel, J. Bray, & M. Heldring (Eds.), *Primary care psychology.* Washington, DC: American Psychological Association.

McLeod, C. C., Budd, M. A., & McClelland, D. C. (1997). Treatment of somatization in primary care. *General Hospital Psychiatry, 19,* 251–258.

Mendlowicz, M. V., & Stein, M. B. (2000). Quality of life in individuals with anxiety disorders. *American Journal of Psychiatry, 157,* 669–682.

Michie, S. (1998). Consultancy. In A. S. Bellack & M. Hersen (Eds.), *Comprehensive clinical psychology,* Vol. 8: *Health psychology* (pp.153–169). Oxford, UK: Pergamon.

Milgrom, J., Burrows, G., & Schwartz, S. (2001). The future of psychology and psychiatry in the medical centre. In J. Milgrom & G. D. Burrows (Eds.), *Psychology and psychiatry: Integrating medical practice* (pp. 297–332). Chichester, UK: Wiley.

Morgan, D. L., & Morgan, R. K. (2001). Single-participant research design. *American Psychologist, 56,* 119–127.

Neal, D. L., & Calarco, M. M. (1999). Mental health providers: Role definitions and collaborative practice issues. In M. B. Riba & R. Balon (Eds.), *Psychopharmacology and psychotherapy: A collaborative approach* (pp. 65–109). Washington, DC: American Psychiatric Press.

Nicholas, M. K., & Wright, M. (2001). Management of acute and chronic pain. In J. Milgrom & G. D. Burrows (Eds.), *Psychology and psychiatry: Integrating medical practice* (pp. 127–154). Chichester, UK: Wiley.

Radley, A., & Chamberlain, K. (2001). Health psychology and the study of the case: From method to analytic concern. *Social Science and Medicine, 53,* 321–332.

Schuster, J. M., Kern, E. E., Kane, V., & Nettleman, L. (1994). Changing roles of mental health clinicians in multidisciplinary teams. *Hospital and Community Psychiatry, 45,* 1187–1189.

Skjørshammer, M. (2001). Cooperation and conflict in a hospital: Interprofessional differences in perception and management of conflicts. *Journal of Interprofessional Care, 15,* 7–18.

Strain, J. J., & Horne, D. J. deL. (2001). Management of medical and surgical patients: Consultation-liaison (C-L) psychiatry and clinical health psychology. In J. Milgrom & G. D. Burrows (Eds.), *Psychology and psychiatry: Integrating medical practice* (pp. 93–126). Chichester, UK: Wiley.

Stulp deGroot, C., Price, D. W., & Leslie, B. (1998). Lessons learned: A collaborative care demonstration project. *Families, Systems, and Health, 16,* 127–138.

Todd, T. (1994). *Surviving and prospering in the managed mental health care environment.* Sarasota, FL: Professional Resources Press.

Winefield, H. R. (1998). Teaching and training other health disciplines. In A. S. Bellack & M. Hersen (Eds.), *Comprehensive clinical psychology,* Vol. 8: *Health psychology* (pp. 171–187). Oxford, UK: Pergamon.

Winefield, H. R. (2003). Work stress and its effects in general practitioners. In M. F. Dollard, A. H. Winefield, & H. R. Winefield (Eds.), *Occupational stress in the human services professions* (pp. 187–207). London: Taylor & Francis.

CHAPTER 4

Motivational Enhancement Interventions and Health Behaviors

Thad R. Leffingwell

Most behavioral health specialists are interested in how to encourage change in health behaviors among their patients. These behavior changes might include reductions or cessations of behaviors harmful to health, such as tobacco use and excessive alcohol use, or adoption/enhancement of new or infrequent behaviors that may improve or protect health, such as adhering to a special diet and increasing physical activity. Certainly, an individual's motivation to make a behavior change may determine whether or not change is attempted or implemented successfully. If motivation for change in important, the question for the behavior health specialist becomes "How can I *motivate* my patients to make important behavior changes?" This chapter describes approaches to enhancing motivation and encouraging behavior change based on principles of motivational interviewing, a patient-centered counseling approach (Miller & Rollnick, 2002). Rather than focusing on "pure" motivational interviewing alone, this chapter focuses on a variety of similar approaches and strategies that are consistent with the principles and spirit of motivational interviewing. A variety of interventions that alter the structure and setting of the intervention, while retaining the fundamental principles and spirit of motivational interviewing, have been developed and tested (Dunn, Deroo, & Rivara, 2001; Rollnick et al., 2002).

Before considering interventions for enhancing motivation, it would be helpful to discuss what motivation is. Motivation is a complex concept that has intrigued psychologists for years. Motivation has most often been described as a property of an individual. From this perspective, motivation may either be state-like (e.g., driven by transitory states of deprivation or need) or trait-like (e.g., something a client either had or lacked). Both of these perspectives place the responsibility for modifying motivation in the hands of the patient (if motivation can be modified at all) and offer little guidance on how to enhance this critical ingredient for change. The guiding conceptualization of motivation in this chapter is more complex and is based on an assumption that motivation is dynamic and can be modified by social interactions (Miller, 1985, 1999). From this perspective, motivation is conceptualized as a product of an interpersonal process between patient and provider, and certainly the job of the provider is to create conditions that maximize motivation (Miller & Rollnick, 2002).

Two other fundamental issues deserve mention at the outset. First, the motivational enhancement interventions described in this chapter focus on reducing ambivalence about behavior change as a means to enhance motivation. With most health behaviors, the patient typically feels more than one way about changing the status quo; part of the patient wants to change, and another part does not. It is this ambivalence that has the patient stuck in his or her current patterns of behavior. The practitioner can intervene in certain ways with the ambivalent patient to "tip the scales" in favor of change. Second, contemporary models of behavior change have moved beyond simple doing/not doing conceptualizations of change and now acknowledge several stages in the change process (Prochaska, DiClemente, & Norcross, 1992). These stages not only include various active stages of attempting change, such as preparation, action, and maintenance, but also include differentiations among individuals not actively involved in change, such as precontemplation and contemplation. This transtheoretical model is well known to most behavioral health specialists and now guides most research and clinical practice regarding health behavior change. The interventions described in this chapter are consistent with this model in that they provide means for intervening appropriately with patients in nonactive stages and maximize the probability of moving patients along the stages of change—ultimately toward successful change.

HISTORICAL BACKGROUND

Clinical Development of Approach

Although the principles of motivational interviewing are seen today as generalizable to many health behavior problems, they were initially developed in the substance abuse field. At the time, the prevailing conceptualization of motivation to change addictive behaviors was based on a belief in trait-like motivation, and resistance and denial were seen as common symptoms of substance dependence. The principles and techniques of motivational interviewing with alcoholics were first described during the early 1980s. Building on social-cognitive processes and a Rogerian counseling style, Miller (1983) described a new approach to patient motivation and a counseling style that offered a compelling alternative to the prevailing model. Miller described client motivation as a product of the interpersonal process or as "a product of the way in which counselors have chosen to interact with problem drinkers" (p. 150). This recasting of client motivation and related behaviors of resistance and denial required a different kind of approach to counseling from the existing approach of direct persuasion, confrontation, and the "breaking through" of denial (e.g., DiCicco, Unterberger, & Mack, 1978). Furthermore, this new approach essentially implicated the confrontational interpersonal approaches typically used by counselors for the frequent observation of resistance and denial with ambivalent individuals. Clearly, motivational interviewing was a radical innovation for encouraging change in patient health behavior. The motivational interviewing approach quickly gained popularity, perhaps due to frustration with then current approaches or the attractiveness of the less confrontational style of the approach.

Since its inception, motivational interviewing has undergone significant refinement and adaptation. The first text describing the approach in great detail appeared in 1991 (Miller & Rollnick, 1991). Subtitled *Preparing People to Change Addictive Behaviors,* this manual focused specifically on how to effectively prepare individuals with substance abuse and dependence problems to make self-directed or assisted changes. This innovative new approach was also described in a Treatment Improvement Protocol (TIP) series manual distributed by the U.S. Department of Health and Human Services (Miller, 1999), and a treatment manual was prepared for the motivational enhancement condition of Project MATCH (National Institute on Alcohol Abuse and Alcoholism, 1995). Building on work to develop a brief method of motivational interviewing for physicians counseling patients (Butler et al., 1999; Rollnick, Heather, & Bell, 1992), Rollnick, Mason, and Butler (1999) published a text describing a model of brief motivational enhancement intervention for physicians that retains the spirit of motivational interviewing while simplifying the technique for applications in more brief encounters. Finally, Miller and Rollnick (2002) produced an extensive revision of the original motivational interviewing text, this time reflecting the broad popularity of the negotiating style by describing the approach as a more general strategy applicable to patients who might be ambivalent about *any* behavior change, not just changing addictive behavior.

Empirical Support

Since the release of the original detailed manual (Miller & Rollnick, 1991), numerous clinical trials investigating motivational interviewing interventions or related adaptations have appeared in the literature. A regularly updated comprehensive bibliography of motivational interviewing literature lists more than 60 reports of clinical outcome studies, and most of these are randomized trials (www.motivationalinterview.org). Although the majority of these reports focus on applications with substance use, applications of brief motivational enhancement interventions to other behavioral problems include problem gambling (Hodgins, Currie, & el-Guebaly, 2001), nutrition (Resnicow,

Jackson, Wang, Dudley, & Baranowski, 2001; Resnicow et al., 2000), medication compliance (Schmaling, Blume, & Afari, 2001), HIV infection protective behaviors (Carey et al., 2000), tobacco use (Butler et al., 1999), mammography screening (Ludman, Curry, Meyer, & Taplin, 1999), engagement in treatment for bulimia nervosa (Treasure et al., 1999), weight control (Smith, Heckemeyer, Kratt, & Mason, 1997), diabetes self-care (Trigwell, Grant, & House, 1997), and even water disinfecting practices for individuals living near unsafe water sources (Thevos, Quick, & Yanduli, 2000).

Reviews of the available motivational interviewing literature are challenging because motivational interviewing is more of a counseling *style* than a *set of techniques* or a collection of *tasks*. This means that interventions may vary significantly in form, including the setting for the intervention (e.g., emergency room, therapy office, physician's exam room) and structure (e.g., duration of interaction), while still retaining the *style* or *spirit* of motivational interviewing. Although this flexibility almost certainly accounts for some of the popularity of the motivational interviewing approach as a clinical tool, it creates difficulties for making inferences about exactly which interventions have which effects. Nonetheless, three reviews of this literature have been attempted.

Noonan and Moyers (1997) performed a qualitative review of the available clinical trials that applied motivational interviewing to substance use problems. They reviewed 11 randomized trials and concluded that 9 studies supported the efficacy of motivational interviewing for substance abuse and dependence problems.

A more comprehensive review was conducted by Dunn and colleagues (2001). They attempted to capture the diverse nature of motivational interviewing approaches while retaining internal validity of the interventions by defining Adaptations of Motivational

Interviewing (AMIs). To qualify as an AMI, an intervention had to claim to adhere to basic principles of motivational interviewing. Consistent with a definition of motivational interviewing offered by Rollnick and Miller (1995), this meant that the intervention had to use a client-centered empathic style to reduce resistance, develop motivational discrepancies, and support the patient's self-efficacy. A structure most often used in AMIs incorporates some sort of review of assessment feedback as the focus of the interview, while the counselor uses an interpersonal style and strategies consistent with motivational interviewing to facilitate the processing of the feedback and to elicit self-motivational statements (e.g., Miller, Sovereign, & Krege, 1988). Using this definition of AMIs and other exclusion criteria regarding study design and outcome measurement, Dunn and colleagues (2001) found 29 studies for inclusion in their review.

The Dunn and colleagues (2001) review included applications of AMIs in four different behavioral change contexts: substance use, tobacco use, HIV risk behaviors, and diet/exercise. These investigators found that 60% of the studies reviewed had significant effect sizes favoring the AMI. The most consistent evidence for AMI effectiveness was observed where the AMI was used as an enhancement to standard treatment for substance use when delivered at the onset of a treatment episode. The findings for applications for tobacco use, HIV risk, and diet/exercise were more mixed but still encouraging, and more research was recommended.

The third review of the motivational interviewing literature was conducted by Burke, Arkowitz, and Dunn (2002). Using a similar approach to that used by Dunn and colleagues (2001), but with slightly more restrictive inclusion criteria, these investigators identified 26 randomized trials of an AMI for review. This review reached similar conclusions, with the most impressive findings emerging for AMIs as both a treatment adjunct to standard

treatment and a stand-alone treatment for patients with alcohol problems. Studies of AMIs applied to problems of tobacco use, illicit drug use, diet/exercise, and eating disorders were reported to be encouraging but too sparse to make strong findings or recommendations. No support was found for the use of AMIs to reduce HIV risk behaviors. The authors concluded that reasonable evidence supports the use of AMIs as both a stand-alone intervention and a treatment adjunct at the onset of other treatment. Although the data are fairly consistent that AMIs are efficacious, the data are very unclear as to how, why, and for whom the interventions work.

VARIATIONS OF MOTIVATIONAL ENHANCEMENT INTERVENTIONS

As noted previously, motivational interviewing rarely exists in "pure" form in the empirical literature, and it seems likely that this is also reflected in clinical practice. For example, the 29 studies reviewed by Dunn and colleagues (2001) used eight different labels other than "motivational interviewing" to describe their interventions. Furthermore, the durations of the interventions ranged from 5 to 360 minutes. Clinicians in practice, receiving little direct guidance from the heterogeneous empirical literature, are likely to create motivational enhancement motivations customized to their patient populations, behavioral problems encountered, and settings. The purpose of this section is to introduce a few prevailing models of motivational enhancement interventions and to introduce key principles from motivational interviewing that would be required to capture the spirit of the motivational interviewing style.

Rollnick and colleagues (2002) attempted to add clarity to the varieties of AMIs that exist in the literature and in practice. According to their framework, brief motivational enhancement interventions could be categorized as one of three general types of intervention: (a) brief advice, (b) behavior change counseling, and (c) motivational interviewing. What these share in common could be considered the core of effective motivational enhancement interventions—a nonconfrontational style and a goal of eliciting change from within the patient rather than imposing from the outside via blaming, coercion, or direct persuasion. The approaches may differ on several domains, including the duration of the consultation, the role of the practitioner, the use of confrontation, and the use of direct information. Rollnick and colleagues also attempted to describe the skill sets necessary for each of these types of intervention, with more complex and varied skills necessary for the longer and more complex interaction of motivational interviewing.

Brief Advice

Rollnick and colleagues (2002) described brief advice as a typically brief (less than 15 minutes) opportunistic intervention delivered by nonspecialists in behavior change counseling. The goals are typically to raise awareness of a behavioral problem and to initiate at least contemplation of change. Information exchange is largely one-way, from practitioner to patient. Goals for behavior change are often suggested rather than elicited. Although the inequality of roles is not consistent with motivational interviewing, the practitioner can maximize the motivational impact of the information and advice by carefully choosing a good opportunity for the intervention, presenting information in a respectful and compassionate manner, and using at least some open-ended questions and reflections.

Behavior Change Counseling

Behavior change counseling, as described by Rollnick and colleagues (2002) is an approach somewhere between brief advice and "pure" motivational interviewing. The consultation is typically longer in duration and may involve more than one problem area. The practitioner and the patient typically share a more equal role in the decision-making and goal-setting process. Using a person-centered approach, the practitioner often uses open-ended questions and reflection to understand the patient's perspective and to check for understanding. Information typically flows in both directions between the practitioner and the patient, in contrast to the one-way flow seen with brief advice. Most often, the goal is to elicit a decision and plan for change in a more pragmatic sense than in motivational interviewing, where one tries to enhance the quality and commitment of the plans for change as well.

Rollnick and colleagues (1999) described a model of behavior change counseling based on earlier work trying to develop "brief motivational interviewing" (Rollnick et al., 1992). Designed for nonspecialists working in time-pressured settings such as primary care clinics, this model simplifies the goals and strategies of the behavior change consultation. After establishing basic rapport and setting an agenda for the consultation, the practitioner's task is to explore the patient's feelings about a behavior change using two dimensions: importance and confidence. In this model, these two dimensions adequately capture the nature of ambivalence, and enhancing both increases the likelihood of both a change attempt and a successful outcome. Throughout the consultation, the practitioner may exchange information (as in brief advice) or use interpersonal strategies to reduce resistance (as in motivational interviewing).

One very creative technique recommended as part of this intervention model is the use of scaled questions (e.g., 1 to 100) for assessing the importance of a behavior change and confidence in making a change. For example, the practitioner might ask "If 0 is 'not important at all' and 100 is 'very important,' what number would you say represents how important it is to you *now* to change ____?" Whatever answers a patient might provide to these types of questions, the answers provide great fodder for reflection, amplification, and investigation. The patient typically will give a number somewhere between the extremes. For the question of importance, this would allow the practitioner to follow up this answer to identify concerns the patient may have about his or her behavior (e.g., "You said '40'. Why not lower? What makes it '40' in importance?") or to identify gaps in knowledge/awareness or other priorities the patient may have (e.g., "Why is the number not higher? What would it take for you to increase the importance of this change?"). For the response to a scaled question about confidence, the practitioner may follow up with questions or reflections to explore barriers perceived by the patient (e.g., "You rated your confidence as '60'. Why not '70' or '80'?") or to identify skills or resources the patient may have available to support a change effort (e.g., "You rated your confidence as '40'. You must feel that there is some chance you could do it if you tried. Why?").

The Rollnick and colleagues (1999) brief intervention model includes several other strategies for exploring importance, building confidence, assessing readiness for change, and making strategies for change. As with all brief behavior change counseling AMIs, practitioners are encouraged to capture the spirit of motivational interviewing in their interactions with clients by using a supportive and nonconfrontational style to minimize and respond to resistance. Practitioners are encouraged to choose from the menus of strategies to create an adaptation that fits their needs and settings rather than adopting a formulaic treatment approach.

Motivational Interviewing

Rollnick and colleagues (2002) described "pure" motivational interviewing as the most complex and involved approach to brief motivational enhancement. Applications of motivational interviewing are typically less opportunistic planned encounters that normally last longer than 30 minutes and often span more than one session. Motivational interviewing requires the full complement of skills and strategies as well as adherence to the core principles of motivational interviewing (Miller & Rollnick, 2002). Confrontational style is always avoided, and direct advice is usually provided only when directly requested by the patient. Communication is used more strategically, with the goal of creating motivational discrepancies, resolving ambivalence, and eliciting self-motivational statements (or "change talk") from the patient.

Miller and Rollnick (2002) defined motivational interviewing as "a client-centered, directive method for enhancing intrinsic motivation to change by exploring and resolving ambivalence" (p. 25). Motivational interviewing has also been described as "a counseling *style* rather than a set of techniques applied to or on people" (Rollnick, 2001, p. 1769, emphasis added). Although a number of techniques and strategies are recommended as consistent with motivational interviewing, other strategies could be used so long as they are consistent with the principles and style of motivational interviewing. In fact, adaptation and creative application of the principles are encouraged. Motivational interviewing in practice, unlike other manualized treatments, might not necessarily have a structured beginning, middle, and end but instead may occur at various times during a treatment relationship between practitioner and patient. It may be left and revisited or may be integrated with an ongoing treatment plan. Motivational interviewing is not something to be done *to* patients but rather is a way of *being with* patients (Miller, 2002).

Fundamentals of Motivational Interviewing

Essential Spirit. Miller and Rollnick (2002) described the spirit of motivational interviewing as "understanding and experiencing the human nature that gives rise to that way of being" and as absolutely fundamental to any intervention that might claim to be motivational interviewing or a reasonable adaptation. How the practitioner thinks about the patient and the process is as important as any technique in determining the nature of the intervention. Miller and Rollnick further described the spirit of motivational interviewing as captured by three fundamental considerations: (a) a collaborative relationship, rather than an authoritarian or prescriptive relationship, between the practitioner and the patient; (b) an eliciting evocative approach rather than a persuasive or educative stance; and (c) a commitment to the ultimate autonomy of the patient to make decisions about change and to marshal personal resources for change. These considerations are mutually consistent in their respect for the patient's freedom of choice as well as competence and expertise in his or her own life.

Phases of the Interview. A comprehensive and complete motivational interview would include two overlapping phases: increasing motivation for change (Phase 1) and strengthening commitment to a decision for change (Phase 2) (Miller & Rollnick, 2002). Phase 1 typically involves strategies for building rapport; increasing problem recognition; and identifying, exploring, and resolving the various aspects of patient ambivalence. Phase 2 typically involves tasks such as goal setting, making behavioral plans, and negotiating time lines while being careful to avoid roadblocks to a successful change attempt (e.g., unrealistic goals, underestimated effort, shallow commitment).

Four Principles. Refinements to Miller's (1983) original description of motivational interviewing have resulted in the distillation of four fundamental principles (Miller & Rollnick, 2002). These principles help to translate the spirit of motivational interviewing into

behavioral strategies to guide the practitioner. The principles are not necessarily meant to be initiated in order or in equal amounts but rather are intended to be skillfully and elegantly woven together during and throughout the process of the interview.

The first principle is *expressing empathy*. Probably nowhere is it more important than here that one believes in the spirit of motivational interviewing. This principle builds on classic work by Rogers (1951, 1961) and assumes that acceptance of patients as they are paradoxically makes it easier for them to change. As with Rogers's approach, careful reflective listening is the key to communicating empathy to the client. The practitioner may use a number of familiar listening skills, including open-ended questions, a variety of reflective statements, and nonverbal behaviors. Reflective listening simultaneously accomplishes several goals, including encouraging elaboration by the patient (which aids in understanding by the practitioner by eliciting data) and communicating to the patient both an effort to understand and ultimately greater understanding for the practitioner of the patient. This behavior often prevents resistance from the outset of the interview because typical behaviors that would be likely to elicit resistance (e.g., direct persuasion, confrontation, appeals to authority) are avoided altogether.

How one thinks about the nature of ambivalence is a key to demonstrating empathy in motivational interviewing. Ambivalence about behavior change is normal and natural, and it occurs for most behavior changes involving habitual behavior patterns, including changing addictive behaviors. Change is difficult. The status quo is comfortable. Patients have frequently had either direct or modeled failure experiences involving behavior change. If one sees ambivalence about change as normal and natural rather than as a sign of pathology, immorality, or other undesirable personality characteristics, it immediately becomes much easier to be comfortable with understanding and exploring that experience.

The second principle, *developing discrepancies,* involves understanding and amplifying differences between the patient's current behavior and his or her goals, values, and/or self-image (Miller & Rollnick, 2002). This discrepancy serves as a motivating force that can be used to elicit self-motivational statements. If an individual perceives a behavior as inconsistent with other important goals, the probability of change increases. Enhancing motivational discrepancies may involve decreasing the importance of current unhealthy behaviors; increasing the importance of behaviors, values, or goals inconsistent with this current behavior; or both. The patient's current behavioral patterns are seen as the result of a balancing attempt among various behaviors, goals, and values that are often conflicting. The practitioner's goal is to tip that balance in the direction of change.

The third principle, *responding to resistance,* is a hallmark principle that truly separates motivational interviewing from most other approaches and is probably the most innovative aspect of the approach. As mentioned previously, resistance is viewed as the result of the interpersonal process, or the way in which the practitioner is interacting with the patient at that moment, rather than as a characteristic of the patient himself or herself. Interactions *create* resistance; people *are not* resistant. From this perspective, it follows that the practitioner holds responsibility for creating conditions in the interpersonal interaction to reduce resistance. When resistance is encountered in the interview, the practitioner sees that as a signal to change strategies rather than as a signal to press onward as in confrontational or persuasive approaches. Because of the paramount importance and complexity of the task of responding to resistance, Miller and Rollnick (2002) offered several strategies for accomplishing this task. These are summarized in Table 4.1.

The final principle, *supporting self-efficacy,* refers to communicating a belief in the patient's ability to be an agent of change on his or her own behalf. This principle is sometimes manifest subtly by the practitioner's implicit belief in the patient's role in the change process. When the patient is treated as the ultimate decision maker and as a collaborative partner in exploring change, a belief in the patient's ability to change is assumed. Also, when the practitioner inquires in a sincere way as to how a patient might go about making a change, this implies a belief in the patient's own resources and ideas. A number of more explicit strategies can also be employed, including reviewing past successes or models, amplifying personal strengths, brainstorming new ideas, and even occasionally giving direct advice (Miller & Rollnick, 2002).

Use of Feedback. Although not inherent to motivational interviewing itself, most investigations of motivational enhancement approaches have used assessment feedback as part of the process (Dunn et al., 2001). Feedback may include information about health status, presence or absence of disease states, and comparisons with normative data. These data provide a useful start to conversations about change. Reviewing personalized feedback with a patient provides many opportunities to explore concerns a patient may have about his or her current behavior or health status. This type of feedback happens frequently in behavior medicine settings, providing practitioners with numerous rich opportunities to use motivational enhancement strategies. Objective feedback alone, especially if it contains bad or anxiety-provoking news, is likely to be experienced by the patient as confrontive and to elicit resistance. Use of a motivational interviewing style and strategies when reviewing the feedback can aid in the patient's ability to process the information and use it effectively to motivate change.

Table 4.1   Examples of Various Useful Methods for Responding to Resistance

Method	Description	Example
Reflective methods		
Simple reflection	Statement that reflects observed resistance	"You would rather not talk about your weight."
Amplified reflection	Restatement of what was heard in exaggerated form	"You would rather *never* talk about your weight. It doesn't concern you *at all*."
Double-sided reflection	Restatement of both sides of ambivalence	"On the one hand, it's embarrassing to talk about your weight, and on the other, you are worried about it and would like to ask for help."
Strategic methods		
Shift focus	Change in focus of interaction	"Let's not worry about what I think right now; let's just talk about any concerns *you* might have."
Reframe	Giving new interpretation to patient's perspective	"You say you've tried and failed many times. It sounds like you have tremendous persistence and courage to keep trying."
Agree with a twist	Agreeing with part of patient's message while reframing another part	"Food is your favorite form of recreation, and it's important to enjoy life, even if it is causing you health problems."
Emphasize personal control	Reaffirming patient's ultimate freedom of choice	"Of course it's up to you what to do next. No one can make the decision for you."
Coming alongside	Taking patient's side of the ambivalence to encourage him or her to voice the other side	"You're right that it would be difficult to change—maybe impossible."

SOURCE: Miller and Rollnick (2002). Reprinted with permission.

Training in Motivational Enhancement Interventions

The varieties of motivational enhancement interventions require a diverse set of skills that vary in complexity depending on the type of intervention employed (Rollnick et al., 2002). For very brief advice encounters, basic knowledge about risks of the current behavior, behavior change strategies, and rudimentary appreciation for the spirit of motivational interviewing likely are all that are required. The more complex interventions, including behavior change counseling and motivational interviewing, require more complex skills and strategies that can probably be learned only through training and supervision. Reflective listening alone is a deceptively complex set of skills to master and is made even more complex by the strategic use of listening in motivational interviewing. In motivational interviewing, the practitioner is not simply expected to mindlessly parrot open-ended questions and reflections for the sake of ongoing dialogue but rather is expected to ask *particular* questions and make *selective* reflective statements to promote motivation for change (Rollnick et al., 2002).

Limited information is available in the empirical literature on appropriate training or on the effects of training. Of 29 studies reviewed by Dunn and colleagues (2001), only 10 reported the durations of training provided to practitioners in the studies, and the durations of that training ranged from 2 to 31 hours. In addition, 11 of the studies reported providing training but offered few details, and 8 of the studies did not include any information about training. Two other studies have examined the effects of training on the knowledge and skills of trainees directly. The first study found that professional participants did demonstrate increases in knowledge about motivational interviewing and basic listening skills in a simple pre-post design (Rubel, Sobell, & Miller, 2000). A second study found that a 2-day workshop on motivational interviewing had significant effects on self-reports of motivational interviewing by trainees and had modest gains in skill use demonstrated on observed practice samples, but expected changes in client behavior were not observed (Miller & Mount, 2001). Unfortunately, although participants in this study did modestly increase their frequency of motivational interviewing consistent strategies, they did not necessarily decrease their use of *inconsistent* strategies. This is of great concern because it may take only very few confrontational interactions to resurrect resistance and spoil the potential gains of motivational strategies. These preliminary results are encouraging but insufficient to make recommendations on empirical grounds for a necessary amount of training for competent practice. Further research is warranted and would be aided by the development of reliable and valid methods for assessing skill acquisition (Barsky & Coleman, 2001).

Unlike the originators of many other empirical treatments, the originators of motivational interviewing have devoted a good deal of thought and energy to training. Both versions of the motivational interviewing text (Miller & Rollnick, 1991, 2002) included sections on teaching and learning the approach. Over the past several years, Miller and Rollnick have annually provided intensive training for professionals already proficient in the method to become trainers in the technique. Members of this group also stay in regular contact with each other via an e-mail listserv, a regular newsletter, and an annual meeting. A list of these "trained trainers" is available on the motivational interviewing Web site (www.motivationalinterview.org).

Miller (2002) proposed a tiered system of training as shown in Table 4.2. This system would allow individuals to tailor the necessary training for their setting and patient needs. Individuals interested in applying the approach to a specific behavioral domain and narrowly defined patient population could do with less training than those interested in a more broad application of the approach and certainly could do with less training than those interested in having the expertise to provide training.

At a minimum, any practitioner interested in applying an approach based on the principles of motivational interviewing should read one or more of the available manuals described earlier. Further training could be obtained via introductory workshops available at many national and regional professional conferences. More intensive training could be arranged from one of the network of trainers. The best possible training will occur with opportunities for practice with feedback, both with role-play exercises and with actual cases (Miller & Rollnick, 2002). Finally, even after formal training in motivational interviewing, a great deal of learning can occur by carefully observing the effect of one's counseling approach on clients. Miller (1996) described motivational interviewing as an approach he "had learned from [his] clients" (p. 835).

Table 4.2   Miller's Proposed Tiered System for Levels of Training in Motivational Interviewing

Type of Training	Goals	Approximate Length
Introduction to motivational interviewing	Learn about the basics of motivational interviewing and decide level of interest in learning more.	2 hours to 1 day
Application of motivational interviewing	Learn about more specific applications of motivational interviewing, including direct practice with a particular application.	1 hour to 1 day
Clinical training	Learn basic style of motivational interviewing, including extended practice. Strengthen empathic listening skills. Learn to recognize client cues for resistance and change talk.	2 to 3 days or several 4- to 8-hour seminars
Advanced training	Learn advanced clinical usefulness of motivational interviewing. Receive individual feedback on intensive practice. Learn methods of evaluating motivational interviewing. Update knowledge of research developments.	2 to 3 days (plus prior minimum proficiency)
Training for trainers	Learn a flexible range of skills for helping others learn motivational interviewing. Learn to assess needs of trainees and adapt accordingly. Update knowledge of research developments.	3 days

SOURCE: Miller (2002). Reprinted with permission.

SUMMARY

Motivational enhancement interventions based on the style and principles of motivational interviewing have enjoyed increasing popularity over the past decade. Some have even expressed concern that the clinical popularity of the approach may be inappropriate given the young nature of the empirical literature (Dunn et al., 2001). Although the extant empirical literature is encouraging and largely supportive of the effectiveness of motivational enhancement interventions, much more research is needed to better understand how, why, when, and for whom the approach can be effective.

The clinical popularity of this approach is expected to continue. Practitioners interested in applying the principles of motivational interviewing with their patients are cautioned that the approach is deceptively complex and intricate, and training and supervision are recommended for individuals interested in developing proficiency in the methods. Creative adaptations are encouraged, but caution is also warranted before implementing radical departures (e.g., group motivational interviewing, computer-guided motivational interviewing) until further research can evaluate whether these innovative adaptations can demonstrate similar efficacy. Practitioners are further cautioned that if aspects of current intervention attempts with patients are inconsistent with motivational interviewing style, it is unlikely that simply adding new strategies to the repertoire will be effective. For some, it may be necessary to abandon old strategies of confrontation, coercion, and persuasion to achieve better outcomes with motivating patient health behavior change.

REFERENCES

Barsky, A., & Coleman, H. (2001). Evaluating skill acquisition in motivational interviewing: The development of an instrument to measure practice skills. *Journal of Drug Education, 31*, 69–82.

Burke, B. L., Arkowitz, H., & Dunn, C. (2002). The efficacy of motivational interviewing and its adaptations: What we know so far. In W. R. Miller & S. Rollnick (Eds.), *Motivational interviewing: Preparing people for change* (pp. 217–250). New York: Guilford.

Butler, C., Rollnick, S., Cohen, D., Russell, I., Bachmann, M., & Stott, N. (1999). Motivational consulting versus brief advice for smokers in general practice: A randomised trial. *British Journal of General Practice, 49*, 611–616.

Carey, M. P., Braaten, L. S., Maisto, S. A., Gleason, J. R., Forsyth, A. D., Durant, L. E., & Jaoworski, B. C. (2000). Using information, motivational enhancement, and skills training to reduce the risk of HIV infection for low-income urban women: A second randomized clinical trial. *Health Psychology, 19*, 3–11.

DiCicco, L., Unterberger, H., & Mack, J. E. (1978). Confronting denial: An alcoholism intervention strategy. *Psychiatric Annals, 8*, 596–606.

Dunn, C., Deroo, L., & Rivara, F. P. (2001). The use of brief interventions adapted from motivational interviewing across behavioral domains: A systematic review. *Addiction, 96*, 1725–1742.

Hodgins, D. C., Currie, S. R., & el-Guebaly, N. (2001). Motivational enhancement and self-help treatments for problem gambling. *Journal of Consulting and Clinical Psychology, 69*, 50–57.

Ludman, E. J., Curry, S. J., Meyer, D., & Taplin, S. H. (1999). Implementation of outreach telephone counseling to promote mammography. *Health Education and Behavior, 26*, 689–702.

Miller, W. R. (1983). Motivational interviewing with problem drinkers. *Behavioural Psychotherapy, 11*, 147–172.

Miller, W. R. (1985). Motivation for treatment: A review with special emphasis on alcoholism. *Psychological Bulletin, 98*, 84–107.

Miller, W. R. (1996). Motivational interviewing: Research, practice, and puzzles. *Addictive Behaviors, 21*, 835–842.

Miller, W. R. (Ed.). (1999). *Enhancing motivation for change in substance abuse treatment* (Treatment Improvement Protocol Series, No. 35, DHHS Publication No. (SMA) 00-3460). Rockville, MD: Center for Substance Abuse Treatment.

Miller, W. R. (2002, January 1). From the desert. *Motivational Interviewing Newsletter: Update, Education, and Training*, pp. 1–2. (Albuquerque, NM: Motivational Learning Network of Trainers)

Miller, W. R., & Mount, K. A. (2001). A small study of training in motivational interviewing: Does one workshop change clinician and client behavior? *Behavioral and Cognitive Psychotherapy, 29*, 457–471.

Miller, W. R., & Rollnick, S. (1991). *Motivational interviewing: Preparing people to change addictive behaviors*. New York: Guilford.

Miller, W. R., & Rollnick, S. (2002). *Motivational interviewing: Preparing people for change*. New York: Guilford.

Miller, W. R., Sovereign, R. G., & Krege, B. (1988). Motivational interviewing with problem drinkers: II. The Drinker's Check-Up as a preventive intervention. *Behavioural Psychotherapy, 16*, 251–268.

National Institute on Alcohol Abuse and Alcoholism. (1995). *Motivational enhancement therapy manual: A clinical research guide for therapists treating individuals with alcohol abuse and dependence* (Project MATCH Monograph

Series, NIH Publication No. 94-3723). Rockville, MD: U.S. Department of Health and Human Services.

Noonan, W. C., & Moyers, T. B. (1997). Motivational interviewing: A review. *Journal of Substance Misuse, 2,* 8–16.

Prochaska, J. O., DiClemente, C. C., & Norcross, J. C. (1992). In search of how people change: Applications to addictive behaviors. *American Psychologist, 47,* 1102–1114.

Resnicow, K., Jackson, A., Wang, T., Dudley, W., & Baranowski, T. (2001). A motivational interviewing intervention to increase fruit and vegetable intake through black churches: Results of the Eat for Life trial. *American Journal of Public Health, 91,* 1686–1693.

Resnicow, K., Wallace, D. C., Jackson, A., Digirolamo, A., Odom, E., Wang, T., Dudley, W. N., Davis, M., Mitchell, D., & Baranowski, T. (2000). Dietary change through African American churches: Baseline results and program description of the Eat for Life trial. *Journal of Cancer Education, 15,* 156–163.

Rogers, C. R. (1951). *Client-centered therapy.* Boston: Houghton Mifflin.

Rogers, C. R. (1961). *On becoming a person.* Boston: Houghton Mifflin.

Rollnick, S. (2001). Enthusiasm, quick-fixes and premature controlled trials. *Addiction, 96,* 1769–1770.

Rollnick, S., Allison, J., Ballasiotes, S., Barth, T., Butler, C., Rose, G. S., & Rosengren, D. B. (2002). In W. R. Miller & S. Rollnick (Eds.), *Motivational interviewing: Preparing people for change* (pp. 270–283). New York: Guilford.

Rollnick, S., Heather, N., & Bell, A. (1992). Negotiating behaviour change in medical settings: The development of brief motivational interviewing. *Journal of Mental Health, 1,* 25–37.

Rollnick, S., Mason, P., & Butler, C. (1999). *Health behavior change.* London: Churchill Livingstone.

Rollnick, S., & Miller, W. R. (1995). What is motivational interviewing? *Behavioural and Cognitive Psychotherapy, 23,* 325–334.

Rubel, E. C., Sobell, L. C., & Miller, W. R. (2000). Do continuing education workshops improve participants' skills? Effects of a motivational interviewing workshop on substance-abuse counselors' skills and knowledge. *The Behavior Therapist, 23,* 73–77.

Schmaling, K. B., Blume, A. W., & Afari, N. (2001). A randomized controlled pilot study of motivational interviewing to change attitudes to medications for asthma. *Journal of Clinical Psychology in Medical Settings, 8*(3), 167–172.

Smith, D. E., Heckemeyer, C. M., Kratt, P. P., & Mason, D. A. (1997). Motivational interviewing to improve adherence to a behavioral weight-control program for older obese women with NIDDM: A pilot study. *Diabetes Care, 20,* 53–54.

Thevos, A. K., Quick, R. E., & Yanduli, V. (2000). Application of motivational interviewing to the adoption of water disinfection practices in Zambia. *Health Promotion International, 15,* 207–214.

Treasure, J. L., Katzman, M., Schmidt, U., Troop, N., Todd, G., & de Silva, P. (1999). Engagement and outcome in the treatment of bulimia nervosa: First phase of a sequential design comparing motivation enhancement therapy and cognitive behavioural therapy. *Behaviour Research and Therapy, 37,* 405–418.

Trigwell, P., Grant, P. J., & House, A. (1997). Motivation and glycemic control in diabetes mellitus. *Journal of Psychosomatic Research, 43,* 307–315.

CHAPTER 5

Brief Psychotherapies and Group Treatments in General Health Care Settings

Deborah J. Wiebe, Lindsey Bloor, and Timothy W. Smith

Over the past 30 years, evidence has continued to accumulate demonstrating that medical conditions both affect and are affected by psychosocial factors. Behavioral habits of daily life, such as physical activity, smoking, and diet, clearly affect the risk of developing the most common sources of morbidity and mortality (e.g., coronary heart disease, cancer, diabetes) as well as the course of such conditions. Other psychosocial factors, such as stressful life circumstances, social support, personality characteristics, and chronic negative emotions, affect the development and course of these same conditions through more direct psychobiological mechanisms. Finally, most acute and chronic medical conditions influence emotional adjustment, personal relationships, work and other aspects of functional activity, and overall quality of life.

One clear implication of the bidirectional associations between psychosocial factors and physical health is that psychosocial interventions might be useful in the prevention and management of medical conditions. This clinical application of basic research in behavioral medicine and health psychology has itself been the focus of an expanding body of research. Although the findings are not uniformly supportive, there is clear evidence that psychotherapy and other approaches to behavior change can be useful additions to routine medical care, both in the reduction of unhealthy risky behavior and in the management of the psychosocial impacts of medical conditions (Smith, Kendall, & Keefe, 2002). In some cases, such interventions are useful as primary or secondary treatments for the underlying medical conditions themselves.

This chapter reviews the conceptual approach that underlies such intervention efforts (i.e., the biopsychosocial model [Engel, 1977]) and provides examples of the wide variety of brief and group interventions used across medical conditions and settings. A comprehensive review is clearly beyond the current scope, but the chapter does describe the nature and use of such interventions in general health care settings and also reviews evidence of their efficacy and effectiveness. The skills and training necessary for the translation of traditional brief psychotherapy and group treatment interventions into the unique culture and context of medical care are also discussed. The chapter begins with a brief history of the developments that have created the opportunity—and even demand—for the expansion of general health care to include interventions traditionally conceptualized as mental health services.

HISTORICAL DEVELOPMENTS

The growth in the importance of psychosocial interventions for the prevention and management of medical conditions was set into motion by changing patterns of disease over the last half of the 20th century. Until that time, acute medical conditions (e.g., infectious diseases) were the leading cause of death in the United States (National Office of Vital Statistics, 1947). By the end of the 20th century, chronic conditions had come to account for more than 70% of all deaths, primarily due to the effects of coronary heart disease, cancer, and cerebrovascular disease (Centers for Disease Control and Prevention, 1999). Certain behaviors (e.g., smoking, activity levels) contribute to the risk of these diseases, and given advances in medical care, patients suffering from these conditions can expect to live long enough that coping with their many impacts will become an important challenge. Finally, the management of these and other increasingly prevalent chronic conditions typically involves many behavioral processes (e.g., adherence to prescribed regimens, exercise-based rehabilitation, stress management interventions). Hence, patterns of morbidity and mortality have changed over the past century in such a way as to make psychosocial interventions an important component of current health care. The parallel rise in health care expenditures has created additional incentives for effective additions to traditional medical care (Kaplan & Groessl, 2002).

In an influential critique of the prevailing biomedical model as too simplistic and reductionistic to accommodate this increasing role of psychological and social factors in the major sources of morbidity and mortality, Engel (1977) argued that a *biopsychosocial* alternative is more appropriate. In this view, based in part on the general systems theory of Von Bertalanffy (1968), health and illness are seen as emerging from the reciprocal interplay of hierarchically arranged levels of analysis, ranging from the molecular to the individual to the sociocultural, with several levels in between. From a biopsychosocial perspective, understanding the source of illness and designing optimal approaches to medical care requires this multisystem analysis. In this expanded conceptual model, psychosocial interventions have an obvious place.

Influential predecessors to the current array of psychosocial interventions began to appear early in the development of the fields of behavioral medicine and clinical health psychology. Growing epidemiological evidence of the role of smoking, excess body weight, and physical inactivity in cardiovascular disease and cancer prompted the application of existing behavior change techniques to these health-relevant targets (e.g., Shapiro, Tursky, Stuart, & Shnidman, 1971; Stuart, 1967). Advances in the physiology of stress and its role in the development of several medical disorders (e.g., hypertension) combined with the available operant behavioral change methods to form the basis of early biofeedback treatments for several chronic conditions (e.g., Pickering & Miller, 1977). Early research demonstrating that the preoperative psychological state (e.g., anxiety, coping behaviors) influenced the postoperative course of surgical patients prompted the development of brief, structured psychosocial interventions for this population (Janis, 1958). Similarly, operant concepts and behavior change technology were successfully applied to the conceptualization and treatment of chronic pain (Fordyce, 1976).

Table 5.1   Outline for the Clinical Application of the Biopsychosocial Model

I. Illness Factors

    A. Pathophysiology
    B. Risk factors
    C. Prognosis
    D. Diagnostic procedures
    E. Treatment procedures

II. Patient Factors

    A. DSM conditions (Axis I and Axis II)
    B. Impact of illness on distress, social and occupational functioning, and quality of life
    C. Conceptualization of disease and treatment
    D. Personality traits and coping styles
    E. Educational and vocational status

III. Social, Family, and Cultural Factors

    A. Quality of marital and family relationships
    B. Use and efficacy of social support
    C. Relationships with the health care team
    D. Cultural background

IV. Health Care System Factors
    A. Health care setting and culture
    B. Insurance coverage and disability benefits for medical condition
    C. Geographical, social, psychological, and monetary barriers to accessing services

SOURCE: Adapted from Smith and Nicassio (1995). Copyright © 1995 by the American Psychological Association. Adapted with permission.

Together, these and other brief interventions provided clear evidence of the promise of extending traditional medical care to include psychotherapy and other behavior change approaches. As reviewed in what follows, the subsequent 30 years of research has produced many examples of innovative and valuable extensions of this prior work (Smith, Nealey, & Hamann, 2000).

Clinical Application of the Biopsychosocial Model

To be feasible and effective, any brief psychosocial intervention with medical patients must begin with an assessment based on the biopsychosocial model. The results of such an assessment identify not only important targets for intervention but also important moderating factors and contextual issues. An outline for this assessment is presented in Table 5.1 (Smith & Nicassio, 1995). This outline is not a formal procedural protocol but instead provides a general orientation or viewpoint that guides more specific informal and formal assessment procedures.

The first category involves information about the patient's specific illness or condition. The pathophysiology, relevant risk factors, natural history and prognosis of the condition, and diagnostic and treatment procedures typically comprising its medical management are essential elements of the patient's context and may help to prioritize specific intervention targets that could be usefully addressed through psychosocial interventions. Through general experience and specific collaborative discussions with other members of the multidisciplinary health care team, the clinical health psychologist must acquire adequate knowledge of the general condition and its typical management as well as of the patient's specific case.

Similarly, characteristics of the patient can guide the identification of specific, potential intervention targets (e.g., depression, limitations in functional activity, knowledge of the disease and its medical/surgical management) or can suggest important moderators of the likely impact of the condition (e.g., coping styles, vocational history and status). This information, in turn, guides the selection and implementation of specific interventions.

Although often overlooked in traditional medical assessments, the patient's social, family, and cultural contexts can also identify potential targets for intervention (e.g., social isolation, serious relationship conflict) or resources to maximize the benefits of other interventions (e.g., social support). The strengths and weaknesses of the patient's relationships with key members of the health care team and the patient's skills for managing and improving those relationships (e.g., assertiveness) are also important considerations in selecting targets or methods for intervention. The patient's cultural/ethnic background is also an important consideration, especially if it is different from that of key members of the health care team given that it can complicate effective communication and collaboration over the long periods of time typically involved in the care of chronic disease.

Finally, the specific health care setting (e.g., inpatient vs. outpatient care, brief vs. prolonged hospitalization) is likely to make some interventions more feasible than others, as are prevailing attitudes toward psychosocial interventions among members of the health care team within the culture of a specific clinic or medical service. Insurance coverage and a variety of potential barriers to psychosocial intervention (e.g., access to safe, adequately supervised exercise facilities) are essential considerations in treatment planning. Only after a thorough consideration of each of these four general categories of the patient's "biopsychosocial presentation" can appropriate interventions be identified and implemented in a manner most likely to maximize their potential benefits to the patient.

Intervention Options for Psychologists in Health Care Settings

Clinical health psychologists choose interventions from the full range of therapeutic options available to professional psychology, but unique features of the medical setting can challenge the psychologist and shape the form that interventions take. The diversity of medical and psychological problems seen across health care settings, each of which is associated with a complex bundle of biopsychosocial issues, requires the psychologist to be a broadly trained generalist. The time demands of health care settings and the cost containment features of the health care system push the clinician to be increasingly brief, efficient, and accountable. The interdisciplinary nature of care and the psychologist's place in the medical hierarchy challenge the psychologist to be collaborative and resourceful in the delivery of services. These features have resulted in a strikingly heterogeneous and creative array of treatments. As outlined in Table 5.2, this sometimes daunting set of treatment issues and options can be structured by considering the level and mode of treatment in the context of one's goals for intervening.

Goals of Intervention

Psychologists working in health care settings intervene to improve patients' health and well-being across three broad and interrelated domains: (a) reducing the risk of developing disease among healthy individuals, (b) improving disease outcomes among those with developed illnesses, and (c) enhancing the quality of life and emotional health of those experiencing

Table 5.2   Intervention Options in General Health Care Settings

I. Reasons for Intervention

    A. Risk reduction

    B. Disease outcomes

    C. Maximizing functioning/quality of life

II. Levels of Intervention

    A. Individual

    B. Couples/Family

    C. Group

    D. Health care team

III. Modes of Intervention

    A. Psychoeducation

    B. Cognitive behavioral therapies

    C. Interpersonal/Social support interventions

---

illness. Given compelling evidence that behavioral and psychosocial processes are integral to the development and course of many physical conditions, psychologists may intervene to reduce the incidence or progression of major illnesses. However, because illness can create profound psychosocial challenges, the goals of clinical health psychologists extend beyond attempts to improve physical health to maximize the daily functioning of patients and their families.

Levels of Intervention

These goals can be met by intervening at a variety of levels. Individual therapy remains a strong option for clinical health psychologists, but interventions involving larger social units are increasingly common. The family unit is an important focus because illnesses can have adverse effects on families, and risk reduction and illness management occur within this broader family context. Family conflict and marital strife appear to be particularly disruptive to managing illness and maintaining quality of life among medical patients (e.g., Schafer, Keith, & Schafer, 2000; Zautra, Burleson, Matt, Roth, & Burrows, 1994) and may even pose a risk for future morbidity and mortality (e.g., Coyne et al., 2001). Hence, interventions that involve families or spouses may be more effective than those that focus solely on the individual (e.g., Anderson, Ho, Brackett, & Laffel, 1999; Epstein, Valoski, Wing, & McCurley, 1990; Keefe et al., 1996).

Group psychotherapy is also fairly common in medical settings. Group psychotherapies tend to be cost- and time-efficient because many educational, behavioral, and interpersonal issues can be addressed readily in a group format (Spira, 1997). Groups have the additional benefits of bestowing a sense of belonging for individuals dealing with the common stress of illness and providing important sources of support, information, and accountability for behavior change (Spira, 1997; Spiegel & Diamond, 2001). Although support groups have the potential to be iatrogenic (e.g., Helgeson, Cohen, Schulz, & Yasko, 2000), there is evidence that well-conducted, structured groups can be as effective as, or more effective than, individual therapy at promoting and maintaining behavior change (e.g., Wing & Jeffery, 1999).

A level that may be somewhat unique to medical settings involves interventions focusing on the health care team. As we witness a gradual shift away from an "acute medical intervention" model toward a "chronic illness management" model, patients are required to assume new responsibilities for day-to-day illness management, and health care professionals are compelled to incorporate behavioral interventions into medical practice (Gonder-Frederick, Cox, & Ritterband, 2002). Health care professionals might need the behavior change expertise of psychologists to do this effectively. Furthermore, because health care providers can be an efficient and powerful source of advice and counseling for patients, interventions to promote physicians' communication skills and enhance the doctor-patient relationship can have broad effects. Finally, the continuing need for pragmatic, cost-effective interventions may result in the training of nonpsychologists for the delivery of brief psychological interventions.

Modes of Intervention

Given the range of issues and problems likely to be encountered across health care settings, psychologists cannot be wedded to any particular therapeutic orientation. This chapter focuses on three broad modes of intervention that can be used across individual, group, or family formats: psychoeducation, cognitive-behavior therapy (CBT), and interpersonal/social support. Psychoeducation generally provides patients with information (e.g., information about health risks, illness, treatments, or coping skills) to alter their attitudes and behaviors in a direction that will improve adjustment. Psychoeducation can provide patients with a medically accurate understanding of their condition and may be sufficient for some patients to adapt to the complex demands of managing illness.

CBT is pervasive in medical settings. These interventions include a myriad of specific behavioral and cognitive techniques that are often combined in a multicomponent fashion. Multicomponent CBT begins with education but commonly adds in skill-building features such as goal setting, self-monitoring, problem solving, stimulus control, relaxation and stress management, and cognitive restructuring. It is also increasingly common to include interpersonal skill acquisition such as assertion training and developing social support. CBT overlaps with psychoeducation to the extent that both modes teach specific skills (e.g., relaxation training), but CBT is delivered in a more progressive, individualized, and interactive manner to help patients not only reconceptualize their health problems and develop new coping skills but also consolidate (e.g., via rehearsal and role-play) and maintain these skills (e.g., relapse prevention).

Given compelling evidence on the importance of social relationships for one's physical health and psychological well-being, interpersonal/social support interventions are also commonly used in medical settings. Aside from some well-defined interpersonal therapies, however, many of these interventions have not been described or studied systematically (Hogan, Linden, & Najarian, 2001). Some social support interventions focus on providing support during therapy per se. This may occur by direct support provision from the therapist; by simply including family, friends, and/or peers in therapy; or by including therapeutic activities that engage or promote support from important others. Other support interventions focus on developing patients' social skills, which can then be used to nurture and strengthen their naturally occurring social support networks. Support interventions can occur at any level but most commonly capitalize on the supportive features of group therapy.

EXAMPLES OF BRIEF PSYCHOLOGICAL INTERVENTIONS IN HEALTH CARE SETTINGS

This section describes how these three modes of intervention—psychoeducation, CBT, and interpersonal/social support—have been used to achieve the three treatment goals in clinical health psychology, namely reducing risk, improving disease outcomes, and enhancing quality of life. This structure is one of convenience and should not be interpreted as implying independence across domains. For example, health behavior interventions are discussed in the context of risk reduction but may also improve disease outcomes (e.g., smoking cessation to reduce vascular complications among individuals with diabetes [Gonder-Frederick et al., 2002]) and enhance quality of life (e.g., exercise interventions to reduce depression with cancer [Andersen, 2002]). The approach taken for this limited review is to provide general themes from the most well-developed literatures (e.g., interventions tested with randomized clinical trials) as well as salient examples across the range of interventions. This section emphasizes brief interventions but occasionally discusses more intensive therapies if their effects are particularly impressive. Finally, despite clear advances in research on the efficacy of behavioral medicine interventions over the past decade, one should note that the interventions discussed here have often not been adequately tested in the health care settings in which they are likely to be used. Hence, for all of these interventions, there is more evidence of their efficacy in controlled trials than of their effectiveness in the conditions and contexts of their typical clinical use during medical care.

Reducing Risk of Developing Disease

It is well known that modifiable risk factors, such as smoking, inactivity, obesity, and risky sexual behaviors, play a major role in the health of the U.S. population. Behavioral interventions to reduce obesity or stop smoking are supported well enough that they are recommended options in the clinical practice guidelines emanating from federal agencies (e.g., Fiore et al., 1996; National Institutes of Health [NIH], 1997). This external validation of what behavioral scientists have known for years may increase the demands for integrating lifestyle change interventions into general health care. Psychosocial variables, such as personality, stress, negative emotions, and impaired social relationships, are also emerging as important factors in the development of illness. Thus, although they are not fully established, interventions to improve psychosocial risk profiles may become increasingly relevant for risk reduction.

Psychoeducation

Education and self-help information are mainstays of most effective risk reduction interventions. In health care settings, psychoeducation can occur in person or via telephone, print, or computer-generated information delivered to at-risk individuals or groups. Although generally considered necessary for risk reduction, education in isolation has fairly modest and short-term effects (Blumenthal, Sherwood, Gullette, Georgiades, & Tweedy, 2002; Dubbert, 2002; Niaura & Abrams, 2002). There is reason to believe that effectiveness can be improved by including family members in educational efforts (e.g., Morisky, DeMuth, Field-Fass, Green, & Levine, 1985), and by tailoring the information to the patients' level of readiness to change (Dubbert, 2002). For example, Strecher and colleagues (1994) found that smoking family practice patients reported a doubling of 6-month quit rates when they received individually tailored smoking cessation letters rather than standard cessation letters (but see Curry, McBride, Grottos, Louie, & Wagner, 1995, for differing results).

A promising educational approach to risk reduction involves training physicians and other health care professionals to provide lifestyle change advice and counseling. Health care providers may be particularly persuasive messengers for risk reduction given their frequency of contact with high-risk individuals and the importance of physician advice in motivating interest to change. Controlled clinical trials suggest that physician advice and written or telephone follow-up are effective at increasing physical activity (e.g., Writing Group for the Activity Counseling Trial, 2001) and smoking cessation (e.g., Ockene et al., 2000; Pieterse, Seydel, DeVries, Mudde, & Kok, 2001). There is also evidence that interventions delivered by other health care providers (e.g., nurses, physician assistants) are effective and additive (Burns, Cohen, Gritz, & Kottke, 1994).

An area of emerging interest involves incorporating motivational interviewing into risk reduction advice and counseling (see Chapter 4 for more details on motivational interviewing). Originally developed to enhance motivation to address addiction, motivational interviewing represents a style of providing personalized behavior change feedback in an empathic, nonconfrontive, and empowering manner (Miller & Rollnick, 1991). Although somewhat mixed, preliminary data suggest that motivational interviewing has the potential to be useful across a range of health behaviors (for reviews, see Dunn, Deroo, & Rivara, 2001; Resnicow et al., 2002). If additional research supports these promising initial data, motivational interviewing may be well suited to medical settings because it is brief and appears to be transportable across behavioral domains and health care professionals.

Cognitive-Behavioral Therapy

Fairly standard group and individual CBT treatment programs are available for a variety of health behaviors. Multicomponent CBT shows substantial improvement over minimal education interventions for improving HIV risk behaviors (Kelly & Kalichman, 2002; NIH, 1997), physical inactivity (Dubbert, 2002), and smoking cessation (Compas, Haaga, Keefe, Leitenberg, & Williams, 1998; Niaura & Abrams, 2002). The importance

of such interventions for preventing the development of disease was demonstrated dramatically in the Diabetes Prevention Trial (National Institute of Diabetes, Digestive, and Kidney Disease, 2001). Although the intervention was not brief, this multicenter, randomized clinical trial clearly demonstrated that behaviorally based lifestyle interventions can be as effective as, or more effective than, medications at preventing the development of diabetes among high-risk individuals.

Although impressive, such data must be interpreted and applied cautiously. In most cases, the interventions represent a bundle of educational, behavioral, and cognitive strategies, making it impossible to evaluate which components are most important for reducing risks. At best, this creates an inefficient approach to providing therapy in the time constraints of many health care settings (cf. Coyne & Racioppo, 2000). Second, although multicomponent CBT appears to be quite effective at promoting initial behavior change, there is a serious problem with relapse. More intensive interventions (e.g., more therapy sessions, multicomponent vs. single-component therapy, medication) appear to produce more prolonged changes (e.g., Blumenthal et al., 2002; Naiura & Abrams, 2002; NIH, 1997; Ockene et al., 2000). On the surface, such findings challenge the brief therapy environment of medical care. However, Wadden, Brownell, and Foster (2002) found that monthly 15-minute sessions conducted during patients' regular medication checks maintained weight loss as effectively as did a more traditional behavioral group therapy program, suggesting that prolonged behavioral interventions can be creatively incorporated into health care settings.

Interpersonal/Social Support Interventions

Risk reduction interventions often include procedures to enhance social support.

Although the methodology and resulting data are quite varied, there may be benefits to socially based interventions for risk reduction. For example, obesity treatments that include spouses result in more weight loss for up to 3 months posttreatment (but not beyond) compared with those that do not (Black, Gleser, & Kooyers, 1990). Similarly, Epstein and colleagues' (1990) family-based behavioral treatment for childhood obesity has produced remarkably sustained reductions in obesity and improvements in physical activity for up to 10 years. Such studies demonstrate the utility of embedding risk reduction into the broader social contexts in which risk behaviors occur.

There also may be benefits to reducing risk behaviors by promoting social support more directly. Wing and Jeffery (1999) found that support enhancement procedures (e.g., recruitment with friends, intragroup activities, provision and receipt of support, intergroup competitions) improved the effectiveness of behavioral group therapy for weight loss. In a very different context, Kelly and colleagues (1993) found that depressed patients with HIV responded to a supportive-expressive group intervention with reductions in depression, maladaptive interpersonal insecurities, and unsafe sex as compared with controls with no treatment.

Improving Disease Outcomes

Psychosocial interventions with medical patients may also be aimed at improving hard indicators of disease outcomes (e.g., mortality, cardiac events, blood glucose levels, immune functioning) by targeting behavioral or psychosocial risk. Because behaviors are integral to the treatment of many medical conditions, psychologists may be called on to improve adherence to medical interventions or to help patients meet the complex self-regulatory and lifestyle demands of chronic illness (e.g., diabetes self-management, home dialysis skills).

At a different level, psychobiological processes related to stress, negative emotions, and social relationships also influence disease progression. Thus, psychologists in medical settings may be in a position to alter disease by intervening to reduce stress, minimize negative emotions, or enhance social support.

Psychoeducation

Psychoeducation is a necessary component in the comprehensive treatment of chronic illnesses. Such interventions provide information about the cause, course, and treatment of diseases as well as stress management (e.g., relaxation), coping, and illness management skills. Although not sufficient for all patients, psychoeducation improves adherence to treatment recommendations and, to a lesser extent, improves health outcomes (for a review, see Roter et al., 1998). Such interventions have been reported to yield clinically meaningful improvement in indexes of blood glucose control among patients with type 2 diabetes (i.e., at a magnitude that reduces serious diabetes complications [Norris, Lau, Smith, Schmid, & Engelgau, 2002]) and to decrease fatal and nonfatal myocardial infarction over a 10-year period among those with coronary heart disease (Dusseldorp, van Elderen, Maes, Meulman, & Kraaij, 1999). Dusseldorp and colleagues (1999) specifically found that psychoeducation improved disease outcomes among coronary heart disease patients primarily if it altered the behavioral or psychosocial risk factors hypothesized to mediate intervention effects. Psychoeducation appears equally beneficial across group or individual formats and when delivered by different health care providers (e.g., Linden, Stossel, & Mourice, 1996; Norris et al., 2002; Roter et al., 1998).

These impressive findings are qualified by evidence that it is difficult to maintain positive outcomes over time and that such interventions are more effective with more intensive or prolonged interventions (cf. Norris et al.,

2002; Roter et al., 1998). Innovative methods to maximize efficiency without limiting effectiveness are currently being explored. Brief office-based interventions that can readily be incorporated into routine visits are now appearing, sometimes taking advantage of interactive computer technology. For example, Glasgow and colleagues (1997) reported that having the health care team review individualized, computer-generated information regarding patient goals and motivation for dietary behaviors resulted in reduced serum cholesterol levels over a 1-year period among patients with type 2 diabetes.

Cognitive-Behavioral Therapy

Several highly publicized studies have demonstrated that intensive, long-term CBT can improve disease processes. For example, Ornish and colleagues (1990, 1998) found that a multicomponent behavioral intervention for CHD patients (i.e., stress management, group therapy, and intensive changes in diet and exercise) resulted in regression of coronary atherosclerosis and reductions in the recurrence of coronary events compared with usual care. Friedman and colleagues' (1986) well-known Recurrent Coronary Prevention Project randomized cardiac patients to group CBT consisting of relaxation training, stress management, and cognitive restructuring to reduce coronary-prone behavior. The intervention yielded diminished Type A behavior and a 44% reduction in the recurrence of nonfatal cardiac events compared with usual care.

The intensity of these interventions makes it unlikely they can be used on a wide-scale basis, but their success has spurred attempts to identify briefer interventions to improve disease outcomes. Although single-component stress management interventions (e.g., relaxation) are not broadly effective at altering disease progression (Linden & Chambers, 1994), they do appear to enhance the effectiveness of standard medical rehabilitation programs

(Linden et al., 1996). In addition, brief group therapy employing multicomponent, cognitive-behavioral stress management (CBSM) (e.g., six to eight sessions of illness education, cognitive restructuring, coping skills training, relaxation or anxiety management, and/or provision of social support) appears to be quite promising. As examples, group CBSM has been found to (a) enhance blood glucose control at 1-year follow-up among patients with type 2 diabetes (Surwit et al., 2002), (b) reduce 6-year mortality rates among those with malignant melanomas (Fawzy et al., 1993), and (c) promote more positive emotional and immunological functioning among individuals infected with HIV (e.g., Antoni et al., 2000; Ironson et al., 1994). These intriguing data are qualified by notable non-replications and mixed results in the broader literature. Miller and Cohen (2001) suggested that psychotherapy may have stronger effects when patients are highly distressed and when the disease condition is not overwhelming the psychobiological process. This possibility suggests that psychosocial interventions to improve disease outcomes should occur while the biological system is still malleable among patients who are seriously distressed.

Brief CBT for depression (Beck, Rush, Shaw, & Emery, 1979) is also important for medical populations. Although many patients adapt well to disease, depression is fairly common among primary care patients (Katon & Schulberg, 1992) and is clearly associated with poorer disease progression (e.g., Frasure-Smith, Lesperance, & Talajic, 1995). Brief CBT effectively reduces depression among medical patients (Coyne, Thompson, Klinkman, & Nease, 2002; Schulberg et al., 1996), with some evidence that it also improves medical outcomes. Lustman, Griffith, Kissel, and Clouse (1998), for example, found that 10 weeks of individual CBT for depression among patients with diabetes improved blood glucose control over the subsequent 6 months compared with diabetes education. Nevertheless, there are disturbing nonreplications of the medical effects of CBT for depression. In a recently completed multicenter trial, cardiac patients who met criteria for depression or low social support were randomized to CBT or usual care (National Heart, Lung, and Blood Institute, 2001). The intervention lessened depression and improved social support but did not have an overall effect on subsequent cardiac events.

Interpersonal/Social Support Interventions

Interpersonal therapy for depression (Klerman, Weissman, Rounsaville, & Chevron, 1984) also reduces depression among primary care patients (Schulberg et al., 1996). To the extent that such reductions can alter important biobehavioral or psychobiological processes, interpersonal therapy may eventually prove to be useful for improving the health of medical patients. At a broader level, provision of social support is a common feature of the multicomponent CBSM therapies described earlier and is hypothesized to be vital to the success of CBSM in improving physical health. This possibility, however, has not been carefully evaluated; the effects of support enhancement on disease outcomes have primarily been studied in the context of multicomponent therapies designed to improve psychosocial adjustment. There are, of course, dramatic demonstrations that support interventions can improve disease. Goodkin and colleagues (1999) recently reported that HIV-positive gay men who randomly received 10 weeks of group-based bereavement counseling were buffered against the increase in HIV viral load displayed by the normal care control. Spiegel, Bloom, Kraemer, and Gottheil (1989) found that women with metastatic breast cancer who engaged in 1 year of supportive-expressive group therapy had longer survival times than did those in the control group. Nevertheless, a large randomized clinical trial to replicate this effect recently revealed that supportive-expressive group therapy improved

psychosocial adjustment but did not prolong survival (Goodwin et al., 2001). Additional research will be necessary to determine whether and when social support interventions in general, and supportive-expressive group therapy in particular, improve disease outcomes.

Maximizing Functioning and Improving Quality of Life

The adaptive demands of medical illnesses and treatments can be burdensome for patients and their families, exacting high costs in their emotional, social, occupational, and financial well-being. The experience of illness and its treatments may cause pain and disability, alter important social and occupational roles, erode financial and coping resources, and engender hopelessness, fear, and depression. In some cases, improved medical management of illnesses yields comparable declines in patients' quality of life. In other cases, illnesses cannot be changed, but suffering and disability can be reduced. Thus, psychologists working in health care settings are often called on to improve patients' emotional well-being (e.g., decrease depression and anxiety), symptom management (e.g., reduce pain or treatment side effects), and more general quality of life (e.g., return to activities of daily living, decreased isolation).

Psychoeducation

Educational interventions are commonly used as a first step toward improving the functioning of patients dealing with chronic or life-threatening illnesses. These brief interventions seek to improve patients' capacities for coping by enhancing their understanding of the cause, treatment, and course of their diseases as well as of their coping options. Although the literature is difficult to evaluate given heterogeneity in method and quality, there is reason to believe that educational interventions are useful. Psychoeducation groups have been reported to have positive effects on emotional and functional adjustment and/or pain and discomfort among patients with cancer (Bottomley, 1997; Helgeson & Cohen, 1996; Meyer & Mark, 1995), diabetes (Clement, 1995), and coronary heart disease (Linden et al., 1996) as well as potentially many others. At least in the context of cancer, these interventions appear to be more effective among those who are most in need (e.g., highly distressed) and when they are delivered early in the disease process (Helgeson & Cohen, 1996; Kiecolt-Glazer, McGuire, Robles, & Glaser, 2002), suggesting that early screening to identify and then treat vulnerable patients may be useful.

Psychoeducational approaches have also been developed to improve patients' reactions to stressful medical procedures and to inter-acting more generally with the health care system. It is well established, for example, that orienting patients to painful and difficult medical procedures (e.g., surgery, chemo-therapy) via sensory, procedural, and coping information results in improved recovery (e.g., reduced hospital stays, pain medication, and anxiety [Contrada, Leventhal, & Anderson, 1994]). Educational interventions to improve patients' interactions with health care profes-sionals have also shown benefits for patient adjustment. Brief interventions to improve physician communication (Rutter, Iconomou, & Quine, 1996) and to help health care pro-fessionals empower patients (Anderson et al., 1995; Gonder-Frederick et al., 2002) may increase patient satisfaction and minimize disease-induced functional limitations.

Cognitive-Behavioral Therapy

Medical patients often experience painful or debilitating symptoms associated with medical treatments and illness. Behavioral and cognitive techniques have been used with success to improve symptom management, often more effectively than education alone.

For example, techniques such as relaxation, biofeedback, guided imagery, and hypnosis appear to be useful for reducing pain and nausea associated with cancer treatments (Compas et al., 1998). Specific behavioral techniques, such as relaxation, CBT, and some forms of biofeedback, have been deemed to be efficacious for treating migraine and tension headache pain (Holroyd, 2002), and multicomponent CBT (i.e., relaxation, cognitive restructuring, coping skills training, and goal setting) appear to be effective at improving pain, physical activity, and psy-chological distress among patients with arthritis (for reviews, see Compas et al., 1998; Keefe et al., 2002).

In contrast to their qualified success at improving disease outcomes, CBT for depres-sion and the multicomponent CBSM group therapies described earlier consistently improve patients' psychosocial well-being. CBT is effective at treating major depression among patients who seek treatment in pri-mary care, regardless of whether or not there is a concomitant presenting medical condition (Schulberg et al., 1996). Similarly, CBSM appears to enhance emotional functioning, coping abilities, functional abilities, and/or quality of life among patients coping with cancer (Meyer & Mark, 1995) and HIV (e.g., Lutgendorf et al., 1998). We are also begin-ning to document the psychosocial processes through which CBSM appears to be effective. Lutgendorf and colleagues (1998) found that the effects of CBSM on depression were medi-ated by altered coping (i.e., increased cognitive coping and social support) in a sample of HIV-positive gay men.

Interpersonal/Social Support Interventions

There is a large enough literature with cancer patients to conclude that professionally run support groups can improve patient qual-ity of life (Compas et al., 1998; Hogan et al.,

2001; Bottomley, 1997). In particular, supportive-expressive group therapy (e.g., encouragement of emotional expression, provision and receipt of emotional support, hypnosis for pain management) has been found to improve mood and pain reports among those with metastatic breast cancer (Goodwin et al., 2001; Spiegel, Bloom, & Yalom, 1981), and to be more effective than CBT at reducing mood disturbance among patients with HIV (Kelly et al., 1993). Broadly speaking, however, data on the effectiveness of support groups are fairly inconsistent. This may be because of heterogeneity in how support groups are conducted. For example, there is reason to believe that peer-run support groups can yield negative outcomes. Helgeson and colleagues (2000) developed a group education intervention for cancer patients that was delivered either with or without peer discussion and opportunities for peer support. Relative to controls, the peer support group displayed impaired psychosocial adjustment (e.g., increased negative affect and conflict with family and friends) that was maintained over 6 months.

Some treatments have focused on improving emotional well-being and quality of life by intervening more directly with interpersonal processes. For example, interpersonal therapy for depression enhances recovery from postpartum depression (O'Hara, Stuart, Goman, & Wenzel, 2000), a finding that is particularly important given that postpartum depression causes great individual and family suffering and impairs infant development but often is not treated pharmacologically if women are breast-feeding. Relatedly, interventions that promote spousal caregiving or couples skills (e.g., communication, problem solving, engaging in the caregiving role) have the potential to aid in managing pain and reducing depression (Keefe et al., 1996), and an intervention to promote teamwork between adolescents with diabetes and their mothers lessens family conflict and improves diabetes management (Anderson et al., 1999).

SPECIALIZED TRAINING AND SKILLS

Given the complexity of issues that psychologists encounter when working in general health care settings and the array of treatment options that may be used to meet these challenges, how does one learn to translate traditional psychological interventions into the unique context of medical care? Excellent guidelines for the training and skills necessary to function effectively as a clinical health psychologist are available elsewhere (e.g., Belar & Deardorff, 1995; Belar et al., 2001; McDaniel, Belar, Schroeder, Hargrove, & Freeman, 2002) and are described in detail in Table 5.3. The knowledge and skills most unique to the brief therapy environment of health care settings are highlighted here.

A biopsychosocial perspective is fundamental to providing brief psychosocial treatments in medical settings. Although specific clinical assessment and intervention skills are necessary, they are woefully insufficient if delivered without consideration of this broader context. Patients enter the medical system for a variety of reasons, some of which may be only tangentially related to their presenting complaints. Assessing patients as part of a biopsychosocial system helps the psychologist to untangle the complex web of issues that often present as medical symptoms. Through this process, the psychologist can more effectively evaluate the need and prioritize the goals for psychological interventions and then implement the most appropriate level and mode of intervention. A biopsychosocial perspective is developed not only through didactic knowledge of the biological, psychological, and sociocultural aspects of health and illness but also through mentored experiences in health care settings serving various medical populations. Such experiential learning can be crucial to solidifying a sophisticated understanding of the dynamic interrelationships among biomedical, psychological, and sociocultural processes in

Table 5.3   Specialized Skills and Training for Providing Brief Interventions in
Health Care Settings

 I. In-Depth Knowledge of the Biopsychosocial Model

   A. Biological aspects of health and illness
   B. Psychological aspects of health and illness

      1. Cognitive aspects of health and illness (e.g., illness models, irrational beliefs)
      2. Affective aspects of health and illness (e.g., bidirectional associations between depression and disease)
      3. Behavioral aspects of health and illness
      4. Developmental aspects of health and illness

   C. Sociocultural aspects of health and illness
   D. Knowledge of the dynamic interrelationships among A, B, and C

 II. Knowledge of Common Conditions and Issues Seen Across Health Care Settings

   A. Pathophysiology
   B. Risk factors
   C. Presenting signs and symptoms
   D. Diagnostic and treatment procedures
   E. Prognosis
   F. Biopsychosocial issues involved in A to E

III. Skills in the Biopsychosocial Assessment of Common Medical Conditions

   A. Traditional psychological assessment skills and knowledge of their limitations
   B. Skill at detecting mental health problems among medical patients
   C. Knowledge of specialized instruments (e.g., relevant personality traits, coping styles, patient conceptualizations of illness, disease-specific adjustment)
   D. Knowledge of medical assessment procedures
   E. Brief interviewing skills
   F. Triage skills

IV. Clinical Skills for Brief Interventions in Health Care

   A. Individual, couples, family, and group therapy skills
   B. Psychoeducation knowledge and skills

      1. Social learning theory
      2. Motivational interviewing

   C. Multicomponent cognitive behavioral therapy

      1. Relaxation training/stress management
      2. Problem solving and coping skills training
      3. Assertiveness training
      4. Cognitive restructuring
      5. Brief motivational interventions
      6. Relapse prevention

   D. Supportive therapy skills
   E. Interpersonal and family systems theory/therapy
   F. Crisis management

 V. Interdisciplinary Collaboration Skills

   A. Well-developed and positive professional identity as a psychologist
   B. Understanding the training, goals, and perspectives of other disciplines
   C. Familiarity with the languages of other disciplines
   D. Communication and social skills

VI. Awareness of Sociopolitical Issues Across Health Care Settings

---

SOURCE: Adapted from McDaniel, Belar, Schroeder, Hargrove, and Freeman (2002).

general as well as their specific instantiation with a given patient. Mentored experiences across health care settings also provide invaluable training on how to navigate the numerous challenges of functioning as a clinical health psychologist in the culture of medicine (e.g., communicating with physicians, getting paid for psychological services).

Clinical health psychologists must also develop a detailed understanding of the medical conditions commonly encountered across health care settings and their associated diagnostic and treatment procedures. Such information is integral to the patient's context and allows psychologists to identify important biobehavioral or psychobiological processes that may become targets for intervention, to anticipate stressful transitions in the disease and treatment process, and to work more collaboratively with the interdisciplinary health care team. Nevertheless, clinical health psychologists must embed this knowledge in the broader biopsychosocial context and not lose sight of their unique perspective on the psychosocial aspects of medical care.

The delivery of effective psychosocial interventions in health care settings requires psychologists to work collaboratively with members of an interdisciplinary health care team—who themselves have unique and sometimes opposing perspectives on patient care—in the context of a health care system that might not fully appreciate the systemic approach. Although good social skills and knowledge of the training and perspectives of other professions are important, the development of a solid professional identity as a psychologist may be most crucial to accomplishing this difficult task (cf. McDaniel et al., 2002).

In this context, one must remember that the specialized skills of the clinical health psychologist emerge out of general core training in the broader discipline of psychology and its traditional applications to mental health. Mental health problems are common in health care settings, and clinical health psychologists who have not developed this broader expertise may encounter patient problems that they are unequipped to handle (cf. Smith, in press). Patients with diabetes who have comorbid eating disorders require more than illness management interventions, and serious pathology among family members can completely undermine the best that psychotherapy has to offer if it is not recognized or addressed. Developing this broad expertise in traditional areas of clinical psychology can be difficult due to competing demands and the daunting challenges of learning a rapidly expanding literature and developing skills at the interface of psychology and medicine. The importance of doing so, however, has been recognized in the training guidelines for health psychology (e.g., McDaniel et al., 2002).

CONCLUSION

Clinical health psychologists have made remarkable strides in integrating a biopsychosocial perspective into medical care and in developing novel approaches to meet the unique challenges of health care settings. As reviewed in this chapter, brief and group psychotherapies hold considerable promise in this endeavor. Although the emerging literature evaluating these interventions is favorable, there are nagging inconsistencies with few examples of programmatic support for specific interventions and few tests of their effectiveness in the medical contexts where they are typically used. In this climate of hope and caution, the biopsychosocial model provides an invaluable framework. This model does not provide a prescriptive blueprint for working with medical patients. Rather, its strength lies in its flexibility to be useful across patients and health care settings, its ability to accommodate rapidly changing medical technology and treatments, and the often necessarily novel and creative clinical interventions that emerge from its application.

REFERENCES

Andersen, B. L. (2002). Biobehavioral outcomes following psychological interventions for cancer patients. *Journal of Consulting and Clinical Psychology, 70,* 590–610.

Anderson, B. J., Ho, J., Brackett, J., & Laffel, L. M. (1999). An office-based intervention to maintain parent-adolescent teamwork in diabetes management: Impact on parent involvement, family conflict, and glycemic control. *Diabetes Care, 22,* 713–721.

Anderson, R. M., Funnell, M. M., Butler, P. M., Arnold, M. S., Fitzgerald, J. T., & Feste, C. C. (1995). Patient empowerment: Results of a randomized controlled trial. *Diabetes Care, 18,* 943–949.

Antoni, M. H., Cruess, D. G., Cruess, S., Lutgendorf, S., Kumar, M., Ironson, G., Klimas, N., Fletcher, M. A., & Schneiderman, N. (2000). Cognitive-behavioral stress management intervention effects on anxiety, 24-hr urinary norepinephrine output, and T-cytotoxic/suppressor cells over time among symptomatic HIV-infected gay men. *Journal of Consulting and Clinical Psychology, 68,* 31–45.

Beck, A. T., Rush, A. J., Shaw, B. F., & Emery, G. (1979). *Cognitive therapy of depression.* New York: Guilford.

Belar, C. D., Brown, R. A., Hersch, L. E., Hornyak, L. M., Rozensky, R. H., Sheridan, E. P., Brown, R. T., & Reed, G. W. (2001). Self-assessment in clinical health psychology: A model for ethical expansion of practice. *Professional Psychology: Research and Practice, 32*(2), 135–141.

Belar, C. D., & Deardorff, W. W. (1995). *Clinical health psychology in medical settings: A practitioner's guidebook.* Washington, DC: American Psychological Association.

Black, D. R., Gleser, L. J., & Kooyers, K. J. (1990). A meta-analytic evaluation of couples weight-loss programs. *Health Psychology, 9,* 330–347.

Blumenthal, J. A., Sherwood, A., Gullette, E. C. D., Georgiades, A., & Tweedy, D. (2002). Biobehavioral approaches to the treatment of essential hypertension. *Journal of Consulting and Clinical Psychology, 70,* 569–589.

Bottomley, A. (1997). Cancer support groups: Are they effective? *European Journal of Cancer Care, 6,* 11–17.

Burns, S., Cohen, S., Gritz, E., & Kottke, T. (1994). *Tobacco and the clinician: Interventions for medical and dental practice* (Vol. 5). Bethesda, MD: U.S. Department of Health and Human Services.

Centers for Disease Control and Prevention. (1999). *Chronic diseases and their risk factors: The nation's leading causes of death.* Washington, DC: U.S. Department of Health and Human Services.

Clement, S. (1995). Diabetes self-management education. *Diabetes Care, 18,* 1204–1214.

Compas, B. E., Haaga, D. A., Keefe, F. J., Leitenberg, H., & Williams, D. A. (1998). Sampling of empirically supported psychological treatments from health psychology: Smoking, chronic pain, cancer, and bulimia nervosa. *Journal of Consulting and Clinical Psychology, 66,* 89–112.

Contrada, R. J., Leventhal, E. A., & Anderson, J. R. (1994). Psychological preparation for surgery: Marshalling individual and social resources to optimize self-regulation. *International Review of Health Psychology, 3,* 219–266.

Coyne, J. C., & Racioppo, M. W. (2000). Never the twain shall meet? Closing the gap between coping research and clinical intervention research. *American Psychologist, 55,* 655–664.

Coyne, J. C., Rohrbaugh, M. J., Shoham, V., Sonnega, J. S., Nicklas, J. M., & Cranford, J. A. (2001). Prognostic importance of marital quality for survival of congestive heart failure. *American Journal of Cardiology, 88,* 526–529.

Coyne, J. C., Thompson, R., Klinkman, M. S., & Nease, D. E., Jr. (2002). Emotional disorders in primary care. *Journal of Consulting and Clinical Psychology, 70,* 798–809.

Curry, S. J., McBride, C., Grottos, L. C., Louie, D., & Wagner, E. H. (1995). A randomized trial of self-help materials, personalized feedback, and telephone counseling with nonvolunteer smokers. *Journal of Consulting and Clinical Psychology, 63,* 1005–1014.

Dubbert, P. M. (2002). Physical activity and exercise: Recent advances and current challenges. *Journal of Consulting and Clinical Psychology, 70,* 526–536.

Dunn, C., Deroo, L., & Rivara, F. (2001). The use of brief interventions adapted from motivational interviewing across behavioral domains: A systematic review. *Addiction, 96,* 1725–1742.

Dusseldorp, E., van Elderen, T., Maes, S., Meulman, J., & Kraaij, V. (1999). A meta-analysis of psychoeducational programs for coronary heart disease patients. *Health Psychology, 18,* 506–519.

Engel, G. L. (1977, April 8). The need for a new medical model: A challenge for biomedicine. *Science, 196,* 129–136.

Epstein, L. H., Valoski, A., Wing, R. R., & McCurley, I. (1990). Ten-year follow-up of behavioral, family-based treatment for obese children. *Journal of the American Medical Association, 264,* 2519–2523.

Fawzy, F. I., Fawzy, N., Hyun, C. S., Elashoff, R., Guthrie, D., Fahey, J. L., & Morton, D. (1993). Malignant melanoma: Effects of a structured psychiatric intervention, coping, affective state, and immune parameters on recurrence and survival six years later. *Archives of General Psychiatry, 50,* 681–689.

Fiore, M., Bailey, W., Cohen, S., Dorfman, S. F., Goldstein, M. G., Gritz, E. R., Heyman, R. G., Holbrook, J., Jaen, C. R., Kottke, T. E., Lando, H. A., Mecklenburg, R., Mullen, P. D., Nett, L. M., Robinson, L., Stitzer, M. L., Tommasello, A. C., Villejo, L., & Wewers, M. E. (1996). *Smoking cessation: Clinical Practice Guideline No. 18* (DHHS Publication No. (ADM) 96-0692). Bethesda, MD: Public Health Service, Agency for Health Case Policy and Research.

Fordyce, W. E. (1976). *Behavioral methods in chronic pain and illness.* St. Louis, MO: C. V. Mosby.

Frasure-Smith, N., Lesperance, F., & Talajic, M. (1995). Depression and 18-month prognosis after myocardial infarction. *Circulation, 91,* 999–1005.

Friedman, M., Thoreson, C. E., Gill, J. J., Ulmer, D., Powell, L. H., Price, V. A., Brown, B., & Thompson, L. (1986). Alteration of Type-A behavior and its effects on cardiac recurrences in post-myocardial infarction patients: Summary results of the Recurrent Coronary Prevention Project. *American Heart Journal, 112,* 653–665.

Glasgow, R. E., La Chance, P. A., Toobert, D. J., Brown, J., Hampson, S. E., & Riddle, M. C. (1997). Long-term effects and costs of brief behavioral dietary intervention for patients with diabetes delivered from the medical office. *Patient Education & Counseling, 32,* 175–184.

Gonder-Frederick, L. A., Cox, D. J., & Ritterband, L. M. (2002). Diabetes and behavioral medicine: The second decade. *Journal of Consulting and Clinical Psychology, 70,* 611–625.

Goodkin, K., Blaney, N. T., Feaster, D. J., Baldewicz, T., Burkhalter, J., & Leeds, B. (1999). A randomized controlled clinical trial of a bereavement support group intervention in human immunodeficiency virus type 1-seropositive and -seronegative homosexual men. *Archives of General Psychiatry, 56,* 52–59.

Goodwin, P. J., Leeszcz, M., Ennis, M., Koopmans, J., Vincent, L., Guther, H., Drysdale, E., Hundleby, M., Chochinor, H. M., Navaro, M., Speca, M., & Hunter, J. (2001). The effect of group psychosocial support on survival in metastatic breast cancer. *New England Journal of Medicine, 345,* 1719–1726.

Helgeson, V. S., & Cohen, S. (1996). Social support and adjustment to cancer: Reconciling descriptive, correlational, and intervention research. *Health Psychology, 15,* 135–148.

Helgeson, V. S., Cohen, S., Schulz, R., & Yasko, J. (2000). Group support interventions for women with breast cancer: Who benefits from what? *Health Psychology, 19,* 107–114.

Hogan, B. E., Linden, W., & Najarian, B. (2001). Social support interventions: Do they work? *Clinical Psychology Review, 22,* 381–440.

Holroyd, K. A. (2002). Assessment and psychological management of recurrent headache disorders. *Journal of Consulting and Clinical Psychology, 70,* 656–677.

Ironson, G., Friedman, A., Klomas, N., Antoni, M. H., Fletcher, M. A., Simoneau, J., LaPerriere, A., & Schneiderman, N. (1994). Distress, denial, and low adherence to behavioral interventions predict faster disease progression in HIV-1 infected gay men. *International Journal of Behavioral Medicine, 1,* 90–105.

Janis, I. L. (1958). *Psychological stress.* New York: John Wiley.

Kaplan, R. M., & Groessl, E. J. (2002). Applications of cost-effectiveness methodologies in behavioral medicine. *Journal of Consulting and Clinical Psychology, 70,* 482–493.

Katon, W., & Schulberg, H. (1992). Epidemiology of depression in primary care. *General Hospital Psychiatry, 14,* 237–247.

Keefe, F. J., Caldwell, D. S., Baucom, D., Salley, A., Robinson, E., Timmons, K., Beaupre, P., Weisberg, J., & Helms, M. (1996). Spouse-assisted coping training in the management of osteoarthritic knee pain. *Arthritis Care and Research, 9,* 279–291.

Keefe, F. J., Smith, S. J., Buffington, A. L. H., Gibson, J., Studts, J. L., & Caldwell, D. S. (2002). Recent advances and future directions in the biopsychosocial assessment and treatment of arthritis. *Journal of Consulting and Clinical Psychology, 70,* 640–655.

Kelly, J. A., & Kalichman, S. C. (2002). Behavioral research with HIV/AIDS primary and secondary prevention: Recent advances and future directions. *Journal of Consulting and Clinical Psychology, 70,* 626–639.

Kelly, J. A., Murphy, D., Bahr, G., Kalichman, S., Morgan, M., Stevenson, L., Koob, J. J., Brasfield, T. L., & Bernstein, B. M. (1993). Outcome of cognitive-behavioral and support group brief therapies for depressed persons diagnosed with HIV infection. *American Journal of Psychiatry, 150,* 1679–1686.

Kiecolt-Glaser, J. K., McGuire, L., Robles, T. F., & Glaser, R. (2002). Psychoneuroimmunology: Psychological influences on immune function and health. *Journal of Consulting and Clinical Psychology, 70,* 537–547.

Klerman, G. L., Weissman, M. M., Rounsaville, B. J., & Chevron, E. S. (1984). *Interpersonal psychotherapy of depression.* New York: Basic Books.

Linden, W., & Chambers, L. (1994). Clinical effectiveness of non-drug treatment for hypertension: A meta-analysis. *Annals of Behavioral Medicine, 16,* 35–45.

Linden, W., Stossel, C., & Mourice, J. (1996). Psychosocial interventions for patients with coronary artery disease: A meta-analysis. *Archives of Internal Medicine, 156,* 745–752.

Lustman, P. J., Griffith, L. S., Kissel, S. S., & Clouse, R. E. (1998). Cognitive behavioral therapy for depression in type 2 diabetes mellitus: A randomized, controlled trial. *Annals of Internal Medicine, 129,* 613–621.

Lutgendorf, S. K., Antoni, M. H., Ironson, G., Starr, K., Costello, N., Zuckerman, M., Klimas, N., Fletcher, M. A., & Schneiderman, N. (1998). Changes in cognitive coping skills and social support during cognitive behavioral stress management intervention and distress outcomes in somatic HIV seropositive gay men. *Psychosomatic Medicine, 60,* 204–214.

McDaniel, S. H., Belar, C. D., Schroeder, C., Hargrove, D. S., & Freeman, E. L. (2002). A training curriculum for professional psychologists in primary care. *Professional Psychology: Research and Practice, 33,* 65–72.

Meyer, T. J., & Mark, M. M. (1995). Effects of psychosocial interventions with adult cancer patients: A meta-analysis of randomized experiments. *Health Psychology, 14,* 101–108.

Miller, G., & Cohen, S. (2001). Psychological interventions and the immune system: A meta-analytical review and critique. *Health Psychology, 20,* 47–63.

Miller, W., & Rollnick, S. (1991). *Motivational interviewing: Preparing people to change addictive behavior.* New York: Guilford.

Morisky, D. M., DeMuth, N. M., Field-Gass, M., Green, L. W., & Levine, D. M. (1985). Evaluation of family health education to build social support for long-term control of high blood pressure. *Health Education Quarterly, 12,* 35–50.

National Heart, Lung, and Blood Institute. (2001). *Study finds no reduction in deaths or heart attacks in heart disease patients treated for depression and low social support.* [Online]. Retrieved on January 20, 2003, from www.nhlbi.niv.gov/new/press/ 01-11-13.htm.

National Institute of Diabetes, Digestive, and Kidney Disease. (2001). *Diet and exercise dramatically delay Type 2 diabetes: Diabetes medication Metformin also effective.* [Online]. Retrieved on January 20, 2003, from www.niddk. nih.gov/welcome/ releases/8_8_01.htm

National Institutes of Health. (1997). *NIH consensus statement: Interventions to prevent HIV risk behaviors.* Bethesda, MD: U.S. Public Health Service.

National Office of Vital Statistics. (1947). *Deaths and death rates for the 10 leading causes of death by sex.* Washington, DC: U.S. Department of Health and Human Services.

Niaura, R., & Abrams, D. B. (2002). Smoking cessation: Progress, priorities, and prospectus. *Journal of Consulting and Clinical Psychology, 70,* 494–509.

Norris, S. L., Lau, J., Smith, S. J., Schmid, C. H., & Engelgau, M. (2002). Self-management education for adults with type 2 diabetes: A meta-analysis of the effects on metabolic control. *Diabetes Care, 25,* 1159–1171.

Ockene, J. K., Emmons, K. M., Mermelstein, R. J., Perkins, K. A., Bonollo, D. S., Voorhees, C. C., & Hollis, J. F. (2000). Relapse and maintenance issues for smoking cessation. *Health Psychology, 19,* 17–31.

O'Hara, M. W., Stuart, S., Gorman, L. L., & Wenzel, A. (2000). Efficacy of interpersonal psychotherapy for postpartum depression. *Archives of General Psychiatry, 57,* 1039–1045.

Ornish, D., Brown, S. E., Scherwitz, L. W., Billings, J. H., Armstrong, W. T., Ports, T. A., Gould, K. L., McLanahan, S. M., Kirekeeide, R. L., & Brand, R. J. (1990). Can lifestyle changes reverse coronary heart disease? The Lifestyle Heart Trial. *Lancet, 336,* 129–133.

Ornish, D., Scherwitz, L. W., Billings, J. H., Brown, S. E., Gould, K. L., & Merritt, T. A. (1998). Intensive lifestyle changes for reversal of coronary heart disease. *Journal of the American Medical Association, 280,* 2001–2007.

Pickering, T. G., & Miller, N. E. (1977). Learned voluntary control of heart rate and rhythm in two subjects with premature ventricular contractions. *British Heart Journal, 39,* 152–159.

Pieterse, M. E., Seydel, E. R., DeVries, H., Mudde, A. N., & Kok, G. J. (2001). Effectiveness of a minimal contact smoking cessation program for Dutch general practitioners: A randomized controlled trial. *Preventive Medicine, 32,* 182–190.

Resnicow, K., Dilorio, C., Soet, J. E., Borelli, B., Hecht, J., & Ernst, D. (2002). Motivational interviewing in health promotion: It sounds like something is changing. *Health Psychology, 21,* 444–451.

Roter, D. L., Hall, J. A., Merisca, R., Nordstrom, B., Cretin, D., & Svarstad, B. (1998). Effectiveness of interventions to improve patient compliance: A meta-analysis. *Medical Care, 36,* 1138–1161.

Rutter, D. R., Iconomou, G., & Quine, L. (1996). Doctor-patient communication and outcome in cancer patients: An intervention. *Psychology and Health, 12,* 57–71.

Schafer, R. B., Keith, P. M., & Schafer, E. (2000). Marital stress, psychological distress, and healthful dietary behavior: A longitudinal analysis. *Journal of Applied Social Psychology, 30,* 1639–1656.

Schulberg, H. C., Block, M. R., Madonia, M. J., Scott, C. P., Rodriguez, E., Imber, S. D., Pere, I. J., Lave, J., Houck, P. R., & Loulehan, J. L. (1996). Treating major depression in primary care practice: Eight-month clinical outcomes. *Archives of General Psychiatry, 53,* 913–919.

Shapiro, D., Tursky, B., Schwartz, G. E., & Shnidman, S. R. (1971). Smoking on cue: A behavioral approach to smoking reduction. *Journal of Health and Social Behavior, 12,* 108–113.

Smith, T. W. (in press). On being careful when you get what you wish for: Commentary on "Self-Assessment in Clinical Health Psychology." *Prevention and Treatment.*

Smith, T. W., Kendall, P. C., & Keefe, F. J. (Eds.). (2002). Behavioral medicine and clinical health psychology [special issue]. *Journal of Consulting and Clinical Psychology, 70*(3).

Smith, T. W., Nealey, J. R., & Hamann, H. A. (2000). Health psychology. In C. R. Snyder & R. E. Ingram (Eds.), *Handbook of psychological change: Psychotherapy processes and practices for the 21st century* (pp. 562–590). New York: John Wiley.

Smith, T. W., & Nicassio, P. M. (1995). Psychological practice: Clinical application of the biopsychosocial model. In P. M. Nicassio & T. W. Smith (Eds.), *Managing chronic illness: A biopsychosocial perspective* (pp. 1–34). Washington, DC: American Psychological Association.

Spiegel, D., Bloom, J. R., Kraemer, H. C., & Gottheil, E. (1989). Effect of psychosocial treatment on survival of patients with metastatic breast cancer. *Lancet, 2,* 888–901.

Spiegel, D., Bloom, J. R., & Yalom, I. (1981). Group support for patients with metastatic cancer: A randomized outcome study. *Archives of General Psychiatry, 38,* 527–533.

Spiegel, D., & Diamond, S. (2001). Psychosocial interventions in cancer group therapy techniques. In A. Baum & B. L. Andersen (Eds.), *Psychosocial interventions for cancer* (pp. 215–234). Washington, DC: American Psychological Association.

Spira, J. L. (1997). *Group psychotherapy for medically ill patients.* New York: Guilford.

Strecher, V. J., Kreuter, M., DenBoer, D. J., Kobrin, S., Hospers, H. J., & Skinner, C. S. (1994). The effects of computer-tailored smoking-cessation messages in family practice settings. *Journal of Family Practice, 39,* 262–270.

Stuart, R. B. (1967). Behavioral control of overeating. *Behavioral Research and Therapy, 5,* 357–365.

Surwit, R. S., van Tilburg, M. A. L., Zucker, N., McCaskill, C. C., Parekh, P., Feinglos, M., Edwards, C. L., Williams, P., & Lane, J. D. (2002). Stress management improves long-term glycemic control in type 2 diabetes. *Diabetes Care, 1,* 30–37.

Von Bertalanffy, L. (1968). *General systems theory.* New York: Braziller.

Wadden, T. A., Brownell, K. D., & Foster, G. D. (2002). Obesity: Responding to the global epidemic. *Journal of Consulting and Clinical Psychology, 70,* 510–525.

Wing, R. R., & Jeffery, R. W. (1999). Benefits of recruiting participants with friends and increasing social support for weight loss and maintenance. *Journal of Consulting and Clinical Psychology, 67,* 132–138.

Writing Group for the Activity Counseling Trial. (2001). Effects of physical activity counseling in primary care. *Journal of the American Medical Association, 286,* 677–687.

Zautra, A. J., Burleson, M. H., Matt, K. S., Roth, S., & Burrows, L. (1994). Interpersonal stress, depression, and disease activity in rheumatoid arthritis and osteoarthritis patients. *Health Psychology, 13,*139–148.

Part II

BEHAVIORS THAT COMPROMISE OVERALL HEALTH STATUS

Introduction to Part II

The next seven chapters switch focus from practical issues that clinical health psychologists face in the workplace to patient behaviors that may impair their overall health status. More than 25 years of research, clinical practice, and community-based interventions have shown that positive behavioral changes help people to feel better physically and emotionally, improve their health status, increase their self-care skills, and improve their ability to live with chronic illness. Behavioral medicine interventions have been shown to reduce health-compromising behaviors and improve clinical outcomes in patients with a variety of medical problems. This part of the handbook targets specific health-compromising behaviors, such as alcohol and nicotine use, as well as more general health-compromising behaviors that are important to virtually all service areas, such as dealing with medication-seeking behavior and adherence to medical recommendations.

In Chapter 6, Erblich and Earleywine review what is known about genetic, constitutional, and environmental factors that have been implicated in the development of alcohol dependence. In addition, they discuss the available yet imperfect treatment options for those suffering from alcohol dependence. It is noted that until recently, progress in this field was impeded by the lack of transdisciplinary idea sharing and collaboration among behavioral scientists, molecular geneticists, and neuroscientists. Clearly, for a complete and balanced understanding of this classic biobehavioral phenomenon, expertise from each of these fields is required. From the standpoint of clinicians, working with individuals suffering from alcohol dependence can be quite difficult, yet many have improved their health status by eliminating the problems related to alcohol use.

In Chapter 7, Cohen and his colleagues describe and define the construct of nicotine dependence and provide guidance on intervention strategies for treating individuals addicted to nicotine. They note that nicotine dependence appears to develop via the interaction between neurobiological substrates and cognitive, behavioral, and emotional domains. Given this multifaceted presentation, clinicians are encouraged to employ a stepped care approach, which begins with brief interventions and progresses to more intensive interventions. Given the pervasiveness of tobacco use disorders among various patient populations and the health consequences associated with these disorders, treatment of nicotine dependence is one area in which clinical health psychologists can have a positive impact on their patients' overall health status.

In Chapter 8, Faith and Thompson explore current etiological models, assessment strategies, and intervention methodologies that inform the behavioral management of obesity. In addition, they highlight the importance of targeting body image disturbances in the treatment of obesity given that many obese individuals do not achieve their desired weight loss. Thus, clinicians are encouraged to be honest about the weight loss their patients can expect, and they need to address goals that seem unachievable. Clinicians are encouraged to be sensitive to their patients' motivation and to collaboratively establish attainable weight loss goals that will foster a sense of mastery and self-efficacy. Ultimately, such treatment can lead to personal satisfaction, self-respect, and healthy interpersonal relationships.

In Chapter 9, Barbour, Houle, and Dubbert review the evidence suggesting that physical activity is beneficial in terms of the prevention and treatment of disease. Despite such benefits, physical inactivity continues to be a pervasive problem that requires consideration of environmental factors (e.g., decreases in activity required on the job, consuming larger portions during meals) in addition to individual factors. The authors also point out that a weakness in this field is the scarcity of research examining underrepresented populations. This is a major problem given that certain diseases are more prevalent among ethnic minorities. Clinicians are encouraged to promote physical activity in their practice because this could significantly reduce the prevalence of chronic disease and could improve the quality of life of their patients.

In Chapter 10, Collins and his colleagues define the complex construct of stress, highlighting the key models addressing this health concern, and incorporate how these models can be translated into treatment. Although they note that stress in itself may not cause disease, stress has been established as a significant risk factor in the development of numerous illnesses and has been implicated in aggravating existing diseases. The authors note that stress is a significant problem facing clinical health psychologists given that it has been shown to reduce patient compliance, which directly affects treatment outcomes. They also include an overview of the available treatments for the stress disorders, including cognitive strategies as well as techniques designed to lower and control physiological arousal, anxiety, and muscular tension.

In Chapter 11, Gulliver, Wolfsdorf, and Michas define the problem of medication seeking, propose a conceptual framework for understanding this construct, and describe assessments and treatments designed to address this troublesome behavior. They point out that clinical health psychologists are frequently called on to intervene not only with patients but also with providers and health care systems to effectively extinguish the problem behavior. The chapter concludes with a synopsis of what is known and what still needs to be explored so as to meet the field's broad objective of optimal clinical care.

Finally, in Chapter 12, Berlant and Pruitt expand the traditional conceptualization of adherence to include multiple levels, including patients, providers, and health care organizations. They note that there are numerous influences on patients' behavior within each of these levels that could make the challenge of improving adherence appear to be overwhelming. As a result, the case study in the chapter focuses on a multilevel approach to treatment. The authors conclude that although it is impossible to have complete control of patients' behavior, consistent consideration of the significance of events that precede and follow behavior at the three levels mentioned will advance adherence enhancement efforts and ultimately affect health outcomes.

CHAPTER 6

Alcohol Problems
Causes, Definitions, and Treatments

JOEL ERBLICH AND MITCH EARLEYWINE

What causes alcoholism? Or, put another way, why is it that although so many people consume alcohol on a regular basis, only a small minority become dependent? This seemingly straightforward question has bewitched clinicians and researchers for centuries. Only recently, with generous help from the disciplines of molecular genetics and neuroscience, have behavioral scientists begun to piece together this age-old puzzle. Part of the problem lies in the way in which alcohol dependence is defined and conceptualized. Another concern is that we have yet to identify the proverbial "switch"—that functional entity (biological, psychological, or otherwise) that "transforms" a nondependent consumer of alcohol into one who is alcoholic. But perhaps most critically, the parallel paths of behavioral scientists, molecular geneticists, and neuroscientists have until recently severely limited the transdisciplinary idea sharing and collaborations that are essential to gaining a complete and balanced understanding of the etiology of this classic *biobehavioral* phenomenon. This chapter attempts to provide some unifying themes that appear to be common to all

etiologic models of addiction and to review what is known about some of the more common genetic, constitutional, and learned/environmental factors that have been implicated in the pathogenesis of alcohol dependence. A rapprochement of these diverse factors may result in a clinically useful working model of understanding the risk for alcoholism.

DEFINITIONS AND DESCRIPTION OF ALCOHOLISM

A nosologic consensus is the outcome of clarifying an etiologic disease pathway. Unfortunately, the classification of alcoholism, like many other multisymptomatic behavioral disorders, has been a matter of some debate. The classic medical approach employs the categorical disease model in which alcoholism is conceptualized as being qualitatively distinct relative to normal "social" drinking (Meyer, 2001). Theorists espousing a categorical point of view would consider abstinence/nonuse, use, abuse, and dependence as conceptually distinct states. Also consistent with this approach is Cloninger and colleagues' (1988) classic description of "types" of alcoholics, an approach that has received only mixed empirical support (Sannibale & Hall, 1998). Concerns regarding the limited nature of such categorical approaches have led many to adopt a quantitative approach, which stresses that alcohol use lies on a continuum from nonuse to dependence (Meyer, 2001). Factors such as quantity of alcohol consumed, frequency of consumption, and variability (i.e., regularity with which drinking occurs) move people along this continuum, the extreme of which is alcohol dependence (Streissguth, Martin, & Buffington, 1976). Recent discussions about the existence of a "switch" that is responsible for transforming a "normal drinker" into an "alcoholic" (e.g., Tsuang, Bar, Harley, & Lyons, 2001), as well as data suggesting that there is great individual variability within the subset of alcoholics, have led to a blending of the two approaches. By the prevailing view, alcoholism is seen as a qualitatively distinct state, but there is a continuum of symptom severity within the subgroup of alcoholics (Meyer, 2001). In addition, quantitative drinking factors (e.g., quantity, frequency, variability) are necessary predictors of the development of alcoholism. That being said, it must also be acknowledged that the putative switch has not yet been identified, and as such, most researchers have relied on studying quantitative drinking factors as a reasonable surrogate. Therefore, the preponderance of theoretical grist has aimed at understanding why some would drink more than others rather than at directly addressing why some people become alcoholics. For now, the proverbial lamppost shines down on the quantitative approach.

Alcohol Dependence

The DSM-IV (*Diagnostic and Statistical Manual of Mental Disorders,* fourth edition) (American Psychiatric Association, 1994) defines drug dependence as a collection of any three of seven symptoms. All must create

meaningful distress and occur within the same year. The diagnosis requires judgment on the clinician's part, but the symptoms tend to be obvious. Each symptom reflects the idea that a person requires the drug to function and makes maladaptive sacrifices to use it. The current diagnosis focuses on consequences rather than on the amount or frequency of consumption. These consequences are (a) tolerance and (b) withdrawal, which were once considered the hallmarks of dependence. The additional symptoms are (c) use that exceeds initial intention, (d) persistent desire for the drug or failed attempts to decrease consumption, (e) loss of time related to use, (f) reduced activities because of consumption, and (g) continued use despite problems.

Tolerance serves as a hallmark of physiological dependence. It occurs when repeated use of the same dose no longer produces the same effect. This symptom often indicates extensive drinking and may motivate continued consumption. People do not grow tolerant to a drug; rather, they grow tolerant to its effects. After repeated use, some of the effects of a drug may decrease, whereas others may not. Tolerance to the desired effects of alcohol may encourage people to drink more, and increased use may coincide with a greater chance for problems.

The second symptom of dependence, withdrawal, refers to the discomfort associated with an absence of the drug. No two people experience withdrawal in the same way. Hallmark signs can range from mild irritability to full-blown hallucinations. Alcohol withdrawal frequently includes tremor, anxiety, craving, and troubled sleep. A severe, palsy-like tremor with frequent perceptual aberrations, known as delirium tremens, often accompanies severe withdrawal.

The DSM-IV distinguishes between dependence with physiological aspects and dependence without physiological aspects. If tolerance or withdrawal appears among the three required symptoms, a diagnosis of physiological dependence is appropriate. Nevertheless, even without the presentation of tolerance or withdrawal, individuals may still receive a diagnosis of alcohol dependence without the specifier "with physiological dependence." This change in procedure has made the diagnosis of alcohol dependence potentially more common.

The third symptom of dependence involves use that exceeds initial intention. This symptom suggests that individuals may plan to have only a couple of drinks but then drink markedly more once they become intoxicated. Use that exceeds intention was once known as "loss of control." Many people misinterpreted the idea of loss of control, suggesting that it referred to an unstoppable compulsion to drink everything available. Based on this interpretation, people who drank to the point of blackout but still had liquor in the house the next morning might have claimed that they did not show loss of control. Today, use that exceeds intention does not imply this dramatic unconscious consumption. This symptom simply suggests that dependent users may have trouble drinking only a small amount if that is what they intend to do. Ironically, people who never intend to drink a small amount might not get the opportunity to qualify for this symptom.

Dependence also includes failed attempts to decrease use, or a constant desire for the drug, as the fourth symptom. An inability to reduce drinking despite a wish to do so certainly suggests that the drug has altered behavior meaningfully. Yet people with no motivation to quit would likely never qualify for failed attempts. Thus, people who have not attempted to quit may still qualify for this symptom if they show a persistent continuous craving. An inability to stop drinking or a constant desire to consume alcohol suggests dependence.

The fifth symptom of dependence involves loss of time related to use. The time lost can be devoted to experiencing intoxication, recovering from it, or seeking the drug. Because alcohol is legal, users might not spend considerable time in search of it. Hence, the number of hours required to qualify for a meaningful loss of time remains unclear, making this symptom quite subjective. A clear-cut case would be anyone whose day is devoted to obtaining alcohol, drinking to the point of intoxication, and recovering from the effects of alcohol. An individual who spends even a portion of the day (e.g., a few hours) on these activities would also qualify. In contrast, an individual who consumes several drinks an hour before going to bed each night might argue that he or she has lost little time and should not qualify for this symptom. Thus, subjective assessment of a meaningful amount of time may contribute to problems with the diagnosis of dependence.

The sixth symptom of dependence is reduced activities because of drinking. This symptom focuses on work, relationships, and leisure. The presence of this symptom suggests that alcohol has taken over so much of one's daily life that the user would qualify as dependent. Any impairment in job performance because of intoxication, hangover, or devoting work hours to obtaining alcohol would qualify for this symptom. Individuals missing work every Monday to recover from weekend binges might also qualify. Sufficient functioning at work, however, does not indicate that one is not dependent. Even with phenomenal job performance, impaired social functioning may be indicative of problems. If a drinker's only friends are drinking buddies and they only socialize while intoxicated, the substance has obviously had a marked impact on friendships. Recreational functioning is also important to the diagnosis. A decrease in leisure activities suggests impaired recreation. A drinker who formerly enjoyed hiking, reading, and theater but who now spends all of his or her free time intoxicated in front of the television would qualify for this symptom. This approach to the diagnosis implies that drinkers who are not experiencing multifaceted lives can improve the way in which they function by drinking less.

The final symptom of dependence requires continued use despite problems. People who persist in using the drug despite obvious negative consequences would qualify for this symptom. Recurrent use regardless of continued occupational, social, interpersonal, psychological, and/or health problems obviously shows dependence. Many of these difficulties involve meaningful others in the drinker's life. Continued consumption despite conflicts with loved ones, employers, and/or family members might qualify for this symptom. This situation supports the idea that anyone who continues to use despite negative consequences (e.g., stomach ulcers, feelings of guilt, loss of self-respect) must have a strong commitment to alcohol.

Alcohol Abuse

A subset of individuals may experience negative consequences from alcohol that do not qualify for a diagnosis of dependence but that meet criteria for a diagnosis of abuse. This diagnosis requires significant impairment or distress directly related to drinking. A diagnosis of alcohol abuse requires only one of the four symptoms that appear in the DSM-IV: (a) interference with major obligations, (b) intoxication in unsafe settings, (c) legal problems, and (d) continued use in the face of problems. Each of these signs requires some interpretation on the part of the individual making a diagnosis; however, most experienced diagnosticians agree on who meets criteria for substance abuse and who does not (Üstün et al., 1997). Abuse remains distinctly separate from dependence, which requires different symptoms and more of them. Although a diagnosis of abuse clearly serves as a sign of genuine troubles, many clinicians consider dependence to be more severe. Thus, those who qualify for dependence would not receive the diagnosis of abuse.

The first symptom of abuse, interference with major obligations, requires impaired performance at work, home, and/or school. Impairments may arise due to intoxication, recovery from intoxication, and/or time devoted to searching for liquor. The definition is necessarily broad so as to include people with a variety of responsibilities. Specifically, this symptom applies to employees who miss work because they have hangovers, students who fail tests because they attend classes intoxicated, and parents who neglect their children so that they can spend time in bars.

The second symptom requires intoxication in unsafe settings. The DSM-IV specifically lists driving a car and operating machinery as hazardous situations in which intoxication could create dangerous negative consequences. Many experienced drinkers claim that their intoxicated driving differs little from their sober driving. Such statements may reflect poorly on their driving abilities in general, but people who tremble as a result of withdrawal might actually drive better after a couple of drinks. Despite this fact, driving a car while drunk, even for only a few blocks, qualifies as alcohol abuse.

The intoxicated performance of any task can lead to a diagnosis of abuse if impairment may lead to negative consequences. This action need not be as elaborate as scaling a skyscraper or handling a firearm. Driving a forklift or using power tools might qualify. Note that no negative consequences actually need to occur; their increased likelihood alone can qualify for abuse. Thus, those who drive drunk but never receive tickets or have accidents would still qualify for abuse due to the fact that they increase their likelihood of experiencing negative consequences.

The third symptom included in the diagnosis of alcohol abuse concerns legal problems. This symptom may say as much about society's values as it does about an individual's behavior (Brecher, 1972; Grilly, 1998). Any legal troubles related to public intoxication, driving while intoxicated, drunk and disorderly behavior, alcohol-related aggression, or underage drinking would qualify.

Finally, the fourth symptom of alcohol abuse concerns consistent use despite problems. Note that recurrent use in the face of occupational, social, interpersonal, psychological, and/or health problems qualifies as abuse.

Alcohol Problems

Describing alcohol-related difficulties as addiction, abuse, or dependence creates certain misunderstandings. All three words may sound deprecating (Eddy, Halbach, Isbell, & Seevers, 1965; Miller, Gold, & Smith, 1997), and each lacks clarity; however, addiction has no accepted definition. As noted previously, abuse and dependence have formal definitions, but the specific diagnosis does not reveal an individual's actual problems. Anyone who qualifies for abuse may have one or more of the four symptoms required, meaning that an individual with such a diagnosis could be experiencing any one of more than a dozen combinations of symptoms. Likewise, dependence requires three of seven symptoms, providing more than 30 potential combinations of symptoms. These terms may also encourage the minimization of problems that do not qualify for a diagnosis, and this can interfere with treatment.

People experiencing negative consequences from alcohol may prove to be unwilling to limit consumption if they do not qualify for addiction, abuse, or dependence. This limitation has inspired an approach that emphasizes problems rather than diagnoses or diseases. Thus, instead of worrying about whether a specific user qualifies for a disorder, time might be better spent identifying individual problems related to drinking. For example, a client may report frequent stomach pains. A survey of this person's drinking may reveal that the pain often follows a binge. Although this problem might not interfere enough to qualify for abuse, the client may benefit from drinking less or quitting. This emphasis on problems may allow the clinician to avoid pointless arguments about whether or not someone is an addict. Instead, the clinician and the client can focus on reducing the harm that alcohol may cause.

MODELS OF ALCOHOLISM

As with many other topics in psychology, there are nearly as many theories of the development of alcohol problems as there are theorists. By and large, however, there is agreement that people drink alcohol because it makes them feel good. Principles of operant conditioning suggest that either positive reinforcement, negative reinforcement, or a combination of the two play a role in drinking behavior. Some data support the role of positive reinforcement in alcohol consumption. For example, Newlin and Thomson (1990) argued that individuals with a positive family history for alcoholism may be more sensitive to the positive/stimulant effects of alcohol, and several studies support this supposition (e.g., Erblich, Earleywine, Erblich, & Bovbjerg, in press). Research in this area has also underscored the importance of negative reinforcement in understanding alcohol consumption. Nearly a half century ago, Conger (1956) advanced the now classic "tension reduction hypothesis," which speaks broadly to alcohol's negatively reinforcing properties. More recent modifications to the tension reduction hypothesis have focused on alcohol's ability to dampen the human stress response (Levenson, Sher, Grossman, Newman, & Newlin, 1980), and further modifications have demonstrated that stress response dampening may be mediated by alcohol's impairment of cognitive processes (Erblich & Earleywine, 1995; Josephs & Steele, 1990). Regardless of the mechanism, reinforcement appears to play a central role in the initiation and maintenance of drinking behavior.

Over the past two decades, Schuckit and colleagues (e.g., Schuckit, 1994; Schuckit, Tsuang, Anthenelli, Tipp, & Nurnberger, 1996) have presented considerable empirical evidence (both cross-sectional and longitudinal) indicating that drinkers who experience lower levels of response to alcohol consumption are more likely to experience problem drinking. They have suggested that such individuals may need to drink more than others to achieve a desirable level of reinforcement or that such individuals' lower interoceptive responses to the substance make it more difficult for them to regulate intake appropriately. Conversely, others have suggested that those who experience higher levels of response to alcohol consumption are more likely to develop problem drinking (e.g., Nagoshi & Wilson, 1987). These theorists have proposed that the more reinforcing the effects of alcohol, the more likely one is to consume. Newlin and Thomson (1990) proposed that both may be the case; that is, lower levels of response to the aversive effects of alcohol, coupled with higher levels of response to its positive effects, create a "double whammy" risk factor for problem drinking. Subsequent empirical studies have provided some support for their model (e.g., Erblich et al., in press). The prevailing view remains that the reinforcement value of alcohol figures prominently in understanding problem drinking. A critical question, by extension, would be the following: What factors contribute to differential levels of alcohol's reinforcement value?

Specific Genetic Factors

Quantitative genetic studies have demonstrated in a compelling fashion that alcoholism has a substantial, but not an exhaustive, heritable component. Cadoret, Troughton, O'Gorman, and Heywood (1986) estimated that up to 60% of the population's variability in alcoholism is attributable to genetic factors. Other epidemiological studies have established that individuals who have an alcoholic parent are three to four times more likely to develop alcoholism themselves. Although exogenous (i.e., nongenetic) factors may account for some of the observed intergenerational transmissibility of alcoholism, the confluence of these epidemiological and quantitative genetic studies suggests a preeminent role of genetics in conferring vulnerability to problem drinking.

In 1990, Blum and colleagues became the first to discover a relationship between a specific genotype and alcoholism. A long tradition of research in neuroscience has implicated dopamine as the central nervous system (CNS) neurotransmitter of reward, and studies have demonstrated that drug use is associated with increased CNS dopamine release. Based on this research, Blum and colleagues (1990) tested the possibility that polymorphisms (i.e., genotypic variants) in the dopamine D_2 receptor gene (DRD2) would be related to alcoholism. Indeed, they found that severe alcoholics were significantly more likely to carry the DRD2 "A1" allele compared with controls. They suggested that this locus may be related to a lower number of D_2 receptors, resulting in hypodopaminergic function that could be alleviated by, among other things, alcohol consumption. This suggestion may be consistent with the overall reinforcement model of risk for alcoholism, such that carriers of this polymorphism may find consuming alcohol more rewarding than do noncarriers. Whether or not this is the case remains to be seen. Strikingly, studies of genetics have typically not included assessments of perceived levels of reinforcement, so that intuitive relations between genotype and reinforcement remain largely speculative. Another concern is that molecular biology has, to date, procured only sketchy evidence that the DRD2 polymorphism is functional; that is, carrying the A1 allele does not necessarily translate to fewer D_2 receptors. Therefore, the mechanism through which DRD2-A1 confers increased risk for alcoholism remains unclear.

Nevertheless, Blum and colleagues' (1990) initial findings have spurred an intensive search for other candidate genotypes that may predict problem drinking. Blum and colleagues (2000) have since tested other dopamine-related genotypes, including polymorphic loci on DRD4 and SLC6A3, a gene that generates the protein responsible for regulating presynaptic dopamine reuptake. Other candidate genes (e.g., SLC6A4, 5HT-1B, GABA-A, muOR, PENK) include those related to serotonin function, GABA function, and opioid release (for a review, see Blum et al., 2000). Studies have provided mixed results, and even the positive studies account for only a small proportion of variance in alcoholism or drinking, with substantial heterogeneity. Findings underscore the importance of polygenic or gene-environment interactions in better understanding this complex behavioral disorder. Indeed, early biochemical research (Davis & Walsh, 1970) has suggested that by-products of alcohol's metabolism (i.e., tetrahydroisoquinolines) may cause a cascade that directly impinges on opioid receptors but that also indirectly affects the breakdown and availability of synaptic dopamine. Although not yet tested, work by Berridge and Robinson (1998) raised the possibility that genes related to dopamine function may operate by increasing the motivational salience of the substance (e.g., craving or "wanting"), whereas relevant polymorphisms in opioid genes may operate by increasing the hedonic value of consumption (e.g., actual reward or "liking"). Although perhaps a way off, possession of these genotypes may suggest distinct loci of intervention (i.e., craving management therapy for carriers of dopamine-related high-risk genotypes vs. opiate antagonist therapy or counterconditioning for carriers of opioid-related high-risk genotypes).

Along similar lines, recent studies characterizing the dysregulation of CNS functional systems through chronic alcohol use have demonstrated striking down-regulation of both the D_1 and D_2 receptor systems (Self & Nestler, 1998). To the extent that genetics may play a role in receptor density, a potential gene-environment interaction may exist that

renders some drinkers particularly susceptible to chronic hypodopaminergic states. This possibility is particularly intriguing as data emerge suggesting that, within the dopamine system, the D_1 subsystem is associated with liking, whereas D_2 is more associated with wanting (Berridge & Robinson, 1998; Self, 1998). The convergence of these data may suggest that psychopharmacological agents with differential affinities to D_1 and D_2 may prove to be selectively efficacious depending on the particular need of the drinker (e.g., a D_2 genetically "vulnerable" person may need more craving management).

A final set of candidate genotypes that has been examined include those genes responsible for generating alcohol metabolic enzymes (e.g., alcohol dehydrogenase, acetaldehyde dehydrogenase, P450 liver enzymes in the cytochrome system) (Higuchi, Muramatsu, Matsushita, Murayama, & Hayashida, 1996). Polymorphic loci on these genes (e.g., ALDH2, ADH2, ADH3, CYP2E1) are subjects of continued scrutiny and may also relate to the magnitude of the hedonic response to alcohol consumption. Because stress is a potent antecedent of alcohol consumption, examination of genetic factors that relate to the stress response (e.g., cortisol regulation) may be a promising avenue in the future. Clearly, the preliminary search for candidate genotypes has yielded only modest results. Genome-wide microarray technology may prove to be highly useful in elucidating the roles of multiple genes in animal models of alcoholism.

Cognitive Factors

There is currently a large body of research demonstrating that individuals with a genetic predisposition to alcoholism display substantial cognitive and neuropsychological deficits. Giancola and Moss (1998) argued that cognitive and neuropsychological deficits, especially those related to executive functioning that predate drinking experiences (e.g., attention, planning, cognitive flexibility, appropriate inhibition), may somehow be related to the development of alcoholism. For example, Alterman, Gerstley, Goldstein, and Tarter (1987) reported that "children of alcoholics" perform more poorly on tasks that putatively assess frontal lobe functioning such as the Stroop task, the Trail Making task, and the Wisconsin Card Sort task. Studies of stimulus-evoked potentials, especially the P300 component (Rodriguez, Porjesz, Chorlian, Polich, & Begleiter, 1999), have provided converging biological support for the notion that children of alcoholics display poorer attentional capacities than do other children. In contrast to the predictors mentioned previously, these cognitive predictors do not necessarily directly operate through differential reinforcement. A likely explanation is that although drinkers with cognitive deficits experience comparable levels of reinforcement from alcohol to those of drinkers without such deficits, the former lack the cognitive resources to regulate their intake or to say "no" when offered a drink. This problem may become particularly pronounced when high-risk drinkers, who are already mildly cognitively deficient, become intoxicated, further undermining their ability to process information or to attend to internal or external intake regulation cues. The possibility also exists that cognitive deficits are epiphenomenal to a broader relation between chronic hypofrontality (which may, in fact, be related to the reinforcement value of alcohol) and future drinking behavior. Alternatively, Erblich and Earleywine (1999) suggested that such deficits may also stem from the more general effects of growing up with an alcoholic parent. Poorer nutrition, educational opportunities, and physical abuse have been reported among children of alcoholics (Rao, Begum, Venkataramana, & Gangadharappa, 2001). One could speculate that growing up in such an environment may lead to the observed cognitive deficits and, as indicated previously, may be an important mechanism through which problem drinking develops. Speculation aside, the precise mechanism through which cognitive and neuropsychological deficits lead to alcoholism remains unclear. In addition, whether these deficits are genetic or environmental in origin is also unclear. Nevertheless, these factors are important to consider when developing an etiologic model of alcoholism.

Characterologic Factors

It is now well established that specific personality factors are strongly predictive of drinking behavior. Nearly four decades ago, MacAndrew (1967) identified clusters of items on the Minnesota Multiphasic Personality Inventory (MMPI), primarily related to deviance proneness, that significantly differentiated alcoholics from nonalcoholics. This early research was one of the first systematic investigations of the potential role of personality characteristics in problem drinking. Since then, the MacAndrew Alcoholism Scale and the Holmes Alcoholism Scale have become mainstays of risk assessment for alcoholism. Recent modifications have found that shorter versions of these scales (7 to 13 items) may be even more strongly related to alcoholism (Conley & Kammeier, 1980; Hoffman, Lumry, Harrison, & Lessard, 1984). Problem drinking has been related to other measures of deviance proneness as well. For example, several studies have found that problem drinkers, alcoholics, and children of alcoholics score significantly more pathologically on the Socialization scale of the California Personality Inventory (e.g., Finn, Sharkansky, Brandt, & Turcotte, 2000). In addition, symptoms of antisocial and borderline personality disorders are common among problem drinkers, alcoholics, and children of alcoholics. Indeed, Sher and Trull (2002) reviewed the literature on personality disorders and concluded that although substance abuse is related to many personality symptoms, including those of paranoid and avoidant personality disorder, the largest consistent set of findings is in antisocial and borderline symptoms.

Problem drinking appears to be related to other personality constructs as well. Studies have demonstrated repeatedly that high scores on Zuckerman's Sensation Seeking Scale (and other similar scales) predict drinking behavior (e.g., Finn, Earleywine, & Pihl, 1992). Other studies of novelty seeking using similar instruments provide additional support for such a relation (Hesselbrock & Hesselbrock, 1992). A longitudinal study of children's novelty seeking found that those who scored highly were more likely to become alcoholics as adults (Cloninger et al., 1988). Interestingly, one of the relatively few transdisciplinary studies performed (Laine, Ahonen, Rasanen, & Tiihonen, 2001) revealed that individuals high in novelty-seeking personality traits also have higher densities of CNS dopamine transporter (DAT). This finding is consistent with genetic hypotheses that high levels of DAT (which clears dopamine from the synapse) would relate to problem drinking.

Still other studies have examined the role of traits such as disinhibition, reward dependence, external locus of control, and negative self-concept and have found significant relations with drinking behavior (e.g., Hesselbrock & Hesselbrock, 1992). Interestingly, neurophysiological studies have linked many of these personality traits, especially sensation seeking, disinhibition, and deviance, to chronic hypoperfusion of the orbitofrontal cortex (Friedman, Cycowicz, & Gaeta, 2001). Theorists have suggested that these personality traits may represent part of a broader syndrome related to cortical underarousal (Brennan & Raine, 1997). The localization of these traits in the CNS is particularly intriguing because the orbitofrontal cortex is precisely the area involved in the cognitive deficits mentioned previously. Furthermore, this region of the brain is highly dopaminergic. The physiological convergence of these biogenetic, cognitive, and personality factors speaks to the preeminent role of a "hungry" brain in dramatically increasing the incentive salience and reward value of alcohol consumption.

Exogenous Factors

Stress is the most consistently reported antecedent to drinking behavior. Naturalistic studies of stress have found strong relations between a number of stressors (e.g., social, medical, trauma) and drinking behaviors. As one example, Seeman and Seeman (1992) found that chronic stress associated with work predicted later alcoholism. Indeed, anecdotal clinical reports consistently support the contention that acute stress is a powerful proximal determinant of drinking episodes. To ascertain a causal relation between stress and drinking, investigators have employed laboratory-based studies of experimental stressors (Stewart, 2000). Findings have demonstrated that social, cognitive, and physical stressors can induce alcohol craving, potentiate the hedonic impact of consumption, and increase the amount of alcohol consumed post-stressor (Stewart, 2000). Interestingly, the magnitudes of stress reactions also predict drinking behavior, such that the previously mentioned drinking parameters are more severe for those who have stronger stress reactions (Sinha & O'Malley, 1999). This finding is important because it suggests not only that stress is a predictor of drinking but also that some who are predisposed to more powerful stress reactions (through some genetic factor or otherwise) are at a particularly high risk for problem drinking. The classic stress vulnerability model may be particularly appropriate for understanding alcoholism. Specifically, constitutional factors, such as genetics, personality characteristics, neuropsychological dysfunction, and stress reactivity, may render some individuals particularly vulnerable to the effects of stress and place them at high risk for dependence.

If stress predicts drinking behavior, coping skills should moderate the degree to which stress has an impact. Indeed, studies have demonstrated that coping skills can buffer the effects of stress on drinking behavior (Wills, Sandy, & Yaeger, 2002). Darwin, Freud, and (most recently) Bandura have underscored the importance of coping in adapting to stressful situations. The Darwinian model of homeostatic maintenance would predict that an organism would consume alcohol to return to a baseline "pre-stress state" (Darwin, 1859/1998). Indeed, ethologists have speculated that animals may take laborious detours from traditional migratory paths to find psychoactive substances. It is thought that this may serve to maintain homeostasis during the stressful process of migration. Freud (1901) formulated the role of coping in terms of "defense mechanisms." He argued that those who are "orally fixated" (i.e., those who experienced some sort of developmental arrest in early life when oral pleasure dominated) might use alcohol to cope with stressors in favor of other healthier coping mechanisms. Finally, Bandura (1969) argued in his social learning theory that use of alcohol as a coping mechanism may stem from imitative learning processes. Drinkers may have observed their parents use alcohol as a method of "unwinding" after a long day, or they may have observed similar media representations of alcohol (e.g., "Miller time"). All of these theorists share the notion that management of stress is a critical moderator of drinking behavior and must be considered when trying to understand the effects of stress on the development of alcoholism.

Another major predictor of drinking behavior is one's expectations of the consequences of drinking (e.g., Keane, Lisman, & Kreutzer, 1980). The more one expects alcohol consumption to lead to positive outcomes (e.g., better social performance, better sexual performance, more tension reduction, euphoria), the more one will drink. Similarly, the less one expects alcohol consumption to lead to negative consequences (e.g., hangover; excessive sedation; sluggishness; trouble with family,

friends, work, and the law), the more one will drink. Studies have shown repeatedly that the Alcohol Expectancy Questionnaire, a classic instrument used to assess positive expectancies, predicts drinking behavior (e.g., Williams & Ricciardelli, 1996). Similarly, the more recently developed Negative Alcohol Expectancy Questionnaire has been found to negatively correlate with drinking variables (McMahon & Jones, 1994). Recent innovations have identified powerful ingrained cognitive schemata that underlie these expectations (Rather, Goldman, Roehrich, & Brannick, 1992), and these are especially strong among those at risk for alcoholism (Erblich, Earleywine, & Erblich, 2001). In an intriguing study, Smith (1994) found that expectations of favorable drinking consequences predated drinking experiences, suggesting that such expectancies may be learned relatively early in life and are not simply a readout of people's actual experiences with alcohol.

Modeling is another critical component in the development of drinking behavior, according to Bandura's social learning theory. Children and teens often rely on role models when developing behavioral repertoires, especially regarding health behaviors (Yancey, Siegel, & McDaniel, 2002). Observing parents, siblings, and other peers consume alcohol may play a powerful role in shaping future behavior (Roski et al., 1997). Other role models, including those seen in advertisements, television programs, and movies, can have a profound influence as well. Thompson and Yokota (2001) found that although the trend has been decreasing, a substantial number of G-rated movies depict alcohol and/or drug use.

Social support is yet another factor found to be involved in the development of problem drinking. Individuals who report low levels of social support are more likely to report problem drinking than are others (Green, Freeborn, & Polen, 2001). In a longitudinal study, Schuckit and Smith (2001) found that even among individuals at high risk for alcoholism, high levels of social support protected against developing alcoholism 15 years later. Marlatt (1996) discussed numerous "proximal determinants" or factors that contribute to the decision to consume alcohol "in the moment." He suggested that those individuals with poor social skills, especially those who are uncomfortable with saying "no," are more likely to consume alcohol (see also Smith & McCrady, 1991). In addition, those who have lower levels of self-efficacy, especially regarding the willpower to abstain or moderate drinking behavior, are more likely to consume alcohol. Taken together, stress, coping, expectancies, modeling, social support, social skills, and self-efficacy can be conceptualized as necessary, but not sufficient, moderators of risk for developing alcoholism, such that the presence of these factors may determine whether or not someone who is vulnerable (by virtue of genetics, personality, or cognitive functioning) will develop alcoholism. It should be noted that although these concepts are being presented independently, there is a sizable literature suggesting complex interrelationships between factors that is beyond the scope of this chapter. An illustration of this point is that coping, social skills, and self-efficacy all may be related and may be affected by expectancies (Marlatt & Gordon, 1985). Nevertheless, we believe that the current body of literature on predictors of drinking behavior points to a classic stress vulnerability model, whereby constitutional factors such as genetics, personality, and cognitive capacities can render an individual vulnerable to the effects of numerous exogenous factors. In sum, the available data suggest that the stress vulnerability approach provides a clinically useful working model of the pathogenesis of alcoholism.

PSYCHOLOGICAL TREATMENTS FOR ALCOHOL PROBLEMS

At least three different approaches have shown considerable promise in minimizing the negative consequences of alcohol: cognitive-behavioral therapy (CBT), motivational interviewing, and 12-step facilitation. CBT focuses on changing the thoughts and situations that previously led to the use of alcohol. Motivational interviewing uses assessments and interpersonal interactions to enhance decisions to alter problem behaviors. Finally, 12-step facilitation employs specific techniques to help people make good use of 12-step treatment.

Each treatment has its strengths. An enormous project that contrasted the outcomes of these three treatments for alcohol-dependent individuals found that all three were comparably effective (Project MATCH Research Group, 1998). The treatments share several factors, and this may help to explain their similar outcomes. Each emphasizes the client's responsibility for change, each treats alcohol use as a phenomenon independent of the individual's value as a person, and each stresses regular attendance and active participation in treatment.

Descriptions of these therapies do not reveal all of their nuances, and even the best attempt to reduce a treatment to a few pages of text invariably fails. Academic descriptions of psychotherapy often miss its potential for intimate and curative interactions, whereas stereotypical depictions of the process often emphasize education, empathy, encouragement, and occasional insights. Ideally, these descriptions combine to alter actions, diminish problems, and increase happiness. The techniques and rationales of each of the treatments discussed in what follows provide only a limited picture of the ways in which they actually proceed.

Although treatments differ in their methods and strategies, most require a meaningful relationship with a therapist. Therapists often believe that techniques create change, but the relationship may serve as an equally important contributor (Strupp, 1989). The idea that the relationship is more important than specific strategies may help to explain some of the similar outcomes created by different therapies

(Wampold et al., 1997). Manualized treatments, which clearly delineate specific material for each session, can lead to different outcomes with different therapists. Although the therapeutic relationship may account for these differences, it does not mimic the friendship and coaching common outside of therapy. Data clearly support psychotherapy's efficacy, but the mechanisms that lead to success remain unclear (Dawes, 1994).

Space limitations preclude a lengthy description of all available treatments for alcohol-related problems. Given the widespread familiarity and availability of 12-step programs, this chapter focuses on CBT and motivational interviewing. The reader who is interested in facilitating participation in 12-step programs is encouraged to read the work of Nowinski and Baker (1992).

Cognitive-Behavioral Therapy

CBT for alcohol problems focuses on altering environments, thoughts, and actions associated with drinking. Different environments may trigger undesired problematic consumption. These triggers involve both external and internal factors. External factors include any person, location, or object associated with alcohol. A beer mug, a rock song, or a swizzle stick may easily trigger a desire to drink. Internal factors include thoughts and feelings linked to alcohol. Some triggers are direct and some are indirect. Direct factors, such as craving and urges, are close to drinking. Indirect factors also increase the chance of drinking, but their import is less obvious. These include frustration, anger, and even delight. CBT suggests that problem drinkers learn to use alcohol in reaction to these triggers in much the same way as people learn any behavior. Therefore, they can learn to engage in new behaviors instead of problematic drinking by altering environments, thoughts, and actions (Beck, Wright, Newman, & Liese, 1993).

The situations that precede drinking often appear to be diverse. For example, an assessment might reveal dramatic drinking at a sporting event, after conflict at home, and every Friday night. The commonalities among these situations are obscure. The cognitive-behavioral model suggests that thoughts about the situations may contribute more to drinking than do the circumstances themselves. Thus, each environment may elicit specific thoughts. A common thought in all of these situations might be that "alcohol is the only way in which to enhance this experience." These types of thoughts are probably easier to alter than are the situations, so the thought rather than the environment becomes the focus of CBT.

The cognitive-behavioral model suggests that people carry a set of underlying beliefs into each situation. Certain situations activate these beliefs, eliciting specific thoughts that subsequently lead to action. For example, a problem drinker might believe that alcohol provides the only way in which to relax. The drinker may interpret a situation as stressful, leading to the activation of the belief that he or she needs alcohol to relax. This belief would likely lead to thoughts of drinking, which might inspire all of the actions required to get a drink. In CBT, the client would learn to challenge his or her beliefs in an effort to minimize or eliminate drinking. Thus, the client may develop skills enabling him or her to see the situation as less stressful, thereby altering the belief that drinking is the only effective way in which to relax (Beck et al., 1993). Instead of drinking, the client might listen to music, meditate, or exercise.

Therapists have developed many techniques for altering these beliefs. Most require identifying the underlying belief and then looking for evidence to support or dispute it. A common strategy that cognitive-behavioral therapists employ includes Socratic questioning, a method by which therapists guide clients through a series of questions so that they might arrive at their own answers. Instead of providing information, this strategy teaches a process for discovery. Eventually, clients can learn to ask these sorts of questions of themselves so that they can maintain sobriety without therapists.

This process also elicits the thoughts and feelings most important to clients. For example, those who believe that alcohol provides the only way in which to relax might respond particularly well to questions about alternative ways in which to unwind. Questions about restful recreation in general may prove helpful. Queries about favorite activities before clients began drinking may also work. As clients generate their own list of preferred ways in which to soothe themselves without alcohol, the belief that alcohol is the sole source of relaxation weakens. It is important to note that clients find their own examples more compelling than any list of relaxation techniques that therapists might generate. This approach also respects clients' ability to present evidence to alter their beliefs (Overholser, 1987). In sum, changing the thoughts about situations that previously led to drinking can help to decrease problematic consumption.

CBT relies on other techniques that are too numerous to list here, but one key set of strategies concerns relapse prevention. Many people can quit drinking briefly but cannot maintain abstinence. Thus, many cognitive-behavioral techniques focus not only on quitting but also on avoiding relapse to alcohol. Thoughts and beliefs remain important in preventing relapse given their relevance to a phenomenon known as the abstinence violation effect. The abstinence violation effect concerns the way in which people cope with backsliding once they have committed to altering their alcohol consumption.

Most people who decide to eliminate or decrease their use of alcohol subsequently make mistakes. They use alcohol when they intended to quit, or they use more than their established

limits. The abstinence violation effect may occur when a small thoughtless sip of beer turns into a full weekend binge. It is as if people say, "Well, I wrecked my abstinence, so I might as well drink the whole bottle." Minimizing the impact of small slips is essential to relapse prevention. Although many believe that the pharmacology of alcohol makes a single dose inevitably turn into a relapse, changes in thinking can actually prevent these slips from creating further problems. In fact, it has been shown that the interpretation of the slip appears to contribute more to relapse than does the actual occurrence of the slip itself (Marlatt & Gordon, 1985).

There is no doubt that intoxicated individuals can make poor decisions about continued drinking and that the pharmacological effects of alcohol contribute to these decisions. Nevertheless, many individuals who relapse report abstinence violation effects that occurred at extremely low doses. A single sip of liquor or smell of wine often lead to the decision to binge. Pharmacology might not play a particularly strong role in these relapses. Marlatt, Demming, and Reid (1973) revealed that alcoholics who drank alcohol but were not aware of doing so did not show the abstinence violation effect and did not continue drinking after the initial dose. In contrast, alcoholics given a placebo believed to be alcohol did show the abstinence violation effect and did consume considerably more alcohol after the placebo. These findings indicate that thoughts also play an important role in relapse prevention.

In sum, CBT relies on the principles of learning theory to treat alcohol-related problems. The treatment may work by altering beliefs about alcohol use and its consequences. It also focuses on the prevention of relapse by identifying situations that may increase the risk of drinking and then teaching alternative ways in which to act under those conditions.

Motivational Interviewing

Motivational interviewing involves brief interactions with a therapist to help the client decrease alcohol-related problems. The treatment enhances motivation before attempting any changes in behavior because in the absence of motivation, any efforts to teach techniques for limiting alcohol consumption are typically an inefficient use of time for both the client and the therapist. Motivational interviewing focuses on identifying clients' own reasons to quit. Once these reasons help to increase desire, clients often develop their own strategies for eliminating alcohol from their lives. Many people stop drinking on their own, and motivational interviewing essentially enhances the chances that a client will join this group. (For a more detailed discussion of motivational interviewing, see Chapter 4.)

Motivational interviewing relies on principles designed to help the client decrease alcohol problems. First, the therapist behaves in a manner that will increase the likelihood of change such as listening attentively without judgment or blame. Second, the therapist employs the "stages of change" model, which views change as a fluid process that requires a different intervention for each stage of the client's willingness to act. In motivational interviewing, the behaviors employed by the therapist that are most likely to induce behavior change on the part of the client (e.g., empathy, nonpossessive warmth, genuineness) were originally emphasized in client-centered therapy (Rogers, 1950).

THE STAGES OF CHANGE MODEL

As mentioned in the previous section, empathy, warmth, and genuineness lay the foundation for any productive therapeutic interaction. Many therapies rely on these aspects of the therapeutic relationship to help support growth. Motivational interviewing combines these qualities with the stages of change model to decrease problem drinking. The stages of change model describes specific steps that individuals appear to take when they alter problem behaviors (Prochaska & DiClemente, 1983). The researchers proposed six stages: (a) precontemplation, (b) contemplation, (c) determination, (d) action, (e) maintenance, and (f) relapse (Prochaska, Norcross, & DiClemente, 1994).

Precontemplation describes the period before individuals consider altering behavior. Drinkers in precontemplation have never considered cutting down or quitting. An adept therapist would not waste time attempting to teach these individuals how to quit because they currently lack the motivation to do so. Instead, the therapist assesses clients' quantity and frequency of drinking in an effort to get them to contemplate change. The best approach for this assessment is the time line "followback" (Sobell & Sobell, 1995), a calendar technique that asks drinkers to go through each day for the previous 3 months and list the number of drinks consumed. The therapist would also ask about any associated consequences such as negative emotions, fatigue, hangovers, accidents, and liver troubles. This assessment often leads clients to make the connection between their drinking and the consequences of their drinking. If these connections are made and they lead clients to consider change in any way, clients have entered the contemplation stage.

Contemplation includes the weighing of the pros and cons of altering actions or continuing the same behavior. The motivational interviewer encourages drinkers in this stage to candidly report all of the positive and negative experiences they attribute to their use of alcohol. Initial assessments of pros and cons often reveal ambivalence, that is, strong desires to continue drinking as well as equally strong desires to stop. Ambivalence serves as a common important component of contemplation. Other approaches to treatment may see ambivalence as denial. The stages of change model emphasizes ambivalence as an inherent part of change. During further discussion, the therapist respectfully reflects drinkers' concerns back to them, emphasizing the negative consequences that they generated earlier. This process often leads problem drinkers to a decision to change. A firm decision to change qualifies as a step toward determination.

Determination begins with a clearly stated desire to alter actions. This stage serves as the appropriate time for drinkers to formulate a plan for limiting alcohol consumption. The plan often stems from brainstorming between the interviewer and the drinkers and may include any options that look promising. For example, the strategy for change may rely on techniques from CBT such as altering beliefs and preventing relapse. In addition, drinkers may decide that membership in a 12-step program sounds appropriate.

Once clients regularly limit their drinking or abstain, they have entered the action stage. They no longer merely consider change; they actually make the desired change. This stage proves to be particularly informative as the genuine experience of new habits and actions reveal valuable information unanticipated during the contemplation and determination stages. Clients may find some situations to be easier or more difficult than they expected. The motivational interviewer will offer reassurance about the process becoming less difficult with the passing of time and more practice. The interviewer helps clients to solve problems related to their alcohol use and listens attentively to clients' detailed descriptions of their difficulties and successes.

After a steady period of action, clients may report increased confidence in their skills. This sense of efficacy, an optimism in their own ability to continue the new behaviors, serves as a hallmark of the maintenance stage. Self-efficacy and sustained change are the keys to maintenance. The therapist and the clients will now work together to prevent relapse. They identify situations that put the drinkers at high risk for relapse, and they plan ways in which to avoid problematic alcohol use in these circumstances. For example, clients may decide to avoid parties where alcohol is present. They may role-play refusing drinks if they are offered them. They may practice relaxation techniques if tension often precedes their drinking. They may call a hotline or a friend during times of temptation. It is important to note that these techniques for preventing relapse are consistent with 12-step and CBT approaches.

Occasional backsliding occurs in many efforts to alter maladaptive drinking behavior. The stages of change model considers lapses and relapses as another category of change. Discussing this fact with clients may help to normalize the occasional slip. Considering lapses as a part of the change process may decrease the chances of an abstinence violation effect transforming a slip into a full-blown relapse. The key to the lapse stage parallels the key to the maintenance stage—preventing relapse. Lapses require immediate action. Lapsing drinkers can prevent relapse by rapidly exiting the situation and removing the chance of continued drinking. Many who lapse berate themselves, but their time and energy may be better spent in identifying the precursors to the slips. A frank examination may reveal a new high-risk situation, providing the opportunity to formulate a plan for how to handle this predicament in the future. For example, a former drinker may find himself or herself lapsing after a fight with a family member. This situation might not be one that the drinker had identified as high risk before. Now the drinker knows that he or she needs to plan new ways in which to deal with conflict. The drinker can turn this lapse into a learning experience to prevent future drinking. Thus, lapses remain a part of the change process, and planning for them may minimize problems.

CASE STUDY

"Bob," a 54-year-old Caucasian male truck driver, came to a Veterans Administration hospital after falling in his driveway. He had seriously injured his face and hands. A breath alcohol monitor suggested that his blood alcohol level was approximately .20. Surgeons removed small rocks from his face and hands and referred him to the chemical dependency treatment program. Assessment revealed that Bob had been drinking alcohol regularly for 41 years, since the age of 13 years, and had his first drink at age 10 years. A time line followback assessment suggested that Bob had consumed between 20 and 24 beers per day over the past 90 days, a pattern he said went back for at least 7 years. He had been in treatment twice previously, once in his late 20s and once approximately 8 years ago. He had maintained complete abstinence for approximately a year each time. Both treatments focused on 12-step interventions, but Bob was unwilling to return to meetings or inpatient treatment. He did, however, agree to attend a 1-hour outpatient appointment the following week.

Bob missed the first outpatient meeting, rescheduled after a telephone call, and missed the second meeting as well. A phone call after his second missed appointment revealed that he was willing to discuss the pros and cons of attending an outpatient appointment. Bob confessed that he thought that the hospital only offered 12-step interventions and that he thought he would be "strong-armed" into going back to "God meetings." With the promise that there would be no discussion of steps or deities, he agreed to attend an outpatient interview the following week. The fact that he was willing to reschedule illustrates the importance of follow-up calls after missed appointments. Bob would have undoubtedly never returned to treatment if he had not been phoned after missing appointments.

Bob arrived promptly at an afternoon appointment with a breath alcohol concentration of .06. He stated that he had consumed 4 beers at lunch but that he was doing much better than he had been doing when he came to the hospital after his fall. He claimed to drink 12 beers per day over the previous 3 weeks and again declined inpatient treatment. On reflection, he admitted that he had cut down to 12 beers per day in the past but had eventually increased back to his usual case of 24 per day. He was unwilling to discuss abstinence but agreed to list the pros and cons of decreasing his drinking to 6 beers per day. This approach is consistent with motivational interviewing interventions for people in the contemplation stage.

Bob was surprised when the therapist asked him to first list the disadvantages of drinking only 6 beers per day. The most salient disadvantage to him was that he would be forced to drink them all at once on an empty stomach to notice any subjective effects. He also mentioned that he might receive ribbing from cronies for not "keeping up" when they watched sporting events or went fishing. The only advantages to decreasing to 6 beers per day that Bob could generate were financial. With some prompting, he decided that he might also have fewer conflicts with his adult children if he decreased his drinking. The therapist pointed out several other potential advantages. Specifically, Bob's liver enzymes suggested the potential for medical problems, and these would eventually improve with a decrease (although they would not improve as much as they would with abstinence). In addition, Bob would be less likely to run into problems while driving his truck for work. Mentioning this potential advantage prompted several tales of bravado about his tolerance. With reflection, these eventually turned to a revealing disclosure about a blackout experience. Bob had arrived in a location more than 300 miles from his home and could not recall any aspect of the trip. He feared that he could have had an accident and killed another driver or himself. He expressed considerable shame, guilt, and fear. Reflection of these emotions appeared to inspire a willingness to limit consumption to 6 beers per day and to drink these only during the evening when it was unlikely that he would drive. Bob also agreed to three more outpatient visits during the next 3 weeks.

The therapist called Bob after 4 days to confirm his next appointment. When asked how he was doing, Bob replied, "If I can't have a 12-pack, I really don't see the point of drinking at all." When asked to elaborate, Bob explained that 6 beers provided little change in his state of mind. He agreed to stick to the limit but implied that he might experiment with an occasional day of abstinence. When he arrived for his next appointment, his breath alcohol was .00. He had consumed 6 beers per day on each day, but he drank only 1 during the evening that the therapist had called. When asked why, Bob said that he felt "silly" drinking at all after what he had said about requiring 12 beers to feel any subjective effects. When asked what subjective effects of alcohol he preferred, Bob focused on tension reduction. The session then turned to standard progressive muscle relaxation training. Bob found relaxing in session to be a bit cumbersome but agreed to listen to a relaxation tape at home.

The following week, Bob decreased his drinking to an average of 4 beers per day, with 1 day of abstinence. When asked how he felt about it, he claimed little change in his own experience but some tentative changes in those around him. His adult children had commented that it was nice to see him drinking less. He said that this did not matter to him much, but his affect certainly seemed improved. He had been listening to the relaxation tape daily and agreed to discuss complete abstinence. The therapist reviewed some relapse prevention strategies and sent Bob home with a list of responses he had generated himself for handling difficult situations. He had focused on drink refusal with friends and stressful situations as his target high-risk situations. Bob generated the expression "I've already had my share" as a response for refusing drinks when offered. He also agreed to listen to the relaxation tape daily in an effort to reduce stress. He discussed looking at things differently in an effort to cope, and he agreed to attend a stress management seminar conducted in another area of the hospital.

At 1 month follow-up, Bob had lapsed one time. He attended a barbecue where an acquaintance handed him an open 40-ounce bottle of beer. Bob stated that he took a drink from the bottle automatically. He then reported that he excused himself to go to the bathroom and poured most of the beer into the sink. He reported that he then carried the partially empty bottle around the party for a while for reasons he could not explain. Bob exhibited signs of disappointment regarding this event. The therapist emphasized that it was a single slip, that Bob had not turned it into an excuse to start a binge, and that Bob did not drink again. Bob seemed happy with the interpretation. He agreed to go back to his favorite "I've already had my share" response if a similar experience arose in the future. The therapist called once the following week to confirm abstinence. At 3 months, Bob reported no new lapses and was happy to report that his liver enzymes had improved. At 9 months, he had continued his abstinence and reported even more improvement on his liver enzymes. Although 9 months of follow-up is not a long time, these initial results were encouraging for this combined approach of motivational interviewing and CBT.

CONCLUSIONS

Alcohol can create numerous problems in the lives of drinkers. Different genetic and environmental factors interact in the creation of alcohol abuse, dependence, and problems. A family history of alcoholism, a combination of personality traits, and a set of cognitive factors all can combine with various life stressors to lead people to turn to alcohol for relief of stress. Consistent use of large quantities may lead to alcohol abuse. It can further lead to alcohol dependence or to other life problems. Three imperfect but useful treatments have proved to be effective in alleviating alcohol problems for many individuals: CBT, motivational interviewing, and 12-step facilitation. These therapies have many overlapping characteristics but also employ techniques specific to each approach that are designed to decrease alcohol-related problems. Although the road to sobriety is fraught with difficulties, many people have changed their lives by eliminating the problems related to their continued alcohol use. Putting an end to problem drinking can have a dramatic impact on health and happiness.

REFERENCES

Alterman, A. I., Gerstley, L. J., Goldstein, G., & Tarter, R. E. (1987). Comparisons of the cognitive functioning of familial and nonfamilial alcoholics. *Journal of Studies on Alcohol, 48,* 425–429.

American Psychiatric Association. (1994). *Diagnostic and statistical manual of mental disorders* (4th ed.). Washington, DC: Author.

Bandura, A. (1969). Social learning of moral judgments. *Journal of Personality and Social Psychology, 11,* 275–279.

Beck, A. T., Wright, F. D., Newman, C. F., & Liese, B. S. (1993). *Cognitive therapy of substance abuse.* New York: Guilford.

Berridge, K. C., & Robinson, T. E. (1998). What is the role of dopamine in reward: Hedonic impact, reward learning, or incentive salience? *Brain Research Reviews, 28,* 309–369.

Blum, K., Braverman, E. R., Holder, J. M., Lubar, J. F., Monastra, V. J., Miller, D., Lubar, J. O., Chen, T. J., & Comings, D. E. (2000). Reward deficiency syndrome: A biogenetic model for the diagnosis and treatment of impulsive, addictive, and compulsive behaviors. *Journal of Psychoactive Drugs, 32*(Suppl.), 1–112.

Blum, K., Noble, E. P., Sheridan, P. J., Montgomery, A., Ritchie, T., Jagadeeswaran, P., Nogami, H., Briggs, A. H., & Cohn, J. B. (1990). Allelic association of human dopamine D_2 receptor gene in alcoholism. *Journal of the American Medical Association, 263,* 2055–2060.

Brecher, E. M. (1972). *Licit and illicit drugs.* Boston: Little, Brown.

Brennan, P. A., & Raine, A. (1997). Biosocial bases of antisocial behavior: Psychophysiological, neurological, and cognitive factors. *Clinical Psychology Review, 17,* 589–604.

Cadoret, R. J., Troughton, E., O'Gorman, T. W., & Heywood, E. (1986). An adoption study of genetic and environmental factors in drug abuse. *Archives of General Psychiatry, 43,* 1131–1136.

Cloninger, C. R., Sigvardsson, S., Gilligan, S. B., von Knorring, A. L., Reich, T., & Bohman, M. (1988). Genetic heterogeneity and the classification of alcoholism. *Advances in Alcohol and Substance Abuse, 7,* 3–16.

Conger, J. J. (1956). Reinforcement theory and the dynamics of alcoholism. *Quarterly Journal of Studies on Alcohol, 17,* 296–305.

Conley, J. J., & Kammeier, M. L. (1980). MMPI item responses of alcoholics in treatment: Comparisons with normal and psychiatric patients. *Journal of Consulting and Clinical Psychology, 48,* 668–669.

Darwin, C. R. (1998). *The origin of species.* New York: Random House. (Original work published 1859)

Davis, V. E., & Walsh, M. J. (1970). Alcohol addiction and tetrahydropapaveroline. *Science, 169,* 1105–1106.

Dawes, R. M. (1994). *House of cards.* New York: Free Press.

Eddy, N. B., Halbach, H., Isbell, H., & Seevers, M. H. (1965). Drug dependence: Its significance and characteristics. *Bulletin of the World Health Organization, 32,* 721–733.

Erblich, J., & Earleywine, M. (1995). Distraction does not impair memory during intoxication: Support for the attention-allocation model. *Journal of Studies on Alcohol, 56,* 444–448.

Erblich, J., & Earleywine, M. (1999). Children of alcoholics exhibit attenuated cognitive impairment during an ethanol challenge. *Alcoholism, Clinical and Experimental Research, 23,* 476–482.

Erblich, J., Earleywine, M., & Erblich, B. (2001). Positive and negative associations with alcohol and familial risk for alcoholism. *Psychology of Addictive Behaviors, 15,* 204–209.

Erblich, J., Earleywine, M., Erblich, B., & Bovbjerg, D. H. (in press). Biphasic stimulant and sedative effects of ethanol: Are children of alcoholics really different? *Addictive Behaviors.*

Finn, P. R., Earleywine, M., & Pihl, R. O. (1992). Sensation seeking, stress reactivity, and alcohol dampening discriminate the density of family history of alcoholism. *Alcoholism, Clinical and Experimental Research, 16,* 585–590.

Finn, P. R., Sharkansky, E. J., Brandt, K. M., & Turcotte, N. (2000). The effects of familial risk, personality, and expectancies on alcohol use and misuse. *Journal of Abnormal Psychology, 109,* 122–133.

Freud, S. (1901). *Psychopathology of everyday life.* London: T. Fisher Unwin.

Friedman, D., Cycowicz, Y. M., & Gaeta, H. (2001). The novelty of P3: An event-related brain potential (ERP) sign of the brain's evaluation of novelty. *Neuroscience and Biobehavioral Reviews, 25,* 355–373.

Giancola, P. R., & Moss, H. B. (1998). Executive cognitive functioning in alcohol use disorders. *Recent Developments in Alcoholism, 14,* 227–251.

Green, C. A., Freeborn, D. K., & Polen, M. R. (2001). Gender and alcohol use: The roles of social support, chronic illness, and psychological well-being. *Journal of Biobehavioral Medicine, 24,* 383–399.

Grilly, D. M. (1998). *Drugs and human behavior.* Boston: Allyn & Bacon.

Hesselbrock, M. N., & Hesselbrock, V. M. (1992). Relationship of family history, antisocial personality disorder, and personality traits in young men at risk for alcoholism. *Journal of Studies on Alcohol, 53,* 619–625.

Higuchi, S., Muramatsu, T., Matsushita, S., Murayama, M., & Hayashida, M. (1996). Polymorphisms of ethanol-oxidizing enzymes in alcoholics with inactive ALDH2. *Human Genetics, 97,* 431–434.

Hoffman, N. G., Lumry, A. E., Harrison, P. A., & Lessard, R. J. (1984). Brief Minnesota Multiphasic Personality Inventory scales to screen for substance abuse. *Drug and Alcohol Dependence, 14,* 209–214.

Josephs, R. A., & Steele, C. M. (1990). The two faces of alcohol myopia: Attentional mediation of psychological stress. *Journal of Abnormal Psychology, 99,* 115–126.

Keane, T. M., Lisman, S. A., & Kreutzer, J. (1980). Alcoholic beverages and their placebos: An empirical evaluation of expectancies. *Addictive Behaviors, 5,* 313–328.

Laine, T. P., Ahonen, A., Rasanen, P., & Tiihonen, J. (2001). Dopamine transporter density and novelty seeking among alcoholics. *Journal of Addictive Diseases, 20,* 91–96.

Levenson, R. W., Sher, K. J., Grossman, L. M., Newman, J., & Newlin, D. B. (1980). Alcohol and stress response dampening: Pharmacological effects, expectancy, and tension reduction. *Journal of Abnormal Psychology, 89,* 528–538.

MacAndrew, C. (1967). Self-reports of male alcoholics: A dimensional analysis of certain differences from nonalcoholic male psychiatric outpatients. *Quarterly Journal of Studies on Alcohol, 28,* 43–51.

Marlatt, G. A. (1996). Taxonomy of high-risk situations for alcohol relapse: Evolution and development of a cognitive-behavioral model. *Addiction, 91*(Suppl.), S37–S49.

Marlatt, G. A., Demming, B., & Reid, J. B. (1973). Loss of control drinking in alcoholics: An experimental analogue. *Journal of Abnormal Psychology, 81,* 233–241.

Marlatt, G. A., & Gordon, J. R. (1985). *Relapse prevention: Maintenance strategies in the treatment of addictive disorders.* New York: Guilford.

McMahon, J., & Jones, B. T. (1994). Social drinkers' negative alcohol expectancy relates to their satisfaction with current consumption: Measuring motivation for change with the NAEQ. *Alcohol and Alcoholism, 29,* 687–690.

Meyer, R. E. (2001). Finding paradigms for the future of alcoholism research: An interdisciplinary perspective. *Alcoholism, Clinical and Experimental Research, 25,* 1393–1406.

Miller, N. S., Gold, M. S., & Smith, D. E. (1997). *Manual of therapeutics for addictions.* New York: John Wiley.

Nagoshi, C. T., & Wilson, J. R. (1987). Influence of family alcoholism history on alcohol metabolism, sensitivity, and tolerance. *Alcoholism, Clinical and Experimental Research, 11,* 392–398.

Newlin, D. B., & Thomson, J. B. (1990). Alcohol challenge with sons of alcoholics: A critical review and analysis. *Psychological Bulletin, 108,* 383–402.

Nowinski, J., & Baker, S. (1992). *The twelve-step facilitation handbook.* New York: Lexington Books.

Overholser, J. C. (1987). Clinical utility of the Socratic method. In C. Stout (Ed.), *Annals of clinical research* (pp. 1–7). Des Plaines, IL: Forest Institute.

Prochaska, J. O., & DiClemente, C. C. (1983). Stages and processes of self-change in smoking: Toward an integrative model of change. *Journal of Consulting and Clinical Psychology, 5,* 390–395.

Prochaska, J. O., Norcross, J. C., & DiClemente, C. C. (1994). *Changing for good.* New York: Avon Books.

Project MATCH Research Group. (1998). Matching patients with alcohol disorders to treatments: Clinical implications from Project MATCH. *Journal of Mental Health UK, 7,* 589–602.

Rao, K. N., Begum, S., Venkataramana, V., & Gangadharappa, N. (2001). Nutritional neglect and physical abuse in children of alcoholics. *Indian Journal of Pediatrics, 68,* 843–845.

Rather, B. C., Goldman, M. S., Roehrich, L., & Brannick, M. (1992). Empirical modeling of an alcohol expectancy memory network using multidimensional scaling. *Journal of Abnormal Psychology, 101,* 174–183.

Rodriguez, H. S., Porjesz, B., Chorlian, D. B., Polich, J., & Begleiter, H. (1999). Visual P3a in male subjects at high risk for alcoholism. *Biological Psychiatry, 46,* 281–291.

Rogers, C. (1950). A current formulation of client-centered therapy. *Social Service Review, 24,* 442–450.

Roski, J., Perry, C. L., McGovern, P. G., Williams, C. L., Farbakhsh, K., & Veblen-Mortenson, S. (1997). School and community influences on adolescent alcohol and drug use. *Health Education Research, 12,* 255–266.

Sannibale, C., & Hall, W. (1998). An evaluation of Cloninger's typology of alcohol abuse. *Addiction, 93,* 1241–1249.

Schuckit, M. A. (1994). Low level of response to alcohol as a predictor of future alcoholism. *American Journal of Psychiatry, 151,* 184–189.

Schuckit, M. A., & Smith, T. L. (2001). A comparison of correlates of DSM-IV alcohol abuse or dependence among more than 400 sons of alcoholics and controls. *Alcoholism, Clinical and Experimental Research, 25,* 1–18.

Schuckit, M. A., Tsuang, J. W., Anthenelli, R. M., Tipp, J. E., & Nurnberger, J. I., Jr. (1996). Alcohol challenges in young men from alcoholic pedigrees and control families: A report from the COGA project. *Journal of Studies on Alcohol, 57,* 368–377.

Seeman, M., & Seeman, A. Z. (1992). Life strains, alienation, and drinking behavior. *Alcoholism, Clinical and Experimental Research, 16,* 199–205.

Self, D. W. (1998). Neural substrates of drug craving and relapse in drug addiction. *Annals of Medicine, 30,* 379–389.

Self, D. W., & Nestler, E. J. (1998). Relapse to drug-seeking: Neural and molecular mechanisms. *Drug and Alcohol Dependence, 51,* 49–60.

Sher, K. J., & Trull, T. J. (2002). Substance use disorder and personality disorder. *Current Psychiatry Reports, 4,* 25–29.

Sinha, R., & O'Malley, S. S. (1999). Craving for alcohol: Findings from the clinic and the laboratory. *Alcohol and Alcoholism, 34,* 223–230.

Smith, D. E., & McCrady, B. S. (1991). Cognitive impairment among alcoholics: Impact on drink refusal skill acquisition and treatment outcome. *Addictive Behaviors, 16,* 265–274.

Smith, G. T. (1994). Psychological expectancy as mediator of vulnerability to alcoholism. *Annals of the New York Academy of Sciences, 708,* 165–171.

Sobell, L. C., & Sobell, M. B. (1995). *Alcohol timeline followback instructional training video.* Toronto: Addiction Research Foundation.

Stewart, J. (2000). Pathways to relapse: The neurobiology of drug- and stress-induced relapse to drug taking. *Journal of Psychiatry and Neuroscience, 25,* 125–136.

Streissguth, A. P., Martin, D. C., & Buffington, V. E. (1976). Test-retest reliability of the three scales derived from a quantity-frequency-variability assessment of self-reported alcohol consumption. *Annals of the New York Academy of Sciences, 273,* 458–466.

Strupp, H. H. (1989). Psychotherapy: Can the practitioner learn from the researcher? *American Psychologist, 44,* 717–724.

Thompson, K. M., & Yokota, F. (2001). Depiction of alcohol, tobacco, and other substances in G-rated animated feature films. *Pediatrics, 107,* 1369–1374.

Tsuang, M. T., Bar, J. L., Harley, R. M., & Lyons, M. J. (2001). The Harvard twin study of substance abuse: What we have learned. *Harvard Review of Psychiatry, 9,* 267–279.

Üstün, B., Compton, W., Mager, D., Babor, T., Baiyewu, O., Chatterji, S., Cottler, L., Goegues, A., Mavreas, V., Peters, L., Pull, C., Saunders, J., Smeets, R., Stipec, M. R., Vrasti, R., Hasin, D., Room, R., Van den Brink, W., Regier, D., Blaine, J., Grant, B. F., & Sartorius, N. (1997). WHO study on the reliability and validity of the alcohol and drug use disorder instruments: Overview of methods and results. *Drug and Alcohol Dependence, 47,* 161–169.

Wampold, B. E., Mondin, G. W., Moody, M., Stich, F., Benson, K., & Ahn, H. (1997). A meta-analysis of outcome studies comparing bona fide psychotherapies: Empirically, "all must have prizes." *Psychological Bulletin, 122,* 203–215.

Williams, R. J., & Ricciardelli, L. A. (1996). Expectancies relate to symptoms of alcohol dependence in young adults. *Addiction, 91,* 1031–1039.

Wills, T. A., Sandy, J. M., & Yaeger, A. M. (2002). Moderators of the relation between substance use level and problems: Test of a self-regulation model in middle adolescence. *Journal of Abnormal Psychology, 111,* 3–21.

Yancey, A. K., Siegel, J. M., & McDaniel, K. L. (2002). Role models, ethnic identity, and health-risk behaviors in urban adolescents. *Archives of Pediatrics and Adolescent Medicine, 156,* 55–61.

CHAPTER 7

The Etiology and Treatment of Nicotine Dependence

A Biopsychosocial Perspective

LEE M. COHEN, DENNIS E. MCCHARGUE,
MONICA CORTEZ-GARLAND, ERIC H. PRENSKY,
AND SADIE EMERY

Chronic use of tobacco-containing products, particularly cigarettes, remains one of the most avoidable causes of death and illness in the United States and claims the lives of more than 430,000 individuals each year (U.S. Department of Health and Human Services [DHHS], 1999). The number of tobacco-related deaths alone exceeds that of deaths due to AIDS, murders, other drugs, alcohol, car crashes, fires, and suicides combined (Centers for Disease Control and Prevention [CDC], 2002). Illnesses associated with tobacco use include, but are not limited to, laryngeal cancer, oral cancer, esophageal cancer, obstructive pulmonary disease, cardiovascular disease, intrauterine growth retardation, and low birth weight (DHHS, 1999). Evidence of significant health risks due to environmental tobacco smoke has also been documented. Adverse health risks caused by exposure to "secondhand" tobacco smoke include lung cancer, asthma, respiratory infections, and decreased pulmonary function (DHHS, 1999). Despite public health efforts to reduce tobacco use in the United States, adult prevalence rates have not changed significantly, and in some cases increases were observed during the 1990s (CDC, 2002). For example, the overall rate of adult cigarette smokers has decreased slightly from 25.0% to 23.3% across all age groups except that of 18- to 24-year-olds (CDC, 2002), whereas the use of smokeless (spit) tobacco and cigars has increased substantially (U.S. Department of Agriculture, 1997). To date, 65.5 million Americans continue to use tobacco products on a regular basis (CDC, 2002) and appear to be more difficult to treat than their counterparts of the 1970s and 1980s (Irvin & Brandon, 2000). As such, tobacco use continues to represent an important health behavior that faces health care professionals.

DEFINITIONS AND DESCRIPTION
OF NICOTINE DEPENDENCE

The addictive process associated with tobacco use has been studied primarily with cigarette smoking, but there is a growing body of literature examining this process in spit tobacco (e.g., Hatsukami & Severson, 1999; McChargue & Collins, 1998) and cigar use (e.g., Henningfield, Fant, Radzius, & Frost, 1999). The DSM-IV-TR (*Diagnostic and Statistical Manual of Mental Disorders,* fourth edition, text revision [American Psychiatric Association, 2000]) classifies chronic tobacco use as a significant clinical impairment because of the psychological and neurobiological effects caused by nicotine—the presumed addictive ingredient found in tobacco products (Henningfield & Heishman, 1995; Robinson & Pritchard, 1992). As a clinical disorder, chronic tobacco use is classified as *nicotine dependence* when three of seven criteria are met within the same 12-month period. In particular, the four most prominent criteria of nicotine dependence are (a) developing a tolerance to nicotine, (b) experiencing nicotine withdrawal, (c) showing a persistent desire or unsuccessful efforts to quit or cut down the use of nicotine, and (d) continuing to use nicotine despite the development of physical or psychological problems that are likely to have been caused or exacerbated by tobacco products (American Psychiatric Association, 2000). Other general criteria for nicotine dependence include using larger amounts over a longer period of time; spending a great deal of time in activities necessary to obtain, use, or recover from nicotine; and experiencing impaired functioning (American Psychiatric Association, 2000).

Tolerance

Simply stated, tolerance is viewed as a diminished response or an adaptation to a given dose after repeated use (Balfour, 1991; Benowitz, 1990). Subjective, behavioral, and physiological adaptation has been shown following repeated exposure to nicotine (Balfour, 1991). For example, dizziness, nausea, and vomiting are associated with initial exposure to cigarette smoking; however, these symptoms disappear rapidly following habitual exposure (Benowitz, 1990). For the most part, tolerance to nicotine develops quickly, sometimes within 35 minutes of administration (Porchet, Benowitz, & Sheiner, 1988). Once tolerance is developed, certain effects (e.g., dizziness) are more transient and dissipate rapidly following a short period of abstinence (Benowitz, 1990), whereas tolerance to most of the subjective and behavioral effects appears to be more long term (Perkins et al., 2001). Researchers have suggested that the rapid "re-sensitization" of the more transient effects, such as the "rush" one experiences from the first cigarette of the day, may partially explain why tobacco users tend to show stable use patterns without progressively increasing their dose amounts over time (Benowitz, 1990).

Nicotine Withdrawal

Nicotine withdrawal is defined as the manifestation of behavioral, subjective, physiological, and biochemical changes that occur when a person abruptly cuts down or quits using nicotine-containing products (Hughes, Higgins, & Hatsukami, 1990). The withdrawal syndrome includes four or more of the following symptoms: (a) dysphoric or depressed mood; (b) insomnia; (c) irritability, frustration, or anger; (d) anxiety; (e) difficulty in concentrating; (f) restlessness; (g) decreased heart rate; and (h) increased appetite or weight gain (American Psychiatric Association, 2000). In addition, these symptoms cause clinically significant distress or impairment in social, occupational, or other important areas of functioning, and the symptoms are not better accounted for by another mental disorder (American Psychiatric Association, 2000).

Declining blood levels of nicotine have been associated with the onset of nicotine withdrawal; however, it is not clear whether the duration and severity of these symptoms are entirely attributable to the rate at which nicotine dissipates from a person's system. For example, nicotine reaches the brain within 10 to 19 seconds after smoking a cigarette, with brain levels of nicotine declining rapidly over 20 to 30 minutes (Benowitz, 1990). On the other hand, nicotine levels in the brain from spit tobacco tend to increase gradually, reaching their peak about 30 minutes after administration, and decline slowly over 2 hours or more (Benowitz, Porchet, & Jacob, 1990). Despite the differing rates of nicotine absorption and depletion observed across these two modes of administration, spit tobacco users consistently report similar experiences of withdrawal, both in terms of the types of symptoms experienced (Hatsukami, Gust, & Keenan, 1987; McChargue & Collins, 1998; McChargue, Collins, & Cohen, 2002) and in terms of the level of severity (McChargue & Collins, 1998). Thus, the severity of withdrawal symptoms may be dictated by a variety of individual differences, including tobacco use patterns (Killen, Fortmann, Newman, & Varady, 1991), psychiatric comorbidities (Pomerleau, Marks, & Pomerleau, 2000), and personality factors (Gilbert & Gilbert, 1995; Madden et al., 1997).

In general, nicotine withdrawal occurs within 24 hours of abruptly reducing or quitting nicotine use, peaks between 48 hours (Hughes & Hatsukami, 1986) and 2 weeks (Shiffman, Paty, Guys, Kassel, & Elash, 1995; West, Hajek, & Belcher, 1989), and resolves after 1 month of abstinence (Hughes, 1992). However, similar to withdrawal severity, the duration of withdrawal patterns are also variable. For example, increases in hunger and weight gain are the most persistent symptoms, lasting as long as 6 months to 1 year (Hughes, 1992; Klesges et al., 1997). In addition, individuals who quit using nicotine-containing products do not always report increased anxiety; however, in cases where anxiety is reported, it could be a function of brief lapses in their abstinence (e.g., periodically smoking one cigarette and then resuming abstinence [West & Hajek, 1997]). Finally, depressive symptoms may persist beyond 1 month, especially among people who have experienced a major depressive episode in the past (Borrelli et al., 1996). In fact, data suggest that there is at least a 33% chance that people with a history of major depression will experience clinically significant levels of depressive symptoms at any time across the first 12 months of nicotine abstinence (Borrelli et al., 1996; Tsoh et al., 2000).

Other Prominent Criteria for Nicotine Dependence

Individuals who use nicotine-containing products also show signs and symptoms associated with the remaining criteria for nicotine dependence. Specifically, a strong and persistent desire to use tobacco maintains use patterns (Baker, Morse, & Sherman, 1986; Tiffany, 1990) and contributes to difficulties in quitting (e.g., Tracy, 1994). Researchers question whether nicotine's ability to alter emotions (Baker et al., 1986; Carmody, 1990; Hall, Munoz, Reus, & Sees, 1993) drives the motivation to use tobacco products or whether this increased motivation is more automatic (Tiffany, 1990) and independent from emotion (Robinson & Berridge, 2000). Nevertheless, nicotine administration appears to create an intense motivation to use tobacco products that is difficult to break regardless of the mechanism that promotes the powerful desire to continue tobacco use.

Individuals who use tobacco also tend to experience extreme difficulty in quitting, and unsuccessful efforts usually are made before they are able to quit permanently. In fact, less than 5% of individuals who meet criteria for nicotine dependence are able to quit on their own (Fiore et al., 1990). This percentage increases to as high as 30% with assisted treatment for nicotine dependence (Fiore et al.,

2000). As stated earlier, fewer and fewer people have quit using tobacco products over the past decade (CDC, 2002) as compared with previous decades (Emmons, Kawachi, & Barclay, 1997). The apparent plateau of cigarette smoking rates and the increase of spit tobacco and cigar use may suggest that today's tobacco users are more resistant to treatment efforts and may even possess underlying vulnerabilities that further establish tobacco use patterns (Gilbert & Gilbert, 1995).

Finally, it is not uncommon for nicotine-dependent individuals to continue to use tobacco products despite physical or psychological problems that may result from chronic nicotine exposure. Familiar examples include the patient with emphysema who continues to smoke while attached to an oxygen tank despite the inherent danger of doing so and the patient who smokes through a tracheotomy tube. Overall, there is anecdotal and empirical evidence suggesting that many patients with cardiovascular disease, chronic obstructive pulmonary disease, and/or cancer—all of which are related to chronic tobacco use (DHHS, 1999)—continue their patterns of use (Gritz, Kristeller, & Burns, 1993). Moreover, continued use is associated with a heightened mortality rate, whereas cessation post-disease diagnosis may improve prognoses (Gritz et al., 1993).

A BIOPSYCHOSOCIAL LEARNING MODEL OF NICOTINE DEPENDENCE

Nicotine dependence is a complex biopsychosocial phenomenon that originates from learning theory. The most parsimonious explanation is that nicotine's effects on neurobiological substrates interact with behavioral, emotional, and cognitive domains to create dependence. Evidence also suggests that chronic use patterns may produce secondary conditioning of the pharmacological effects on

the brain (Rose & Levin, 1991) and sensitization of some neurobiological systems (Robinson & Berridge, 2000; Watkins, Koob, & Markou, 2000). In general, tobacco use behaviors are maintained by nicotine's ability to enhance desirable effects (positive reinforcement) and to dispel undesirable effects (negative reinforcement). Over time, frequent and repeated use of tobacco products in specific situations, environments, and emotional states may automatically trigger tobacco use (secondary conditioning and sensitization) (Rose & Levin, 1991; Shiffman, 1991). For example, a person who typically smokes while talking on the phone may light another cigarette when the phone rings without realizing that he or she already had a cigarette lit.

Positive Reinforcement and Sensitization: A Story of Rewarding Properties

The most widely studied neurobiological substrate associated with nicotine-related positive reinforcement is dopamine (Wise, 1998). The mesolimbic dopamine system has long been touted as the reward center of the brain that shapes goal-directed behavior (Olds & Milner, 1954; Stein, Belluzzi, Ritter, & Wise, 1974), including drug use behavior (Di Chiara, 1998; Koob & Le Moal, 1997). Consistent with the reward hypothesis of dopamine, nicotine's preferential binding to nicotinic cholinergic receptors within the mesolimbic dopamine system (Clarke & Pert, 1985) and nicotine's reliable activation of dopamine release within the same system (Pomerleau & Pomerleau, 1984) suggest that nicotine produces powerful rewarding effects for people who use tobacco.

The rewarding effects of nicotine become more powerful over time due to the biphasic nature of nicotine's influence on dopamine release. During nicotine administration, the dopaminergic system becomes sensitized rather than habituated (e.g., tolerance)

(Robinson & Berridge, 2000; Watkins et al., 2000). In other words, dopamine release is enhanced, rather than diminished, from repeated exposure to nicotine. As levels of nicotine are depleted during abstinence, dopamine also shows neuroadaptive effects. Neuroadaptation reflects the progressive blunting of naturally occurring dopamine (Epping-Jordan, Watkins, Koob, & Markou, 1998). The ever-growing disparity between sensitized dopamine release from nicotine administration and blunted naturally occurring dopamine release during nicotine abstinence is hypothesized to alter reward thresholds (Watkins et al., 2000), presumably making it very difficult for tobacco users to experience pleasure without the aid of nicotine.

Glutamate functioning also appears to play an important role in the positive reinforcement of nicotine via its symbiotic relationship with dopamine. As discussed earlier, dopaminergic functioning is regarded as the primary mechanism that accounts for the rewarding properties of nicotine. However, glutamate may actually strengthen nicotine's rewarding properties and permanently implant the effect of such reward into long-term memory. For instance, nicotine administration has been shown to increase glutamate release within the mesolimbic dopamine system (Garcia-Munoz, Patino, Young, & Groves, 1996) as well as within hippocampal neurons associated with memory and learning (Radcliffe, Fisher, Gray, & Dani, 1999). Given that glutamate is strongly linked to learning and memory (Goda & Stevens, 1996), it has been hypothesized that the simultaneous activation of the hippocampal and dopaminergic systems solidifies the rewarding properties of nicotine (Mansvelder & McGehee, 2000). Even after long periods of abstinence, the responsiveness of these systems to nicotine remains abnormal, suggesting that these neurotransmitters play a substantial role in the long-lasting, enduring changes associated with nicotine dependence (Pulvirenti & Diana, 2001).

These long-lasting memories may help to explain the incongruent psychosocial findings related to the reward obtained from nicotine administration. A standard assumption has been that self-reported pleasure (e.g., positive affect or euphoria) acts as a substitute for the rewarding effects of nicotine. However, empirical evidence has not consistently produced data to support this assumption. If self-reported pleasure mimicked the neurobiological substrates, one would expect that pleasure would show sensitizing effects (i.e., more and more pleasure from repeated exposure) after nicotine administration and would show acute decreases in pleasure during nicotine abstinence. Although research shows the expected decrease in pleasure following nicotine abstinence (Hughes & Hatsukami, 1986), euphoric effects during nicotine administration are minimal (Pomerleau & Pomerleau, 1992) and may further diminish, rather than increase, with repeated exposure (Robinson & Berridge, 2000). If pleasure diminishes with chronic nicotine use and is not linked with dopamine sensitization, memories about the pleasure-enhancing effects of nicotine may be sufficient for continued motivation to self-administer nicotine.

As noted earlier, the rewarding effects of nicotine are long-lasting in a tobacco user's memory system. A plausible psychosocial mechanism that takes into account these embedded reward effects is positive smoking expectancies or the belief that smoking will lead to a positive outcome (e.g., relaxation). For decades, positive drug expectancies have been shown to reflect long-term drug use patterns (Vuchinich & Tucker, 1988). In fact, a recent study showed that smoking outcome expectancies combine with one's tendency to experience negative affective states to predict smoking behavior over time (Cohen, McCarthy, Brown, & Myers, 2002). These findings indicate that at least part of the commonly observed relationship between negative affect and smoking behavior can be explained by smoking expectancies.

Negative Reinforcement: A Story of Emotion Regulation

When considering negative reinforcement associated with tobacco use disorders, nicotine administration is believed to have negative mood-alleviating properties via its manipulation of neurotransmitters such as serotonin (Carmody, 1990; Hall et al., 1993). Specifically, low levels of serotonin have been strongly associated with negative mood states (Maes & Meltzer, 1995), and nicotine administration appears to increase levels of this neurotransmitter (Kenny, File, & Neal, 2000). In fact, nicotine's ability to elevate serotonin levels may partially explain why people report that using nicotine-containing products alleviates negative affective states (Carmody, 1990; Hall et al., 1993). Consistent with the serotonin hypothesis of nicotine dependence, when one abstains from nicotine, medications that improve the efficiency of serotonin (e.g., serotonin reuptake inhibitors such as fluoxetine) prolong short-term abstinence (Niaura et al., 2002), particularly among smokers with high baseline levels of depression (Hitsman et al., 1999). Moreover, once people abstaining from nicotine are taken off of this type of medication, there is an increased likelihood that they will experience a major depressive episode (e.g., Borrelli et al., 1996). Hence, this depressive vulnerability during nicotine abstinence is particularly salient for depression-prone individuals.

Although many people report using tobacco products due to their negative mood-alleviating properties (Spielberger, Foreyt, Reheiser, & Poston, 1998), psychosocial research investigating this hypothesis is mixed. It is clear that after short-term abstinence, nicotine administration will reverse any negative affective symptoms associated with the nicotine withdrawal syndrome. However, it remains unclear whether nicotine has the same effect on negative affect that is not associated with nicotine withdrawal. In some studies, administration of nicotine exhibits the expected mood-alleviating properties.

Specifically, older heavy smokers show dose-dependent relief from stress and anxiety following nicotine administration (Gilbert, Robinson, Chamberlin, & Spielberger, 1989), with higher doses of nicotine producing the greatest mood relief (Gilbert et al., 1989; Perkins et al., 1993). In addition, nicotine replacement therapy produces clinically significant reductions in symptoms of depression among nonsmokers suffering from major depression (Salin-Pascual, Rosas, Jimenez-Genchi, & Rivera-Meza, 1996). Nevertheless, mood responses that are not shown to be related to nicotine withdrawal are highly variable. For instance, some evidence actually indicates that nicotine creates higher levels of anxiety and stress (Parrott, 1999; Piasecki & Baker, 2000). Similarly, smoking in response to depression may increase, rather than decrease, symptoms of depression among smokers with a ruminative coping style (Richmond, Spring, Sommerfeld, & McChargue, 2001).

Despite the apparent inconsistencies shown among studies examining negative mood relief from nicotine administration, the importance of the negative reinforcing properties of nicotine should not be minimized. In fact, if only a fraction of individuals achieve negative mood relief from the administration of nicotine, negative affect's role in the maintenance of tobacco use behaviors remains quite salient. For example, both baseline and post-quit negative affect predict relapse (Pomerleau, Adkins, & Pertschuk, 1978; Swan, Ward, & Jack, 1996; West et al., 1989). Furthermore, a large portion of tobacco users suffer from psychological problems that are associated with affective dysregulation (Breslau, 1995). Finally, personality traits that increase the likelihood of experiencing frequent and persistent bouts of negative affect predict tobacco use behaviors and relapse (Gilbert & Gilbert, 1995). Although it remains unclear as to the properties of nicotine that negatively reinforce tobacco use, there is sufficient evidence to implicate the importance of negative reinforcement in nicotine dependence.

Classical Conditioning: A Story of Automatic Processes

Classical conditioning occurs when nicotine administration (unconditioned stimulus) produces psychological and physiological states (unconditioned response) that are repeatedly paired with neutral stimuli (conditioned stimulus). In other words, chronic nicotine administration elicits many reinforcing properties that eventually become conditioned to environmental and psychological stimuli (Iwamoto, Fudala, Mundy, & Williamson, 1987; Rose & Levin, 1991). Over time, the repeated pairings between the once neutral stimuli and nicotine administration produce conditioned responses that initiate and maintain tobacco use behavior (Rose & Levin, 1991). Conditioned responses from emotional and environmental cues reflect the activation of cognitive (Tiffany, 1990), emotional (Baker et al., 1986), and physiological (Robinson & Berridge, 2000) domains. Exposure to such cues evokes strong tobacco use motivation or urges. Some researchers hypothesize that this increase in motivation reflects the desire to evoke a pleasant feeling or to take away unpleasant states (Baker et al., 1986), whereas others view this increased motivation as more automatic (Tiffany, 1990), that is, driven by sensitized neurobiological systems (Robinson & Berridge, 2000).

OTHER IMPORTANT FACTORS IN NICOTINE DEPENDENCE RESEARCH

Genetics

The development of nicotine dependence cannot result entirely from random interactions between neurobiological and psychosocial factors. It has been suggested that individuals who use tobacco and become nicotine dependent may be different from individuals who do not use tobacco because of biologically based predispositions that produce qualitatively different reinforcement from nicotine administration (Pomerleau & Kardia, 1999). Evidence supporting the notion that genetic factors dictate who is likely to become nicotine dependent comes from a variety of sources. For example, twin studies have shown greater concordance rates in monozygotic twins than in dizygotic twins, with heritability estimates of 53% for tobacco use (see review by Hughes, 1986). In addition, certain individuals may be more sensitive to nicotinic properties than are others. A selective sensitivity to nicotine is hypothesized to produce more rapid tolerance and more extensive self-administration patterns (Pomerleau, 1995). As such, genetic factors may help to explain why certain subgroups of smokers become more dependent at earlier ages (e.g., Madden et al., 1999) and have extreme difficulties in quitting (e.g., Lerman et al., 1999).

Gender and Ethnicity

Rates of nicotine dependence appear to differ across gender and ethnic groups. In addition, the proportions of men and women who use tobacco products vary greatly in some countries, such as Japan and Greece, but not in others, such as the United States and the United Kingdom (Grunberg, Winders, & Wewers, 1991). Thus, it may be that tobacco use is reinforced differently for women in countries where as many women use tobacco products as do men. In addition, certain minority populations (e.g., African Americans) within the United States report higher rates of tobacco use than do Caucasians (CDC, 1999), and women and minorities appear to be less successful at quitting (Piper, Fox, Welsch, Fiore, & Baker, 2001). Therefore, these individuals are at greater risk for contracting smoking-related illnesses, making it very important to consider how gender and ethnicity influence the recruitment, retention, and treatment of nicotine-dependent individuals (Piper et al., 2001).

More is known about the etiology and treatment of nicotine dependence for women than for different ethnic groups. The scarcity of research on minorities that use tobacco products has led many researchers and practitioners to examine nicotine dependence among minority populations. Contemporary knowledge regarding what motivates U.S. women to use tobacco products, particularly cigarettes, has focused on two primary issues: (a) affect regulation and (b) weight control. In general, women are more affectively vulnerable than men, and it is believed that this vulnerability is well suited for nicotine's mood-alleviating effects. As such, women may receive greater mood regulatory benefits from smoking than do men, and this is believed to partially explain why women have more difficulty in quitting (Piper et al., 2001). In addition, women frequently express concern about gaining weight after they quit smoking (Klesges & Klesges, 1988). This concern is not surprising given that individuals who are abstinent for 1 year will gain an average of 13 pounds (Klesges et al., 1997).

Comorbid Personality and Psychopathology

The influence of personality on tobacco use is based on the belief that traits predispose people to frequent and persistent aversive mood states (Cloninger, 1987; Tellegen, 1985; Tomkins & McCarter, 1964). As such, many theorize that chronic exposure to mood dysregulation provides ample opportunity for people to learn that tobacco products are an efficient source of relief from these problematic affective states. Traits that are associated with compromised affective systems and tobacco use behavior include sensation seeking, neuroticism, extroversion, and psychoticism (Gilbert & Gilbert, 1995; Spielberger & Jacobs, 1982).

Contemporary research has identified an overwhelming proportion of patients with psychiatric mood, anxiety, and psychotic problems as possessing high levels of comorbid nicotine dependence (Hughes, Hatsukami, Mitchell, & Dahlgren, 1986). Comorbid psychopathology represents an important issue to address in nicotine dependence research because these individuals report excessive dependence levels and have extreme difficulty in quitting (Hughes et al., 1986; McChargue, Gulliver, & Hitsman, 2002a, 2002b). Moreover, psychiatric smokers are at a heightened risk of smoking and psychiatric-related health problems as compared with nonsmoking psychiatric patients and nonpsychiatric smokers (Jeste, Gladsjo, Lindamer, & Lacro, 1996; Linkins & Comstock, 1990). Prevalence rates of smoking among this population range from 31% to 90%, depending on the psychiatric disorder (Beckham et al., 1997; de Leon et al., 1995; Hughes et al., 1986).

It has been hypothesized that chronic tobacco use observed among individuals with psychopathological problems reflects self-medicating behaviors. According to the self-medication hypothesis, psychiatric patients smoke in part because nicotine helps to regulate their symptomatology (Gilbert & Gilbert, 1995). For example, patients with major depression may smoke to improve depressed mood states (Hall et al., 1993). Similarly, patients with schizophrenia may find that smoking helps to reduce negative symptoms such as anhedonia, apathy, blunted affect, and emotional withdrawal (McChargue et al., 2002a, 2002b). Finally, patients with posttraumatic stress disorder and other anxiety disorders may smoke to cope with emotional and physiological distress (Beckham et al., 1997).

This self-medication process transforms tobacco use into an extremely rewarding behavior for psychiatric individuals as compared with nonpsychiatric cohorts who report similar tobacco use patterns (Spring, Pingitore, & McChargue, in press). As such, the goal of complete abstinence might not be initially possible for some psychiatric subgroups (e.g., individuals diagnosed with schizophrenia). These individuals may require a stepped care approach that focuses on reducing exposure to tobacco toxins until the individuals are able to stabilize lower rates of tobacco use and learn adequate coping skills (McChargue et al., 2002a, 2002b).

ASSESSMENT AND TREATMENT

As discussed earlier, nicotine dependence is maintained by many factors across diverse patient populations. Another issue that leads to difficulties in the treatment and assessment of nicotine dependence is the pervasive nature of tobacco use. Specifically, the widespread use of tobacco products forces clinical health psychologists to address issues related to this construct in a variety of settings and situations. Hence, clinicians are encouraged to be mindful of the settings or situations in which they deliver their interventions (Collins et al., 1999). Overall, it is recommended that a multidisciplinary approach to the assessment and treatment of nicotine dependence be used if long-term abstinence is to be achieved (Fagerström, 1991).

Assessment of Nicotine Dependence

The assessment of nicotine dependence may take many forms at differing levels of intensity within behavioral medicine settings. For example, the approach to assessments of nicotine dependence in an emergency room is likely to differ from the approach to assessments used in outpatient settings. Therefore, the assessment should be tailored to the specific setting. Prior to beginning an assessment, the clinician should consider the purpose for the assessment, the environment where the assessment will take place, and the form of intervention conducive to the setting.

Pretreatment Assessments

To provide adequate treatment, it is essential that the clinician conduct the most comprehensive evaluation possible. The evaluation should include the assessment of physiological, psychological, and social factors that appear to influence the patient's tobacco use patterns (Ockene, Kristeller, & Donnelly, 1999). Pertinent information may be acquired via a clinical interview, self-report measures, a chart review, and corroboration from behavioral medicine staff. Ockene and colleagues (1999) noted that, at the very least, an assessment of nicotine dependence starts with a clinical interview. During this interview, physiological assessment questions should include past quit attempts, withdrawal symptoms experienced during past quit attempts, and the patient's perceived addiction to nicotine. Questions within the social domain should include the number of friends, family members, and coworkers who use tobacco products; the expected amount of social support or nonsupport; and the degree to which the patient can be assertive at rebuffing pressure from others to smoke (Ockene et al., 1999) . Included within the psychological assessment should be questions related to emotional problems (e.g., stress, depression), behavioral indexes (e.g., extent to which person will go to have a cigarette), and cognitive factors (e.g., self-efficacy beliefs about quitting [Ockene et al., 1999]). Ockene and colleagues (1999) also noted that gathering information about a patient's smoking history, as well as having the patient self-monitor his or her smoking behavior, can provide useful data that may aid in treatment specificity. Finally, health factors that may be a consequence of chronic use patterns should also be assessed, and patients who present with physical complaints (e.g., shortness of breath) should be referred to a physician (Ockene et al., 1999).

Pretreatment assessment can be as brief as a 10-minute clinical interview or as long as a 2½-hour structured assessment. Again, the setting and purpose of the assessment should dictate the type of assessment administered. For a relatively brief assessment or for information that will be incorporated within a larger assessment, there are a variety of standardized self-report measures that can be used to assess level of dependence, self-efficacy, readiness to quit, general reasons for use, and perceptions of what tobacco products do for the person. For more comprehensive interviews, several structured and semistructured interviews are available, including the Diagnostic Interview Schedule (Malgady, Rogler, & Tryon, 1992) and the Structured Clinical Interview for the DSM-IV Axis I Disorders–Clinician Version (First, Spitzer, Gibbon, & Williams, 1997).

Most self-report measures have adequate psychometric properties and have been used with a variety of populations. Although a detailed description of all tobacco-related measures available is beyond the scope of this chapter, the following measures are recommended.

1. *The Fagerström Test of Nicotine Dependence* (Heatherton, Kozlowski, Frecker, & Fagerström, 1991): This is a 6-item, self-report questionnaire designed to assess various components of smoking behavior, including an estimate of daily intake, difficulty in refraining, and other aspects related to the pattern of intake.

2. *The Smoking Self-Efficacy Questionnaire* (Colletti, Supnick, & Payne, 1985): This is a 17-item questionnaire designed to assess respondents' beliefs about their ability to control their urges to smoke in a variety of situations.

3. The Smoking Consequences Questionnaire (Brandon & Baker, 1991): The Smoking Consequences Questionnaire (SCQ) is a 50-item measure designed to assess expectations associated with cigarette smoking. It has four factors: negative consequences (e.g., health risks), positive reinforcement/sensory satisfaction (e.g., taste, relaxation), negative reinforcement/negative affect reduction (e.g., reduction of sadness and anxiety), and appetite/weight control. The SCQ-Adult (Copeland, Brandon, & Quinn, 1995) is an extension of the SCQ for use with an older population of dependent smokers.

4. *The Contemplation Ladder* (Biener & Abrams, 1991): This is a measure of readiness to consider tobacco cessation. It is designed to assess a tobacco user's position on a continuum ranging from having no thoughts of quitting to being engaged in action to change one's tobacco use. The ladder is consistent with Prochaska and DiClemente's (1983) model, which states that tobacco cessation is the culmination of an extended process of behavior change. The measure employs a picture of a ladder, where each rung has an associated number that the patient is instructed to circle representing where he or she is in thinking about quitting.

Posttreatment Assessments

Posttreatment assessment allows the clinician to measure and adjust treatment efforts as necessary. Issues that may arise include treatment compliance, sudden exacerbation of clinical disorders (e.g., major depression), severe tobacco withdrawal, intense and persistent urges to use nicotine, weight gain, brief smoking lapses, and abstinence status. Many of these issues can be assessed using clinical interviews. A supplementary self-report measure is the Minnesota Nicotine Withdrawal Scale (Hughes & Hatsukami, 1986), which assesses withdrawal severity. This measure may be used repeatedly to assess withdrawal across time.

For purposes of assessing treatment compliance, lapsing, and abstinence status, the clinician may assess tobacco use daily, weekly, or at designated follow-up times. Self-reported lapses and relapses in isolation or combined with biochemical verification have been used. A detailed description of the utility of biochemical markers of tobacco and cessation as well as recommendations for their application in clinical practice is beyond the scope of this chapter. However, the Society for Research on Nicotine and Tobacco Subcommittee on Biochemical Verification (2002) recently published an overview of this subject. In general, the committee noted that there are currently three biomarkers used to assess whether a person has been abstinent from nicotine: thiocyanate (SCN), cotinine, and expired carbon monoxide (CO). SCN and cotinine are metabolites of nicotine that indicate tobacco use over the past week, and CO (as obtained via expired air) indicates smoked tobacco use within the past 24 hours. The committee also noted that the standard indication of tobacco use has been cotinine levels above 15 nanograms per milliliter, carbon monoxide levels above 8 to 10 parts per million, and SCN levels of 78 to 84 micromoles per liter. (For a more in-depth review of biochemical verification recommendations, see Society for Research on Nicotine and Tobacco Subcommittee on Biochemical Verification, 2002.)

Treatment of Nicotine Dependence

The treatment of nicotine dependence should be viewed as a multidisciplinary stepped care approach. The stepped care approach starts with the assessment of the patient's motivation to quit and progresses to the implementation of brief interventions. For example, routine screening and brief counseling (less than 3 minutes) within emergency rooms increase long-term abstinence rates from 3% (usual care) to 8% to 11% (Bernstein & Becker, 2002). If the patient is unmotivated to quit, the clinician should incorporate motivational enhancing techniques within the brief intervention. Only after brief interventions are unsuccessful should the clinician refer the patient to more intensive treatments. As discussed in the next two subsections, all recommendations for brief and intensive interventions are consistent with the clinical practice guidelines for treating nicotine dependence (Fiore et al., 2000). It should be noted that both brief and intensive interventions recommend the inclusion of pharmacological treatment. However, pharmacological agents associated with treating nicotine dependence are discussed in a separate subsection.

Brief Interventions

Brief interventions are designed to be used in a variety of settings and should not take more than 3 to 10 minutes. Brief interventions include assessing tobacco use patterns and willingness to quit, advising the patient to make a quit attempt, assisting the patient in quitting, and scheduling follow-up sessions (Fiore et al., 2000). Unfortunately, not all tobacco-using patients are highly motivated to quit. In cases where the patient is not so motivated, it is recommended that the clinician use an empathetic therapeutic style that avoids arguments, increases self-efficacy, and encourages adaptive skills at quitting (Prochaska & Goldstein, 1991). Confrontational and punitive styles may have the opposite effect by further decreasing the patient's motivation to quit (Miller & Rollnick, 2002).

Brief assistance that has been shown to increase abstinence rates may be as simple as providing the patient with self-help material combined with recommending approved pharmacological treatment (Killen, Fortmann, Newman, & Varady, 1990). Other brief techniques include (a) helping to identify upcoming challenges, (b) processing helpful skills from prior quit attempts, (c) reducing alcohol consumption during the first month of abstinence, (d) encouraging others who use tobacco within the same household to quit as well, (e) providing social support within the clinical environment, and (f) helping the patient to find another supportive environment (Fiore et al., 2000).

The first follow-up session should be scheduled approximately 1 week after the quit date, with the second scheduled 1 to 3 weeks later (Fiore et al., 2000). During the follow-up, the clinician should remain supportive, highlight successes (no matter how small), and encourage problem solving. The patient may have a tendency to overemphasize an aspect of the quit attempt that is linked to failure (Shiffman et al., 1996). If so, the clinician should try to reframe the perceived failure as a learning experience and reengage the patient in problem solving (Fiore et al., 2000).

Intensive Treatments

It is recommended that intensive treatments be offered to all tobacco users because, on average, such interventions are more effective than brief interventions (Fiore et al., 2000). This recommendation, however, might not be feasible. Thus, for each individual who wishes to quit, the clinician is encouraged to use a stepped care approach that starts brief and progressively increases in intensity. The reason for this is that, under certain circumstances, brief interventions can be more effective than intensive interventions (Smith et al., 2001), and brief interventions are more practical in a variety of settings (e.g., primary care facilities).

Treatment Format for Intensive Treatments. To qualify as an intensive treatment, there must be a minimum of four sessions lasting more than 10 minutes each (Fiore et al., 2000). If feasible, group sessions of 8 to 10 people are recommended over individual sessions because the group setting fosters social support (Ockene et al., 1999). Sessions should be scheduled on a weekly basis during the initial 4 weeks of treatment and then biweekly for the next 4 weeks (Ockene et al., 1999). Finally, posttreatment follow-ups should be scheduled 6 to 12 months after the quit date (Kozlowski, Henningfield, & Brigham, 2001).

Treatment Components. Many of the psychosocial components used in tobacco cessation treatment packages are cognitive-behavioral in nature. The purpose of these components is to break the association between smoking and other life activities and to increase the patient's ability to cope during abstinence. As stated earlier, pharmacological therapies are highly recommended in conjunction with these psychosocial interventions.

Before a patient attempts to quit, the patient is encouraged to gather as much about his or her smoking habit as possible. The patient is asked to pay attention to specific triggers that he or she believes will challenge the attempt at quitting. Tobacco-related triggers include situations, emotions, thoughts, and places that evoke strong urges to use tobacco. Self-monitoring smoking behavior prior to a quit attempt often will help the patient to identify tobacco-related triggers that are relevant to his or her life. However, it is not atypical for many other "unexpected" triggers to arise once the patient has achieved abstinence. Thus, it is important to continue monitoring triggers long after the quit date. It is also suggested that the clinician provide the patient with education regarding the withdrawal symptoms that he or she may experience as well as the addictive nature of tobacco because this information can aid the patient in understanding the process of addiction (Fiore et al., 2000; Kozlowski et al., 2001). For example, skills training focused on problem solving and symptom management are helpful (Fiore et al., 2000). In addition, there are several nonspecific treatment factors that the clinician should provide during treatment. These treatment factors include discussing and eliciting positive expectancies, being supportive and understanding, and providing a time line for the quit attempt (Fiore et al., 2000; Kozlowski et al., 2001).

Once the patient quits, he or she may experience a variety of nicotine withdrawal symptoms that undermine quit attempts. It is important for the clinician to assist the patient in coping with these symptoms, particularly during the first month of abstinence. The clinician should encourage the patient to use the skills he or she learned during the pre-quit sessions. For example, encouraging the use of relaxation techniques (e.g., removing oneself from stressful situations, deep breathing) provides an alternative means by which to cope with stressful situations and negative affect associated with tobacco withdrawal

(Dziegielewski & Eater, 2000; Hatsukami & Lando, 1999). The use of accessible substitutes, such as chewing gum, may also help the patient to cope with withdrawal symptoms (Cohen, Britt, Collins, al'Absi, & McChargue, 2001; Cohen, Britt, Collins, Stott, & Carter, 1999; Cohen, Collins, & Britt, 1997). In addition, encouraging the patient to avoid situations where tobacco use is likely to occur (e.g., bars, bowling alleys) as well as to engage in healthy alternative behaviors (e.g., exercise) may help to prolong abstinence (Dziegielewski & Eater, 2000; Ockene et al., 1999).

Finally, working with the patient to develop the requisite skills to elicit social support from others outside of treatment is integral to successful tobacco cessation (Fiore et al., 2000). One type of social support outside of therapy that should be suggested is Nicotine Anonymous (NicA). These mutual-help groups provide social and emotional support for many sufferers of addictive disorders through personal sharing on a weekly basis (Lichtenstein, 1999). It has been suggested that NicA may be most effective for highly dependent smokers or those who also abuse another substance (e.g., alcohol). At the very least, patients who do not have a significant outside support system may need more frequent contact from a clinician to support them during their quit attempts (Ockene et al., 1999).

Pharmacological Interventions

According to the *Clinical Practice Guidelines* (Fiore et al., 2000), many first-line medications exist for the treatment of nicotine dependence, as do several second-line medications. First-line medications have been established as efficacious through clinical trials and have been approved by the Food and Drug Administration (FDA) for use with nicotine dependence. First-line medications include nicotine replacement products (e.g., gums, patches, nasal sprays, inhalers) and buproprion-SR (sustained release). With the exception of nicotine gum, these interventions

have been shown to approximately double abstinence rates when compared with placebo treatments.

Second-line treatments have also been found to be efficacious, but the use of these medications is limited due to the lack of FDA approval as treatment for nicotine dependence as well as concerns about potential side effects. Second-line treatments include fluoxetine, clonidine, nortriptyline, and a combination of nicotine replacement therapies. Mention of second-line therapies is limited to this paragraph because such therapies are not viable treatment options at this time. Thus, this subsection limits further discussion of pharmacology to first-line treatments.

Nicotine Replacement Therapy. Nicotine replacement therapy (NRT) is intended to break the conditioning of nicotine with environmental cues by making nicotine intake independent of events in the environment (Glover & Glover, 2001). Although NRT provides lower doses of nicotine than do other tobacco products, it can be used to decrease the severity of withdrawal symptoms by providing a slow consistent dose of nicotine through an alternate administration route (Jarvis & Sutherland, 1998). NRT comes in many different forms, including gums, patches, nasal sprays, and inhalers.

Nicotine Polacrilex (gum) was the first NRT approved by the FDA (Jarvis & Sutherland, 1998). The absorption rate is fairly rapid, and peak nicotine levels are reached within 20 to 30 minutes (Hatsukami & Lando, 1999). Use is recommended for 3 months (Hatsukami & Lando, 1999). Although nicotine gum can be used on an as-needed basis to control tobacco urges, a fixed schedule has been shown to be more effective in dealing with withdrawal symptoms (Ockene et al., 1999). Nicotine gum is dispensed in 2- or 4-milligram doses, with the 4-milligram dose recommended for heavily dependent smokers (Fiore et al., 2000).

The nicotine patch has a passive delivery system. The absorption of nicotine is slower than with the gum (Jarvis & Sutherland, 1998), resulting in peak levels of nicotine 4 to 9 hours after administration (Hatsumaki & Lando, 1999). The patch is available in either 24-hour (Habitrol, Nicoderm, and Nicoderm CQ) or 16-hour doses (Nicotrol). Typically, 24-hour patches have 21 or 22 milligrams of nicotine, whereas patches designed for 16-hour use have 15 milligrams of nicotine (Hatsukami & Lando, 1999; Ockene et al., 1999).

A nicotine nasal spray is available with a prescription (Fiore et al., 2000) and decreases craving within minutes of use due to rapid absorption rates (Hatsukami & Lando, 1999; Jarvis & Sutherland, 1998; Ockene et al., 1999). Treatment is typically 6 to 8 weeks but can be extended to 3 months in severe cases (Hatsukami & Lando, 1999; Ockene et al., 1999). It is important to note that the nasal spray may be more effective in situations where instant relief from nicotine craving is a priority (Hurt et al., 1998).

Finally, the nicotine inhaler dispenses 10 milligrams of nicotine per inhaler cartridge (Eissenberg, Stitzer, & Henningfield, 1999; Hatsukami & Lando, 1999). A unique feature of the inhaler is that it provides oral and tactile reinforcement because it consists of a mouthpiece and a nicotine cartridge as well as nicotine (Hatsukami & Lando, 1999; Ockene et al., 1999).

Non-nicotine Therapies. Buproprion is an antidepressant medication that has been shown to aid in the management of nicotine withdrawal symptoms (Johnston, Robinson, Adams, Glassman, & Covey, 1999). Although the mechanism of buproprion is not completely clear (Johnston et al., 1999), it is presumed to block neural reuptake of dopamine and/or norepinephrine (Fiore et al., 2000). Buproprion remains the only non-nicotine medication used in tobacco cessation programs that is approved by the FDA (Fiore et al., 2000; Johnston et al., 1999).

If All Else Fails. . .

If all else fails, the clinician is advised to lower tobacco use behavior when abstinence appears to be initially unattainable (McChargue et al., 2002a, 2002b) and/or pharmacological therapies are not suitable (Ockene et al., 1999). Reducing tobacco use may be accomplished via nicotine fading. Nicotine fading involves switching to a brand with lower nicotine levels as well as gradually decreasing the quantity of tobacco used (Ockene et al., 1999). For example, once cigarette consumption has been decreased to 5 to 10 cigarettes per day and has been stabilized at this level, a quit date should be reestablished (Ockene et al., 1999).

CONCLUSIONS

Chronic use of tobacco products has been linked to a number of serious health problems that affect many people throughout the world. It appears that nicotine dependence develops via the interaction between neurobiological substrates and cognitive, behavioral, and emotional domains. Although there are a variety of factors that contribute to the development of nicotine dependence, once people are dependent, it is clear that they have extreme difficulty in quitting. For the most part, treatment of nicotine dependence takes a stepped care approach, which begins with brief interventions and progresses to more intensive interventions. The goal of this chapter was to increase knowledge about nicotine dependence and to provide guidance on intervention strategies for treating individuals with nicotine dependence. Given the pervasiveness of tobacco use disorders among various patient populations and the health consequences associated with these disorders, treatment of nicotine dependence is one area in which clinical health psychologists can have a positive impact on their patients' overall health status.

CASE STUDY

This case study illustrates an intensive smoking treatment. The client, "Betty," was a 67-year-old Caucasian female who was referred by her primary care physician for individual smoking treatment. Betty presented with complaints of having "no control" over her smoking behavior but having a strong desire to quit smoking. She also reported that her health was "failing" and that her physician would not perform "a necessary medical procedure" unless she quit. Specifically, Betty noted that she suffered from numerous medical problems, including chronic bronchitis, asthma, and emphysema. Medical concerns had reduced her independence by causing her to rely on a motorized scooter for community mobility. Betty reported that she lived in an apartment by herself and noted that she had very little local social support. She did indicate, however, that she had several relatives who lived "out of state" with whom she talked via phone on a weekly basis.

During Betty's intake session, she was asked to exhale into a CO monitor and to complete the Fagerström Test of Nicotine Dependence. Results revealed a CO reading of 48 parts per million (indicating heavy smoking rates) and a test score of 9 (indicating a high level of nicotine dependence). In addition to these measures, a detailed account of her smoking history and quit attempts was obtained via clinical interview. In sum, Betty reported smoking her first cigarette at the age of 12 years and progressing to daily cigarette smoking by the age of 14 years. She noted that when she was smoking at her heaviest rate, she smoked two packs (40 cigarettes) per day, but she was currently smoking 25 cigarettes per day. Betty reported that she had tried unsuccessfully to quit smoking many times in her life, noting that she could recall four occasions when she made "serious attempts" to quit by using group smoking cessation programs, using nicotine replacement patches, and stopping "cold turkey." Betty made it clear to the therapist that she did not want to use nicotine replacement patches this time because she had "vivid disturbing dreams" the last time she had used them. She noted that her previous quit attempts resulted in temporary cessation, with her longest period of abstinence being a little more than 1½ years. She also noted, on a scale of 1 to 10, that she had a strong desire to quit smoking (10/10), that it was very important that she quit smoking (10/10), but that she was only somewhat confident in her ability to quit (5/10).

Betty agreed to attend weekly sessions for the next 8 weeks. Betty and the therapist collaboratively planned to reduce her nicotine intake and to have her learn more about her smoking behavior (e.g., when she smoked, where she smoked, why she smoked) during the first 4 weeks of treatment. A quit date was set for Week 5, and during Weeks 6 to 8 it was decided that the focus of treatment would be on issues related to relapse prevention. Betty left the intake session with two "homework" assignments, namely (a) to attempt to reduce smoking intake by 10% during the week and (b) to keep a written record of her smoking behavior. Specifically, each time she was about to smoke a cigarette, Betty was asked to write down the time of day, any emotions she was feeling at the time, and the situational circumstances that occurred just prior to her smoking.

Betty presented for her second session on time and indicated that she had reduced her smoking intake successfully and kept accurate records of her smoking behavior. She was eager to report that by the end of the week, she was able to reduce her smoking to 10 cigarettes per day (a far greater reduction than the agreed-on 10%). She also noted that she wanted to smoke more frequently than she actually did; however, she "got sick" of writing down all of the requested information before each cigarette. She noted that tracking her smoking behavior allowed her to cut out many cigarettes that she did not "really need." She also indicated that in reducing her smoking intake, she learned that the "cravings" she had to smoke throughout the day would not "last forever" and in fact passed rather quickly, usually within 10 to 15 minutes. After praising Betty on the progress she had made during the past week, the therapist reviewed the "smoking record sheets" that Betty had completed in an attempt to identify commonalities in her smoking behavior. Examination of the smoking record sheets revealed that Betty smoked most often after eating meals and during times of perceived stress. In an attempt to aid Betty during these difficult times, urge control strategies were discussed.

One of the keys to success in smoking cessation is learning how to get through urges or cravings to smoke. Given that Betty had already learned how to get through some of her urges to smoke, the therapist enlisted Betty's help to get a sense of what worked for her during the past week. Betty noted that if she just waited long enough, her urge to smoke would go away (although she was quick to point out that the urges would return). Building on Betty's success, the therapist noted that delaying smoking might not work in all situations and taught Betty a number of other urge control strategies that might prove to be useful in situations where delaying smoking was too difficult. The therapist outlined five basic strategies that Betty could pull from her "tool box" when faced with difficult urges: (a) *d*elaying smoking, (b) *e*scaping from situations or events that may contribute to the urge, (c) *a*voiding situations where the temptation to smoke may be too great, (d) *d*istracting herself by thinking about or doing other things that she enjoys doing, and (e) *s*ubstituting something else for a cigarette such as sugarless gum, candy, or sunflower seeds. (All of these strategies can be remembered by the simple yet appropriate acronym of DEADS.) The therapist encouraged Betty to continue doing what worked for her the previous week and to try some of the other strategies that were taught when the urge to smoke surfaced. For "homework," Betty was again encouraged to reduce her smoking by 10%. The therapist also encouraged Betty to pick a "smoking place" in her home where she usually did not smoke and did not engage in other activities such as talking on the phone, socializing, eating, watching television, and reading mail. It was suggested that she smoke only in this place, with the idea being that she would not associate smoking in this place with any other kind of activity. Also, it would mean that she would have to stop what she was doing so as to smoke a cigarette.

During the third and fourth weeks of treatment, Betty was able to reduce her smoking to 4 cigarettes per day using the strategies discussed earlier. In anticipation of the Week 5 quit date, most of the fourth session was centered on preparing Betty for her quit attempt. She was instructed to have her final cigarette no later than before she went to bed on the night before she was to attend her fifth session. She was also encouraged to "seek out and destroy" all of the cigarettes that remained in her apartment that evening so as to be sure that there would not be any cigarettes readily available to her when she woke up the next morning. She was also educated about what types of withdrawal symptoms she might expect (e.g., depressed mood, irritability, anxiety) so that they would not catch her "off guard." In addition, detailed plans were made outlining how she would deal with her cravings to smoke so that she had a "plan of attack" if a craving surfaced. She was also encouraged to start thinking about how to reward herself once she quit.

During the fifth session, Betty was not as animated as she had been during the previous 4 weeks of treatment. She reported that she had not smoked a cigarette since before she went to bed the previous evening; however, she noted that she "really wanted one." The therapist reinforced Betty for all of her hard work and reminded her that her cravings would pass and that the intensity and frequency of the cravings would dissipate over time. The remainder of the session was spent discussing the health benefits that she could expect over the next several weeks (e.g., decrease in coughing and sinus congestion, increase in overall energy level). Finally, Betty was informed that she might "slip" and smoke a cigarette during the course of the next week. She was told that this is "normal" and that if it happens, she should look at it as just a "slip," not a "total relapse." She was encouraged to get back to being "smoke free" after the slip rather than to give herself permission to smoke as many cigarettes as she wanted and view her efforts as a failure.

Sessions 6 to 8 began with Betty exhaling into the CO monitor to show her that her CO levels were decreasing, thereby increasing the amount of oxygen that was circulating throughout her body. Her readings were 11, 8, and 7, respectively. In addition, these sessions centered on ways in which Betty could prevent relapse. She had done exceptionally well and did not experience a slip during these 3 weeks. Betty and the therapist worked on anticipating difficult situations and planned ahead as to how she would cope with these situations if and when they arose. Betty was particularly concerned about what she would do in stressful situations that were bound to arise in the future. It was discussed how she could take a "time out," removing herself from the situation, taking deep breaths, and/or thinking of something fun she had recently done rather than smoking. At the end of Session 8, Betty was commended for her hard work, given information about local support groups (in case she desired additional help), and was scheduled for three "booster sessions" 1, 3, and 6 months later.

At 1-month follow-up, Betty reported that she had one slip during the holidays as she was caught off guard by her "emotions." She noted that she recognized what she was doing and immediately put out the cigarette and did not allow herself to smoke again. She noted that she repeatedly reminded herself of her hard work and told herself that she refused to "go back to Square One." She also noted that this slip was a "reality check" and reminded her that she should not get overconfident about her progress and that she had to continue to work on her addiction to nicotine. Betty admitted that she "would be lying" if she said she did not want a cigarette. But she added that the cravings were not occurring as often and that they were not as severe when they did occur. Betty was praised by the therapist and was encouraged to "keep her guard up." At the 3- and 6-month follow-ups, Betty reported that she had not slipped again and that her energy levels were up. At the 6-month follow-up, she reported that it looked as though her physician was considering performing the medical procedure she needed.

REFERENCES

American Psychiatric Association. (2000). *Diagnostic and statistical manual of mental disorders* (4th ed., text revision). Washington, DC: Author.

Baker, T. B., Morse, E., & Sherman, J. E. (1986). The motivation to use drugs: A psychobiological analysis of urges. In C. Rivers (Ed.), *The Nebraska Symposium on Motivation: Alcohol Use and Abuse* (pp. 257–323). Lincoln: University of Nebraska Press.

Balfour, D. J. (1991). Neural mechanisms underlying nicotine dependence. *Addiction, 89,* 1419–1423.

Beckham, J. C., Kirby, A. C., Feldman, M. E., Hertzberg, M. A., Moore, S. D., Crawford, A. L., Davidson, J. R. T., & Fairbank, J. A. (1997). Prevalence and correlates of heavy smoking in Vietnam veterans with chronic posttraumatic stress disorder. *Addictive Behaviors, 22,* 637–647.

Benowitz, N. L. (1990). Pharmacokinetic considerations in understanding nicotine dependence. In *The biology of nicotine dependence* (pp. 186–209). Chichester, UK: Wiley.

Benowitz, N. L., Porchet, H., & Jacob, P., III. (1990). Pharmacokinetics, metabolism, and pharmacodynamics of nicotine. In S. Wonnacott, M. A. H. Russell, & I. P. Stolerman (Eds.), *Nicotine psychopharmacology: Molecular, cellular, and behavioural aspects* (pp. 112–157). Oxford, UK: Oxford University Press.

Bernstein, S. L., & Becker, B. M. (2002). Preventive care in the emergency department: Diagnosis and management of smoking and smoking-related illness in the emergency department—A systematic review. *Academic Emergency Medicine, 9,* 720–729.

Biener, L., & Abrams, D. B. (1991). The contemplation ladder: Validation of a measure of readiness to consider smoking cessation. *Health Psychology, 10,* 360–365.

Borrelli, B., Niaura, R., Keuthen, N., Goldstein, M., Depue, J., Murphy, C., & Abrams, D. B. (1996). Development of major depressive disorder during smoking cessation treatment. *Journal of Clinical Psychiatry, 57,* 534–538.

Brandon, T. H., & Baker, T. B. (1991). The Smoking Consequences Questionnaire: The subjective expected utility of smoking in college students. *Psychological Assessment, 3,* 484–491.

Breslau, N. (1995). Psychiatry comorbidity of smoking and nicotine dependence. *Behavioral Genetics, 25,* 95–101.

Carmody, T. P. (1990). Affect regulation, nicotine addiction, and smoking cessation. *Journal of Psychoactive Drugs, 24,* 111–122.

Centers for Disease Control and Prevention. (1999). Cigarette smoking among adults: United States, 1997. *Morbidity and Mortality Weekly Report, 48,* 993–996.

Centers for Disease Control and Prevention. (2002). Cigarette smoking among adults: United States, 2000. *Morbidity and Mortality Weekly Report, 51,* 642–645.

Clark, P. B., & Pert, A. (1985). Autoradiographic evidence for nicotine receptors on nigrostriatal and mesolimbic dopaminergic neurons. *Brain Research, 348,* 355–358.

Cloninger, C. R. (1987). A systematic method for clinical description and classification of personality variates: A proposal. *Archives of General Psychiatry, 44,* 573–588.

Cohen, L. M., Britt, D. M., Collins, F. L., Jr., al'Absi, M., & McChargue, D. E. (2001). Multimodal assessment of the effect of chewing gum on nicotine withdrawal. *Addictive Behaviors, 26,* 289–295.

Cohen, L. M., Britt, D. M., Collins, F. L., Jr., Stott, H. D., & Carter, L. C. (1999). Chewing gum affects smoking topography. *Experimental and Clinical Psychopharmacology, 7,* 444–447.

Cohen, L. M., Collins, F. L., Jr., & Britt, D. M. (1997). The effect of chewing gum on tobacco withdrawal. *Addictive Behaviors, 22,* 796–763.

Cohen, L. M., McCarthy, D. M., Brown, S. A., & Myers, M. G. (2002). Negative affect combines with smoking outcome expectancies to predict smoking behavior. *Psychology of Addictive Behaviors, 16,* 91–97.

Colletti, G., Supnick, J. A., & Payne, T. J. (1985). The Smoking Self-Efficacy Questionnaire (SSEQ): Preliminary scale development and validation. *Behavioral Assessment, 7,* 249–260.

Collins, F. L., Jr., Britt, D. M., Cohen, L. M., McChargue, D. E., Larson, M. E. M., Leftwich, M. J. T., & Stott, H. D. (1999). Treating nicotine dependence. In L. VandeCreek & T. L. Jackson (Eds.), *Innovations in clinical practice: A source book* (Vol. 17, pp. 135–151). Sarasota, FL: Professional Resources Press.

Copeland, A. L., Brandon, T. H., & Quinn, E. P. (1995). The Smoking Consequences Questionnaire–Adult: Measurement of smoking outcome expectancies of experienced smokers. *Psychological Assessment, 7,* 484–494.

de Leon, J. D., Dadvand, M., Canuso, C., White, A. O., Stanilla, J. K., & Simpson, G. M. (1995). Schizophrenia and smoking: An epidemiological survey in a state hospital. *American Journal of Psychiatry, 152,* 453–455.

Di Chiara, G. (1998). A motivational learning hypothesis of the role of mesolimbic dopamine in compulsive drug use. *Journal of Psychopharmacology, 12,* 54–67.

Dziegielewski, S. F., & Eater, J. A. (2000). Smoking cessation: Increasing practice understanding and time-limited intervention strategy. *Families in Society, 81,* 246–255.

Eissenberg, T., Stitzer, M. L., & Henningfield, J. E. (1999). Current issues in nicotine replacement. In D. F. Seidman & L. S. Covey (Eds.), *Helping the hardcore smoker: A clinician's guide* (pp. 137–158). Mahwah, NJ: Lawrence Erlbaum.

Emmons, K. M., Kawachi, I., & Barclay, G. (1997). Tobacco control: A brief review of its history and prospects for the future. *Hematological Oncology Clinics of North America, 2,* 177–195.

Epping-Jordan, M. P., Watkins, S. S., Koob, G. F., & Markou, A. (1998). Dramatic decreases in brain reward function during nicotine withdrawal. *Nature, 393,* 6–79.

Fagerström, K. O. (1991). Towards better diagnoses and more individual treatment of tobacco dependence. *British Journal of Addiction, 86,* 543–547.

Fiore, M. C., Bailey, W. C., Cohen, S. J., Dorfman, S. F., Goldstein, M. G., Gritz, E. R., Heyman, R. B., Jaén, C. R., Kottke, T. E., Lando, H. A., Mecklenburg, R. E., Mullen, P. D., Nett, L. M., Robinson, L., Stitzer, M. L., Tommasello, A. C., Villejo, L., & Wewers, M. E. (2000). *Clinical practice guidelines: Treating tobacco use and dependence.* Washington, DC: U.S. Department of Health and Human Services, Public Health Service.

Fiore, M. C., Novotny, T. E., Pierce, J. P., Giovino, G. A., Hatziandreu, E. J., Newcomb, P. A., Surawicz, T. S., & Davis, R. M. (1990). Methods used to quit smoking in the United States. *Journal of the American Medical Association, 263,* 2760–2765.

First, M. B., Spitzer, R. L., Gibbon, M., & Williams, J. B. W. (1997). *Structured Clinical Interview for DSM-IV Axis I Disorders–Clinician's Version (SCID-CV).* Washington, DC: American Psychiatric Association.

Garcia-Munoz, M., Patino, P., Young, S. J., & Groves, P. M. (1996). Effects of nicotine on dopaminergic nigrostriatal axons requires stimulation of presynaptic glutamatergic receptors. *Journal of Pharmacology & Experimental Therapeutics, 277,* 1685–1693.

Gilbert, D. G., & Gilbert, B. O. (1995). Personality, psychopathology, and nicotine response as mediators of the genetics of smoking. *Behavior Genetics, 25*(2), 133–147.

Gilbert, D. G., Robinson, J. H., Chamberlin, C. L., & Spielberger, C. D. (1989). Effects of smoking/nicotine on anxiety, heart rate, and lateralization of EEG during a stressful movie. *Psychophysiology, 26,* 311–320.

Glover, E. D., & Glover, P. N. (2001). Pharmacologic treatments for the nicotine dependent smoker. *American Journal of Health Behavior, 25,* 179–182.

Goda, Y., & Stevens, C. F. (1996). Synaptic plasticity: The basis of particular types of learning. *Current Biology, 6,* 375–378.

Gritz, E. R., Kristeller, J. L., & Burns, D. M. (1993). Treating nicotine addiction in high-risk groups and patients with medical co-morbidity. In C. T. Orleans & J. S. Slade (Eds.), *Nicotine addiction: Principles and management* (pp. 279–309). New York: Oxford University Press.

Grunberg, N. E., Winders, S. E., & Wewers, M. E. (1991). Gender differences in tobacco use. *Health Psychology, 10,* 143–153.

Hall, S. M., Munoz, F., Reus, V. I., & Sees, K. L. (1993). Nicotine, negative affect, and depression. *Journal of Consulting and Clinical Psychology, 61,* 761–767.

Hatsukami, D. K., Gust, S. W., & Keenan, R. M. (1987). Physiologic and subjective changes from smokeless tobacco withdrawal. *Clinical Pharmacology Therapy, 41,* 103–107.

Hatsukami, D. K., & Lando, H. (1999). Smoking cessation. In P. J. Ott, R. E. Tarter, & R. T. Ammerman (Eds.), *Sourcebook on substance abuse: Etiology, epidemiology, assessment, and treatment* (pp. 399–415). Boston: Allyn & Bacon.

Hatsukami, D. K., & Severson, H. H. (1999). Oral spit tobacco: Addiction, prevention, and treatment. *Nicotine and Tobacco Research, 1,* 21–44.

Heatherton, T. F., Kozlowski, L. T., Frecker, R. C., & Fagerström, K. O. (1991). The Fagerström Test for Nicotine Dependence: A revision of the Fagerström Tolerance Questionnaire. *British Journal of Addiction, 86,* 1119–1127.

Henningfield, J. E., Fant, R. V., Radzius, A., & Frost, S. (1999). Nicotine concentration, smoke pH, and whole tobacco aqueous pH of some cigar brands and types popular in the United States. *Nicotine and Tobacco Research, 1,* 163–168.

Henningfield, J. E., & Heishman, S. J. (1995). The addictive role of nicotine in tobacco use. *Psychopharmacology, 117,* 11–13.

Hitsman, B., Pingitore, R., Spring, B., Mahableshwarkar, A., Mizes, J. S., Segraves, K. A., Kristeller, J. L., & Xu, W. (1999). Antidepressant pharmacotherapy helps some cigarette smokers more than others. *Journal of Consulting and Clinical Psychology, 67,* 547–554.

Hughes, J. R. (1986). Genetics of smoking: A brief review. *Behavior Therapy, 17,* 335–345.

Hughes, J. R. (1992). Tobacco withdrawal in self-quitters. *Journal of Consulting and Clinical Psychology, 60,* 689–697.

Hughes, J. R., & Hatsukami, D. (1986). Signs and symptoms of tobacco withdrawal. *Archives of General Psychiatry, 43,* 289–294.

Hughes, J. R., Hatsukami, D., Mitchell, J. E., & Dahlgren, L. A. (1986). Prevalence of smoking among psychiatric outpatients. *American Journal of Psychiatry, 143,* 993–997.

Hughes, J. R., Higgins, S. T., & Hatsukami, D. (1990). Effects of abstinence from tobacco: A critical review. In L. T. Kozlowski, H. Annis, H. D. Cappell, F. Glaser, M. Goodstadt, Y. Israel, H. Kalant, E. M. Sellers, & J. Vingilis (Eds.), *Research advances in alcohol and drug problems.* (pp. 317–398). New York: Plenum.

Hurt, R. D., Offord, K. P., Croghan, I. T., Croghan, G. A., Gomez-Dahl, L. C., Wolter, T. D., Dale, L. C., & Moyer, T. P. (1998). Temporal effects of nicotine nasal spray and gum on nicotine withdrawal symptoms. *Psychopharmacology, 140,* 98–104.

Irvin, J. E., & Brandon, T. H. (2000). The increasing recalcitrance of smokers in clinical trials. *Nicotine and Tobacco Research, 2,* 79–84.

Iwamoto, E. T., Fudala, P. J., Mundy, W. R., & Williamson, E. C. (1987). Nicotine actions in models of learning/memory and reward. In W. R. Martin, G. R. Van Loon, E. T. Iwamoto, & L. Davis (Eds.), *Tobacco smoking and nicotine: A neurobiological approach* (pp. 101–111). New York: Plenum.

Jarvis, M., & Sutherland, G. (1998). Tobacco smoking. In D. W. Johnston & M. Johnston (Eds.), *Comprehensive clinical psychology* (pp. 645–674). New York: Elsevier Science.

Jeste, D. V., Gladsjo, J. A., Lindamer, L. A., & Lacro, J. P. (1996). Medical comorbidity in schizophrenia. *Schizophrenia Bulletin, 22,* 413–430.

Johnston, A., Robinson, M. D., Adams, D. P., Glassman, A. H., & Covey, L. S. (1999). Nonnicotine medications for smoking cessation. In D. F. Seidmean & L. S. Covey (Eds.), *Helping the hard-core smoker: A clinician's guide* (pp. 159–173). Mahwah, NJ: Lawrence Erlbaum.

Kenny, P. J., File, S. E., & Neal, M. J. (2000). Evidence for a complex influence of nicotinic acetylcholine receptors on hippocampal serotonin release. *Journal of Neurochemistry, 75,* 2409–2414.

Killen, J. D., Fortmann, S. P., Newman, B., & Varady, A. (1990). Evaluation of a treatment approach combining nicotine gum with self-guided behavioral treatments for smoking relapse prevention. *Journal of Consulting and Clinical Psychology, 58,* 85–92.

Killen, J. D., Fortmann, S. P., Newman, B., & Varady, A. (1991). Prospective study of factors influencing the development of craving associated with smoking cessation. *Psychopharmacology, 105,* 191–196.

Klesges, R. C., & Klesges, L. M. (1988). Cigarette smoking as a dieting strategy in a university population. *International Journal of Eating Disorders, 7,* 413–419.

Klesges, R. C., Winders, S. E., Meyers, A. W., Eck, L. H., Ward, K. D., Hultquist, C. M., Ray, J. W., & Shadish, W. R. (1997). How much weight gain occurs following smoking cessation? A comparison of weight gain using both continuous and point prevalence abstinence. *Journal of Consulting and Clinical Psychology, 65,* 286–291.

Koob, G. F., & Le Moal, M. (1997). Drug abuse: Hedonic homeostatic dysregulation. *Science, 278,* 52–58.

Kozlowski, L. T., Henningfield, J. E., & Brigham, J. (2001). *Cigarettes, nicotine, and health: A biobehavioral approach.* Thousand Oaks, CA: Sage.

Lerman, C., Caporaso, N. E., Audrain, J., Main, D., Bowman, E. D., Lockshin, B., Boyd, N. R., & Shields, P. G. (1999). Evidence suggesting the role of specific genetic factors in cigarette smoking. *Health Psychology, 18,* 19–34.

Lichtenstein, E. (1999). Nicotine Anonymous: Community resource and research implications. *Psychology of Addictive Behaviors, 13,* 60–68.

Linkins, R. W., & Comstock, G. W. (1990). Depressed mood and development of cancer. *American Journal of Epidemiology, 132,* 962–972.

Madden, P. A. F., Bucholz, K. K., Dinwiddie, S. H., Slutske, W. S., Beirut, L. J., Statham, D. J., Dunne, M. P., Martin, N. G., & Heath, A. C. (1997). Nicotine withdrawal in women. *Addiction, 92,* 889–902.

Madden, P. A. F., Heath, A. C., Pedersen, N. L., Kaprio, J., Koskenvuo, M. J., & Martin, N. G. (1999). The genetics of smoking persistence in men and women: A multicultural study. *Behavior Genetics, 29,* 423–431.

Maes, M., & Meltzer, H. Y. (1995). The serotonin hypothesis of major depression. In F. E. Bloom & D. J. Kupfer (Eds.), *Psychopharmacology: The fourth generation of progress* (pp. 933–944). New York: Raven.

Malgady, R. G., Rogler, L. H., & Tryon, W. W. (1992). Issues of validity in the Diagnostic Interview Schedule. *Journal of Psychiatric Research, 26,* 59–67.

Mansvelder, H. D., & McGehee, D. S. (2000). Long-term potentiation of excitatory inputs to brain reward areas by nicotine. *Neuron, 27,* 349–357.

McChargue, D. E., & Collins, F. L. (1998). Differentiating withdrawal patterns between smokers and smokeless tobacco users. *Experimental and Clinical Psychopharmacology, 6,* 205–208.

McChargue, D. E., Collins, F. L., & Cohen, L. M. (2002). Effect of non-nicotinic moist snuff replacement and lobeline on withdrawal symptoms during 48-hour smokeless tobacco deprivation. *Nicotine and Tobacco Research, 4,* 195–200.

McChargue, D. E., Gulliver, S. B., & Hitsman, B. (2002a). A reply to the commentaries on schizophrenia and smoking treatment: More research is needed. *Addiction, 97,* 785–793.

McChargue, D. E., Gulliver, S. B., & Hitsman, B. (2002b). Would smokers with schizophrenia benefit from a more flexible approach to smoking treatment? *Addiction, 97,* 799–800.

Miller, W. R., & Rollnick, S. (2002). *Motivational interviewing: Preparing people for change.* New York: Guilford.

Niaura, R., Spring, B., Borrelli, B., Hedeker, D., Goldstein, M. G., Keuthen, N., DePue, J., Kristeller, J., Ockene, J., Prochazka, A., Chiles, J. A., & Abrams, D. B. (2002). Multicenter trial of fluoxetine as an adjunct to behavioral smoking cessation treatment. *Journal of Consulting and Clinical Psychology, 70,* 887–896.

Ockene, J. K., Kristeller, J. L., & Donnelly, G. (1999). Tobacco. In M. Galanter & H. D. Kleber (Eds.), *The American Psychiatric Press textbook of substance abuse treatment* (2nd ed., pp. 215–238). Washington, DC: American Psychiatric Association.

Olds, J., & Milner, P. (1954). Positive reinforcement produced by electrical stimulation of septal area and other regions of rat brain. *Journal of Comparative Physiological Psychology, 47,* 419–427.

Parrott, A. C. (1999). Does cigarette smoking cause stress? *American Psychologist, 54,* 817–820.

Perkins, K. A., Gerlach, D., Broge, M., Sanders, M., Grobe, J., Fonte, C., Cherry, C., Wilson, A., & Jacob, R. (2001). Quitting cigarette smoking produces minimal loss of chronic tolerance to nicotine. *Psychopharmacology, 158,* 7–17.

Perkins, K. A., Grobe, J. E., Epstein, L. H., Caggiula, A., Stiller, R. L., & Jacob, R. G. (1993). Chronic and acute tolerance to subjective effects of nicotine. *Pharmacology Biochemistry and Behavior, 45,* 375–381.

Piasecki, T. M., & Baker, T. (2000). Does smoking amortize negative affect? *American Psychologist, 55,* 1156–1157.

Piper, M. E., Fox, B. J., Welsch, S. K., Fiore, M. C., & Baker, T. B. (2001). Gender and racial/ethnic differences in tobacco-dependence treatment: A commentary and research recommendations. *Nicotine and Tobacco Research, 3,* 291–297.

Pomerleau, C. S., Marks, J. L., & Pomerleau, O. F. (2000). Who gets what symptom? Effects of psychiatric cofactors and nicotine dependence on patterns of smoking withdrawal symptomatology. *Nicotine and Tobacco Research, 2,* 275–280.

Pomerleau, C. S., & Pomerleau, O. F. (1992). Euphoriant effects of nicotine in smokers. *Psychopharmacology, 108,* 460–465.

Pomerleau, O. F. (1995). Individual differences in sensitivity to nicotine: Implications for genetic research on nicotine dependence. *Behavior Genetics, 25,* 161–177.

Pomerleau, O., Adkins, D., & Pertschuk, M. (1978). Predictors of outcome and recidivism in smoking cessation treatment. *Addictive Behaviors, 3,* 65–70.

Pomerleau, O. F., & Kardia, S. L. R. (1999). Introduction to the featured section: Genetic research on smoking. *Health Psychology, 18,* 3–6.

Pomerleau, O. F., & Pomerleau, C. S. (1984). Neuroregulators and the reinforcement of smoking: Towards a biobehavioral explanation. *Neuroscience and Biobehavioral Reviews, 8,* 503–513.

Porchet, H. C., Benowitz, N. L., & Sheiner, L. B. (1988). Pharmacodynamic model of tolerance: Application to nicotine. *Journal of Pharmacology and Experimental Therapeutics, 244,* 231–235.

Prochaska, J. O., & DiClemente, C. C. (1983). Stages and processes of self-change of smoking: Toward an integrative model of change. *Journal of Consulting and Clinical Psychology, 51,* 390–395.

Prochaska, J., & Goldstein, M. G. (1991). Process of smoking cessation. Implications for clinicians. *Clinical Chest Medicine, 12,* 727–735.

Pulvirenti, L., & Diana, M. (2001). Drug dependence as a disorder of neural plasticity: Focus on dopamine and glutamate. *Reviews in the Neurosciences, 12,* 141–158.

Radcliffe, K. A., Fisher, J. L., Gray, R., & Dani, J. A. (1999). Nicotinic modulation of glutamate and GABA synaptic transmission of hippocampal neurons. *Annals of the New York Academy of Sciences, 868,* 591–610.

Richmond, M., Spring, B., Sommerfeld, B. K., & McChargue, D. E. (2001). Rumination and cigarette smoking: A bad combination for depressive outcomes? *Journal of Consulting and Clinical Psychology, 69,* 836–840.

Robinson, J. H., & Pritchard, W. S. (1992). The role of nicotine in tobacco use. *Psychopharmacology, 108,* 397–407.

Robinson, T. E., & Berridge, K. C. (2000). The psychology and neurobiology of addiction: An incentive-sensitization view. *Addiction, 95,* S91–S117.

Rose, J. E., & Levin, E. D. (1991). Inter-relationships between conditioned and primary reinforcement in the maintenance of cigarette smoking. *British Journal of Addiction, 86,* 605–609.

Salin-Pascual, R. J., Rosas, M., Jimenez-Genchi, A., & Rivera-Meza, B. L. (1996). Antidepressant effect of transdermal nicotine patches in nonsmoking patients with major depression. *Journal of Clinical Psychiatry, 57,* 387–389.

Shiffman, S. (1991). Refining models of dependence: Variations across persons and situations. *British Journal of Addiction, 86,* 611–615.

Shiffman, S., Hickcox, M., Paty, J. A., Guys, M., Kassel, J. D., & Richards, T. J. (1996). Progression from a smoking lapse to relapse: Prediction from abstinence violation effects, nicotine dependence, and lapse characteristics. *Journal of Consulting and Clinical Psychology, 64,* 993–1002.

Shiffman, S., Paty, J. A., Guys, M., Kassel, J. D., & Elash, C. (1995). Nicotine withdrawal in chippers and regular smokers: Subjective and cognitive effects. *Health Psychology, 14,* 301–309.

Smith, S. S., Jorenby, D. E., Fiore, M. C., Anderson, J. E., Mielke, M. M., Beach, K. E., Piasecki, T. M., & Baker, T. B. (2001). Strike while the iron is hot: Can stepped-care treatments resurrect relapsing smokers? *Journal of Consulting and Clinical Psychology, 69,* 429–439.

Society for Research on Nicotine and Tobacco Subcommittee on Biochemical Verification. (2002). Biochemical verification of tobacco use and cessation. *Nicotine and Tobacco Research, 4,* 149–159.

Spielberger, C. D., Foreyt, J. P., Reheiser, E. C., & Poston, W. S. C. (1998). Motivational, emotional, and personality characteristics of smokeless tobacco users compared with cigarette smokers. *Personality and Individual Differences, 25,* 821–832.

Spielberger, C. D., & Jacobs, G. A. (1982). Personality and smoking behavior. *Journal of Personality Assessment, 46,* 396–403.

Spring, B., Pingitore, G., & McChargue, D. E. (in press). Reward value of cigarette smoking for comparably heavy smoking schizophrenic, depressed, and nonpatient smokers. *American Journal of Psychiatry.*

Stein, L., Belluzzi, J. D., Ritter, S., & Wise, C. D. (1974). Self-stimulation reward pathways: Norepinephrine vs. dopamine. *Journal of Psychiatric Research, 11,* 115–124.

Swan, G. E., Ward, M. M., & Jack, L. M. (1996). Abstinence effects as predictors of 28-day relapse in smokers. *Addictive Behaviors, 21,* 481–490.

Tellegen, A. (1985). Structures of mood and personality and their relevance to assessing anxiety, with an emphasis on self-report. In H. Tuma & J. Maser (Eds.), *Anxiety and anxiety disorders* (pp. 681–706). Hillsdale, NJ: Lawrence Erlbaum.

Tiffany, S. T. (1990). A cognitive model of drug urges and drug-use behavior: Role of automatic and nonautomatic processes. *Psychological Reviews, 97,* 147–168.

Tomkins, S., & McCarter, R. (1964). What and where are the primary affects? Some evidence for a theory. *Perception and Motor Skills, 18,* 119–156.

Tracy, J. I. (1994). Assessing the relationship between craving and relapse. *Drug and Alcohol Review, 13,* 71–77.

Tsoh, J. Y., Humfleet, G. L., Munoz, R. F., Reus, V. I., Hartz, D. T., & Hall, S. M. (2000). Development of major depression after treatment for smoking cessation. *American Journal of Psychiatry, 157,* 368–374.

U.S. Department of Agriculture. (1997). *Tobacco situation and outlook report* (Series TBS, No. 239). Washington, DC: U.S. Department of Agriculture, Economic Research Service,

U.S. Department of Health and Human Services. (1999). Tobacco Use: United States, 1900–1999. *Morbidity and Mortality Weekly Report, 48,* 986–993.

Vuchinich, R. E., & Tucker, J. A. (1988). Contributions from behavioral theories of choice to an analysis of alcohol abuse. *Journal of Abnormal Psychology, 97,* 181–195.

Watkins, S. S., Koob, G. F., & Markou, A. (2000). Neural mechanisms underlying nicotine addiction: Acute positive reinforcement and withdrawal. *Nicotine and Tobacco Research, 2,* 19–37.

West, R., & Hajek, P. (1997). What happens to anxiety levels on giving up smoking? *American Journal of Psychiatry, 154,* 1589–1592.

West, R., Hajek, P., & Belcher, M. (1989). Severity of withdrawal symptoms as a predictor of outcome of an attempt to quit smoking. *Psychological Medicine, 19,* 981–985.

Wise, R. A. (1998). Drug-activation of brain reward pathways. *Drug and Alcohol Dependence, 51,* 13–22.

CHAPTER 8

Obesity and Body Image Disturbance

MYLES S. FAITH AND J. KEVIN THOMPSON

Obesity in the United States and other countries is a significant and growing public health problem. The U.S. surgeon general recently released a report referring to the current rates of obesity as a "public health epidemic" (Centers for Disease Control and Prevention, 2002). Obesity among adults, adolescents, and children is increasingly encountered in clinical settings, and an awareness of current etiological models, assessment strategies, and intervention methodologies is necessary for the optimal management of this important health problem. This chapter explores these issues, with an emphasis on the practical strategies that may inform the behavioral management of obesity. It also provides a brief discussion of targeting body image in obesity treatment.

DEFINITIONS AND DESCRIPTION OF OBESITY

A consensus has emerged during recent years that one of the best methods for clinically defining obesity is the body mass index (BMI). The formula for BMI is weight in kilograms divided by the square of height in meters (w/h^2). This method is also referred to as Quetelet's index (Garrow & Webster, 1985). BMI can also be computed from pounds and inches: weight (in pounds) divided by height (in inches) times 704.5. BMI cutoffs for weight classification are presented in Table 8.1. Note that a BMI between 25.0 and 29.9 connotes an overweight status, with BMIs greater than 30 indicating obesity.

Despite its widespread use, there are limits to BMI as a measure of weight status (Heymsfield et al., 2000). For instance, it cannot be used as a specific indicator of the level of body fat on the individual, and it is influenced by factors such as age, gender, and exercise status (i.e., sedentary vs. active). Specifically, women tend to have a higher percentage of body fat than do men given the same BMI. In addition, older individuals tend to have a higher percentage of body fat than do younger individuals for a given BMI, and people who work out regularly (especially those who lift weights) may have a lower percentage of body fat than do individuals who are less athletic for a specific BMI.

Table 8.1   Classification of Overweight and Obesity by BMI

	Obesity Class	BMI
Underweight		< 18.5
Normal		18.5–24.9
Overweight		25.0–29.9
Obesity	I	30.0–34.9
	II	35.0–39.9
Extreme obesity	III	≥ 40.0

SOURCE: NIH/NHLBI (1998).

Prevalence statistics reported during the past few years reveal an astonishing increase in the level of overweight and obese individuals in the United States (Centers for Disease Control and Prevention, 2002; Mokdad, Bowman, & Ford, 2001; Mokdad, Serdula, & Dietz, 1999, 2000). Currently, 61% of U.S. adults ages 20 to 74 years are either overweight or obese. The level of obesity increased from 12% of the U.S. population in 1991 to 19.8% in 2000. Thus, an estimated 38.8 million adults in the United States met the BMI cutoff of 30.0 for obesity in the year 2000. Table 8.2 displays these data by gender and ethnicity. These data reflect the particularly high levels of obesity in African American and Hispanic populations.

PHYSICAL AND PSYCHOLOGICAL PROBLEMS ASSOCIATED WITH OBESITY

Physical Problems

A wide variety of health problems are associated with obesity. It has been estimated that 325,000 deaths could be attributed to obesity each year (Allison, Fontaine, Manson, Stevens, & VanItallie, 1999). An overweight or obese status has been linked to such seemingly disparate health problems as heart disease, cancer, type 2 diabetes, stroke, arthritis, breathing problems (sleep apnea), high blood pressure, high blood cholesterol, gout, and gallstones (Field, Barnoya, & Colditz, 2002). (More information on physical problems relevant to the assessment of obesity can be found later in this chapter.)

Psychological and Psychosocial Problems

A wide variety of psychological problems have been examined as a concomitant of obesity, and perhaps even more research efforts during recent years have focused on the psychosocial "consequences" of obesity. Psychosocial consequences entail the specific interpersonal, social, and occupational problems encountered by the obese individual specifically due to an elevated weight status such as being teased about one's size, facing societal prejudice against obesity (which may have economic consequences), and encountering physical barriers (e.g., plane seats that are too small).

Somewhat surprisingly, the common assumption that an elevated weight must necessarily be associated with a plethora of psychological problems is not supported by the literature (Faith & Allison, 1996). Early work in the area did not confirm the expected finding that obese individuals were more depressed than nonobese individuals. Recently, however, a nationally representative sample of more than 40,000 people were evaluated via structured interviews for level of depression (Carpenter, Hasin, Allison, & Faith, 2000). Obese women were 37% more likely to have met DSM-IV (*Diagnostic and Statistical Manual of Mental Disorders,* fourth edition) criteria (American Psychiatric Association, 1994) for major depression during the previous year compared with women of average weight. On the other hand, obese men had a significantly reduced risk for depression. Interestingly, for men, being underweight was associated with greater depression. Research into the reasons behind such a dramatic gender difference in the psychosocial consequences of obesity is an active area of inquiry.

Table 8.2   Increasing Adult Obesity Prevalence: Obesity Trends (percentages)

Sample	*1991*	*1995*	*1998*	*2000*
Total	12.0	15.3	17.9	19.8
Gender				
Men	11.7	15.6	17.7	20.2
Women	12.2	15.0	18.1	19.4
Ethnicity				
White, non-Hispanic	11.3	14.5	16.6	18.5
Black, non-Hispanic	19.3	22.6	26.9	29.3
Hispanic	11.6	16.8	20.8	23.4

SOURCE: Mokdad, Bowman, Ford, Vinicor, Marks, and Koplan (2001).

The comorbidity of eating disturbances with obesity has been a controversial area. Obesity is not a diagnosable psychiatric condition, and it is not listed as an eating disorder in the DSM-IV (nor has it been labeled as such in previous editions of the DSM). However, the association of a particular type of eating disturbance—binge eating—has been noted as an associate of obesity for many years (Stunkard, 2002). During recent years, binge eating disorder has been proposed as a new entry in the DSM and is currently included in the DSM-IV as a disorder in need of further study. The issue is relevant for obesity because perhaps 30% to 40% of individuals with binge eating disorder are also obese (Johnson & Torgrud, 1996). In addition, individuals with binge eating disorder have higher levels of depression than do non-binge eating controls (Wadden, Womble, Stunkard, & Anderson, 2002). Recently, Bulik, Sullivan, and Kendler (2002) examined the prevalence of binge eating and obesity in a population-based sample of female twins. Obese women with binge eating disorder had higher levels of health dissatisfaction, major medical disorders, major depression, panic disorder, phobias, and alcohol dependence.

One of the most consistent findings related to body image dissatisfaction is that obese individuals are more dissatisfied with their appearance than are nonobese individuals. One possible reason for the greater dissatisfaction of obese individuals is, of course, that they live in a society that glorifies the antithesis of obesity— a slender, nonfat, "ideal" body (Thompson, Heinberg, Altabe, & Tantleff-Dunn, 1999). Pressure and information related by the media, family, and peers may be a constant reminder of the unacceptable nature of the physicality of obese individuals. For instance, negative verbal commentary in the form of teasing or criticism of appearance is a common experience of obese individuals. Some studies have shown that more than 90% of obese individuals have been teased about their appearance (Thompson & Smolak, 2001). Interestingly, teasing may be a more direct influence on body dissatisfaction than is weight. In fact, Thompson, Coovert, Richards, Johnson, and Cattarin (1995) found that BMI had no direct effect on body image but was mediated through teasing history. That is, only those individuals with an elevated BMI who had been teased developed body dissatisfaction.

Occupational and social discrimination against obese individuals is also widely supported by survey and laboratory studies. Gortmaker, Must, Perrin, Sobol, and Dietz (1993) evaluated more than 10,000 overweight and normal-weight adolescents for 7 years. At the conclusion of the study, overweight females were less likely to be married and also had lower incomes, whereas overweight males were only less likely to be married. Experimental designs have also demonstrated that job applicants' weight has a powerful effect on factors such as selection for a particular job, promotion, and dismissal (e.g., Pingitore, Dugoni, Tindale, & Spring, 1994; Roehling, 1999).

MODELS OF OBESITY

Genetic, metabolic, environmental, and developmental models have been offered to explain the onset and maintenance of obesity. To date, evidence supports each as a potentially relevant factor. There is, however, a great deal of variability across individuals, making unitary models limited in their explanatory value. Given the tremendous increase in the prevalence of obesity over the past 10 years, it is understandable that environmental causes have received considerable examination (Hill & Peters, 1998).

Environmental Factors

Environmental models address factors that promote the intake of excessive energy (calories) as well as those variables that promote a reduction of energy expenditure via exercise. The ready availability of energy-dense foods, advent of larger portion sizes at restaurants, increased use of fast foods, and decreased preparation of meals are environmental factors that may promote weight gain (French, Story, & Jeffery, 2001). In addition, there have been numerous environmental modifications as a result of technological advances that have enhanced the sedentary nature of many individuals' lifestyles both at home and in the workplace. Computers, video games, and television are often selected to the exclusion of recreational activities that burn calories (Dowda, Ainsworth, Addy, Saunders, & Riner, 2001), whereas physical education is increasingly eliminated or downsized in schools due to liability concerns or increased emphasis on classroom activities to enhance standardized testing

scores. Finally, urban planning and sprawl often do not include sidewalks or bike paths to encourage exercise, and residents who perceive their neighborhoods to be unsafe may be reluctant to leave their homes.

Horgen and Brownell (2002) referred to the "toxic environment" as a primary cause of the emerging problem of obesity. Support for this position is enhanced not only by the recent epidemic in the United States but also by the burgeoning problem worldwide, leading the World Health Organization (1998) to declare that a global epidemic exists. Obesity now appears to be increasing in every country that has been surveyed. Migration, urbanization, and affluence, coupled with the "Americanization" of food selections and eating habits in other countries, have been suggested as dominant, large-scale, environmental factors (VanItallie, 1994). In the United States, the pervasiveness of the "toxic environment" is apparent from even a superficial examination of the strategies of food marketing. Fast-food restaurants offer options to "bigger size" one's meals, inducing even greater consumption of meals already high in fat content.

Genetic Factors

Mapping of the human genome has generated interest in studying the genetic factors for a variety of psychological and physical disorders. Analysis of the genomic regions with linkage to obesity is at a relatively early stage of scientific development (Price, 2002), although molecular studies are identifying an ever-growing list of genes that may confer increased risk for obesity in humans (Rankinen et al., 2002). More traditional work in this area has focused on the analysis of familial/genetic influence by examining monozygotic and dizygotic twins. Specifically, examination of body composition among twins has revealed that monozygotic twins have correlations ranging from .60 to .70, higher than the .20 to .30 observed among dizygotic twins (Price, 2002).

Recent summaries of the work in this area suggest that 67% of the variation in BMI among monozygotic twins may be attributable to genetics (Price, 2002; Tataranni & Ravussin, 2002). This genetic influence may manifest in physiological and behavioral effects such as different resting metabolic rates, reduced physical activity (e.g., fidgeting), and excessive food consumption. Although a "thrifty" gene has long been hypothesized to lie at the roots of the elevated obesity rates in some subgroups (e.g., among the Pima Indians), no such single gene has been detected. Even among such subgroups, however, rates of obesity have increased along the lines of other population groups over the past 50 years, suggesting more than a genetic influence (Price, Charles, Pettitt, & Knowler, 1993). Hence, obesity is most likely a "polygenic trait," influenced by multiple genes that interact among themselves as well as by environmental inputs (Comuzzie & Allison, 1998).

An interesting question in this area is whether genes have a direct biological effect on obesity *and* perhaps drive an individually based response to specific environmental factors (e.g., low activity, excessive eating) (Faith, Johnson, & Allison, 1997; Keller, Pietrobelli, Must, & Faith, 2002). Put more clearly, are genes partly responsible for those gaining the most weight in our toxic environment? Bouchard and colleagues (2000) overfed identical twins for 3 months and found that although there were large differences in the levels of weight added across pairs, within-pair gains were similar. Therefore, it is possible that gene-environment interactions exist with respect to weight gain.

Developmental Factors

There is strong support for the prediction of obese status in adulthood from an examination of the weight of the individual during childhood and adolescence (Thompson & Smolak, 2001). Overweight adolescents have a 70% chance of becoming overweight or obese adults. Interestingly, the contribution of the parents' weight, along with the child's weight, may depend on the child. For instance, Whitaker, Wright, Pepe, Seidel, and Dietz (1997) looked at the weight of both the parents and the child to determine whether one or both contributed to the development of obesity in the child. They found that very young children (ages 1 to 2 years) who were obese and had an overweight parent had a fourfold risk for adult obesity as compared with overweight children of the same age who had average-weight parents. However, by age 10 years, the effect was independent of the parents' weight.

Other early developmental factors that have received examination include type of infant feeding (breast vs. bottle), feeding style, and parental control over feeding. Each of these areas is receiving a great deal of attention, and the findings are often inconclusive. However, it appears that, despite the widely held view to the contrary, there is no difference between breast-feeding and bottle-feeding in terms of the later development of obesity (Berkowitz & Stunkard, 2002). Feeding style involves the study of factors such as rapid eating and the vigor of the sucking response during infancy. Findings in this area are intriguing. For example, Stunkard, Berkowitz, Stallings, and Schoeller (1999) found that the infant offspring of overweight mothers had a more vigorous sucking style than did the infants of control mothers. Importantly, the authors also found that they could predict level of fatness at age 1 year by an examination of the sucking style. Finally, parental control is the degree to which a parent, typically the mother, attempts to manage or direct the child's intake. Birch and colleagues have pioneered work in this area and found intriguing results suggesting that parental control may influence not only weight gain but, in certain circumstances, restriction of intake as well (Fisher & Birch, 2001).

Summary

Prevalence rates of obesity have increased drastically during the past few decades in children, adolescents, and adults as well as among both genders and all ethnicities evaluated. This "epidemic" has generated a wealth of research into associated health and physical conditions as well as strategies to understand causal variables. To date, etiological models are inconclusive, but compelling epidemiological evidence points toward a "toxic" environment that sets the stage for the development and perpetuates the maintenance of obesity.

ASSESSMENT AND TREATMENT OF OBESITY

This section summarizes approaches for the assessment and treatment of obesity in adults. General guidelines and strategies are provided here; however, more detailed descriptions are provided elsewhere (Foreyt & Goodrick, 1992; Kirschenbaum, 1994; Wadden & VanItallie, 1992). In particular, clinicians specializing in this area are encouraged to read the seminal report, *Clinical Guidelines on the Identification, Evaluation, and Treatment of Overweight and Obesity in Adults* (National Institutes of Health/National Heart, Lung, and Blood Institute [NIH/NHLBI], 1998). This report provides the most authoritative, comprehensive, and empirically based guidelines to date for obesity treatment. Most of the guidelines provided herein are adapted from these expert recommendations.

This section is broken down into assessment and treatment. Within treatment, behavioral/lifestyle interventions and brief updates on pharmacological and surgical interventions are discussed. This is followed up with a discussion of the role of body image enhancement in obesity treatment.

Assessment

With approximately half of the U.S. population overweight or obese, it is important to determine when treatment is warranted. Two measurements that are practical for clinical settings are recommended as first-step screening instruments: BMI and the waist circumference. As described previously (Table 8.1), BMI can be used to define degree of obesity. Waist circumference, as determined by a tape measure, is suggested because BMI alone does not provide an informative index of so-called "abdominal fat." Abdominal fat is important for assessment because higher levels of abdominal fat are an independent predictor of health complications related to obesity (Pi-Sunyer, 1993). Hence, an individual who is "overweight" but has excess abdominal fat may be at greater risk for various diseases (e.g., cardiovascular disease, type 2 diabetes) than is another individual who is "obese" with lower levels of abdominal fat.

Waist circumference is measured by a standard protocol (NIH/NHLBI, 1998) and should be performed by trained staff. Expert guidelines suggest that waist circumference measurements should be taken among persons with BMIs between 25.0 and 34.9. For individuals with BMIs greater than or equal to 35.0, or who are "short" in stature, waist circumference may be minimally informative beyond BMI alone (NIH/NHLBI, 1998). Among adults with BMIs between 25.0 and 34.9, waist circumferences greater than 102 centimeters (40 inches) in men and greater than 88 centimeters (35 inches) in women have been proposed as "high-risk" cutoffs for disease. Elevated waist circumferences are associated with increased risk for type 2 diabetes, dyslipidemia, hypertension, and cardiovascular disease. Table 8.3 summarizes the relative risk of disease as a function of BMI and waist circumference profiles and illustrates how abdominal fat levels can amplify or attenuate the health risks associated with elevated BMI.

Table 8.3 Risk of Type II Diabetes, Hypertension, and Cardiovascular Disease as a Function of Weight Class and Waist Circumference

Weight Class	*"Normal"* Waist Circumference	*"High-Risk"* Waist Circumference
Underweight	—	—
Normal	—	—
Overweight	Increased	High
Obesity-I	High	Very high
Obesity-II	Very high	Very high
Extreme obesity	Extremely high	Extremely high

SOURCE: Adapted from NIH/NHLBI (1998).

Beyond BMI and waist circumference assessment, expert guidelines pinpoint additional clinical markers that may indicate individuals at a "very high absolute risk" of disease. The presence of one or more of these conditions may suggest the need for more aggressive obesity intervention. Table 8.4 summarizes these diseases or target organ damages that should be considered when evaluating obese patients (NIH/NHLBI, 1998).

Treatment

Obesity Treatment Algorithm

The NIH/NHLBI (1998) report provides a concrete algorithm to guide the obesity evaluation-treatment interface, and is depicted in Figure 8.1.

The heuristic begins with assessment of family history of obesity. If there is no history of obesity, experts recommend 2-year intervals for the assessment of changes in BMI. At 2-year assessments (or more frequent assessments if obesity is familial), health professionals are advised to calculate BMI as well as to measure weight, height, and waist circumference. For patients who are overweight or obese, *or* who have a high-risk waist circumference (greater than 88 centimeters in females, greater than 102 centimeters in males), a thorough medical assessment is warranted that assesses the conditions listed in Table 8.4. For patients who are obese, are

overweight, or have a high risk waist circumference *in conjunction with* at least two risk factors, development of a treatment plan for weight control and risk factor reduction is warranted. Individuals who meet these criteria but do not want to lose weight may be advised to maintain their current weight or address concurrent risk factors until they are sufficiently motivated to lose weight. Treatment generally encompasses dietary, physical activity, and lifestyle changes, with appropriate assessment of barriers to treatment and periodic weight checks.

Intervention Components

A well-established literature indicates that behavioral/lifestyle approaches to obesity treatment are effective for inducing weight loss, although relapse is very common (Faith, Fontaine, Cheskin, & Allison, 2000; Wadden, Sternberg, Letizia, Stunkard, & Foster, 1989). Enhanced dietary quality is a hallmark feature of behavioral treatment, as patients are traditionally prescribed a "low-calorie diet" that is generally 800 to 1,500 calories per day. Features of the American Heart Association's Low-Calorie Step I Diet are summarized in Table 8.5 (NIH/NHLBI, 1998).

Reducing total caloric intake by 500 to 1,000 calories per day, assuming no changes in physical activity levels, is expected to induce weight loss of approximately 1 to 2 pounds per week. Reducing total caloric intake by 300 to

Table 8.4   Diseases and Target Organ Damages for Potential Assessment in Obese Adults

---

 1. Identification of patients at very high absolute risk:

1a. Established CHD

> History of myocardial infraction
> History of angina pectoris (stable or unstable)
> History of coronary artery surgery
> History of coronary artery procedures (angioplasty)

1b. Presence of other atherosclerotic disease

> Peripheral arterial disease
> Abdominal aortic aneurysm
> Symptomatic carotid artery disease
> Type 2 diabetes
> Sleep apnea

 2. Identification of other obesity-associated diseases:

2a. Gynecological abnormalities

2b. Osteoarthritis

2c. Gallstones and their complications

2d. Stress incontinence

 3. Identification of cardiovascular risk factors that impart a high absolute risk (patients can be classified as being at high absolute risk for obesity-related disorders if they have three or more of the multiple risk factors listed below):

3a. Cigarette smoking

3b. Hypertension: A patient is classified as having hypertension if systolic blood pressure is > 140 millimeters of mercury or diastolic blood pressure is > 90 millimeters of mercury *or* if the patient is taking antihypertensive agents.

3c. High-risk LDL cholesterol: A high-risk LDL cholesterol is defined as a serum concentration of > 160 milligrams per deciliter. A borderline high-risk LDL cholesterol (130 to 159 milligrams per deciliter), together with two or more other risk factors, also confers high risk.

3d. Low HDL cholesterol: A low HDL cholesterol is defined as a serum concentration of < 35 milligrams per deciliter.

3e. Impaired fasting glucose: The presence of clinical type 2 diabetes (fasting plasma glucose of > 126 milligrams per deciliter or 2 hours postprandial plasma glucose of > 200 milligrams per deciliter) is a major risk factor for CVD, and its presence alone places a patient in the category of very high absolute risk. Impaired fasting glucose (fasting plasma glucose 110 to 125 milligrams per deciliter) is considered by many authorities to be a risk factor for cardiovascular disease.

3f. Family history of premature CHD

3g. Age (males > 45 years or females > 55 years or postmenopausal)

 4. Other risk factors:

4a. Physical inactivity

4b. High triglycerides (400 to 1,000 milligrams per deciliter = "high", > 1,000 milligrams per deciliter = "very high")

SOURCE: NIH/NHLBI (1998).

NOTE: CHD = coronary heart disease; LDL = low-density lipoprotein; HDL = high-density lipoprotein; CVD = cardiovascular disease.

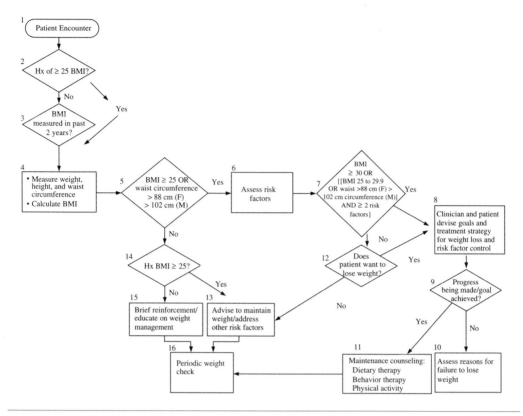

Figure 8.1   The Obesity Evaluation-Treatment Interface

SOURCE: National Institutes of Health/National Heart, Lung, and Blood Institute (1998).

500 calories per day (the equivalent of approximately two soft drinks) is expected to induce weight loss of ½ to 1 pound per week, assuming no changes in physical activity. For these reasons, obese adults are typically prescribed to consume 1,000 to 1,200 calories per day (women) or 1,200 to 1,500 calories per day (men) to achieve weight loss.

Physical activity is another pillar of obesity treatment. Physical activity without concurrent improvements in diet quality will have a less potent effect on weight loss than will changes in diet plus physical activity (NIH/NHLBI, 1998). During recent years, research has focused on the beneficial effects of so-called "lifestyle activity" changes compared with more regimented and structured exercise programs. Lifestyle programs teach individuals how to program physical activity changes into

everyday living. Examples include parking farther away in the parking lot so that one needs to walk farther to the office/shop, taking daily walks, cleaning the house regularly, moving while talking on the phone, and taking stairs instead of elevators whenever one has a choice. A study by Andersen and colleagues (1999) compared weight loss among 40 obese women who were randomized to a weight loss group that incorporated a structured aerobic exercise regimen versus a lifestyle activity regimen. Although the two groups lost comparable amounts of weight during the 16-week intervention, the aerobic exercise group regained significantly more weight on average (1.6 kilograms) than did the lifestyle intervention group (0.08 kilograms). Data from the Women's Healthy Lifestyle Project Clinical Trial (Kuller, Simkin-Silverman, Wing, Meilahn, & Ives,

Table 8.5   Low-Calorie Step I Diet

Nutrient	Recommended Intake
Calories	Approximately 500 to 1,000 calories per day reduction from usual intake
Total fat	≤ 30% of total calories
Saturated fatty acids	8% to 10% of total calories
Monounsaturated fats	≤ 15% of total calories
Polyunsaturated fats	≤ 10% of total calories
Cholesterol	< 300 milligrams per day
Protein	Approximately 15% of total calories
Carbohydrates	55% or more of total calories
Sodium chloride	No more than 100 millimoles per day (approximately 2.4 grams of sodium or approximately 6 grams of sodium chloride)
Calcium	1,000 to 1,500 milligrams
Fiber	20 to 30 grams

SOURCE: NIH/NHLBI (1998).

2001) also confirm that prescriptions for lifestyle physical activity, in conjunction with the aforementioned dietary prescriptions, can prevent excess weight gain and elevations in low-density lipoprotein (LDL) cholesterol among women as they progress from perimenopause to postmenopause.

On a practical level, increasing daily physical activity can be personally tailored to accommodate individual lives. "Moderate" intensity physical activity is conceptualized as activities that translate to an energy deficit of 150 calories per day, which would sum to 1,000 calories per week (NIH/NHLBI, 1998). The amount of time needed to achieve this deficit each day will depend on the nature of the activity and the individual's weight. Expert guidelines suggest that initially the obese patient should engage in moderate activity levels for 30 to 45 minutes per day on 3 to 5 days per week (NIH/NHLBI, 1998). According to the surgeon general's report, most adults should ultimately strive to accumulate at least 30 minutes of moderate-intensity physical activity on most, if not all, days of the week. Table 8.6 illustrates the different ways in which an adult can achieve moderate physical activity levels each day, varying the time spent doing the activity and the strenuousness of the activity.

Behavioral Techniques

Descriptions of the behavioral treatment of obesity can be traced back to classical articles by Ferster, Nurnberger, and Levitt (1962) and Stuart (1967). Between the 1970s and the 1990s, classical experiments tested behavioral treatments for obesity among a range of obese patients. As the methodological rigor of these studies (including sample sizes, treatment lengths, and follow-up lengths) improved over time, so did the efficacy of treatment (Faith et al., 2000; Wadden & Foster, 2000). Whereas intervention studies published in 1974 achieved a mean weight loss of 3.8 kilograms (or approximately 8.5 pounds), those published between 1985 and 1987 achieved a mean weight loss of 8.4 kilograms (or approximately 18.5 pounds). Unfortunately, a cardinal disappointment of these same weight loss studies—and a finding that transcends decades of research—is an excessive rate of recidivism (Wadden et al., 1989; Wilson, 1994).

Specific components of the behavioral treatment of obesity have been outlined in detail elsewhere (Foreyt & Goodrick, 1992; Kirschenbaum, 1994; Wadden & VanItallie, 1992). Critical concepts reviewed by expert guidelines (NIH/NHLBI, 1998) include the following.

Table 8.6   Examples of Moderate Amounts of Physical Activity

Activity	Requirements
Washing or waxing a car for 45 to 60 minutes	Less vigorous/More time
Washing windows or floors for 45 to 60 minutes	
Playing volleyball for 45 minutes	
Playing touch football for 30 to 45 minutes	
Gardening for 30 to 45 minutes	
Wheeling self in wheelchair for 30 to 40 minutes	
Walking 1¾ miles in 35 minutes	
Playing basketball for 30 minutes	
Bicycling 5 miles in 30 minutes	
Dancing fast (socially) for 30 minutes	
Pushing a stroller 1½ miles in 30 minutes	
Raking leaves for 30 minutes	
Walking 2 miles in 30 minutes	
Engaging in water aerobics for 30 minutes	
Swimming laps for 20 minutes	
Playing a basketball game for 15 to 20 minutes	
Bicycling 4 miles in 15 minutes	
Jumping rope for 15 minutes	More vigorous/Less time
Running 1½ miles in 15 minutes	
Shoveling snow for 15 minutes	
Stair walking for 15 minutes	

Self-Monitoring of Eating Habits and Physical Activity. Recording in detail what one eats every day can provide revealing insights into the environmental, emotional, and/or interpersonal circumstances that may prompt intake of particular foods. Keeping such recordings with standard paper-and-pencil methods or with novel palm computers can bring patterns of eating and inactivity to consciousness and help make them the target of treatment.

Stress Management. Stress can prompt overeating in certain obese individuals, especially those with binge eating tendencies (Faith, Allison, & Geliebter, 1997). Teaching obese individuals coping strategies to deal with stress without eating can be an important component of treatment. Exercise can be an effective stress management technique that also confers benefits for weight management.

Stimulus Control. Unhealthy food selections and/or overeating can be stimulated by foods that are more readily accessible and conveniently ready for eating. For example, homes that do not keep an ample supply of fresh fruits and vegetables for snacking are less conducive to weight control than are homes in which these foods are readily available.

Therefore, behavioral interventions focus on barriers to restructuring the environment in ways that stimulate healthy eating and physical activity.

Contingency Management. Rewards for behavioral changes can be an effective component of treatment. Rewards can be tangible gifts for oneself or praise from family members and friends (i.e., social support).

Cognitive Restructuring. Positive self-statements that challenge defeating self-statements can be effective for teaching obese patients to cope with treatment "failures" (e.g., periods of weight regain) or other unexpected challenges during treatment. These matters can be especially important for obese patients lacking in self-acceptance or self-esteem due to limited weight loss or weight regain (Wilson, 1996). Recent advances in treatment are focusing on promotion of more realistic weight loss expectations to promote better psychological well-being and perhaps even weight loss.

Pharmacological Therapy

Detailed reviews of the drug treatment literature have been published elsewhere (e.g., Haddock, Poston, Dill, Foreyt, & Ericsson, 2002). There are currently two prescription medications that are approved by the Food and Drug Administration (FDA) for obesity treatment: sibutramine (Meridia) and orlistat (Xenical). Sibutramine is an anorexiant (or appetite suppressant) that exerts its effect by inhibiting the reuptake of norepinephrine, dopamine, and serotinin in the brain. Controlled clinical trials document the clinical effectiveness of sibutramine for weight loss (Berube-Parent, Prudhomme, St-Pierre, Doucet, & Tremblay, 2001; Fanghanel, Cortinas, Sanchez-Reyes, & Berber, 2001; Wirth & Krause, 2001). On the other hand, a major concern surrounding sibutramine is the potential for increased heart rate and blood pressure (Bray et al., 1996). For these reasons, individuals with a history of high blood pressure, coronary heart disease, congestive heart failure, arrhythmias, or stroke should not take sibutramine. All patients taking the medication are encouraged to have their blood pressure monitored regularly (NIH/NHLBI, 1998).

Orlistat exerts its effects by inhibiting pancreatic lipase and thereby decreasing fat absorption. The effectiveness of orlistat for inducing long-term (i.e., 2-year) weight loss compared with controls was documented in two sets of multisite studies: one conducted in Europe (Rossner, Sjöström, Noack, Meinders, & Noseda, 2000) and one conducted in the United States (Davidson et al., 1999). Orlistat can also have beneficial effects on blood glucose levels and diabetes-related risk factors (Heymsfield et al., 2000). The fact that orlistat's principal mechanism of action does not involve brain neurotransmitters represents a distinct advantage over sibutramine. On the other hand, orlistat has its own adverse effects, including a decrease in absorption of fat-soluble vitamins, soft stool and anal leakage in some individuals, and a possible link to breast cancer (NIH/NHLBI, 1998).

In sum, there are currently two FDA-approved drug options for obese individuals who may need additional help to achieve weight loss. However, these pharmacological agents can have adverse effects and so require careful medical supervision if they are to be taken. Expert guidelines propose these alternatives as possible options only after a patient has tried 6 months of behavioral intervention, including diet and exercise, without success. Even then, these alternatives are recommended only for patients with BMIs greater than or equal to 30 *without* obesity-related risk factors or diseases or for patients with BMIs greater than or equal to 27 *with* concomitant obesity-related risk factors or diseases (NIH/NHLBI, 1998).

Surgical Approaches

Surgical approaches to obesity are generally recommended only for the most severe cases in which other behavioral and pharmacological approaches have failed. These approaches are recommended only for individuals with BMIs greater than or equal to 40 or for individuals with BMIs greater than or equal to 35 *plus* comorbid medical conditions (NIH/NHLBI, 1998). Current surgical approaches include so-called "gastric restriction" (vertical gastric banding) and "gastric bypass" (Roux-en Y), which can achieve sizable weight loss and improvements in comorbidities. The most striking data documenting these effects come from the Swedish Obesity Study, initiated in 1987, that has prospectively followed 1,000 obese patients who underwent surgical treatment compared with 1,000 obese patients who received conventional nonsurgical intervention. A decade after the treatment was initiated, long-term results provided compelling data favoring surgical treatment. Surgical patients lost an average of 28 kilograms (or approximately 61 pounds) compared with 0.5 kilograms (or approximately 1 pound) lost by nonsurgical controls. Compared with the control group, surgical patients had a 32-fold reduction in 2-year diabetes incidence and a 5-fold reduction at 8-year follow-up (Torgerson & Sjöström, 2001). Surgical patients were also more likely to show reduced time on sick leave and disability pension (Narbro et al., 1999).

At the same time, surgery-related complications can be common and should be monitored. Side effects noted in one surgical study (Pories et al., 1995) included Vitamin B deficiency (39.9% of patients), depression (23.7% of patients), gastritis (13.2% of patients), and dehydration/malnutrition (5.8% of patients).

Targeting Body Image in Obesity Treatment

Body image disparagement, or dissatisfaction with one's body, is one of the more common psychological hardships of obesity (Faith & Allison, 1996; Friedman & Brownell, 1995). This is readily understandable given the numerous prejudices and forms of discrimination that confront obese individuals (Puhl & Brownell, 2001). To this end, consideration of a patient's body image both at the beginning and over the course of treatment is an important consideration. There are at least two ways in which body image issues might be built into treatment programs: (a) body image as an outcome measure index to be targeted in addition to other traditional health risk factors and (b) body image and size acceptance as a potential mediator of weight change.

Body Image as a Treatment Outcome. Assessing body image changes is justified based on the frequency with which obese individuals report dissatisfaction with their bodies. A detailed list of validated body image measures for obese individuals is available elsewhere (Thompson et al., 1999). Results from behavioral interventions indicate that body image is significantly enhanced when patients lose weight (Foster, Wadden, & Vogt, 1997; Sarwer, Wadden, & Foster, 1998). Hence, clinicians can anticipate improvement in body image as an additional benefit of weight loss. Given the challenges of achieving weight loss, other investigators have attempted to develop cognitive-behavioral interventions that target psychological well-being and body image without necessarily inducing weight loss. Many of these treatments stem from the so-called "anti-diet" framework. Examples include Ciliska's (1990) program, which attempted to help patients "reestablish normal eating, improve self-esteem, and learn to deal with negative messages about our body shape in order to be more accepting of ourselves" (p. 49), and Polivy and Herman's (1992) "Undieting" program.

In one of the most comprehensive programs to date, Rosen and colleagues (Rosen, 1996; Rosen, Orosan, & Reiter, 1995) developed a treatment that targeted negative body image among obese women. Individuals were assigned to either a no-treatment control group or a cognitive-behavioral intervention that

Table 8.7   Sample Questions to Probe Patient Weight Loss Expectations

1. What is your target weight loss goal? Why?
2. What would you consider to be an acceptable weight loss goal? Why?
3. What would you consider to be a disappointing but somewhat acceptable weight loss goal? Why?
4. What would you consider to be your dream weight loss goal? Why?
5. How would you feel about a weight loss of [10%]? Why?

SOURCE: These questions were modeled after Foster, Wadden, Vogt, and Brewer (1997).

included exploration of the social consequences of obesity, factors that cause and maintain negative body image, stress management surrounding physical appearance, cognitive restructuring surrounding assumptions of physical appearance, and body image exposure in stressful social situations. Results indicated that the treatment group showed significant improvements on most psychological and body image measures as compared with the control group. Details of this treatment protocol are provided elsewhere (Rosen et al., 1995); however, these data indicate that body image enhancement can be a viable treatment goal for certain obese patients.

Body Image and Size Acceptance as Possible Mediators of Weight Loss. Studies by Foster and colleagues revealed that many obese patients hold vastly unrealistic expectations about the amount of weight loss they can achieve through current intervention approaches (Foster, Wadden, Phelan, Sarwer, & Sanderson, 2001; Foster, Wadden, Vogt, & Brewer, 1997). Obese individuals enrolling in a university-based weight loss program were asked to define the amounts of weight loss they defined as a goal or target weight loss, acceptable but not particularly happy weight loss, and disappointing weight loss. Results indicated that most patients brought unrealistic weight loss goals to treatment. (See Table 8.7) Patients defined a 32% reduction in weight as their target goal. A 25-kilogram (or approximately

55-pound) weight loss was considered to be an acceptable but not particularly happy weight loss, and a 17-kilogram (or approximately 37.5-pound) weight loss was considered to be a disappointment. At the end of treatment, none of the patients had achieved his or her "dream" weight, 9% had attained a "happy weight," 20% had attained a "disappointing" weight, 24% had attained an "acceptable" weight, and 47% had lost less weight than what they defined as a disappointing weight. To put these numbers into context, behavioral interventions currently strive to induce weight loss of approximately 8% to 10%. Although a 10% weight reduction is less than what patients might desire, it can confer important health benefits (NIH/NHLBI, 1998).

Based on these data, Foster, Wadden, Vogt, and Brewer (1997) concluded, "It seems more appropriate to help patients *accept more modest weight loss outcomes* rather than attempt to devise treatments to increase weight loss" (p. 85, emphasis in original). Indeed, Cooper and Fairburn (2001) called for novel behavioral treatments that assess patients' baseline treatment expectations and that use cognitive strategies to promote more realistic treatment goals. The underlying hypothesis is that helping patients to adopt more realistic treatment expectations will ultimately promote better treatment outcomes given that frustrations associated with modest weight loss will be reduced. This hypothesis awaits empirical evaluation.

CASE STUDY

The case of "Virginia M." is a useful one that illustrates the many facets of human obesity and reminds us that obese individuals are no different from nonobese individuals in many respects. Obese individuals lead complicated and busy lives, and they desire professional success and achievement as well as gratifying interpersonal relationships. Obese individuals have a genetic constitution, however, that makes weight gain easier when they engage in behaviors that favor excess energy intake (overeating high-fat foods) and reduced energy expenditure (being sedentary).

Virginia's background fits this description reasonably well. A 37-year-old divorced attorney, Virginia is a professionally active woman who "lives on the run" and perceives there to be limited time to lead a healthier life. Weighing 200 pounds (or approximately 91 kilograms) and measuring 5 feet 5 inches in height, her BMI is 33.3, putting her in the Obesity-I category. Virginia has a waist circumference of 92 centimeters, putting her at elevated risk for obesity-related complications (according to the guidelines reviewed herein). Obesity runs on the maternal side of her family but not on the paternal side. Although Virginia says that she feels fine, a recent medical examination suggested slightly elevated total and LDL ("bad") cholesterol and blood pressure. Based on the treatment algorithm reviewed herein, Virginia would benefit from weight loss.

When Virginia was asked what her "ideal" weight would be, she indicated 185 pounds. Such a 15-pound weight loss (from 200 to 185 pounds) would represent an 8% weight reduction, which is reasonable given current behavioral interventions. Fortunately, her expectations do not appear to be unrealistically high, and this can be used clinically to enhance her motivation to make changes. If Virginia had defined her ideal weight to be 160 pounds, it might have been necessary to explore more attainable goals before beginning treatment.

Virginia sought behavioral therapy, and a treatment program was developed that targeted healthier eating, increased physical activity, and reduced job stress. One of the most critical themes in her treatment was that of building structure into her life. Structure was operationalized as planning and preparing appropriate meals ahead of time (something Virginia avoided previously), planning ways in which to increase lifestyle physical activity that would be compatible with her active professional goals, and joining and working out in a gym. To modify her diet, Virginia began keeping a food record and self-monitored her dietary intake several days each week. Keeping this record revealed important patterns (e.g., snacking on high-fat foods during afternoons when she skipped lunch, eating fast foods when she was feeling lonely during the evenings). Based on these insights, she began to structure lunches more regularly, even when she was busy. She also began to find substitute activities during the evening to replace snacking (e.g., movies, walks, social events for singles). In terms of physical activity, she began 30 minutes of fast-pace walking 3 days per week, and this was gradually increased to 5 days per week before she joined a gym. She also began lessons in relaxation training and began reading books on time management to better balance her daily activities.

To date, Virginia has lost nearly 10 pounds and continues toward her goal. She recognizes that "treatment" will require lifelong lifestyle modification. Given that Virginia's job is central to her self-image, she will continue to work hard; however, she recognizes the potential health complications of her weight and will be especially attentive to cardiovascular disease and type 2 diabetes symptoms. These serious medical conditions cannot be discarded. At the same time, Virginia better prioritizes personal happiness and relationships. She is increasingly recognizing that beauty, like body weight, can come in different sizes.

Collectively, these data speak to the utility of assessing patients' expectations about weight loss goals. Health care professionals should be candid about the types of weight loss that patients can expect, given the current data, and may wish to address weight loss goals that seem unattainable. At the same time, clinicians should be sensitive to patients' motivations and should collaboratively establish attainable weight loss goals that will foster a sense of mastery and self-efficacy. Table 8.7 illustrates questions that clinicians may wish to ask as part of an assessment of weight loss expectation.

CONCLUSIONS

Obesity is one of the most pressing public health disorders confronting Western societies. It is a multifaceted problem in terms of its causes and consequences. Obesity is determined by genetic and environmental factors that are poorly understood. It seems apparent that one's genetic background will affect weight gain in response to eating. Certain individuals inherit a propensity to resist weight gain, whereas others readily put on weight in response to modest elevations in daily caloric intake. On a broader environmental level, changes appear to be occurring that put the entire population at increased risk for obesity. Indeed, the population prevalence of obesity has increased dramatically during the past several decades.

The diagnosis and treatment of obesity starts at the simplest level with assessment of BMI, although this is hardly the place to stop. Because obesity is associated with many health complications, it is important that these be assessed especially among the heaviest individuals. High blood pressure, elevated total and LDL cholesterol, and type 2 diabetes are just a few of the health complications that must be considered. Psychosocial factors, such as poor self-esteem and poor body image, also deserve consideration. Because body image and obesity are so strongly intertwined, it is important that the overall life satisfaction of obese individuals be assessed.

Behavioral treatments that target lifestyle changes compatible with everyday life, promote healthier food choices and reduced fat intake, and increase physical activity most days of the week are generally the first intervention strategy. Pharmacological agents can be used to assist with weight loss, although potential side effects need to be considered carefully. Each of the two current FDA-approved drugs, sibutramine and orlistat, has its own side effects that render it prohibitive for many obese adults. Surgical treatments have encouraging outcome results for severe obesity. For those morbidly obese individuals who have obesity-related complications and cannot lose weight through other prescribed methods, surgery may be a consideration when evaluated judiciously.

The high recidivism rate for obesity treatment indicates that many obese individuals will not achieve their desired weight loss. This underscores the importance of helping obese individuals to achieve personal satisfaction, self-respect, and healthy interpersonal relationships through the highs and lows of weight management.

REFERENCES

Allison, D. B., Fontaine, K. R., Manson, J. E., Stevens, J., & VanItallie, T. B. (1999). Annual deaths attributable to obesity in the United States. *Journal of the American Medical Association, 282,* 1530–1538.

American Psychiatric Association. (1994). *Diagnostic and Statistical Manual of Mental Disorders* (4th ed.). Washington, DC: Author.

Andersen, R. E., Wadden, T. A., Bartlett, S. J., Zemel, B., Verde, T. J., & Franckowiak, S. C. (1999). Effects of lifestyle activity vs. structured aerobic exercise in obese women: A randomized trial. *Journal of the American Medical Association, 281,* 335–340.

Berkowitz, R. I., & Stunkard, A. J. (2002). Development of childhood obesity. In T. A. Wadden & A. J. Stunkard (Eds.), *Handbook of obesity treatment* (pp. 515–531). New York: Guilford.

Berube-Parent, S., Prudhomme, D., St-Pierre, S., Doucet, E., & Tremblay, A. (2001). Obesity treatment with a progressive clinical tri-therapy combining sibutramine and a supervised diet-exercise intervention. *International Journal of Obesity & Related Metabolic Disorders, 25,* 1144–1153.

Bouchard, C., Rankinen, T., Chagnon, Y. C., Rice, T., Perusse, L., Gagnon, J., Borecki, I., An, P., Leon, A. S., Skinner, J. S., Wilmore, H. H., Province, M., & Rao, D. C. (2000). Genomic scan for maximal oxygen uptake and its response to training in the HERITAGE Family Study. *Journal of Applied Physiology, 88,* 551–559.

Bray, G. A., Ryan, D. H., Gordon, D., Heidingsfelder, S., Cerise, F., & Wilson, K. (1996). A double-blind randomized placebo-controlled trial of sibutramine. *Obesity Research, 4,* 263–270.

Bulik, C. M., Sullivan, P. F., & Kendler, K. S. (2002). Medical and psychiatric morbidity in obese women with and without binge eating. *International Journal of Eating Disorders, 32,* 72–78.

Carpenter, K. M., Hasin, D. S., Allison, D. B., & Faith, M. S. (2000). Relationships between obesity and DSM-IV major depressive disorder, suicide ideation, and suicide attempts: Results from a general population study. *American Journal of Public Health, 90,* 251–257.

Centers for Disease Control and Prevention. (2002). *Surgeon general's report on obesity.* Atlanta, GA: Author. Retrieved on January 20, 2003, from www.cdc.gov

Ciliska, D. (1990). *Beyond dieting: Psychological interventions for chronically obese women—A non-dieting approach.* New York: Brunner/Mazel.

Comuzzie, A. G., & Allison, D. B. (1998). The search for human obesity genes. *Science, 280,* 1374–1377.

Cooper, Z., & Fairburn, C. G. (2001). A new cognitive behavioural approach to the treatment of obesity. *Behaviour Research & Therapy, 39,* 499–511.

Davidson, M. H., Hauptman, J., DiGirolamo, M., Foreyt, J. P., Halsted, C. H., Heber, D., Heimburger, D. C., Lucas, C. P., Robbins, D. C., Chung, J., & Heymsfield, S. B. (1999). Weight control and risk factor reduction in obese subjects treated for 2 years with orlistat: A randomized controlled trial. *Journal of the American Medical Association, 281,* 235–242.

Dowda, M., Ainsworth, B. E., Addy, C. L., Saunders, R., & Riner, W. (2001). Environmental influences, physical activity, and weight status in 8- to 16-year-olds. *Archives of Pediatric and Adolescent Medicine, 155,* 711–717.

Faith, M. S., & Allison, D. B. (1996). Assessment of psychological status in obese persons. In J. K. Thompson (Ed.), *Body image, eating disorders, and obesity: A practical guide for assessment and treatment* (pp. 365–387). Washington, DC: American Psychological Association.

Faith, M. S., Allison, D. B., & Geliebter, A. (1997). Emotional eating and obesity: Theoretical considerations and practical recommendations. In S. Dalton (Ed.), *Obesity and weight control: The health professional's guide to understanding and treatment* (pp. 439–465). Gaithersburg, MD: Aspen.

Faith, M. S., Fontaine, K. R., Cheskin, L. J., & Allison, D. B. (2000). Behavioral approaches to the problems of obesity. *Behavior Modification, 24,* 459–493.

Faith, M. S., Johnson, S. L., & Allison, D. B. (1997). Putting the "behavior" into the behavior genetics of obesity research. *Behavior Genetics, 27,* 423–439.

Fanghanel, G., Cortinas, L., Sanchez-Reyes, L., & Berber, A. (2001). Second phase of a double-blind study clinical trial on sibutramine for the treatment of patients suffering essential obesity: Six months after treatment cross-over. *International Journal of Obesity & Related Metabolic Disorders, 25,* 741–747.

Ferster, C. B., Nurnberger, J. I., & Levitt, E. E. (1962). The control of eating. *Journal of Mathematics, 1,* 87–109.

Field, A. E., Barnoya, J., & Colditz, G. A. (2002). Epidemiology and health and economic consequences of obesity. In T. A. Wadden & A. J. Stunkard (Eds.), *Handbook of obesity treatment* (pp. 3–18). New York: Guilford.

Fisher, J. A., & Birch, L. (2001). Early regulation of eating behavior. In J. K. Thompson & L. Smolak (Eds.), *Body image, eating disorders, and obesity in youth: Assessment, treatment, and prevention* (pp. 23–39). Washington, DC: American Psychological Association.

Foreyt, J. P., & Goodrick, G. K. (1992). *Living without dieting.* New York: Time Warner.

Foster, G. D., Wadden, T. A., Phelan S., Sarwer D. B., & Sanderson, R. S. (2001). Obese patients' perceptions of treatment outcomes and the factors that influence them. *Archives of Internal Medicine, 161,* 2133–2139.

Foster, G. D., Wadden, T. A., & Vogt, R. A. (1997). Body image in obese women before, during, and after weight loss treatment. *Health Psychology, 16,* 226–229.

Foster, G. D., Wadden, T. A., Vogt, R. A., & Brewer, G. (1997). What is a reasonable weight loss? Patients' expectations and evaluations of obesity treatment outcomes. *Journal of Consulting and Clinical Psychology, 65,* 79–85.

French, S. A., Story, M., & Jeffery, R. W. (2001). Environmental influences on eating and physical activity. *Annual Review of Public Health, 22,* 309–335.

Friedman, M. A., & Brownell, K. D. (1995). Psychological correlates of obesity: Moving to the next research generation. *Psychological Bulletin, 117,* 3–20.

Garrow, J. S., & Webster, J. (1985). Quetelet's index (w/h^2) as a measure of fatness. *International Journal of Obesity, 9,* 147–153.

Gortmaker, S. L., Must, A., Perrin, J. M., Sobol, A. M., & Dietz, W. H. (1993). Social and economic consequences of overweight in adolescence and young adulthood. *New England Journal of Medicine, 329,* 1008–1112.

Haddock, C. K., Poston, W. S., Dill, P. L., Foreyt, J. P., & Ericsson, M. (2002). Pharmacotherapy for obesity: A quantitative analysis of four decades of published randomized clinical trials. *International Journal of Obesity, 26,* 262–273.

Heymsfield, S. B., Segal, K. R., Hauptman, J., Lucas, C. P., Boldrin, M. N., Rissanen, A., Wilding, J. P., & Sjöström, L. (2000). Effects of weight loss with orlistat on glucose tolerance and progression to Type 2 diabetes in obese adults. *Archives of Internal Medicine, 160,* 1321–1326.

Hill, J. O., & Peters, J. C. (1998). Environmental contributions to the obesity epidemic. *Science, 280,* 1371–1374.

Horgen, K. B., & Brownell, K. D. (2002). Confronting the toxic environment: Environmental public health actions in a world crisis. In T. A. Wadden & A. J. Stunkard (Eds.), *Handbook of obesity treatment* (pp. 95–106). New York: Guilford.

Johnson, W. G., & Torgrud, L. J. (1996). Assessment and treatment of binge eating disorder. In J. K. Thompson (Ed.), *Body image, eating disorders, and obesity: An integrative guide for assessment and treatment* (pp. 321–343). Washington, DC: American Psychological Association.

Keller, K. L., Pietrobelli, A., Must, S., & Faith, M. S. (2002). Genetics of eating and its relation to obesity. *Current Atherosclerosis Reports, 4,* 176–182.

Kirschenbaum, D. S. (1994). *Weight loss through persistence.* Oakland, CA: New Harbinger.

Kuller, L. H., Simkin-Silverman, L. R., Wing, R. R., Meilahn, E., & Ives, D. G. (2001). Women's Healthy Lifestyle Project: A randomized clinical trial—Results at 54 months. *Circulation, 103,* 32–37.

Mokdad, A. H., Bowman, B. A., & Ford, E. S. (2001). The continuing of obesity and diabetes in the United States. *Journal of the American Medical Association, 286,* 1195–1200.

Mokdad, A. H., Bowman, B. A., Ford, E. S., Vinicor, F., Marks, J. S., & Koplan, J. P. (2001). *Journal of the American Medical Association, 286,* 1195–1200.

Mokdad, A. H., Serdula, M., & Dietz, W. (1999). The spread of the obesity epidemic in the United States. *Journal of the American Medical Association, 282,* 1519–1522.

Mokdad, A. H., Serdula, M., & Dietz, W. (2000). The continuing obesity epidemic in the United States. *Journal of the American Medical Association, 284,* 1650–1651.

Narbro, K., Agren, G., Jonsson, E., Larsson, B., Naslund, I., Wedel, H., & Sjöström, L. (1999). Sick leave and disability pension before and after treatment for obesity: A report from the Swedish Obese Subjects (SOS) study. *International Journal of Obesity & Related Metabolic Disorders, 23,* 619–624.

National Institutes of Health/National Heart, Lung, and Blood Institute. (1998). *Clinical guidelines on the identification, evaluation, and treatment of overweight and obesity in adults.* Bethesda, MD: Author. Retrieved on January 20, 2003, from www.nhlbi.nih.gov/ guidelines/obesity/practgde.htm

Pingitore, R., Dugoni, B. L., Tindale, R. S., & Spring, B. (1994). Bias against overweight job applicants in a simulated employment interview. *Journal of Applied Psychology, 79,* 909–917.

Pi-Sunyer, F. X. (1993). Medical hazards of obesity. *Annals of Internal Medicine, 119,* 655–660.

Polivy, P., & Herman, C. P. (1992). Undieting: A program to help people stop dieting. *International Journal of Eating Disorders, 11,* 261–268.

Pories, W. J., Swanson, M. S., MacDonald, K. G., Long, S. B., Morris, P. G., Brown, B. M., Barakat, H. A., deRamon, R. A., Israel, G., & Dolezal, J. M. (1995). Who would have thought it? An operation proves to be the most effective therapy for adult-onset diabetes mellitus. *Annals of Surgery, 222,* 339–350.

Price, R. A. (2002). Genetics and common obesities: Background, current status, strategies, and future prospects. In T. A. Wadden & A. J. Stunkard (Eds.), *Handbook of obesity treatment* (pp. 73–94). New York: Guilford.

Price, R. A., Charles, M. A., Pettitt, D. J., & Knowler, W. C. (1993). Obesity in Pima Indians: Large increases among post-World War II birth cohorts. *American Journal of Physiological Anthropology, 92,* 473–479.

Puhl, R., & Brownell, K. D. (2001). Bias, discrimination, and obesity. *Obesity Research, 9,* 788–805.

Rankinen, T., Perusse, L., Weisnagel, S. J., Snyder, E. E., Chagnon, Y. C., & Bouchard, C. (2002). The human obesity gene map: The 2001 update. *Obesity Research, 10,* 196–249.

Roehling, M. V. (1999). Weight-based discrimination in employment: Psychological and legal aspects. *Personnel Psychology, 52,* 969–1016.

Rosen, J. C. (1996). Improving body image in obesity. In J. K. Thompson (Ed.), *Body image, eating disorders, and obesity: An integrative guide for assessment and treatmenr* (pp. 425–440). Washington, DC: American Psychological Association.

Rosen, J. C., Orosan, P., & Reiter, J. (1995). Cognitive behavior therapy for negative body image in obese women. *Behavior Therapy, 26,* 25–42.

Rossner, S., Sjöström, L., Noack, R., Meinders, A. E., & Noseda, G. (2000). Weight loss, weight maintenance, and improved cardiovascular risk factors after 2 years treatment with orlistat for obesity: European Orlistat Obesity Study Group. *Obesity Research, 8,* 49–61.

Sarwer, D. B., Wadden, T. A., & Foster, G. D. (1998). Assessment of body image dissatisfaction in obese women: Specificity, severity, and clinical significance. *Journal of Consulting and Clinical Psychology, 66,* 651–654.

Stuart, R. B. (1967). Behavioral control of overeating. *Behaviour Research and Therapy, 5,* 357–365.

Stunkard, A. J. (2002). Binge-eating disorder and night-eating syndrome. In T. A. Wadden & A. J. Stunkard (Eds.), *Handbook of obesity treatment* (pp. 107–121). New York: Guilford.

Stunkard, A. J., Berkowitz, R. I., Stallings, V. A., & Schoeller, D. A. (1999). Energy intake, not energy output, is a determinant of body size in infants. *American Journal of Clinical Nutrition, 69,* 524–530.

Tataranni, P. A., & Ravussin, E. (2002). Energy metabolism and obesity. In T. A. Wadden & A. J. Stunkard (Eds.), *Handbook of obesity treatment* (pp. 42–72). New York: Guilford.

Thompson, J. K., Coovert, M., Richards, K. J., Johnson, S., & Cattarin, J. (1995). Development of body image, eating disturbance, and general psychological functioning in female adolescents: Covariance structure modeling and longitudinal investigations. *International Journal of Eating Disorders, 18,* 221–236.

Thompson, J. K., Heinberg, L. J., Altabe, M. N., & Tantleff-Dunn, S. (1999). *Exacting beauty: Theory, assessment, and treatment of body image disturbance.* Washington, DC: American Psychological Association.

Thompson, J. K., & Smolak, L. (2001). *Body image, eating disorders, and obesity in youth: Assessment, treatment, and prevention.* Washington, DC: American Psychological Association.

Torgerson, J. S., & Sjöström, L. (2001). The Swedish Obese Subjects (SOS) Study: Rationale and results. *International Journal of Obesity & Related Metabolic Disorders, 25,* S2–S4.

VanItallie, T. B. (1994). Worldwide epidemiology of obesity. *Pharmacoeconomics, 5,* 1.

Wadden, T. A., & Foster, G. D. (2000). Behavioral treatment of obesity. *Medical Clinics of North America, 84,* 441–446.

Wadden, T. A., Sternberg, J. A., Letizia, K. A., Stunkard, A. J., & Foster, G. D. (1989). Treatment of obesity by very low calorie diet, behavior therapy, and their combination: A 5-year perspective. *International Journal of Obesity, 13,* 39–46.

Wadden, T. A., & VanItallie, T. B. (1992). *Treatment of the severely obese patient.* New York: Guilford.

Wadden, T. A., Womble, L. G., Stunkard, A. J., & Anderson, D. A. (2002). Psychosocial consequences of obesity and weight loss. In T. A. Wadden & A. J. Stunkard (Eds.), *Handbook of obesity treatment* (pp. 144–169). New York: Guilford.

Whitaker, R. C., Wright, J. A., Pepe, M. S., Seidel, K. D., & Dietz, W. H. (1997). Predicting obesity in young adulthood from childhood and parental obesity. *New England Journal of Medicine, 337,* 869–873.

Wilson, G. T. (1994). Behavioral treatment of obesity: Thirty years and counting. *Advances in Behavioural Research and Therapy, 16,* 3331–3375.

Wilson, G. T. (1996). Acceptance and change in the treatment of eating disorders and obesity. *Behavior Therapy, 27,* 417–439.

Wirth, A., & Krause, J. (2001). Long-term weight loss with sibutramine: A randomized controlled trial. *Journal of the American Medical Association, 286,* 1331–1339.

World Health Organization. (1998). *Obesity: Preventing and managing the global epidemic* (Publication No. WHO/NUT/NCD/98.1). Geneva: Author.

CHAPTER 9

Physical Inactivity as a Risk Factor for Chronic Disease

KRISTA A. BARBOUR, TIMOTHY T. HOULE, AND PATRICIA M. DUBBERT

T he health benefits of physical activity have been demonstrated repeatedly over the past several decades, and engaging in regular physical activity has been recommended as one effective way in which to decrease both morbidity and mortality (U.S. Department of Health and Human Services, 1996). Unfortunately, current guidelines for leisure time physical activity are not met by the majority of individuals in the United States. Indeed, a significant percentage of the population is considered sedentary or insufficiently active (Centers for Disease Control and Prevention [CDC], 2001). Because of its status as a primary risk factor in the development of chronic disease, *physical inactivity* must be addressed in any effort to reduce rates of illness and early mortality.

DEFINITIONS AND DESCRIPTIONS OF PHYSICAL ACTIVITY AND INACTIVITY

In 1996, the U.S. surgeon general issued a report outlining the importance of physical activity for good health. The report included recommendations for the intensity, duration, and frequency of physical activity sufficient for meeting the goal of disease *prevention* in the general population. A primary conclusion of the report was that a moderate level of activity (e.g., 30 minutes of walking on most days of the week) is an appropriate goal for most Americans in terms of realizing health benefits. However, the report also emphasized that 60% of American adults are not physically active on a regular basis and that 25% are sedentary (e.g., report no leisure time physical activity). A recent, population-based telephone survey of American adults found that rates of physical activity remained stable during the years of 1990 to 1998 (CDC, 2001), a finding that was disappointing and somewhat surprising given the increased emphasis on public health initiatives to increase physical activity rates in the United States.

Perhaps even more discouraging are the results of studies focusing on demographic differences in the prevalence of regular physical activity. These findings indicate that the percentage of active adults is considerably smaller among ethnic minorities (particularly Hispanic Americans) relative to Caucasians. In addition, women are generally less physically active than men, and physical activity decreases with age. Other predictors of an inactive lifestyle include lower income, lesser educational attainment, and living in the southern or midwestern United States (Schoenborn & Barnes, 2002).

According to an American College of Sports Medicine (1998) position stand, healthy adults should engage in 20 to 60 minutes (which may be continuous or accumulated in several shorter bouts) of aerobic activity 3 to 5 days per week to improve cardiorespiratory fitness. For most people, a moderate intensity level of physical activity is recommended to decrease the likelihood of exercise-induced injury. In addition to aerobic exercise, individuals are encouraged to incorporate both resistance (e.g., set of exercises that are designed to condition major muscle groups two or three times per week) and flexibility (e.g., stretch major muscle groups two or three times per week) training into their exercise programs.

However, as already noted, most American adults do not meet this level of physical activity. Given this unfortunate fact, it is important to consider the potential negative consequences of physical *inactivity*. For example, a lack of physical activity has been clearly linked to an increased risk of all-cause mortality (see, e.g., Blair et al., 1989; Wei et al., 1999). In addition, a sedentary lifestyle has been shown to predict the nation's number one cause of death: cardiovascular disease (CVD) (Farrell et al., 1998). Indeed, a large percentage of the population is at increased risk of disease morbidity and mortality because of insufficient physical activity. The surgeon general's report and the body of scientific knowledge it represents suggest that many individuals will acquire illnesses that can be prevented by physical activity. In addition, it is possible that the progression of many diseases and conditions can be slowed or halted by

becoming active if one is sedentary or by increasing one's activity level. For most of the remainder of the chapter, the focus will shift from physical activity as a primary prevention strategy to physical activity as it relates to specific chronic diseases.

To discuss the role that physical activity plays in chronic disease, it is useful to first address the issue of *assessment* of physical activity. This includes the methods commonly used to measure activity as well as recent trends in assessment (for a review of the major developments in physical activity research during the past decade, see Dubbert, 2002). The following section addresses the numerous ways in which physical activity has been conceptualized by researchers.

OVERVIEW OF RESEARCH IN THE ASSESSMENT OF PHYSICAL ACTIVITY

The measurement of physical activity has received increasing attention during the past several decades. The task of quantifying physical activity across various populations, settings, and purposes has proved to be particularly daunting. In the subsections that follow, the methods that have been used to measure physical activity in both the laboratory and community settings are summarized, with special emphasis on each method's particular strengths and weaknesses. The issues involved with the assessment of physical activity in specialized populations and settings are also discussed along with future directions of physical activity assessment.

Physical Activity: What to Measure?

Physical activity has been characterized as "any bodily movement resulting in energy expenditure above resting levels" (Freedson & Miller, 2000, p. 21; see also Caspersen, 1989).

This definition logically leads to the goal of quantifying energy expenditure as the target of measurement. Indeed, the methods described in this section are often compared with simultaneous measures of energy expenditure as indexes of validity. However, physical activity is more accurately conceptualized as multidimensional in nature, with frequency, intensity, duration, and circumstance as relevant variables (Bassett, 2000). This is intuitively the case given that two very different activities, such as swimming and walking, may have the same net energy expenditure for a given time; even if one is of greater intensity, the other can be engaged in for longer duration or greater frequency.

Given the multidimensional nature of physical activity, no single assessment method provides valid and reliable measurement over the possible range of populations, settings, and uses (Wood, 2000). These limitations are made more complex when combined with the current limitations of technology and logistical concerns, which preclude the use of certain methods when assessing certain activities. Thus, when selecting a method for the assessment of physical activity, a researcher must clearly define the purpose of measurement and the application for which it is to be used.

Methods for Assessing Physical Activity

Self-Report. Self-report instruments are the most widely used instruments in the assessment of physical activity (Sallis & Saelens, 2000). These instruments include measures such as activity logs, self-administered questionnaires, interview-administered questionnaires, and proxy reports (for detailed lists and reviews, see Kriska & Caspersen, 1997; Montoye, Kemper, Saris, & Washburn, 1996; Sallis, 1991; Sallis & Saelens, 2000). Many of these measures have adequate reliability and validity and also provide assessment of multiple activity modalities over a range of situations at a low

cost. In a recent review of self-report measures used during the 1990s, Sallis and Saelens (2000) found that, in general, adult self-report measures were more valid for reports of vigorous activity than for reports of moderate intensity activity. In addition, they found that interview measures had stronger psychometric properties than did self-administered measures and that self-report measures did not provide accurate estimates of absolute amounts of physical activity; in fact, most self-report measures overestimated absolute amounts of physical activity. In general, simple self-report measures, although known to be less than perfectly accurate, remain extremely valuable in many public health surveys and particularly in clinical applications.

Pedometer. A pedometer measures vertical acceleration using a spring-loaded lever arm that records motion either mechanically or by closing an electrical circuit. Sophisticated pedometers have a digital output that can represent activity either in number of steps or in mileage estimates. Electronic pedometers are extremely portable and are available for less than $20 (for a list and review, see Freedson & Miller, 2000). Recent studies have shown that pedometers are fairly accurate at counting steps but cannot distinguish between walking and running (Bassett, 2000). Furthermore, pedometers have little data storage capabilities and do not allow for the recording of specific activity patterns throughout the day. Despite these limitations, pedometers are widely used as a low-cost method of collecting objective physical activity data and in interventions that target increased walking- and running-type activities.

Accelerometer. Accelerometers measure acceleration in either the vertical (uniaxial) or three-dimensional (triaxial) plane. The fundamental assumption behind an accelerometer is that acceleration is directly proportional to muscle forces; the greater the acceleration of the limb, torso, or the like, the more energy expended by the organism. Accelerometers are extremely portable but can be quite expensive, with triaxial accelerometers costing more than $500 (for a list and review, see Freedson & Miller, 2000). Accelerometers have large capacities for data storage and are able to record the amount and intensity of activity as well as the specific activity patterns over days or weeks. Although too expensive for many clinical applications, accelerometers might be of value in specialized programs such as for treatment of chronic pain and cardiopulmonary rehabilitation.

Heart Rate Monitor. Heart rate monitors generally consist of a chest strap transmitter and a wristwatch receiver for storage. Monitors vary in quality but can be purchased for between $200 and $500 (for a list and review, see Freedson & Miller, 2000). Under normal conditions, heart rate is linearly related to energy expenditure, but many sources of error can elevate heart rate even at rest and can obscure the relationship between energy expenditure and heart rate (Freedson & Miller, 2000). Good heart rate monitors have storage capacity to record heart rate over extended periods of time and allow for patterns of activity over time. These monitors might not be practical for many clinical applications but could be valuable for cardiac patients.

Table 9.1 highlights the strengths and weaknesses of each type of field measure described in this section. Recently, researchers aware of the limitations of any single type of assessment modality have focused on combining the methods to sample more of the qualities of physical activity. The use of multiple modalities and complex calibration techniques can increase measurement accuracy, and they are often recommended for the assessment of physical activity.

The complex and multidimensional nature of various forms of physical activity is sufficient to complicate the accurate assessment of physical activity. However, recent attention has been given to the special assessment problems presented by certain subgroups and especially lifestyle-related activities. For example, the assessment of physical activity in older adults using self-report instruments is made more complicated by the fact that this group tends to engage in primarily light- and moderate-intensity activity (Bernstein et al., 1998; Washburn, 2000). There is as yet a paucity of age-specific questionnaires to assess this population (Washburn, 2000). The combination of the types of activities engaged in by older adults, the measures used to assess them, and the potential unreliability of recall for these types of activities supports the need for more refined assessment tools for older adults.

Traditional assessment of physical activity has focused on participation in structured, time-limited bouts of activity (i.e., "exercise"). For example, researchers may measure the number of miles walked on the treadmill or the number of minutes spent on a stationary bicycle. More recently, however, the definition of what should constitute physical activity has been broadened. One such change has been to challenge the notion that physical activity must occur in one episode of long duration (i.e., 20 to 30 minutes) to be beneficial. It is now generally agreed that the accumulation of activity throughout one's day may be sufficient to realize improved health. Such activities may include walking the stairs instead of riding the elevator and walking short distances instead of driving a car.

In addition to the more inclusive definition of physical activity, other difficulties remain in measurement. For example, occupational activity is often neglected in surveys of physical activity. Because most occupations today are primarily sedentary, most physical activity questionnaires inquire about leisure time activity only. This is problematic because those individuals most likely to be characterized as sedentary during leisure time are also more likely to engage in job-related physical activity

Table 9.1 Field Methods for the Assessment of Physical Activity

Modality	Cost	Patterns of Activity?	Accuracy	Comments
Self-report	Low	Yes	Good for relative amounts	Many different options available
Pedometer	Low	No	Good for walking	Unable to distinguish instensity of physical activity
Accelerometer Uniaxial	Medium	Yes	Measures both amount and intensity	Might not measure light activities in multiple planes
Triaxial	High	Yes	As above	Measures multiple planes of movement
Heart rate	Medium-High	Yes	Good	Multiple sources of measurement error

(CDC, 2001). Thus, it may be that some respondents who are classified as sedentary are actually active, but only on the job. The failure of many studies to capture physical activity obtained through employment is a weakness that needs to be addressed in future research.

PHYSICAL ACTIVITY INTERVENTION IN CHRONIC DISEASE

Cardiovascular Disease and Physical Activity

Physical activity has clearly been shown to reduce the risk of cardiovascular morbidity and mortality (e.g., Berlin & Colditz, 1990) and, as a result, has been recommended in the primary prevention of CVD. However, because most Americans do not acquire a level of physical activity that is sufficient to decrease the risk of CVD, research has focused on *secondary* prevention following cardiovascular events (e.g., chest pain, heart attack). The purpose of secondary prevention is to prevent further cardiac events in individuals who already manifest some degree of CVD.

Traditionally, individuals who had experienced heart attacks were prescribed bed rest as a significant part of their cardiac rehabilitation. However, as the medical and psychological benefits of being active were documented for this population (for a review of this evidence, see Dubbert, Rappaport, & Martin, 1987), physical activity became a primary focus of treatment for those with CVD. The recommended intensity, duration, and frequency of physical activity to be prescribed in cardiac rehabilitation programs are described in Leon (2000). In sum, sessions of aerobic exercise should include both warm-up and cool-down periods and should be of an intensity of between 40% and 85% of VO_{2max} (a widely used measure of maximal oxygen consumption at a given workload). These sessions should occur three times per week and last for at least 20 to 60 minutes each session. When health psychologists consider physical activity in CVD rehabilitation, they must keep in mind that participation in a physical activity program should be supervised by a medical expert such as a physician or an exercise professional (American Association of Cardiovascular and Pulmonary Rehabilitation, 1999; Dubbert et al., 1987). This is a necessity because although events are infrequent, patients with CVD are at increased risk for experiencing cardiac events as a result of participation in physical activity relative to their disease-free counterparts.

Many observational studies have demonstrated a significant relationship between physical activity and cardiovascular mortality. In a large-scale prospective investigation, Wannamethee, Shaper, and Walker (2000) examined the association between physical activity and mortality in older men with CVD. These men were followed up approximately 13 years subsequent to a baseline assessment. Men who participated in physical activity experienced significant reductions in both all-cause and cardiovascular mortality relative to sedentary individuals. Importantly, several types of physical activity (e.g., gardening, walking) were shown to have a beneficial effect on mortality rates. In addition, those men who were sedentary at baseline but who later became active demonstrated significantly lower levels of mortality than did those men who remained inactive throughout the follow-up period.

Randomized clinical trials of physical activity in the treatment of CVD have generally shown that physical activity is effective at reducing cardiovascular mortality (for a review of these studies, see Oldridge, Guyatt, Fischer, & Rimm, 1988). In addition, physical activity interventions have resulted in increased exercise endurance, decreased chest pain, and reduced progression of atherosclerosis (Leon, 2000). Finally, as discussed elsewhere in this chapter, physical activity also improves several conditions that are known risk factors for CVD such as obesity and hypertension.

In conclusion, physical activity has been shown to be effective in the secondary prevention of CVD (i.e., reduction of cardiac events). Regular physical activity should be recommended for all individuals with CVD who do not have conditions that would limit or prohibit their participation. Because most cardiac rehabilitation research has focused on Caucasian men, future research should address the effectiveness of physical activity in ethnic minorities and women who have developed CVD. (For a more complete discussion of coronary heart disease, see Chapter 15.)

Hypertension and Physical Activity

Hypertension, or elevated blood pressure (BP), affects approximately 50 million adults in the United States (Kaplan, 1998). Hypertension is a major health issue in the United States, representing the most significant risk factor for the development of CVD, including both coronary heart disease and stroke (MacMahon et al., 1990). Current guidelines (Joint National Committee on Detection, Evaluation, and Treatment of High Blood Pressure [JNC], 1997) dictate that the optimal level of BP should be 120/80 mm Hg (millimeters of mercury) or lower. Values of 140/90 or higher are considered to be high or in the hypertensive range.

Given that many hypertensive patients' BP levels are not consistently controlled with antihypertensive medication (most likely due to poor compliance with medications [Mancia, Sega, Milesi, Cesana, & Zanchetti, 1997]), decades of research have been devoted to the investigation of the non-pharmacological treatment of hypertension. Examples of widely studied treatments include relaxation, biofeedback, and stress management (for a review of these treatments, see Linden & Chambers, 1994).

Physical activity has also been examined as a treatment for hypertension. It has been recommended that for individuals classified as mildly hypertensive, initial treatment consisting of "lifestyle changes," including physical activity, should be implemented for the first 6 to 12 months (JNC, 1997). In this subsection, the efficacy of physical activity for the treatment of hypertension is explored. In general, the desired outcome of a physical activity intervention would be the decreased use of medications used to control BP or the elimination of the need for antihypertensive medication altogether, along with a possible improvement in other CVD risk factors related to physical activity.

In a recent review of 15 studies of exercise training in hypertensive individuals, Hagberg, Park, and Brown (2000) found that approximately 75% of participants experienced significant decreases in BP. In addition, the hypotensive effect of physical activity was shown to occur quickly (within 1 to 10 weeks) and at low to moderate levels of intensity. Interestingly, the reduction in BP levels was not related to the amount of weight lost during the various training programs.

In a meta-analysis of 29 randomized clinical trials of aerobic physical activity, it was demonstrated that participation in a training program averaging 19 weeks resulted in a 4-point decrease in systolic BP and a 3-point decrease in diastolic BP (Halbert et al., 1997). Although this change in BP was significantly more than that achieved by participants in the control groups, it is lower than that reported in other studies. Consistent with the Hagberg and colleagues (2000) review, however, the improvement in BP levels occurred in the absence of weight loss.

Thus, aerobic exercise training appears to have a beneficial effect on reducing BP in individuals with hypertension. (However, not all studies have found significant effects [Blumenthal, Siegal, & Appelbaum, 1991; Nami et al., 2000].) Although the majority of training programs examined have aerobic exercise (e.g., walking, cycling), recent evidence suggests that *nonaerobic* forms of physical activity, such as resistance training, may also be useful in the treatment of hypertension. A recent meta-analysis (Kelley & Kelley, 2000) showed a small but statistically significant decrease in BP following resistance training two to five times per week for an average of 14 weeks.

The ability of a physical activity program to decrease BP may depend, in part, on individual characteristics such as gender and ethnicity (Lesniak & Dubbert, 2001). Regarding gender differences in the effectiveness of physical activity in treating hypertension, the data have generally shown no significant differences between women and men. Studies examining the effectiveness of physical activity in lowering BP in African Americans are particularly important because of the high prevalence of hypertension within this group. In addition, hypertension in African Americans is more severe and less well controlled relative to other ethnic groups. Unfortunately, the relationship between hypertension and physical activity in African Americans has not been studied adequately (Lesniak & Dubbert, 2001). Encouragingly, the data that do exist suggest that physical activity is an effective treatment for hypertension in African Americans (e.g., Kokkinos et al., 1995).

In summary, physical activity has been shown to be an effective treatment for hypertension. However, it should also be noted that the hypotensive effect of physical activity has been shown to be modest in several studies (for a review, see Blumenthal, Sherwood, Gullette, Georgiades, & Tweedy, 2002). Although the BP reduction achieved by physical activity may appear to be minimal, epidemiological data indicate that small drops in BP are accompanied by an impressive decrease in the risk of stroke and CVD. For example, a 5- to 6-point reduction in diastolic BP has been associated with a 35% to 40% decrease in stroke and with a 20% to 25% decrease in heart disease (Collins et al., 1990). (For a more complete discussion of hypertension, see Chapter 14.)

Chronic Obstructive Pulmonary Disease and Physical Activity

Chronic obstructive pulmonary disease (COPD) is a condition in which there is an impaired ability of the lungs to take in sufficient air. The primary symptoms of the disease consist of difficulty in breathing and a long-term cough. COPD may result from a variety of lung disorders such as asthma and emphysema. A common corollary of COPD is exercise intolerance. This often is a result of a vicious cycle in which the individual, on experiencing breathing difficulties (dyspnea) while exercising, perceives the dyspnea as threatening and so avoids engaging in physical activity. Eventually, deconditioning occurs and leads to exercise intolerance.

In an effort to target the exercise intolerance that often accompanies the disease, many treatment programs for COPD include a physical activity component. The physical activity offered is typically in the context of a pulmonary rehabilitation program (which might also include topics such as health education and stress management). There is much evidence showing that physical activity improves the exercise tolerance of COPD patients. In addition, improvement can be demonstrated after 4 weeks of training (Lacasse et al., 1996). Specifically, physical activity decreases dyspnea, decreases leg fatigue, and enhances health-related quality of life (for a review of this literature, see Bourjeily & Rochester, 2000).

COPD is a disease that is characterized by intermittent exacerbations (e.g., upper and lower respiratory tract infections). In general, the available evidence suggests that participation in a pulmonary rehabilitation program that includes a physical activity component is associated with a reduction in COPD-related exacerbations and hospitalizations (Berry & Walschlager, 1998). Unfortunately, it has been difficult to identify the specific components of rehabilitation programs that may lead to this improvement in health. Further research is necessary to determine whether or not physical activity alone leads to better health outcomes.

In addition to the physical limitations experienced by COPD patients, impaired cognitive functioning is sometimes associated with the disease (Prigatano, Parsons, Wright, Levin, & Hawryluk, 1983) and may result from decreased blood oxygenation levels (Grant et al., 1987).

Physical activity has been shown to improve the cognitive test performance in COPD patients. For example, Emery, Schein, Hauck, and MacIntyre (1998) found that, in addition to improvement in exercise endurance, some aspects of cognitive functioning (e.g., verbal fluency) were improved in a sample of community adults (over age 50 years) diagnosed with COPD. In this study, the physical activity component consisted of 45 minutes of aerobic activity on 5 days per week for 5 weeks (followed by a 5-week period of lower intensity activity on 3 days per week). As with the improvement exhibited in physical health, these changes in cognitive functioning were demonstrated after a relatively brief physical activity intervention.

In sum, the evidence clearly supports the use of physical activity in the treatment of COPD. Inclusion of a physical activity component in pulmonary rehabilitation programs has been shown repeatedly to increase exercise endurance and may result in fewer complications and hospitalizations related to the disease. In addition, there is some evidence to suggest that physical activity improves the cognitive functioning of individuals with COPD. Further research is needed to determine the optimal dose of physical activity necessary to produce sufficient improvements in both physical health and cognitive performance.

OBESITY AND PHYSICAL ACTIVITY

Obesity in the United States has achieved the status of a public health crisis (for a recent review of the problem, see Wadden, Foster, & Brownell, 2002). This is due to the fact that excess weight represents a major risk factor for chronic disease development (e.g., hypertension, CVD, type 2 diabetes mellitus). Most clinicians are now encouraged to evaluate weight status using the body mass index (BMI). BMI, the most commonly used measure of healthy versus unhealthy weight, assesses body weight in relation to height and is defined as weight in kilograms divided by height in meters squared. Current guidelines define "overweight" as BMI values in the range of 25.0 to 29.9, with "obesity" considered to be any value of 30.0 or higher (National Institutes of Health, 1998). It has been estimated that approximately 50% of U.S. adults are overweight or obese (World Health Organization, 1998), and the prevalence appears to be rising (Bouchard, 2000).

Body weight is determined by energy (food) intake and energy expenditure; however, this is a simplified definition of an extremely complex set of biological, behavioral, and environmental variables (the complexities of the issue are addressed in Salbe & Ravussin, 2000). If energy intake and expenditure are in balance, no significant weight loss or gain should occur. However, a situation in which food intake is consistently higher than energy expended will result in weight gain. Two primary contributors to the energy imbalance evident in the United States are a sedentary lifestyle and poor dietary habits. The focus of the remainder of this section is on the relationship between obesity and the *expenditure* of energy, that is, physical activity (or exercise).

Observational studies have demonstrated a significant relationship between physical activity and obesity, with more active individuals being less likely to be obese. In addition, there exist prospective studies suggesting that a lack of physical activity is a predictor of obesity (for a review, see Jebb & Moore, 1999). However, isolating the effects of physical activity interventions for obesity is difficult because most studies also include a dietary modification component such as a low-calorie diet. It has been shown that weight loss programs using physical activity alone are effective in producing modest weight loss (as compared with control groups) but do not result in as much weight loss as does exercise combined with dietary changes (Wing, 1999). One possible explanation for the relatively minimal effect of physical activity alone on body weight is the duration of most exercise programs. It may be that the 4 to 6 months of training typical of physical activity studies is not sufficient for realizing the benefits of physical activity (Wing, 1999). Findings from longitudinal investigations of physical activity and weight have suggested that long-term physical activity is effective in slowing and minimizing subsequent weight gain (but might not result in weight loss or even prevent weight gain [Grundy et al., 1999]).

Thus, *maintaining* participation in an exercise program is key to successful weight loss. In general, treatment programs for obesity (typically including physical activity accompanied by dietary changes) induce an initially rapid weight loss followed by a steady reduction in the amount of weight lost long term (Jeffery et al., 2000). Perri and colleagues (2001) compared a standard weight loss intervention (20 weeks of educational sessions, dietary changes, and moderate-intensity physical activity) with extended treatment. Extended treatment occurred for 12 months following the completion of the standard intervention and included the use of exercise diaries. It was found that participants assigned to extended treatment (after completing the standard program) maintained the weight lost during the standard treatment, whereas those completing the standard treatment alone regained approximately half of the weight initially lost (Perri et al., 2001).

There is also evidence that tailoring a physical activity program to an individual's specific needs may result in higher levels of exercise maintenance. For example, Bock, Marcus, Pinto, and Forsyth (2001) found that participants who received individualized feedback regarding their exercise program were significantly more likely to maintain treatment levels of physical activity at follow-up (12 months) than were participants who completed a standard physical activity intervention.

In conclusion, weight loss programs that include a physical activity component have generally been shown to lead to a clinically significant weight reduction. However, the challenge of maintaining this weight loss following treatment remains. Future research should focus on the factors related to continued participation in physical activity. For example, understanding the behavioral variables that differentiate individuals who maintain physical activity (and weight loss) from those who regain the weight initially lost during treatment is a high priority (Marcus et al., 2000). (A more complete discussion of obesity and body image disturbances was provided in Chapter 8.)

OSTEOARTHRITIS AND PHYSICAL ACTIVITY

Arthritis is one of the leading causes of chronic pain and often results in disability and decreased quality of life. Osteoarthritis can be divided into two conceptual types: primary osteoarthritis, which is thought to be related to aging and heredity, and secondary osteoarthritis, which is caused by conditions such as obesity, joint trauma, and repetitive joint use (Cheng et al., 2000). It is estimated that the prevalence of arthritis is increasing, with 15.0% of the population affected in 1990 but an expected prevalence of 18.2% by 2020 (Wang, Helmick, Macera, Zhang, & Pratt, 2001). Furthermore, the disability rates produced from arthritis also appear to be growing, with those affected reporting more suffering from arthritis (Wang et al., 2001; Yelin, 1992).

Traditionally, physicians have suggested the avoidance of vigorous activity and encouraged physical inactivity for the treatment of osteoarthritis, reflecting a belief that joint use exacerbates the condition. This "wear-and-tear" hypothesis persists even today, as studies examining the role of physical activity in producing osteoarthritis have been somewhat inconsistent (Sutton, Muir, Mockett, & Fentem, 2001). The potential role of physical activity in the development of osteoarthritis has increased in importance with the surgeon general's report calling for adults to increase their levels of physical activity (U.S. Department of Health and Human Services, 1996).

Recent research has shown that engaging in low- to moderate-intensity levels of physical activity does not increase the risk of the development of osteoarthritis in the knee or hip (Cheng et al., 2000; Sutton et al., 2001). The risk of developing osteoarthritis from high-intensity activities is not so clear, however, with some studies showing increased risk (Cheng et al., 2000; Cooper et al., 1998; Cooper, McAlindon, Coggon, Egger, & Dieppe, 1994) and others not showing increased risk (White, Wright, & Hudson, 1993). What is clear from the studies involving intense physical activity is that joint injury greatly increases the risk of osteoarthritis (Cheng et al., 2000; Sutton et al., 2001) and that perhaps the higher risk of developing osteoarthritis associated with intense physical activities may be explained by those activities' greater association with injury.

There are several reasons to believe that increased physical activity is beneficial in preventing and reducing the symptoms of osteoarthritis (Cheng et al., 2000). Activity strengthens the muscular support surrounding joints and consequently reduces the risk of injury. Furthermore, physical activity improves and maintains joint mobility. Physical activity is also effective at reducing many of the other risk factors of osteoarthritis such as obesity, hypertension, hypercholesterolemia, and high blood glucose (Hart, Doyle, & Spector, 1995). Finally, physical activity increases the nourishment of joint cartilage through the diffusion of nutrients via joint fluid (Cheng et al., 2000; Hall, Urban, & Gehl, 1991).

In 1999, the Arthritis Foundation, CDC, and 90 other organizations released the *National Arthritis Action Plan: A Public*

Health Strategy (Meenan, Callahan, & Helmick, 1999; Wang et al., 2001). Among the recommendations included in this publication was the need to decrease the rates of physical inactivity in adults with arthritis (34.8%), which are higher than those in adults without arthritis (27.7%) (Wang et al., 2001). Others have also recommended the use of physical activity in the management of osteoarthritis, and its positive effects have received empirical support (Ettinger & Afable, 1994; Ettinger et al., 1997; Minor, 1991).

CANCER AND PHYSICAL ACTIVITY

Recently, Friedenreich (2001) summarized the current literature about the association between physical activity and cancer. She concluded that there is growing evidence for a protective effect resulting from physical activity. However, the evidence considered was entirely dependent on epidemiological research. Friedenreich expounded on the need for randomized, controlled intervention trials, which will allow the underlying mechanisms of the association between physical activity and cancer to be better understood. Yet even with the lack of controlled research, the negative association between physical activity and certain cancers supports the role of physical activity in the prevention of many forms of cancer.

The strongest evidence of the negative association between physical activity and cancer exists for colon cancer and, to a somewhat lesser degree, breast cancer (Friedenreich, 2001). In both forms of cancer, the risk reduction for the most physically active has been as high as 70% (for reviews, see Colditz, Cannuscio, & Frazier, 1997; Friedenreich, 2001; Friedenreich, Thune, Brinton, & Albanes, 1998; Gammon, John, & Britton, 1998; Lattika, Pukkala, & Vihko, 1998). The average risk reduction in colon cancer is 40% to 50%, with risk for both forms of cancer

showing a negative dose-response to increasing levels of physical activity (Friedenreich, 2001).

The evidence supporting risk reduction from physical activity in other cancers is not as compelling, but there is substantial evidence supporting the association with prostate cancer (Friedenreich, 2001). Furthermore, preliminary evidence has been gathering to indicate that physical activity may be negatively related to lung cancer, testicular cancer, ovarian cancer, and endometrial cancer (Friedenreich, 2001). However, there is also compelling evidence to indicate that physical activity is not at all associated with rectal cancer (Friedenreich, 2001).

The role of exercise in cancer treatment has not been well researched, yet physical activity can help to reduce the loss of lean muscle mass during treatment, improve functional capacity, increase appetite, and enhance quality of life (for a review, see Oliveria & Christos, 1997). Furthermore, physical activity has been shown to be helpful in reducing other forms of risk in the development of cancer such as obesity and other lifestyle-related health conditions.

DIABETES MELLITUS AND PHYSICAL ACTIVITY

Diabetes is a heterogeneous group of disorders characterized by hyperglycemia or higher than normal levels of blood glucose. Type 1 diabetes, commonly referred to as "insulin-dependent diabetes," occurs as a result of autoimmune destruction of the pancreas, leading to a deficiency in insulin production (Peirce, 1999). Type 2 diabetes, which accounts for 90% to 95% of all diabetic cases in the United States (Kriska, Blair, & Pereira, 1994), occurs as a result of altered insulin secretion, elevated hepatic glucose production, and/or diminished glucose use in skeletal muscle (Wallberg-Henriksson, Rincon, & Zierath, 1998). Prolonged hyperglycemia leads to the glycation of tissues, causing organ damage and other negative health effects.

The past decade witnessed an increase in the prevalence of diabetes. It is estimated that in 1995, 4.0% of the world's population was afflicted, and this prevalence was projected to increase to 5.4% by 2025 (Peirce, 1999). However, these reported case estimates may be low given that there may be no symptoms at the onset of the disease, causing many early cases to elude detection (Kriska et al., 1994). The incidence of type 2 diabetes increases with age and is greatly increased in obese individuals, with a reported 60% to 90% of type 2 diabetic patients being obese at onset (Kriska et al., 1994).

Physical inactivity has been shown to affect the physiological mechanisms thought to underlie diabetes. A total of 35 days of induced physical inactivity caused a decrease in glucose tolerance in eight healthy males (Lipman et al., 1972). Furthermore, individuals with spinal cord injury had higher blood glucose levels than did age-matched controls (Duckworth et al., 1980). Although a complete review of the physiological effects of physical activity on glucose regulation is beyond the scope of this chapter, substantial evidence exists supporting the use of physical activity in the management and prevention of type 2 diabetes (for reviews, see Peirce, 1999; Wallberg-Henriksson et al., 1998).

Exercise has been shown to lower blood glucose levels in diabetics (Hubinger, Franzen, & Gries, 1987; Peirce, 1999). It is estimated that 90% of glucose clearance occurs in skeletal muscle, and this process can be greatly enhanced with increased energy use created through physical activity (Peirce, 1999). Exercise can enhance insulin-independent transport of glucose into cells (Peirce, 1999) and can increase insulin sensitivity (Burstein, Epstein, Shapiro, Charuzi, & Karnieli, 1990). Furthermore, regular exercise programs have been shown to improve metabolic control, especially in the young (Wallberg-Henriksson, 1992). Exercise-related decrease in body weight

can also have a beneficial effect on glucose regulation (Wallberg-Henriksson et al., 1998).

Increasing physical activity in patients with type 1 diabetes is a complicated issue because of the necessary self-regulation of insulin levels. Hypoglycemia is a potentially life-threatening state that can be induced after exercise. Thus, the use of physical activity in the regulation of type 1 diabetes must be conducted with careful consideration of the potential for exercise-induced hypoglycemia or ketosis. However, exercise has been shown to decrease the daily insulin regimens of type 1 diabetics by increasing insulin-independent glucose transport and by increasing insulin sensitivity (Peirce, 1999).

An overwhelming body of evidence exists to suggest that increased physical activity should be recommended not only as a fundamental management strategy for physician-diagnosed diabetes but also as a strategy for the prevention of type 2 diabetes. (For a more complete discussion of type 2 diabetes, see Chapter 16.)

PSYCHOLOGICAL FUNCTIONING AND PHYSICAL ACTIVITY

In addition to the widely studied effects of physical activity on physical functioning, participation in physical activity has been shown to play a role in emotional well-being. When discussing the relationship between physical activity and emotions, it is necessary to consider both acute and chronic effects. Regarding the improvement of mood (e.g., depression) following a single bout of exercise, the evidence is mixed, with some studies finding no effect and others demonstrating significantly enhanced mood. However, the results do indicate that *dose* of exercise (i.e., physical activity of varying intensities) does play a role in subsequent mood (for a review of these studies, see Rejeski, 1994).

In addition to mood improvement, one must consider the possible inducement of negative mood following a session of physical activity. Results of several studies have shown that high-intensity exercise bouts may lead to an increase in feelings of anxiety and depressed mood in some individuals (Rejeski, 1994). There is some evidence to suggest that individuals who are predisposed to negative mood states are more likely to experience anxiety as a result of engaging in physical activity (Cameron & Hudson, 1986). However, this issue is complex, and further research is needed to increase our understanding of the role that physical activity plays in short-term changes in mood. It has been found that in women with normal mood at baseline, mood after exercise improves most for those who felt worse previous to engaging in physical activity (Rejeski, Gauvin, Hobson, & Norris, 1995).

Given that the U.S. population is aging, the treatment of depressive disorders in older adults is becoming increasingly important. Blumenthal and colleagues (1999) examined the use of physical activity as a treatment for major depressive disorder in older adults. In their work, they compared participation in a physical activity program with the use of a commonly prescribed antidepressant medication (sertraline hydrochloride). Participants in the study were randomly assigned to receive either the medication, a physical activity intervention, or a combination of physical activity and medication. The 16-week physical activity treatment consisted of three 45-minute sessions of aerobic activity per week. It was found that both the medication group and the physical activity group experienced a reduction in their levels of depression (Blumenthal et al., 1999). The two types of treatment did not differ significantly from one another in effectiveness. These results suggest that physical activity is a viable alternative to medication in the treatment of depression in older adults.

In a 6-month follow-up study of the same participants, it was demonstrated that those individuals who were assigned to the physical activity treatment experienced lower rates of depression than did those receiving medication (30% vs. 50%, respectively). In addition, participants in the physical activity group were significantly more likely to have recovered from major depressive disorder (partially or fully) than were those in the medication group (Babyak et al., 2000). Regarding maintenance of physical activity, 64% of participants who received the physical activity treatment continued to exercise following completion of the 16-week program.

In sum, it appears that physical activity has the potential to improve mood both immediately following a bout of exercise (i.e., acute effects) and after participation in a long-term program (i.e., chronic effects). Thus, physical activity may be an effective means of enhancing mental health as well as physical health. In individuals experiencing a mood disorder (e.g., depression), physical activity has been shown to be a practical alternative to medication and should be recommended as either a primary treatment or an adjunctive treatment (assuming no physical limitations that would contraindicate exercise).

CONCLUSIONS

The purpose of this chapter was to review the evidence that physical activity is beneficial in terms of the prevention and treatment of disease. It was shown that the literature supports engaging in physical activity as an effective means to reducing morbidity and mortality. Unfortunately, most individuals do not achieve an adequate level of physical activity. Understanding this pervasive lack of physical activity participation requires consideration of the role that environmental factors play in our society.

As indicated in a recent review (Dubbert et al., 2002), it is clear that the inactive lifestyle that characterizes many individuals in the United States is due partly to a decrease in activity required on the job as well as to the

CASE STUDY

"L. B." was a 56-year-old married Caucasian male who was referred for evaluation by his primary care physician. At the time of the evaluation, L. B. was 40 pounds overweight and was at the borderline of requiring medication to control his blood glucose levels. He was also experiencing low to moderate levels of chronic pain in his lower back, and this pain was reportedly aggravated by exertion. He was referred for evaluation of potential behavioral and lifestyle interventions to place his blood sugar levels under better control and help him to lose weight.

L. B. was screened for depression, anxiety, and other psychopathology during his initial visit using a standard battery of self-report assessment instruments in combination with a clinical interview. The assessment revealed that L. B. was generally well adjusted but that he was reporting low levels of dysphoria and poor mood. Specifically, he reported a lack of energy, difficulty in sleeping, and a loss of interest in pleasurable activities. These symptoms were severe enough to warrant discussion but appeared to be on the sub-threshold of a clinical diagnosis. L. B. appeared to be motivated to address his current medical problems, stating that he was quite concerned about developing diabetes.

L. B.'s lifestyle was initially assessed during the interview using questions such as "Describe a typical day." From this line of questioning, it was apparent that his lifestyle largely consisted of eating meals out, working long hours at his desk, and enjoying his weekend and after-work time by watching sports and being sedentary. When asked about his levels of physical activity, L. B. reported that he used to enjoy being active but that his lower back pain had forced him to "take it easy" because it usually hurt when he engaged in even moderate levels of activity. To further examine his levels of physical activity, he was given a pedometer to wear throughout the next week and was instructed to engage in his usual schedule. It should be noted that L. B.'s primary care physician had cleared him medically for all forms of physical activity and that L. B. had no detectable structural damage in his lower back. In addition, circulation and sensation in his lower extremities and feet were not impaired (walking ability may be limited in those with foot complications secondary to diabetes). He agreed to record the number of steps each evening in a log as well as to keep a food diary.

Figure 9.1 displays L. B.'s baseline levels of physical activity as recorded by a pedometer. These baseline levels of activity were discussed in the session, and L. B. reported surprise at the low levels of activity in which he was engaging. His beliefs about increasing his levels of physical activity were discussed. The rationale behind the positive benefits of physical activity for mood, glucose regulation, and chronic pain was explained. L. B. felt that walking would not aggravate his back and stated that he was willing to begin a walking regimen. It was decided that L. B. would attempt to walk during his lunch hour but that if he were unable to do so, he would walk after work with his wife. He also agreed to continue to monitor his activity but decided to discontinue his food log.

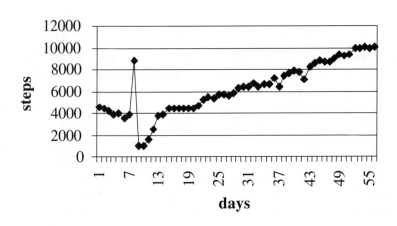

Figure 9.1   L. B.'s Steps as a Function of Time

L. B. called the clinic after his first day of walking to report that he had greatly increased pain (which he described as 8 on a 10-point scale) and that he wanted to discontinue the regimen. He further stated that he was not wearing the pedometer (he had called in sick to work because of the pain) and that he planned on not moving for the remainder of the day. After a discussion of some of L. B.'s frustrations, he was persuaded to continue to wear the pedometer for the remainder of the week, even if he did not continue to implement a walking regimen.

At the next clinic visit, L. B.'s log was reviewed, and as can be seen in Figure 9.1, his increased pain was attributed to his "overdoing it" on the first day of his regimen. Many of his pain beliefs regarding his physical limitations were discussed in the context of pacing himself. L. B. was persuaded to attempt his walking regimen again, but this time with some restrictions set by the therapist. Specifically, during the first week, he should not walk beyond 4,500 steps (as indicated on the pedometer). He agreed to this but felt that this walking regimen was too little to be of benefit.

Throughout the next few weeks, L. B.'s therapist-imposed upper limits of pedometer readings were allowed to increase (Figure 9.1). L. B. reported success with the regimen, stating that it allowed him extra time with his wife, who was also enjoying walking with him. The goal of 10,000 steps daily was discussed, and L. B. felt that this goal could be accomplished. He soon reached the goal and discontinued recording his activity, although he purchased his own pedometer. He was also implementing changes in his diet that greatly facilitated his sense of efficacy in changing his lifestyle.

By the end of treatment, L. B. had succeeded in losing 15 pounds and was extremely proud of this accomplishment. He had increased his activity to 10,000 steps daily, with no increase in lower back pain. (It should be noted that individuals with foot or knee pain might not be able to attain this level of activity.) In fact, he reported that his back "has not felt better in 15 years." Furthermore, his primary care physician believed that if L. B. were able to maintain his lifestyle changes, he would not have to pharmacologically manage L. B.'s blood sugar levels. L. B. was confident that he would be able to maintain his increased levels of physical activity, stating that he particularly liked the accompanying increased levels of energy and would like to lose more weight.

availability of sedentary leisure time activities for both children and adults. Americans are also dining out more often and are consuming larger portions during meals. In addition, the physical environment plays a role in physical activity participation. For example, in a sample of women age 40 years or over, it was found that the lack of enjoyable scenery and hills in the neighborhood was associated with less leisure time activity (King et al., 2000).

Although more recent studies have included men and women of color, the majority of research has been with Caucasians. Because certain diseases are more prevalent in ethnic minorities (e.g., hypertension in African Americans), it is crucial to focus attention on these groups. In addition, consideration should be given to subgroups *within* ethnic minority groups. Crespo, Smit, Carter-Pokras, and Andersen (2001) found that degree of acculturation (i.e., the extent to which an ethnic group adopts the customs and traditions of the majority culture) was associated with leisure time physical activity in Mexican Americans. Specifically, it was shown that inactivity was significantly more likely in those individuals who spoke primarily Spanish in the home (a sign of less acculturation to American society). In contrast, those who spoke primarily English had physical activity rates that were similar to those of the general (majority) population. Thus, it may be useful to tailor physical activity promotion in such a way as to target less acculturated individuals (e.g., by increasing the availability of informational materials in languages other than English).

Recent studies have examined physical *activity* versus physical *fitness*. Researchers have attempted to make this distinction because it is possible, for example, that two individuals engaging in the same dose (including intensity, duration, and frequency) of physical activity may have different levels of physical fitness. Blair, Cheng, and Holder (2001) sought to address the issue of whether physical activity or fitness is more important for good health. After reviewing the evidence from 67 studies that assessed physical activity, fitness, and a health outcome, they concluded that it is not possible to determine whether activity or fitness is more important in terms of producing health benefits. Instead, they found a consistent dose-response relation between physical activity and fitness and health outcomes across studies included in the review. That is, at both higher activity and fitness levels, there was a reduction in disease morbidity and mortality.

Blair and colleagues (2001) recommended that researchers begin to define more specifically the nature of the dose-response relationship. For example, what would be the difference in health outcomes in an individual who exercises for 15 minutes per day versus an individual who engages in 60 minutes of physical activity per day? Whether or not such a difference in activity duration translates into significantly different health outcomes is unknown. In addition, although the focus has been on cardiorespiratory fitness, other possible types of fitness should be considered and studied more widely. These might include metabolic, flexibility, cognitive functioning, and mental health. As other types of fitness become better defined, it may be possible to tailor physical activity to an individual's needs. For example, an individual might be prescribed a specific type of physical activity to address his or her particular risk factors.

Another important area of continued research should focus on the maintenance of physical activity. Why is it so difficult to maintain this behavior? Why is engaging in physical activity pleasurable for some individuals but not for others? One step in answering the question of why some individuals are more likely to maintain a program of physical activity might be to examine emotions related to exercise. Although much has been written of the emotions that occur as a result of physical activity participation, one aspect of the relationship between physical activity and emotion that has received little attention is the importance of the emotional changes that occur *during* physical activity (Rejeski, 1994).

Researchers should also continue to investigate the role of medical professionals in physical activity participation. In a recent telephone survey of nearly 2,000 U.S. adults, only 28% of the respondents reported receiving advice from their physicians to increase physical activity (Glasgow, Eakin, Fisher, Bacak, & Brownson, 2001). Although there has been increased interest in this area and several studies have been published, further examination of the factors that may increase physician prescription of physical activity is needed.

Finally, more research is needed on effective strategies for promoting physical activity in adults. As illustrated in the preceding case study, cognitive-behavioral strategies such as self-monitoring and goal setting can be very effective in helping individuals to change physical activity behaviors. In behavioral medicine settings with chronic disease patients, health psychologists work with exercise professionals and other experts who prescribe the appropriate activity regimens. Psychologists are often responsible for assisting patients in developing motivational strategies and self-management programs to build physical activity into their lifestyles and sustain the change over time. Psychologists may also assist with assessing mood and cognitive states that could affect ability to carry out prescribed physical activity programs.

Recent reviews (e.g., Blair & Morrow, 1998; Dubbert, 2002; Sallis & Owen, 1998; U.S. Department of Health and Human Services, 1996) have described successful physical activity promotion projects and intervention strategies in a variety of populations and settings. Participation in physical activity is a powerful tool in the prevention of many of the diseases covered in this chapter. By increasing the numbers of individuals who regularly engage in physical activity, we could significantly reduce the chronic disease burden and improve the quality of life of millions of Americans.

REFERENCES

American Association of Cardiovascular and Pulmonary Rehabilitation. (1999). *Guidelines for cardiac rehabilitation and secondary prevention programs* (3rd ed.). Champaign, IL: Human Kinetics Press.

American College of Sports Medicine. (1998). The recommended quantity and quality of exercise for developing and maintaining cardiorespiratory and muscular fitness and flexibility in healthy adults. *Medicine & Science in Sports & Exercise, 30,* 975–991.

Babyak, M., Blumenthal, J. A., Herman, S., Khatri, P., Doraiswamy, M., Moore, K., Craighead, W. E., & Baldewicz, T. T. (2000). Exercise treatment for major depression: Maintenance of therapeutic benefit at 10 months. *Psychosomatic Medicine, 62,* 633–638.

Bassett, D. R. (2000). Validity and reliability issues in objective monitoring of physical activity. *Research Quarterly for Exercise and Sport, 71*(2), 30–36.

Berlin, J. A., & Colditz, G. A. (1990). A meta-analysis of physical activity in the prevention of coronary heart disease. *American Journal of Epidemiology, 132,* 612–628.

Bernstein, M., Sloutskis, D., Kumanyika, S., Sparti, A., Schultz, Y., & Morbiana, A. (1998). Data-based approach for developing a physical activity frequency questionnaire. *American Journal of Epidemiology, 147,* 147–154.

Berry, M. J., & Walschlager, S. A. (1998). Exercise training and chronic obstructive pulmonary disease: Past and future research directions. *Journal of Cardiopulmonary Rehabilitation, 18,* 181–191.

Blair, S. N., Cheng, Y., & Holder, J. S. (2001). Is physical activity or physical fitness more important in defining health benefits? *Medicine & Science in Sports & Exercise, 33,* S379–S399.

Blair, S. N., Kohl, H. W., Paffenbarger, R. S., Clark, D. G., Cooper, K. H., & Gibbons, L. W. (1989). Physical fitness and all-cause mortality. *Journal of the American Medical Association, 262,* 2395–2401.

Blair, S. N., & Morrow, J. R. (1998). Cooper Institute/American College of Sports Medicine 1997 Physical Activity Conference. *American Journal of Preventive Medicine, 15,* 255–256.

Blumenthal, J. A., Babyak, M. A., Moore, K. A., Craighead, W. E., Herman, S., Khatri, P., Waugh, R., Napolitano, M. A., Forman, L. M., Appelbaum, M., Doraiswamy, M., & Krishnan, R. (1999). Effects of exercise training on older patients with major depression. *Archives of Internal Medicine, 159,* 2349–2356.

Blumenthal, J. A., Sherwood, A., Gullette, E. C. D., Georgiades, A., & Tweedy, D. (2002). Biobehavioral approaches to the treatment of essential hypertension. *Journal of Consulting and Clinical Psychology, 70,* 569–589.

Blumenthal, J. A., Siegal, W. C., & Appelbaum, M. (1991). Failure of exercise to reduce blood pressure in patients with mild hypertension. *Journal of the American Medical Association, 266,* 2098–2104.

Bock, B. C., Marcus, B. H., Pinto, B. M., & Forsyth, L. H. (2001). Maintenance of physical activity following an individualized motivationally tailored intervention. *Annals of Behavioral Medicine, 23,* 79–87.

Bouchard, C. (2000). Introduction. In C. Bouchard (Ed.), *Physical activity and obesity.* Champaign, IL: Human Kinetics Press.

Bourjeily, G., & Rochester, C. L. (2000). Exercise training in chronic obstructive pulmonary disease. *Clinics in Chest Medicine, 21,* 763–780.

Burstein, R., Epstein, Y., Shapiro, Y., Charuzi, I., & Karnieli, E. (1990). Effect of an acute bout of exercise on glucose disposal in human obesity. *Journal of Applied Physiology, 69,* 299–304.

Cameron, O. G., & Hudson, C. J. (1986). Influence of exercise on anxiety level in patients with anxiety disorders. *Psychosomatics, 27,* 720–723.

Caspersen, C. J. (1989). Physical activity epidemiology: Concepts, methods, and applications to exercise science. In K. Pandolf (Ed.), *Exercise and sports science reviews* (Vol. 17, pp. 423–473). Baltimore, MD: Williams & Wilkins.

Centers for Disease Control and Prevention. (2001). Physical activity trends: United States, 1990–1998. *Morbidity and Mortality Weekly Report, 50,* 166–169.

Cheng, Y., Macera, C. A., Davis, D. R., Ainsworth, B. E., Troped, P. J., & Blair, S. N. (2000). Physical activity and self-reported, physician-diagnosed osteoarthritis: Is physical activity a risk factor? *Journal of Clinical Epidemiology, 53,* 315–322.

Colditz, G. A., Cannuscio, C. C., & Frazier, A. L. (1997). Physical activity and reduced risk of colon cancer: Implications for prevention. *Cancer Causes Control, 8,* 649–667.

Collins, R., Peto, R., MacMahon, S., Hebert, P., Fiebach, N. H., Eberlein, K. A., Godwin, J., Qizilbash, N., Taylor, J. O., & Hennekens, C. H. (1990). Blood pressure, stroke, and coronary heart disease:, II. Short term reductions in blood pressure: Overview of randomised drug trials in their epidemiological context. *Lancet, 335,* 827–838.

Cooper, C., Inskip, H., Croft, P., Campbell, L., Smith, G., McLaren, M., & Coggon, D. (1998). Individual risk factors for hip osteoarthritis: Obesity, hip injury, and physical activity. *American Journal of Epidemiology, 147,* 516–522.

Cooper, C., McAlindon, T., Coggon, D., Egger, P., & Dieppe, P. (1994). Occupational activity and osteoarthritis of the knee. *Annals of Rheumatic Disease, 53*(2), 90–93.

Crespo, C. J., Smit, E., Carter-Pokras, O., & Andersen, R. (2001). Acculturation and leisure-time physical inactivity in Mexican American adults: Results from NHANES III, 1988–1994. *American Journal of Public Health, 91,* 1254–1257.

Dubbert, P. M. (2002). Physical activity and exercise: Recent advances and current challenges. *Journal of Consulting and Clinical Psychology, 70,* 526–536.

Dubbert, P. M., Carithers, T., Sumner, A. E., Barbour, K., Clark, B., Hall, J. E., & Crook, E. (2002). Obesity, physical inactivity, and risk for cardiovascular disease. *American Journal of Medical Science, 324,* 116–126.

Dubbert, P. M., Rappaport, N. B., & Martin, J. E. (1987). Exercise in cardiovascular disease. *Behavior Modification, 11,* 329–347.

Duckworth, W. C., Solomon, S. S., Jallepalli, P., Heckemeyer, C., Finnern J., & Powers, A. (1980). Glucose intolerance due to insulin resistance in patients with spinal cord injuries. *Diabetes, 29,* 906–910.

Emery, C. F., Schein, R. L., Hauck, E. R., & MacIntyre, N. R. (1998). Psychological and cognitive outcomes of a randomized trial of exercise among patients with chronic obstructive pulmonary disease. *Health Psychology, 17,* 232–240.

Ettinger, W. H., & Afable, R. F. (1994). Physical disability from knee osteoarthritis: The role of exercise as an intervention. *Medicine & Science in Sports & Exercise, 26,* 1435–1440.

Ettinger, W. H., Jr., Burns, R., Messier, S. P., Applegate, W., Rejeski, W. J., & Morgan, T. (1997). A randomized trial comparing aerobic exercise and resistance exercise with a health education program in older adults with knee osteoarthritis: The Fitness Arthritis and Seniors Trial (FAST). *Journal of the American Medical Association, 277,* 25–31.

Farrell, S., Kampert, J. B., Kohl, H. W., Barlow, C. E., Macera, C. A., Paffenbarger, R. S., Gibbons, L. W., & Blair, S. N. (1998). Influences of cardiorespiratory fitness levels and other predictors on cardiovascular disease mortality in men. *Medicine & Science in Sports & Exercise, 30,* 899–905.

Freedson, P. S., & Miller, K. M. (2000). Objective monitoring of physical activity using motion sensors and heart rate. *Research Quarterly for Exercise and Sport, 71*(2), 21–29.

Friedenreich, C. M. (2001). Physical activity and cancer prevention: From observational to interventional research. *Cancer, Epidemiology, Biomarkers, & Prevention, 10,* 287–301.

Friedenreich, C. M., Thune, I., Brinton, L. A., & Albanes, D. (1998). Epidemiologic issues related to the association between physical activity and breast cancer. *Cancer, 83,* 600–610.

Gammon, M. D., John, E. M., & Britton, J. A. (1998). Recreational and occupational physical activities and risk of breast cancer. *Journal of the National Cancer Institute, 90,* 100–117.

Glasgow, R. E., Eakin, E. G., Fisher, E. B., Bacak, S. J., & Brownson, R. C. (2001). Physician advice and support for physical activity. *American Journal of Preventive Medicine, 21,* 189–196.

Grant, I., Prigatano, G. P., Heaton, R. K., McSweeney, A. J., Wright, E. C., & Adams, K. M. (1987). Progressive neuropsychologic impairment and hypoxemia. *Archives of General Psychiatry, 44,* 999–1006.

Grundy, S. M., Blackburn, G., Higgins, M., Lauer, R., Perri, M. G., & Ryan, D. (1999). Physical activity in the prevention and treatment of obesity and its comorbidities. *Medicine & Science in Sports & Exercise, 31,* S502–S508.

Hagberg, J. M., Park, J., & Brown, M. D. (2000). The role of exercise training in the treatment of hypertension. *Sports Medicine, 30,* 193–206.

Halbert, J. A., Silagy, C. A., Finucane, P., Withers, R. T., Hamdorf, P. A., & Andrews, G. R. (1997). The effectiveness of exercise training in lowering blood pressure: A meta-analysis of randomised controlled trials of 4 weeks or longer. *Journal of Human Hypertension, 11,* 641–649.

Hall, A. C., Urban, J. P. G., & Gehl, K. A. (1991). The effects of hydrostatic pressure on matrix synthesis in articular cartilage. *Journal of Orthopedic Research, 9,* 1–10.

Hart, D. J., Doyle, D. V., & Spector, T. D. (1995). Association between metabolic factors and knee osteoarthritis in women. *Journal of Rheumatology, 22,* 1118–1123.

Hubinger, A., Franzen, A., & Gries, F. A. (1987). Hormonal and metabolic response to physical exercise in hyperinsulinemic and non-hyperinsulinemic Type 2 diabetics. *Diabetes Research, 4*(2), 57–61.

Jebb, S. A., & Moore, M. S. (1999). Contribution of a sedentary lifestyle and inactivity to the etiology of overweight and obesity: Current evidence and research issues. *Medicine & Science in Sports & Exercise, 31,* S534–S541.

Jeffery, R. W., Drewnowski, A., Epstein, L. H., Stunkard, A. J., Wilson, G. T., Wing, R. R., & Hill, D. R. (2000). Long-term maintenance of weight loss: Current status. *Health Psychology, 19,* 5–16.

Joint National Committee on Detection, Evaluation, and Treatment of High Blood Pressure. (1997). The sixth report of the Joint National Committee on Detection, Evaluation, and Treatment of High Blood Pressure (JNC-VI). *Archives of Internal Medicine, 157,* 2413–2446.

Kaplan, N. W. (1998). *Clinical hypertension* (7th ed.). Baltimore, MD: Williams & Wilkins.

Kelley, G. A., & Kelley, K. S. (2000). Progressive resistance exercise and resting blood pressure: A meta-analysis of randomized controlled trials. *Hypertension, 35,* 838–843.

King, A. C., Castro, C., Wilcox, S., Eyler, A. A., Sallis, J. F., & Brownson, R. (2000). Personal and environmental factors associated with physical inactivity among different racial-ethnic groups of U.S. middle-aged and older-aged women. *Health Psychology, 19,* 354–364.

Kokkinos, P. F., Narayan, P., Coleran, J. A., Pittaras, M., Notargiacomo, A., Reda, D., & Papademetriou, V. (1995). Effects of regular exercise on blood pressure and left ventricular hypertrophy in African-American men with severe hypertension. *New England Journal of Medicine, 333,* 1462–1467.

Kriska, A. M., Blair, S. M., & Pereira, M. A. (1994). The potential role of physical activity in the prevention of non-insulin-dependent diabetes mellitus: The epidemiological evidence. *Exercise and Sport Science Review, 22,* 121–143.

Kriska, A. M., & Caspersen, C. J. (Eds.). (1997). A collection of physical activity questionnaires for health related research. *Medicine & Science in Sports & Exercise, 29,* S1–S205.

Lacasse, Y., Wong, E., Guyatt, G. H., King, D., Cook, D. J., & Goldstein, R. S. (1996). Meta-analysis of respiratory rehabilitation in chronic obstructive pulmonary disease. *Lancet, 348,* 1115–1119.

Lattika, P., Pukkala, E., & Vihko, V. (1998). Relationship between the risk of breast cancer and physical activity. *Sports Medicine, 26,* 133–143.

Leon, A. S. (2000). Exercise following myocardial infarction. *Sports Medicine, 29,* 301–311.

Lesniak, K. T., & Dubbert, P. M. (2001). Exercise and hypertension. *Current Opinion in Cardiology, 16,* 356–359.

Linden, W., & Chambers, L. (1994). Clinical effectiveness of non-drug treatment for hypertension: A meta-analysis. *Annals of Behavioral Medicine, 16,* 35–45.

Lipman, R. L., Raskin, P., Love, T., Triebwasser, J., Lecocq, F. R., & Schnure, J. J. (1972). Glucose intolerance during decreased physical activity in man. *Diabetes, 21*(2), 101–107.

MacMahon, S., Peto, R., Cutler, J., Collins, R., Sorlie, P., Neaton, J., Abbott, R., Godwin, J., Dyer, A., & Stamler, J. (1990). Blood pressure, stroke, and coronary heart disease: I. Prolonged differences in blood pressure: Prospective observational studies corrected for the regression dilution bias. *Lancet, 335,* 765–774.

Mancia, G., Sega, R., Milesi, C., Cesana, G., & Zanchetti, A. (1997). Blood-pressure control in the hypertensive population. *Lancet, 349,* 454–457.

Marcus, B. H., Dubbert, P. M., Forsyth, L. H., McKenzie, T. L., Stone, E. J., Dunn, A. L., & Blair, S. N. (2000). Physical activity behavior change: Issues in adoption and maintenance. *Health Psychology, 19,* 32–41.

Meenan, R. F., Callahan, L. F., & Helmick, C. G. (1999). The National Arthritis Action Plan: A public health strategy for a looming epidemic. *Arthritis Care Research, 12,* 79–81.

Minor, M. A. (1991). Physical activity and management of arthritis. *Annals of Behavioral Medicine, 13,* 117–124.

Montoye, H. J., Kemper, H. C. G., Saris, W. H. M., & Washburn, R. A. (1996). *Measuring physical activity and energy expenditure.* Champaign, IL: Human Kinetics Press.

Nami, R., Mondillo, S., Agricola, E., Lenti, S., Ferro, G., Nami, N., Tarantino, M., Glauco, G., Spano, E., & Gennari, C. (2000). Aerobic exercise training fails to reduce blood pressure in non-dipper-type hypertension. *American Journal of Hypertension, 13,* 593–600.

National Institutes of Health. (1998). Clinical guidelines on the identification, evaluation, and treatment of overweight and obesity in adults: The evidence report. *Obesity Research, 6,* S51–S209.

Oldridge, N. B., Guyatt, G. H., Fischer, M. E., & Rimm, A. A. (1988). Cardiac rehabilitation after myocardial infarction: Combined experience of randomised clinical trials. *Journal of the American Medical Association, 260,* 945–950.

Oliveria, S. A., & Christos, P. J. (1997). The epidemiology of physical activity and cancer. *Annals of the New York Academy of Sciences, 833,* 79–90.

Peirce, N. S. (1999). Diabetes and exercise. *British Journal of Sports Medicine, 33,* 161–172.

Perri, M. G., Nezu, A. M., McKelvey, W. F., Shermer, R. L., Renjilian, D. A., & Viegener, B. J. (2001). Relapse prevention training and problem-solving therapy in the long-term management of obesity. *Journal of Consulting and Clinical Psychology, 69,* 722–726.

Prigatano, G. P., Parsons, O., Wright, E., Levin, D. C., & Hawryluk, G. (1983). Neuropsychological test performance in mildly hypoxemic patients with chronic obstructive pulmonary disease. *Journal of Consulting and Clinical Psychology, 51,* 108–116.

Rejeski, W. J. (1994). Dose-response issues from a psychosocial perspective. In C. Bouchard, R. T. Shephard, & T. Stephens (Eds.), *Physical activity, fitness, and health* (pp. 1040–1055). Champaign, IL: Human Kinetics Press.

Rejeski, W. J., Gauvin, L., Hobson, M. L., & Norris, J. L. (1995). Effects of baseline responses, in-task feelings, and duration of activity on exercise-induced feeling states in women. *Health Psychology, 14*, 350–359.

Salbe, A. D., & Ravussin, E. (2000). The determinants of obesity. In C. Bouchard (Ed.), *Physical activity and obesity* (pp. 69–102). Champaign, IL: Human Kinetics Press.

Sallis, J. F. (1991). Self-report measures of children's physical activity. *Journal of School Health, 61*, 215–219.

Sallis, J. F., & Owen, N. (1998). *Physical activity and behavioral medicine.* Thousand Oaks: CA: Sage.

Sallis, J. F., & Saelens, B. E. (2000). Assessment of physical activity by self-report: Status, limitations, and future directions. *Research Quarterly for Exercise and Sport, 71*(2), 1–14.

Schoenborn, C. A., & Barnes, P. M. (2002). *Leisure-time physical activity among adults: United States, 1997–98* (advance data from Vital and Health Statistics, No. 325). Hyattsville, MD: National Center for Health Statistics.

Sutton, A. J., Muir, K. R., Mockett, S., & Fentem, P. (2001). A case-control study to investigate the relation between low and moderate levels of physical activity and osteoarthritis of the knee using data collected as part of the Allied Dunbar National Fitness Survey. *Annals of Rheumatic Disease, 60*, 756–764.

U.S. Department of Health and Human Services. (1996). *Physical activity and health: Report of the surgeon general.* Washington, DC: U.S. Department of Health and Human Services, Centers for Disease Control and Prevention, National Center for Chronic Disease Prevention and Health Promotion.

Wadden, T. A., Foster, G. D., & Brownell, K. D. (2002). Obesity: Responding to the global epidemic. *Journal of Consulting and Clinical Psychology, 70*, 510–525.

Wallberg-Henriksson, H. (1992). Interaction of exercise and insulin in type 2 diabetes mellitus. *Diabetes Care, 15*, 1777–1782.

Wallberg-Henriksson, H., Rincon, J., & Zierath, J. R. (1998). Exercise in the management of non-insulin-dependent diabetes mellitus. *Sports Medicine, 25*(1), 25–35.

Wang, G., Helmick, C. G., Macera, C., Zhang, P., & Pratt, M. (2001). Inactivity-associated medical costs among U.S. adults with arthritis. *Arthritis Care & Research, 45*, 439–445.

Wannamethee, S. G., Shaper, A. G., & Walker, M. (2000). Physical activity and mortality in older men with diagnosed coronary heart disease. *Circulation, 102*, 1358–1363.

Washburn, R. A. (2000). Assessment of physical activity in older adults. *Research Quarterly for Exercise and Sport, 71*(2), 79–88.

Wei, M., Kampert, J. B., Barlow, C. E., Nichaman, M. Z., Gibbons, L. W., Paffenbarger, R. S., Gibbons, L. W., & Blair, S. N. (1999). Relationship between low cardiorespiratory fitness and mortality in normal weight, overweight, and obese men. *Journal of the American Medical Association, 282*, 1547–1553.

White, J. A., Wright, V., & Hudson, A. M. (1993). Relationship between habitual physical activity and osteoarthritis in aging women. *Public Health, 107*, 459–470.

Wing, R. R. (1999). Physical activity in the treatment of the adulthood overweight and obesity: Current evidence and research issues. *Medicine & Science in Sports & Exercise, 31*, S547–S552.

Wood, T. M. (2000). Issues and future directions in assessing physical activity: An introduction to the conference proceedings. *Research Quarterly for Exercise and Sport, 71*(2), ii–vii.

World Health Organization. (1998). *Obesity: Preventing and managing the world epidemic.* Geneva: Author.

Yelin, E. (1992). The cumulative impact of a common chronic condition. *Arthritis Rheum, 33,* 750–755.

CHAPTER 10

Stress and Health

Frank L. Collins, Jr., Kristen H. Sorocco, Kimberly R. Haala, Brian I. Miller, and William R. Lovallo

Although stress may not cause disease, it has been established that stress may be a risk factor for the development of disease, may aggravate an existing disease, and may reduce a compliance and treatment success. As a result, many health professionals frequently refer clients to clinical health psychologists for help in dealing with stress-related issues. Clients referred in this manner frequently have a basic understanding that emotional and psychological factors influence health (often seen as the mind influencing the body); however, they frequently do not understand the mechanisms involved in this process. Likewise, clinical health psychologists may have an in-depth understanding of effective treatment methods for reducing stress while having only an elementary understanding of the physiological foundations that can help to guide a more sophisticated conceptualization and treatment for these disorders. The major goals of this chapter are to (a) provide health professionals with a model to use with clients, (b) review the literature on models of coping, and (c) provide information assessment and treatment strategies.

WHAT EXACTLY IS STRESS?

To understand the complexities of the construct we call stress, it is important to have a basic understanding of how the body is organized. The body is a complex machine that functions in a hierarchical manner. At the most basic level, individual organs and tissues have self-regulating properties that allow the body to maintain normal function (homeostasis) when external conditions are constant. However, individual organs and tissues are not able to respond to rapid changes (challenges) in the environment or coordinate their responses with other bodily systems. Therefore, higher levels in the nervous system modulate the self-regulation of tissues and organs when homeostasis is threatened. Modulation in self-regulatory functioning is achieved through the receipt of sensory inputs, integrated control over target tissues, endocrine outflow, and autonomic function. This process is discussed in further detail later in this chapter.

In its simplest form, stress involves a stressor and stress response that challenge the body's ability to maintain homeostasis. A stressor is any physical or mental challenge to the body that threatens homeostasis. Physical stressors are events that challenge the body to function beyond normal capacity (McEwen, 2000). Examples of physical stressors include bodily injury, physical exertion, noise, overcrowding, and excessive heat or cold. Physical stressors are generated through internal mechanisms and are a bottom-up process. Alternatively, psychological stressors are top-down processes that challenge an individual's mental capacity. Psychological stressors include challenges such as time-pressured tasks, speech tasks, mental arithmetic, interpersonal conflict, overcrowding, isolation, and traumatic life events. Therefore, both a physical stressor, such as being trapped outside in below-freezing temperatures, and a psychological stressor, such as participating in a public speaking task, can challenge the homeostasis of the body.

A stress response may consist of both a behavioral response and physiological response. A behavioral response is any action taken on the environment, such as quickly leaving a dangerous situation or implementing a coping skill, whereas a physiological response is an alteration in physiological functioning that serves to restore an imbalance in homeostatic functioning. Examples of physiological responses include an increase in blood pressure, elevated heart rate, impaired memory and decision-making abilities, and altered metabolism. Both behavioral and physiological responses to a stressor may be associated with a negative affective state for the individual.

Most individuals can identify stressors they experience in their daily lives as well as how they experience the negative effects of stress. However, what goes on between the stressor and the stress response in terms of physiology is less clearly understood by clients with whom health professionals come into contact. By educating clients on the psychological and physiological mechanisms of stress, health professionals can teach clients the adaptive role of the stress response to episodic stressors and the detrimental physical and psychological effects caused by chronic long-term stress.

Physiology of the Psychological Stress Response

After any external event occurs, sensory information related to the event is processed within the corticolimbic system (Figure 10.1). In general, the corticolimbic system is responsible for threat appraisals and the processing of emotions. The corticolimbic system is composed of multiple brain structures, including the thalamus, sensory cortex, prefrontal cortex, memory system, and amygdala. As an individual experiences an external event in the environment, sensory information is relayed from the thalamus to the sensory cortex. From the sensory cortex, the information is relayed to the prefrontal cortex, which is responsible for decision making and planning. Interestingly, the prefrontal cortex is tied to the person's memory system, so incoming information is evaluated based on his or her prior memories. The appraisal process is completed in the prefrontal cortex, which communicates with the amygdala, the region in the brain where emotions are processed.

One of the main functions of the corticolimbic system during the stress response is the appraisal of potential threats in the environment. Lazarus and Folkman's (1984) model of coping distinguishes between two types of appraisals that occur during a stress response. A primary appraisal is responsible for determining the magnitude of the threat such as immediate danger. If a threat appraisal is made, secondary appraisals help an individual to evaluate ways in which to cope with the stressor. For example, if a threat appraisal indicates immediate danger, the corticolimbic system immediately activates the peripheral nervous system to signal the body to engage in behaviors that initiate movement.

After primary and secondary appraisals have been made indicating a threat, the corticolimbic system also sends a message to the hypothalamus in addition to the message that was sent to the peripheral nervous system

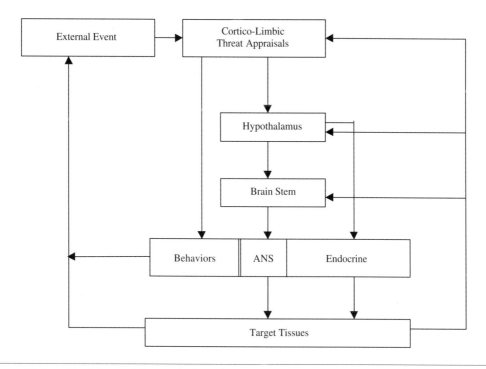

Figure 10.1 Physiology of the Psychological Stress Response

NOTE: ANS = autonomic nervous system.

signaling the body to move. The hypothalamus is responsible for coordinating the nervous system and controls the autonomic nervous system via the brain stem. The autonomic nervous system is divided into three main branches: the sympathetic nervous system, the parasympathetic nervous system, and the entric nervous system. For the purposes of this chapter, only the sympathetic and parasympathetic nervous systems are discussed. Both the sympathetic and parasympathetic nervous systems are involved in maintaining homeostasis. The sympathetic nervous system is usually responsible for increasing the activation of bodily systems (flight-fight response), whereas the parasympathetic nervous system is responsible for feeding, energy storage, and reproduction. The brain stem itself can initiate changes in the autonomic nervous system in single organs and tissues but is not efficient at coordinating across organs or between systems. The role of the autonomic nervous

system in the stress response is to prepare the body to respond to the stressor.

The hypothalamus, as a coordinator between systems, also communicates with the endocrine system during a stress response. There are two main endocrine functions during a stress response: the adrenocortical response and the adrenomedullary response. The adrenocortical response releases cortisol into the body during a stress response. Cortisol is released through multiple steps. First, the paraventricular nucleus of the hypothalamus releases corticotropin-releasing factor (CRF), which travels to the pituitary gland. CRF causes the secretion of adrenocorticotropin in the anterior pituitary gland and the secretion of cortisol in the adrenal cortex. Cortisol is then released from the adrenal cortex. Cortisol as a hormone is always present in the body, indicating its importance in normal functioning, but the levels vary due to both time of day (diurnal pattern) and current stressors. Cortisol is responsible for increasing sympathetic nervous system function, releasing stored glucose and fats for energy, and suppressing immune function.

Another stress hormone that is important to the stress response is epinephrine, also known as adrenaline. The adrenomedullary response releases epinephrine into general circulation in response to the increase in sympathetic nervous system activity caused by the release of cortisol. Epinephrine increases relative to the stress response and assists in coordinating bodily systems to make both behavioral and metabolic changes necessary to deal with the stressor. More specifically, epinephrine stimulates heart muscles, increasing heart rate and oxygen levels to prepare the body to respond to the stressor.

After the first three components of a stress response occur, regulation of the autonomic nervous system and endocrine system is maintained by negative feedback. Information on cortisol and epinephrine output is sent from tissues and organs to the brain stem, hypothalamus, and corticolimbic system, where the decision to continue production of cortisol and epinephrine is made. If production of these hormones is no longer needed, messages are sent to the pituitary and adrenal glands to discontinue output.

Negative Physiological Impacts of Chronic Stress

Walter Cannon, a physiologist who first introduced the term *stress,* distinguished between short-term and long-term stressors (Carlson, 1999). He discussed the fact that physiologically we were built to deal with episodic stressors rather than chronic stressors. The stress response is designed to deal efficiently with episodic stressors; however, there are negative physiological and psychological consequences when an individual is under chronic stress. The negative physiological consequences resulting from chronic stress are due to the prolonged activation of the stress response, which cannot be easily eliminated by behavioral and psychological mechanisms.

If we reexamine the physiology of the stress response, some of the negative consequences of chronic stress become evident. To begin with, cortisol and epinephrine, the hormones released during the stress response, have detrimental effects when they are released continuously. For example, one of the roles of cortisol is to suppress the immune function, which episodically is fine but which over a long period of time leaves an individual susceptible to illness (Lovallo, 1997). Chronic stress also increases the amount of time it takes for a wound to heal. For example, Kiecolt-Glaser, Marucha, Malarkey, Mercado, and Glaser (1995) examined the length of time it took for punch biopsy wounds to heal in individuals caring for a relative with Alzheimer's disease and found that wounds took significantly longer to heal in caregivers under chronic stress in comparison with control participants. The continuous release of cortisol also might be related to the sleep problems commonly reported among individuals experiencing chronic stressors. As was mentioned earlier, cortisol is released diurnally two times per day: once during the morning and then again after lunch. Researchers have found that the continuous release of cortisol decreases rapid eye movement (REM) sleep, which is essential to normal sleep cycles (Vgontzas, Bixler, & Kales, 2000).

In addition, the release of epinephrine during the stress response can put individuals experiencing chronic stress at risk for cardiovascular disease (Pollard, 2000). Epinephrine stimulates cardiac muscles, resulting in an increased heart rate and potentially hypertension. Epinephrine also is involved in increasing blood platelet adhesiveness and in reducing clotting time, both of which are risk factors for myocardial infarctions and cerebrovascular accidents (Markovitz & Matthews, 1991).

Chronic stressors also can negatively affect individuals psychologically. As discussed previously, the second stage in the stress response after experiencing a stressor is the appraisal process. During the appraisal process, emotions are generated, and emotions in turn influence an individual's mood. Chronic stress can lead to a negative mood state such as depression or anxiety. Negative mood states can influence how a person appraises situations by serving as a filter through which he or she interprets information from the environment. How the person appraises environmental events influences the duration of the stress response because it can be considered the highest level of control over homeostatic functioning (Lovallo, 1997).

Although the human body is designed to deal with episodic stressors, chronic stress can negatively affect both the physiological and psychological functioning of an individual. However, individual differences resulting from both genetics and life experiences influence how individuals respond to stressors. In fact, two individuals who experience the same traumatic event might react to the stressor completely differently depending on each individual's access to coping resources. By studying how individuals respond to stress, researchers have been able to develop coping models for stress and to identify effective treatment interventions designed to help individuals develop coping skills.

MODELS OF STRESS

As noted previously, at the most basic level, stress involves two processes: an environmental event (stressor) and a physiological response (stress response). Over the years, models of stress have differentially focused on these two components, with most contemporary models focusing on stress as a transactional process (Cassidy, 1999). A comprehensive review of the strengths and weaknesses of each model is beyond the scope of this chapter; however, clinical health psychologists need to have familiarity with these major approaches

and how these models are translated into treatment options.

Stimulus Models

Stimulus models focus on environmental events that produce demand on the organism. Early research in this area (cf. Brown & Harris, 1978; Holmes & Rahe, 1967) led to a focus on negative life events as a major source of stress. Intervention efforts focused on learning to deal more effectively with these demands (coping) or on learning to predict and (where appropriate) minimize exposure to negative life events. Cassidy (1999) argued that these models primarily served a classification role, providing researchers and clinicians with necessary tools for identification of individuals experiencing stress. Intervention, particularly stress management strategies, has moved beyond stimulus models.

Response Models

Stress is frequently identified by the presence of specific symptoms that include overt behavioral, physiological, and cognitive symptoms. These symptoms are the natural consequences of demand, and although one cannot separate stress responses from stressors, focus on response models has played a major role in the development of treatment strategies typically labeled "stress management" (cf. Lehrer & Woolfolk, 1993).

These models use a bottom-up explanation rather than a top-down basis as in the appraisal models. Much of the theory behind these models comes out of biofeedback and relaxation research as well as from Eastern philosophy. The basic premise of these models is that stress can be influenced by a person's level of autonomic arousal. In other words, if a person is experiencing high levels of arousal, the person will feel as though he or she is under more stress. If the arousal is reduced, the person will subjectively experience lower amounts of stress. This may occur even if the demands on the person have not been reduced or changed.

In relation to this, it is believed that the perception of controllability of arousal may also influence stress levels. People who experience high levels of arousal and do not feel as though they can control that arousal may report more stress than do people who experience the same levels of arousal but feel as though they have control over their arousal.

Appraisal Models

Appraisal models view psychological stress as a process whereby an individual interprets or views environmental events and perceived coping ability that in turn shapes his or her emotional, behavioral, and physiological responses to events. Appraisal theories suggest that the person "appraises" an event in an attempt to discern its meaning in the context of his or her experiences. These appraisals lead to decisions regarding whether or not the event is viewed as threatening or harmful and what actions would be appropriate under the circumstances.

Appraisal models are a natural outgrowth of stimulus and response models. Appraisal of an event by definition requires that an event occur. Thus, it should be no surprise that many events that would be labeled as stressors are in fact appraised as high demand. Likewise, when a person appraises an event as high demand, the natural consequence of such an appraisal is behaviors, emotions, and/or cognitions that fit the definition of a stress response.

Lazarus's model (Lazarus, 1966, 1999; Lazarus & Folkman, 1984) is the most widely accepted stress model. As noted previously, Lazarus divided the appraisal process into two distinct parts: primary and secondary. Primary appraisals are intended to determine the threat value of an event. They take into consideration the familiarity of the event, the beliefs of the person, and commitments. An event can be perceived as stressful or benign. Stress appraisals, whether positive or negative, lead to autonomic arousal.

Lazarus proposed three types of stress appraisals: harm/loss, threat, and challenge. Harm/loss appraisals occur in cases where damage has already occurred. For instance, a harm/loss appraisal would occur when a person has become ill or injured, lost a loved one, or suffered a blow to his or her self-esteem. Threat appraisals occur when harm or loss can be anticipated but has not yet occurred. These are different from harm/loss appraisals mainly in that threat appraisals allow the person to plan and adapt to minimize or alleviate some of the harm before it occurs. The third type of stress appraisal is challenge. Challenge appraisals are more positive in that the focus is on opportunity to achieve growth or to gain something from the event. These categories are not necessarily exclusive. There may be, and often are, situations in which threat and challenge appraisals are experienced from the same event.

Once primary appraisal determines that an event is stressful, a person must choose what he or she is going to do about the situation. This is where secondary appraisals come in. Secondary appraisals evaluate the person's available options for coping with a stressful event and the possible consequences of those actions. These appraisals take into account personal resources and the limitations of the environment.

Appraisals rarely occur in this linear fashion. Rather, primary and secondary appraisals may occur almost simultaneously, and changes in the event, new information, and/or changes in the level of perceived threat may alter a person's appraisals. Lazarus referred to these new appraisals as reappraisals. A person reappraises an event when there are changes that may affect the stressfulness of the event or his or her ability to cope with it.

Coping responses are generated from the appraisal process. According to Lazarus, coping refers to constantly changing cognitive and behavioral efforts to manage specific external and/or internal demands that are appraised as taxing or exceeding the resources of the person. Coping can be divided into two types of responses: problem focused and emotion focused. Problem-focused responses operate directly on the situation itself and may include behaviors aimed at increasing personal resources, altering the event, and/or generating alternative solutions. Emotion-focused coping is directed at lessening the emotional distress caused by the event. Little or no effort is devoted to changing the event that caused the distress. This type of coping includes strategies such as avoidance, reappraising the situation, distancing, and selective attention. As with the division between types of appraisals, the boundary between problem-focused coping and emotion-focused coping is somewhat blurred. People often engage in a coping strategy that serves both purposes or use more than one strategy at the same time to serve both purposes.

Problem-focused strategies can be costly early on because of the energy and time that they require. However, they can lead to alterations in the event that lessen its stress value and so lessen the amount of coping that continues to be needed. Emotion-focused strategies are not as costly early on, but if the situation remains stressful, these coping responses can lead to a continued drain on resources. Once a coping response has been used, the situation is reappraised taking into account changes a person has made to the situation or his or her response to it. In this way, the appraisal process is circular and recurrent.

SYMPTOMS OF CHRONIC STRESS

Chronic exposure to stress can lead to a variety of impairments in many domains. People who are under chronic stress report a number of symptoms. Some of these symptoms are vague and do not greatly affect their functioning, whereas others can be quite severe and troubling to patients. Stress can lead to emotional impairments such as inappropriate crying, nervousness, edginess, anger, and irritability. In addition, patients experiencing chronic stress may feel overwhelmed, powerless, and isolated. They may report general feelings of unhappiness and dissatisfaction. They may report feeling that life has no meaning anymore. Some patients may appear cynical or apathetic. They may report that they feel empty or directionless, and they may have a strong urge to try to prove themselves.

People experiencing chronic stress often exhibit cognitive problems such as foggy thinking, distractibility, and forgetfulness. They often say that they cannot stop worrying. Some patients report that they cannot seem to be creative anymore or have no sense of humor. Chronic stress can also lead to behavioral problems and trouble in relationships. Stressed people may be bossy and critical of others and themselves. They may take up alcoholism or smoking, or they may begin to eat or chew gum compulsively. Spouses or partners of stressed individuals often report that their significant others grind their teeth in their sleep, have a lowered sex drive, and have "clammed up." Stressed people may also seem resentful or intolerant of others and may isolate themselves.

In addition to these impairments in a wide range of functioning, people experiencing chronic stress may experience a number of physical symptoms. Patients commonly report headaches, fatigue, restlessness, and sleep disturbances. Patients also report unexplained backaches, painful muscle tension, and gastrointestinal discomfort such as stomachaches and indigestion. Patients may also have an increased heart rate and increased blood pressure.

Effects of Stress on Health

As noted earlier, stress increases the risk of disease. This can occur via the numerous symptoms just described or through the effects of stress on the immune system. In addition, stress can exacerbate already existing disease states or can impede recovery from an illness. Although the effects of stress on health have been widely studied, there has been little conclusive evidence on the mechanism by which these effects occur.

Immune Function. The immune function is very complex, involving many different antibodies and activities. One of the acute effects of stress is to suppress immune functioning and thereby increase infection susceptibility. Stress leads to increased adrenaline secretion, which suppresses the production of some antibodies, decreases macrophage activity, and decreases interleukin production. Reduced immune function can increase a person's chances of viral and bacterial infection, which may lead to illnesses such as the common cold and mononucleosis. For instance, Cohen, Tyrrell, and Smith (1991) placed a cold virus in the nasal passages of participants. They found that participants who had reported high levels of stress within the past year were much more likely to become infected than were those who reported low levels of stress.

Cardiovascular Disease. Stress may also exacerbate or lead to cardiovascular disease. Chronic stress elevates blood pressure and serum cholesterol levels. In addition, some evidence suggests that chronic central nervous system hyperactivity reduces the body's sensitivity to insulin, and this also increases blood pressure.

Gastrointestinal Disorders. Stress also affects the gastrointestinal tract. It can increase colonic contractions or can lead to spasms in the colon. There may also be increased muscle tension in the abdominal area as well as throughout the body. Stress may also increase pain sensitivity. Consequently, people who experience chronic stress may be seen for disorders such as irritable bowel syndrome, Chron's disease, and general gastric discomfort.

Sleep Disorders. As listed previously, some of the symptoms of stress include nervousness and constant worrying. These symptoms, as well as other stress effects, can lead to interruptions in sleep patterns. Stress often leads to insomnia and frequent nighttime waking. Sleep efficiency is usually lowered, and people may report feeling tired and worn out even after receiving a full night's sleep.

Anxiety and Depression. As can be seen from the list of symptoms earlier, stress often leads to feelings of anxiety and depression, and this can become a problem in itself for some patients.

Substance Abuse. Some substances have a stress-relieving effect, and some patients may resort to substance abuse as a way of coping with their high stress levels.

ASSESSMENT OF STRESS AND TREATMENT OF STRESS

The exclusion of "stress disorders" from the DSM-IV (*Diagnostic and Statistical Manual of Mental Disorders,* fourth edition [American Psychiatric Association, 1994]) as a distinct category has led to a wide variety of methods used in the measurement of stress. From the clinical health psychologist's perspective, the most important criterion for diagnosing a given complaint as a clinical stress problem is the judgment that it is amenable to improvement by changing the way in which the person perceives or manages his or her transactions with the immediate environment. Therefore, the diagnosis of a clinical stress problem has less to do with the etiology or severity of the problem itself than with the prediction of its responsiveness to the teaching of coping skills.

Assessment

One of the primary ways in which the physician assesses preliminary signs of stress is the patient's self-report via questionnaires and/or a clinical interview. Self-report questionnaires typically allow the patient to rate whether a symptom is present or absent as well as the severity of the symptom. Clinical interviews are often designed to allow the physician to use a checklist format for quick and efficient diagnoses.

Two of the more frequently used scales to assess stressors are the Life Events Survey (Sarason, Johnson, & Siegel, 1978) and the Daily Hassles and Uplifts Scale (Kanner, Coyne, Schaefer, & Lazarus, 1981). The Life Events Survey consists of 57 items, and the client checks each event that has ever happened to him or her. Then the client rates each of these items positively or negatively in terms of desirability and impact at the time the event occurred. Each item is rated on a 7-point scale from −3 to +3, with the sum indicating the client's life events experience. Sarason and colleagues (1978) noted that negative scores are the best predictor of health problems.

The Daily Hassles and Uplifts Scale was developed to address more minor events in a person's life. This 143-item survey has generated enormous numbers of research studies focusing on the types of stressors found for individuals with various disease states (e.g., VanHoudenhove et al., 2002) as well as on differences in stressful experiences of particular high-risk populations (e.g., McCallum, Arnold, & Bolland, 2002). In addition, psychometric research evaluating the questionnaire indicates that for some populations, the order in which items are presented influences ratings. Specifically, events are rated as less uplifting when they follow hassle items than when they precede hassle items (Mayberry et al., 2002).

Life events can also be measured as part of a structured or unstructured interview. Brown and Harris (1978) developed a structured interview format called the Bedford College Interview for Life Events and Difficulties, which has been found to be both reliable and potentially more useful because it allows trained raters to evaluate contextual factors surrounding specific life events. For example, someone who lost a parent following a prolonged illness that preceded the death may view the "loss of a parent" event quite differently from someone who lost a parent in an unexpected accident.

Symptoms of stress can be measured using common emotional scales, including the Spielberger anxiety (Spielberger, Gorsuch, Lushene, Vagg, & Jacobs, 1983) and anger (Spielberger, 1996) scales (for a review, see Spielberger, Sydeman, Owen, & Marsh, 1999), the Beck inventories (Beck Depression Inventory-II [Beck, Steer, & Brown, 1996] and Beck Anxiety Inventory [Beck, 1990]), and broad-based measures such as the Symptom Checklist 90–Revised (Derogatis, 1975).

Treatment

The treatment of stress disorders often falls into one of two types: treatments aimed at reducing central nervous system activation and treatments designed to address problems in appraisal or coping skills. Treatment techniques that involve the alteration of appraisals often incorporate cognitive strategies to alter and improve the competitiveness-readiness level, whereas central nervous system activation reduction techniques focus on lowering or controlling physiological arousal, anxiety, and muscular tension. It should be noted that the term *stress management* is typically used to describe a number of treatment techniques designed to reduce stress rather than referring to any one specific method. Lehrer and Woolfolk provided detailed chapters on the methods and approaches that fit this broad category of "stress management" (Lehrer & Woolfolk, 1993; Woolfolk & Lehrer, 1984). In the current chapter, several of the most common methods are merely outlined.

Training in these individual techniques should be done under close supervision as part of a formal training program.

Treatments That Focus on Central Nervous System Reduction

Relaxation methods encompass a range of techniques, each with unique properties; however, all share the goal of creating a relaxation response. This response is designed to activate the parasympathetic nervous system, resulting in a decrease in oxygen consumption, heart rate, respiration, and skeletal muscle activity along with an increase in skin resistance and alpha brain waves. Four factors have been identified as important for eliciting a relaxation response: a mental device (a word, a phrase, or an object to shift attention inward), a passive attitude, decreased muscle tonus, and a quiet environment. The ultimate goal of relaxation training is to evoke the relaxation response to counter situational stress.

Progressive Relaxation. Modern progressive relaxation techniques were derived from Edmond Jacobson's work during the early part of the 20th century. The main premise of his approach was that it is impossible to be nervous or tense when skeletal muscles are completely relaxed. Jacobson noted that relaxation is a fundamental physiological occurrence that consists of systematically learning to elongate muscle fibers. For this reason, the use of suggestion by the progressive relaxation instructor should be abandoned given that the perception of relaxation is not so important as actual physiological relaxation (McGuigan, 1993).

Jacobson's full progressive relaxation procedure involves systematically tensing and relaxing specific muscle groups in a predetermined order and was described in great detail by McGuigan (1993). The individual is instructed to tense a muscle before relaxing it to help him or her recognize the difference between tension and relaxation. To first become familiar with the sensation of tension, the learner is instructed to lie on his or her back with arms at the sides and to bend the wrist up at a 90-degree angle. The learner perceives tension in the forearm. Next the learner performs much of the same task except that this time the wrist is bent at a 45-degree angle, producing less tension. This method is repeated again at increasingly smaller angles. Using this method of diminishing tensions teaches the learner to detect not only high tension but even the most minute tension.

Relaxation begins with the instructor explaining the basic physiology of neuromuscular circuits and the nature of tension and relaxation. The learning environment can be quite varied; classrooms, gymnasiums, and conference rooms all provide learners with something soft to lie on such as mats, blankets, or thick carpets. In clinical treatment, individual rooms with cots, pillows, and blankets are often provided. It should be noted that complete elimination of external distraction is not desired because the normal environment in which the individual will be relaxing can be quite noisy. Relaxation starts with the muscles of the left arm and proceeds to the right arm, left and right legs, abdomen, back, chest, and shoulder muscles and then concludes with the neck and face muscles. The starting position is with the learner lying on his or her back, with the arms by the sides. Only one position is practiced each hour. The control signal, which for the position with the hand bent back is the vague sensation in the upper surface of the forearm, is observed three times during each period. This is the critical signal that the individual is to learn and recognize. The tensed position is held for a minute or so, and then the "power goes off" (relaxing the signal away) for a few minutes.

During this initial session, the learner will make a few common mistakes, and it is the instructor's crucial job to catch and correct these mistakes. These include misidentifying a control signal as a strain and making an effort to relax by working the hand down to a "resting" position, which is merely adding more tension, instead of allowing the hand to simply collapse.

The amount of time required to learn progressive relaxation may seem excessive from a naive learner's point of view. Attempts to shorten the process have not yielded satisfactory results. Jacobson explained that a body that has been practicing overtension for decades will not be able to reverse the process in brief sessions. Children, however, have been shown to learn progressive relaxation quite rapidly, probably because they have not had as many years practicing maladaptive tension habits.

Abbreviated Progressive Relaxation Training. Condensed versions of progressive relaxation have been linked to the work of Wolpe (1958), who developed a "short" version of progressive relaxation for treating phobias (Bernstein & Carlson, 1993). Abbreviated progressive relaxation was standardized and popularized by Bernstein and Borkovec (1973) in their classic text, *Progressive Relaxation Training,* and is the source citation for many clinical intervention studies using progressive relaxation (Hillenberg & Collins, 1982).

Bernstein and Carson (1993) provided a detailed review of abbreviated procedures, which are summarized here. In the initial training session, 16 muscle groups are the focus of tension release procedures. The client is typically asked to recline during the introduction. The order in which the muscle groups are taught is standardized, and the therapist demonstrates the tensing methods and then paces the client through the series of tension release procedures. The client is encouraged to practice relaxation skills twice a day, 15 to 20 minutes each time, with continued training in sessions paced by the therapist.

Autogenic Training. Autogenic training was developed by Johannes Heinrich Schultz following his own observations of individuals under hypnosis and Oskar Vogt's observations in brain research (Linden, 1993). Schultz noticed that hypnotized patients would report a heaviness of the limbs and a warmth sensation. Hypnosis was believed to be something that patients allowed to happen to themselves, not something that the therapist did to them. The objective of autogenic training is to permit self-regulation in either direction (deep relaxation or augmentation of a physiological activity) through "passive concentration," also described as "self-hypnosis." Training can be taught individually or in groups. The ideal setting should be one at room temperature, slightly darkened, with a couch or exercise mats and pillows.

Biofeedback Methods. In general, biofeedback systems operate by detecting changes in the biological environment and conveying this information to the client in the form of visual and auditory signals (Stoyva & Budzynski, 1993). The client then synthesizes this information with a trial-and-error strategy to cause the signals to change in the desired direction; thus, the client learns how to control the biological response system. It is further intended that the client will be gradually weaned away from the biofeedback signal, allowing for the transfer of control into everyday life.

The most common form of biofeedback used in stress management is electromyographic (EMG) feedback. EMG feedback operates by detecting biological signals and providing visual or auditory signals linked to this biological system via amplification of the psychophysiological measures. This immediate feedback is thought to facilitate learning to control or reduce arousal through trial-and-error strategies designed to produce changes in the signal in a desired direction (Stoyva & Budzynski, 1993).

EMG feedback offers a number of specific advantages as compared with traditional non-biofeedback relaxation therapies in that it provides a direct measure of client learning through the monitoring of muscular activity rather than depending on the client's verbal report of relaxation. EMG data quantify physiological relationships and operationalize the concept of relaxation. Some drawbacks associated with biofeedback are that the client may become dependent on the machine and that it provides minimal training in coping strategies for reducing tension.

Yoga-Based Stress Management. Yoga methods have had the most popularity in the treatment of hypertension (Patel, 1993). This technique appears to reduce stress in part by helping the client to reframe the stressor in a nonthreatening fashion. Yoga, which means "union," is an Indian philosophy that presents various values, techniques, and disciplines to teach ways of establishing harmony by developing the mind among the various sides of life. The sides of human life are both material (body) and nonmaterial (mind and soul). Different techniques or combinations are used depending on whether one's intellect, emotions, or actions dominate. The main components of yoga include 14 breathing exercises (which facilitate regulation of the mind and body), 200 balanced physical postures (which help to prevent musculoskeletal deterioration), and exercises for awakening "kundalini" (the energy reservoir at the base of the spinal cord). Yoga is based on a belief that life can be conceptualized as a gaseous exchange that takes place between "inspired" (oxygenated) air and the blood circulating in the lungs. Deep muscle relaxation, visualization, and meditation all are components of yoga-based therapies, further illustrating yoga's emphasis ranging from the physical to the spiritual in nature. For a more in-depth review of yoga methods, the reader is referred to Patel (1993), who provides a detailed summary of these methods.

Meditation. Although meditation is often viewed as a yoga-based technique, Carrington (1978) introduced a "clinically standardized meditation procedure" that appears to be useful for reducing stress symptoms in a range of health-related disorders (see also Carrington, 1993). Meditation can be divided into two distinct forms: concentrative and nonconcentrative. The concentrative forms of meditation are simple to learn. The techniques are often practiced in a quiet environment, with the object of the meditator's attention being a mentally repeated sound, the meditator's breath, or some other appropriate focal sound (e.g., running water). If attention is found to be wandering, the meditator is directed back to the attentional object in an unforceful manner. A nonconcentrative technique expands the meditator's attentional field to include as much of his or her conscious mental activity as possible. In this sense, the specific techniques of meditation are secondary to the actual experience of meditation in bringing about therapeutic change.

In summary, there are many paths to the reduction of sympathetic nervous system activation, producing a shift toward lower arousal characterized by parasympathetic nervous system dominance. Because the stress response is characterized by a heightened sympathetic tone, shifting autonomic dominance to the parasympathetic nervous system should be effective in moderating stress and anxiety reactions regardless of the methods used. Schwartz (1993) pointed out that although numerous methods are available for stress management, client characteristics may lead the therapist to consider alternative strategies that might best fit clients' life histories and experiences and that might be more appealing to clients. Therapists who develop skills in multiple methods will be in a better position to provide clients with methods that are both evidence based and philosophically consistent with client expectations.

COGNITIVE APPROACHES TO STRESS

Cognitive approaches conceptualize stress as the result of an active cognitive set that includes successive appraisals of environmental demands and the risks, costs, and gains of specific coping responses. When an individual's vital interests appear to be challenged, cognitive processes provide a selective conceptualization of what is occurring. Beck (1993) provided an in-depth review of cognitive approaches to stress management that are summarized in the current chapter.

The initial appraisal of an event can be considered a quick scan to determine whether it is pleasant, neutral, or noxious. When the vital interests (harm or enhancement) of an individual (egocentric view) are assessed to be affected, a critical response ensues. An emergency critical response is activated when the individual perceives a threat to his or her survival, domain, individuality, or status. This response is critical to the development of stress reactions. At the same time the situation is evaluated as a threat, the individual is assessing his or her resources for dealing with the ensuing problem. This assessment is labeled "secondary appraisal" (Lazarus, 1966).

The basic rationale behind the treatment of stress from a cognitive perspective is that certain idiosyncratic cognitive patterns become hyperactive and lead to the overmobilization of the voluntary nervous system and autonomic nervous system. When this occurs, the protective buffers and adaptive functions (e.g., objectivity, perspective, reality testing) are rendered ineffective against the cognitive constellation that has been triggered. This overmobilization directly results in reactive syndromes (e.g., anxiety, hostility) or psychosomatic syndromes. In the long term, these physical effects can lead to dysfunction of specific systems or organs (e.g., musculoskeletal, cardiovascular, gastrointestinal). Therefore, the ultimate goal of therapy is to reduce the dominance of the controlling constellation of cognitions and to allow the protective buffers' adaptive functions to take over.

An initial treatment approach often includes directly reducing the exposure of the stressful stimuli to the individual. This serves to reduce the intensity of the cognitive constellations, reduce the mobilization of the neuromuscular endocrine system, and increase perspective and objectivity. This sets the stage for the individual to now reflect on his or her reactions, test other options, and adopt a broader and more realistic view of the situation. The specific terms for the previously described treatment are as follows: identifying automatic thoughts ("What am I thinking now?"), recognizing and correcting cognitive distortions ("It does not have to mean this; it is probably that"), and identifying the broad beliefs and assumptions that underlie the hyperactive constellations ("I'm a bad person and I don't deserve good things"). The process described previously outlines the process known as cognitive restructuring or the ABC approach. The premise is that the antecedent or event leads to thoughts and feelings that ultimately drive the individual's behavior. By changing the way in which the individual thinks about the events, the person will be able to change his or her behavior. In respect to this chapter, the individual will be able to reduce the stress response by "seeing the problem in another light" using this systematic approach.

Stress Inoculation Training

Stress inoculation training is based on the premise that bolstering (inoculating) an individual's repertoire of coping responses to milder stressors can serve to defuse responses to major life stressors (for a more extensive review, see Meichenbaum, 1993). This is accomplished with the use of an overlapping three-phase intervention approach. The goal of the initial phase is to establish a relationship between the trainer and the client to help the client better understand the nature of stress and its effects on emotions and behavior. Similarly to the cognitive approach, this initial phase focuses on getting the client to appreciate how he or she appraises both events and on his or her ability to cope with the events. In addition, alternative explanations and alternatives are explored. At the end of the initial phase, a reconceptualization of the client's problems is made.

The second phase focuses on coping skills acquisition and rehearsal of these skills. Attention is paid to removing factors that may interfere with adequate coping such as maladaptive beliefs and feelings of low self-efficacy. The skills are practiced initially in the training setting, with gradual introduction in vivo.

The final phase of stress inoculation training calls for the client to apply the variety of learned coping skills across increasing levels ("inoculation") of stressors on a graduated basis. This is accomplished by imagery and behavioral rehearsal, modeling, role-playing, and graded in vivo exposure. Attention is also allocated to relapse prevention. The client is taught how to handle a lapse and not allow for it to become a relapse. In summary, stress inoculation training combines client self-monitoring, cognitive restructuring, problem solving, self-instructional and relaxation training, behavioral and imagined rehearsal, and environmental change, with the goal of enabling the client to be flexible in his or her coping repertoire and to have the confidence to cope resourcefully.

Summary

As this brief review illustrates, there are many approaches to stress management. Cognitive approaches focus on a "top-down" method, with the primary goal being the reduction of cognitions that, if unchecked, begin a cascade of behavioral and biological processes that include autonomic nervous system arousal and endocrine activation. Through the modification of appraisal processes, an individual is able to minimize threat and demand, thereby reducing levels of the stress response. Treatments that focus on central nervous system reduction directly can be conceptualized as "bottom-up" methods that directly influence behavioral and biological processes. In addition, some central nervous system reduction methods have been shown to directly influence cognitive processes that show up as enhanced coping and reduced perception of demand based on the individual's "knowing" that he or she now has the skill to reduce arousal directly. The following case study illustrates this point.

CONCLUSIONS

This chapter has provided an overview of the biological and psychosocial factors related to stress. A great deal of attention was given to the biological mechanisms involved in the stress response because this is an aspect of training that is often lacking. As the case study illustrates, assessment and treatment may at times focus on behavioral and cognitive factors; however, knowledge of the biology of stress may help clients to accept psychological treatment.

The treatment methods presented in this chapter were, by necessity, merely summarized. Therapists who have not used relaxation or other anxiety reduction methods should seek out supervised experiences before using these with clients. What at times seems very easy to do can in fact be much more complicated than it appears. As should be noted from both the case study and the early work of Jacobson, it takes a great deal of therapist time to successfully train relaxation skills. Merely sending clients home with a taped session is not sufficient. Likewise, the cognitive interventions require systematic training and should not be attempted without supervised experiences.

CASE STUDY

"Jane M." was referred by her physician for treatment of stress that was thought to be linked to her frequent headaches. Jane had recently been promoted to a managerial position with her company, and the new position required that she visit regional offices in nearby states on a frequent basis. She was on the road several days each week, and for the past 6 months she reported constant fatigue and frequent headaches. While fatigued and tired, she found it difficult to relax at night while on the road.

Baseline assessment included the Daily Hassles and Uplifts Scale, the Spielberger State-Trait Anger Inventory, the Beck Depression Inventory-II, and a clinical interview. Results indicated mild levels of depression and moderate to severe levels of anger. The anger appeared to be most linked to Jane's dissatisfaction with the staff at many of the hotels where she stayed and her inability to be "treated with the respect that she deserved" when problems arose. There were few life events rated as positive, with many minor annoyances receiving very negative ratings.

Although it seemed clear that Jane's stress levels were at times generated by her perceptions of events and expectations that she "should" be treated more respectfully, it was also obvious from early sessions that she was physiologically very tense and quite concerned that her physician believed her problems were all "mental." The therapist spent a great deal of time discussing how negative events start a chain of physiological processes that lead to heightened arousal that for some people result in headaches or other physical problems. For some clients, merely learning to reduce this arousal can be useful. Jane showed a strong interest in learning how to reduce physical arousal, and a treatment plan was developed that initially focused on learning relaxation skills.

The relaxation method used was a form of abbreviated progressive relaxation training developed by Charles R. Carlson (Carlson, Collins, Nitz, Sturgis, & Rogers, 1990; Carlson, Ventralla, & Sturgis, 1987; Kay & Carlson, 1992) called stretch-based relaxation. Stretch-based relaxation focuses on stretching of muscles, facilitating a differentiation of muscle sensations that contributes to a recognition of muscle tension and fosters relaxation of the muscles.

Training was conducted over an 8-week period, with in-session relaxation training taking between 30 and 40 minutes of each session. The remaining time was spent discussing the application of stretch-based relaxation to Jane's daily routine and fine-tuning home practice. Her initial response was that she could not produce the levels of relaxation at home that she experienced in sessions, and these concerns and expectations were addressed with a reminder that she would improve with continued practice. At Session 5, she reported feeling much more effective at home, and in-session training switched from being therapist-led training to client-paced training with the therapist observing Jane's performance.

At Session 6, Jane reported a critical incident where she was checking into a hotel and the night clerk could not find her reservation. It took some time for the clerk to come up with a suitable room, and in the past she would have become physically tense and extremely angry and would have developed a headache that would keep her from sleeping well. She remembered thinking to herself that if she got tense from this "incompetent clerk," she would just use her relaxation skills to calm down once she was in her room and could avoid getting a headache. Not only did she not get a headache that evening, she did not even feel tense while waiting. Discussion with her therapist indicated that the knowledge that she "knew what to do if she got tense" seemed to ward off feelings of tension. She began to entertain the idea that it was not merely the situation that "got her tense"; rather, it was her reaction to the situation (including the expectancy that a headache would ensue) that contributed to her tension.

Sessions 7 and 8 involved a minor review of stretch-based relaxation, with a great deal of the sessions devoted to discussion of how Jane planned to implement this new skill in her life to keep herself more relaxed. Readministration of the Daily Hassles and Uplifts Scale indicated that the number of situations did not change but that the perception of the situations as negative was greatly improved. Headaches had dropped off significantly with more relaxed sleep and energy. Jane was encouraged to continue formally practicing relaxation on at least a weekly basis.

REFERENCES

American Psychiatric Association. (1994). *Diagnostic and statistical manual of mental disorders* (4th ed.). Washington, DC: Author.

Beck, A. T. (1990). *Manual for the Beck Anxiety Inventory.* San Antonio, TX: Psychological Corporation.

Beck, A. T. (1993). Cognitive approaches to stress. In P. M. Lehrer & R. L. Woolfolk (Eds.), *Principles and practice of stress management* (2nd ed., pp. 333–372). New York: Guilford.

Beck, A. T., Steer, R. A., & Brown, G. K. (1996). *Manual for the Beck Depression Inventory-II.* San Antonio, TX: Psychological Corporation.

Bernstein, D. A., & Borkovec, T. D. (1973). *Progressive relaxation training: A manual for the helping professions.* Champaign, IL: Research Press.

Bernstein, D. A., & Carlson, C. R. (1993). Progressive relaxation: Abbreviated methods. In P. M. Lehrer & R. L. Woolfolk (Eds.), *Principles and practice of stress management* (2nd ed., pp. 53–88). New York: Guilford.

Brown, G. W., & Harris, T. O. (1978). *Social origins of depression: A study of psychiatric disorder in women.* London: Tavistock.

Carlson, C. R., Collins, F. L., Nitz, A. J., Sturgis, E. T., & Rogers, J. L. (1990). Muscle stretching as an alternative relaxation training procedure. *Journal of Behavior Therapy and Experimental Psychiatry, 21,* 29–38.

Carlson, C. R., Ventralla, M. A., & Sturgis, E. T. (1987). Relaxation training through muscle stretching procedures: A pilot case. *Journal of Behavior Therapy and Experimental Psychiatry, 18,* 121–126.

Carlson, N. R. (1999). *Foundations of physiological psychology* (4th ed.). Boston: Allyn & Bacon.

Carrington, P. (1978). *Clinically standardized meditation (CSM) instructor's kit.* Kendall Park, NJ: Pace Educational Systems.

Carrington, P. (1993). Modern forms of meditation. In P. M. Lehrer & R. L. Woolfolk (Eds.), *Principles and practice of stress management* (2nd ed., pp. 139–168). New York: Guilford.

Cassidy, T. (1999). *Stress, cognition, and health.* New York: Routledge.

Cohen, S., Tyrrell, D. A. J., & Smith, A. P. (1991). Psychological stress and susceptibility to the common cold. *New England Journal of Medicine, 325,* 606–612.

Derogatis, L. R. (1975). *The Symptom Checklist 90–Revised.* Minneapolis, MN: NCS Assessments.

Hillenberg, J. B., & Collins, F. L. (1982). A procedural analysis and review of relaxation training research. *Behaviour Research and Therapy, 20,* 251–260.

Holmes, T. H., & Rahe, R. (1967). The Social Readjustment Rating Scale. *Journal of Psychosomatic Research, 14,* 213–218.

Kanner, A. D., Coyne, J. C., Schaefer, C., & Lazarus, R. S. (1981). Comparison of two modes of stress measurement: Daily hassles and uplifts versus major life events. *Journal of Behavioral Medicine, 4,* 1–39.

Kay, J. A., & Carlson, C. R. (1992). The role of stretch-based relaxation in the treatment of chronic neck tension. *Behavior Therapy, 23,* 423–431.

Kiecolt-Glaser, J. K., Marucha, P. T., Malarkey, W. B., Mercado, A. M., & Glaser, R. (1995). Slowing of wound healing by psychological stress. *Lancet, 346,* 1194–1196.

Lazarus, R. S. (1966). *Psychological stress and the coping process.* New York: McGraw-Hill.

Lazarus, R. S. (1999). *Stress and emotion: A new synthesis.* New York: Springer.

Lazarus, R. S., & Folkman, S. (1984). *Stress, appraisal, and coping.* New York: Springer.

Lehrer, P. M., & Woolfolk, R. L. (1993). *Principles and practice of stress management* (2nd ed.). New York: Guilford.

Linden, W. (1993). The autogenic training method of J. H. Schultz. In P. M. Lehrer & R. L. Woolfolk (Eds.), *Principles and practice of stress management* (2nd ed., pp. 205–230). New York: Guilford.

Lovallo, W. R. (1997). *Stress and health: Biological and psychological interactions.* Thousand Oaks, CA: Sage.

Markovitz, J. H., & Matthews, K. A. (1991). Platelets and coronary heart disease: Potential psychophysiologic mechanisms. *Psychosomatic Medicine, 53,* 643–668.

Mayberry, D., Mayberry, M., Bresnan, R., Croft, B., Graham, R., Macaulay, J., McQualter, S., Mitchell, E., Sherwell, K., & Szakacs, E. (2002). Responding to daily event questionnaires: The influence of the order of hassle and uplift scales. *Stress and Health: Journal of the International Society of the Investigation of Stress, 18,* 19–26.

McCallum, D. M., Arnold, S. E., & Bolland, J. M. (2002) Low-income African-American women talk about stress. *Journal of Social Distress and the Homeless, 11,* 249–263.

McEwen, B. S. (2000). Stress, definitions and concepts of. In G. Fink (Ed.), *The encyclopedia of stress* (Vol. 3, pp. 508–509). San Diego: Academic Press.

McGuigan, F. J. (1993). Progressive relaxation: Origins, principles, and clinical applications. In P. M. Lehrer & R. L. Woolfolk (Eds.), *Principles and practice of stress management* (2nd ed., pp. 17–52). New York: Guilford.

Meichenbaum, D. (1993). Stress inoculation training: A 20-year update. In P. M. Lehrer & R. L. Woolfolk (Eds.), *Principles and practice of stress management* (2nd ed., pp. 373–406). New York: Guilford.

Patel, C. (1993). Yoga-based therapy. In P. M. Lehrer & R. L. Woolfolk (Eds.), *Principles and practice of stress management* (2nd ed., pp. 89–138). New York: Guilford.

Pollard, T. M. (2000). Adrenaline. In G. Fink (Ed.), *The encyclopedia of stress* (Vol. 3, pp. 52–58). San Diego: Academic Press.

Sarason, I. G., Johnson, J. H., & Siegel, J. M. (1978). Assessing the impact of life changes: Development of the Life Experiences Survey. *Journal of Consulting and Clinical Psychology, 46,* 932–946.

Schwartz, G. E. (1993). Foreword: Biofeedback is not relaxation is not hypnosis. In P. M. Lehrer & R. L. Woolfolk (Eds.), *Principles and practice of stress management* (2nd ed., pp. vii–viii). New York: Guilford.

Spielberger, C. D. (1996). *Manual for the State-Trait Anger Expression Scale.* Odessa, FL: Psychological Assessment Resources.

Spielberger, C. D., Gorsuch, R. L., Lushene, R., Vagg, P. R., & Jacobs, G. A. (1983). *The State-Trait Anxiety Inventory.* Palo Alto, CA: Mind Garden.

Spielberger, C. D., Sydeman, S. J., Owen, A. E., & Marsh, B. J. (1999). The State-Trait Anxiety Inventory (STAI) and State-Trait Anger Expression Inventory (STAXI). In M. E. Marush (Ed.), *The use of psychological tests for treatment planning and outcome assessment* (2nd ed., pp. 993–1021). Mahwah, NJ: Lawrence Erlbaum.

Stoyva, J. M., & Budzynski, T. H. (1993). Biofeedback methods in the treatment of anxiety and stress disorders. In P. M. Lehrer & R. L. Woolfolk (Eds.), *Principles and practice of stress management* (2nd ed., pp. 263–300). New York: Guilford.

VanHoudenhove, B., Neerincky, E., Onghene, P., Vingerhoets, A., Roeland, L., & Vertommen, H. (2002). Daily hassles reported by chronic fatigue syndrome and fibromyalgia patients in tertiary care: A controlled quantitative and qualitative study. *Psychotherapy and Psychosomatics, 71,* 207–213.

Vgontzas, A. N., Bixler, E. O., & Kales, A. (2000). Sleep, sleep disorders, and stress. In G. Fink (Ed.), *The encyclopedia of stress* (Vol. 3, pp. 449–457). San Diego: Academic Press.

Wolpe, J. (1958). *Psychotherapy by reciprocal inhibition.* Stanford, CA: Stanford University Press.

Woolfolk, R. L., & Lehrer, P. M. (1984). *Principles and practice of stress management.* New York: Guilford.

CHAPTER 11

Management of Inappropriate Medication-Seeking Behavior

SUZY BIRD GULLIVER, BARBARA A. WOLFSDORF, AND ALEXANDER MICHAS

Perhaps one of the largest occupational challenges faced by clinical health psychologists is that of addressing the unhealthy and/or inappropriate use of medications. The problem of medication seeking is made all the more complex because medication-seeking behavior is not solely the responsibility of the patient who is actively engaged in the behavior. The prescribing providers, the health care system in which the patient seeks treatment, and (most recently) the cyber-community for pharmaceuticals all constitute potentially active participants in this high-risk, maladaptive behavior.

Clinical health psychologists are frequently called on to intervene not only with patients but also with providers and the system to effectively extinguish the problem behavior. Indeed, referral sources for evaluation and treatment of medication-seeking behavior are nearly as common as the types of drugs that patients seek. For example, a clinical health psychologist may become aware of medication seeking in a patient being treated for another disorder, the psychologist may receive consult requests from care providers who have identified medication seeking in a patient or in a group of patients, or the psychologist may be required to intervene with a provider or a group of providers whose prescribing practices are suspect. Regardless of how the medication-seeking behavior is identified, multidimensional assessment and treatment plans are the keys to successful amelioration of the difficulty. This chapter defines the problem of medication seeking, proposes a conceptual framework for understanding medication seeking, and describes assessment plans as well as treatment development to address this behavior. A descriptive case study is also presented to illustrate these ideas. Finally, the chapter concludes with a synopsis of what is known and what still needs to be explored to meet the field's overarching objective of optimal clinical care.

DEFINITIONS AND DESCRIPTION OF MEDICATION-SEEKING BEHAVIOR

Definitions of medication-seeking behavior (also known as drug-seeking behavior) are often incomplete, vague, or lacking in the literature addressing the phenomenon. For the purposes of this chapter, the term *medication-seeking behavior* is used to highlight the pursuit of legal prescription medications rather than illicit "drugs." Medication-seeking behavior is defined as a pervasive pattern of requesting medications that have either little or no therapeutic efficacy for the presenting problem and/or in dosages exceeding therapeutic limits. This definition is consistent with that offered by Pankratz, Hickam, and Toth (1989), who defined drug-seeking behavior as "any attempt to influence a physician to prescribe excessive medication or to obtain abusable medications through illegal activities" (p. 115).

Notably, medication-seeking behavior may occur within several contexts. For example, this maladaptive behavior may manifest within a somatoform disorder in which the patient has a genuine conviction of his or her illness and requests medication "appropriate" for the believed illness (Singh, 1998). Alternatively, medication seeking may occur within the presence of an addiction that began with appropriate treatment of a valid medical or psychological illness, in which case the behavior represents an attempt to prevent withdrawal symptoms or loss of functioning and may or may not be sincerely driven. Finally, this behavior may be largely manipulative in nature and be motivated by the desire for a "high," for thrill seeking, or for the street value and concomitant financial rewards of possessing desirable medications. Clearly, these contexts for medication-seeking behavior are not mutually exclusive.

Furthermore, a number of distinct health care professionals may be affected by medication-seeking patients and subsequently may call on health psychologists to intervene. Physicians are likely the most frequently targeted group (although this assertion has yet to be evaluated empirically), but patients may also look to nurse practitioners in their attempts to obtain medications. In addition, patients may target psychologists, case managers, nurses, pharmacists, and other providers seen as "gatekeepers" to prescribing physicians. For instance, within the chapter authors' outpatient mental health clinic, the psychiatric Walk-In Clinic (WIC) operates each afternoon of the business week. The WIC is staffed by psychology and social work trainees, licensed mental health care providers, and supervising clinical health psychologists. Medication evaluations (with the possibility of immediate prescriptions) are provided 3 days a week for 1 hour by nurse practitioners and psychiatrists. One of the principal tasks in the WIC is to identify medication seeking and make appropriate treatment plans. The multidisciplinary team is ideally suited for this task, as is described in greater detail later. The health psychologist, as a senior supervisor, must be aware of the different contexts within which medication-seeking behavior may occur and must be prepared to work with a multitude of different professionals relative to this issue. Although much discussion within this chapter centers on the prescribing physician, the issues raised are equally important for all health care providers who come in contact with medication-seeking patients.

The pervasiveness of medication-seeking behavior, as defined here, is as yet unknown. Very little clean data exist that would yield meaningful conclusions regarding its incidence and prevalence. However, in addition to the clinical lore that most practicing health psychologists will endorse, some national statistics are useful. For instance, the American Medical Association (AMA) stated, "The abuse of prescription drugs results in more injuries and deaths to Americans than all illegal drugs combined. Prescription drugs are involved in more than 60% of all drug-related emergency room visits and 70% of all drug-related deaths" (Weiss & Greenfield, 1986, cited in Lewis & Gaule, 1999, p. 838). The National Institute on Drug Abuse (NIDA, 2001) reported that approximately 9 million Americans over age 12 years used prescription medications for nonmedical reasons in 1999, and the incidence of prescription drug abuse seems to be increasing. For example, according to the 1999 National Household Survey on Drug Abuse, nonmedical use of prescriptions increased for nearly all medication classes from 1990 to 1998. Pain relief medication initiation increased by 181%, tranquilizer use increased by 132%, sedative use increased by 90%, and stimulant use increased by 165%. In fact, the street value of abused (but prescribed) medications was second only to cocaine sales between 1987 and 1997 (AMA, 1988).

Although the published data addressing medication seeking are not clear and distinct, indirect measures of the scope and intensity of the problem can be divided into the following categories: challenges for the patient, challenges for the physician, challenges for the medical system, and challenges for the culture.

Challenges for the Patient

Multiple negative medical consequences may result from medication seeking on the part of the patient. First, there is the risk of medication complications, such as overdose, and the ongoing concern of polypharmacy. Second, when patients with physiological addictions are unable to meet their medication needs, the possibility of triggering an acute withdrawal syndrome exists. Third, patients who chronically medicate might not observe or report symptoms that need assessment and additional treatment.

In addition, patients who attain the medications of choice begin a cycle of negative reinforcement that is ultimately likely to increase the symptoms for which the medications are prescribed. For instance, Silberstein (1992) noted that medication abuse can result in increased headaches in patients who previously had intermittent headaches. The tremendous power of the negative reinforcement cycle is well documented in problems that are primarily psychogenic in nature (e.g., anxiety disorders,

addiction). Pain syndromes are frequently maintained, at least in part, by the negative reinforcement achieved through narcotic medications. Although some data argue persuasively that a cycle of overuse cannot be instated when patients are faced with scheduled dosing for a pain syndrome, certain subgroups of patients are at increased risk for negative sequelae from as-needed dosing (Poling & Byrne, 2000). That is, patients who have a known history of prior addictions (perhaps with the exception of tobacco use disorder) are more likely to be noncompliant with a fixed dosing schedule and are at increased risk for a craving response and possible relapse to the drug of choice while on a fixed dosing schedule.

The final negative consequences of medication-seeking behavior to patients are societal. Patients who become labeled as *medication seeking* suffer the slings and arrows of social disapproval, often inspiring dislike among care providers. As described previously, many patients began the cycle of medication seeking while under care for documented medical or psychological illnesses; therefore, they are in part correct in their assertions that they are ill and in need of medication. Yet the attitude of hostility and dislike toward these patients, and the subsequent conflictual relationships with health care providers, may result in increased "doctor shopping" and/or increased likelihood of the acquisition of prescriptions from providers motivated to avoid conflict (e.g., Longo, Parran, Johnson, & Kinsey, 2000). These possible consequences in turn decrease the likelihood of appropriate patient care and are largely iatrogenic because these patients are likely in need of more—not less—clinical management.

Challenges for the Physician

The drug-seeking patient presents multiple challenges for the physician. First, the patient's behavior places the patient's life in danger, and this places attendant liability on the physician. Patients suspected of medication seeking are difficult to assess and even more challenging to treat. In addition, the assessment of such patients treads very closely to accusing them of dishonesty, and this violates the basic premise of the physician-patient relationship. Patients facing an evaluation of medication-seeking behavior frequently become hostile and angry. This response is generally experienced as punishing to the care provider, and it decreases the chances that the provider will confront similar patients in the future.

Second, in most instances, the physician has been trained in a "cure" model. Therefore, when a disease that cannot be cured (e.g., chronic pain syndrome) presents at a clinic, the appropriate response within this model of training is to attempt to increase the dose or intensity of the treatment so as to better help the patient. If the patient does not respond to the increased care, the physician's confidence in the mode of treatment declines, and the physician is left to either "blame the healer or blame the patient."

Third, the physician's behavior is shaped by the patient's response, and this presents two difficulties. The patient, who may immediately become more pleasant and manageable at the sight of a prescription pad, reinforces providing medication. In contrast, the unhappy patient can create a rather large disturbance in the course of a busy schedule. The physician learns quickly that the provision of medication will allow him or her to return to other patients who are less aversive, so an additional negative reinforcement loop emerges.

The controversy over medication-seeking behavior and the concomitant responses of physicians is not complete without acknowledgment that practices of overprescribing are only half of the story. Inadequate pharmacological treatment of legitimate medical and psychological illnesses presents an equally problematic (although less widely discussed) issue. In keeping with the medical code of ethics, it is at least as problematic to underprescribe medication as it is to overprescribe

medication. For instance, much of the focus of changing physician prescribing practices has been in the area of decreasing the prescription of "drugs of abuse." However, Parran (1997) stated that the systematic undertreatment of acute pain and undertreatment of malignant pain is pervasive and unnecessary. Also of note is the fact that medications with exceedingly low abuse liability (e.g., antibiotics) are overprescribed, and this creates a new category of abuse. With the advent of antibiotic-resistant bacteria, overprescription of other medications has also been called into question.

Challenges for the System

Perhaps the most pervasive systemic problem with medication seeking is the amount of time and resources that is consumed by medication misuse, both in terms of treating these patients appropriately and inappropriately and in terms of attempting to intervene in these complex behavioral interactions. Systems must establish mechanisms by which to identify offending patients and physicians. They must track both groups for a sufficient duration to establish patterns of behavior and legitimacy of claims, and they must create a remediation plan. These are costly measures in terms of both fiscal implications and systemic morale. That is, health care providers working within systems plagued by medication seeking are likely unhappy with the position of "medication police" and face additional scrutiny by a community that may perceive differential "fault." Furthermore, reports of medication mismanagement in the media are likely to send more patients to alternative sources of health care, and this taxes the system in new ways (e.g., decreased revenues, increased acute illness of unknown etiology due to patient having nontraditional care that may have only placebo effects or even be iatrogenic). Finally, systems are aware of bona fide medication prescriptions for dependents being used by medication-seeking caregivers (e.g., parents using their children's Ritalin, adult children of terminally ill patients using parental pain medications to the detriment of genuine pain management of the ill parents).

Challenges for the Culture

The problem of medication seeking also has implications for the culture. Specifically, problems of increased mortality of patients, decreased confidence and hope in medicine (thereby driving health care providers away from patient care), and increased costs to the system all combine to create significant threats to public safety. Determining appropriate interventions requires further consideration of the legal implications for liability, responsibility, and potential prosecution.

In sum, the problem of medication seeking is large and complex and has the potential for widespread harm that far exceeds the dynamics of a small number of individual patients who greatly tax a small number of physicians. A handful of scientists and practitioners have started to explore a number of intervention tactics for this problem. This literature is described next.

OVERVIEW OF RESEARCH IN MEDICATION SEEKING

Very little empirical work on medication seeking is available in the literature today. A literature search using the *Psychlit* databases, including publications between 1972 and 2002 and using the terms "medication seeking" and "drug seeking," yielded 38 citations, of which only 6 were directly relevant to this chapter. A similar *Medline* search using the same terms and years of literature yielded 19 citations, of which only 4 were relevant to this chapter. When the search was expanded to include "prescription drug abuse" and "medication noncompliance" for the same time frame, an additional 4 relevant citations were found using *Psychlit* and an additional 12 relevant citations were found using *Medline*. Finally, 26 additional articles were identified from the reference sections of the articles mentioned previously. Thus, an extensive review of 29 years of published, peer-reviewed literature yielded 52 available articles that were directly or peripherally related to this issue (a rate of less than 2 pertinent publications per year).

These literature search results are consistent with the one published evaluation that could be located addressing the methodology of the existing literature (Nichol, Venturini, & Sung, 1999). Nichol and colleagues (1999) surveyed a computerized *Medline* search from 1980 to 1996 using "patient compliance" as a major term and "drug therapy" as a subheading term. Of the random subset of the 719 identified articles, the majority of research articles on medication compliance (a behavioral neighbor of drug seeking) were descriptive in nature (63.9% of the articles reviewed). Most (41.7%) used a sample of convenience, and the overall quality of the published research was evaluated as very poor. Thus, the amount of empirical literature available to inform this section is quite limited.

With that cautionary note, there are three areas in which published data exist: (a) epidemiological data on prescription drug abuse, (b) content and case reviews of physicians, and (c) evaluation reports regarding the usefulness of systemic interventions to change the reinforcement of medication seeking by decreasing prescriptions, particularly among medications with higher abuse potential. One published evaluation of methods to alter physician skill levels in assessing and responding to medication seeking was available but showed no significant gains as a result of training (Taverner, Dodding, & White, 2000). No data beyond a handful of case descriptions were available on the nonmedical treatment of medication seekers in an individual or group setting.

Epidemiological Data

As noted previously, few data from epidemiological studies tracking the use and misuse of prescription medications are available.

The most recent National Household Survey on Drug Abuse (NIDA, 2001) indicates that drugs other than caffeine, alcohol, nicotine, cannabis, stimulants, and heroin were used by about 8% of the general population during the month immediately preceding the trial. Given the sampling biases of the National Household Survey (e.g., homeless individuals, itinerant workers, and school truants are not captured in the sample), actual drug use may be greater in the population at large.

Among drugs that are coded as Schedule II (high abuse potential with severe dependence liability [e.g., narcotics]) or Schedule III (less abuse potential than Schedule I and Schedule II but containing small amounts of certain narcotic agents [e.g., acetaminophen with codeine]), no published estimates of use or abuse could be found. Schedule IV medications (less abuse potential than Schedule III medications, including drugs such as benzodiazepines) do have drug-specific use figures. Specifically, the Task Force on Benzodiazepine Dependency of the American Psychiatric Association reported that 10% to 12% of the population use benzodiazepines each year but that only 1% to 2% of the population take these drugs on a long-term basis (Gold, Miller, Stennie, & Populla-Vardi, 1995; Salzman, 1990).

Perhaps the most instructive data are drawn from populations of hospitalized patients. These data demonstrate that addictions affect up to 50% of this population. In addition, 15% to 30% of patients seen in primary care settings meet criteria for addiction (Longo et al., 2000). Among psychiatric patients, estimates of comorbid addictions are even higher. Given that most abuse (upward of 80% in the example of benzodiazepine abuse) of Schedule IV drugs occurs within the context of polysubstance abuse or dependence (Longo et al., 2000), the problem of drug abuse is likely to be a significant red flag for identification of populations at increased risk for medication seeking.

Content and Case Reviews of Physicians

According to Kofoed, Bloom, Williams, Rhyne, and Resnick (1989), the problem of inappropriate prescribing is the largest single category of complaints filed against physicians. Interestingly, only a small percentage of physicians are responsible for most inappropriate prescriptions. For example, results from Maronde, Seibert, and Katzoff (1972) suggest that less than 5% of the staff accounted for 50% of the inappropriate prescriptions written in one hospital.

Kofoed and colleagues (1989) reviewed the cases of reported inappropriate prescribing that were deemed substantive and pursued to some degree by the Oregon Board of Medical Examiners between 1981 and 1986. Results indicated that more than half (51%) of the complaints resulting in informal interviews with the investigative committee of the board involved inappropriate prescription writing. (This is in contrast to the second most frequent category of complaints, habitual or excessive use of intoxicants, which accounted for only 13% of such investigations.) Furthermore, complaints of inappropriate prescribing involved an average of approximately 2 drugs, most frequently including opiates and/or benzodiazepines. In fact, 9 of the 10 most frequently cited inappropriately prescribed medications belonged to one of these two categories of drugs.

In addition to the identification of specific types of medications that may be inappropriately prescribed, Kofoed and colleagues (1989) identified types of patients who may be prescribed medications inappropriately. Nearly 80% of patients identified in complaints of inappropriate prescribing were pain patients (55%) or drug-seeking patients (24%). In addition, slightly more than half of the physicians under investigation for any reason between 1981 and 1986 had a history of at least one other investigation during the previous 4 to 9 years; of those previous complaints, 70% were for inappropriate prescription writing.

Perhaps most important is the assertion by Kofoed and colleagues (1989) that inappropriate prescribing is unlikely to be a problem of intentional deceit. In fact, less than 5% of physicians under investigation appeared to be clearly dishonest. Rather, the large proportion of physicians under investigation were guilty of possessing inadequate pharmacological knowledge or of being "pseudobenevolent overprescribers." These last-mentioned overprescribers are characterized by a strong need to help their patients, grandiose thoughts about their own importance in treating particular patients, an orientation toward immediate symptom relief rather than long-term outcomes, and an inability to handle their own emotions if the medication is withheld. Unfortunately, the phenomena of inadequate knowledge and pseudobenevolent overprescribing may co-occur.

With only a general sense of the categories of patients who may be using prescription medications inappropriately, and a similarly general idea regarding the health care professionals who provide such prescriptions, intervention may seem to be a daunting task. Of particular importance is the choice of targets for intervention. Should the target be the patient, the prescriber, the system, or some combination thereof? These options are discussed in greater detail within the context of a biopsychosocial model for understanding medication-seeking behavior. However, it may be useful to first review interventions (all systemic in nature) that have been described in the literature.

Descriptions of Systemic Interventions

According to NIDA, five types of systemic interventions have been developed to address medication misuse on a systemic level. Each

of these methods may indirectly affect medication-seeking behavior by the disruption of drug diversion (Cooper, Czechowicz, Molinari, & Petersen, 1993). The Automated Reports and Consolidated Orders System (ARCOS), Drug Investigational Units (DIU), Electronic Point of Sale Systems (EPOS), Medicaid Fraud and Abuse System (MFAS), and Multiple Copy Prescription Program (MCPP) all are available to decrease medication diversion. An expert panel at NIDA evaluated the clinical utility of these systems and published its findings in 1993. It was found that although each system had its own advantages and disadvantages, the differences in applications of each method made an empirical evaluation of all systems impossible. Nonetheless, each system did have some impact.

MacLeod and Swanson (1996) described the systemic intervention made in the emergency departments of four Canadian hospitals to better manage chronic pain without inappropriate prescribing practices or the reinforcement of medication-seeking behavior. These hospitals operationally define medication seeking as any patient coming in to any department 10 or more times during the previous 12-month period and requesting opioids for a chronic pain problem. Once a patient is identified in this manner, treatment is refused unless the patient is registered in the chronic pain registry, where he or she undergoes a systematic evaluation for pain syndrome and treatment planning. Once on the registry, the patient receives only one care provider. This primary care physician becomes the only recognized prescriber. In addition, the patient is allowed to visit only one emergency department (to further limit attempts to doctor shop or the "splitting" of treatment providers). Primary care providers see the patient once every 9 weeks for evaluation of the home care prescribed by the consulting physician. This thoughtfully designed system has not yet been evaluated empirically. The results of such an investigation would be particularly useful to other systems attempting to change maladaptive prescribing practices and medication-seeking behavior as well as to improve patient care.

Another example of an innovative systemic intervention for the problem of medication seeking can be found in the Tripler Army Medical Center's sole provider program (Lewis & Gaule, 1999). Similar to the intervention described by MacLeod and Swanson (1996), the sole provider program focuses on the systemic monitoring of prescriptions for controlled substances and access to, as well as communication among, health care providers as important means by which to reduce medication-seeking behavior. In this system, a patient can be enrolled in the sole provider program either through a referral from a health care professional or through identification during twice-annual reviews of all prescriptions for controlled substances. In the latter case, a multidisciplinary sole provider subcommittee reviews prescriptions for controlled substances written to patients within the Tripler Army Medical Center. Patients who are identified as having suspicious patterns of prescriptions (e.g., unusual numbers, large quantities, or multiple providers of prescriptions) are reviewed closely by the subcommittee. If no legitimate explanation for a patient's prescriptions can be identified, the patient is provided with one physician (usually his or her primary care manager), who acts as the patient's point of contact for all prescriptions. The patient is also provided with an alternative provider (usually the head of the group within which the sole provider works) for situations in which the sole provider is not available.

All providers who have previously written prescriptions for identified patients are informed of these patients' entry into the program via written communication (i.e., confidential, closed-loop e-mail and letter). Patients are encouraged to address any questions or concerns to their sole provider. The prescription use of patients in the sole provider program is monitored on an ongoing basis, with decreasing frequency over time. Formal and widely accessible computerized files are established and continually updated to reflect any and all attempts on the part of these patients to procure prescriptions (both successful appropriate attempts and those conceptualized as maladaptive medication seeking). This facilitates prescription monitoring and communication among the health care providers. Hence, when a patient presents to a provider, all potential prescribers are armed with the knowledge of the individual's prescription history and potential difficulties associated with that history.

As in the previous example, such a system integrates patient care, facilitates easy and efficient communication among health care providers, and improves delivery of service to the patient. Although anecdotal evidence supports the success of this program, it also awaits empirical evaluation. With these examples in mind, a biopsychosocial model of understanding medication seeking is offered next. Based on this model, additional targets for intervention may be elucidated.

UNDERSTANDING MEDICATION-SEEKING BEHAVIOR AND IDENTIFYING TARGETS FOR INTERVENTION: A BIOPSYCHOSOCIAL MODEL

Although the paucity of empirical literature precludes the development of a data-driven model for understanding and intervening with medication-seeking behavior, the existing theoretical and clinical literature provides a starting point for the development of such a model. Specifically, biological, psychological, and social (including environmental) variables all play important roles in the development and maintenance of medication seeking (e.g., the biopsychosocial model of behavior [Engel, 1977]). As seen in Figure 11.1, these variables

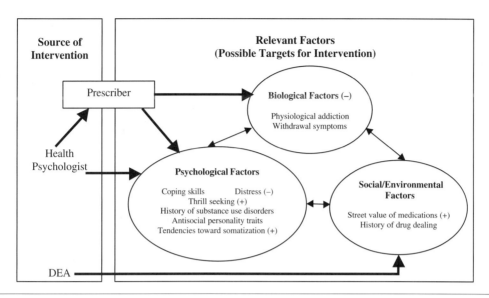

Figure 11.1   Medication-Seeking Behavior: A Framework for Understanding and Intervention

NOTE: DEA = Drug Enforcement Agency. Minus sign (–) indicates negatively reinforced factors. Plus sign (+) indicates positively reinforced factors.

may be interrelated and form both positive and negative reinforcement loops for medication-seeking behavior.

Of greatest relevance to the health psychologist are the psychological factors associated with (and often reinforced by) the medication-seeking behavior as well as the role of the prescriber (usually a physician but alternatively a nurse practitioner or another prescribing health care professional) in the cycle of medication seeking.

Patient Targets

The medication-seeking patient may be characterized by a number of psychological characteristics, including ineffective and/or maladaptive coping skills (of which self-medication may be just one), high levels of distress, a tendency toward thrill seeking, a predisposition to addiction based on a history of substance use disorders, antisocial personality traits (i.e., tendencies toward manipulation for the patient's own gain such as pleasure

associated with medication misuse, reversal of withdrawal symptoms associated with medication misuse, and/or financial gains associated with black market prescription medication sales), and a tendency to manifest psychological distress as physical symptoms (as in the case of somatoform disorders or subclinical somatization [Longo et al., 2000]). Interestingly, no studies that used psychometrically sound assessments of patients characterized as medication seeking were discovered in the current review of the literature. Research measures of illicit drug use, abuse, and dependence are likely too unwieldy to be clinically useful. Future research is needed to establish efficient, valid, and reliable means of assessing medication-seeking behavior. Ideally, such measurement development will allow comparisons to be made between baseline measures of medication seeking and postintervention assessment of such maladaptive behaviors. Currently, the description of patient characteristics must be based on descriptive reports and clinical experience.

Patients may engage in a number of different medication-seeking behaviors. Specifically, Parran (1997) identified 11 such behaviors, including *overreporting or manufacturing symptoms* to procure prescription medication and *endorsing multiple somatic complaints or vague somatic complaints*. These vague exaggerated reports often include descriptions of pain (with no organic origin), anxiety, and/or insomnia. In addition, because the street value of certain medications is higher (e.g., Percocet and drugs with known intoxicating effects are worth more than non-narcotic medications), and because brand-name medications carry a higher street value than do generic medications (perhaps because brand names are easily verified as such by the buyer), medication-seeking patients may *insist on specific medications* or *refuse a generic equivalent*. Additional medication-seeking behaviors include *making arguments about pharmacology, making demands for multiple prescription medications* (i.e., polypharmacy) *or demands for controlled substances on a first visit*, and *making assertions that patients have a high tolerance* for the medication (and therefore need a higher or more frequent dosage).

Particularly uncomfortable for the health care professional are medication-seeking behaviors that involve excessive manipulation and/or dishonesty. Examples of such behaviors include patients who seek medication via *veiled threats* to the prescriber, clinic staff, or hospital and those who seek medication via *excessive flattery* preceding a prescription request (Parran, 1997). In addition, Parran and colleagues (Longo et al., 2000; Parran, 1997) described typical scams used by patients to procure prescriptions. Examples of these scams include claims that patients spilled a bottle of medication or that the bottle was somehow lost or stolen. At its most extreme, medication-seeking behavior may take the form of altering prescriptions written by physicians or stealing prescription pads and forging prescriptions.

A final patient behavior that is particularly difficult to assess and to intervene with is the phenomenon of "doctor shopping." Patients doctor shop when they use a minimum of two (but often many more) physicians, medical centers, or multidisciplinary clinics, either professing dissatisfaction with the previous prescriber or claiming to have no other care providers. Patients quickly become aware of which facilities, as well as which physicians, are less likely to identify doctor shopping.

These psychological factors and forms of medication-seeking behavior suggest numerous interventions on the part of the health psychologist and physician (or other prescribing clinician). In the chapter authors' own clinical environment, health psychologists often act as "gatekeepers" to psychiatric medication management. Therefore, they interact directly with medication-seeking patients and have the opportunity to intervene relative to psychological factors before the patients even reach the potential prescribers. In instances where the patient is an ongoing patient of the health psychologist, beliefs about prescription medication use and misuse can be identified, examined, and challenged. In addition, alternative coping strategies can be taught and practiced, relapse prevention approaches can be implemented, and somatic complaints can be placed in the context of existing distress. Furthermore, with a therapeutic alliance in place, the health psychologist is better equipped to challenge antisocial behaviors (e.g., manipulation) and to set clear limits regarding appropriate use of prescribed medication. Finally, and perhaps most important, in an ongoing therapeutic relationship, the health psychologist can (and should) be sufficiently familiar with the genuine symptoms and illnesses of the patient so that the psychologist can identify the appropriate role of medication in their treatment. Any appropriate pharmacological intervention may then be delivered within the context of psychosocial treatment (as recommended in the "BRENDA" approach, which combines medication and psychosocial treatments within the context of addiction treatment [Volpicelli, Pettinati, McLellan & O'Brien, 2001]).

Prescriber Targets

In instances where the health psychologist has only a brief interaction with the medication-seeking patient and/or where the health psychologist acts as a consultant to the prescribing physician, educating the prescriber about psychological illness and the influences of psychological factors on physical illness is critical to a successful outcome. In addition, the health psychologist will play an important role in working with prescribers to more comfortably set limits and process conflicts related to medication seeking with their patients as well as in establishing and coordinating systemic interventions to reduce medication-seeking behavior.

A number of suggestions for physicians that have been published by the medical community (Council on Scientific Affairs, 1982) are useful to the health psychologist and can easily extend to other prescribing targets. To facilitate the prevention and management of medication-seeking behavior, prescribing care providers must first identify potential maladaptive medication seeking. As noted by Parran (1997), physicians can learn to recognize common scams, including those described earlier such as the following: "I dropped my medicine off the sink and into the toilet. I had plenty left. I don't know how I can afford to have it refilled, but it's the only thing that helps." Prescribers can be empowered to effectively confront the medication seeker, perhaps through motivational enhancement techniques. Parran described "turning the tables on the scammer" as an effective intervention. In

addition, prescribers are encouraged to be meticulous in their prescription-writing practices, taking extreme care with legibility so as to decrease the likelihood of a medicine dosage or amount being altered. Prescribers should adhere to rational and systematic prescribing practices. In particular, caution with medicines of greater abuse liability should be evident and reflected behaviorally through shorter duration of prescribing and more careful monitoring of use. Finally, firm limits to prescription pad access must be established (Finch, 1993; Longo et al., 2000).

Early work in the health care field by the AMA (1990) led to development of a descriptive taxonomy of the "problem prescriber" known as the "4 D's" (Longo et al., 2000; Parran, 1997; Wesson & Smith, 1990). According to this view, problem prescribers fall into four categories: dated, duped, dishonest, and disabled. In the chapter authors' opinion, the importance of this system is largely historic. Since the paradigm shift brought about by Miller and Rollnick's (1991) seminal work on motivational interviewing, the iatrogenic nature of pejorative labeling processes is understood. The qualities subsumed under the 4 D's can be described more effectively as barriers to physician success in the management of medication seeking. For those physicians who have fallen behind the current knowledge base on prescribing practices, state-mandated continuing education can facilitate change. In response to those individuals whose wish to trust their patients sometimes overwhelms indications of potential medication misuse, introduction to and instruction in the techniques of motivational enhancement will provide the care provider with an empathic stance while addressing behaviors that do not help the patient to receive optimal care. Truly dishonest care providers with prescription privileges are atypical based on reviews of state registries, and legal interventions with these individuals appear to be effective (e.g., Kofoed et al., 1989). Disabled prescribers must be assessed and treated as mandated by the ethical codes of the governing body. Thus, three interventions for problem prescribers are (a) education, (b) training and feedback in effective interventions, and (c) support and reinforcement for adaptive prescribing practices.

Systemwide Interventions

Systemwide interventions actually roll outward from the individual prescriber to the office setting, where clear procedures are mandated, adhered to, and monitored by objective means. For instance, Finch (1993) suggested three office-based policies, namely that (a) refills should be available through only one prescriber, (b) no refills should ever be allowed during off-hours, and (c) a rapid accurate method for tracking refills must be instated and maintained (Finch, 1993).

Approximately 20 years ago, the Florida Medical Association and several county medical societies took steps to reduce medication-seeking behavior. These efforts included an absence of certain controlled substances being routinely stocked in pharmacies and a delay in their delivery (amphetamines or methaqualones), personal verification of all prescriptions of these controlled substances by phone between pharmacists and prescribers, reminders to physicians to safeguard their prescription pads (including avoiding having Drug Enforcement Agency numbers printed on the prescription pads), and assistance by both pharmacy and law enforcement agencies in these efforts (Council on Scientific Affairs, 1982).

Hospital-based programs are thought to be most effective when (a) there is only one prescriber per patient, (b) a systematic yet private marking system for charts is in place to alert other health care providers to the potential for medication noncompliance, and (c) communication between care providers is fostered by staff meetings and scheduled team supervision (Council on Scientific Affairs, 1982; Lewis &

Gaule, 1999; MacLeod & Swanson, 1996). Although outcome data are as yet unavailable, several examples of hospital systems' efforts to implement these steps to reduce medication-seeking behavior have been described in the literature, and outcome measures should become available in the future.

ASSESSMENT AND TREATMENTS OF MEDICATION-SEEKING BEHAVIOR

Assessment

In the chapter authors' opinion, the most pressing diagnostic issue is the lack of a systematic means of assessment for medication-seeking patients. Across what is available in the literature, a number of medical and psychological conditions exist that might prompt careful assessment of the potential for medication seeking. Just a few of the conditions with demonstrated relationships to adaptive and maladaptive medication seeking are chronic pain disorders, addiction, diabetes, cancer, seizure disorders, posttraumatic stress disorder, stress, anxiety disorders, endometriosis, and premenstrual syndrome. Certainly, a new patient presenting with any of these concerns should be screened for medication seeking. In addition, patients for whom medications of choice have significant abuse liability should be monitored carefully to guard against dependence.

Given that a well-developed, psychometrically sound assessment of medication seeking is not available, we suggest that standard clinical interviews be augmented by self-report measures and biochemical validation whenever possible. First, a mini-mental status exam should be conducted. Patients should be asked to list all medicines they take, including over-the-counter preparations, herbal supplements, and teas. Alcohol use, tobacco use, and caffeine use should also be queried. Information regarding past use of medications and medication reactions should be gathered. Illegal drug use, abuse, and dependence can be measured by the Drug Abuse Screening Test (Skinner, 1982). Risky alcohol use can be measured quickly via the Alcohol Use Disorders Identification Test (Reinert & Allen, 2002) or even more quickly via the CAGE (*c*ut down, *a*nnoyed, *g*uilty, *e*ye opener) questionnaire (Buchsbaum, Buchanan, Centor, Schnoll, & Lawton, 1991). If possible, physiological data, such as liver function tests, could be gathered for later use in a motivational enhancement session with medication-seeking patients. All assessment can be conducted under the umbrella of ensuring an accurate and thorough understanding of the patient.

Such assessment procedures are commonly used in the WIC and frequently inform the development of the treatment plan. In addition, this assessment procedure gathers specific data to be used in the context of the intervention to the patient as well as in informing the social support network, the prescribing health care provider, and the health care system.

Treatment

There are four primary goals for treatment. The first goal is to extinguish medication seeking, as defined previously, in patients presenting for treatment. The second goal is to ensure that the bona fide wellness concerns of medication seekers are adequately managed as medically indicated. The third goal is to ameliorate the problems of physicians whose prescribing volitionally or involuntarily contributes to the problem of medication seeking. Finally, interventions should result in sustained systemic support of the identification and management of medication seeking, as described earlier in the Tripler Army system (Lewis & Gaule, 1999).

Strategies for Patients

The chapter authors believe that the most effective treatments from the addictive behaviors

outcome literature will likely generalize to the care of the medication-seeking patient. The compelling data regarding brief interventions delivered in motivational enhancement therapy (MET) (e.g., Miller & Rollnick, 1991) argue persuasively for the use of MET both at the time of the identification and assessment of the problem and during the initial feedback stages.

The second active component in the treatment of medication-seeking behavior involves education about the cycle of negative reinforcement, where the patient is encouraged to identify misuse of medication as allowing escape or avoidance from unpleasant physiological or affective states. The patient can then be taught to see how escape or avoidance reinforces the initial state and will likely increase the occurrence of the presenting symptom.

The next phase of treatment is usually aided by a functional analysis of the antecedents and consequences of the drug-seeking behavior. Functional analysis is presented as a means of helping the patient to identify his or her own "choice points for change," in keeping with both MET and the principles of functional analysis. The patient is then encouraged to make a plan for change that may, depending on the level of physiological dependence to the medications in question, involve a supervised taper and/or medical detoxification. The patient may also accept a referral to appropriate individual and/or group support at this time.

In sum, the treatment provided to the medication-seeking patient is truly a brief intervention that may be elaborated or pared back depending on the setting in which the patient is encountered. Creative application of these techniques is easily construed across settings.

Strategies for Physicians

The overarching strategies of behavior change are perhaps equally effective in conducting an intervention to aid physicians treating medication-seeking patients. An MET approach

(Text continues on page 205)

CASE STUDY

"Geoffrey Van Snewt" was a busy, 48-year-old, married businessman. He initially presented to a clinical health psychologist with his wife of 25 years, who was having some menopausal difficulties. The couple had three children, the oldest of whom was in college. The two younger children were in boarding schools two states away from the family home. Both parents reported that the children were within normal limits psychosocially and were of no inordinate concern to the parents. Neither Mr. nor Mrs. Van Snewt had living parents. Both reported that the marriage had been solid, without any threats to the longevity of the relationship. Financial difficulties were absent. The husband and wife owned their home and could afford the tuition for all three of their children's private educations. Mrs. Van Snewt did not work outside the home but volunteered in the community. Aside from the menopausal symptoms and recent depressive symptoms, neither partner complained of health difficulties, although Mr. Van Snewt mentioned that he was not able to bounce back from athletic injuries as easily and quickly as he had been able to do in the past. Both adults were active and nonsedentary. Neither partner reported smoking cigarettes, and Mr. Van Snewt denied alcohol use beyond the rare social drink while on business. Mrs. Van Snewt reported daily drinking in amounts that were uncomfortable to her and "out of character." She was not drinking to intoxication but was concerned because she had not been a regular drinker before menopause began.

Mrs. Van Snewt presented as the primary patient, although both parties reported extreme distress around the perceived changes in her affect and behavior. Specifically, Mrs. Van Snewt reported symptoms of depression, including loss of interest in shared activities, decreased libido, and increased alcohol use. The couple was advised to seek individual therapy for Mrs. Van Snewt while continuing the conjoint sessions with the clinical health psychologist to increase communication and decrease distress in the relationship. The treating clinical health psychologist made a referral for Mrs. Van Snewt to obtain individual treatment and requested and received permission to speak with Mrs. Van Snewt's gynecologist and primary care physician regarding the time course of her complaints. A brief course of psychoeducation regarding menopause as well as communication skills-oriented marital therapy followed, with good resolution. After five sessions, the couple felt more able to cope with fluctuations in Mrs. Van Snewt's mood and activity levels, and both partners reported that their communication skills had improved. Mrs. Van Snewt continued with individual therapy and reported that it was going well. No additional couples treatment was deemed necessary.

About 3 months after treatment concluded, Mrs. Van Snewt called the clinical health psychologist and stated that she thought her spouse was "in trouble" with his pain medication. She stated that he was unwilling to call for an appointment himself but that he would return to the clinic if the psychologist agreed to see both parties similar to the work done when Mrs. Van Snewt had "her" difficulties. The clinical health psychologist subsequently offered the couple a conjoint assessment session and asked both parties to bring a list of all current medications kept in the home as well as a list of all physicians (including their contact information).

When the couple arrived for their session, Mr. Van Snewt exuded self-confidence. He took his seat in the therapist's office and charmingly thanked the therapist for meeting with the couple so quickly. Mr. Van Snewt said,

> I feel such relief now that it is out on the table. I started on Percocet about a year and a half ago for the plantar fasciitis I developed from running and tennis. As being on the tennis court is imperative for business, I need the medication to keep me on the courts. I'm sure I can get back on track. I've already asked Dr. Galtry to give me a referral to a podiatrist to make me some new orthotics. *Runners* magazine said they are a sure cure for the problem. I came in today because when Sara found those bottles in my gear, she flew off the handle. She was better for a time, but now she's making a mountain out of a molehill. I just had prescriptions from around the country because of my hectic travel schedule. I know that Sara benefited from individual work, but she really got better when we did it together. She didn't keep seeing her psychologist after our work together stopped, and I don't see why I should have to go to individual therapy either. My plan is to have just one person give me medication, only when I really need it.

Mrs. Van Snewt produced lists of the medications that were currently in the couple's home, most of which were unremarkable. The only medication with significant abuse potential was Percocet. Unfortunately, Mrs. Van Snewt had located more than 15 bottles of the narcotic medication, all prescribed to Mr. Van Snewt over the past 18 months. Most bottles were empty; however, Mrs. Van Snewt was concerned because these medications came from seven different walk-in centers in the couple's county. In addition to those seven centers, one bottle (with refills) came from the family physician, and the others came from drop-in clinics from cities Mr. Van Snewt had visited while on business. There was also a large bottle from Mexico that still contained a number of pills. Mrs. Van Snewt said,

> Geoffrey is so smooth, he can talk a hungry dog off a meat truck. Although he says he knows that this isn't normal, I'm having trouble trusting his plan. He hid this from me all this time, and I thought we had no secrets. I guess I was just too wrapped up in my own problems. I think he needs to see someone, but he is afraid that it will damage his career. I tell him that bringing drugs into the country from Mexico would damage his career more than being unable to play tennis, but he just winks and says it will be okay.

Case Conceptualization

Mr. Van Snewt had developed a dependence to Percocet that was maintained by powerful, short-term, positive consequences and a fixed belief that the short-term consequences outweighed any possible long-term negative consequences. That is, he had multiple rapid reinforcers for continued prescription drug use and abuse, including (a) the powerful pain relief offered to him by the narcotic, (b) the immediate success of "scoring" new prescriptions, (c) the euphoric mood associated with narcotic intoxication that aided him during high-intensity business meetings and social interactions, and (d) the avoidance of loss of business "meetings" on the tennis courts. In contrast, he believed that stopping Percocet use would (a) decrease his business success, (b) deprive him of pleasurable activities, and (c) create a perception within his marriage that he had a "problem."

A natural strength motivating Mr. Van Snewt toward change was the potential disruption to the marital relationship. Although he did not see this as an overt mediator in his medication-seeking behaviors, the therapist contemplated the utility of incorporating the marital relationship as a strength to be drawn on in motivating behavioral change. In addition, Mr. Van Snewt valued his status in the business world and had a strong wish to be admired by his children. The potential threat to his status inherent in his high-risk, medication-seeking behaviors (e.g., possessing multiple prescriptions from different prescribers, importing large quantities of medications) was a potential place to build on the discrepancies between the patient's belief that he was not in any danger and the reality that he was. Given Mr. Van Snewt's dedication to athletic pursuits, the health psychologist thought that education about maintenance of physical integrity might also aid in motivating Mr. Van Snewt to see the genuine potential for long-term physical damage that misusing pain medications might cause.

Clearly, the system in which Mr. Van Snewt achieved successful medication procurement needed attention as well. The family physician, who appeared to be very well meaning but not well informed about the pervasiveness of Mr. Van Snewt's use, needed to be involved in the intervention. If necessary, the health maintenance organization (HMO) through which Mr. Van Snewt received his care could be called on to assist. The therapist completed the model in Figure 11.2 for the conceptualization of the case and prepared "pros and cons" worksheets for Mr. Van Snewt to complete.

Treatments Used

At the outset of treatment, the clinical health psychologist determined that strategies of motivational enhancement would be useful. The overall therapeutic framework from which the clinical health psychologist worked was similar to that described by Miller and Rollnick (1991), wherein therapists approach treatment as a collaborative effort with the patient. Mr. Van Snewt's ambivalence regarding changing his Percocet use was to be respected and addressed in an empathic nonjudgmental style. His responsibility and freedom to choose change was emphasized.

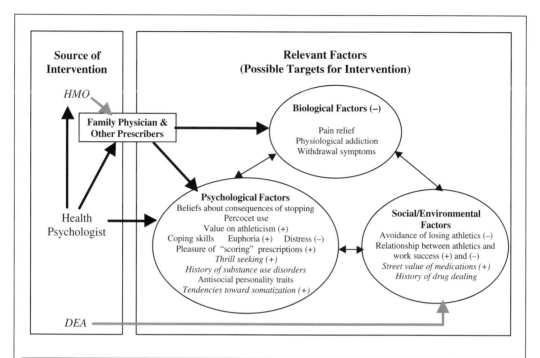

Figure 11.2   Case Conceptualization of Mr. Van Snewt's Medication-Seeking Behavior

NOTE: DEA = Drug Enforcement Agency; HMO = health maintenance organization. Minus sign (–) indicates negatively reinforced factors. Plus sign (+) indicates positively reinforced factors. Relevant aspects of the model are denoted in roman type and black. Aspects of the model inapplicable to this conceptualization are in italic type and gray.

The first session was framed as an assessment session, during which the clinical health psychologist led the couple through a series of questions regarding perceived use, reviewed the medications listed, and gathered contact information for prescribers. While the patient and his wife were present, the clinical health psychologist contacted the primary care physician, who confirmed that Mr. Van Snewt had told him he was having foot problems, had received one prescription for Percocet (refilled twice), and had recently requested a referral for an assessment with a podiatrist. The clinical health psychologist advised the physician that the patient and his wife were present in her office and had given consent for the psychologist to disclose that the patient was overusing his prescription and had received prescriptions from multiple sources. The physician then stated that it was likely that the patient could manage a slow taper off the medication and that he would see the patient to begin the taper that afternoon. The patient was offered an appointment but declined, citing other commitments. The physician was thanked and was assured that communication between treatment providers would continue, with the full consent of Mr. Van Snewt.

At the close of the assessment session, the conceptual model was presented to Mr. and Mrs. Van Snewt, with the therapist highlighting the particular choice points for change, including assessment of actual use, biochemical validation (random and scheduled), continued contact and contracting with the clinical health psychologist, and setting up of a variety of contingency contracts designed to encourage change. The couple was encouraged to contemplate the feedback delivered regarding its medication-seeking patterns and health status and was encouraged to make decisions from an informed perspective. The menu of alternative change methods from which the Van Snewts could choose was offered. The Van Snewts were also provided with information about medically supervised inpatient detoxification in case it proved to be necessary. In keeping with MET and Mr. Van Snewt's stated goals, the therapist's task was to reflect those goals back to the patient by way of recapitulation, reality test their likelihood, and begin to identify the things that would have to change for success to occur.

The Van Snewts accepted another appointment within one business week but canceled the appointment several days later, stating that an unexpected visit from one of their children would preclude their attendance. At the time of cancellation, Mrs. Van Snewt scheduled a new appointment for the following week.

Mrs. Van Snewt attended the rescheduled appointment, reportedly expecting to meet her husband at the clinical health psychologist's office. Mr. Van Snewt telephoned his wife on her mobile phone 10 minutes after the appointment was scheduled to begin, explaining that he was running late at work and that she should "go ahead" without him. Because Mr. and Mrs. Van Snewt were seeing the clinical health psychologist as a couple, the session was ended at that time. Before leaving the office, Mrs. Van Snewt and the clinical health psychologist scheduled an additional appointment for the couple. The morning of the appointment, Mrs. Van Snewt called the clinical health psychologist, explaining in a voice mail message that the problem had been "solved" and that the couple would no longer need to see her. She continued to say that the family physician had tapered Mr. Van Snewt off the Percocet and had refused to provide any additional prescriptions. Mrs. Van Snewt explained that she was pleased with this outcome and was certain that Mr. Van Snewt was "cured." Mr. Van Snewt did not contact the clinical health psychologist again.

Problems Encountered

As can be ascertained from this case example, a substantial systemic challenge exists when treating patients who seek and use prescribed controlled substances inappropriately. Although such patients may exist within a relatively integrated system of care (e.g., a large veterans hospital or other medical center), such individuals often have multiple, relatively disconnected health care providers. When the possibility of cyber-prescriptions is entered into the equation, systemic intervention becomes even more challenging. In this situation, it is essentially impossible to create a treatment team united in the prevention of medication seeking and prescription drug abuse.

In additional to issues at a macro level, more personal factors often play a significant role in the treatment of medication-seeking patients. In this case, Mr. Van Snewt's ambivalence regarding the extent to which his use of Percocet was problematic, as well as Mrs. Van Snewt's investment in believing her husband and avoiding conflict in the marital relationship, intersected in a way that ultimately precluded intervention with the couple directly. Although ambivalence regarding change is a normative characteristic of most patients early in treatment and could have been managed optimally using an MET approach, the couple's presence was obviously a prerequisite for this to occur.

Finally, individual and systemic challenges intersect in this case, where Mr. Van Snewt's considerable financial and work success, high status in the community, and personal charm disarmed potential prescribers. In thinking of "medication-seeking patients," Mr. Van Snewt is unlikely to fit the image conjured up by such professionals. Therefore, these prescribers were likely caught off-guard and were easily convinced of sincere physical pain and the "appropriateness" of providing prescriptions for controlled substances to this "upstanding responsible" man.

will ensure that the physician does not perceive the health psychologist as critical. Education about the pattern of negative reinforcement for both the patient and the physician can be conducted. Specifically, a functional analysis of the conditions in which prescribers are effective versus when they are ineffective will help to clarify the behavior for the physician, both in terms of the patient process of negative reinforcement and in terms of the physician process of negative reinforcement. Finally, the physician needs to have easily accessible information regarding treatment referrals at his or her disposal.

The AMA encourages physicians who are treating medication seekers to have additional training. Such training should include the acquisition and use of chemical dependence screening skills, practice in early and firm limit setting regarding indications for controlled drug prescription, teaching in careful documentation with a firm diagnosis and the ruling out of chemical dependency, and practice. This training should be supervised and have ample role-playing opportunities. Physicians are also encouraged to enlist the support of all the pharmacists given that pharmacists are liable for filling controlled prescriptions along with the physicians who wrote them.

Systemic Interventions

The systemic interventions, as outlined here, are likely to effect change. Future research is needed to address the particular effects of each program as well as the effects of the individual components that make up each program.

CONCLUSIONS

The most compelling conclusion to be drawn from the existing literature and the chapter authors' clinical experience with the problem of medication seeking is that the knowledge base is *extremely* limited. Indeed, health care professionals have no true sense of the prevalence and incidence of medication seeking itself. Neither are they currently equipped to describe the financial, physical, and emotional costs of this behavior. Health care professionals can follow good clinical practice, but they have no means of establishing the utility of programs designed to deal with this problem. The state of the current literature is that they must begin anew. To that end, this chapter concludes with the following suggestions.

First, psychometrically sound assessments of medication seeking need to be developed. Biochemical validation of current use should be considered in the development of such measures. Many interesting questions regarding this project are possible. Specifically, can medication seeking be operationally defined and accurately diagnosed in an efficient and effective manner? Is there a means of taking the guesswork out of it?

Second, psychometrically sound assessments of prescribing practices should be developed and implemented. With national databases of prescription medications easily within the purview of the established medical community and the experience of existing systems designed to track such measures, this possibility should not be difficult.

Finally, educational programs to assist in the identification of inappropriate seeking, as well as inappropriate prescribing, need to be evaluated systematically.

REFERENCES

American Medical Association. (1988). *Balancing the response to prescription drug abuse: Proceedings from the Second White House AMA Symposium on prescribing controlled substances.* Chicago: American Medical Association, Department of Substance Abuse.

American Medical Association. (1990). *Balancing the response to prescription drug abuse: Report of a national symposium on medicine and public policy.* Chicago: American Medical Association, Department of Substance Abuse.

Buchsbaum, D. G., Buchanan, R. G., Centor, R. M., Schnoll, S. H., & Lawton, M. J. (1991). Screening for alcohol use using CAGE scores and likelihood ratios. *Annals of Internal Medicine, 115,* 774–777.

Cooper, J. R., Czechowicz, D. J., Molinari, S. P., & Petersen, R. C. (Eds.). (1993). *Impact of prescription drug diversion control systems on medical practice and patient care* (NIDA Research Monograph No. 131). Bethesda, MD: National Institute on Drug Abuse.

Council on Scientific Affairs. (1982). Drug abuse related to prescribing practices. *Journal of the American Medical Association, 247,* 864–866.

Engel, G. L. (1977). The need for a new medical model: A challenge for biomedicine. *Science, 196,* 129–136.

Finch, J. (1993). Prescription drug abuse. *Primary Care, 20,* 231–239.

Gold, M. S., Miller, N. S., Stennie, K., & Populla-Vardi, C. (1995). Epidemiology of benzodiazepine use and dependence. *Psychiatric Annals, 25,* 146–148.

Kofoed, L., Bloom, J. D., Williams, M. H., Rhyne, C., & Resnick, M. (1989). Physicians investigated for inappropriate prescribing by the Oregon Board of Medical Examiners. *Western Journal of Medicine, 150,* 597–601.

Lewis, P., & Gaule, D. (1999). Dealing with drug-seeking patients: The Tripler Army Medical Center experience. *Military Medicine, 164,* 838–840.

Longo, J. P., Parran, T., Johnson, B., & Kinsey, W. (2000). Addiction: II. Identification and management of the drug-seeking patients. *American Family Physician, 61,* 2401–2408.

MacLeod, B. D., & Swanson, R. (1996). A new approach to chronic pain in the ED. *American Journal of Emergency Medicine, 14,* 323–326.

Maronde, R. F., Seibert, S., & Katzoff, J. (1972). Prescription data processing: Its role in the control of drug abuse. *California Medicine, 117,* 22–28.

Miller, W. R., & Rollnick, S. (1991). *Motivational interviewing.* New York: Guilford.

National Institute on Drug Abuse. (2001). *Prescription drugs: Abuse and addiction* (Research Report Series, NIH Publication No. 01–4881). Washington, DC: U.S. Department of Health and Human Services, National Institutes of Health, National Institute on Drug Abuse.

Nichol, M. B., Venturini, F., & Sung, J. C. (1999). A critical evaluation of the methodology of the literature on medication compliance. *Annals of Pharmacotherapy, 33,* 531–535.

Pankratz, L., Hickam, D. H., & Toth, S. (1989). The identification and management of drug-seeking behavior in a medical center. *Drug and Alcohol Dependence, 24,* 115–118.

Parran, T. P. (1997). Prescription drug abuse: A question of balance. *Medical Clinics of North America, 81,* 967–978.

Poling, A., & Byrne, T. (2000). *Introduction to behavioral pharmacology.* Reno, NV: Context Press.

Reinert, D. F., & Allen, J. P. (2002). The Alcohol Use Disorders Identification Test (AUDIT): A review of recent research. *Alcoholism: Clinical and Experimental Research, 23,* 272–279.

Salzman, C. (1990). *Benzodiazepine dependence, toxicity, and abuse: A task force report of the American Psychiatric Association* (Task Force on Benzodiazepine Dependency). Washington, DC: American Psychiatric Association.

Silberstein, S. D. (1992). Evaluation and emergency treatment of headache. *Headache, 32,* 396–407.

Singh, B. S. (1998). Managing somatoform disorders. *Medical Journal of Australia, 168,* 572–577.

Skinner, H. A. (1982). The Drug Abuse Screening Test. *Addictive Behaviors, 7,* 363–371.

Taverner, D., Dodding, C. J., & White, J. M. (2000). Comparison of methods for teaching clinical skills in assessing and managing drug-seeking patients. *Medical Education, 34,* 285–291.

Volpicelli, J. R., Pettinati, H. M., McLellan, A. T., & O'Brien, C. P. (2001). *The BRENDA method: Combining medication and psychosocial treatments for addiction treatment.* New York: Guilford.

Weiss, R. D., & Greenfield, D. P. (1986). Prescription drug abuse. *Psychiatric Clinics of North America, 9,* 475–490.

Wesson, D. R., & Smith, D. E. (1990). Prescription drug abuse: Patient, physician, and cultural responsibilities. *Western Journal of Medicine, 152,* 613–616.

CHAPTER 12

Adherence to Medical Recommendations

NICOLE E. BERLANT AND SHERI D. PRUITT

T he failure to adhere to medical recommendations is a significant and multifaceted health care problem. Estimates are that 30% to 70% of patients do not fully adhere to the medical advice of their physicians (National Heart, Lung, and Blood Institute, 1998). Moreover, up to 80% of patients are unsuccessful in following recommendations for behavioral changes such as smoking cessation and dietary restrictions.

Adherence is a complex behavioral process that is determined largely by environmental influences on the patient. However, the patient's environment is broad, extending beyond his or her immediate surroundings to encompass associated health care providers and the health care organization in which the patient receives services. Nonadherence is far more than a patient problem, and efforts that focus solely on the patient impede the ability to make meaningful advances in the adherence arena.

The expansion of the conceptualization of adherence to include multiple levels (i.e., patients, providers, and health care organizations), and the realization that there are multiple influences on a patient's behavior within each of these levels, could make the challenge of improving

adherence appear to be insurmountable. Fortunately, behavioral science offers valuable principles, theories, and models that address the determinants of behaviors of patients, providers, and organizations (Pruitt, 2001). These same principles, theories, and models from behavioral science provide a conceptual framework for organizing current knowledge, testing future hypotheses, and developing multilevel interventions for improving patients' adherence to medical recommendations.

DEFINITIONS AND DESCRIPTION OF ADHERENCE

Although adherence has been defined as the extent to which patient behavior corresponds with recommendations from a health care provider (Rand, 1993; Vitolins, Rand, Rapp, Ribisl, & Sevick, 2000), this broad definition belies the complexity of the issue. Adherence is better conceptualized as an acceptable frequency, intensity, and/or accuracy of specific behaviors, given a specific circumstance, that is associated with improved clinical outcomes. Adherence is a process—a behavioral means to the end point of better health status.

The process of adherence is influenced by multiple determinants. These include a variety of factors at the patient, provider, and health care organization levels. Factors at the patient level consist of a person's knowledge and beliefs about illness, degree of motivation and self-efficacy related to illness management behaviors, and expectancies related to the outcomes of adherence or nonadherence. In addition, disease- and treatment-specific issues influence adherence at the patient level. These include (a) the social, physical, psychological, and occupational disabilities resulting from symptoms and treatments; (b) the cultural meanings of diseases and treatments; (c) the disease severity and prognosis; and (d) the complexity, timing, and degree of beneficial and detrimental effects of treatments.

Influential factors at the provider level encompass the knowledge, skills, and attitudes of health care providers as well as the quality of the patient-provider relationship. Health care organization factors involve characteristics of the organization such as access to diagnostic and treatment services, education to manage health problems, coordination and integration of care, and organizational links to community support services (World Health Organization, 2001).

The need for a clear conceptualization of the adherence construct becomes even more evident when measurement and intervention strategies are taken into consideration. For example, provider recommendations range from advice that requires relatively simple and familiar behaviors (e.g., requests for patients to return for follow-up appointments or to obtain inoculations) to recommendations that patients participate in complex and novel regimens (e.g., daily alterations in diet, smoking cessation, increase in physical activity). Measurement and intervention strategies obviously differ according to the circumstances and/or intensity of the recommendations. Nevertheless, it is important to note that adherence is fundamental for successful management of health problems, and patients are asked to follow some degree of recommendations for all medical conditions.

With the possible exception of psychiatric disorders, adherence is not specific to a particular condition or condition regimen (Haynes, 1979). Basic behavioral principles and models of behavior change cut across all medical conditions, rendering a review of each specific condition less important than a grasp of the common themes. Moreover, increasing the effectiveness of adherence interventions may have a far greater impact on the health of the population than would any improvements in specific medical treatments (Haynes et al., 2002).

Although adherence traditionally is discussed as a patient problem (e.g., "The patient is nonadherent"), the time has come to consider the adherence issue within the larger health care organization context. Adherence is a multifaceted construct that spans patients' medical problems, but providers and the health care organization must be considered as similarly responsible for improving adherence rates. Clarifying our conceptualization of the construct could serve to forward intervention efforts. Better interventions are imperative because if significant improvements in adherence are not made, many medical treatments and providers' therapeutic efforts will continue to be inefficient.

THE ROLE OF BEHAVIORAL SCIENCE IN ADHERENCE

The influence of behavior on health has never been as apparent as it is today. Most people living in this century will die from "lifestyle illnesses" or medical conditions resulting from daily habits such as diet, exercise, alcohol consumption, tobacco use, and/or health risk behaviors (Kaplan, Sallis, & Patterson, 1993). In fact, current estimates indicate that daily behavior contributes as much as 50% to an individual's overall health status (Institute for the Future, 2000). Decades of behavioral research provide proven strategies for changing behavior. Integrating this knowledge within the medical arena can help patients to alter their daily patterns and reduce the risks associated with the development of health problems and/or negative consequences of preestablished conditions. Moreover, behavior change strategies can be applied across diverse medical conditions (Dunbar-Jacob, Burke, & Pyczynski, 1995; Nessman, Carnahan, & Nugent, 1980). In addition, the same learning principles that are effective in changing patient behavior are effective in altering the behavior of health care providers (Oxman, Thomson, Davis, & Haynes, 1995) and health care organizations (DeBusk et al., 1994).

Behavioral science is the application of experimental methods to learn about, predict, and explain the observable actions of humans, including not only observable behaviors but also verbal statements about subjective experiences and symptoms. Much of human behavior has been well understood for decades. The most basic yet most powerful principle is the influence of antecedents and consequences on behavior, that is, operant learning (Skinner, 1938, 1953). Antecedents, or preceding events, are internal (thoughts) or external (environmental cues) circumstances that elicit a behavior. Consequences, or expected consequences, that can be conceptualized as rewards or punishments also influence behavior. These principles translate into the ability to predict the probability of a patient, provider, or health care organization initiating or continuing a behavior because such behaviors partially depend on what happens before and after the specific behavior occurs. Although learning theory historically has been criticized for explaining behavior in overly simplistic "stimulus-response" relationships, contemporary learning theory integrates environmental cues and contexts, memory, expectancies, and neurological processes related to learning (Institute of Medicine, 2001).

From a theoretical standpoint, it would be possible to "control" behavior of patients, providers, and health care organizations if the events preceding and following a specific behavior could be controlled. From a practical standpoint, behavioral principles can be used to design interventions that have the potential to shape behavior at each incremental level of influence (patient, provider, and health care organization) to address adherence problems.

Behavioral interventions based on the basic principles of learning (i.e., antecedents and consequences) are quite potent for changing behavior. New behaviors can be learned, and established behaviors can be increased or decreased using these concepts. In fact, a variety of health behaviors have been altered successfully using some variation of operant-based techniques (Brownell & Cohen, 1995; Janis, 1983; Mahoney, 1974). In general, behavioral change strategies that focus on what occurs before and after targeted behaviors have been substantially more effective than other approaches.

The most effective methods for changing behavior are those that teach individuals how to integrate the basic principles of learning into their daily lives (Bandura & Simon, 1977; Matarazzo, 1980). This practice is called "self-management," "self-directed behavior change," or "self-regulation." Specific techniques for changing and maintaining one's health behavior include self-monitoring, goal setting, stimulus control, self-reinforcement, behavioral rehearsal, arranging social support, behavioral contracting, and relapse prevention. The use of behavioral principles in the area of relapse prevention has been particularly well studied in response to the ubiquitously high rates of relapse after health behavior changes such as smoking cessation, reduction in alcohol consumption, and weight loss. Research in relapse prevention has demonstrated the significance of contextual cues (e.g., physical environment, time of day, emotional status) in the maintenance or extinction of health behaviors.

Although the fundamental principles of learning and behavior change appear to be simple, they are deceptively so. Behavior change and maintenance continues to be an enigma, and even the best behavioral techniques are not invariably effective. Nevertheless, a century of behavioral science remains the strongest foundation to guide current efforts in changing behavior to improve health.

The obligation to integrate behavioral science into physical health was recognized 25 years ago when the interdisciplinary field of behavioral medicine was formally defined (Schwartz & Weiss, 1977). The adherence problem is ideally attacked from this interdisciplinary perspective. In fact, researchers in the behavioral medicine arena have developed sophisticated models that envelop the basic principles of learning and apply them to complex health behaviors.

MODELS FOR UNDERSTANDING ADHERENCE BEHAVIOR

Theories and models provide a conceptual framework for organizing thoughts about adherence and other health behaviors. Over the past 100 years, numerous theories about behavior have been proposed. This section briefly reviews some of the more influential models: the social cognitive theory (Bandura & Simon, 1977), the theory of reasoned action (Ajzen & Fishbein, 1980), the health belief model (Rosenstock, 1974), the theory of interpersonal behavior (Triandis, 1977), the transtheoretical model (Prochaska & DiClemente, 1982), and the information–motivation–behavioral skills (IMB) model (Fisher & Fisher, 1992; Fisher, Fisher, Miscovich, Kimble, & Malloy, 1996).

Social Cognitive Theory

Bandura's social cognitive theory (Bandura, 1982; Bandura & Simon, 1977) suggests that behavioral changes are predicated on the belief that a person can successfully complete a desired behavior. This belief is necessary even when all other predictors of behavior would suggest that a person is ready to engage in a particular behavior. For example, a person can feel vulnerable to a disease, understand how to change his or her behavior to be healthier, believe that the new behavior will decrease the likelihood of illness, and feel supported by the social environment. However, if the person lacks conviction in his or her ability to change, the social cognitive theory predicts that the person is unlikely to be successful.

The construct regarding a person's belief about ability to change is called "perceived self-efficacy" and is modified by four sources of information: (a) performance attainment or success with previous tasks, (b) vicarious experience or watching others perform a task, (c) verbal persuasion, and (d) physiological states such as anxiety and relaxation. The social cognitive theory predicts that self-efficacy influences adherence by mediating behaviors in multiple ways, including immediate behavior choices, effort expenditure, thoughts, emotional reactions, and behavior performance. There is empirical support for the theory as it relates to adherence and the maintenance of behavior change, but Bandura's theory is limited by the complexity of quantifying the conceptual elements in the model.

Theory of Reasoned Action

The theory of reasoned action was introduced in an attempt to explain the relationships among beliefs (normative and behavioral), attitudes, intentions, and behaviors. According to this theory, an individual's intent to adopt a behavior is determined by his or her attitude about performing the behavior and social factors such as the perception of attitudes about the behavior held by significant others (Ajzen & Fishbein, 1980). Ajzen and Fishbein (1980) suggested that attitude toward a behavior is a much better predictor of that behavior than is attitude toward the disease that is associated with the behavior. For example, attitude toward mammography should be a better predictor of screening behavior than is attitude toward breast cancer. Personality and sociocultural variables influence the likelihood of adopting a behavior by mediating the attitudes of the individual and of his or her significant others. Both the degree of influence imposed by the person's attitude and his or her perception of other's beliefs vary with each behavior.

Health Belief Model

The health belief model (Becker & Maiman, 1975; Rosenstock, 1974) integrates behavioral and cognitive theories to explain why people fail to adhere to health behaviors by considering the impact of the consequences and expectations related to the behaviors. Specifically, the probability that a person will adopt or maintain a behavior to prevent or control a disease depends on four things: (a) perceived susceptibility, (b) perceived threat, (c) perceived benefits, and (d) perceived barriers. Perceived susceptibility describes the perception of risk to personal health, whereas perceived threat describes the proportion of negative consequences of disease. Perceived benefits and barriers describe the beliefs about the outcomes of recommended behaviors in reducing the perceived threat. It should be noted that the health belief model highlights the fact that adherence to health behaviors often requires people to act to prevent illness even while they are still healthy.

Theory of Interpersonal Behavior

The theory of interpersonal behavior (Triandis, 1977) interrelates a person's intention to perform a behavior, facilitating conditions, and habit. In this model, intention is mediated by a cognitive analysis of the pros and cons of adopting a behavior, an affective analysis of previous positive and negative experiences, the social influence of normative and role beliefs, and personal beliefs about responsibility for one's health. Habit influences the likelihood of behavior when regular behaviors become automatic, at which point the role of intention is reduced.

Transtheoretical Model

The transtheoretical model (Prochaska & DiClemente, 1982) proposes the "stages of change" framework as a comprehensive model of behavioral change in both the positive and negative directions (e.g., the acquisition of a health behavior such as exercise, the reduction or cessation of a risk behavior such as smoking). Originally developed as a smoking cessation tool, the transtheoretical model has been applied to psychotherapy and a variety of health behaviors as a way of matching individuals to their stage of preparedness for behavior change. Cross-sectional studies have supported the existence of five stages (precontemplation, contemplation, preparation, action, and maintenance), but some longitudinal studies have not identified these discrete stages. In addition, a recent investigation has reported the stages to be weak predictors of smoking cessation (Institute of Medicine, 2001). Nevertheless, the finding that many people have low levels of motivation for behavior change has led to interventions specifically intended to increase motivation such as Miller and Rollnick's (2002) motivational interviewing strategies. (A more detailed discussion of motivational interviewing was provided in Chapter 4.)

Information–Motivation–Behavioral Skills Model

Each of the theories just discussed has advantages and disadvantages, yet none of them readily translates into a comprehensive intervention for changing health behavior. The recently developed information–motivation–behavioral skills model (Fisher & Fisher, 1992; Fisher et al., 1996) borrows elements from the earlier theories to construct a conceptually based, generalizable, and parsimonious model to guide thinking about complex health behaviors. Subjected to rigorous empirical investigation, interventions based on this model have demonstrable efficacy in effecting behavioral change across a variety of clinical applications (Carey, Kalichman, Forsyth, Wright, & Johnson, 1997; Fisher & Fisher, 1992; Fisher et al., 1996). In both prospective and correlational studies, the information, motivation, and behavioral skills constructs have accounted for an average of 33% of the variance in behavior change (Fisher et al., 1996).

The IMB model, similar to what has been reported previously, demonstrates that information is a prerequisite but that information in itself is insufficient to alter behavior (see Mazzuca, 1982). It provides evidence that motivation and behavioral skills are critical determinants that are independent of behavior change (Fisher & Fisher, 1992; Fisher et al., 1996). Information and motivation work largely through behavioral skills to affect behavior. However, when the behavioral skills are familiar or uncomplicated, information and motivation can have direct effects on behavior. In this case, a patient might fill a prescription (a simple familiar behavior) based on information given by the provider. The relationship between the information and motivation constructs is weak. In practical terms, a highly motivated person may have little information, or a highly informed person may have low motivation. However, in the IMB model, the presence of both information and motivation increases the likelihood of complex behavior change.

To this point, each of the components of the IMB model has been described. "Information" consists of basic knowledge about a medical condition and effective strategies for managing it. "Motivation" encompasses personal attitudes toward the behavior, perceived social support for such behavior, and the patient's subjective norm or perception of how others with this medical condition might behave. "Behavioral skills" includes ensuring that the patient has the specific behavioral tools or strategies necessary to perform the adherence behavior such as enlisting social support and other self-regulation strategies. Finally, information, motivation, and behavioral skills must pertain directly to the desired behavioral outcome; that is, they must be specific.

Much of the adherence research and interventions applies individual components of the IMB model despite evidence that all three elements are necessary for complex behavior change. The failure to explicitly implement information, motivation, and behavioral skills may be partially attributed to the commonsensical nature of the model. Health care providers often assume that they provide information to patients and motivate them, and providers also recognize the importance of behavioral skills in improving health. However, there is evidence that providers typically give limited information (Waitzkin & Stoeckle, 1976), lack motivational enhancement abilities (Botelho & Skinner, 1995), and lack the knowledge (often leading to frustration) in teaching patients behavioral skills (Alto, 1995).

The expense of intensively educating physicians to improve their information dissemination, motivational interviewing, and behavioral skills training may be prohibitive when considering efficient and effective strategies for improving patient adherence. However, creative education strategies, such as distance learning techniques, have been used successfully to train physicians in basic behavioral concepts to influence adherence (Casebeer, Klapow, Centor, Stafford, & Skrinar, 1999). Training less expensive or more readily available providers in the application of the IMB model may be a more viable option. Pharmacists, case managers, health educators, and any persons involved in patient care should be exposed to these basic concepts.

Nonphysician providers have an incredibly important role and opportunity to improve significantly the health of their patients by specifically targeting patient adherence issues.

More structured, thoughtful, and sophisticated provider-patient interactions are essential if improvements in adherence are to be realized. The generalizable IMB model can be applied to providers to meet this goal. As this empirically based model predicts, when providers have adequate information, motivation, and behavioral skills, they will integrate new behaviors into their practices. Adapted to an organizational level, the same IMB framework can be used to change the behavior of decision makers and administrators toward improved health care organization functioning.

STATE-OF-THE-ART INTERVENTIONS FOR IMPROVING ADHERENCE

Adherence intervention research has focused largely on patient behavior and medication regimens as opposed to targeting provider and health care organization variables. According to several published adherence reviews, no single intervention targeting patient behavior is effective, and the most promising methods of improving adherence behavior use a combination of the following strategies (Houston-Miller, Hill, Kottke, & Ockene, 1997; Haynes et al., 2002; Roter et al., 1998):

- Patient education (Morisky et al., 1983)
- Behavioral skills (Oldridge & Jones, 1983; Swain & Steckel, 1981)
- Self-rewards (Mahoney, Moura, & Wade, 1973)
- Social support (Daltroy & Godin, 1989)
- Telephone follow-up (Taylor, Houston-Miller, Killen, & DeBusk, 1990)

Various combinations of these techniques have been shown to increase adherence behavior and treatment outcomes. However, even the most efficacious patient-focused interventions do not yield substantial effects for adherence behavior over the long term (Haynes, McKibbon, & Kanani, 1996), and few randomized controlled trials targeting patient adherence behavior exist (Haynes et al., 2002).

A recent review of the long-term management of obesity (Perri, 1998) described many of these techniques by examining the status of research concerning adherence and relapse prevention in weight management. A number of strategies to increase adherence to weight control behaviors have been investigated, including continuing therapist contact, formal relapse prevention training, monetary incentives, low-calorie food provision, and peer support. Intensive behavioral therapist contact (beyond 6 months) has been repeatedly demonstrated to prolong the maintenance of weight loss, although contact does not result in greater weight loss (Perri, 1998).

Relapse prevention training has been used successfully as part of a multicomponent maintenance program (Perri, Shapiro, Ludwig, Twentyman, & McAdoo, 1984). Marlatt and Gordon's (1985) "relapse prevention" is defined as a set of techniques designed to keep people from relapsing to prior health habits after initial successful behavior modification, including training and coping skills for high-risk relapse situations and lifestyle rebalancing (Taylor, 1995). In addition, peer support meetings have been associated with greater weight loss maintenance over time. However, neither of these components has been shown to lead to greater behavioral adherence (Perri et al., 1987). Multicomponent maintenance programs lead to greater sustained weight loss than does standard care, but within these programs continued therapist contact appears to be the key component. Perri (1998) hypothesized that the improved outcomes seen in extended treatment programs are due to the maintained adherence to behavior changes. This extended adherence is likely secondary to the ongoing effects of the social pressure of groups, repeated cues for "appropriate" eating and exercise, continued therapist reinforcement and problem solving, and sustained motivation and morale from continued therapeutic support.

Adherence Interventions at the Patient Level

Most people have difficulty in adhering to medical recommendations, especially when the advice entails self-administered care. Consequently, patient characteristics have been the focus of numerous adherence investigations. Efforts to identify stable personality traits of the "nonadherent patient" have been futile. However, mental health problems have been examined in recent reports, and there is evidence that depression and anxiety are predictive of adherence to medical recommendations (Chesney, Chrisman, Luftey, & Pescosolido, 1999; DiMatteo, Lepper, & Croghan, 2000; Lustman et al., 1995; Ziegelstein et al., 2000). Interestingly, providers historically have attributed adherence problems to patients' personalities (Davis, 1966) or attitudes (Stone, 1979). It may be that providers are detecting mental health problems, such as depression, but are inaccurately labeling these problems as "attitudinal" or "personality" faults in their patients. Such misattribution leads to a failure to treat possible underlying mental health disorders that, if treated, can improve patient adherence.

Adherence Interventions at the Provider Level

Because providers play a significant role in adherence, designing interventions to affect their performance seems to be a reasonable strategy, but investigations in this area are few. Providers prescribe the medical regimen, interpret it, monitor clinical outcomes, and provide feedback to patients (Center for the Advancement of Health, 1999). Accordingly, provider communication has been widely examined, and importantly, associations with patient health outcomes have been demonstrated. In a review of randomized controlled trials, Stewart (1996) reported that providers who share information, build partnerships, and provide emotional support to their patients have better outcomes than do providers who do not interact with patients in this manner. Correlational studies reveal a direct relationship between patient adherence and provider communication styles that include providing information, engaging in "positive talk," and asking patients specific questions about adherence (Hall, Roter, & Katz, 1988). Patient satisfaction also plays a role in that those who are satisfied with their providers and medical regimens adhere to recommendations more diligently (Whitcher-Alagna, 1983). Finally, patients who view themselves as partners engaged in their treatment plans have better adherence behavior and health outcomes (Schulman, 1979).

One example of the potential for providers to affect health behavior change is the use of "minimal contact" interventions in primary care to help patients quit smoking. Advice or counseling alone produces increased 6- and 12-month quit rates in biochemically validated studies (e.g., Ockene et al., 2000). The most effective primary care interventions include several core elements such as a strong provider-delivered "quit smoking" message; self-help materials covering motivational, behavioral, and relapse prevention strategies; a prescription for nicotine replacement therapy; brief counseling that includes setting a quit date; and follow-up support (Glasgow & Orleans, 1997). The American Medical Association has recognized the important influence of health care providers in reducing smoking rates and during the early 1990s created guidelines for the treatment of nicotine addiction (American Medical Association, 1993). The guidelines recommend that providers do the following:

- Ask about smoking at every opportunity.
- Advise all smokers to quit.

- Assist smokers to quit through the use of self-help materials and nicotine replacement whenever appropriate.
- Arrange follow-up contacts.

The ask–advise–assist–arrange model has been used successfully for inpatient and outpatient settings and has resulted in quit rates significantly higher than usual-care approaches (Glasgow & Orleans, 1997).

Adherence Interventions at the Health Care Organization Level

Health care organizations have the potential to influence patient adherence behavior as well given that they control access to care. For example, organizations direct providers' schedules, appointment lengths, allocation of resources, fee structures, communication/information systems, and organizational priorities. As such, health care organizations ultimately influence patients' behavior in many ways. Organizations set parameters of care (e.g., appointment length), often leading providers to report that their schedules do not allow enough time to address adherence behavior adequately (Ammerman et al., 1993). Fee structures are determined by organizations, and many systems (e.g., fee-for-service) lack financial reimbursement for patient counseling and education, substantially threatening adherence-focused interventions. The allocation of resources within an organization may result in high stress and increased demands on providers that in turn have been associated with decreased patient adherence behavior (DiMatteo & DiNicola, 1982).

Furthermore, organizations determine continuity of care. Patients demonstrate better adherence behavior when they receive care from the same health care provider over time and when patient information is communicated with other providers (Meichenbaum & Turk, 1987). For example, the ability of clinics

and pharmacies to share information regarding patients' behavior around prescription refills has the potential to improve adherence. This is possible because the information allows health care providers to track patients' use of medication as a proxy of medication adherence. Patients can be contacted if they are using medications at a rate that is too fast or too slow. In addition, organizations determine the level of communication with patients. Ongoing communication efforts (e.g., phone contacts) that help to keep patients engaged in their health care may be the most simple and cost-effective strategy for improving adherence (Haynes et al., 1996).

The "state-of-the-art" interventions in adherence target each level of the adherence problem mentioned previously (patient, provider, and health care organization). Several programs have demonstrated good results using a multilevel team approach (Hypertension Detection and Follow-up Program Cooperative Group, 1979; Multiple Risk Factor Intervention Trial Research Group, 1982; SHEP Cooperative Research Group, 1991). In fact, adequate evidence exists to support the effectiveness of innovative, modified health care teams over traditional, independent physician practice and minimally structured organizations (DeBusk et al., 1994; Peters, Davidson, & Ossorio, 1995).

STATE-OF-THE-ART MEASUREMENT OF ADHERENCE BEHAVIOR

Accurate assessment of adherence behavior is necessary for effective and efficient treatment planning and for ensuring that changes in health outcomes can be attributed to the recommended regimen. In addition, decisions to change recommendations, medications, and/or communication style so as to invoke patient participation depend on valid and reliable measurement of the adherence construct. Indisputably, there is no "gold standard" for measuring adherence behavior (Farmer, 1999; Vitolins et al., 2000). However, a variety of strategies have been reported in the literature.

Subjective Measures of Adherence Behavior

One measurement approach is to ask providers and patients to provide their subjective ratings of adherence behavior. When providers rate the degree to which patients follow their recommendations, providers overestimate adherence behavior (DiMatteo & DiNicola, 1982; Norell, 1981). The validity of patients' subjective reports has been problematic as well. Patients who reveal that they have not followed advice tend to describe their behavior accurately (Cramer & Mattson, 1991), whereas patients who deny their failure to follow recommendations tend to report their behavior inaccurately (Spector et al., 1986). Other subjective rating indicators include standardized, patient-administered questionnaires (e.g., Morisky, Green, & Levine, 1986). These questionnaires have typically been used to assess global patient characteristics or "personality" traits that have proved to be poor predictors of adherence behavior (Farmer, 1999). There are no stable (i.e., trait) factors that reliably predict adherence. However, questionnaires that assess specific behaviors that relate to specific medical recommendations, such as food frequency questionnaires (Freudenheim, 1993) used for measuring eating behavior to improve management of obesity, may be reasonable predictors of adherence behaviors (Sumartojo, 1993).

Objective Measures of Adherence Behavior

Another approach in assessing adherence behaviors is using objective measures. Although objective strategies may initially appear to be an improvement over subjective approaches, both approaches have their drawbacks. For example, remaining dosage units (e.g., tablets) can be counted at clinic visits, but counting inaccuracies are common and typically result in overestimations of adherence behavior (Matsui et al., 1994). In addition, important information, such as the timing of dosages and the patterns of missed dosages, is not captured using this strategy. Recently, electronic monitoring devices, such as the Medication Event Monitoring System (MEMS), have been used to record the time and date that a medication container was opened, thereby giving a better description of the manner in which patients take their medications (Cramer & Mattson, 1991). Unfortunately, the expense of these devices precludes their widespread use. Pharmacy databases can also be used to check when prescriptions are filled initially, refilled over time, and/or discontinued prematurely. However, one problem with this approach is that complete information is difficult to obtain given that patients may use more than one pharmacy or data might not be routinely captured.

Biochemical Measures of Adherence Behavior

Biochemical measurement is a third approach for assessing adherence behavior. Nontoxic biological markers can be added to medications, and their presence in blood or urine can provide evidence that a patient recently received a dose of the medication under examination. This assessment strategy is far from perfect given that findings can be misleading and influenced by a variety of individual factors, including diet, absorption, and rate of excretion (Vitolins, 2000).

In sum, adherence measurement provides useful information that outcome monitoring alone cannot provide, but it remains only an estimation of a patient's actual behavior. Several of the

CASE STUDY

Kaiser Permanente, a large health maintenance organization, is addressing the problem of adherence at the patient, provider, and health care organization levels. Most recently, chronic conditions have been the target of organizational efforts directed toward improving adherence. Specific factors at each level known to influence patients' ability to adhere to medical recommendations are addressed, with the ultimate goal of improving health outcomes in patients with chronic problems.

One strategy for improving adherence rates is to offer a variety of appointment formats and time frames (e.g., individual, group, interdisciplinary team led, telephone) so as to increase the amount of contact between patients and providers. Offering a range of services maximizes opportunities for providers and patients to attend to adherence issues and incorporates professionals other than physicians into clinical contacts. Clinical health educators, registered dieticians, pharmacists, care managers, and clinical health psychologists are examples of nonphysician providers at Kaiser Permanente who augment patient care and serve to increase the frequency of patient contacts within the health care organization. Nonphysician providers have different areas of expertise and different approaches to the adherence problem. Moreover, they can extend physicians' time and influence by supporting physicians' recommendations through additional education, motivation, coordination, and self-management support.

Another strategy for improving adherence at Kaiser Permanente is to ensure the quality of the patient-provider relationship. Patients are assigned a consistent primary care provider (PCP) who oversees and coordinates all medical care. The PCP establishes an ongoing and open relationship with the patient to maintain continuity of care over time and to enhance two-way communication and shared responsibility for chronic condition management. Most Kaiser Permanente PCPs participate in group appointments during which adherence issues are routinely addressed. Patients learn about their conditions, undergo motivational enhancement to initiate and maintain new behaviors, and learn new behavioral skills to implement for the daily management of their health problems.

Sophisticated information systems also help to identify patients having difficulty in adhering to recommendations. Kaiser Permanente's electronic systems facilitate communication among primary care, specialty care, inpatient care, and pharmacy services. PCPs and specialists are able to monitor pharmacy data on prescription refills and use this information as a proxy of adherence to medication regimens. Laboratory results are also readily available to PCPs, and patients' attendance at group appointments or educational classes can be monitored. Treatment protocols specific to different chronic conditions allow for the ongoing monitoring of a number of biological indexes and of adherence to screening and prevention activities.

Finally, there are special efforts to promote continuity and contact with the organization to maximize patients' adherence behavior and to minimize or delay expensive disease complications. Care is planned; follow-up appointments, laboratory tests, and health education group appointments are scheduled. When patients do not adhere to the care protocols, they are contacted through a variety of outreach strategies. These strategies include regular patient newsletters, individualized reminder letters from their PCPs, and telephone calls from care managers.

Patient-centered outcomes continue to improve. Biological indexes have improved across conditions such as heart disease, asthma, and diabetes. Screening and prevention activities have increased, and hospital admissions for patients with chronic conditions have declined.

measurement strategies are extremely costly (e.g., MEMS) or depend on information technology (e.g., pharmacy databases) that is not available in many organizations. Determining the "best" measurement strategy to get an approximation of adherence behavior requires taking all considerations into account. Most important, the strategies employed must meet basic psychometric standards of acceptable reliability and validity (Nunnally & Bernstein, 1994). Additional considerations include meeting the goals of the provider or researcher, the accuracy requirements associated with the regimen, the available resources, the response burden on the patient, and how the results will be used. Finally, because no solitary measurement strategy has been deemed optimal, a multimethod approach that combines feasible self-report and reasonable objective measures is the current state of the art in the measurement of adherence behavior.

CONCLUSIONS

Adherence is behavior. Changing it becomes increasingly more difficult as patients are asked to learn new behaviors, alter their daily routines, and maintain the changes over time

(Malahey, 1966; Marlatt & Gordon, 1985; Zola, 1981). Effective strategies that consistently change and maintain complex behaviors across time might never be discovered. However, substantial evidence exists in the behavioral science arena identifying the most effective strategies for changing behavior. This abundant body of research should guide future intervention efforts. Behavioral science also provides fundamental principles of behavior and empirically evaluated models that can serve as a framework for organizing the conceptualization of the adherence problem.

The fundamental concepts from behavioral science apply to behavior in general, including all medical conditions and the recommendations for their management, health care provider behavior, and the behavior of health care organizations. The conceptual models (e.g., IMB model) provide a framework for these behavioral principles. Given this knowledge, efforts for improving adherence behaviors can be focused and intensified. Moreover, although complete control is impossible, consistent consideration of the significance of events that precede and follow behavior at the patient, provider, and health care organization levels will advance adherence enhancement efforts and ultimately affect health outcomes.

REFERENCES

Ajzen, I., & Fishbein, M. (1980). *Understanding attitudes and predicting social behavior*. Englewood Cliffs, NJ: Prentice Hall.

Alto, W. A. (1995). Prevention in practice. *Primary Care, 22,* 543–544.

American Medical Association. (1993). *How to help patients stop smoking.* Chicago: Author.

Ammerman, A. S., DeVillis, R. F., Carey, T. S., Keyserling, T. C., Strogatz, D. S., Haines, P. S., Simpson, R. J., Jr., & Siskovick, D. S. (1993). Physician-based diet counseling for cholesterol reduction: Current practices, determinants, and strategies for improvement. *Preventive Medicine, 22,* 96–109.

Bandura, A. (1982). Self-efficacy mechanism in human agency. *American Psychologist, 37,* 122–147.

Bandura, A. J., & Simon, K. M. (1977). The role of proximal intentions in self-regulation of refractory behavior. *Cognitive Therapy and Research, 1,* 177–184.

Becker, M. H., & Maiman, L. A. (1975). Sociobehavioral determinants of compliance with health care and medical care recommendations. *Medical Care, 13,* 10–24.

Botelho, R. J., & Skinner, H. (1995). Motivating change in health behavior: Implications for health promotion and disease prevention. *Primary Care, 22,* 565–589.

Brownell, K. D., & Cohen, L. S. (1995). Adherence to dietary regimens: II. Components of effective interventions. *Behavioral Medicine, 20,* 155–164.

Carey, M. P., Kalichman, S. C., Forsyth, A. D., Wright, E. M., & Johnson, B. T. (1997). Enhancing motivation to reduce the risk of HIV infection for economically disadvantaged urban women. *Journal of Consulting and Clinical Psychology, 65,* 531–541.

Casebeer, L., Klapow, J., Centor, R., Stafford, M., & Skrinar, A. (1999). Improving physician skills in patient adherence through a combined CME intervention: Clinical patient outcomes. *Academic Medicine, 74,* 1334–1339.

Center for the Advancement of Health. (1999). *Interventions to improve adherence to medical regimens in the elderly* [Online]. Retrieved on January 20, 2003, from www.cfah.org

Chesney, M., Chrisman, N. J., Luftey, K., & Pescosolido, B. A. (1999, April). *Not what the doctor ordered: Challenges individuals face in adhering to medical advice/treatment.* Paper presented during a symposium conducted at the congressional briefing of the Consortium of Social Science Association, Washington, DC.

Cramer, J. A., & Mattson, R. H. (1991). Monitoring compliance with antiepileptic drug therapy. In J. A. Cramer & B. Spilker (Eds.), *Patient compliance in medical practice and clinical trials* (pp. 123–137). New York: Raven.

Daltroy, L. H., & Godin, G. (1989). The influence of spousal approval and patient perception of spousal approval on cardiac participation in exercise programs. *Journal of Cardiopulmonary Rehabilitation, 9,* 363–367.

Davis, M. S. (1966). Variations in patients' compliance with doctor's advice: Analysis of congruence between survey responses and results of empirical observations. *Journal of Medical Education, 41,* 1037–1048.

DeBusk, R. F., Miller, N. H., Superko, H. R., Dennis, C. A., Thomas, R. J., Lew, H. T., Berger, W. E., III, Heller, R. S., Rompf, J., Gee, D., Kraemer, H. C., Bandura, A., Ghandour, F., Clark, M., Shah, R.V., Fisher, L., & Taylor, C. B. (1994). A case-management system for coronary risk factor modification after acute myocardial infarction. *Annals of Internal Medicine, 120,* 721–729.

DiMatteo, M. R., & DiNicola, D. D. (1982). *Achieving patient compliance.* New York: Pergamon.

DiMatteo, M. R., Lepper, H. S., & Croghan, T. W. (2000). Depression is a risk factor for noncompliance with medical treatment. *Archives of Internal Medicine, 160,* 2101–2107.

Dunbar-Jacob, J., Burke, L. E., & Pyczynski, S. (1995). Clinical assessment and management of adherence to medical regimens. In P. M. Nicassio & T. W. Smith (Eds.), *Managing chronic illness: A biopsychosocial perspective.* Washington, DC: American Psychological Association.

Farmer, K. C. (1999). Methods for measuring and monitoring medication regimen adherence in clinical trials and clinical practice. *Clinical Therapeutics, 31,* 1074–1090.

Fisher, J. D., & Fisher, W. A. (1992). Changing AIDS-risk behavior. *Psychological Bulletin, 111,* 455–474.

Fisher, J. D., Fisher, W. A., Miscovich, S. J., Kimble, D. L., & Malloy, T. E. (1996). Changing AIDS risk behavior: Effects of an intervention emphasizing AIDS risk reduction information, motivation, and behavioral skills in a college student population. *Health Psychology, 15,* 114–123.

Freudenheim, J. L. (1993). A review of study designs and methods of dietary assessment in nutritional epidemiology of chronic disease. *Journal of Nutrition, 123,* 401–405.

Glasgow, R. E., & Orleans, C. T. (1997). Adherence to smoking cessation regimens. In D. S. Gochman (Ed.), *Handbook of health behavior research II: Provider determinants* (pp. 353–377). New York: Plenum.

Hall, J. A., Roter, D. L., & Katz, N. R. (1988). Meta-analysis of correlates of provider behavior in medical encounters. *Medical Care, 26,* 657.

Haynes, R. B. (1979). Determinants of compliance: The disease and the mechanics of treatment. In R. B. Haynes, D. W. Taylor, & D. L. Sackett (Eds.), *Compliance in health care* (pp. 49–62). Baltimore, MD: Johns Hopkins University Press.

Haynes, R. B., McKibbon, K. A., & Kanani, R. (1996). Systematic review of randomised trials of interventions to assist patients to follow prescriptions for medications. *Lancet, 348,* 383–386.

Haynes, R. B., Montague, P., Oliver, T., McKibbon, K. A., Brouwers, M. C., & Kanani, R. (2002). Interventions for helping patients to follow prescriptions for medications. *Cochrane Database of Systematic Reviews, 2.*

Houston-Miller, N., Hill, M., Kottke, T., & Ockene, S. (1997). The multilevel compliance challenge: Recommendations for a call to action. *Circulation, 95,* 1085–1090.

Hypertension Detection and Follow-up Program Cooperative Group. (1979). Five-year findings of the Hypertension Detection and Follow-up Program: I. Reduction in mortality of persons with high blood pressure, including mild hypertension. *Journal of the American Medical Association, 242,* 2562–2571.

Institute for the Future. (2000). *Health and health care 2010: The forecast, the challenge.* San Francisco: Jossey-Bass.

Institute of Medicine. (2001). *Health and behavior: The interplay of biological, behavioral, and societal influences.* Washington, DC: National Academy Press.

Janis, I. L. (1983). The role of social support in adherence to stressful decisions. *American Psychologist, 38,* 143.

Kaplan, R. M., Sallis, J. F., & Patterson, T. L. (1993). *Health and human behavior.* New York: McGraw-Hill.

Lustman, P. J., Griffith, L. S., Clouse, R. E., Freeland, K. E., Eisen, S. A., Rubin, E. H., Carney, R. M., & McGill, J. B. (1995). Effects of Alprazolam on glucose regulation in diabetes: Results of a double-blind, placebo-controlled trial. *Psychosomatic Medicine, 59,* 241–250.

Mahoney, M. J. (1974). Self-reward and self-monitoring techniques for weight control. *Behavior Therapy, 5,* 48–57.

Mahoney, M. J., Moura, N. G. M., & Wade, T. C. (1973). The relative efficacy of self-reward, self-punishment, and self-monitoring techniques for weight loss. *Journal of Consulting and Clinical Psychology, 40,* 404–407.

Malahey, B. (1966). The effects of instructions and labeling in the number of medication errors made by patients at home. *American Journal of Hospital Pharmacy, 23,* 283–292.

Marlatt, G. A., & Gordon, J. R. (1985). *Relapse prevention: Maintenance strategies in addictive behavior change.* New York: Guilford.

Matarazzo, J. D. (1980). Behavioral health and behavioral medicine: Frontiers for a new health psychology. *American Psychologist, 35,* 807–817.

Matsui, D., Hermann, C., Klein, J. J., Berkovitch, M., Olivieri, N., & Koren, G. (1994). Critical comparison of novel and existing methods of compliance assessment during a clinical trial of an oral iron chelator. *Journal of Clinical Pharmacology, 34,* 944–949.

Mazzuca, S. A. (1982). Does patient education in chronic disease have therapeutic value? *Journal of Chronic Diseases, 35,* 521–529.

Meichenbaum, D., & Turk, D. C. (1987). *Facilitating treatment adherence: A practitioner's guidebook.* New York: Plenum.

Miller, W. R., & Rollnick, S. (2002). *Motivational interviewing.* New York: Guilford.

Morisky, D. E., Green, L. W., & Levine, D. M. (1986). Concurrent and predictive validity of a self-reported measure of medication adherence. *Medical Care, 24,* 67–74.

Morisky, D. E., Levine, D. M., Green, L. W., Shapiro, S., Russel, R. P., & Smith, C. R. (1983). Five-year blood pressure control and mortality following health education for hypertensive patients. *American Journal of Public Health, 73,* 153–162.

Multiple Risk Factor Intervention Trial Research Group. (1982). Multiple Risk Factor Intervention Trial: Risk factor changes and mortality results. *Journal of the American Medical Association, 248,* 1465–1477.

National Heart, Lung, and Blood Institute. (1998). *Behavioral research in cardiovascular, lung, and blood health and disease.* Washington, DC: U.S. Department of Health and Human Services.

Nessman, D. G., Carnahan, J. E., & Nugent, C. A. (1980). Increasing compliance: Patient-oriented hypertension groups. *Archives of Internal Medicine, 140,* 1427–1430.

Norell, S. E. (1981). Accuracy of patient interviews and estimates by clinical staff determining medication compliance. *Social Science and Medicine, 15,* 57–61.

Nunnally, J. C., & Bernstein, I. H. (1994). *Psychometric theory* (3rd ed.). New York: McGraw-Hill.

Ockene, J. K., Emmons, K. M., Mermelstein, R. J., Perkins, K. A., Bonollo, D. S., Voorhees, C. C., & Hollis, J. F. (2000). Relapse and maintenance issues for smoking cessation. *Health Psychology, 19,* 17–31.

Oldridge, N. B., & Jones, N. L. (1983). Improving patient compliance in cardiac rehabilitation: Effects of written agreement and self-monitoring. *Journal of Cardiopulmonary Rehabilitation, 3,* 257–262.

Oxman, A. D., Thomson, M. A., Davis, D. A., & Haynes, R. B. (1995). No magic bullets: A systematic review of 102 trials of interventions to improve professional practice. *Canadian Medical Association Journal, 153,* 1423–1431.

Perri, M. G. (1998). The maintenance of treatment effects in the long-term management of obesity. *Clinical Psychology: Science and Practice, 5,* 526–543.

Perri, M. G., McAdoo, W. G., McAllister, D. A., Lauer, J. B., Jordan, R. C., Yancey, D. Z., & Nezu, A. M. (1987). Effects of peer support and therapist contact on long term weight loss. *Journal of Clinical and Consulting Psychology, 65,* 278–285.

Perri, M. G., Shapiro, R. M., Ludwig, W. W., Twentyman, C. T., & McAdoo, W. G. (1984). Maintenance strategies for the treatment of obesity: An evaluation of relapse prevention training and posttreatment contact by mail and telephone. *Journal of Consulting and Clinical Psychology, 52,* 404–413.

Peters, A. L., Davidson, M. B., & Ossorio, R. C. (1995). Management of patients with diabetes by nurses with support of subspecialists. *HMO Practice, 9,* 8–12.

Prochaska, J. O., & DiClemente, C. C. (1982). Transtheoretical therapy: Toward a more integrative model of change. *Psychotherapy: Theory, Research, & Practice, 19,* 276-288.

Pruitt, S. D. (2001). *Adherence to medical recommendations* (commissioned report to WHO, Adherence Project). Geneva: World Health Organization.

Rand, C. (1993). Measuring adherence with therapy for chronic diseases: Implications for the treatment of heterozygous familial hypercholesterolemia. *American Journal of Cardiology, 72,* D68–D74.

Rosenstock, I. M. (1974). Historical origins of the health belief model. *Health Education Monographs, 2,* 1–8.

Roter, D. L., Hall, J. A., Merisca, R., Nordstrom, B., Cretin, D., & Svarstad, B. (1998). Effectiveness of interventions to improve patient compliance. *Medical Care, 36,* 1138–1161.

Schulman, B. A. (1979). Active patient orientation and outcomes in hypertensive treatment. *Medical Care, 17,* 267–280.

Schwartz, G. E., & Weiss, S. M. (1977). *Yale Conference on Behavioral Medicine.* Washington, DC: U.S. Department of Health, Education, and Welfare; National Heart, Lung, and Blood Institute.

SHEP Cooperative Research Group. (1991). Prevention of stroke by antihypertensive drug treatment in older persons with isolated systolic hypertension: Final results of the Systolic Hypertension in the Elderly Program (SHEP). *Journal of the American Medical Association, 265,* 3255–3264.

Skinner, B. F. (1938). *The behavior of organisms.* New York: Appleton-Century-Crofts.

Skinner, B. F. (1953). *Science and human behavior.* New York: Macmillan.

Spector, S. L., Kingsman, R., Mawhinney, H., Sigel, S. C. J., Rachelefsky, G. S., Katz, R. M., & Rohr, A. S. (1986). Compliance of patient with asthma with an experimental aerosolized medication: Implications for controlled clinical trials. *Journal of Allergy and Clinical Immunology, 77,* 65–70.

Stewart, M. A. (1996). Effective physician-patient communication and health outcomes: A review. *Canadian Medical Association, 152,* 1423.

Stone, G. C. (1979). Patient compliance and the role of the expert. *Journal of Social Issues, 35,* 34–59.

Sumartojo, E. (1993). When tuberculosis treatment fails: A social behavioral account of patient adherence. *American Review of Respiratory Disease, 147,* 1311–1320.

Swain, M. S., & Steckel, S. B. (1981). Influencing adherence among hypertensives. *Research Nursing & Health, 4,* 213–222.

Taylor, C. B., Houston-Miller, N., Killen, J. D., & DeBusk, R. F. (1990). Smoking cessation after acute myocardial infarction: Effects of a nurse-managed intervention. *Annals of Internal Medicine, 113,* 118–123.

Taylor, S. E. (1995). *Health psychology.* New York: McGraw-Hill.

Triandis, H. C. (1977). *Interpersonal behavior.* Pacific Grove, CA: Brooks/Cole.

Vitolins, M. Z., Rand, C. S., Rapp, S. R., Ribisl, P. M., & Sevick, M. A. (2000). Measuring adherence to behavioral and medical interventions. *Controlled Clinical Trials, 21,* 1885–1945.

Waitzkin, H., & Stoeckle, J. D. (1976). Information control and the micropolitics of health care. *Social Science and Medicine, 10,* 263–276.

Whitcher-Alagna, S. (1983). Receiving medical help: A psychosocial perspective on patient reactions. In A. Nadler, J. D. Fisher, & B. M. DePaulo (Eds.), *New directions in helping.* New York: Academic Press.

World Health Organization. (2001). *Adherence to long-term therapies: Policy for action* (WHO Adherence Project: Toward Policies for Action). Geneva: Author.

Ziegelstein, R. C., Fauerback, J. A., Stevens, S. S., Romanelli, J., Richter, D. P., & Bush, D. E. (2000). Patients with depression are less likely to follow recommendations to reduce cardiac risk during recovery from a myocardial infarction. *Archives of Internal Medicine, 160,* 1818–1823.

Zola, I. K. (1981). Structural constraints on the doctor-patient relationship: The case of non-compliance. In L. Eisenberg & A. Kleinman (Eds.), *The relevance of social science for medicine* (pp. 241–252). New York: D. Reidel.

Part III

BEHAVIORAL ASPECTS OF MEDICAL PROBLEMS

Introduction to Part III

The next nine chapters epitomize the critical role that psychologists play within health treatment teams across the globe. Whereas Part II focused on unhealthy behaviors that deteriorate health status, this section targets the unhealthy outcomes of certain behaviors and explores adaptive behavioral approaches that improve, prevent, and/or alleviate such deleterious medical conditions. Moreover, the chapters in this section also focus on understanding and addressing psychological problems, such as depression, that result from these medical conditions.

In Chapter 13, Boothby, Kuhajda, and Thorn explore the role of individual difference variables (e.g., biological states, personality), cognitive appraisal, and coping skills in relation to an individual's adjustment to pain. They address these issues within a biopsychosocial framework and note that chronic pain can have a significant impact on how an individual experiences day-to-day life. They also note how chronic pain can create psychological problems that complicate adequate adjustment to their condition. Clinicians working with this population are encouraged to work as valued members of multidisciplinary teams and to positively influence the lives of such patients via cognitive-behavioral techniques.

In Chapter 14, al'Absi and Hoffman define hypertension, discuss the etiological factors that contribute to this health concern, and highlight how to assess and treat this problem. Their underlying message is that hypertension is a silent killer that can be easily overlooked by medical professionals because there are no specific symptoms. As such, body weight, alcohol consumption, low levels of physical activity, and the experience of chronic stress are targeted as factors that may independently and conjointly contribute to hypertension. Clinicians are encouraged to intervene using cognitive-behavioral approaches designed to control weight, reduce or eliminate alcohol consumption, teach more effective ways in which to cope with stress, and foster adherence to medical and psychological treatments.

In Chapter 15, Schwartz and Ketterer provide a practical set of recommendations for working clinically with patients suffering from heart disease. They conceptualize coronary heart disease within a cognitive-behavioral framework and point out the importance of a comprehensive assessment. They note that the assessment and treatment of patients' health risk behaviors, such as smoking, obesity, and lack of exercise, are essential to secondary prevention efforts and are critical for optimal recovery of function and general health. Given the significant influence of negative emotions on the development of heart disease, clinical health psychologists play a vital role in the treatment of such patients by employing cognitive-behavioral interventions with and without pharmacotherapy.

In Chapter 16, Hoff and her colleagues present issues and behavioral strategies associated with the management of type 2 diabetes as well as assessment and treatment recommendations. They describe and discuss etiological factors, including a host of psychological consequences that co-occur with this health problem. They note that clinical health psychologists intervene with diabetic patients in a variety of ways, including making patients more aware of their health-compromising behaviors via self-monitoring and encouraging behavioral changes that lead to a healthier lifestyle. In addition, clinical health psychologists are in a unique position to address the psychological issues that may arise as a result of this chronic condition.

In Chapter 17, Kreitler takes on the awesome task of reviewing the significant body of research examining etiological, assessment, and treatment issues related to cancer. She addresses the psychological phenomena that undermine annual preventive measures, such as screening for cancer, among high-risk groups. She also explores psychological factors that interfere with the adjustment, coping, and preparation of patients at various stages of cancer progression. In addition, Kreitler discusses the assessment of psychological problems that arise from the impact of cancer on a person's life and the subsequent treatment options for such issues. Throughout the chapter, she highlights the impact of cancer not only on the patient but also on family members and health care providers.

In Chapter 18, Garos discusses sexual dysfunctions that may arise due to multiple factors. The chapter begins with a section reviewing the human sexual response, followed by a discussion about the psychological and medical conditions that may initiate or exacerbate sexual dysfunction. Given that males and females suffer from different types of sexual dysfunction, Garos opens with an overall approach to treatment and then breaks down the ensuing assessment and treatment section into various male and female sexual problems. In this section of the chapter, the reader will find prevalence rates and contributing factors for each dysfunction as well as idiosyncratic treatment approaches to each disorder.

In Chapter 19, Blalock and Campos present a thought-provoking piece on human immunodeficiency virus (HIV) and acquired immune deficiency syndrome (AIDS). They describe the various expressions of HIV and the stages at which HIV develops into AIDS.

Next, they highlight the importance of primary prevention and offer prevention strategies for health psychologists and medical personnel. The chapter also includes detailed descriptions of various assessment tools and recommended treatment approaches for psychosocial issues that reduce patients' quality of life. Both psychological and pharmacological treatments for coexisting psychological disorders are presented.

In Chapter 20, Lackner notes the high prevalence of irritable bowel syndrome (IBS) and describes the clinical and diagnostic features associated with this disorder. Next, he points out that this syndrome has historically been viewed as a physical manifestation of a variety of psychiatric conditions. As such, he uses a biopsychosocial model to illustrate the interplay between psychological functioning and IBS. Lackner also emphasizes the importance of comprehensive psychodiagnostic assessments before discussing treatment approaches for patients suffering from IBS. Treatment recommendations explore the contribution of conjunctive therapy that uses pharmacotherapy, cognitive-behavioral, and motivational enhancement approaches.

Finally, in Chapter 21, Wolfe and Pruitt discuss the impact that insomnia and the other sleep disorders have on human functioning and the overall quality of life. They start by describing the basic elements of sleep before delving into the etiology of a variety of sleep disorders. Next, they break down assessment and treatment recommendations by type of sleep disorder. Given the high prevalence and pervasive negative impact of insomnia, much of the treatment section in this chapter focuses on this disorder. Clinical health psychologists are urged *not* to underestimate sleep problems when patients present with such disorders.

CHAPTER 13

Diagnostic and Treatment Considerations in Chronic Pain

Jennifer L. Boothby, Melissa C. Kuhajda, and Beverly E. Thorn

Pain is a perceptual experience that includes sensory and emotional components associated with actual or threatened tissue damage (Merskey & Bogdale, 1994). Virtually everyone experiences pain at some time in his or her life, but for most individuals the pain experience is time limited and does not warrant clinical intervention. However, for some individuals, the pain problem persists and significantly disrupts daily functioning. Pain that persists for longer than 6 months is referred to as "chronic pain" (Keefe, 1982), and chronic pain is often associated with feelings of "demoralization, helplessness, hopelessness, and outright depression" (Turk, 1996, p. 3). The experience of chronic pain can be far-reaching, affecting numerous areas of an individual's life. For example, chronic pain patients often face limited physical functioning, inability or reduced ability to work, financial concerns related to their work situations and medical costs, frequent medical visits, emotional distress, and/or disrupted interpersonal relationships.

Prevalence rates for chronic pain vary depending on the population studied and the site of the pain problem. LeResche and Von Korff (1999) reviewed prevalence rates for back pain across several studies. They reported that approximately 11% to 45% of individuals are affected by persistent back pain. Other researchers found that 17% of men and 20% of women in Australia reported experiencing a chronic pain problem during the previous 6 months (Blyth et al., 2001). Approximately 50% of a sample of U.S. veterans seeking medical treatment reported suffering from at least one chronic pain complaint (Clark, 2002). Prevalence rates for migraine headaches have been reported to range from 3.4% to 17.6% (Breslau, Davis, & Andreski, 1991), and rates of temporomandibular joint pain were found to range from 3% to 15% (LeResche & Von Korff, 1999). Overall, women appear to suffer from higher rates of chronic pain problems than do men, and prevalence rates for many pain complaints increase with age (LeResche & Von Korff, 1999).

Pain is one of the most common reasons for seeking medical care, and for many medical disorders pain is a primary complaint.

For example, rheumatological disorders, cancer, dental problems, gastrointestinal disorders, AIDS, and neurological conditions all share pain as a presenting complaint. In addition, many individuals who sustain injuries experience substantial pain, and for some the pain persists for years. Moreover, pain is not entirely a physiological experience. Decades of research have shown that pain has sensory, affective, and evaluative components (Melzack & Wall, 1965). Thus, understanding pain and understanding its treatment are important areas in which health psychologists should become involved. In fact, a health psychologist would be hard-pressed to work in a medical setting and not confront patients with pain problems on a relatively frequent basis.

BACKGROUND AND ETIOLOGY

Biopsychosocial Model of Pain

Our current understanding of pain perception is consistent with the biopsychosocial model. A useful conceptual heuristic for the biopsychosocial model of pain has been adapted from Lazarus and Folkman's (1984) transactional stress and coping theory (Thorn, Rich, & Boothby, 1999) and is expanded in Figure 13.1. In the expanded model, the influence of individual variables, cognitive appraisal processes, and coping interact to influence ongoing adjustment to the pain experience. Individual variables include biological state (e.g., disease process), dispositional factors (e.g., personality), and stable social roles (e.g., primary relationship issues). Cognitive appraisal processes include both primary appraisal mechanisms (whether a pain-related experience is judged to be stressful or benign, and if it is stressful, whether it is judged to be a threat, a loss, or a challenge) and secondary appraisal processes (cognitions and beliefs about the pain, cognitions and beliefs about the self, and expectations about the utility of certain coping

options). The cognitive appraisal processes influence one's emotional, cognitive, behavioral, and physiological response to the pain experience. Those responses that represent attempts to mitigate the pain experience are called coping attempts. The efficacy of the coping attempt is not what gives it the label of "coping"; rather, it is the effortful intention to manage the stressful pain experience. Coping responses ultimately influence important adaptational outcomes such as social and occupational functioning, morale and mood, and somatic health. Finally, it is crucial to note that the process of appraisal, coping, and adaptation is fluid rather than static; adaptation itself changes the nature of the pain experience, which affects cognitive appraisal processes, thereby influencing coping and adaptation.

The transactional model as adapted for pain is not limited to appraisal of, and coping with, the pain stimulus. Obviously, there are many related aspects of chronic pain such as feelings of dependency, dealing with marital strain or divorce, and losing one's job and income. Each of these environmental challenges contributes to the "stress" of a person with chronic pain. The multifaceted nature of stressors related to pain, and the patient's evolving response to them, is particularly important in the context of coping with chronic pain.

The model just conceptualized is useful from a theoretical perspective but does not offer a format for treatment conceptualization. To this end, the chapter authors have adopted a cognitive conceptualization through which cognitive-behavioral treatment can be delivered. A cognitive formulation fits well with a transactional model of pain because it not only emphasizes the importance of cognitions but also presumes that cognitive factors precede and determine the nature of coping attempts. A cognitive formulation also presumes that altering a person's cognitions results in changes in his or her emotional, behavioral, cognitive, and physiological coping processes. Put another way, the cognitive

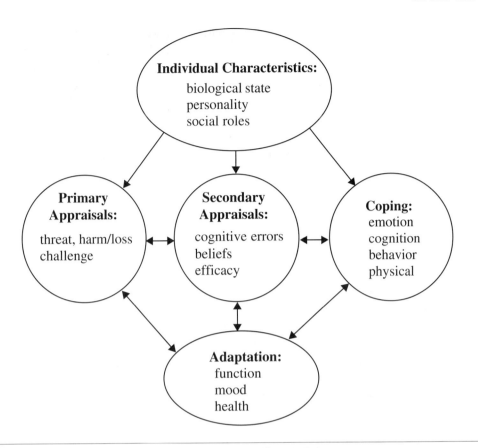

Figure 13.1   Transactional Model of Adjustment to Chronic Pain

formulation assumes that cognitions are the mechanisms through which certain variables have their impact on outcome (i.e., cognitions serve as mediators for adaptive change).

Although it is far from established that cognitive mechanisms are the mediators for adaptive change in pain management, several models of cognitive-affective functioning ascribe antecedent status to cognitive factors in the development of emotional dysfunction (Beck & Emery, 1985; Riskind & Williams, 1999; Vasey & Burkovec, 1992). Vlaeyen and Linton (2000) adopted a cognitive framework to account for pain-related disability, suggesting that catastrophic thinking might represent the cognitive precursor to pain-related behavioral avoidance. Several psychosocial pain researchers have suggested that it may be more

important to reduce negativistic cognitions than to increase coping (Geisser, Robinson, & Riley, 1999; Newton & Barbaree, 1987; Turk & Rudy, 1992). Thorn, Boothby, and Sullivan (2002) suggested that, especially for those individuals who engage in catastrophic thinking about pain and pain-related stressors, it may be important to target treatment toward reducing cognitive errors prior to attempting to increase coping skills. These and other authors (Chaves & Brown, 1987) hypothesized that the change mechanism involved in pain management is the reduction of maladaptive thinking. There are examples in the literature that provide support for this formulation.

Pain-related catastrophizing is a well-researched cognitive factor that is a remarkably robust predictor of pain responsivity and adjustment to chronic painful states. Catastrophizing is consistently related to higher levels of self-reported pain as well as to other measures of pain maladjustment (Geisser, Robinson, & Henson, 1994; Jacobsen & Butler, 1996; Robinson et al., 1997; Sullivan & Neish, 1998; Sullivan, Rouse, Bishop, & Johnston, 1997). Clearly, individuals who catastrophize about their pain are less functional than persons who do not catastrophize. More important to the cognitive formulation described previously, catastrophizing has been shown to mediate certain relations between individual differences (e.g., sex differences) and pain responsivity (Sullivan, Tripp, & Santor, 2000). Relatedly, other negative cognitions associated with pain have been shown to mediate the relation between beliefs about pain and certain outcome measures (Stroud, Thorn, Jensen, & Boothby, 2000). In a recent path analysis of multiple potential predictors of pain, catastrophizing predicted pain over and above measures of fear of pain, trait anxiety, and state anxiety (Sullivan, Stanish, Sullivan, & Tripp, 2002), suggesting that although catastrophizing is related to other variables (in this case emotion), catastrophizing is a separate construct and is more predictive of adjustment to pain than are these other variables.

Although there has been some debate regarding whether catastrophic thinking and other maladaptive cognitions are a manifestation of a personality type (Sullivan et al., 2001), an appraisal process (Thorn et al., 1999), or a coping strategy (Keefe, Lefebvre, & Smith, 1999), using the transactional model described previously, catastrophizing and other negative thoughts could be accommodated at several locations within the model. For example, the trait-like tendencies toward negative affectivity, neuroticism, and emotional vulnerability all have been associated with catastrophic thinking (Affleck, Tennen, Urrows, & Higgins, 1992; Crombez, Eccleston, Van den Broek, Van Doudenhove, & Goubert, 2002; Ward, Thorn, & Clements, 2002). Thus, the dispositional

tendency toward maladaptive cognitions could moderate levels of catastrophic and other negative pain-related thinking. Negative pain-related thoughts could also result from primary threat and loss/harm appraisals, thereby serving as secondary appraisal processes (Thorn et al., 1999). Finally, there has been some suggestion that catastrophic responses could represent a means of seeking support through emotional disclosure (Sullivan et al., 2000). Because social support is often used as a means of coping, it might be that negative cognitive, emotional, and behavioral expressions of pain and its potential consequences may be used to gain social proximity, attention, and/or empathy from others. Although the primary goal of the communal coper may be to gain empathy and support, and not necessarily to reduce pain, the ultimate outcome of such coping behavior might be maladaptive in that such negative thought processes, emotions, and behaviors may contribute to heightened pain experiences (Sullivan et al., 2001).

Diagnostic and Etiological Issues

Clinical Description

"Mary's" story, a description of which follows and which is actually a compilation of the stories of many patients who present for pain management treatment in practice, is not at all dissimilar to what health psychologists see in pain clinics across the United States and abroad. Mary walked slowly and gingerly, in a self-protective manner, from the waiting room into the therapy office and grimaced as she carefully sat in the chair. She said,

> No hard feelings intended, but I really don't want to be here today. My doctor, after having sent me to six different specialists who were unable to help, told me yesterday that there is nothing else he can do for me and that I've just got to learn to live with this pain. He suggested that I come to you, but I don't think I need a shrink! I mean, my pain

is real. I'm not just making it up. I actually had to quit a job I dearly loved, one that I had spent years searching for, but as my pain grew worse, I began to feel fatigued more and more often. I also started having trouble remembering things and would get halfway through a story and forget what it was I was even talking about. It became embarrassing and depressing to think that I might endanger the lives of the people I work with, so I first took a leave of absence but eventually quit. I know I'm depressed, but I wouldn't be if I didn't have this pain.

Mary also described feelings of despair and hopelessness. She explained that her husband, who originally was understanding and supportive, had begun to question the veracity of her condition by saying things such as the following: "Everybody gets pain, especially as they age. You're going to need to toughen up and learn to live with it." Mary was tearful and angry. Not only was her pain negatively affecting her relationship with her husband, but she had noticed that some of her friends had stopped calling— "probably because I had refused many invitations to go shopping and to go to the gym like I did all the time before this pain."

The first several sessions with a health psychologist are primarily devoted to rapport building, ensuring pain patients that the psychologist believes their pain is real, helping patients to understand that feeling depressed about their pain is actually a normal response to an abnormal situation, and beginning the process of educating patients about the important body-mind connection. When patients' bodies hurt and they have been diagnosed with controversial illnesses (e.g., fibromyalgia, chronic fatigue syndrome), they strive to make sense of this experience. They soon may begin to have exaggerated and distorted thoughts about their current condition, and the following may be a common comment: "I'm never going to feel better. My pain is ruining my life." Having catastrophic thoughts leads patients to

feel depressed, anxious, and hopeless. These feelings lead to increased muscle tension and the production of harmful stress hormones, which in turn lead to an increase in pain intensity. Negative and exaggerated thoughts and feelings also influence decisions about activity levels. Inactivity leads to muscle deconditioning, so that when patients attempt activity at a future time, it will be uncomfortable or may be excruciatingly painful, thereby influencing their decision to stay in bed. When patients present for pain treatment, they often have been completely sedentary or perhaps even bedridden for 6 months prior to their first visit.

Diagnostic Considerations

Historically, the health psychologist has looked to the DSM (*Diagnostic and Statistical Manual of Mental Disorders*) for guidance in accurately diagnosing patients with chronic pain conditions. The DSM-II (American Psychiatric Association, 1968) provided no specific diagnosis pertaining to pain. Therefore, pain patients of this era were typically given a DSM-II diagnosis of "psychophysiological disorder," especially when emotional factors were thought to influence their painful condition. Psychogenic pain disorder appeared under the rubric of somatoform disorders in the DSM-III (American Psychiatric Association, 1980). Three major criteria were required for a diagnosis of psychogenic pain disorder: severe and prolonged pain, no known organic pathology, and psychological factors (e.g., pain onset is positively correlated with psychological conflict) that are etiologically involved in the pain.

In the DSM-III-R (American Psychiatric Association, 1987), psychogenic pain disorder was renamed somatoform pain disorder because demonstrating that pain is psychogenic proved to be nearly impossible. Two major criteria were required for a diagnosis of somatoform pain disorder: "preoccupation with pain" for at least 6 months and no known organic pathology (or when organic pathology is found, the complaint of pain and functional [e.g., social, occupational] impairment is not commensurate with physical findings but rather is grossly exaggerated). The DSM-IV subcommittee on pain disorders found that the DSM-III-R somatoform pain disorder diagnosis was rarely used because there appeared to be no consensus on what "preoccupation with pain" meant. In addition, there was difficulty in determining whether the patient's response to pain was being grossly exaggerated. There was also disagreement on the appropriateness of this diagnosis for individuals with disabling pain due to known medical conditions.

In the DSM-IV (American Psychiatric Association, 1994), somatoform pain disorder was renamed as pain disorder. Diagnostic criteria included pain in at least one specific area of the body significant enough to warrant clinical attention, pain that causes distress or functional (e.g., social, occupational) impairment, psychological issues that are thought to play a significant part in important components of the pain (onset, frequency, duration, severity, exacerbation, or maintenance), pain that is not intentionally produced or feigned (as in factitious disorder or malingering), and pain that is not better accounted for by a mood, anxiety, or psychotic disorder and does not meet criteria for dyspareunia.

The DSM-IV pain disorder diagnosis has been criticized for a number of reasons. First, no guidelines are provided for determining when psychological factors significantly affect pain or are sufficient to warrant separate DSM-IV diagnoses in addition to pain disorder. There is a high prevalence of depression and anxiety disorders among chronic pain patients, yet under the DSM-IV criteria, these patients who seemingly would be most appropriate for this diagnostic category could conceivably be excluded due to the criterion that "pain is not better accounted for by a Mood, Anxiety, . . . Disorder." Romano and Turner (1985) reported that anywhere from 10% to

100% of patients with chronic pain have comorbid depression, according to the studies they reviewed. Fishbain, Goldberg, Meagher, Steele, and Rosomoff (1986) found depression and chronic pain to coexist approximately 50% of the time. Panic disorder is diagnosed in 16% to 25% of patients presenting to emergency rooms with chest pain (Beitman et al., 1991; Carney, Freedland, Ludbrook, Saunders, & Jaffe, 1990). Aghabeigi, Feinmann, and Harris (1992) reported that 21% of fibromyalgia patients in their clinic carried a dual diagnosis of pain disorder and posttraumatic stress disorder. Other studies purport that anywhere from 50% to 100% of pain patients entering clinical treatment for pain management have comorbid posttraumatic stress disorder (Kulich, Mencher, Bertrand, & Maciewicz, 2000). It appears to be the case, then, that the DSM-IV pain disorder diagnosis, like its DSM predecessors (somatoform pain disorder and psychogenic pain disorder), remains a diagnosis of exclusion with ambiguous inclusion criteria.

CO-OCCURRING PSYCHOLOGICAL DISORDERS

As indicated previously, chronic pain patients often have symptoms consistent with a mood disorder, namely depression. It is common for these patients to argue that depression is their reaction to the limitations placed on them via their chronic pain condition. In other words, if they did not have chronic pain, they would not be depressed. Whether or not this is true is of little actual consequence in terms of treatment considerations. What health psychologists do know is that alleviating depressive symptoms in chronic pain patients, regardless of the depressive etiology, not only makes their pain more tolerable but also lifts their mood, both of which serve to improve the quality of their lives. On the other hand, chronic pain patients may view a diagnosis of depression (or anxiety) as a sign that their pain is not real—a common concern for pain patients. They may perceive mood and anxiety disorder diagnoses as discounting their pain and may be prone to ask questions such as the following: "Since I have depression, does that mean that my pain is all in my head?" The pain specialist/health professional can typically remedy this misunderstanding by assuring these patients that their depressive or anxious characteristics are actually a normal response to abnormal circumstances.

Substance-induced mood disorder can also occur in chronic pain patients. Due to these patients' compromised health conditions, different physicians frequently prescribe numerous medications. For this reason, it is a good idea to recommend that pain patients maintain a list of all current medications, indicating specific dosages and frequencies with which they take each of them, and to make a point of providing each of their health care providers with this list. Medications known to evoke mood symptoms include, but are not limited to, steroids, anticonvulsants, antihypertensives, anti-Parkinsonian medications, antiulcer medications, cardiac medications, oral contraceptives, and muscle relaxants.

Anxiety disorders, such as panic disorder and posttraumatic stress disorder, are frequently associated with chronic pain disorders. In addition to the studies cited earlier, Stewart, Breslau, and Keck (1994) reported that migraine headaches are more strongly correlated with panic attacks than are any other types of headache. In a community assessment of 10,000 individuals who presented to their primary care physicians with complaints of headache, 15% of females and 13% of males had a history of panic disorder (Sullivan, 2001).

Whether or not pain disorders should be classified as conversion disorders has been, and continues to be, a point of contention among health care professionals. Some do not support the notion that pain conditions can be classified as conversion disorder symptoms because most pain conditions are not neurological in nature

or representative of a deficit or incapacity. Others believe pain to be the most common conversion symptom (Ziegler, Imboden, & Myer, 1960). Sullivan (2001) purported that although there may be some components of conversion disorder present in chronic pain patients (secondary gain), classifying these patients with a conversion disorder is generally not useful.

Although the diagnosis of somatization disorder is rarely used, it warrants a few brief statements. Several specific criteria are required for this diagnosis, and these are detailed in the DSM-IV (American Psychiatric Association, 1994) under somatoform disorders. Prevalence estimates for somatization disorder range from 0.13% to 0.40% in the community (Smith, 1991), from 0.2% to 5.0% in primary care settings (Sullivan, 2001), and from 8% to 12% in pain clinics (Kouyanou, Pither, Rabe-Hesketh, & Wessely, 1998). Sullivan (2001) stated, "Somatization as a process, meaning the somatic experience of distress, is ubiquitous. . . . Somatization disorder is a rare, chronic, and treatment-resistant condition that characterizes the most severely and chronically distressed individuals" (p. 284). Thus, although many chronic pain patients might initially appear to be highly focused and preoccupied on somatic functioning, meeting full criteria for a diagnosis of somatization disorder is relatively rare.

It is imperative for the health psychologist to have at least a basic understanding of common chronic pain conditions (where pain is the primary symptom) and other related health conditions (where pain is an associated symptom but not the primary one) when patients present for clinical pain management. Some common chronic pain conditions include, but are not limited to, fibromyalgia, headache, chronic low back pain, and complex regional pain syndrome. Other related health conditions include chronic fatigue syndrome, multiple chemical sensitivities, and lupus. By and large, the etiology, nature, and treatment of these conditions are considered controversial among health care professionals. Before describing specific aspects of each, it may be useful to look at common challenges that nearly all chronic pain patients face regardless of etiology. Taylor, Friedberg, and Jason (2001) identified the following seven challenges. First, these patients' symptoms and degree of impairment vary significantly across individuals and chronic pain conditions (e.g., one fibromyalgia patient may be working full-time, whereas another is bedridden). Second, treatments (e.g., pharmacological, psychological, physical) for chronic pain conditions are ameliorative in nature and typically do not cure these disorders. Third, these chronic pain conditions are much more prevalent among women than among men (e.g., women comprise approximately 70% of chronic fatigue patients, 90% of fibromyalgia patients, and 75% of multiple chemical sensitivities patients). Fourth, there is high comorbidity among chronic pain conditions (e.g., many fibromyalgia patients have chronic fatigue as well). Fifth, recovery rates are minimal (and that is why they are referred to as chronic conditions). Sixth, patients incur multiple losses of an economic and social nature (e.g., disability and social isolation). Seventh, there is a high level of psychiatric comorbidity (e.g., many patients with fibromyalgia also have depression and anxiety disorders).

In 1990, the American College of Rheumatology officially recognized fibromyalgia as an illness with the following classification criteria: (a) history of widespread muscular pain and (b) tenderness in 11 of 18 "tender points" located in specific areas of the body (Wolfe et al., 1990). Fatigue, disrupted sleep, headache, irritable bowel, and irritable bladder are also characteristic symptoms of this disease. The etiology of fibromyalgia is unknown, but many affected individuals and their health care professionals report that symptoms often appear following surgery, following an injury of a traumatic nature, or following an acute medical illness (Waylonis & Perkins, 1994). Wolfe and colleagues (1990) estimated that

approximately 2% of the population has fibromyalgia.

According to the International Headache Society's "Classification and Diagnostic Criteria for Headache Disorders, Cranial Neuralgias, and Facial Pain" (Headache Classification Committee of the International Headache Society, 1988), migraine and tension-type headaches are the most commonly diagnosed chronic headache disorders. Pain characteristics of tension-type headaches (previously called tension, muscle contraction, stress, or ordinary headaches) include a pressing and/or tightening sensation of a mild to moderate intensity occurring bilaterally, with minimal aggravation by routine physical activity (Rapoport & Sheftell, 1996). Typical pain characteristics for migraine headaches include a throbbing and/or pulsating sensation of moderate to severe intensity occurring unilaterally, with aggravation by routine physical activity. The presence of nausea and/or vomiting along with photophobia and phonophobia is usually characteristic of migraineurs exclusively, although these symptoms may be experienced to a lesser degree by tension-type headache sufferers (Rapoport & Sheftell, 1996). Although the exact cause of headache pain remains a mystery, several theories have been generated. For migraine headaches, Rapoport and Sheftell (1996) reported three major theories, namely that (a) changes occur in cerebral blood flow and electrical cortical activity; (b) neurogenic inflammation, produced by the release of Substance P and other neurotransmitters, impinges on the site where trigeminal nerve endings meet dural arteries; and (c) the size of peripheral blood vessels is altered (e.g., constricted, dilated) in response to some unknown noradrenergic and serotonergic disruption. The etiology of some tension-type headaches involves an increase in pericranial muscle activity (Rapoport & Sheftell, 1996).

The lifetime prevalence of low back pain is estimated to be 70% for individuals in developed countries. Approximately 16% of all workmen's compensation claims are low back pain related, and the estimated cost of lost productivity is enormous (Amundson, 2002). There are many causes of chronic low back pain, including muscle spasm and tightness, whiplash, osteoarthritis (or spondylosis, a degenerative process affecting the normal function and structure of the spine), osteoporosis (degeneration of bone mass), herniated disc, sciatica (pain [lower back, buttocks, radiating down the thighs and sometimes into the feet] that follows the sciatic nerve), compression fracture (vertebral body that is crushed by external force to the spine), spinal stenosis (narrowing of small nerve passageway called foramen, causing nerve compression, swelling, and pain), and osteomyelitis (infection in the spine). It is not unusual for individuals with low back pain to have no structural abnormalities that can be detected on physical examinations, X rays, or magnetic resonance imaging procedures (MRIs). In addition, patients who have undergone repeated back surgeries may have pain from scar tissue that is pressing on nerves.

Complex regional pain syndrome, type 1, also known as reflex sympathetic dystrophy, Sudeck's dystrophy, or hand/shoulder syndrome, is a condition that can develop after traumatic injury to the extremities (Caudill, 2002) but has also been known to develop spontaneously (Bruehl, Steger, & Harden, 2001). A primary symptom is autonomic nervous system dysfunction that includes swelling, increased sweating, blood vessel constriction or dilation, and severe pain in the involved extremity. The diagnosis of complex regional pain syndrome with specific criteria agreed on by the International Association for the Study of Pain was developed in 1994.

Chronic fatigue syndrome, a significant public health concern, lowers the quality of all aspects of life (e.g., social, occupational, interpersonal) for approximately 0.42% of the U.S. population or 800,000 individuals (Anderson & Ferrans, 1997; Jason et al., 1999). Fukuda

and colleagues (1994) described the current U.S. diagnostic criteria as (a) prolonged (at least 6 months) overwhelming fatigue that is not ameliorated with rest, where (b) during the same 6-month period of chronic fatigue, the individual experiences at least four of eight minor symptoms (sore throat, cognitive dysfunction [short-term memory or concentration problems], cervical or axillary lymph node tenderness, muscle pain, joint pain, development of new type of headache, sleep disturbance, or malaise) for at least 24 hours. The etiology of chronic fatigue syndrome is unknown, although medical researchers have speculated for years that viruses such as Epstein-Barr, cytomegalovirus, and herpes simplex virus (Types I and II), or an overactive immune system, may have a role in causing the syndrome.

Multiple chemical sensitivities, a recognized disorder by the American Lung Association, the American Medical Association, the U.S. Environmental Protection Agency, and the U.S. Consumer Product Safety Commission, remains a controversial health condition among many health care professionals. Taylor and colleagues (2001) referred to it as "a chronic condition of irritation or inflammation of sensory organs, gastrointestinal distress, fatigue, and compromised neurological function, including learning and memory deficits, hypersensitivity to unpleasant smells, tingling of nerves, and sensory discomfort" (p. 5). These symptoms appear to be triggered by exposure to certain chemical agents, which Donnay (1998) reported to be primarily pesticides, detergent residues, and perfumes. In California and New Mexico, public health department surveys reveal prevalence rates to be anywhere from 2% to 6% (Taylor et al., 2001).

Lupus, or systemic lupus erythematosus, is thought to be an autoimmune disorder that affects multiple organ systems and that is characterized by skin lesions (butterfly rash) on sun exposure, arthritis and pain in multiple joints, chronic kidney infection, and blood vessel inflammation (causing peripheral neuropathy in hands and feet or causing pain, ulceration, and infection in lungs, heart, and intestines). The etiology may be due at least partially to a genetic defect in B lymphocytes, which produce autoantibodies that attack cells (F. A. Davis, 1997). Although some individuals die from this disease (i.e., with multiple organ system involvement), medical researchers are helping lupus patients to live much longer and higher quality lives than ever before (Lahita, 2001).

ASSESSMENT AND TREATMENT

Pain Assessment

To effectively treat chronic pain, the health psychologist must fully assess the individual's pain experience and also explore variables known to affect treatment response. A general strategy for pain assessment is presented here, with specific examples of assessment instruments and information about how individual variables affect treatment outcome. Evaluation strategies for specific pain problems or medical disorders are not discussed.

Pain Intensity. Self-reported pain intensity is believed to be a good measure of overall pain and suffering. Several methods exist for obtaining this information from patients. For example, numerical rating scales require patients to rate the intensity of their pain using a number, for example, from 0 to 10. Verbal rating scales ask patients to describe their pain with an adjective chosen from a list that can then be quantified. Visual analog scales are straight lines with verbal intensity descriptors on the end points and require patients to rate their pain by placing a mark on the line. Clinicians must then use a ruler to measure where the mark occurs so as to quantify the rating. Each of these methods has its strengths and weaknesses, primarily related to ease of use and ability of patients to conceptualize their pain in the manner requested (Williams, 1996).

Pain Experience. Although assessing pain intensity is an important aspect of any pain evaluation, other aspects of the pain experience are also critical in fully understanding the patient's perspective. Measures such as the McGill Pain Questionnaire (Melzack, 1987), the West Haven–Yale Multidimensional Pain Inventory (Kerns, Turk, & Rudy, 1985), and the Sickness Impact Profile (Roland & Morris, 1983) provide information regarding sensory and emotional components of pain, physical activity level, spouse responses to pain, and overall psychosocial functioning. Pain behaviors can also be included under the rubric of overall pain experience and can be assessed through self-report or observation of the patient. Pain behaviors include grimacing, moaning, limping, lying down, and consuming pain medications. Many pain behaviors are often reinforcing and lead to higher levels of disability. For example, if the spouse of a chronic pain patient attempts to comfort the patient whenever he or she appears to be hurting, the patient may learn that certain pain behaviors result in attention and sympathy. Keefe and Hill (1985) developed a methodology for assessing pain behavior that requires videotaping, whereas other clinicians have developed checklists to evaluate behavioral responses to pain (Waddell, McCulloch, Kummel, & Venner, 1980). Pain assessments that address the broader pain experience have the potential of offering more detailed treatment recommendations and of providing a standard of comparison for patients' posttreatment functioning.

Pain Beliefs and Cognitions. Cognitive factors, such as beliefs, appraisals, and cognitive distortions, play an important role in adjustment to pain and the development of disability (DeGood & Shutty, 1992). For example, the critical role of catastrophizing in altering the pain experience was highlighted earlier in this chapter. In addition to catastrophizing, research has shown other negative cognitions to be associated with poorer functioning among chronic pain patients. For example, DeGood and Shutty (1992) described the importance of low self-efficacy and beliefs that pain is mysterious or out of the individual's control in predicting poor pain treatment response. Fear of pain and reinjury is also associated with poor pain outcomes, and recent research has revealed that anxiety sensitivity exacerbates pain-related fear and leads to avoidance of physical activity (Asmundson, 1996). Fear of pain is associated with selective attentional bias for pain-related information (Keogh, Ellery, Hunt, & Hannent, 2001), potentially resulting in more negative pain experiences for individuals with elevated fears of pain. Finally, several studies have found that cognitive errors (e.g., overgeneralization, selective abstraction) are related to depressive symptoms in chronic pain patients (Lefebvre, 1981; Smith, Christensen, Peck, & Ward, 1994) and that pain treatment that addresses cognitive factors (e.g., cognitive errors) is effective at alleviating depression in this population (Moreno, Cunningham, Gatchel, & Mayer, 1991). Pain research has also revealed that changes in negative cognitions and beliefs more generally are also associated with improvement following multidisciplinary pain treatment (Jensen, Turner, & Romano, 2001).

Many instruments exist for the measurement of pain-related beliefs and cognitive factors. A few of these measures include the Pain Beliefs and Perceptions Inventory (Williams & Thorn, 1989), the Inventory of Negative Thoughts in Response to Pain (Gil, Williams, Keefe, & Beckham, 1990), the Pain Catastrophizing Scale (Sullivan, Bishop, & Pivik, 1995), and the Pain Anxiety Symptoms Scale (McCracken, Zayfert, & Gross, 1992). A variety of similar instruments exist for the assessment of cognitions that are more illness specific.

Pain Coping. Coping consists of cognitive and behavioral efforts undertaken to manage stressful situations. How chronic pain patients cope with the pain experience is related to their physical and psychosocial functioning. Coping attempts that are passive, such as hoping or praying for an end to the pain, are often associated with higher levels of physical disability and psychological dysfunction than are more active strategies for coping (Boothby, Thorn, Stroud, & Jensen, 1999). Catastrophizing is sometimes conceptualized as a coping strategy, and as described previously, catastrophizing is consistently related to poor pain outcomes (Sullivan et al., 2001). Although active coping strategies, such as distraction techniques and using positive coping self-statements, are not generally associated with negative pain outcomes, they are also not consistently correlated with positive outcomes (Boothby et al., 1999). As a result, some pain researchers have suggested that it is more important to decrease passive coping or negative coping attempts rather than to only teach more adaptive, active coping strategies (Geisser et al., 1999; Newton & Barbaree, 1987).

Several measures exist for the assessment of pain coping. The Coping Strategies Questionnaire (Rosenstiel & Keefe, 1983) was specifically developed to assess coping among pain patients, and it is the most frequently used instrument of its kind. The Cognitive Coping Strategies Inventory (Butler, Damarin, Beaulieu, Schwebel, & Thorn, 1989) and the Vanderbilt Pain Management Inventory (Brown & Nicassio, 1987) are also inventories specific to pain coping assessment. Numerous instruments exist for the evaluation of coping strategies more generally. However, it is recommended that a pain-specific instrument be used whenever possible because coping is often conceptualized as situation specific

(Lazarus, 1993) and patients might cope with chronic pain differently from how they approach other stressors.

Emotional Functioning. Individuals with chronic pain often have associated emotional difficulties. Emotional reactions, such as depression and anxiety, are common responses to persistent pain and can serve to compound the original pain problem and lead to more severe impairment and disability. Research has demonstrated consistently that certain types of psychopathology are associated with poorer adjustment to chronic pain and poorer treatment response (Block, 1996; Brennan, Barrett, & Garretson, 1986; Gaskin, Greene, Robinson, & Geisser, 1992).

Rates of depression, anxiety, and anger have been shown to be higher among chronic pain patients than in community samples (Banks & Kerns, 1996; Fernandez & Turk, 1995; Gaskin et al., 1992). Research using the Minnesota Multiphasic Personality Inventory (MMPI) has demonstrated that patients with chronic pain tend to have higher elevations on scales measuring preoccupation with somatic complaints, depression, and the development of physical symptoms in response to stressful situations (Etscheidt, Steger, & Braverman, 1995). Personality disorders are also quite prevalent among chronic pain patients, with one study finding avoidant, dependent, and obsessive-compulsive personality disorders to be particularly common (Elliott, Jackson, Layfield, & Kendall, 1996). Other researchers reported that more than 50% of chronic low back pain patients involved in a functional restoration program met criteria for a personality disorder, with paranoid personality disorder being the most common (Gatchel, Polatin, Mayer, & Garcy, 1994).

Higher levels of psychopathology are commonly associated with poor treatment response and continued disability. Robbins, Moody, Hahn, and Weaver (1996) found that chronic pain patients who did not return to work following multidisciplinary treatment had higher pretreatment levels of depression, anxiety, psychoticism, and overall distress than did patients who returned to work. Gatchel, Polatin, and Mayer (1995) evaluated a large sample of acute low back patients and found higher levels of self-reported pain and disability as well as higher scores on Scale 3 (hysteria) of the MMPI to be associated with a lack of return to work after 1 year. Thus, evaluating patients for the presence of these symptoms and disorders is an important piece in potentially preventing severe disability and in planning effective treatment. The assessment of psychological symptoms and disorders can be undertaken using self-report measures that are common to clinicians in other areas of psychological practice (e.g., MMPI, Symptom Checklist-90–Revised, Beck Depression Inventory).

Acute Pain Management

Health psychologists are involved in the management of acute pain less frequently than they are in the management of chronic pain. Because acute pain is by definition time limited, it is managed primarily with pharmacological agents. However, research has shown that health psychologists can make important contributions to acute pain management. Chapman and Turner (1986) proposed three goals for interventions with patients undergoing painful medical procedures: (a) increasing the patients' knowledge about the procedure, (b) enhancing a sense of control over the procedure and the pain experience, and (c) improving the patients' ability to diminish emotional responses to pain that increase stress responses.

Research has shown that information-based strategies can be effective at reducing fear and anxiety associated with medical procedures as well as at decreasing pain intensity during the procedure (Suls & Wan, 1989). Instructing patients in the use of relaxation techniques serves to decrease sympathetic nervous system arousal and also provides a means of enhancing personal control over the pain experience. Relaxation techniques consist of deep breathing exercises, progressive muscle relaxation, guided imagery, biofeedback, and hypnosis. To date, no one specific relaxation technique has been shown to be significantly more effective than any other for acute pain management (Williams, 1999). Several studies have shown that patients who receive psychological interventions, such as training in relaxation methods, prior to painful medical procedures report less pain, use less opioid analgesics, report less anxiety, and recover more quickly than do patients who receive standard medical management (Gil, 1984; Schultheis, Peterson, & Selby, 1987).

Chronic Pain Management

Pharmacological Interventions. Pharmacological agents are the first line of treatment for acute pain, and these agents are often used aggressively in an effort to bring rapid relief from pain. Centrally acting analgesics are commonly used in the treatment of acute pain. However, the treatment of chronic pain tends to be more complex, with the use of a wider variety of pharmacological agents and with the goal of managing the pain condition for a longer duration. Examples of pharmacological agents used to treat chronic pain include narcotic analgesics (e.g., Lortab, Percodan), nonnarcotic analgesics (e.g., Ibuprofen, Tylenol), muscle relaxants (e.g., Flexeril, Robaxin), topical analgesics (e.g., Zovax), anticonvulsants (e.g., Neurontin, Tegretol), antidepressants (e.g., Paxil, Prozac), and antianxiety medications (e.g., Librium, Ativan).

Although narcotic analgesics are commonly used in the treatment of chronic pain, there are mixed findings regarding their utility. Some studies have found the long-term use of opioids to provide significant pain relief (Portenoy & Foley, 1986) and to increase functional status (Zenz, Strumpf, & Tryba, 1992), whereas others have found opioids to provide only minor pain relief without improvements in activity levels (Jamison, Raymond, Slawsby,

Nedeljkovic, & Katz, 1998; Moulin et al., 1996). Researchers have also suggested that using narcotic analgesics as the sole treatment program without incorporating psychosocial interventions can undermine overall rehabilitation and functional restoration (Turk & Meichenbaum, 1994). Thus, opioids are often combined with other medical and behavioral treatments to manage chronic pain most effectively. Despite strong concerns on the part of medical professionals and patients alike regarding the potential for addiction to opioid medications, there is a relatively low risk of addiction in patients without a history of substance abuse if the drug is administered orally (Merskey & Moulin, 1999). Nevertheless, chronic administration of any drug, particularly multiple analgesic agents, does not enhance function and possibly contributes to pain-related disabilities. It is estimated that 3% to 18% of patients seeking treatment for chronic pain have substance abuse problems (Fishbain, Rosomoff, & Rosomoff, 1992).

Surgical and Other Medical Interventions. A variety of medical interventions exist for the management of chronic pain, ranging from more radical procedures, such as surgery, to more benign types of interventions, such as stimulation therapies. Surgery for chronic pain conditions is most appropriate when nonsurgical methods have failed to provide pain relief and when an individual is severely disabled due to the pain. A psychological evaluation is often a useful precursor to invasive procedures given that studies have found a number of psychosocial risk factors, such as negative affect, certain personality types, catastrophizing, and a history of medicolegal problems, to be predictive of poor surgical outcome (Block, 1996).

Stimulation therapies, such as transcutaneous electrical nerve stimulation (TENS), are another medical intervention for the treatment of pain. Stimulation therapies are based on the concept of counter-irritation, in which large-diameter afferent fibers are stimulated and serve to temper pain transmission by "closing the gate" on the transmission of pain signals (Melzack, 1975). TENS has been shown to be an effective intervention for individuals with low back pain, peripheral nerve damage, and degenerative musculoskeletal disease, among other conditions (Melzack, 1975; Meyler, de Jongste, & Rolf, 1994). However, patients who report high levels of psychological distress do not respond as favorably to TENS (Meyler et al., 1994).

Cognitive-Behavioral Interventions. Because chronic pain reflects more than just physical symptomatology, psychosocial treatments are useful in addressing the psychological and environmental difficulties common to pain patients. Although cognitive-behavioral therapy (CBT) for pain is a multifaceted approach with many goals and objectives, a primary goal of this treatment approach is to assist chronic pain patients in understanding that pain is manageable and that disability and depression are not inevitable consequences of living with a pain condition. Additional treatment goals often focus on developing more adaptive methods of thinking, feeling, and behaving that will result in increased physical activity, improved interpersonal relationships, and decreased psychological distress.

What constitutes a CBT program for pain varies from clinician to clinician. Because CBT is comprised of many techniques and interventions, clinicians often pick and choose from among those techniques that seem most fitting for individual clients. For example, cognitive and behavioral interventions are often quite distinct in their focus but are commonly used in conjunction with one another to treat pain. Frequently used CBT approaches for chronic pain treatment are discussed in what follows, but the reader should bear in mind that many alternative approaches exist.

Muscle tension is a common problem among pain patients because guarding and tensing are often automatic responses to pain sensations. One goal of CBT is to reduce muscle tension through the use of one or more relaxation strategies. Biofeedback, progressive muscle relaxation, and guided imagery all have been shown to be effective at reducing muscle tension. Studies that have attempted to compare the effectiveness of these relaxation techniques have found no significant differences (Holroyd & Penzien, 1985; Spence, Sharpe, Newton-John, & Champion, 1995). The choice of which strategy to use with a specific patient will depend largely on patient characteristics such as age, personality, and overall motivation. For example, the physical tensing and releasing of tension called for in progressive muscle relaxation might fatigue some elderly individuals. Other individuals might believe that the active participation and physical exertion required by this strategy are required to see success, and they have difficulty in grasping the idea that passive interventions, such as guided imagery, will result in improvement. Still other patients will be convinced of a treatment's worth only if the strategy appears to be more "medical" and so will buy into the usefulness of biofeedback as a treatment approach. What appears to be more important than *which* relaxation strategy is incorporated into treatment is how patients perceive the intervention and whether they believe in its utility.

Another behavioral approach common in the treatment of pain is operant conditioning for the reduction of pain behaviors. Operant conditioning relies on extinction paradigms to reduce overt pain behaviors and uses reinforcement strategies to increase well behaviors. For example, to increase a patient's overall activity level, uptime and exercise are gradually increased and the patient is reinforced for this activity. Similarly, to decrease a patient's verbal complaints of pain, treatment providers ignore such instances and instead reinforce the patient for the absence of overt pain behaviors. The cooperation of a patient's spouse or family often is enlisted to apply the operant conditioning methods within the home. Operant methods have been shown to be particularly effective at increasing chronic pain patients' physical functioning and thereby increasing return to work (Fordyce, 1988).

Cognitive interventions for pain management include cognitive restructuring and cognitive coping skills training. Cognitive restructuring is commonly used in the treatment of depression and anxiety, and this approach can be adapted to address cognitive errors accompanying chronic pain. The rationale of cognitive interventions for pain is that changing a person's cognitions results in emotional, behavioral, and physiological changes, and there is evidence that cognitive mechanisms are involved in improvement in adaptive functioning among chronic pain patients. Thorn and colleagues (2002) proposed a cognitive treatment framework for specifically reducing catastrophizing, a common cognitive distortion among pain patients. This treatment approach is based in part on cognitive therapy for depression (Beck, 1995), and it assists patients in first identifying maladaptive thinking patterns and then challenging and replacing those dysfunctional thoughts with more adaptive thinking styles. Although Thorn and colleagues focused specifically on catastrophizing, other maladaptive pain beliefs and attitudes, such as those described earlier in the chapter, can easily be a focus of the intervention. In addition, Thorn and colleagues expanded their treatment approach to address other factors that might maintain catastrophic thinking. For example, patients are introduced to assertiveness skills training as a means of meeting interpersonal needs rather than relying on catastrophizing as a strategy for garnering social support.

Cognitive coping skills training for pain focuses on developing new coping skills to better manage pain. Coping skills training often encompasses many strategies for pain management rather than instruction in any one specific skill. These coping strategies might include distraction techniques, reinterpretation of pain sensations, problem solving, positive coping self-statements, and goal setting. The goal of coping skills training programs is often to arm patients with an arsenal of skills for decreasing pain, increasing functioning, and improving their overall quality of life. As mentioned previously, some pain researchers believe that reducing maladaptive coping attempts is more critical to treatment success than is increasing more positive coping strategies (Geisser et al., 1999; Newton & Barbaree, 1987). However, research has not been conducted to evaluate this issue specifically. Moreover, even if reducing passive or negative coping strategies is critical for patient improvement, most patients would likely benefit to some degree from also learning more active and positive methods for coping with pain.

Multidisciplinary Treatment. Given that the experience of pain is best understood in a biopsychosocial framework, it follows that pain treatment should also address each of these areas—the physical, the psychological, and the environmental. Multidisciplinary pain clinics have been established to provide such comprehensive treatment and are typically staffed by health care professionals from many disciplines, including physicians, nurses, physical therapists, occupational therapists, and psychologists (Turk & Stacey, 1997). The first pain clinic was established at the University of Washington in 1961, and it is estimated that more than 350 multidisciplinary pain centers exist in the United States today (Okifuji, Turk, & Kalauokalani, 1999).

Although multidisciplinary programs vary in their treatment approaches, most include an assessment process that attempts to identify the specific needs of a patient so that treatment can be customized to match the patient's needs (Turk & Stacey, 1997). The objectives of most pain clinics include reduction of pain, elimination (or significant reduction in the use) of opioid medications, reduction in the use of overall medical services, improvement in physical functioning, and improvement in social support (Follick, Ahern, Attanasio, & Riley, 1985). The ultimate goal is not to *eliminate* the pain but rather to rehabilitate patients and improve their quality of life. To achieve these ends, patients might be exposed to physical exercise and physical therapy modalities. They are often educated about the nature of pain and its cognitive, affective, and social correlates. They might participate in individual and group psychotherapy where cognitive and behavioral interventions are used for pain management. Family members are often included in the treatment process to provide support and to assist with maintenance of treatment gains on program completion. Drug detoxification is sometimes necessary to assist patients in reducing their reliance on pain medications. Finally, work-related issues are often addressed, including increasing patients' physical capacity to return to work and removing barriers to obtain employment.

Meta-analyses have shown that chronic pain patients who participate in multidisciplinary pain treatment experience greater pain relief than do patients who receive either no treatment or standard, single-discipline pain treatment (Cutler et al., 1994; Flor, Fydrich, & Turk, 1992). Multidisciplinary treatment was also found to result in significant improvements in mood, activity levels, medication use, pain behaviors, return to work, and overall health care use, and treatment gains persisted over an extended period of time. Research has also shown that multidisciplinary pain clinic treatment costs less than standard medical interventions for pain, with an estimated annual savings of close to $280 million in medical and surgical costs alone (Okifuji et al., 1999). Savings also occur when the number of individuals requiring long-term disability payments is substantially reduced.

CONCLUSIONS

Chronic pain clearly affects the totality of an individual's life experience and often creates additional burdens and stressors that exacerbate the experience of pain. Because pain has sensory, affective, and evaluative aspects, it is best understood and treated from a biopsychosocial perspective with input from health psychologists. Health psychologists have the training and expertise necessary to positively affect patients with chronic pain, helping them to manage pain more effectively and to improve their overall quality of life. Moreover, health psychologists, by nature of their broad-based training in psychosocial complications of many medical conditions, are in the unique position of being able to offer pain management services in a variety of medical contexts.

Multidisciplinary pain clinics are an obvious site for health psychologists to be involved in the treatment of pain. However, other tertiary care settings, such as neurology clinics and cancer treatment centers, provide ample opportunities for health psychologists to play a role in pain management. Although primary care settings are becoming more popular locations for collaborative treatment relationships between psychologists and physicians, they are still a largely untapped source for providing pain interventions. Because many individuals with pain complaints initially visit primary care providers for treatment, health psychologists in these settings would have the opportunity to see patients earlier in the pain experience and could potentially make important contributions to preventing chronic pain and disability from developing. Von Korff (1999) proposed a specific treatment approach for primary care patients presenting with pain problems. This approach addresses common challenges to the treatment of pain in a primary care setting and delineates several foci of treatment that resemble many of the treatment components presented in this chapter. Other psychologists have proposed methods for developing relationships with primary care providers (Bray & Rogers, 1995; Holloway, 1995), although not specifically for the management of pain.

Although our understanding of the pain experience has grown tremendously during recent decades, research on pain continues

CASE STUDY

Earlier in the chapter, a case conceptualization of a hypothetical patient, "Mary," was provided. Over a period of several years, Mary had been diagnosed with fibromyalgia, migraine headaches, and irritable bowel and bladder syndromes. This 42-year-old woman was in her second marriage and had two grown children living out of the house. Although Mary had been gainfully employed as a nurse for 10 years, she was no longer working and had recently begun receiving disability benefits. She no longer drove because she was concerned that her pain level would cause her to lose control of her car. Thus, she was dependent on her husband for her frequent visits to health care providers. Mary's friendships and other social contacts had been slowly eroding as the amount of time she spent in bed or on the couch increased. Mary complained of an inability to concentrate that had reached the point where she could no longer get enjoyment from reading. Although Mary complained that her husband was growing weary of her chronic pain and disability, the chapter authors' observation was that her husband was very solicitous and that part of the partners' marital identity was their conjoint attendance to Mary's needs and visits to health care professionals. Mary's medication regimen included more than 10 daily prescription drugs, with additional prescribed medications as needed for pain and over-the-counter analgesics as she judged to be necessary. Multiple physicians prescribed the medications, and it was unclear at the time of evaluation whether there was sufficient communication among these physicians.

Mary was admitted into the chapter authors' cognitive-behavioral chronic stress and pain management group described elsewhere (Thorn et al., 2002). This 10-week group presents pain as a stress-related illness, formats treatment as a stress management approach, and focuses on both cognitive and behavioral aspects of increasing coping and function despite the pain. The authors believe that group treatment offers the advantage of patient interaction and an opportunity for the patients to learn from one another in addition to modeling appropriate emotional expression and assertive requests regarding pain problems. Mary successfully completed the group and continues to pursue individual therapy regarding underlying social stressors, including an unfulfilling marriage, which she now sees as exacerbating her pain experience and disability. She continues to struggle with issues of assertive expression of her needs rather than the aggressive emotional displays that drive away family members. Although she is still in daily pain and continues to receive disability payments, she is taking fewer medications and her social interactions have improved. The next goal for Mary is to reduce her fears and anxieties regarding physical activity and to motivate her to engage in a gentle, daily exercise regimen.

and will undoubtedly result in greater refinement of current pain models. The role of psychosocial processes in the pain experience demands continued investigation, and with more sophisticated research designs and analyses, those factors most critical for treatment success will also become more apparent.

REFERENCES

Affleck, G., Tennen, H., Urrows, S., & Higgins, P. (1992). Neuroticism and the pain mood relation in rheumatoid arthritis: Insights from a perspective daily study. *Journal of Consulting and Clinical Psychology, 60,* 119–126.

Aghabeigi, B., Feinmann, C., & Harris, M. (1992). Prevalence of post-traumatic stress disorder in patients with chronic idiopathic facial pain. *British Journal of Oral and Maxillofacial Surgery, 30,* 360–364.

American Psychiatric Association. (1968). *Diagnostic and statistical manual of mental disorders* (2nd ed.). Washington, DC: Author.

American Psychiatric Association. (1980). *Diagnostic and statistical manual of mental disorders* (3rd ed.). Washington, DC: Author.

American Psychiatric Association. (1987). *Diagnostic and statistical manual of mental disorders* (3rd ed., rev.). Washington, DC: Author.

American Psychiatric Association. (1994). *Diagnostic and statistical manual of mental disorders* (4th ed.). Washington, DC: Author.

Amundson, G. M. (2002). *Low back pain.* [Online]. Retrieved on June 16, 2002, from www.spineuniverse.com/displayarticle.php/article216.html

Anderson, J. S., & Ferrans, C. E. (1997). The quality of life of persons with chronic fatigue syndrome. *Journal of Nervous and Mental Disease, 185,* 359–367.

Asmundson, G. J. G. (1996). Role of anxiety sensitivity in pain-related fear and avoidance. *Journal of Behavioral Medicine, 19,* 577–586.

Banks, S. M., & Kerns, R. D. (1996). Explaining high rates of depression in chronic pain: A diathesis-stress framework. *Psychological Bulletin, 119,* 95–110.

Beck, A. T., & Emery, G. (1985). *Anxiety disorders and phobias: A cognitive perspective.* New York: Basic Books.

Beck, J. S. (1995). *Cognitive therapy: Basics and beyond.* New York: Guilford.

Beitman, B. D., Kushner, M. G., Basha, I., Lamberti, J., Mukerji, V., & Bartels, K. (1991). Follow-up status of patients with angiographically normal coronary arteries and panic disorder. *Journal of the American Medical Association, 265,* 1545–1549.

Block, A. R. (1996). *Presurgical psychological screening in chronic pain syndromes: A guide for the behavioral health practitioner.* Mahwah, NJ: Lawrence Erlbaum.

Blyth, F. M., March, L. M., Brnabic, A. J., Jorm, L. R., Williamson, M., & Cousins, M. J. (2001). Chronic pain in Australia: A prevalence study. *Pain, 89,* 127–134.

Boothby, J. L., Thorn, B. E., Stroud, M. W., & Jensen, M. P. (1999). Coping with pain. In R. J. Gatchel & D. C. Turk (Eds.), *Psychosocial factors in pain: Critical perspectives* (pp. 343–359). New York: Guilford.

Bray, J. H., & Rogers, J. C. (1995). Linking psychologists and family physicians for collaborative practice. *Professional Psychology: Research and Practice, 26,* 132–138.

Brennan, A. F., Barrett, C. L., & Garretson, H. D. (1986). The prediction of chronic pain outcome by psychological variables. *International Journal of Psychiatry in Medicine, 16,* 373–387.

Breslau, N., Davis, G. C., & Andreski, P. (1991). Migraine, psychiatric disorders, and suicide attempts: An epidemiological study of young adults. *Psychiatry Research, 37,* 11–23.

Brown, G. K., & Nicassio, P. M. (1987). Development of a questionnaire for the assessment of active and passive coping strategies in chronic pain patients. *Pain, 31,* 53–63.

Bruehl, S., Steger, H. G., & Harden, R. N. (2001). Complex regional pain syndrome. In D. C. Turk & R. Melzack (Eds.), *Handbook of pain assessment* (2nd ed., pp. 275–291). New York: Guilford.

Butler, R. W., Damarin, F. L., Beaulieu, C. L., Schwebel, A. I., & Thorn, B. E. (1989). Assessing cognitive coping strategies for acute pain. *Psychological Assessment: A Journal of Consulting and Clinical Psychology, 1,* 41–45.

Carney, R. M., Freedland, K. E., Ludbrook, P. A., Saunders, R. D., & Jaffe, A. S. (1990). Major depression, panic disorder, and mitral valve prolapse in patients who complain of chest pain. *American Journal of Medicine, 89*, 757–760.

Caudill, M. A. (2002). *Managing pain before it manages you* (rev. ed.). New York: Guilford.

Chapman, C. R., & Turner, J. A. (1986). Psychological control of acute pain in medical settings. *Journal of Pain and Symptom Management, 1*, 9–20.

Chaves, J. F., & Brown, J. M. (1987). Spontaneous cognitive strategies for the control of clinical pain and stress. *Journal of Behavioral Medicine, 10*, 263–276.

Clark, J. D. (2002). Chronic pain prevalence and analgesic prescribing in a general medical population. *Journal of Pain and Symptom Management, 23*, 131–137.

Crombez, G., Eccleston, C., Van den Broek, A., Van Doudenhove, B., & Goubert, L. (2002). The effects of catastrophic thinking about pain on attentional interference by pain: No mediation of negative affectivity in healthy volunteers and in patients with low back pain. *Pain Research and Management, 7*, 31–33.

Cutler, R. B., Fishbain, D. A., Rosomoff, H. L., Abdel-Moty, E., Khalil, T. M., & Rosomoff, R. S. (1994). Does nonsurgical pain center treatment of chronic pain return patients to work? A review and meta-analysis of the literature. *Spine, 19*, 643–652.

DeGood, D. E., & Shutty, M. S. (1992). Assessment of pain beliefs, coping, and self-efficacy. In D. C. Turk & R. Melzack (Eds.), *Handbook of pain assessment* (pp. 214–234). New York: Guilford.

Donnay, A. (1998, April 29). *Questionnaire for screening CFS, FMS, and MCS in adults*. Testimony presented to the U.S. Chronic Fatigue Syndrome Coordinating Committee, Washington, DC.

Elliott, T. R., Jackson, W. T., Layfield, M., & Kendall, D. (1996). Personality disorders and response to outpatient treatment of chronic pain. *Journal of Clinical Psychology in Medical Settings, 3*, 219–234.

Etscheidt, M. A., Steger, H. G., & Braverman, B. (1995). Multidimensional Pain Inventory profile classifications and psychopathology. *Journal of Clinical Psychology, 51*, 29–36.

F. A. Davis. (1997). *Taber's cyclopedic medical dictionary* (18th ed.). Philadelphia: Author.

Fernandez, E., & Turk, D. C. (1995). The scope and significance of anger in the experience of chronic pain. *Pain, 61*, 165–175.

Fishbain, D. A., Goldberg, M., Meagher, B. R., Steele, R., & Rosomoff, H. (1986). Male and female chronic pain patients categorized by DSM-III psychiatric diagnostic criteria. *Pain, 26*, 181–187.

Fishbain, D. A., Rosomoff, H. L., & Rosomoff, R. S. (1992). Drug abuse, dependence, and addiction in chronic pain patients. *Clinical Journal of Pain, 8*, 77–85.

Flor, H., Fydrich, T., & Turk, D. C. (1992). Efficacy of multidisciplinary pain treatment centers: A meta-analytic review. *Pain, 49*, 221–230.

Follick, M. J., Ahern, D. K., Attanasio, V., & Riley, J. F. (1985). Chronic pain programs: Current aims, strategies, and needs. *Annals of Behavioral Medicine, 7*, 17–20.

Fordyce, W. E. (1988). Pain and suffering: A reappraisal. *American Psychologist, 43*, 276–283.

Fukuda, K., Straus, S. E., Hickie, I., Sharpe, M. C., Dobbins, J. G., & Komaroff, A. (1994). The chronic fatigue syndrome: A comprehensive approach to its definition and study. *Annals of Internal Medicine, 121*, 953–959.

Gaskin, M. E., Greene, A. F., Robinson, M. E., & Geisser, M. E. (1992). Negative affect and the experience of chronic pain. *Journal of Psychosomatic Research, 36*, 707–713.

Gatchel, R. J., Polatin, P. B., & Mayer, T. G. (1995). The dominant role of psychosocial risk factors in the development of chronic low back pain disability. *Spine, 20,* 2702–2709.

Gatchel, R. J., Polatin, P. B., Mayer, T. G., & Garcy, P. (1994). Psychopathology and the rehabilitation of patients with chronic low back pain disability. *Archives of Physical Medicine and Rehabilitation, 75,* 666–670.

Geisser, M. E., Robinson, M. E., & Henson, C. D. (1994). The Coping Strategies Questionnaire and chronic pain adjustment: A conceptual and empirical reanalysis. *Clinical Journal of Pain, 10,* 98–106.

Geisser, M. E., Robinson, M. E., & Riley, J. L. (1999). Pain beliefs, coping, and adjustment to chronic pain. *Pain Forum, 8,* 161–168.

Gil, K. M. (1984). Coping with invasive medical procedures: A descriptive model. *Clinical Psychology Review, 4,* 339–362.

Gil, K. M., Williams, D. A., Keefe, F. J., & Beckham, J. C. (1990). The relationship of negative thoughts to pain and psychological distress. *Behavior Therapy, 21,* 349–362.

Headache Classification Committee of the International Headache Society. (1988). Classification and diagnostic criteria for headache disorders, cranial neuralgias, and facial pain. *Cephalalgia, 8,* 9–92.

Holloway, R. L. (1995). Building a primary care discipline: Notes from a psychologist in family medicine. *Journal of Clinical Psychology in Medical Settings, 2,* 7–20.

Holroyd, K. A., & Penzien, D. B. (1985). Client variables and the behavioral treatment of recurrent tension headache: A meta-analytic review. *Journal of Behavioral Medicine, 9,* 515–536.

Jacobsen, P. B., & Butler, R. W. (1996). Relation of cognitive coping and catastrophizing to acute pain and analgesic use following breast cancer surgery. *Journal of Behavioral Medicine, 19,* 17–29.

Jamison, R. N., Raymond, S. A., Slawsby, E. A., Nedeljkovic, S. S., & Katz, N. P. (1998). Opioid therapy for chronic noncancer back pain: A randomized prospective study. *Spine, 23,* 2591–2600.

Jason, L. A., Richman, J. A., Rademaker, A. W., Jordan, K. M., Plioplys, A. V., Taylor, R. R., McCready, W., Huang, C. F., & Plioplys, S. (1999). A community-based study of chronic fatigue syndrome. *Archives of Internal Medicine, 159,* 2129–2137.

Jensen, M. P., Turner, J. A., & Romano, J. M. (2001). Changes in beliefs, catastrophizing, and coping are associated with improvement in multidisciplinary pain treatment. *Journal of Consulting and Clinical Psychology, 69,* 655–662.

Keefe, F. J. (1982). Behavioral assessment and treatment of chronic pain: Current status and future directions. *Journal of Consulting and Clinical Psychology, 50,* 896–911.

Keefe, F. J., & Hill, R. W. (1985). An objective approach to quantifying pain behavior and gait patterns in low back pain patients. *Pain, 21,* 153–161.

Keefe, F. J., Lefebvre, J. C., & Smith, S. J. (1999). Catastrophizing research: Avoiding conceptual errors and maintaining a balanced perspective. *Pain Forum, 8,* 176–180.

Keogh, E., Ellery, D., Hunt, C., & Hannent, I. (2001). Selective attentional bias for pain-related stimuli amongst pain fearful individuals. *Pain, 91,* 91–100.

Kerns, R. D., Turk, D., & Rudy, T. E. (1985). The West Haven–Yale Multidimensional Pain Inventory (WHYMPI). *Pain, 23,* 345–356.

Kouyanou, K., Pither, C. E., Rabe-Hesketh, S., & Wessely, S. (1998). A comparative study of iatrogenesis, medication abuse, and psychiatric morbidity in chronic pain patients with and without medically explained symptoms. *Pain, 76,* 417–426.

Kulich, R. J., Mencher, P., Bertrand, C., & Maciewicz, R. (2000). Comorbidity of post-traumatic stress disorder and pain: Implications for clinical and forensic assessment. *Current Review of Pain, 4,* 36–48.

Lahita, R. G. (2001). *What is lupus?* [Online]. Retrieved on July 9, 2002, from www.lupus.org

Lazarus, R. S. (1993). Coping theory and research: Past, present, and future. *Psychosomatic Medicine, 55,* 234–247.

Lazarus, R. S., & Folkman, S. (1984). *Stress, appraisal, and coping.* New York: Springer.

Lefebvre, M. F. (1981). Cognitive distortion and cognitive errors in depressed psychiatric and low back pain patients. *Journal of Consulting and Clinical Psychology, 49,* 517–525.

LeResche, L., & Von Korff, M. (1999). Epidemiology of chronic pain. In A. R. Block, E. F. Kremer, & E. Fernandez (Eds.), *Handbook of pain syndromes: Biopsychosocial perspectives* (pp. 3–22). Mahwah, NJ: Lawrence Erlbaum.

McCracken, L. M., Zayfert, C., & Gross, R. T. (1992). The Pain Anxiety Scale: Development and validation of a scale to measure fear of pain. *Pain, 50,* 67–73.

Melzack, R. (1975). Prolonged relief of pain by brief, intense transcutaneous somatic stimulation. *Pain, 1,* 357–373.

Melzack, R. (1987). The short form McGill pain questionnaire. *Pain, 30,* 191–197.

Melzack, R., & Wall, P. D. (1965). Pain mechanisms: A new theory. *Science, 50,* 971–979.

Merskey, H., & Bogdale, N. (Eds.). (1994). *Classification of chronic pain: Descriptions of chronic pain syndromes and definitions of pain terms.* Seattle, WA: IASP Press.

Merskey, H., & Moulin, D. (1999). Pharmacological treatment in chronic pain. In A. R. Block, E. F. Kremer, & E. Fernandez (Eds.), *Handbook of pain syndromes: Biopsychosocial perspectives* (pp. 149–163). Mahwah, NJ: Lawrence Erlbaum.

Meyler, W. J., de Jongste, M. J. L., & Rolf, C. A. M. (1994). Clinical evaluation of pain treatment with electrostimulation: A study of TENS in patients with different pain syndromes. *Clinical Journal of Pain, 10,* 22–27.

Moreno, R., Cunningham, A. C., Gatchel, R. J., & Mayer, T. G. (1991). Functional restoration for chronic low back pain: Changes in depression, cognitive distortion, and disability. *Journal of Occupational Rehabilitation, 1,* 207–216.

Moulin, D. E., Iezzi, A., Amireah, R., Sharpe, W. K. J., Boyd, D., & Merskey, H. (1996). Randomized trial of oral morphine for chronic non-cancer pain. *Lancet, 347,* 143–147.

Newton, C. R., & Barbaree, H. E. (1987). Cognitive changes accompanying headache treatment: The use of a thought-sampling procedure. *Cognitive Therapy and Research, 11,* 635–651.

Okifuji, A., Turk, D. C., & Kalauokalani, D. (1999). Clinical outcome and economic evaluation of multidisciplinary pain centers. In A. R. Block, E. F. Kremer, & E. Fernandez (Eds.), *Handbook of pain syndromes: Biopsychosocial perspectives* (pp. 77–97). Mahwah, NJ: Lawrence Erlbaum.

Portenoy, R. K., & Foley, K. M. (1986). Chronic use of opioid analgesics in non-malignant pain: Report of 38 cases. *Pain, 25,* 171–186.

Rapoport, A. M., & Sheftell, F. D. (1996). *Headache disorders: A management guide for practitioners.* Philadelphia: W. B. Saunders.

Riskind, J. H., & Williams, N. L. (1999). Specific cognitive content of anxiety and catastrophizing: Looming vulnerability and the looming maladaptive style. *Journal of Cognitive Psychotherapy, 13,* 41–54.

Robbins, R. A., Moody, D. S., Hahn, M. B., & Weaver, M. A. (1996). Psychological testing variables as predictors of return to work by chronic pain patients. *Perceptual and Motor Skills, 83,* 1317–1318.

Robinson, M. E., Riley, J. L., Myers, C. D., Sadler, I. J., Kvaal, S. A., Geisser, M. E., & Keefe, F. J. (1997). The Coping Strategies Questionnaire: A large sample, item level factor analysis. *Clinical Journal of Pain, 13,* 43–49.

Roland, M., & Morris, R. (1983). A study of the natural history of back pain: I. Development of a reliable and sensitive measure of disability in low back pain. *Spine, 8,* 141–144.

Romano, J. M., & Turner, J. A. (1985). Chronic pain and depression: Does the evidence support a relationship? *Psychological Bulletin, 97,* 18–34.

Rosenstiel, A. K., & Keefe, F. J. (1983). The use of coping strategies in chronic low back pain: Relationship to patient characteristics and current adjustment. *Pain, 17,* 33–44.

Schultheis, K., Peterson, L., & Selby, V. (1987). Preparation for stressful medical procedures and person × treatment interactions. *Clinical Psychology Review, 7,* 329–352.

Smith, G. R. (1991). *Somatization disorder in the medical setting.* Washington, DC: American Psychiatric Association.

Smith, T. W., Christensen, A. J., Peck, J. R., & Ward, J. R. (1994). Cognitive distortion, helplessness, and depressed mood in rheumatoid arthritis: A 4-year longitudinal analysis. *Health Psychology, 13,* 213–217.

Spence, S. H., Sharpe, L., Newton-John, T., & Champion, D. (1995). Effect of EMG biofeedback compared to applied relaxation training with chronic, upper extremity cumulative trauma disorders. *Pain, 63,* 199–206.

Stewart, W., Breslau, N., & Keck, P. E., Jr. (1994). Comorbidity of migraine and panic disorder. *Neurology, 44*(10, Suppl. 7), S23–S27.

Stroud, M. W., Thorn, B. E., Jensen, M. P., & Boothby, J. L. (2000). The relation between pain beliefs, negative thoughts, and psychosocial functioning in chronic pain patients. *Pain, 84,* 347–352.

Sullivan, M. D. (2001). Assessment of psychiatric disorders. In D. C. Turk & R. Melzack (Eds.), *Handbook of pain assessment* (2nd ed., pp. 275–291). New York: Guilford.

Sullivan, M. J. L., Bishop, S. R., & Pivik, J. (1995). The Pain Catastrophizing Scale: Development and validation. *Psychological Assessment, 7,* 524–532.

Sullivan, M. J. L., & Neish, N. (1998). Catastrophizing, anxiety, and pain during dental hygiene treatment. *Communicative Dental Oral Epidemiology, 37,* 243–250.

Sullivan, M. J. L., Rouse, D., Bishop, S., & Johnston, S. (1997). Thought suppression, catastrophizing, and pain. *Cognitive Therapy and Research, 21,* 555–568.

Sullivan, M. J. L., Stanish, W., Sullivan, M. E., & Tripp, D. (2002). Differential predictors of pain and disability in patients with whiplash injuries. *Pain Research and Management, 7,* 68–74.

Sullivan, M. J. L., Thorn, B. E., Haythornthwaite, J., Keefe, F., Martin, M., Bradley, L., & Lefebvre, J. C. (2001). Theoretical perspectives on the relation between catastrophizing and pain. *Clinical Journal of Pain, 17,* 52–64.

Sullivan, M. J. L., Tripp, D. A., & Santor, D. (2000). Gender differences in pain and pain behavior: The role of catastrophizing. *Cognitive Therapy and Research, 24,* 121–134.

Suls, J., & Wan, C. K. (1989). Effects of sensory and procedure information on coping with stressful medical procedures and pain: A meta-analysis. *Journal of Consulting and Clinical Psychology, 57,* 372–379.

Taylor, R. R., Friedberg, F., & Jason, L. A. (2001). *A clinician's guide to controversial illnesses: Chronic fatigue syndrome, fibromyalgia, multiple chemical sensitivities.* Sarasota, FL: Professional Resources Press.

Thorn, B. E., Boothby, J. L., & Sullivan, M. J. L. (2002). Targeted treatment of catastrophizing for the management of chronic pain. *Cognitive and Behavioral Practice, 9,* 127–138.

Thorn, B. E., Rich, M. A., & Boothby, J. L. (1999). Pain beliefs and coping attempts: Conceptual model building. *Pain Forum, 8,* 169–171.

Turk, D. C. (1996). Biopsychosocial perspective on chronic pain. In R. J. Gatchel & D. C. Turk (Eds.), *Psychological approaches to pain management: A practitioner's handbook* (pp. 3–32). New York: Guilford.

Turk, D. C., & Meichenbaum, D. (1994). A cognitive-behavioral approach to pain management. In P. D. Wall & R. Melzack (Eds.), *Textbook of pain* (pp. 787–794). London: Churchill Livingstone.

Turk, D. C., & Rudy, T. E. (1992). Cognitive factors and persistent pain: A glimpse into Pandora's box. *Cognitive Therapy and Research, 16,* 99–122.

Turk, D. C., & Stacey, B. R. (1997). Multidisciplinary pain centers in the treatment of chronic pain. In J. W. Frymoyer, T. B. Ducker, N. M. Hadler, J. P. Kostuik, J. N. Weinstein, & T. S. Whitecloud, III (Eds.), *The adult spine: Principles and practice* (2nd ed., pp. 253–274). New York: Raven.

Vasey, M. W., & Burkovec, T. D. (1992). A catastrophizing assessment of worrisome thoughts. *Cognitive Therapy and Research, 16,* 505–520.

Vlaeyen, J. W. S., & Linton, S. J. (2000). Fear-avoidance and its consequences in chronic musculoskeletal pain: A state of the art. *Pain, 85,* 317–332.

Von Korff, M. (1999). Pain management in primary care: An individualized stepped-care approach. In R. J. Gatchel & D. C. Turk (Eds.), *Psychosocial factors in pain: Critical perspectives* (pp. 360–373). New York: Guilford.

Waddell, G., McCulloch, J. A., Kummel, E., & Venner, R. M. (1980). Nonorganic physical signs in low-back pain. *Spine, 5,* 117–125.

Ward, L. C., Thorn, B. E., & Clements, K. L. (2002). *Factor structure of the Personal Attributes Questionnaire: Agency, communion, and emotional vulnerability.* Unpublished manuscript, Department of Veterans Affairs Medical Center, Tuscaloosa, AL.

Waylonis, G. W., & Perkins, R. H. (1994). Post-traumatic fibromyalgia: A long-term follow-up. *American Journal of Physical Medicine and Rehabilitation, 73,* 403–412.

Williams, D. A. (1996). Acute pain management. In R. J. Gatchel & D. C. Turk (Eds.), *Psychological approaches to pain management: A practitioner's handbook* (pp. 55–77). New York: Guilford.

Williams, D. A. (1999). Acute pain (with special emphasis on painful medical procedures). In R. J. Gatchel & D. C. Turk (Eds.), *Psychosocial factors in pain: Critical perspectives* (pp. 151–163). New York: Guilford.

Williams, D. A., & Thorn, B. E. (1989). An empirical assessment of pain beliefs. *Pain, 36,* 351–358.

Wolfe, F., Smythe, H. A., Yunus, M. B., Bennett, R. M., Bombardier, C., Goldenberg, D. L., Tugwell, P., Campbell, S. M., Abeles, M., Clark, P., Fam, A. G., Farber, S. J., Fiechtner, J. J., Franklin, C. M., Gatter, R. A., Hamaty, D., Lessard, J., Lichtbroun, A. S., Masi, A. T., McCain, G. A., Reynolds, W. J., Romano, T. J., Russell, I. J., & Sheon, R. P. (1990). The American College of Rheumatology 1990 criteria for the classification of fibromyalgia. *Arthritis and Rheumatology, 33,* 160–172.

Zenz, M., Strumpf, M., & Tryba, M. (1992). Long-term oral opioid therapy in patients with chronic non-malignant pain. *Journal of Pain and Symptom Management, 7,* 69–77.

Ziegler, F. J., Imboden, J. B., & Myer, E. (1960). Contemporary conversion reaction: A clinical study. *American Journal of Psychiatry, 116,* 901–903.

CHAPTER 14

Hypertension

MUSTAFA AL'ABSI AND RICHARD G. HOFFMAN

Hypertension is a major risk factor of heart disease, the leading cause of death in the United States. It contributes to stroke, the third leading cause of death, and it also contributes to approximately one fourth of kidney failures. These devastating diseases exact a high toll in human suffering, deteriorating quality of life, and financial cost, making a strong case for continuous effort to identify causes and develop means to control hypertension. As is described in more detail later in this chapter, hypertension is one of the risk factors that can be controlled by available behavioral and pharmacological interventions. However, many challenges face clinicians in their efforts to implement and ensure compliance with regimens for this disorder.

The term *hypertension* is used to indicate high blood pressure (BP). Although hypertension can occur at any age, it is more prevalent in adults over age 35 years. It is particularly prevalent among African Americans, middle-aged and elderly people, obese individuals, and heavy drinkers (MacMahon, Cutler, Brittain, & Higgins, 1987; Neaton & Wentworth, 1992; Stamler et al., 1989; Whelton, 1985). However, there is a high heterogeneity in hypertension prevalence related to heterogeneity in underlying pathophysiological processes.

Cultural and psychosocial factors, as well as responsiveness to interventions, may also contribute to differences in hypertension prevalence (Horan & Mockrin, 1992).

Increased risk for hypertension is directly associated with increased risk for premature death due to cardiovascular diseases (Lie, Mundal, & Erikssen, 1985; Neaton & Wentworth, 1992; Stamler et al., 1989). Hypertension increases workload on the heart and contributes to myocardial cell enlargement and left-ventricular hypertrophy. As BP increases, the pumping action of the heart requires more effort and energy. Under the condition of high BP, the arteries carry blood that is moving under greater pressure. Chronically, this state eventually leads to various structural changes in the heart and blood vessels, leading to the hardening of arteries, and other organs may also get directly affected, leading to the sequelae of hypertension, including stroke, congestive heart failure, kidney failure, and heart attack. Another important risk for hypertension is that when it is present with other risk factors (e.g., high blood cholesterol, smoking, diabetes, obesity), the danger of major heart problems or a stroke increases in a manner that exceeds the simple addition of the risk weight of these risk factors.

One in four adults has high BP, and approximately 32% of those with hypertension are not aware that they have it. Approximately 15% of those with hypertension are not on any therapeutic regimen, and about 26% are inadequately treated. Furthermore, hypertension affects about one in three African Americans (Burt et al., 1995). Hypertension develops earlier in life, and is usually more severe, in blacks than in whites. The longer hypertension is left untreated, the more serious its complications can become, and this possibly contributes to the prevalence of the different levels of cardiac adaptation processes and the greater sequelae seen in African Americans with high BP (Burt et al., 1995; Koren, Mensah, Blake, Laragh, & Devereux, 1993).

BACKGROUND AND ETIOLOGY

Diagnosis

When BP is measured, it is defined as two numbers: systolic and diastolic. Systolic BP represents the force at which blood flows when the heart beats. Diastolic BP, on the other hand, is an estimate of the force of blood flow when the heart relaxes (in between heartbeats). Together, these numbers (written as the value of systolic BP divided by the value of diastolic BP, recorded in millimeters of mercury [mm Hg]) compose a person's BP and are used to determine whether or not the pressures are in a healthy range. The Joint National Committee on Detection, Evaluation, and Treatment of High Blood Pressure (JNC, 1997) and the American Heart Association have put forth recommendations on the classification of BP levels. The recommendations are as follows. First, optimal BP is systolic less than 120 mm Hg and diastolic less than 80 mm Hg. Second, normal BP is systolic less than 130 mm Hg and diastolic less than 85 mm Hg. Third, high normal BP is systolic 130 to 139 mm Hg or diastolic 85 to 89 mm Hg. Fourth, Stage 1 (mild) hypertension is

systolic 140 to 159 mm Hg or diastolic 90 to 99 mm Hg. Fifth, Stage 2 (moderate) hypertension is systolic 160 to 179 mm Hg or diastolic 100 to 109 mm Hg. Finally, Stage 3 (higher) hypertension is systolic 180 or higher mm Hg or diastolic 110 mm Hg or higher.

Etiological Issues

Hypertension is a highly heterogeneous disorder with multiple pathogenic mechanisms. The causes for 90% to 95% of hypertension cases (called "essential hypertension") are not known. The remaining 5% to 10% of hypertension (called "secondary hypertension") may be caused by other diseases such as kidney abnormalities, congenital abnormalities in major blood vessels in the body, and abnormalities associated with vasoconstriction of arteries.

Despite no clear identification of the pathophysiology of essential hypertension, the role of psychological variables in hypertension has occupied a prominent position within the field of behavioral medicine (Alexander, 1939). In particular, recent evidence suggests that stress may contribute to the pathophysiology of hypertension (Henry et al., 1993). Researchers propose that exaggerated cardiovascular responses to frequent and persistent stress episodes may be a risk factor and/or a marker for cardiovascular disease (Everson et al., 1997; Light et al., 1999). For example, exposure to stress has been found to accelerate hypertension development in spontaneously hypertensive rats, whereas unstressed rats had a delayed development and milder hypertension (Henry et al., 1993; Yamori, Matsumoto, Yamabe, & Okamoto, 1969). Research has also shown that responses to laboratory stressors predict future BP elevations (Matthews, Woodall, & Allen, 1993; Menkes et al., 1989; Treiber et al., 1996). Individuals who are at high risk for hypertension or who have chronically elevated BP tend to show exaggerated BP responses to behavioral stressors (al'Absi,

Buchanan, & Lovallo, 1996; al'Absi, Lovallo, McKey, & Pincomb, 1994; Everson, Kaplan, Goldberg, & Salonen, 1996). These elevated responses, combined with the high baseline BP, contribute to a high workload on the heart.

As was discussed more thoroughly in Chapter 10, the primary peripheral hormone produced by the adrenal cortex, cortisol, is considered to be the central component of the stress response (Kaplan, 1998). It is proposed that cortisol response to stressful events represents one mechanism through which prolonged stress exerts its hypothesized pathogenic effects on hypertension (Litchfield et al., 1998; Watt et al., 1992). In short, cortisol is essential to the maintenance of normal vascular tone. It has effects on responses to catecholamines and other vasoactive agents such as angiotensin II and vasopressin (Vander, Sherman, & Luciano, 1994). The physical nature of cardiac output and the resistance of the blood vessels to this blood flow determine BP. The control of these activities is mediated by neurohumoral activity, including norepinephrine, epinephrine, acetylcholine, and their receptors, and these agents are modulated by cortisol. Cortisol has ready access to the central nervous system, affecting areas of the brain that are involved in the control of BP (e.g., hypothalamus, limbic system) (Wilson & Foster, 1992). In addition, cortisol enhances sympathetic nervous system activity by increasing adrenergic receptor sensitivity to neurotransmitter activation (Davies & Lefkowitz, 1984). The bolstering of sympathetic nervous system activity is believed to enhance circulating fluid volume by causing fluid to shift from intracellular to extracellular compartments in the kidney (Kaplan, 1990). This results in improved venous return to the heart and increased cardiac output. Cortisol also inhibits the production of prostaglandin and arachidonic acid, bradykinin, serotonin, and histamine (Wilson & Foster, 1992), leading to vasoconstrictive effects. These properties of cortisol increase the effects of cardiovascular activation on the heart and blood vessels. Thus, they may play a role in the development of hypertension.

The relationship among stress, cortisol, and hypertension development bears some parallel in humans. Patients with high levels of cortisol due to Cushing's syndrome show about 80% prevalence of hypertension (Kaplan, 1990). This is often corrected using glucocorticoid antagonists, which also reduce BP (Fallo, Paoletta, Tona, Boscaro, & Sonino, 1993). Furthermore, normotensives who are at high risk for hypertension and borderline hypertensives show enhanced adrenocortical activity (e.g., elevated cortisol) in response to a variety of psychological stressors (al'Absi & Arnett, 2000). For example, prior research has evaluated adrenocortical activity in persons at high risk for hypertension during rest and in response to acute stressors. When at rest in a novel experimental environment, borderline hypertensives showed enhanced adrenocortical activation relative to low-risk controls (al'Absi & Lovallo, 1993) and had larger responses during work on mental arithmetic and psychomotor stress (al'Absi et al., 1994). These tendencies are exaggerated in the presence of psychostimulants such as caffeine. Relative to low-risk controls, caffeine can differentially increase cortisol secretion in unmediated, mildly hypertensive men (al'Absi, Lovallo, Sung, & Wilson, 1995). This suggests that early stages of hypertension may be especially sensitive to caffeine's pituitary-adrenocortical effects when under stressful conditions.

Prior research has also obtained similar results in normotensive persons at high risk for hypertension, defined as having a positive parental history or having mildly elevated BP but not yet medicated (al'Absi, Everson, & Lovallo, 1995). These individuals showed elevated adrenocorticotropin and cortisol concentrations after caffeine ingestion relative to placebo. They also showed an additive effect on adrenocorticotropin and cortisol increases to the acute stress and caffeine. The high-risk group showed earlier and more persistent rises throughout the tasks than did the low-risk group (al'Absi et al., 1998). Neither the behavioral stress nor caffeine alone produced cortisol responses in normotensive men, although significant elevations occurred in the low-risk men after the tasks in the presence of caffeine. This line of work suggests that the previously observed increased activation of the autonomic nervous system (Julius & Nesbitt, 1996) and the cardiovascular control centers of the hypothalamus and medulla may be paralleled by enhanced responses of the adrenocortical system to behavioral stress and to stimulant agents such as caffeine.

The increased cortisol levels and responses in hypertension-prone persons may represent an altered stress response, characterized by heightened hypothalamic-adrenocortical activation. The development of hypertension is accompanied by enhanced activation of the cardiovascular control centers of the hypothalamus and medulla (Bunag & Takeda, 1979; Jin & Rockhold, 1991) as well as by increased sympathetic nervous system function and adrenergic activity (Julius & Nesbitt, 1996). Such activation would predict greater levels of adrenocortical activity, possibly initiated at the hypothalamic level above in the central nervous system. As illustrated in Figure 14.1, adrenocortical activation may contribute independently and in combination with other risk factors to increase BP. Genetic vulnerability may enhance adrenocortical activation both centrally and peripherally. This adrenocortical activation may also be caused by other risk factors known to increase cortisol such as obesity and alcohol intake (Keltikangas-Jarvinen, Raikkonen, Hautanen, & Adlercreutz, 1996; Raikkonen, Hautanen, & Keltikangas-Jarvinen, 1996). Therefore, it is appealing to propose that adrenocortical dysregulation, in combination with environmental factors such as high salt intake and smoking, may represent enhanced risk.

ASSESSMENT AND TREATMENT

Measurement

Hypertension is usually called the silent killer because it has no specific symptoms. Patients may have hypertension for many years without knowing it because there is no specific perceived sensory information associated with high BP. The only way in which to determine whether a person has hypertension is by measuring BP. Measurement of BP is a quick and a reliable way in which to determine levels of risk for hypertension. A screening measurement can be conducted in a hospital clinic, doctor's office, nurse's office, company clinic, or school or at a health fair. If screening suggests high BP, a physician may ask for more detailed BP measurement, including ambulatory monitoring over a 24-hour period. This more detailed assessment is important to have a reliable conclusion of BP levels.

In a clinical setting, BP is measured using an instrument called a sphygmomanometer. During this measurement, a rubber cuff is wrapped around the patient's upper arm. The cuff is then inflated, causing the cuff to compress a large artery in the arm, thereby stopping blood flow in the arm. The pressure is then reduced by releasing the air from the cuff. With the reduced cuff pressure, blood starts to pulse through the artery, making a sound, while the clinician listens with a stethoscope. This pulsing sound continues until the pressure in the artery is higher than the pressure in the cuff. The clinician records BP using a gauge connected to the cuff. Two BPs are recorded. The first is when the first sound is heard. This reflects the systolic BP and indicates pressure related to the blood flow when the heart beats. The second is when the final sound is heard. This reflects the diastolic pressure and indicates the pressure between heartbeats. The unit for the assessment of BP is millimeters of mercury.

There are several factors that might introduce error variance into measurement of BP,

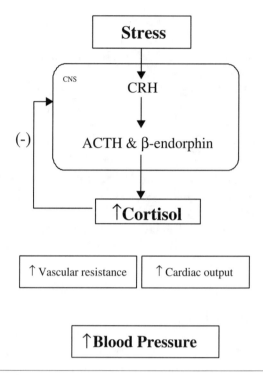

Figure 14.1 Potential Pathways Among Stress, Cortisol, and Hypertension Risk

NOTE: CRH = corticotropin-releasing hormone; ACTH = adrenocorticotropic hormone.

including behavioral and environmental factors. For example, prevailing temperature, health status, prior smoking, consumption of caffeine-containing beverages, and time since last meal all are factors that could artificially affect accuracy of BP measurement. Prior to measurement, the patient should sit in a comfortable chair with his or her feet on the floor for approximately 5 minutes. The patient should have emptied his or her bladder and should not be engaged in conversation during the assessment. Measurement should be conducted multiple times to obtain an average, and intervals between measurement should be more than 1 minute.

Assessment in Clinical Settings: The "White Coat" Effect

One important issue to consider during diagnosis is a phenomenon called "white coat hypertension." This occurs when BP measured in the clinic or in the physician's office is high enough to warrant diagnosis for hypertension, but measurement in the field outside the clinic (e.g., at home) shows a normotensive range of BP (Pickering, Coats, Mallion, Mancia, & Verdecchia, 1999; Pickering et al., 1988). It is estimated that 20% of hypertensives have white coat hypertension (Pickering et al., 1999). It is still not clear what the clinical significance of this discrepancy is or how to address this phenomenon in treatment. Nevertheless, it should be noted that about one in four of those who are considered for antihypertensive medication may actually have white coat hypertension (Myers & Reeves, 1991; Selenta, Hogan, & Linden, 2000). Persons with white coat hypertension differ from true normotensives on several demographic and lifestyle variables. They tend to be male, past smokers, and older and also tend to consume more alcohol.

Some investigators argue that the white coat hypertension is a benign condition (Gosse, Promax, Durandet, & Clementy, 1993; Julius et al., 1990; Verdecchia, Schillaci, Borgioni, Ciucci, & Porcellati, 1997). Others argue that it has clinical significance, including increased cardiovascular risk (Kuwajima, Suzuki, Fujisawa, & Kuramoto, 1993; Weber, Neutel, Smith, & Graettinger, 1994). Because this condition is not associated with sustained BP elevation, it is possible that the harmful effect of this condition is due to high BP variability across settings (Lantelme, Milon, Gharib, Gayet, & Fortrat, 1998). An exaggerated BP lability may contribute to greater organ damage in hypertensives (Parati, Pomidossi, Albini, Malaspina, & Mancia, 1987) and in individuals with white coat hypertension (Cavallini et al., 1995). Individuals with white coat hypertension may represent a subgroup of hypertensives who require a targeted intervention to manage the situational reactivity they exhibit. This is significant in light of the observed negative cardiac abnormalities that have been observed in those with white coat hypertension (Cardillo, De Felice, Campia, & Folli, 1993). Finally, it has been shown that the white coat effect may have a negative prognostic impact, even in the absence of sustained hypertension (Kuwajima et al., 1993; Weber et al., 1994).

Intervention Strategies to Control Hypertension

The treatment of hypertension is a long-term effort that puts a burden on patients and their health care providers. Many patients with hypertension may benefit from behavioral modification techniques such as reducing weight, eating properly, and getting the right amount of exercise. Pharmacotherapy is also widely used for treatment of hypertension. In the following subsections, specific intervention strategies that have been used in the control of hypertension are described and evaluated.

Weight Control, Weight Loss, and Blood Pressure

The Role of Weight Control in Primary Prevention. A clear direct relationship exists between body weight and BP. Overweight individuals (body mass index greater than 27.8 for men and greater than 27.3 for women) have an increased incidence of hypertension (Oparil, 2000), and this relationship between obesity and hypertension appears to be strongest for younger adults (Stone & Kushner, 2000).

The pathogenesis of obesity-induced hypertension is not well characterized but is likely related to hemodynamic alterations, renal dysfunction, and an increase in sympathetic nervous system activity that may be related to insulin resistance (Hall, 1997). The hemodynamic changes are likely due to increases in adipose tissue and expansion of extracellular water and total blood volume, resulting in an augmented stroke volume and increased cardiac output proportional to body size. Abnormal renal sodium and water handling (pressure natriuresis) causes the initiation of hypertension (Stone & Kushner, 2000). Ultimately, eccentric left ventricular hypertrophy may develop as an adaptation to increased vessel wall stress that results from expanded intravascular volumes, venous return, and left ventricular preload increase (Messerli, 1982). Echocardiography studies have demonstrated that a positive correlation exists between percentage overweight and both left ventricular wall thickness and internal dimension, even in the absence of hypertension (Stone & Kushner, 2000). Among the severely obese, duration of obesity is associated with higher left ventricular mass, poorer left ventricular systolic function, and greater impairment of left ventricular diastolic filling, and this ultimately may lead to concentric left ventricular hypertrophy (Alpert & Hashimi, 1993).

The available evidence from multiple echocardiographic studies suggests that weight reduction reduces left ventricular mass in both obese hypertensive and normotensive patients, resulting in a direct hemodynamic effect as a result of the reductions in blood volume, systemic BP, venous return, cardiac output, stroke volume, and oxygen consumption (Himeno, Nishino, Nakashima, Kuroiwa, & Ikeda, 1996; Stone & Kushner, 2000). Because of findings such as these, prevention efforts have focused on weight loss. Data from such efforts demonstrate that weight loss reduces BP in people at risk for developing hypertension (Appel et al., 1997; Stamler et al., 1989; Stevens et al., 1993, 2001). For example, individuals who were placed on a low-saturated fat diet rich in fruits, vegetables, and low-fat dairy foods showed substantial reductions in BP of 5.5 mm Hg relative to control participants (Appel et al., 1997).

As delineated by Stevens and colleagues (1993, 2001), prevention efforts include group and individual counseling focused on dietary change, physical activity, and social support. Dietary interventions target fat, sugar, and alcohol consumption. Graded increases in physical activity are also planned and monitored. Eventually, physical activity should reflect brisk walking at the level of 40% to 55% of heart rate reserve for 35 to 45 minutes per day, 4 to 5 days per week. Interventions also include weekly group meetings used to facilitate social support and enhance nutritional education as well as to motivate behavior change. Specific behavior change techniques include setting explicit short-term goals and developing specific action plans to achieve goals, developing alternative strategies for situations that trigger problem eating, and engaging in self-monitoring via food diaries and graphing of daily physical exercise.

Evidence from three large-scale clinical weight loss and dieting trials has demonstrated a direct relationship between weight loss and BP reduction in normotensive individuals, suggesting that clinically significant long-term reductions in BP and reduced risk for hypertension can be achieved with even modest weight loss.

The Effect of Weight Control and Dieting on Blood Pressure in Hypertensive Patients. The sixth report of the JNC (1997) recommended the following: "All patients with hypertension who are above their ideal weight should be prescribed an individualized, monitored weight reduction program involving caloric restriction and increased physical activity" (p. 2422). Available guidelines suggest that a target weight loss goal of 10% of body weight over 6 months of therapy is appropriate, with combinatory treatment of dietary therapy, physical activity, and behavior therapy. Following NHLBI guidelines, treatment should be initiated with 30 to 45 minutes of moderate physical activity 3 to 5 days per week in addition to a low-calorie diet that produces a 500- to 1,000-calorie-per-day deficit (Stone & Kushner, 2000). A review of the voluminous literature in the behavioral treatment of obesity is beyond the scope of this chapter, but obvious strategies for weight loss with this population would include self-monitoring strategies, weight loss problem solving, urge control, stimulus control interventions, and stress management approaches related to dieting (Bonato & Boland, 1986; Simkin-Silverman, Wing, Boraz, Meilan, & Kuller, 1998; Rapoport, Clark, & Wardle, 2000; Wadden, Berkowitz, Sarwer, Prus-Wisniewski, & Steinberg, 2001).

The available literature from several weight loss studies that have enrolled hypertensive patients suggests that weight reductions of 3% to 9% of body weight, with antihypertensive drug regimens held constant, are likely to yield reductions in systolic BP in the range of 3.0 to 6.8 mm Hg and reductions in diastolic BP in the range of 2.9 to 5.7 mm Hg

(Brand et al., 1998; Corrigan, Raczynski, Swencionis, & Jennings, 1991; Langford et al., 1985; Reisin et al., 1983; Stamler et al., 1989). Trials that allowed adjustment of anti-hypertensive drug regimens generally found that lower doses and/or a fewer number of antihypertensive drugs were required by successful participants in weight reduction programs versus controls, suggesting that weight loss may enhance the efficacy of antihypertensive drugs (Oparil, 2000).

Sodium Intake and Blood Pressure

Primary Prevention and Salt Sensitivity. Epidemiological literature suggests a direct relationship between population BPs and sodium intake, typically expressed as the effect of dietary salt intake (Elliott, 1991; Stamler, 1997). There is also some support in the literature to suggest that the effect of dietary salt intake may vary among subpopulations and that the relationship between dietary sodium and BP may be pronounced in these subgroups. There have been several studies that suggest that older adults and African Americans may be "salt sensitive" and have a greater BP response to dietary sodium intake (e.g., Ishibashi et al., 1994; Weinberger, 1996), and there is at least one report that suggests an increased salt sensitivity in women (Kojima et al., 1992).

To date, it remains unclear whether a restriction in salt intake would have an effect on the incidence of hypertension, even within salt-sensitive subpopulations. Because evidence suggests that the association of sodium intake with cardiovascular mortality and morbidity varies by overweight status (He et al., 1999) and that advice to restrict salt intake is less effective in preventing hypertension in overweight people than is advice on weight reduction (He, Whelton, Appel, Charleston, & Klag, 2000), most current health risk guidelines do not support a restriction of salt intake in the normotensive population (Fodor,

Whitmore, Leenen, & Larochelle, 1999). Instead, weight reduction is viewed as a more desirable target for primary prevention efforts.

The Effect of Salt Restriction on Blood Pressure in Hypertensive Patients. Current guidelines recommend restrictions of dietary sodium to a range of 90 to 130 millimoles per day in hypertensive patients over the age of 44 years (Fodor et al., 1999). This corresponds to about 3 to 7 grams of salt per day. Patients should be counseled to avoid foods high in salt (e.g., prepared foods) and to choose foods low in salt (e.g., fresh fruits and vegetables). Combined salt restriction and diet modification trials have demonstrated a great deal of promise (Sacks et al., 2001; Vollmer et al., 2001). Such trials report decreases in BP of between 7 and 12 mm Hg in systolic BP and at least 5 mm Hg in diastolic pressure for hypertensive patients who were on both a salt restricted diet and the Dietary Approaches to Stop Hypertension (DASH) diet (Vollmer et al., 2001).

Although there is evidence that salt restriction, either alone or in combination with dietary intervention, is effective in lowering BP in short-term clinical trials, there is a clear need for an increased role of behavioral intervention in the long-term maintenance of this benefit. Brunner and colleagues (1997) reported very little change in BPs at 9- to 18-month follow-up of hypertensive patients after dietary advice to reduce salt intake was given by nutritionists or specially trained counselors, and a similar finding was reported by Ebrahim and Davey (1998) at 6-month follow-up, although a 2.1-mm Hg decrease in diastolic pressure was maintained.

Alcohol Intake and Blood Pressure

Primary Prevention and Alcohol. Epidemiological data indicate a direct relationship between excess alcohol consumption and risk of hypertension, with several studies suggesting a linear dose-response relationship starting with an alcohol consumption threshold of three drinks per day (roughly 30 grams of ethanol); more than 2 ounces of alcohol per day significantly increases the risk of becoming hypertensive (e.g., Klatsky, Friedman, Siegelaub, & Gerard, 1977; Treadway, 2000), whereas a daily alcohol intake of less than 1 ounce may result in a modest *decrease* in BP for most people (Gilman, Cook, Evans, Rosner, & Hennekens, 1995) except African American males (Fuchs, Chambless, Whelton, Nieto, & Heiss, 2001). Recent data (Thadhani et al., 2002; Witteman et al., 1990) also suggests that regular consumption of more than one and a half drinks per day, regardless of the type of alcoholic beverage consumed, substantially increases the risk of hypertension for women.

The mechanism of alcohol-induced hypertension is not clearly delineated. Alcohol is hypothesized to affect the renin-angiotensin-aldosterone axis and cortisol secretion in addition to contributing to heart rate variability, disrupting adrenergic nervous system discharge, and affecting insulin sensitivity (Oparil, 2000; Potter & Beevers, 1984). As such, available guidelines suggest that to reduce the relative risk of developing hypertension, those healthy adults who choose to drink should limit alcohol consumption to no more than 2 standard drinks per day, with consumption not exceeding 14 standard drinks per week for men and 9 standard drinks per week for women (Campbell, Ashley, Carruthers, Lacourciere, & McKay, 1999). A standard drink is defined as approximately a 12-ounce glass of beer, a 5-ounce glass of table wine, or a 1.5-ounce glass of distilled spirits (Cushman et al., 1998).

The Effect of Alcohol on Blood Pressure in Hypertensive Patients. Even though the evidence is fairly clear in implicating alcohol consumption as a risk factor for hypertension, the available data related to the effect of reducing alcohol consumption in hypertensive patients

suggest a relatively modest effect on BP (Xin et al., 2001). For example, high normal to slightly hypertensive heavy drinkers (more than 21 drinks per week), who showed an average decrease in alcohol consumption of 1.3 drinks per day, reduced their BP by only 1.2/0.7 mm Hg following a cognitive-behavioral outpatient alcohol reduction program (Cushman et al., 1998). Moreover, meta-analytic data from 15 alcohol reduction trials involving 2,234 total patients demonstrated an overall reduction in BP attributable to alcohol reduction of only 3.31 mm Hg systolic and 2.04 mm Hg diastolic (Xin et al., 2001). Although these effects are modest, a dose-response relationship was observed between mean percentage of alcohol reduction and mean BP reduction. Regardless of the modest reductions in BP with concomitant alcohol reduction, available guidelines suggest that hypertensive nondrinkers should continue to abstain from consuming alcohol. For hypertensive alcohol drinkers, alcohol intake should be limited to no more than 1 ounce of alcohol (2 ounces of 100-proof whiskey, 8 ounces of wine, or 24 ounces of beer) per day in most men and half that amount in women and smaller men (Oparil, 2000).

Exercise and Blood Pressure

Primary Prevention and Exercise. In 1995, the Centers for Disease Control and Prevention and the American College of Sports Medicine jointly issued a recommendation regarding the primary prevention of cardiovascular disease, stating that "every U.S. adult should accumulate 30 minutes or more of moderate-intensity physical activity on most, preferably all, days of the week," with moderate physical activity defined as equivalent to brisk walking at 3 to 4 miles per hour for healthy adults (Pate et al., 1995). Current recommendations were based on findings that moderate- to high-intensity exercise, if sustained, leads to a lowering of BP in normotensive individuals and an apparent reduction in the relative risk of developing hypertension (Braith, Pollock, Lowenthal, Graves, & Limacher, 1994; Paffenbarger, Jung, Leung, & Hyde, 1991). For example, regularly scheduled moderate physical activity, such as swimming or brisk walking for 30 minutes, has been reported to decrease both systolic and diastolic BP from 4 to 8 mm Hg, with an average reduction of 6 to 7 mm Hg (Arrol & Beaglehole, 1992; Fagard, 1995), and this level of activity may be more effective in lowering BP than more vigorous activity such as jogging (Jennings, 1997).

The Effect of Exercise on Blood Pressure in Hypertensive Patients. The available evidence suggests that regular rhythmic physical exercise of the lower extremities by hypertensive individuals decreases both systolic and diastolic BP (in about 75% of such individuals) by as much as 11 mm Hg and 8 mm Hg, respectively, independent of weight loss, alcohol intake, and sodium intake (Hagberg, Montain, Martin, & Ehsani, 1989; Kelly & McClellan, 1994; Martin, Dubbert, & Cushman, 1990). Although the mechanism of action is not well understood in all cases, there is some evidence that exercise training may result in regression of pathological left ventricular hypertrophy in at least some hypertensive patients (Hagberg, Park, & Brown, 2000). In some cases, a consistent exercise regimen may also obviate the need for medication in mildly hypertensive patients (Kelemen, Effron, Valenti, & Stewart, 1990).

The effect of exercise in this population appears to be more pronounced in women than in men, and middle-aged people may derive more benefit than either younger or older people. Exercise reduces BP more consistently in Asian and Pacific Islander patients than in Caucasian patients, especially when systolic BP is examined (Hagberg et al., 2000). There is some evidence to suggest that apoE, ACE, and LPL genotypes may identify hypertensive patients who are most likely to improve BP, lipoprotein lipids, and cardiovascular disease risk the most with exercise training (Hagberg, Ferrell, Dengel, & Wilund, 1999). This may account for some of the variation in BP responses to exercise, including the 25% or so of hypertensive patients who show very little response to exercise (Blumenthal, Siegel, & Appelbaum, 1991; Cooper, 2000). Although most of the work in this area has examined the effect of moderate-intensity exercise, there is some evidence to suggest a possible beneficial role of light aerobic exercise in the reduction of BP in older patients. Young, Appel, Jee, and Miller (1999) reported decreases of 7.0 mm Hg systolic BP and 2.4 mm Hg diastolic BP in a sample of 62 sedentary older adults with high normal or Stage 1 hypertension who had completed a 12-week program of t'ai chi, an Eastern form of relaxation and exercise.

The sixth report of the JNC (1997) recommended that hypertensive patients follow the physical activity guidelines outlined in the surgeon general's report for lowering resting BP, which consists of moderately intense aerobic exercise at 40% to 60% of maximum oxygen consumption. This can be achieved, for example, by 30 to 45 minutes of brisk walking several times per week. The most recent recommendations of the Canadian Medical Association are consistent with these guidelines, specifically recommending that individuals with mild hypertension should engage in 50 to 60 minutes of moderate rhythmic exercise of the lower limbs, such as brisk walking or cycling, three to four times per week (Cleroux, Feldman, & Petrella, 1999). The Canadian Medical Association guidelines also suggest that exercise should be prescribed as adjunctive therapy for individuals who require pharmacotherapy for hypertension, especially those who are not receiving beta blockers.

Stress Management and Blood Pressure

Primary Prevention and Stress Management. There is very little evidence in the literature to date to suggest that successful stress management prevents hypertension despite the implication that chronic psychosocial stress may play a role in the etiology of hypertension (e.g., Anderson, Myers, & Pickering, 1989; Lucini, Norbiato, Clerici, & Pagani, 2002). For example, Phase 1 of the Trials of Hypertension Prevention project (Trials of Hypertension Prevention Collaborative Research Group, 1992) examined the effect of a multimodality stress management program, which included progressive relaxation, on the BP of 562 individuals in the general population with normal to high normal BP and found no statistically or clinically significant changes in BP following this intervention relative to matched controls (Batey et al., 2000). However, further investigation in this area is needed to investigate the efficacy of highly individualized stress management programs as a preventive measure in at-risk target populations of normotensive individuals with high levels of chronic psychosocial stress.

The Effect of Stress Management on Blood Pressure in Hypertensive Patients. A variety of meta-analyses have been conducted to test the hypothesis that stress management interventions effectively reduce BP among hypertensive patients (Eisenberg et al., 1993; Jacob, Chesney, Williams, Ding, & Shapiro, 1991; Kaufman et al., 1988; Linden & Chambers, 1994). A conservative interpretation of such meta-analytic findings is that individualized, multicomponent stress management treatment appears to be more effective in lowering BP than do single-component, standardized relaxation interventions (Johnston, Gold, & Kentish, 1993; Linden & Chambers, 1994; Ward, Swan, & Chesney, 1987). In fact, the results were negligible in most cases when a single stress management technique was used. Therefore, the Canadian Medical Association has tentatively recommended that if stress is viewed as a prominent contributor to a patient's high BP, an individualized stress management intervention that uses multiple components should be considered (Spence, Barnett,

Linden, Ramsden, & Taenzer, 1999). In particular, it has been suggested that a stress management intervention should include some or all of the following components: skills training in adaptive mood management, communication, problem solving, and relaxation/reduction of sympathetic arousal as well as training in the reevaluation of negative life events and increased awareness of stressors and stress responses.

Linden and Chambers (1994) compared the effect sizes of single-method relaxation, multimethod relaxation, and individualized, cognitive-behavioral treatment therapies to reduce BP. They reported observed mean decreases of 9.7 mm Hg in systolic BP and 7.2 mm Hg in diastolic BP with such interventions. Individualized, cognitive-behavioral treatment therapies were found to reduce BP at a level comparable in effect size to BP medications and weight reduction/physical exercise, with observed mean decreases of 15.2 mm Hg in systolic BP and 9.2 mm Hg in diastolic BP. The individualized, cognitive-behavioral treatment therapies included studies focusing on marital communication training for hypertensive patients (Ewart, Taylor, Kraemer, & Agras, 1984), cognitive restructuring and behavioral intervention programs (Bosley & Allen, 1989; Chesney, Black, Swan, & Ward, 1987; Jorgensen, Houston, & Zurawski, 1981), anger management interventions (Achmon, Granek, Golomb, & Hart, 1989), and individualized stress management that included the recognition of somatic cues for stress (Richter-Heinrich et al., 1981). Similar, very encouraging results were reported by Schneider and colleagues (1995) and Linden, Lenz, and Con (2001).

Pharmacological Interventions

Hypertension is treated pharmacologically by several categories of medications called antihypertension medications (Table 14.1). Although details into the specific pharmacology

Table 14.1   Examples of Categories of Medications Used in the Treatment of
High Blood Pressure

Class of Medications	Generic Name Examples	Brand Name Examples
ACE inhibitors		
	Captopril	Capoten
	Fosinopril sodium	Monopril
	Moexipril	Univasc
	Ramipril	Altace
Alpha blockers		
	Doxazosin mesylate	Cardura
	Prazosin hydrochloride	Minipress
	Terazosin hydrochloride	Hytrin
Angiotensin II receptor blockers		
	Candesartan	Candesartan
	Irbesartan	Irbesartan
	Losartan potassium	Losartan potassium
	Valsartan	Valsartan
Beta blockers		
	Acebutolol	Sectral
	Atenolol	Tenormin
	Betaxolol	Kerlone
	Bisoprolol fumarate	Zebeta
	Carteolol hydrochloride	Cartrol
	Metoprolol tartrate	Lopressor
	Metoprolol succinate	Toprol-XL
	Nadolol	Corgard
	Penbutolol sulfate	Levatol
	Pindolol	Visken
	Propranolol hydrochloride	Inderal
	Timolol maleate	Blocadren
Calcium channel blockers		
	Amlodipine besylate	Norvasc
	Diltiazem hydrochloride	Cardizem, Dilacor-XR, Tiazac
	Felodipine	Plendil
	Isradipine	DynaCirc
	Nicardipine	Cardene
	Nifedipine	Adalat, Procardia
	Nisoldipine	Sular
	Verapamil hydrochloride	Calan, Covera-HS, Isoptin, Verelan
Central agonists		
	Alpha methyldopa	Aldomet
	Clonidine hydrochloride	Catapres
	Guanabenz acetate	Wytensin
	Guanfacine hydrochloride	Tenex

(Continued)

Table 14.1   (Continued)

Class of Medications	Generic Name Examples	Brand Name Examples
Diuretics		
	Chlorthalidone	Hygroton
	Chlorthalidone	Hygroton
	Furosemide	Lasix
	Hydrochlorothiazide	Esidrix, hydroDIURIL, microzide
	Indapamide	Lozol
	Metolazone	Mykrox, Zaroxolyn

of these categories of medications are beyond the scope of this chapter, familiarity with these classes and specific generic and brand names may be helpful for psychologists who work in primary medical care settings. Furthermore, information about side effects of these medications should enhance the expertise of behavioral therapists in their efforts to help other medical professionals and patients, drawing better outcomes from pharmacotherapy and increasing compliance.

One class of medication that is used to treat hypertension is diuretics. These medications work by helping the body remove excess fluids and sodium salt. Beta blockers work by reducing the heart rate and thereby reducing the volume of blood ejected by the heart (cardiac output). Because the sympathetic nervous system innervates the heart, arteries, and other parts of the body, activation of this system can increase heart work or constrict arteries, leading to increased BP. Therefore, a class of medications called sympathetic nerve inhibitors works by inhibiting sympathetic nerves on blood vessels. Vasodilators work by causing blood vessel walls and muscles to relax, leading to dilation of the vessels and reducing their pressure. The angiotensin-converting enzyme (ACE) inhibitors work by interfering with the production of angiotensin. Angiotensin is a vasoconstricting chemical. The angiotensin II receptor blockers block the effects of angiotensin. The calcium antagonists (calcium channel blockers) reduce BP by reducing heart rate and relaxing blood vessels.

Pharmacological interventions introduce another complication, namely side effects. Clinicians can help to reduce the negative effects of side effects on compliance by educating their patients about these side effects, helping them to learn ways in which to minimize side effects or to adjust medication dosages in coordination with their prescribers after achieving normal BP.

Multicomponent Approach

As noted earlier, there are well-documented lifestyle modifications with proven efficacy (e.g., weight control, diet, exercise, alcohol control, sodium restriction, at least some stress management interventions). A significant proportion of all available health care resources are expended for the treatment of hypertension. Hypertension accounts for about 30 million physician visits per year in the United States alone and is the second most common reason for outpatient physician visits in the country (Knight et al., 2001). Despite this staggering number of physician visits, and despite the impressive array of pharmacological and nonpharmacological interventions that are available for the management of hypertension, it is estimated (Berlowitz et al., 1998; Hyman & Pavlik, 2001; Mulrow, 1998) that fewer than one third of U.S. patients with hypertension have controlled BP (less than 140/90 mm Hg). In one large sample of 1,394 New York City health care workers, only 12% of those patients who were treated for hypertension had BP controlled at less than 140/90 mm Hg despite having comprehensive medical insurance and full access to health care (Stockwell, Madhaven, Cohen, Gibson, & Alerman, 1994). Of equal or greater concern, a recent study that employed electronic monitoring of patients with long-standing serious hypertension suggested that fully 61% of these patients failed to take their antihypertensive medication as prescribed (Lee et al., 1996).

Multiple factors have been implicated as contributing to poor BP control, including the lack of primary care physicians in some populations (Shea, Misra, Ehrlich, Field, & Francis, 1992), the cost of antihypertensive medication (Ahluwalia, McNagny, & Rask, 1997), medication side effects, presence or absence of comorbid illness, age of the patient, severity of the disease, health habits, intensity of care, physician compliance with established guidelines (Oliveria et al., 2002), complexity of the medication regimen, patient knowledge base and understanding of the seriousness of uncontrolled hypertension, and patient behavior related to compliance and adherence (Knight et al., 2001; Oliveria et al., 2002). The remainder of this section focuses on the role of educational interventions, multicomponent behavioral programs, and interventions related to compliance and adherence for hypertensive patients given that patient adherence has been identified as one of the main reasons why BP therapy fails (Miller, Hill, Kottke, & Ockene, 1997).

General guidelines for physicians related to improving patients' adherence to antihypertensive therapy have been published by the JNC (1997) and elaborated by Kaplan (1998). Table 14.2 represents a compilation of the recommendations from both of these sources. Most of these recommendations rest on solid behavioral principles from the behavioral medicine adherence literature. For example, self-monitoring is a cornerstone of assessing adherence, and the recent guidelines

of the American Society of Hypertension Ad Hoc Panel (Pickering, 1995) describe the role of patient self-monitoring of BP both in assessing the response to antihypertensive medications more accurately and in potentially improving patient compliance and involvement in patients' own health care. In a similar fashion, Gonzalez-Fernandez, Rivera, Torres, Quiles, and Jackson (1990) reported a 60% increase in compliance and decreases of 14/11 mm Hg systolic/diastolic BP at 8-week follow-up after a brief, four-session, inpatient educational program administered to a sample of 57 middle-aged to elderly hypertensive patients.

There are additional intervention strategies that may be useful to consider in an effort to maximize patient compliance and minimize adherence problems. The use of reminders and prompts, including medication reminder calendars or alerts, specialized medication dispensers, and reminder calls regarding physician or clinic appointments, is very useful for many patients. Behavioral contracting has a clear role in the management of hypertensive patients, particularly in maintaining adherence to nonpharmacological interventions. Stepwise introduction of antihypertensive interventions is recommended, that is, using a graduated approach of introducing more easily attainable goals early in treatment so as to shape subsequent adherence behavior. Similarly, interventions designed to enhance the medical office visit experience have been documented to increase adherence. These include using a scheduling system that minimizes waiting time for patients, providing adequate opportunity for patients to communicate with health care personnel (including liberal call-in or on-call with clinic staff), and other interventions designed to provide a personalized patient experience in a physically attractive and positive medical office environment.

A recent meta-analysis of the medical adherence literature completed by Roter and colleagues (1998) of 153 intervention strategies

Table 14.2 General Guidelines to Improve Patient Adherence to Antihypertensive Therapy

1. Be aware of signs of patient nonadherence to antihypertensive therapy.
2. Establish the goal of therapy: to reduce blood pressure to nonhypertensive levels with minimal or no adverse side effects.
3. Educate patients about the disease, and involve them and their families in its treatment.
   a. Have patients measure blood pressure at home.
4. Maintain contact with patients.
   a. Consider telecommunications.
5. Keep care inexpensive and simple.
   a. Integrate pill taking into routine activities of daily living.
6. Encourage lifestyle modifications.
7. Prescribe medications according to pharmacological principles, favoring long-acting formulations.
   a. Continue to add effective and tolerated drugs, stepwise, in sufficient doses to achieve the goals of therapy.
   b. Be willing to stop unsuccessful therapy and to try a different approach.
   c. Anticipate side effects, and adjust therapy to ameliorate side effects that do not disappear spontaneously.
8. Encourage a positive attitude about achieving therapeutic goals.
9. Consider using nurse case management.

SOURCE: Joint National Committee on Detection, Evaluation, and Treatment of High Blood Pressure (1997).
NOTE: Cortisol response is initiated by the release of corticotropin releasing factors (CRF) from neuronal cell bodies of the paraventricular nucleus (PVN). CRF acts on the corticotrope cells of the anterior pituitary, stimulating synthesis of proopiomelanocortin (POMS), and leading to the subsequent release of ACTH and β–endorphin into the systemic circulation. Upon reaching the adrenal cortex, ACTH leads to the synthesis and release of cortisol. Cortisol, through direct and indirect cardiovascular mechanisms, contributes to increased blood pressure. These effects, as discussed in the text, seem to be stronger in hypertension-prone individuals.

designed to promote patient adherence to medical regimens suggests that adherence strategies that combine educational, behavioral, and affective components may be more effective than single-focus interventions. For example, Clifford, Tan, and Gorsuch (1991) reported significant improvements in weight, percentage body fat, exercise adherence, and systolic and diastolic BP in middle-aged overweight patients who were given social support and taught several cognitive-behavioral techniques that applied to exercise adherence, weight reduction/maintenance, and stress management relative to an assessment-only control group.

Similarly, Boulware and colleagues' (2001) meta-analysis of 15 behavioral interventions for hypertension involving 4,072 patients noted that educational interventions plus counseling interventions achieved a higher level of hypertension control than did either intervention alone. The best method to increase compliance and adherence is likely to involve highly individualized approaches to each patient. For example, patients who characteristically have active styles of coping with illness and treatment-related issues may benefit from self-control-based strategies such as self-monitoring, self-evaluation, and self-reinforcement of adherence behaviors (Haynes et al., 1976). Patients with more passive styles may benefit from more structured adherence interventions such as behavioral contracting, direct instruction by health care providers, and external inducements or rewards (Christensen & Johnson, 2002).

CASE STUDY

The patient, "George Richards," is a 42-year-old married Caucasian male who works as a certified public accountant in Minneapolis, Minnesota. He had received episodic medical care over the course of the past 15 years, although he has had excellent health benefits through his company. He had seldom been sick and had not seen any reason to visit a doctor. He was last seen medically 4 years ago, at age 38 years, when he visited his family physician for a physical examination prior to scheduled surgery for repair of a hernia that he had sustained while helping a friend move some furniture. This had been George's only surgery, and up to that point he had experienced no chronic illnesses of any sort. At that time, he was 5 feet 7 inches tall and weighed 170 pounds. He was a nonsmoker and social drinker, averaging four to six glasses of wine per week. He had few hobbies and was a self-professed "workaholic" who typically worked 60 hours or more per week in a very stressful work environment. At that doctor visit, George's BP was 145/95. He had no known family history of either hypertension or cardiovascular disease. His cholesterol was within or below the average range at 172, and his lipid profile was within normal limits. No electrocardiogram (ECG) was done. He was told by the family physician to lose 10 pounds and to try to get into some sort of exercise program. He was also advised to try to do something for relaxation and to cut back his hours at work. He was advised that his BP would be checked on each subsequent visit back to see the doctor.

After George was fully recovered from his noneventful hernia surgery, he bought an exercise bicycle but found that he seldom had time to use it and also found this to be a relatively boring activity for him. He began walking with his wife when he could fit it into his work schedule, which typically was one time per week or less and usually was a mile or so at a time unless the couple was interrupted by a call on George's cell phone. He tried to watch his weight initially, but he frequently ate in restaurants with business clients and eventually went back to a traditional "meat and potatoes" diet. His alcohol intake increased to two to three drinks per day, usually in an attempt to "unwind" after a long day at the office. He had been promoted to a supervisory position in his office, and this increased his workload and job-related stress; however, with two children in college, he felt that he had no other option than to work longer and longer hours. He developed some occasional sleep onset insomnia but otherwise convinced himself that he "felt just fine" and saw no reason to see his physician.

Because of changes in his company's health maintenance organization insurance plan, George was recently assigned to a different medical practice with a new physician, and an initial physical was recommended by that medical plan. Although he saw no reason to see this new physician either, George reluctantly made an appointment for a physical exam. He had recently become a partner in his firm and had considerable difficulty in fitting a visit to the physician into his busy schedule. At this initial visit, George's BP averaged 175/105 over three separate readings. His weight was 185 pounds. An ECG done in the office showed a normal rate and rhythm but revealed an axis deviation consistent with mild left ventricular hypertrophy. George was informed that his BP was in the range of Stage 2 hypertension, which required initial nonpharmacological intervention and BP monitoring every 2 weeks by the clinic nursing staff. A "no added salt" diet (3 to 4 grams per day) was prescribed that was low in saturated fat and rich in fruits, vegetables, and low-fat dairy products. He was advised to limit his alcohol intake to 1 ounce per day. Because his office building had a health club, he was encouraged to purchase a membership and schedule time for exercise at least three times per week. He was told that if his BP did not normalize within 2 to 3 months, a full dose of a first-line antihypertensive medication would be necessary.

Subsequent to this office visit, George's BPs averaged 165/100 in clinic BP checks over the course of the next 6 weeks. George had lost about 4 pounds but was having difficulty in sticking to his diet. Although he did purchase a health club membership, he found exercising there to be as boring as it had been using the exercise bicycle, and he had used his membership on only two brief occasions. He did cut back his alcohol intake to one to two drinks per day but discovered that he had trouble unwinding and had significant problems with insomnia when he had fewer drinks than that. When George saw his physician at 6-week follow-up, the decision was made to refer him to a local behavioral medicine clinic to attempt to bolster the nonpharmacological interventions prescribed to that point. A psychologist at the behavioral medicine clinic saw George 2 weeks later. At the request of this psychologist, George was seen with his wife. An individualized exercise plan was crafted for him, including daily walking with his wife or walking on a treadmill placed in front of the family's large-screen television at increasing rates and distances that he would self-monitor and report back on subsequent weekly visits. George and his wife were given copies of a modified version of the DASH diet that would fit their lifestyle and were asked to keep dietary intake records. At a subsequent visit 2 weeks later, a behavioral intervention program for George's insomnia was devised. George was enrolled in a stress management course that included relaxation tapes that he could use to help with his sleep onset problems as well as training in life management skills that he could apply in his place of business.

George was seen again by his family physician after attending six weekly sessions at the behavioral medicine clinic. His weight was now 174 pounds, and his BP was 150/95. He was walking 1 to 2 miles an average of five times per week, and his alcohol consumption was down to one to two glasses of wine per week. His physician started him on a low dose of an ACE inhibitor (Lisinopril, 5 milligrams per day) as an adjunct to the behavioral interventions. At 1 month follow-up, George's BP had stabilized at 130/85, his total cholesterol was 191, his weight had stabilized at 170 pounds, and he was continuing in monthly maintenance sessions at the behavioral medicine clinic.

CONCLUSIONS

Hypertension is a major risk factor for many devastating illnesses, including coronary heart disease, stroke, and kidney failure. Efforts to develop effective means for diagnosing and treating hypertension have been in the forefront of public health research. These efforts have led to greater recognition of the importance of frequent screening of BP and for implementing reliable means for measuring BP, including the use of ambulatory monitoring for diagnosing this disorder.

A strong movement toward promoting preventive efforts has also characterized public health work over the past two decades. The greater awareness of hypertension has also led to a more comprehensive view of the etiological factors of this disorder, consequently leading to a greater emphasis on a menu of strategies targeting BP control. To that end,

behavioral medicine research has contributed significantly toward expanding available intervention methods. Because of the long-term nature of interventions, behavioral researchers have focused their efforts on developing diverse behavioral modification techniques, targeting factors such as weight, eating habits, physical activity, and substance use. In addition to behavioral and psychosocial methods, advancement has been made in available pharmacological treatment options.

Although advancement has been made in developing effective control strategies, many challenges in implementing them remain. These include compliance with regimens and consistency in applying interventions over a long period of time. Behavioral medicine scientists and clinicians are in the forefront of trying to maximize patients' cooperation and chances for success in controlling hypertension.

REFERENCES

Achmon, J., Granek, M., Golomb, M., & Hart, J. (1989). Behavioral treatment of essential hypertension: A comparison between cognitive therapy and biofeedback of heart rate. *Psychosomatic Medicine, 51,* 152–164.

Ahluwalia, J. S., McNagny, S. E., & Rask, K. J. (1997). Correlates of controlled hypertension in indigent, inner-city hypertensive patients. *Journal of General Internal Medicine, 12,* 7–14.

al'Absi, M., & Arnett, D. K. (2000). Adrenocortical responses to psychological stress and risk for hypertension. *Biomedical Pharmacotherapy, 54,* 234–244.

al'Absi, M., Buchanan, T., & Lovallo, W. R. (1996). Pain perception and cardiovascular responses in men with positive parental history for hypertension. *Psychophysiology, 33,* 655–661.

al'Absi, M., Everson, S., & Lovallo, W. R. (1995). Hypertension risk factors and cardiovascular reactivity to mental stress in men. *International Journal of Psychophysiology, 20,* 155–160.

al'Absi, M., & Lovallo, W. R. (1993). Cortisol concentrations in serum of borderline hypertensive men exposed to a novel experimental setting. *Psychoneuroendocrinology, 18,* 355–363.

al'Absi, M., Lovallo, W. R., McKey, B., & Pincomb, G. (1994). Borderline hypertensives produce exaggerated adrenocortical responses to mental stress. *Psychosomatic Medicine, 56,* 245–250.

al'Absi, M., Lovallo, W. R., McKey, B., Sung, B. H., Whitsett, T. L., & Wilson, M. F. (1998). Hypothalamic-pituitary adrenocortical responses to psychological stress and caffeine in men at high and low risk for hypertension. *Psychosomatic Medicine, 60,* 521–527.

al'Absi, M., Lovallo, W. R., Pincomb, G. P., Sung, B. H., & Wilson, M. F. (1995). Adrenocortical effects of caffeine and behavioral stress on adrenocortical responses in hypertension-prone men. *International Journal of Behavioral Medicine, 2,* 263–275.

Alexander, F. (1939). Emotional factor in essential hypertension. *Psychosomatic Medicine, 1,* 173–179.

Alpert, M. A., & Hashimi, M. W. (1993). Obesity and the heart. *Journal of Medical Science, 306,* 117.

Anderson, N. B., Myers, H. F., & Pickering, T. (1989). Hypertension in blacks: Psychosocial and biological perspectives. *Journal of Hypertension, 7,* 161–172.

Appel, L. J., Moore, T. J., Obarzanek, E., Vollmer, W. M., Svetkey, L. P., Sacks, F. M., Bray, G. A., Vogt, T. M., Cutler, J. A., Windhauser, M. M., Lin, P. H., & Karanja, N. (1997). A clinical trial of the effects of dietary patterns on blood pressure: DASH Collaborative Research Group. *New England Journal of Medicine, 336,* 1117–1124.

Arroll, B., & Beaglehole, R. (1992). Does physical activity lower blood pressure? A critical review of the clinical trials. *Journal of Clinical Epidemiology, 45,* 439–447.

Batey, D. M., Kaufmann, P. G., Raczynski, J. M., Hollis, J. F., Murphy, J. K., Rosner, B., Corrigan, S. A., Rappaport, N. B., Danielson, E. M., Lasser, N. L., & Kuhn, C. M. (2000). Stress management intervention for primary prevention of hypertension: Detailed results from Phase I of Trials of Hypertension Prevention (TOHP-I). *Annals of Epidemiology, 10*(1), 45–58.

Berlowitz, D. R., Ash, A. S., Hickey, E. C., Friedman, R. H., Glickman, M., Kader, B., & Moskowitz, M. A. (1998). Inadequate management of blood pressure in a hypertensive population. *New England Journal of Medicine, 339,* 1957–1963.

Blumenthal, J. A., Siegel, W. C., & Appelbaum, M. (1991). Failure of exercise to reduce blood pressure in patients with mild hypertension: Results of a randomized controlled trial. *Journal of the American Medical Association, 266,* 2098–2104.

Bonato, D. P., & Boland, F. J. (1986). A comparison of specific strategies for long-term maintenance following a behavioural treatment program for obese women. *International Journal of Eating Disorders, 5,* 949–958.

Bosley, F., & Allen, T. W. (1989). Stress management training for hypertensives: Cognitive and physiological effects. *Journal of Behavioral Medicine, 12,* 77–89.

Boulware, L. E., Daumit, G. L., Frick, K. D., Minkovitz, C. S., Lawrence, R. S., & Powe, N. R. (2001). An evidence-based review of patient-centered behavioral interventions for hypertension. *American Journal of Preventive Medicine, 21,* 221–232.

Braith, R. W., Pollock, M. L., Lowenthal, D. T., Graves, J. E., & Limacher, M. C. (1994). Moderate- and high-intensity exercise lowers blood pressure in normotensive subjects 60–79 years of age. *American Journal of Cardiology, 73,* 1124–1128.

Brand, M. B., Mulrow, C. D., Chiquette, E., Angel, L., Cornell, J. E., Summerhill, C., & Grem, R., Jr. (1998). Weight-reducing diets for control of hypertension in adults. *The Cochrane Library, 4.* (Oxford, UK: Update Software)

Brunner, E., White, I., Thorogood, M., Bristow, A., Curle, D., & Marmot, M. (1997). Can dietary interventions change diet and cardiovascular risk factors? A meta-analysis of randomized controlled trials. *American Journal of Public Health, 87,* 1415–1422.

Bunag, R. D., & Takeda, K. (1979). Sympathetic hyperresponsiveness to hypothalamic stimulation in young hypertensive rats. *American Journal of Physiology, 237,* R39–R44.

Burt, V. L., Whelton, P., Roccella, E. J., Brown, C., Cutler, J. A., Higgins, M., Horan, M. J., & Labarthe, D. (1995). Prevalence of hypertension in the U.S. adult population: Results from the Third National Health and Nutrition Examination Survey, 1988–1991. *Hypertension, 25,* 305–313.

Campbell, N. R., Ashley, M. J., Carruthers, S. G., Lacourciere, Y., & McKay, D. W. (1999). Lifestyle modifications to prevent and control hypertension: III. Recommendations on alcohol consumption. *Canadian Medical Association Journal, 160*(9, Suppl.), S13–S20.

Cardillo, C., De Felice, F., Campia, U., & Folli, G. (1993). Psychophysiological reactivity and cardiac end-organ changes in white coat hypertension. *Hypertension, 21,* 836–844.

Cavallini, M. C., Roman, M. J., Pickering, T. G., Schwartz, J. E., Pini, R., & Devereux, R.B. (1995). Is white coat hypertension associated with arterial disease or left ventricular hypertrophy? *Hypertension, 26,* 413–419.

Chesney, M. A., Black, G. W., Swan, G. E., & Ward, M. M. (1987). Relaxation training for essential hypertension at the worksite: I. The untreated mild hypertensive. *Psychosomatic Medicine, 49,* 250–263.

Christensen, A. J., & Johnson, J. A. (2002). Patient adherence with medical treatment regimens: An interactive approach. *Current Directions in Psychological Science, 11*(3), 94–97.

Cleroux, J., Feldman, R. D., & Petrella, R. J. (1999). Lifestyle modifications to prevent and control hypertension: IV. Recommendations on physical exercise training. *Canadian Medical Association Journal, 160*(9, Suppl.), S21–S28.

Clifford, P. A., Tan, S., & Gorsuch, R. L. (1991). Efficacy of a self-directed behavioral health change program: Weight, body composition, cardiovascular fitness, blood pressure, health risk, and psychosocial mediating variables. *Journal of Behavioral Medicine, 14,* 303–323.

Cooper, A. R. (2000). What is the magnitude of blood pressure response to a programme of moderate intensity exercise? Randomised controlled trial among sedentary adults with unmedicated hypertension. *British Journal of General Practice, 50,* 958–962.

Corrigan, S. A., Raczynski, J. M., Swencionis, C., & Jennings, S. G. (1991). Weight reduction in the prevention and treatment of hypertension: A review of representative clinical trials. *American Journal of Health Promotion, 5,* 208–214.

Cushman, W. C., Cutler, J. A., Hanna, E., Bingham, S. F., Follmann, D., Harford, T., Dubbert, P., Allender, P. S., Dufour, M., Collins, J. F., Walsh, S. M., Kirk, G. F., Burg, M., Felicetta, J. V., Hamilton, B. P., Katz, L. A., Perry, H. M., Willenbring, M. L., Lakshman, R., & Hamburger, R. J., for the PATHS Group. (1998). Prevention and Treatment of Hypertension Study (PATH): Effects of an alcohol treatment program on blood pressure. *Archives of Internal Medicine, 158,* 1197–1207.

Davies, A. O., & Lefkowitz, R. J. (1984). Regulation of beta-adrenergic receptors by steroid hormones. *Annual Review of Physiology, 46,* 119–130.

Ebrahim, S., & Davey, S. G. (1998). Lowering blood pressure: A systematic review of sustained effects of non-pharmacological interventions. *Journal of Public Health, 2,* 441–448.

Eisenberg, D. M., Delbanco, T. L., Berkey, C. S., Kaptchuk, T. J., Kupelnick, B., Kuhl, J., & Chalmers, T. (1993). Cognitive behavioral techniques for hypertension: Are they effective? *Annals of Internal Medicine, 118,* 964–972.

Elliott, P. (1991). Observational studies of salt and blood pressure. *Hypertension, 17*, 3–8.

Everson, S. A., Kaplan, G. A., Goldberg, D. E., & Salonen, J. T. (1996). Anticipatory blood pressure response to exercise predicts future high blood pressure in middle-aged men. *Hypertension, 27*, 1059–1064.

Everson, S. A., Lynch, J. W., Chesney, M. A., Kaplan, G. A., Goldberg, D. E., Shade, S. B., Cohen, R. D., Salonen, R., & Salonen, J. T. (1997). Interaction of workplace demands and cardiovascular reactivity in progression of carotid atherosclerosis: Population based study. *British Medical Journal, 314*, 553–558.

Ewart, C. K., Taylor, C. B., Kraemer, H. C., & Agras, W. S. (1984). Reducing blood pressure reactivity during interpersonal conflict: Effects of marital communication training. *Behavior Therapy, 15*, 473–484.

Fagard, R. H. (1995). The role of exercise in blood pressure control: Supportive evidence. *Journal of Hypertension, 13*, 1223–1227.

Fallo, F., Paoletta, A., Tona, F., Boscaro, M., & Sonino, N. (1993). Response of hypertension to conventional antihypertensive treatment and/or steroidogenesis inhibitors in Cushing's syndrome. *Journal of Internal Medicine, 234*, 595–598.

Fodor, J. G., Whitmore, B., Leenen, F., & Larochelle, P. (1999). Lifestyle modifications to prevent and control hypertension: V. Recommendations on dietary salt. *Canadian Medical Association Journal, 160*(Suppl. 9), S29–S34.

Fuchs, F. D., Chambless, L. E., Whelton, P. K., Nieto, F. J., & Heiss, G. (2001). Alcohol consumption and the incidence of hypertension: The Atherosclerosis Risk in Communities Study. *Hypertension, 37*, 1242–1250.

Gilman, M. W., Cook, N. R., Evans, D. A., Rosner, B., & Hennekens, C. H. (1995). Relationship of alcohol intake with blood pressure in young adults. *Hypertension, 25*, 1106–1110.

Gonzalez-Fernandez, R. A., Rivera, M., Torres, D., Quiles, J., & Jackson, A. (1990). Usefulness of a systemic hypertension in-hospital educational program. *American Journal of Cardiology, 65*, 1384–1386.

Gosse, P., Promax, H., Durandet, P., & Clementy, J. (1993). White coat hypertension: No harm for the heart. *Hypertension, 22*, 766–770.

Hagberg, J. M., Ferrell, R. E., Dengel, D. R., & Wilund, K. R. (1999). Exercise training-induced blood pressure and plasma lipid improvements in hypertensives may be genotype dependent. *Hypertension, 34*, 18–23.

Hagberg, J. M., Montain, S. J., Martin, W. H., & Ehsani, A. A. (1989). Effect of exercise training in 60- to 69-year-old persons with essential hypertension. *American Journal of Cardiology, 64*, 348–353.

Hagberg, J. M., Park, J. J., & Brown, M. D. (2000). The role of exercise training in the treatment of hypertension: An update. *Sports Medicine, 30*(3), 193–206.

Hall, J. E. (1997). Mechanisms of abnormal renal sodium handling in obesity hypertension. *American Journal of Hypertension, 10*, S49.

Haynes, R. B., Sackett, D. L., Gibson, E. S., Taylor, D. W., Hackett, B. C., Roberts, R. S., & Johnson, A. L. (1976). Improvement of medication compliance in uncontrolled hypertension. *Lancet, 1*, 1265–1268.

He, J., Ogden, L. G., Vupputuri, S., Bazzano, L. A., Loria, C., & Whelton, P. K. (1999). Dietary sodium intake and subsequent risk of cardiovascular disease in overweight adults. *Journal of the American Medical Association, 282*, 2027–2034.

He, J., Whelton, P. K., Appel, L. J., Charleston, J., & Klag, M. J. (2000). Long-term effects of weight loss and dietary sodium reduction on incidence of hypertension. *Hypertension, 35*, 544–549.

Henry, J. P., Liu, Y. Y., Nadra, W. E., Qian, C., Mormede., P., Lemaire, V., Ely, D., & Hendley, E. D. (1993). Psychosocial stress can induce chronic hypertension in normotensive strains of rats. *Hypertension, 21,* 714–723.

Himeno, E., Nishino, K., Nakashima, Y., Kuroiwa, A., & Ikeda, M. (1996). Weight reduction regresses left ventricular mass regardless of blood pressure level in obese subjects. *American Heart Journal, 131,* 313.

Horan, M. J., & Mockrin, S. C. (1992). Heterogeneity of hypertension. *American Journal of Hypertension, 5,* S110–S113.

Hyman, D. J., & Pavlik, V. N. (2001). Characteristics of patients with uncontrolled hypertension in the United States. *New England Journal of Medicine, 345,* 479–486.

Ishibashi, K., Oshima, T., Matsuura, H., Watanabe, M., Ishida, M., Ishida, T., Ozono, R., Kajiyama, G., & Kanbe, M. (1994). Effects of age and sex on sodium chloride sensitivity: Association with plasma rennin activity. *Clinical Nephrology, 42,* 376–380.

Jacob, R. G., Chesney, M. A., Williams, D. M., Ding, Y., & Shapiro, A. P. (1991). Relaxation therapy for hypertension: Design effects and treatment effects. *Annals of Behavioral Medicine, 13,* 5–17.

Jennings, G. L. (1997). Exercise and blood pressure control: Walk, run, or swim? *Journal of Hypertension, 15,* 567–569.

Jin, C. B., & Rockhold, R. W. (1991). Sympathoadrenal control by paraventricular hypothalamic beta-endorphin in hypertension. *Hypertension, 18,* 503–515.

Johnston, D. W., Gold, A., & Kentish, J. (1993). Effect of stress management on blood pressure in mild primary hypertension. *British Medical Journal, 306,* 963–966.

Joint National Committee on Detection, Evaluation, and Treatment of High Blood Pressure. (1997). The sixth report of the Joint National Committee on Prevention, Detection, Evaluation, and Treatment of High Blood Pressure. *Archives of Internal Medicine, 157,* 2413–2446.

Jorgensen, R. S., Houston, B. K., & Zurawski, R. M. (1981). Anxiety management training in the treatment of essential hypertension. *Behaviour Research and Therapy, 19,* 467–474.

Julius, S., Mejia, A., Jones, K., Krause, L., Schork, N., Van de Ven, C., Johnson, E., Petrin, J., Sekkarie, M., Kjedsen, S. E., Schmouder, R., Gupta, R., Ferraro, J., Nazzaro, P., & Weissfeld, J. (1990). "White coat" versus "sustained" borderline hypertension in Tecumseh, Michigan. *Hypertension, 16,* 617–623.

Julius, S., & Nesbitt, S. (1996). Sympathetic overactivity in hypertension: A moving target. *American Journal of Hypertension, 9,* S113–S120.

Kaplan, N. M. (1990). *Clinical hypertension* (5th ed.). Baltimore, MD: Williams & Wilkins.

Kaplan, N. M. (Ed.). (1998). *Clinical hypertension* (7th ed.). Baltimore, MD: Williams & Wilkins.

Kaufmann, P. G., Jacob, R. G., Ewart, C. K., Chesney, M. A., Muenz, L. R., Doub, N., & Mercer, W. (1988). Hypertension intervention pooling project. *Health Psychology, 7*(Suppl.), 209–224.

Kelemen, M. H., Effron, M. B., Valenti, S. A., & Stewart, K. J. (1990). Exercise training combined with antihypertensive drug therapy. *Journal of the American Medical Association, 263,* 2766.

Kelly, G., & McClellan, P. (1994). Antihypertensive effects of aerobic exercise: A brief meta-analytic review of randomized controlled trials. *American Journal of Hypertension, 7,* 115–119.

Keltikangas-Jarvinen, L., Raikkonen, K., Hautanen, A., & Adlercreutz, H. (1996). Vital exhaustion, anger expression, and pituitary and adrenocortical hormones:

Implications for the insulin resistance syndrome. *Arteriosclerosis, Thrombosis, & Vascular Biology, 16,* 275–280.

Klatsky, A. L., Friedman, G. D., Siegelaub, A. B., & Gerard, M. J. (1977). Alcohol consumption and blood pressure: Kaiser-Permanente Multiphasic Health Examination data. *New England Journal of Medicine, 296,* 1194–1200.

Knight, E. L., Bohn, R. L., Wang, P. S., Glynn, R. J., Mogun, H., & Avorn, J. (2001). Predictors of uncontrolled hypertension in ambulatory patients. *Hypertension, 38,* 809–814.

Kojima, S., Murakami, K., Kimura, G., Sanai, T., Yoshida, K., Imanishi, M., Abe, H., Kawamura, M., Kawano, Y., & Ashida, T. (1992). A gender difference in the association between salt sensitivity and family history of hypertension. *American Journal of Hypertension, 5,* 1–7.

Koren, M. J., Mensah, G. A., Blake, J., Laragh, J. F., & Devereux, R. B. (1993). Comparison of left ventricular mass and geometry in black and white patients with essential hypertension. *American Journal of Hypertension, 6,* 815–823.

Kuwajima, I., Suzuki, Y., Fujisawa, A., & Kuramoto, K. (1993). Is white coat hypertension innocent? Structure and function of the heart in the elderly. *Hypertension, 22,* 826–831.

Langford, H. G., Blaufox, M. D., Oberman, A., Hawkins, C. M., Curb, J. D., Cutter, G. R., Wasserthell-Smoller, S., Pressel, S., Babcock, C., Abernethy, J. D., Hotchkiss, J., & Tyler, M. (1985). Dietary therapy slows the return of hypertension after stopping prolonged medication. *Journal of the American Medical Association, 253,* 657–664.

Lantelme, P., Milon, H., Gharib, C., Gayet, C., & Fortrat, J. O. (1998). White coat effect and reactivity to stress: Cardiovascular and autonomic nervous system responses. *Hypertension, 31,* 1021–1029.

Lee, J. Y., Kusek, J. W., Greene, P. G., Bernhard, S., Norris, K., Smith, D., Wilkening, B., & Wright, J. T. (1996). Assessing medication adherence by pill count and electronic monitoring in the African American Study of Kidney Disease and Hypertension (AASK) pilot study. *American Journal of Hypertension, 9,* 719–725.

Lie, H., Mundal, R., & Erikssen, J. (1985). Coronary risk factors and incidence of coronary death in relation to physical fitness: Seven-year follow-up study of middle-aged men and elderly men. *European Heart Journal, 6,* 147–157.

Light, K. C., Girdler, S. S., Sherwood, A., Bragdon, E. E., Brownley, K. A., West, S. G., & Hinderliter, A. L. (1999). High stress responsivity predicts later blood pressure only in combination with positive family history and high life stress. *Hypertension, 33,* 1458–1464.

Linden, W., & Chambers, L. (1994). Clinical effectiveness of non-drug treatment for hypertension: A meta-analysis. *Annals of Behavioral Medicine, 16,* 35–45.

Linden, W., Lenz, J. W., & Con, A. H. (2001). Individualized stress management for primary hypertension: A randomized trial. *Archives of Internal Medicine, 161,* 1071–1080.

Litchfield, W. R., Hunt, S. C., Jeunemaitre, X., Fisher, N. D., Hopkins, P. N., Williams, R. R., Corvol, P., & Williams, G. H. (1998). Increased urinary free cortisol: A potential intermediate phenotype of essential hypertension. *Hypertension, 31,* 569–574.

Lucini, D., Norbiato, G., Clerici, M., & Pagani, M. (2002). Hemodynamic and autonomic adjustments to real life stress conditions in humans. *Hypertension, 39,* 184–188.

MacMahon, S., Cutler, J., Brittain, E., & Higgins, M. (1987). Obesity and hypertension: Epidemiological and clinical issues. *European Heart Journal, 8*(Suppl. B), 57–70.

Martin, J. E., Dubbert, P. M., & Cushman, W. C. (1990). Controlled trial of aerobic exercise in hypertension. *Circulation, 81,* 1560–1567.

Matthews, K. A., Woodall, K. L., & Allen, M. T. (1993). Cardiovascular reactivity to stress predicts future blood pressure status. *Hypertension, 22,* 479–485.

Menkes, M. S., Matthews, K. A., Krantz, D. S., Lundberg, U., Mead, L. A., Qaqish, B., Liang, K. Y., Thomas, C. B., & Pearson, T. A. (1989). Cardiovascular reactivity to the cold pressor test as a predictor of hypertension. *Hypertension, 14,* 524–530.

Messerli, F. H. (1982). Cardiovascular effects of obesity and hypertension. *Lancet, 1,* 1165.

Miller, N. H., Hill, M., Kottke, T., & Ockene, I. S. (1997). The multi-level compliance challenge: Recommendations for a call to action—A statement for healthcare professionals. *Circulation, 95,* 1085–1090.

Mulrow, P. J. (1998). Detection and control of hypertension in the population: The United States experience. *American Journal of Hypertension, 11,* 744–746.

Myers, M. G., & Reeves, R. A. (1991). White coat phenomenon in patients receiving antihypertensive therapy. *American Journal of Hypertension, 4,* 844–849.

Neaton, J. D., & Wentworth, D. (1992). Serum cholesterol, blood pressure, cigarette smoking, and death from coronary heart disease: Overall findings and differences by age for 316,099 white men. *Archives of Internal Medicine, 152,* 56–64.

Oliveria, S. A., Lapuerta, P., McCarthy, B. D., L'Italien, G. J., Berlowitz, D. R., & Asch, S. M. (2002). Physician-related barriers to the effective management of uncontrolled hypertension. *Archives of Internal Medicine, 162,* 413–420.

Oparil, S. (2000). Arterial hypertension. In R. L. Cecil, J. C. Bennett, & L. Goldman (Eds.), *Cecil textbook of medicine* (21st ed., pp. 258–273). Philadelphia: W. B. Saunders.

Paffenbarger, R. S., Jung, D. L., Leung, R. W., & Hyde, R. T. (1991). Physical activity and hypertension: An epidemiologic view. *Annals of Medicine, 23,* 319–327.

Parati, G., Pomidossi, G., Albini, F., Malaspina, D., & Mancia, G. (1987). Relationship of 24-hour blood pressure mean and variability to severity of target-organ damage in hypertension. *Journal of Hypertension, 5,* 93–98.

Pate, R. R., Pratt, M., Blair, S. N., Haskell, W. L., Macera, C. A., Bouchard, C., Buchner, D., Ettinger, W., Heath, G. W., & King, A. C. (1995). Physical activity and public health: A recommendation from the Centers for Disease Control and Prevention and the American College of Sports Medicine. *Journal of the American Medical Association, 273,* 402–407.

Pickering, T. (1995). Recommendations for the use of home (self) and ambulatory blood pressure monitoring: American Society of Hypertension Ad Hoc Panel. *American Journal of Hypertension, 9,* 1–11.

Pickering, T. G., Coats, A., Mallion, J. M., Mancia, G., & Verdecchia, P. (1999). Blood pressure monitoring: Task Force V—White-coat hypertension. *Blood Pressure Monitoring, 4,* 333–341.

Pickering, T. G., James, J. D., Boddie, C., Harshfield, G. A., Blank, S., & Laragh, J. H (1988). How common is white coat hypertension? *Journal of the American Medical Association, 259,* 225–228.

Potter, J. F., & Beevers, D. G. (1984). Pressor effect of alcohol in hypertension. *Lancet, 1,* 119–122.

Raikkonen, K., Hautanen, A., & Keltikangas-Jarvinen, L. (1996). Feelings of exhaustion, emotional distress, and pituitary and adrenocortical hormones in borderline hypertension. *Journal of Hypertension, 14,* 713–718.

Rapoport, L., Clark, M., & Wardle, J. (2000). Evaluation of a modified cognitive-behavioural programme for weight management. *International Journal of Obesity, 24,* 1726–1737.

Reisin, E., Frolich, E. D., Messerli, F. H., Dreslinski, G. R., Dunn, F. G., Jones, M. M., & Batson, H. M., Jr. (1983). Cardiovascular changes after weight reduction in obesity hypertension. *Annals of Internal Medicine, 98,* 315–319.

Richter-Heinrich, E., Homuth, V., Heinrich, B., et al. (1981). Long term application of behavioral treatments in essential hypertensives. *Physiology and Behavior, 26,* 915–920.

Roter, D. L., Hall, J. A., Mersica, R., Nordstrom, B., Cretin, D., & Svarstad, B. (1998). Effectiveness of interventions to improve patient compliance: A meta-analysis. *Medical Care, 36,* 1138–1161.

Sacks, F. M., Svetkey, L. P., Vollmer, W. M., Appel, L. J., Bray, G. A., Harsha, D., Obarzanek, E., Conlin, P. R., Miller, E. R., III, Simons-Morton, D. G., Karanja, N., & Lin, P. H., for DASH-Sodium Collaborative Research Group. (2001). Effects on blood pressure of reduced dietary sodium and the Dietary Approaches to Stop Hypertension (DASH) diet: DASH-Sodium Collaborative Research Group. *New England Journal of Medicine, 344,* 3–10.

Schneider, R. H., Staggers, F., Alexander, C., Sheppard, W., Rainforth, M., & Kodwani, K. (1995). A randomized controlled trial of stress reduction for hypertension in older African-Americans. *Hypertension, 26,* 820–827.

Selenta, C., Hogan, B. E., & Linden, W. (2000). How often do office blood pressure measurements fail to identify true hypertension? An exploration of white-coat normotension. *Archives of Family Medicine, 9,* 533–540.

Shea, S., Misra, D., Ehrlich, M. H., Field, L., & Francis, C. K. (1992). Predisposing factors for severe, uncontrolled hypertension in an inner-city minority population. *New England Journal of Medicine, 327,* 776–781.

Simkin-Silverman, L. R., Wing, R. R., Boraz, M. A., Meilan, E. N., & Kuller, L. H. (1998). Maintenance of cardiovascular risk factor changes among middle-aged women in a lifestyle intervention trial. *Women's Health: Research on Gender, Behaviour, and Policy, 4,* 255–271.

Spence, J. D., Barnett, P. A., Linden, W., Ramsden, V., & Taenzer, P. (1999). Lifestyle modifications to prevent and control hypertension: VII. Recommendations on stress management. *Canadian Medical Association Journal, 160*(9, Suppl.), S46–S50.

Stamler, J. (1997). The INTERSALT study: Background, methods, findings, and implications. *American Journal of Clinical Nutrition, 65,* S626–S642.

Stamler, R., Stamler, J., Gosch, F. C., Civinelli, J., Fishman, J., McKeever, P., McDonald, A., & Dyer, A. R. (1989). Primary prevention of hypertension by nutritional-hygienic means: Final report of a randomized, controlled trial. *Journal of the American Medical Association, 262,* 1801–1807.

Stevens, V. J., Corrigan, S. A., Obarzanek, E., Bernauer, E., Cook, N. R., Hebert, P., Mattfeldt-Beman, M., Oberman, A., Sugars, C., & Dalcin, A. T. (1993). Weight loss intervention in Phase 1 of the Trials of Hypertension Prevention: The TOHP Collaborative Research Group. *Archives of Internal Medicine, 153,* 849–858.

Stevens, V. J., Obarzanek, E., Cook, N. R., Lee, I., Appel, L. J., West, D. S., Milas, N. C., Mattfeldt-Beman, M., Belden, L., Bragg, C., Millstone, M., Raczynski, J., Brewer, A., Singh, B., & Cohen, J., for Trials for the Hypertension Prevention Research Group. (2001). Long-term weight loss and changes in blood pressure: Results of the Trials of Hypertension Prevention, Phase II. *Annals of Internal Medicine, 134,* 1–11.

Stockwell, D. H., Madhaven, S., Cohen, H., Gibson, G., & Alerman, M. H. (1994). The determinants of hypertension awareness, treatment, and control in an insured population. *American Journal of Public Health, 84,* 1768–1774.

Stone, N. J., & Kushner, R. (2000). Risk factor modification for cardiac disease: Effects of dietary modification and treatment of obesity—Emphasis on improving vascular outcomes. *Medical Clinics of North America, 84*(1), 95–122.

Thadhani, R., Camargo, C. A., Stampfer, M. J., Curhan, G. C., Willett, W. C., & Rimm, E. B. (2002). Prospective study of moderate alcohol consumption and risk of hypertension in young women. *Archives of Internal Medicine, 162,* 569–574.

Treadway, K. (2000). Management of hypertension. In A. H. Goroll, A. G. Mulley, & L. A. May (Eds.), *Primary care medicine: Office evaluation and management of the adult patient* (4th ed., pp. 149–164). Philadelphia: Lippincott/Williams & Wilkins.

Treiber, F. A., Turner, J. R., Davis, H., Thompson, W., Levy, M., & Strong, W. B. (1996). Young children's cardiovascular stress responses predict resting cardiovascular functioning 2½ years later. *Journal of Cardiovascular Risk, 3,* 95–100.

Trials of Hypertension Prevention Collaborative Research Group. (1992). The effects of non-pharmacologic interventions on blood pressure of persons with high normal levels: Results of the Trials of Hypertension Prevention, Phase 1. *Journal of the American Medical Association, 267,* 1213–1220.

Vander, A. J., Sherman, J. H., & Luciano, D. S. (1994). *Human physiology* (6th ed.). New York: McGraw-Hill.

Verdecchia, P., Schillaci, G., Borgioni, C., Ciucci, A., & Porcellati, C. (1997). Prognostic significance of the white coat effect. *Hypertension, 29,* 1218–1224.

Vollmer, W. M., Sacks, F. M., Ard, J., Appel, L. J., Bray, G. A., Simons-Morton, D. G., Conlin, P. R., Svetkey, L. P., Erlinger, T. P., Moore, T. J., & Karanja, N. (2001). Effects of diet and sodium intake on blood pressure: Subgroup analysis of the DASH-Sodium Trial. *Annals of Internal Medicine, 135,* 1019–1028.

Wadden, T. A., Berkowitz, R. I., Sarwer, D. B., Prus-Wisniewski, R., & Steinberg, C. (2001). Benefits of lifestyle modification in the pharmacologic treatment of obesity: A randomized trial. *Archives of Internal Medicine, 161,* 218–227.

Ward, M. M., Swan, G. E., & Chesney, M. A. (1987). Arousal reduction treatments for mild hypertension: A meta-analysis of recent studies. In S. Julius & D. R. Bassett (Eds.), *Behavioral factors in hypertension* (pp. 285–302). Amsterdam: Elsevier North-Holland.

Watt, G. C., Harrap, S. B., Foy, C. J., Holton, D. W., Edwards, H. V., Davidson, H. R., Connor, J. M., Lever, A. F., & Fraser, R. (1992). Abnormalities of glucocorticoid metabolism and the renin-angiotensin system: A four-corners approach to the identification of genetic determinants of blood pressure. *Journal of Hypertension, 10,* 473–482.

Weber, M. A., Neutel, J. M., Smith, D. H. G., & Graettinger, W. F. (1994). Diagnosis of mild hypertension by ambulatory blood pressure monitoring. *Circulation, 90,* 2291–2298.

Weinberger, M. H. (1996). Salt sensitivity of blood pressure in humans. *Hypertension, 27,* 481–490.

Whelton, P. K. (1985). Blood pressure in adults and the elderly. In W. H. Birkenhäger & J. L. Reid (Eds.), *Handbook of hypertension* (pp. 51–69). Amsterdam: Elsevier Science.

Wilson, J. D., & Foster, D. W. (1992). *Williams textbook of endocrinology* (8th ed.). Philadelphia: W. B. Saunders.

Witteman, J. C., Willett, W. C., Stampfer, M. J., Colditz, G. A., Kok, F. J., Sacks, F. M., Speizer, F. E., Rosner, B., & Hennekens, C. H. (1990). Relation of moderate alcohol consumption and risk of systemic hypertension in women. *American Journal of Cardiology, 65,* 633–637.

Xin, X., He, J., Frontini, M. G., Ogden, L. G., Motsamai, O. I., & Whelton, P. K. (2001). Effects of alcohol reduction on blood pressure: A meta-analysis of randomized controlled trials. *Hypertension, 38*, 1112–1117.

Yamori, Y., Matsumoto, M., Yamabe, H., & Okamoto, K. (1969). Augmentation of spontaneous hypertension by chronic stress in rats. *Japanese Circulation Journal, 33*, 399–409.

Young, D. R., Appel, L. J., Jee, S., & Miller, E. R. (1999). The effects of aerobic exercise and t'ai chi on blood pressure in older people: Results of a randomized trial. *Journal of the American Geriatrics Society, 47*, 277–284.

CHAPTER 15

Coronary Heart Disease

Behavioral Cardiology
in Clinical Practice

STEVEN M. SCHWARTZ AND
MARK W. KETTERER

Heart disease continues to be the number one killer of men and women in the United States, where myocardial infarctions (MIs) occur at a rate of about 1.5 million per year. For about 30% of these patients, death is sudden and the first "symptom" they experience. Ischemic heart disease or coronary heart disease (CHD) is predicted to remain the leading cause of death worldwide through 2020. Despite these compelling statistics, the survival rate from acute coronary events continues to improve, and more than 1 million people survive acute coronary events annually in the United States. Thus, issues pertaining to psychological functioning, behavioral risk, and quality of life are increasingly relevant as heart patients face more favorable prospects for recovery and rehabilitation. Assessing and treating these patients' health risk behaviors, such as smoking, obesity, fatty diet, lack of exercise, nonadherence to medical regimen, social isolation, and emotional status

(e.g., depression, anger, anxiety) is essential to secondary prevention efforts and is critical for optimal recovery of function and general health.

The modern evolution of behavioral cardiology arguably began during the mid-1970s with the work of Friedman and Rosenman (1974) on "Type A behavior." Since that time, behavioral scientists and clinicians in collaboration with medical colleagues have considerably expanded and refined our understanding of the relationship among psychological, emotional, psychophysiological, and behavioral factors in the development, maintenance, and exacerbation of CHD. Given the increasing clinical role of behavioral clinicians in managing heart patients, this chapter provides (a) a brief review of the etiology of heart disease, (b) a cognitive-behavioral case conceptualization of CHD, and (c) a pragmatic presentation of the clinical issues for assessing and treating patients with coronary artery disease.

PSYCHOPHYSIOLOGICAL AND BIOMEDICAL ASPECTS OF THE CHD PATIENT

Atherosclerosis

Atherosclerosis is defined as the buildup of plaques (e.g., "blockages," "stenoses," "lesions," "occlusions") typically composed of lipids, complex carbohydrates, and blood products along artery walls. The development of atherosclerosis is multidetermined and progressive unless the condition is vigorously treated. By the time a cohort reaches middle age, half or more will have some amount of atherosclerosis. However, some people reach advanced ages of 80 years or more with little or no clinically significant atherosclerosis. Therefore, although a number of etiological risk factors have been identified, our understanding of the etiology remains incomplete. However, most of the currently accepted risk factors (aside from family history, sex, and age) are modifiable by medication, changes in lifestyle, or both.

When patients have lesions at one site (e.g., coronary arteries), it is highly probable that they will have lesions at other sites (e.g., carotid, femoral, or renal arteries). Blockages that are large enough to threaten blood supply, and thus to threaten oxygen flow to critical areas (e.g., heart, brain, kidney, legs), produce transient ischemia (i.e., reversible oxygen supply/demand deficit) or permanent damage secondary to infarction (i.e., tissue death due to cessation of blood supply). Large plaques (50% or greater blockage) are associated with a higher risk of infarction. Interestingly, although large plaques may threaten adequate blood flow locally, chronic deprivation of an adequate blood supply to the heart can provoke the development of collateral arteries around the occluded sites as a remarkable biological compensatory strategy. These collateral arteries then provide natural bypasses in the event of infarction of the main trunk. Also of note, although large blockages are more likely to produce an infarct, the much higher prevalence of "small" lesions (less than 50% occlusion) means that most MIs (absolute number) actually occur at sites with low-level occlusion.

Atherosclerosis will follow a "stuttering" course marked by periods of growth, stasis, and (sometimes) regression. Plaques may be fibrous and stable, or they may be unstable, containing a pool of dead cells and lipids covered by a thin membrane or cap and eccentric in shape. When this cap ruptures, the contents of the pool are thought to provoke thrombus formation (i.e., clot), sometimes self-resolving (but perhaps provoking angina) and sometimes evolving into a full blockage of the artery (MI). Fully 85% to 90% of infarctions are believed to be caused by this sequence. The cause of plaque instability is thought to be chronic recurring inflammation, perhaps with some causal contribution from genetic factors and/or infection with *Chlamydia pneumoniae* (Ridker, Hennekens, Buring, & Rifai, 2000; Ross, 1999).

Precisely what triggers a rupture remains a matter of debate (Allen & Scheidt, 1996), although it has been hypothesized that elevated emotional states may be one triggering mechanism secondary to emotion-aggravated contractility of the heart, blood pressure changes, increased blood viscosity, vasoconstriction, and/or localized vasospasm. Thrombogenesis is certainly encouraged by various psychobiochemicophysical events, including via stress reactivity pathways. For example, elevated circulating catecholamines and platelet aggregation are associated with states of acute fear or anger (Markovitz, 1998). Heart rates and diastolic and systolic blood pressures rise, sometimes precipitously, in response to even mild transient and contrived stressors in the laboratory (Goldberg et al., 1996; Ketterer, Freedland, et al., 2000). Daily life stress is typically more meaningful and chronic, provoking more intense and prolonged emotional burden on patients. This has been measured with in vivo monitoring studies (e.g., Polk, Kamarck, & Shiffman, 2002).

Note that even when accounting for all of the factors in epidemiological studies, only about half of cases of ischemic heart disease can be explained (Farmer & Gotto, 1997). Although most infarctions are probably the result of unstable plaque rupture, 2% to 10% of all infarctions in the human heart occur in the absence of any atherosclerosis, and another 5% to 10% occur in a part of the coronary vascular tree without plaque. Thus, acute thrombus formation can occur independent of plaque rupture. It is now believed that the occurrence of a MI requires something beyond atherosclerosis.

Depending on location (which determines the amount of heart muscle affected by cessation of blood flow) and the presence of collateral circulation and/or anatomical variants in the coronary vascular tree, the size and significance of an infarction can vary widely. MIs considered large will generally decrease the heart's pumping function (i.e., ejection fraction [EF]). A normal EF (i.e., the proportion of blood ejected from the left ventricle during systole) will average about 66% in the heart of a healthy adult but includes values above 50%. Unless the patient engages in strenuous physical activity, EFs above 40% may be undetectable by the patient. EFs below 40% define heart failure, and this generally affects routine physical function (i.e., dyspnea, fatigue, and/or dependent edema). With EFs below 20%, the patient may be considered for a transplant.

Angina

Angina pectoris refers to transient chest pain or discomfort resulting from ischemia of heart muscle. The discomfort occurs secondary to an oxygen supply/demand deficit. Hence, strenuous physical activity that increases the heart's workload is a common trigger. Most commonly experienced as chest "discomfort" (e.g., pain, pressure, fullness, squeezing), angina sometimes manifests as arm pain, jaw pain, lower back pain, headache, nausea/vomiting/upset stomach, cognitive confusion, dyspnea (i.e., shortness of breath), dizziness, syncope/near syncope, and/or weakness. Stable angina has well-delineated triggers (typically physical exertion and sometimes stress) and responds well to nitrates. Unstable angina is far less predictable and is often accompanied by severe and prolonged pain. The presence of unstable angina is clinically considered an acute coronary event requiring emergent care because it may be caused by plaque rupture.

Angina is generally presumed to result from ischemia, but this "causal" relationship is less than perfect (e.g., Krantz et al., 1994). Importantly, the symptoms of angina are shared by a wide range of other conditions, including acute emotional states, psychiatric disorders, and other medical conditions, making differential diagnosis difficult at times (Richter, 1992; Schwartz, Trask, & Ketterer, 1999). Most episodes of ischemia captured on Holter monitoring in both laboratory testing and in vivo settings are not associated with chest pain/pressure or other symptoms, typically referred to as silent myocardial ischemia. (A Holter monitor is a small portable device that collects electrocardiogram [ECG] data on a continuous basis during daily life.) Furthermore, most episodes of chest pain are not associated with ischemia as measured by surface ECG ("atypical" or "noncardiac" chest pain). In fact, recurrent emergency room visits by cardiac patients for chest discomfort without evidence of ischemia/infarction are quite common.

Angina is strongly associated with depression/anxiety, and cognitive-behavioral treatment of emotional distress has been found to reduce episodes of angina and ischemia (Blumenthal et al., 1997; Ketterer, Fitzgerald, et al., 2000; Lewin, 1997). Pain intolerance secondary to depression/anxiety, or ischemia/angina provocation secondary to fear/anger, increases chest discomfort (Ketterer, Fitzgerald, et al., 2000; Ketterer et al., 1998; Schwartz et al., 1999), and chest discomfort provokes treatment seeking and aggressive diagnostic/ treatment decisions by physicians. Thus, if not directly affecting disease progression, emotional distress will still affect quality of life, illness behavior, and disease management in adverse ways.

Because angina is the major driving force behind medical system use, treatment of emotional distress may reduce this use (Black, Allison, Williams, Rummans, & Gau, 1998; Davidson, 2000; Frasure-Smith & Lesperance, 1998). Recently, Schwartz and colleagues (1999) proposed a spectrum approach to chest pain management (e.g., pain and palpitations) that includes presentations consistent with pain/anxiety, Syndrome X/nonischemic chest pain, Prinzmetal's angina, and angina pectoris. Because psychological and behavioral problems are similar in angina and other forms of chest discomfort regardless of the underlying cause, disease management strategies should be multidisciplinary. The rise of "chest pain" clinics for nonemergent chest pain attests to greater recognition of this overlapping and complex problem.

Arrhythmias

The heart contracts and relaxes in a highly orchestrated fashion or rhythm to efficiently move blood from the venous compartment (deoxygenated blood) to the arterial compartment (oxygenated blood). This is a two-phase process in which the heart fills during the relaxation phase (diastole) and then the heart forcefully empties during the contraction phase (systole). This orchestration is electrochemical in nature and is maintained by a specialized cluster of cells collectively called the sinoatrial node or natural pacemaker. Disruption of this sequencing is referred to as an arrhythmia. Arrhythmias can range from benign to malignant. Of particular clinical significance are *sustained*

ventricular tachycardia and *ventricular fibrillation,* the presumed causal culprits in sudden cardiac death. Note that the ventricular portion of the heart is the primary pumping chamber for the brain and general body. There are a number of factors (e.g., drugs, disease, infarction, emotional distress) that can produce abnormal rhythms, many of which can be serious or even life threatening. In severe instances, blood flow may slow sufficiently to cause acute brain failure (syncope). When the heart has been thrown into inefficient sequencing of its contractions, cardioversion (transthoracic electrical shock) is used to achieve a normal sinus rhythm.

Patients at high risk for future life-threatening arrhythmias will likely receive antiarrhythmic medications that regulate heartbeat, pacemakers, and (in severe cases) implantable cardioverter defibrillators. This latter device, like the pacemaker, is placed inside the body and can function as an "onboard" crash cart that greatly improves both sudden cardiac death and all-cause mortality relative to medication management alone (Gilkson & Friedman, 2001). However, there is growing evidence that the device itself can produce problems of behavioral or psychological maladjustment in a significant subgroup of patients (for an excellent review, see Sears, Todaro, Lewis, Sotile, & Conti, 1999).

Behavioral clinicians are particularly familiar with the *sinus tachycardias* most characteristic of panic attacks and other acute anxiety and mood states. Importantly, clinicians must be aware that patients can and do develop anxious presentations from more dangerous heart rhythms as well (Schwartz et al., 2002). Also, there is considerable evidence that the subjective symptom of palpitation correlates poorly with underlying cardiac rhythm (Barsky, 2001; Barsky, Cleary, Barnett, Christiansen, & Ruskin, 1994), as was described previously for chest pain. Although it is generally acknowledged that panic spectrum disorders can and do masquerade as cardiac problems, the reverse is also true. To illustrate the complexity among anxiety, palpitations, and cardiac rhythm, Lessmeier and colleagues (1997) found that 67% of patients presenting for treatment of paroxysmal supraventricular tachycardia (PSVT) met criteria for panic and that PSVT went unrecognized in 55% of the patients even after an initial medical evaluation. Equally striking, 86% of patients displayed resolution of anxiety symptoms with antiarrhythmic therapy.

Hemodynamics

This chapter has already alluded to the notion that the heart can develop compensatory strategies in the presence of heart dysfunction/disease (e.g., development of collateral arteries as a natural bypass). Hemodynamics is the study of the forces involved in the movement of blood through the circulatory system. It is through the study of these processes that one can understand the physical and functional changes that occur in the diseased heart as it attempts to maintain homeostasis in the body. A simplified version of the process is as follows. As the EF of the heart declines in heart failure, or with infarct-related heart muscle damage, the heart begins to struggle to push blood out into the body, creating a variety of physical changes in the heart's structure over time. This process, referred to as *remodeling*, can be characterized by heart enlargement, thickening of the heart walls, and leaking heart valves that regurgitate blood as the heart becomes more inefficient. This inefficiency is manifest in wall motion abnormalities. Wall motion abnormalities can be visualized by blood pool radionuclide imaging (technetium sestamibi) or on echocardiogram. Localized perfusion defects can be visualized by uptake of radioactively labeled glucose (technetium pyrophosphate or thallium). This type of diagnostic testing is thought to reflect impairment of blood flow to an area of heart muscle. This impairment can be reversible when the patient is not being stressed, or it is "fixed" (present when the patient is both at rest and stressed), implying

permanent tissue death ("infarction"). Likewise, certain patterns on the ECG (*ST segment depression*) reflect ischemia or infarction. Table 15.1 presents some of the common cardiac diagnostic and treatment procedures.

Cognitive-Behavioral Case Conceptualization of CHD

Understanding the factors that contribute to both acute and chronic aspects of CHD would be incomplete without consideration of the psychological, emotional, and behavioral characteristics of the patient or the patient population. The clinical study of these unique risk factors and their modification is at the very "heart" of behavioral cardiology. Given what is currently supported by the evidentiary literature, a general cognitive-behavioral conceptualization of cardiovascular disease development and rehabilitation can be constructed on the following assumptions:

1. Many of the biological processes that underlie cardiovascular disease develop over time out of health risk behaviors and lifestyles. These risk factors for CHD are relevant to disease development, maintenance, and exacerbation and also contribute to related and complicating conditions such as emphysema, type 2 diabetes, pulmonary hypertension, and heart failure.

2. Lifestyle and behavioral risks are generally immediately and highly gratifying. The powerful reward value of these risk behaviors causes them to become habitualized as a consequence of frequent and persistent practice, thereby making them particularly resistant to intervention. For example, a pack-a-day smoker receives 70,000 infusions of nicotine during the course of a year; that is a number of "hits" unparalleled by any other recreational drug.

3. The negative, debilitating health consequences of these behaviors typically develop slowly over time, allowing the person to accommodate to many of the

Table 15.1   Common Cardiac Diagnostic and Treatment Procedures

ECG:	Monitors the electrical activity in the heart to past or present heart attack, the location of the heart affected, and the rhythm of the heart; can be used with or without exercise (treadmill testing) and in vivo with Holter monitoring (continuous monitoring) or event monitoring (event-specific recordings)
Echocardiogram:	Ultrasound evaluation of the heart allowing for an imaging of the working heart to be captured, including chambers, valves, and heart muscle walls; can also be done in conjunction with exercise or use of a medication (e.g., Dobutamine) that increases heart rate
Cardiac catheterization:	Invasive procedure that is performed by inserting a catheter (tube-like device) into an artery (typically in the groin) and advancing through the arterial system into the heart, with the catheter able to measure pressures inside the heart chambers and, when equipped with a camera, able to take video of the heart in action
Percutaneous transluminal coronary angioplasty (PTCA)/ directional coronary atherectomy (DCA):	Advancing a catheter up to a blockage in a critical artery and reducing the occlusion by expanding a small balloon or using a plaque-cutting device, with stents (stainless steel mesh tubes) sometimes being put into place to prevent re-occlusion
Coronary artery bypass graft:	Surgical procedure that takes blood vessels from another part of the body (typically in the legs or chest) and then stitches them around the blocked coronary artery

symptoms of physiological degradation and reduced function.

4. The individual's cognitive and emotional status mediates lifestyle risk factors and also contributes more directly to disease development, maintenance, and exacerbation through the autonomic nervous system's stress reactivity pathways associated with fight/flight and psychoneuroimmunological pathways.

5. The biological, psychological, and behavioral factors noted previously, as well as environmental factors, influence one another in a bidirectional or reciprocal fashion.

ASSESSMENT OF THE CHD PATIENT

Screening

Identification and triaging of emotionally distressed patients from cardiac settings often requires the use of an objective, psychometrically sound questionnaire to aid clinical staff in recognizing distress. There are a number of well-validated self-report measures for assessing CHD patients, and most focus on emotional status, functionality, and/or quality of life. Table 15.2 lists some of the commonly used tools and the underlying constructs they purport to measure. Any of the psychometric instruments validated as prospective predictors of cardiac outcomes could be used, but they are clearly redundant in terms of their predictive utility (Ketterer et al., 2002). Because of brevity, nonstigmatizing content, and ease of administration and scoring (many CHD patients will become frustrated with lengthy questionnaires or test batteries), the Hospital Anxiety and Depression Scale (HADS). with a cutoff of 13 or greater, is recommended (Herrman, 1997). The chapter authors suspect that

Table 15.2 Self-Report Measures for the Cardiac Patient

Hospital Anxiety and Depression Scale

Symptom Checklist-90–Revised (Brief Symptom Inventory)

Beck Depression Inventory

State-Trait Anxiety Inventory

Crown-Crisp

Cook-Medly Hostility Scale

Ketterer Stress Symptom Frequency Checklist

Millon Behavioral Health Inventory

Toronto Alexithymia Scale

SF36

Seattle Angina Questionnaire

Minnesota Living With Heart Failure Questionnaire

Cardiac Anxiety Questionnaire

screening will eventually require an instrument designed for completion by a significant other so as to circumvent denial (Ketterer et al., 1996, 1998, 2002), but this remains to be proven in prospective studies.

Clinical Interviewing (Functional Analysis)

Evaluation should, as always, include a thorough psychosocial history, mental status exam, and review of cardiovascular risk factors (Table 15.3 lists the domains to consider in an initial evaluation). Importantly, this evaluation should include identification of barriers to change as well as cardiovascular risk factors. Behavioral assessment models have long been used in the functional analysis of problem behaviors (Barrios, 1988), including illness behavior (Schwartz, Gramling, & Mancini, 1994). Because the modifiable risk factors for CHD are deeply embedded in the psychology and behavior of the patient, approaching the initial assessment of the patient can be greatly facilitated by using a functional-analytic framework. The Stimulus–Organismic–Response–Consequence (SORC)

model (Goldfried & Sprafkin, 1976) is one of several common models and is used here for illustration purposes.

The Stimulus (patient triggers or hot buttons). The *stimulus* portion of the SORC model refers to the triggers or cues that evoke health risk behavior. Stimulus control variables relate to cardiovascular risk in a number of ways. Overt behaviors such as substance abuse (e.g., nicotine, alcohol, cocaine), lack of exercise, and acute emotional reactions can have a broad range of environmental and cognitive triggers. For example, it is not unusual for the mere presence of a critical supervisor to trigger acute autonomic arousal and concomitant emotional distress (e.g., anxiety, anger, irritation, worry), even when there is no current overt conflict. Therefore, it is imperative to identify the patient's triggers (or buttons), noting that patients may vary greatly in their understanding of or insight into the functional relationships between triggers and emotional or behavioral responses.

Organismic Variables. Organismic variables are the dispositional characteristics of the patient (e.g., genetic, physiological, temperamental,

Table 15.3   An Evaluation Checklist for CHD Patients

Frequency and triggers for chest pain

Disease-specific worries (often grief over disease-imposed role changes or limitations)

Disease-specific knowledge (what the patient knows about his or her condition and recovery)

Physical activity level (including activities such as walking and gardening)

Smoking (e.g., number of cigarettes per day, smoking history in years)

Eating habits (e.g., high-risk foods with high fat content, salt, sugar; eating behaviors such as binging, rapid eating, stress/emotional eating)

Alcohol intake (e.g., number of drinks per day/week, drinking history, CAGE questions)

Interpersonal conflicts (particularly focusing on work and marital relationships)

Job stress (e.g., deadlines, responsibilities)

Sleep habits (e.g., apnea, insomnia, restless leg syndrome)

Emotional status (e.g., depression, grief, anxiety, anger/hostility, alexithymia)

Comorbid medical conditions (e.g., diabetes, heart failure, chronic obstructive pulmonary disease)

---

experiential) that are peculiar to the individual. The familial aspects of cardiovascular disease reflect both genetic factors and early learning experiences. Of particular interest may be the early modeling of cardiovascular risk behaviors such as smoking, angry acting out, and a maladaptive emphasis on competition and/or achievement at the expense of other important aspects of development.

The Response. The response describes the target risk behavior itself (e.g., eating a fatty meal). The response can also be operationalized as a nonbehavior (i.e., failure to act) such as an inability or unwillingness to engage in regular exercise. In addition, behavioral risk includes not only overt acts or failures to act but also covert behaviors such as certain cognitions. Table 15.4 lists some of the common maladaptive cognitions to assess in the CHD patient.

Consequences. There are several factors that affect the power of a consequence to shape behavior. Many of the risk behaviors seen in the CHD patient are highly overlearned, habitualized, and/or otherwise resistant to

change. Understanding the ways in which these behaviors are reinforced or maintained is critical to the secondary prevention process. Timing is particularly important in health risk behavior. As a general rule, temporal proximity of behavior and consequence will wield greater influence over the behavior. As noted previously, many risk behaviors provide immediate gratification. In particular, it is important to view the CHD patient's actions as maintained by relief from negative affective states.

Emotional Status

There are several emotional domains that have consistently proven themselves to have robust relationships to cardiac outcome and/or are relevant to individual work with the CHD patient (for an excellent review, see Rozanski, Blumenthal, & Kaplan, 1999). Assessment of depression/dysphoria, anger/hostility, stress, anxiety, and alexithymia is essential in a thorough evaluation of the CHD patient. It is important to note that many patients may present with subclinical levels of emotional distress (relative to cutoffs for traditional psychiatric patients), and these levels may still be clinically

Table 15.4   Common Cognitive Errors in CHD Patients

Chronic and excessive worry or anger about uncontrollable events (e.g., "catastrophizing" finances of retirement, allowing kids to sink or swim, confronting boss) is a chronic stressor for many patients. In many cases, patients have difficulty in discriminating the degree of control present in any stressful situation.

Inaccurate understanding of "normal" is common, particularly among Type A or assertiveness-impaired patients. Unrealistic expectations regarding their own behavior or others' behavior can cause chronic aggravation or feelings of being unloved (commonly accompanied by the "shoulds" or a set of rigidly held obligations or responsibilities).

"Anyone would react as I did" is probably a variant of the misunderstanding of "normal" and can be assessed using the "Rule of 100" test.[a]

Malevolent attributions are present in many cases. Often, patients will make attributions regarding the motives and intentions of others as malevolent (e.g., a car cuts them off on the highway, thereby provoking rage because the other driver was "obviously" stupid, irresponsible, and/or dangerous).

Surreptitious arrogance in interpersonal interactions is often characterized by overt politeness but dismissal of others' desires/opinions and devaluation of their feelings.

Inability to trust is frequently present and may have its origins in malevolent attributions or deeper insecurities that patients might not acknowledge or even be aware of fully.

Catastrophizing lateness/"unproductive" time is part of the time urgency characteristic of the Type A personality. Often, patients will have a profound intolerance for "downtime." Various forms of self-pacing exercises requiring the patient to go slower are helpful.

Confusing "right" with "harmful" might also be called the "just world hypothesis," in which patients will get very angry over perceived injustices, slights, or inequities. They believe that if they can "prove" their case, the world would have to come into compliance. In fact, it often does not matter whether one is right or not, and anger will still kill. Is this worth dying for?

Importance of "things" over persons, that is, what is regretted on deathbeds is time not spent with family/friends rather than time not spent at the office.

---

a. The clinician should ask himself or herself, "If 100 people were in this situation, what proportion would react in this way?" Thus, the clinician's sense of normative behavior can be used to gauge how "normal" the patient's reaction is.

significant, related to important clinical outcomes, and worthy of treatment even if they do not meet formal DSM (*Diagnostic and Statistical Manual of Mental Disorders,* fourth edition [American Psychiatric Association, 1994]) diagnostic criteria. In many cases, patients will "somatize" their distress (i.e., report only the physical symptoms and deny or minimize the affective/cognitive symptoms). Therefore, emphasizing the concrete benefits of improved sleep or energy, or of reduced chest pain, can help the patient to accept treatment.

Obtaining two or three adjectives for affect, and then obtaining concrete examples where these imply chronic conflict, for each significant other (e.g., parent, sibling, spouse/lover, child, boss) facilitates efforts toward mapping the patient's psychosocial stressors. This can also provide some clues as to how the patient construes and responds to others and as to the success of these coping patterns. Of particular importance are overlearned/automatized coping responses (which are presumably learned early in life and are often outside the patient's awareness) and whether they succeed at merely reducing distress but not stress (maladaptive) or at reducing both distress and stress (adaptive). Testing the patient's history against the "Rule of Three" may be a useful exercise. If the patient has made the same mistake three times or more (e.g., getting fired, marrying an abusive alcoholic), it is highly likely that this is a deeply ingrained pattern that the patient does not perceive regarding himself or herself. It should become a goal of treatment to raise the patient's awareness of this pattern, define a face-saving way of construing the pattern, and then develop more adaptive alternative responses. For example, instead of framing the problem as "I'm an angry guy," it may be more acceptable and constructive to frame it as "I care too much and have too high a set of expectations, and therefore I get frustrated a lot."

Depression. There are now numerous published reports linking depression and depressive symptoms to adverse cardiac outcomes (e.g., Booth-Kewley & Friedman, 1987; Carney, Freedland, Eisen, Rich, & Jaffe, 1995; Cassem & Hackett, 1973; Frasure-Smith, Lesperance, & Talajic, 1993). Based on this evidence, depression should now be considered an established independent risk factor for CHD outcomes (Glassman & Shapiro, 1998). Unfortunately, there are not yet any randomized controlled trials of sufficient methodological rigor to demonstrate a reduction in CHD morbidity or mortality as a result of treating depression either psychotherapeutically or psychopharmacologically. However, SADHART (Zoloft vs. placebo) and ENRICHD (stress management plus a selective serotonin reuptake inhibitor [SSRI] vs. standard care) are ongoing clinical trials targeting depression in CHD. What can be said with some certainty is that CHD/depression comorbidity does affect patient functionality, compliance, and quality of life such that assessment and aggressive treatment where indicated is an essential part of comprehensive care regardless of the impact on CHD-specific morbidity and mortality.

Anger. The work of Friedman and Rosenman (1974) on the Type A personality identified a number of characteristics that tended to cluster together and appeared to be associated with cardiovascular prognosis. Apart from ambition, "busyness," and constant effort, these characteristics include cynicism/mistrust, stubbornness/opinionated, perfectionism/demanding, alexithymia, controlling/overcontrolled, impatient, and worrier/obsessional. Importantly, not one of these characteristics can be argued as pathognomonic of the syndrome, nor does any appear to have a direct effect on the genesis or exacerbation of CHD. Rather, these characteristics are of importance because they tend to foster a hostility complex or "AIAI" (*a*ggravation, *i*rritation, *a*nger, and *i*mpatience).

Although the literature has been marred by inconsistent operational definitions, psychometric problems with self-report measures, and a more complex relationship between the AIAI construct and CHD than was originally conceived, it nevertheless remains prudent to assess the patient's ability to modulate anger. AIAI has been proved to be a causal factor for CHD in a randomly assigned, controlled clinical trial of cognitive/behavioral stress management that targeted AIAI and reduced death/MI rates by 37% relative to placebo controls (Dusseldorp, van Elderen, Maes, Meulman, & Kraaij, 1999; Friedman et al., 1986, 1987).

A related issue concerns *confrontation avoidance*, where conflict with either family members or coworkers often leads to "stewing" (anger) or chronic anxiety. This has been conceptualized as the "anger in/anger out" issue. This can occur for a variety of reasons, including the Type A who despises but will not discuss conflicts with his or her boss and the Type A's spouse who is afraid of expressing his or her disagreement over even trivial matters due to the consequent verbal assault (e.g., "that's so stupid") or cold shoulder. One common example seen is the cardiac patient who has living with him or her a late adolescent who is not working, going to school, or contributing to the workload at home and who may be abusing drugs or even being verbally abusive with the parents.

Anxiety. The data supporting a relationship between anxiety and CHD is perhaps more complex and less compelling than those supporting depression. As stated previously, acute anxiety might play an acute role in plaque ruptures, arrhythmias, and blood pressure. Anxiety has been implicated as a major risk factor for CHD in multiple prospective risk factor studies, particularly for death or sudden death (Kamarck & Jennings, 1991; Ketterer, 1999; Kubzansky, Kawachi, Weiss, & Sparrow, 1998). Unfortunately, no large-scale randomized control trials exist, nor are any under way, to examine treatment in this population and cardiac outcomes. It should be noted that acute digoxin toxicity (e.g., tremor, loss of appetite, confusion) may mimic anxiety.

Alexithymia. Many CHD patients are found to display some degree of alexithymia, which refers to difficulty in identifying and/or labeling emotional states in self and others. Patients with this disorder will display a poverty of vocabulary in reporting their feelings and describing other people's personalities, and they will typically not explore psychosocial circumstances as possible causes of their problems. They will present as emotionally concrete (as opposed to metaphorical) in talking about what appear to be emotionally charged situations. When exploring their psychosocial circumstances, it is necessary to gently probe for concrete event/behavioral details because these patients rarely volunteer information spontaneously because they frequently view it as irrelevant. Alexithymia can make it difficult for many patients to benefit

from traditional psychological intervention, although they are typically good at complying with behavioral assignments.

Substance Use

Assessment of substance use, particularly tobacco products, is particularly important in any evaluation. Smoking is a powerful predictor for many diseases, including CHD. If the patient is an active or recent smoker, immediate referral for Zyban or an SSRI and possible nicotine replacement should be facilitated (Edwards, Murphy, Downs, Ackerman, & Rosenthal, 1989; Ketterer, Pickering, Stoever, & Wansley, 1987; Murphy, Edwards, Downs, Ackerman, & Rosenthal, 1990). Smoking is such a potent predictor of outcomes that hesitation is not prudent unless the patient insists on thinking it over. The patient should be taught techniques to avoid smoking cues (e.g., bars, sitting around after meals) and to disrupt smoking habits (e.g., smoke with the opposite hand, change brands, smoke menthol), and should be taught relaxation procedures to help control acute urges prior to setting a contracted quit date (preferably during a psychosocially quiescent period). Giving the patient 24-hour-per-day access to the clinician during the first month of cessation is a privilege that will rarely be used or abused, and it seems to assist some patients in managing their impulses.

Although not a common problem in this population, chemical dependency (e.g., cocaine, alcohol) should be ruled out. It is a futile exercise to try to treat emotional distress in someone whose central nervous system is under assault by fluctuating levels of psychoactive substances. Detoxification may be necessary before further treatment can proceed. Note that prolonged alcohol abuse can result in cardiomyopathy. Prevalence rates for cocaine abuse in CHD do not exist, but it is clear that chronic cocaine use, particularly when smoking is the route of administration, can lead to early heart disease. Because cocaine can provoke coronary vasoconstriction, chest pain, and MI as well as depression, it is important to consider this in the history of the patient. Cocaine use is probably the most common single factor precipitating MI in young people (e.g., under age 40 years), so a drug screen may help to account for early CHD.

Sleep Apnea

Sleep apnea is a periodic cessation of breathing during sleep that is an underappreciated comorbidity in CHD. Clinicians should suspect sleep apnea when there are signs of persistent nightly snoring, bed partner complaints or descriptions of choking/gasping/cessation of breathing, and/or chronic fatigue ("excessive daytime sleepiness"). Patients may also manifest subtle signs of cognitive dysfunction or mood symptoms. Suspected apnea should result in referral for evaluation to a sleep center. It is not clear whether treatment of sleep apnea lowers the risk of MI/death, but this seems likely to be the case (Ketterer, Brymer, Rhoads, Kraft, & Kenyon, 1994). Because many apneics develop a reactive depression due to self-attributions regarding their "laziness," treatment of sleep apnea can improve mood (Dahlof, Ejnell, Hallstrom, & Hdner, 2000).

Cognitive Dysfunction

Of particular importance in this population, particularly given advanced age, are consideration of whether the patient displays any cognitive impairment (often subtle and in the absence of waxing/waning arousal and attention). The use of a cognitive screening tool or procedure (e.g., month, year, three items immediate and delayed, counting backward) at initial evaluation is important. Because of the patient's vascular disease and/or arrhythmias (particularly those patients who have atrial fibrillation), the likelihood of mild-moderate,

early-stage, multi-infarct dementia (often manifesting on magnetic resonance imaging/computerized tomography [MRI/CT] as "periventricular leukomalacia" or "ischemic white matter changes") is elevated. Although the patient may still be highly functional, irritability/frustration over subtle memory-related problems may be an aggravating factor if he or she externalizes causality. Ruling out alternative, potentially arrestable causes (e.g., a thyroid-stimulating hormone for thyroid problems, a venereal disease research laboratory or a rapid plasma regain test for neurosyphilis) is important, but such causes are only rarely found. Patients often fear a large cerebrovascular accident more than they fear a heart attack. Because prophylaxis of cerebrovascular accidents is the same as the regimen followed for MIs, patients can be reassured that all reasonable steps are being taken, and their concern can be used to further motivate "taking care of themselves."

The Importance of Collateral Clinical Data

Because of the high rate of denial/minimization/alexithymia present in this patient population, the clinician should be somewhat skeptical about the patient's version of his or her life and circumstances. Although it is important to understand how the patient attributes meaning to events, psychological "holes" in narration (e.g., "Gee, I don't know why she left me") should be seen as important and indicative of a chronic coping problem.

Significant others should always be used as collateral sources of information when evaluating a patient or tracking response to treatment. Sometimes, this can be accomplished by simply asking the patient, "How does your wife [husband] think you are doing?" Other times, it is necessary to obtain independent contact with the significant other because of the patient's denial/alexithymia or other lack of insight. Often, it is necessary to obtain this data out of the patient's hearing range given that many spouses report "walking on eggshells" so as not to provoke the patient's ire. One prudent tactic is to simply tell the patient that "it's always helpful to have another person's perspective on how you're doing." At a later point in time, the clinician can encourage the patient to use an appropriate significant other as a "monitor" under the mutual contract that the spouse should not be punished for providing accurate but unwelcome feedback.

As an adjunct to interviewing significant others, the Spouse/Friend Ketterer Stress Symptom Frequency Checklist (KSSFC) (Ketterer et al., 1996, 1998, 2002) is recommended for obtaining a significant other's assessments of the patient's emotional status. The KSSFC is unique in this feature of allowing both patient self-ratings and ratings by significant others. The spouse/friend KSSFC can be administered by sending it home with minimal written instructions and a stamped addressed envelope to "someone who knows you well." The patient and significant other should be encouraged to not discuss the questionnaire until after it has been mailed back. If the clinician is seeking direct input from a spouse/significant other on the patient's routine emotional functioning, it is critical that the conversation occur without the patient being present. It has been demonstrated that spouse/friend-reported depression using the KSSFC is a stronger correlate of coronary artery disease severity (by angiography) than is self-report and that denial of depression (spouse/friend minus self-ratings) is an even stronger correlate (Ketterer et al., 1996). Furthermore, spouse/friend ratings (and not self-ratings) of anxiety were the only predictor of angina at 5-year follow-up, and it was shown that denial of distress (particularly AIAI) is a very strong predictor of mortality (Ketterer et al., 1998). For this reason, the chapter authors routinely send their male patients home with a questionnaire about themselves to be given to "someone who

knows you well" to complete and return independently by mail *before* discussions with the patients. Although not yet documented, it will be interesting to see whether this relationship holds true for female patient/male significant other dyads.

TREATMENT AND CLINICAL PRACTICE

Stress and Coping Framework

Stress is a concept that most people, including those with CHD, readily accept and for which they have some intuitive understanding. Framing any psychological or behavioral problems within a diathesis stress model rather than using more traditional or formal psychiatric nomenclature (e.g., "crankiness" rather than "anger," feeling "down" rather than feeling "depressed," "worried" or "stressed" rather than "anxious") will typically provoke the least resistance and help to facilitate a therapeutic alliance. Clinicians working within a traditional psychiatric context and looking to develop cardiac referrals will face resistance from patients even before their first visits. Ideally, treatment should be done as part of a multidisciplinary cardiac team or consultation service rather than removed in a separate psychiatric setting to maximize destigmatization. Table 15.5 summarizes some of the treatment studies focusing on stress reduction.

Here the transactional model of Lazarus and Folkman (1984) works nicely. In the most general sense, coping efforts can be presented to patients as taking one of two tacks: problem-focused coping or emotion-focused coping. For heuristic purposes, these two coping efforts can be discussed as if they are separate, independent coping methods, whereas in vivo they most often interact in dynamic fashion and over time the patient will need to integrate them more effectively. Problem-focused coping, or efforts aimed at defining the problem,

Table 15.5 Benefits of Treating "Stress" in Ischemic Heart Disease

Proven (i.e., at least one intervention study published)	
Improved quality of life	Dusseldorp et al. (1999)
Decreased myocardial infarction and death	Dusseldorp et al. (1999); Ketterer (1993)
Reduction of ambulatory ischemia	Blumenthal et al. (1997); Friedman et al. (1996)
Decreased smoking relapse	Dusseldorp et al. (1999); Hall et al. (1994, 1998)
Decreased chest pain/pressure	Blumenthal et al. (1997); Gallacher et al. (1997); Ketterer, Fitzgerald, et al. (2000); Lewin (1997)
Reduction of moderate-level hypertension	Dusseldorp et al. (1999); Linden and Chambers (1994)
Probable (i.e., demonstrated to correlate with stress)	
Greater compliance to medications	Carney et al. (1995)
Greater compliance to exercise recommendations	Dusseldorp et al. (1999); Stetson et al. (1997)
Greater compliance to glucose control	Cox and Gonder-Frederik (1992)
Decreased medical system use	Allison et al. (1995); Black et al. (1998); Frasure-Smith & Lesperance (1998)
Possible (i.e., mechanistically plausible)	
Decreased infection/ulceration/ destabilization of plaque by *Chlamydia pneumoniae*?	
Decreased need for revascularization secondary to decreased chest pain	
Decreased treatment-seeking delay	
Increased heart rate variability	

its solution, and implementation of instrumental actions designed to bring about resolution, is often highly developed in CHD patients. Despite their good problem-solving skills, CHD patients may display poor discrimination skills in situations where problem solving is likely to be ineffective. Consequently, they may manifest an inability to profit from experience (e.g., banging their heads against a brick wall) in apparent defiance of punishing consequences. Repeated failures may lead to AIAI. Consequently, feeling trapped in stressful circumstances is a common experience.

Reliance on problem-focused coping strategies often comes at the expense of good, constructive, emotion-focused coping skills. Issues such as poor self-pacing, inability to relax or

tolerate "downtime," and substance use are indicative of poor emotion-focused coping.

It is usually useful to teach some form of relaxation to new patients. Acute reductions in heart rate and blood pressure, and the subjective benefits (e.g., calming, reduced worry, reduced chest pain, reduced headache, easier sleep onset) that accompany these exercises, provide an immediately perceived sense of control over previously "uncontrollable" events and so reinforce instructions regarding stress and CHD. The chapter authors use such a procedure prior to all group sessions because it also seems to foster psychological mindedness, permitting possible alteration of pathogenic cognitive attributions. Helping patients to master abbreviated relaxation methods, such as a "cleansing breath," is important in the transfer of relaxation skills to in vivo stressors.

The core goal of stress management in coronary artery disease patients is to reduce the frequency/intensity/duration (or "density") of emotional distress (or "stress"). The clinician should consider whether the patient's psychosocial environment is unusually stressful (i.e., triggers) and should identify one chronic stressor (or a few) and use ongoing life events to alter habitual cognitions/behaviors ("coping"). An alcoholic spouse, a demanding or abusive boss, and kids who are abusing drugs and sponging off the patient all require a different nexus of the intervention. For example, the chapter authors have seen a half dozen cases where getting an angry spouse on an SSRI resolved a patient's chest pain.

Frequently recurring stressors that lead to problematic emotions/behaviors should be identified and reviewed at each session to see whether the patient is attempting suggested alternatives and whether the alternatives are "working" (i.e., reducing the density of emotional distress). By attacking the largest stressors first, the patient is most likely to succeed at having a big effect quickly. The only exception to this strategy is when the patient is too overwhelmed (fearful) of attempting an alternative response or when response-specific skills deficits are present and require time to remediate. For example, the patient might not know how to behave assertively and/or might not be able to appropriately discriminate between assertive and aggressive behaviors. For such a patient, time must be spent reviewing events and teaching and even role-playing skills until the patient begins to perceive the unavoidability of facing the "dragon" (usually a boss, parent, child, or spouse) and has attained adequate skills. If such attempts are unsuccessful, consideration should be given to involving the dragon in treatment.

The clinician should assess and begin to challenge self/other perceptions ("I'm/He's the kind of person who . . . "). Many cardiac patients, while readily labeling others, seem to have lived unexamined lives. This means that the uniqueness (and maladaptiveness) of one's own personality often is not part of the way in which the patient attributes meaning to events. Once the clinician has a firm grasp on the patient's habitual ways of thinking/responding, it is critical to find a positive (or humorous) or pragmatic way in which to frame this trait. Thus, an obsessional person can be described as "thorough" or "careful," or he or she can be described as "picky." The former will generally be received by the patient as a positive trait (perhaps carried too far at times), whereas the latter will evoke defensiveness. Once rapport is established, teasing/humor can be a powerful tool for getting the patient to cast himself or herself in a new light and for diffusing angry or resentful emotional responses. The locus of the problem then is no longer "out there" but at least partly "in here." Well-written readings (generally full of stories/cases) on topics such as Type A behavior (Friedman & Ulmer, 1984), assertiveness (Alberti & Emmons, 1975), panic attacks (Sheehan, 1983), and nurturant communication (Gordon, 1970) can be helpful in getting the patient to think about his or her life, beliefs, and behavior. Without such rich biographical examples, the patient tends to restrict his or her perspective (e.g., "I'm right, dammit, and that SOB is going to admit it") so as to win the battle while losing the war. The clinician who can bring a rich body of personal, historical, or clinical vignettes to bear will teach the patient more quickly than will the clinician who deals only in abstractions (Friedman, 1979).

It is important to review weekly/monthly stressful events with the patient to ascertain frequency of stressors, the cognitive/behavioral response of the patient, whether a suggested alternative response was tried, and the success/failure of the response as well as to encourage alteration of future events. It is common for patients to not recognize that a "new" event is in fact the same as, or at least similar to, a previous pattern. Thus, helping the patient to perceive the similarities is necessary before he or she will experience familiarity and so the opportunity for a new choice. Some patients are deliberately evasive or seem to be truly unable to recall examples of stressful interactions from their own lives. Some such patients will offer relatively trivial or minor events, avoiding discussion of the major stressors. If a patient is reluctant/unable to offer examples from daily life, the clinician should use clinical stories or examples from his or her own life to destigmatize/normalize and provide examples of situations that the clinician thinks are applicable to the patient's situation. The chapter authors have observed many such patients who, despite no discussion of the significant stressors in their own lives, nonetheless benefited from hearing the counselors' or others' stories in group sessions. Indirect feedback (usually from a spouse) indicates that the patient is attempting to alter his or her habitual way of thinking/coping.

Optimizing Self-Management: Using a Family Practice Model

The goal of the therapist is generally to make himself or herself obsolete as soon as possible, although the idea of a "cure" in any psychotherapeutic relationship is untenable (Hoyt, 1995). The chapter authors find the family practice model (Hoyt, 1995; Morrill, 1978) attractive for the CHD patient. In this light, they find it helpful to think of themselves as "coaches" rather than as "doctors" or "therapists" who serve as periodic resources for reality testing and problem solving. Although the initial stages of therapy may follow a more traditional pathway, the course of treatment is best conceived of as intermittent but longitudinal, with the ultimate treatment goal of assisting the patient in fitting disease self-management into the unique circumstances of his or her own life.

Treatment episodes evolve into "tune-up" or "booster" sessions that reinforce skills already

acquired or focus narrowly, in a problem-solving manner, on current stressors with which the patient is stuck. The therapy should also secondarily serve to support and reinforce adherence to secondary prevention efforts given that long-term adherence rates in cardiac rehabilitation are generally poor (Burke, Dunbar-Jacobs, & Hill, 1997). This is an often neglected aspect of the coaching role. It is critical to recognize, accept, and work within the patient's cognitive, emotional, behavioral, intellectual, fiscal, and life structure limitations so as to help him or her reengineer a healthier lifestyle. One issue in particular pertains to helping the patient to distinguish between a lapse (i.e., momentary slip in behavior) and a relapse (return to baseline level of the problem behavior). It is not uncommon for patients to have lapses, and these should be normalized for the patient. The intent here is to circumvent the patient from allowing lapses to evolve into relapses (e.g., "Well, I already smoked two cigarettes, so I might as well smoke the whole pack").

Psychopharmacology

Behavioral clinicians are often less familiar with the types of medications used in treating cardiac diseases. Thus, Table 15.6 provides a list of the classifications of the most common medications along with a summary of the functions associated with each medication type. Importantly, patients can develop tolerance to these drugs, rendering them less effective over time with frequent use.

The advent of the newer antianxiety/antidepressive agents (mostly serotonin and noradrenalin reuptake inhibitors but also atypicals such as Buspar and Wellbutrin) has revolutionized psychopharmacotherapy in CHD patients. Although these new agents are no more effective at treating anxiety/depression than are the older agents, the older agents (tricyclic or heterocyclic antidepressants) have anticholinergic properties (e.g., dry mouth, blurry vision, orthostatic hypotension) that

Table 15.6   Common Cardiac Medications Listed by Function

Nitrates (e.g., Sublingual nitroglycerin, Nitropatch, Isordil, Sorbitrate, Ismo, Imdur): Drugs that produce vasodilation, used particularly for the relief of angina

ACE inhibitors (e.g., Capoten/Vasotec, Monopril, Destril, Prinivil, Altace, Accupril): Vasodilators that are used as antihypertensives

Beta blockers (e.g., Inderal, Lopressor, Toprol, Corgard, Sectral): Drugs that serve as beta-division adrenergic blockers, thereby reducing heart rate, blood pressure, and strength of heart contraction used for hypertension and relief of angina

Calcium channel blockers (e.g., Cardizem, Dilacor, Procardia, Norvasc, Isoptin): Central and peripheral vasodilators that serve as antihypertensives and anti-ischemics used to treat chest pain, hypertension, and irregular heartbeats

Digoxin (e.g., Lanoxin, Digitoxin): Decreases the strength of heart contractions and allows the heart to keep beating regularly; used for arrhythmias

Diuretics (e.g., Lasix, Dyazide, Esidrix): Medications to increase urinary output and decrease fluids in the body and cardiovascular system; particularly used in heart failure

Anticoagulants (e.g., asprin, Coumadin, Ticlid, Persantine, Plavix, Lovenox, Ecotrin, Heparin): Change the blood's viscosity by acting as blood "thinners"

Antilipidemics (e.g., Lipitor, Zocor, Mevacor, Lopid, Lescol, Niacin): Medications that affect blood lipids by reducing low-density lipoprotein (LDL, bad cholesterol) and total cholesterol and by increasing high-density lipoprotein (HDL, good cholesterol)

Antiarrhythmics (e.g., Quinidine, Betapace, Amniodarone, Norpace, Rythmol): Help to prevent both atrial and ventricular arrhythmias

make adherence problematic. In CHD patients, these agents prolong the "QRS" interval that is thought to place some patients at risk for possibly fatal arrhythmias. However, in the only (nonrandomized) comparison of patients on tricyclic antidepressants (TCAs), death rates were actually lower (Pratt et al., 1996).

The use of SSRIs in the treatment of stress among CHD patients requires thorough initial instructions, careful monitoring of side effects, comparatively low dosing, and consideration of possible drug-drug complications. Doses typically used in this population are at or below the generally recognized therapeutic range in psychiatric patients. Thus, 10 to 20 milligrams of Celexa or 25 to 50 milligrams of Zoloft is adequate for perhaps 90% of this population. Because the delay in onset is slow and variable, the adage "start low, go slow" is advisable. Many patients will stop the medication if no change is observed during the first few days unless the importance of at least a 1-month trial is emphasized repeatedly. With some SSRIs (e.g., Paxil, Remeron), there often is an immediate soporific effect, and these should initially be tried at night. Otherwise, the medications are taken in the morning to avoid interfering with sleep and with food to minimize gastrointestinal distress (i.e., abdominal cramping or diarrhea). Most of the improvements will "sneak up" on patients over 10 days to 6 weeks. Indeed, it is common for patients to say "I don't feel any different" but for family members and/or coworkers to notice a change in the patients. Prepping patients about the subtle effects of these medications can go a long way toward circumventing unrealistic expectations and potential nonadherence. Tracking a symptom (e.g., chest pain, fatigue, sleep onset delay, nocturnal awakening) in an empirical fashion can help to document improvements. Patients may be inclined to attribute improvements to other factors. It is critical that clinicians indicate their belief that the medication is probably the cause.

Common side effects within 24 to 48 hours of starting therapy include diarrhea/ abdominal cramping (about 10% of patients). Half of those experiencing diarrhea/abdominal cramping are only mildly affected, and it should resolve within 10 days. The remainder must be tried on other agents. Headache occurs in about 3% of patients and generally resolves within 10 days. In addition, intense anxiety occurs in about 1% of patients. Over several weeks, about one quarter of patients develop loss of libido or erectile problems. Alternative agents, or referral to a psychiatrist for additional agents, should be considered. Some weight gain (7 to 10 pounds) may occur.

The chapter authors have observed several adverse effects of SSRIs that are unique to this population. Some patients, usually with a history of prior atrial fibrillation, may develop *worsened* atrial fibrillation on SSRIs. The authors believe that consultation with a psychiatrist is necessary to select a safe and effective agent (e.g., Buspar, Wellbutrin). Likewise, because of the effect of some SSRIs on cytochrome P450 metabolic pathways in the liver, some drugs will be removed from the bloodstream more slowly, thereby raising bioavailability. Management can include reduced dosing of the affected agent or use of another SSRI that is less likely to have this effect. Celexa and Zoloft are minimally likely to interfere with other medications and so are generally first-choice agents. Among the medications potentially affected in cardiac patients are digoxin and beta blockers. *Digoxin toxicity* can result in confusion/cognitive impairment, loss of appetite, and a resting tremor. *Potentiation of beta blockers* by use of an SSRI can result in lowered heart rate and blood pressure. Clinically, patients will complain of worsened fatigue or tiredness, dizziness, or light-headedness. Because of the effects on the liver, *hepatic strain* will sometimes result from use of an SSRI. This is most common in patients with prior liver injury (e.g., history of alcohol abuse or hepatitis) or in patients receiving other hepatically difficult medications (e.g., lipid-lowering agents). In severe enough cases, weakness, nausea, and loss of appetite will indicate low-level hepatic failure and should result in immediate cessation of the drug until liver function tests can be obtained. Some SSRIs may be less likely to have this effect.

Many patients will resist referral to a psychiatrist but will accept these agents from a cardiologist or a primary care physician. If one is attempting a first trial, working with the cardiologist/primary care physician may be adequate. But if special circumstances occur (e.g., nonresponse, intolerance of two agents, multiple or problematic side effects such as sexual dysfunction, need for larger doses, recent history of substance abuse, propensity for somatization), referral to a psychiatrist should become a goal of psychological treatment.

Another option may be to use the herbal St. John's wort, which is widely used in Europe for the treatment of depression. Several dozen randomized clinical trials on St. John's wort have demonstrated an effectiveness equivalent to that of TCAs (and therefore presumably SSRIs) but with fewer side effects than TCAs (Linde & Mulrow, 1999), although other reports have called these data into question. Preparations by reputable manufacturers (e.g., Centrum, Quanterra) should be used because smaller sources have not carefully standardized source or dose given that these supplements are not regulated by the U.S. Food and Drug Administration. Because St. John's wort is not viewed as "artificial" or a "psychiatric medication," patients will sometimes try it (or even insist on it) rather than the better understood

CASE STUDY

The case of "Harriet R." is a useful one that illustrates many of the psychological aspects of CHD. Harriet was a 46-year-old, white, married mother of three children who was referred for stress management by her cardiologist after she had experienced an MI 6 months earlier. No risk factors were detected other than her constant stress.

Harriet lived with constant tension over avoiding confronting her sometimes outspoken and opinionated husband. One of the early examples of tension was that her husband frequently "forgot" to do things he was supposed to do, and Harriet was resentful that she had to remind her husband to do things and was often criticized by him for her constant reminding (which he described as "nagging"). For example, she reported that she always had to remind him to take his hymnal to choir practice. Not only did she feel angry over always having to remind him, but she frequently experienced chest pain when thinking about these interactions. Harriet's husband seemed quite concerned but was not able to empathize with her. Rather, he too would get angry when she reminded him to do things.

Following suggestions from the therapist, Harriet agreed to "deliberately not remind" her husband for a week. He "spontaneously" began remembering things himself, and it became apparent to Harriet that her worry/resentment was totally wasted energy. Not only did it seem that she did not need to remind her husband so often, but the number of negative interactions that the couple experienced went down and the frequency with which Harriet experienced angina was greatly reduced.

At this point, discussions with Harriet's therapist shifted her concerns to the belief that her daughter might be gay and that her husband would ban the daughter from the family if he found out. Like her experiences with "reminding her husband," whenever she began to worry about her daughter's sexual orientation, Harriet experienced frequent angina. After reviewing why Harriet thought her daughter was gay, the therapist agreed that it was likely and encouraged her to discuss this with her daughter. Pointing out that Harriet had previously sold her husband short, the therapist coached the patient on how to approach the topic with her husband. He responded with surprise and disappointment, but after pondering the possibility for a few days, he stated that he would still love her and want her in the family.

These experiences helped Harriet learn that much of her concern and worry were generated by her own expectations and that her perceived negative outcomes were not always as predictable as she had once believed. Over the course of treatment, Harriet became better at recognizing the role of her beliefs and expectations in her stress levels, and she was able to greatly reduce the frequency with which she became angry at others. This resulted in remarkable reductions in the frequency and severity of her angina. Harriet reported to her therapist that when she would begin to feel any anger, she could quickly assess the potential "validity" of what was making her angry, and most of the time the anger went away immediately when she realized that the situation was not as negative as she had initially thought.

and tested SSRIs. Importantly, St. John's wort is known to decrease digoxin levels by about 25% to 33%.

The chapter authors have not yet found it necessary to refer a patient for electroconvulsive therapy (ECT). But if a patient presents an otherwise intractable depression, special considerations are necessary. Heart failure, aneurysm, and arrythmias are considered contraindications to ECT.

SUMMARY AND CONCLUSIONS

There is mounting evidence that psychological and behavioral factors play an independent and critical role in the development, maintenance, and exacerbation of CHD. The clinical behavioral sciences, including health psychologists of all stripes, have played a significant role in moving this scientific literature forward. More recent trends have allowed for practitioners to play more central roles in clinical settings such as Phase II cardiac rehabilitation and consultation services targeting cardiology patients. These trends are likely to continue, thereby allowing greater and more varied practice opportunities with this patient population. This chapter has attempted to provide an experienced and practical set of recommendations for working clinically with the CHD patient. There is a continued need for more practice-based writing in this arena that combines evidence-based literature with clinical experience. In addition, novel methods of integration into service delivery behavioral interventions must be explored for all manner of secondary prevention targets (Trask et al., 2002).

REFERENCES

Alberti, R. E., & Emmons, M. L. (1975). *Stand up, speak out, talk back!* New York: Pocket Books.

Allen, R., & Scheidt, S. (1996). Empirical basis of cardiac psychology. In R. Allen & S. Scheidt (Eds.), *Heart and mind: The practice of cardiac psychology* (pp. 63–123). Washington, DC: American Psychological Association.

Allison, T. G., Williams, D. E., Miller, T. D., Patten, C. A., Bailey, K. R., Squires, R. W., & Gau, G. T. (1995). Medical and economic costs of psychologic distress in patients with coronary artery disease. *Mayo Clinic Proceedings, 70,* 734–742.

American Psychiatric Association. (1994). *Diagnostic and statistical manual of mental disorders* (4th ed.). Washington, DC: Author.

Barrios, B. (1988). On the changing nature of behavioral assessment. In M. Hersen & A. S. Bellack (Eds.), *Behavioral assessment: A practical handbook* (pp. 3–41). New York: Pergamon.

Barsky, A. J. (2001). Palpitations, arrhythmias, and awareness of cardiac activity. *Annals of Internal Medicine, 134,* 832–837.

Barsky, A. J., Cleary, P. D., Barnett, M. C., Christiansen, C. L., & Ruskin, J. N. (1994). The accuracy of symptom reporting by patients complaining of palpitations. *American Journal of Medicine, 97,* 214–221.

Black, J. L., Allison, T. G., Williams, D. E., Rummans, T. A., & Gau, G. T. (1998). Effect of intervention for psychological distress on rehospitalization rates in cardiac rehabilitation patients. *Psychosomatics, 39,* 134–143.

Blumenthal, J. A., Jiang, W., Babyak, M. A., Krantz, D. S., Frid, D. J., Coleman, R. E., Waugh, R., Hanson, M., Appelbaum, M., O'Connor, C., & Morris, J. J. (1997). Stress management and exercise training in cardiac patients with myocardial ischemia. *Archives of Internal Medicine, 157,* 2213–2223.

Booth-Kewley, S., & Friedman, H. S. (1987). Psychological predictors of heart disease: A quantitative review. *Psychological Bulletin, 101,* 343–362.

Burke, L. E., Dunbar-Jacobs, J. M., & Hill, M. N. (1997). Compliance with cardiovascular disease prevention strategies: A review of the research. *Annals of Behavioral Medicine, 19,* 239–263.

Carney, R. M., Freedland, K. E., Eisen, S. A., Rich, M. W., & Jaffe, A. S. (1995). Major depression and medication adherence in elderly patients with coronary artery disease. *Health Psychology, 14,* 88–90.

Cassem, N. H., & Hackett, T. P. (1973). Psychological rehabilitation of myocardial infarction patients in the acute phase. *Heart & Lung, 2,* 382–388.

Cox, D., & Gonder-Frederik, L. (1992). Major developments in behavioral diabetes research. *Journal of Consulting and Clinical Psychology, 60,* 628–638.

Dahlof, P., Ejnell, H., Hallstrom, T., & Hdner, J. (2000). Surgical treatment of the sleep apnea syndrome reduces associated major depression. *International Journal of Behavioral Medicine, 7,* 73–88.

Davidson, K. W. (2000). Dose-response relations between hostility reductions and cardiac-related hospitalizations. *Psychosomatic Medicine, 62,* 149 (Abstract 1430).

Dusseldorp, E., van Elderen, T., Maes, S., Meulman, J., & Kraaij, V. (1999). A meta-analysis of psychoeducational programs for coronary heart disease patients. *Health Psychology, 18,* 506–519.

Edwards, N. B., Murphy, J. K., Downs, A. D., Ackerman, B. J., & Rosenthal, T. L. (1989). Doxepin as an adjunct to smoking cessation: A double-blind pilot study. *American Journal of Psychiatry, 146,* 373–376.

Farmer, J. A., & Gotto, A. M. (1997). Dyslipidemia and other risk factors for coronary artery disease. In E. Braunwald (Ed.), *Heart disease: A textbook of cardiovascular medicine.* Philadelphia: W. B. Saunders.

Frasure-Smith, N., & Lesperance, F. (1998). Depression and anxiety increase physician costs during the first post-MI year. *Psychosomatic Medicine, 60,* 99.

Frasure-Smith, N., Lesperance, F., & Talajic, M. (1993). Depression following myocardial infarction. *Journal of the American Medical Association, 270,* 1819–1825.

Friedman, M. (1979). Qualities of therapist required for successful modification of coronary-prone (Type A) behavior. *Psychiatric Clinics of North America, 2,* 243–248.

Friedman, M., Breall, W. S., Goodwin, M. L., Sparagon, B. J., Ghandour, G., & Fleischman, N. (1996). Effect of Type A behavioral counseling on frequency of episodes of silent myocardial ischemia in coronary patients. *American Heart Journal, 132,* 333–337.

Friedman, M., Powell, L. H., Thoreson, C. E., Ulmer, D., Price, V., Gill, J. J., Thompson, L., Rabin, D. D., Brown, B., Breall, W. S., Levy, R., & Bourg, E. (1987). Effect of discontinuance of Type A behavioral counseling on Type A behavior and cardiac recurrence rate of post myocardial infarction patients. *American Heart Journal, 114,* 483–490.

Friedman, M., & Rosenman, R. H. (1974). *Type A behavior and your heart.* New York: Alfred A. Knopf.

Friedman, M., Thoreson, C. E., Gill, J. J., Ulmer, D., Powell, L. H., Price, V. A., Brown, B., Thompson, L., Rabin, D. D., Breall, W.S., Bourg, E., Levy, R., & Dixon, T. (1986). Alteration of Type A behavior and its effect on cardiac recurrences in post myocardial infarction patients: Summary results of the Recurrent Coronary Prevention Project. *American Heart Journal, 112,* 653–665.

Friedman, M., & Ulmer, D. (1984). *Treating Type A behavior and your heart.* New York: Alfred A. Knopf.

Gallacher, J. E. J., Hopkinson, C. A., Bennett, P., Burr, M. L., & Elwood, P. C. (1997). Effect of stress management on angina. *Psychology & Health, 12,* 523–532.

Gilkson, M., & Friedman, P. A. (2001). The implantable cardioverter defibrillator. *Lancet, 357,* 1107–1117.

Glassman, A. H., & Shapiro, P. A. (1998). Depression and the course of coronary artery disease. *American Journal of Psychiatry, 55,* 683–690.

Goldberg, A. D., Becker, L. C., Bonsall, R., Cohen, J. D., Ketterer, M. W., Kaufman, P. G., Krantz, D. S., Light, K. C., McMahon, R. P., Noreuil, T., Pepine, C. J., Raczysnki, J., Stone, P. H., Strother, D., Taylor, H., & Sheps, D. S., for the PIMI Investigators. (1996). Ischemic, hemodynamic, and neurohormonal responses to mental and exercise stress: Experience from the Psychophysiological Investigations of Myocardial Ischemia study (PIMI). *Circulation, 94,* 2402–2409.

Goldfried, M. R., & Sprafkin, J. N. (1976). Behavioral personality assessment. In J. T. Spence, R. C. Carson, & J. W. Thibaut (Eds.), *Behavioral approaches to therapy* (pp. 295–321). Morristown, NJ: General Learning.

Gordon, T. (1970). *P.E.T.: Parent Effectiveness Training.* New York: Peter H. Wyden.

Hall, S. M., Munoz, R. F., & Reus, V. I. (1994). Cognitive-behavioral intervention increases abstinence rates for depressive history smokers. *Journal of Consulting and Clinical Psychology, 62,* 141–146.

Hall, S. M., Reus, V. I., Munoz, R. F., Sees, K. L., Humfleet, G., Hartz, D. T., Frederik, S., & Triffleman, E. (1998). Nortriptyline and cognitive-behavioral therapy in the treatment of cigarette smoking. *Archives of General Psychiatry, 55,* 683–690.

Herrman, C. (1997). International experiences with the Hospital Anxiety and Depression Scale: A review of validation data and clinical results. *Journal of Psychosomatic Research, 42,* 17–41.

Hoyt, M. F. (1995). *Brief therapy and managed care: Readings for contemporary practice.* San Francisco: Jossey-Bass.

Kamarck, T. W., & Jennings, J. R. (1991). Biobehavioral factors in sudden cardiac death. *Psychological Bulletin, 109,* 42–75.

Ketterer, M. W. (1993). Secondary prevention of ischemic heart disease: The case for aggressive behavioral monitoring and intervention. *Psychosomatics, 34,* 478–484.

Ketterer, M. W. (1999). Cognitive/Behavioral therapy of anxiety in the medically ill: Cardiac settings. *Seminars in Clinical Neuropsychiatry, 4*(2), 148–153.

Ketterer, M. W., Brymer, J., Rhoads, K., Kraft, P., & Kenyon, L. W. (1994). Snoring and the severity of coronary artery disease in males. *Psychosomatic Medicine, 56,* 232–236.

Ketterer, M. W., Denollet, J., Goldberg, A. D., McCullough, P. A., John, S., Farha, A. J., Clark, V., Keteyian, S., Chapp, J., Thayer, B., & Deveshwar, S. (2002). The big mush: Psychometric measures are confounded and nonindependent in their association with age at initial diagnosis of ICHD. *Journal of Cardiovascular Risk, 9,* 41–48.

Ketterer, M. W., Fitzgerald, F., Keteyian, S., Thayer, B., Jordan, M., McGowan, C., Mahr, G., Manganas, A., & Goldberg, A. D. (2000). Chest pain and the treatment of psychosocial/emotional distress in CAD patients. *Journal of Behavioral Medicine, 23,* 437–450.

Ketterer, M. W., Freedland, K. E., Krantz, D. S., Kaufmann, P. G., Forman, S., Greene, A., Raczynski, J., Knatterud, G., Light, K., Carney, R. M., Stone, P., Becker, L., & Sheps, D., for the PIMI Investigators. (2000). Psychological correlates of mental stress induced ischemia in the laboratory: The Psychophysiological Investigation of Myocardial Ischemia (PIMI) study. *Journal of Health Psychology, 5,* 75–85.

Ketterer, M. W., Huffman, J., Lumley, M. A., Wassef, S., Gray, L., Kenyon, L., Kraft, P., Brymer, J., Rhoads, K., Lovallo, W. R., & Goldberg, A. D. (1998). Five year follow-up for adverse outcomes in males with at least minimally positive angiograms: Importance of "denial" in assessing psychosocial risk factors. *Journal of Psychosomatic Research, 44,* 241–250.

Ketterer, M. W., Kenyon, L., Foley, B. A., Brymer, J., Rhoads, K., Kraft, P., & Lovallo, W. R. (1996). Denial of depression as an independent correlate of coronary artery disease. *Journal of Health Psychology, 1,* 93–105.

Ketterer, M. W., Pickering, E., Stoever, W. W., & Wansley, R. A. (1987). Smoking prevention, cessation, and maintenance: A review for the primary care physician. *Journal of the American Osteopathic Association, 87,* 248–257.

Krantz, D. S., Hedges, S. M., Gabbay, F. H., Klein, J., Falconer, J. J., Merz, C. N., Gottdiener, J. S., Lutz, H., & Rozanski, A. (1994). Triggers of angina and st-segment depression in ambulatory patients with coronary artery disease: Evidence for an uncoupling of angina and ischemia. *American Heart Journal, 128,* 703–712.

Kubzansky, L. D., Kawachi, I., Weiss, S. T., & Sparrow, D. (1998). Anxiety and coronary heart disease: A synthesis of epidemiological, psychological, and experimental evidence. *Annals of Behavioral Medicine, 20,* 47–58.

Lazarus, R. S., & Folkman, S. (1984). *Stress, appraisal, and coping.* New York: Springer.

Lessmeier, T. J., Gamperling, D., Johnson-Liddon, V., Fromm, B. S., Steinman, R. T., Meissner, M. D., & Lehmann, M. H. (1997). Unrecognized paroxysmal supraventricular tachycardia: Potential for misdiagnosis of panic disorder. *Archives of Internal Medicine, 157,* 537–543.

Lewin, B. (1997). The psychological and behavioral management of angina. *Journal of Psychosomatic Research, 43,* 453–462.

Linde, K., & Mulrow, C. D. (1999). St. John's wort is more effective than placebo for treating depressive disorders. *ACP Journal Club, 130,* 60–80.

Linden, W., & Chambers, L. (1994). Clinical effectiveness of nondrug treatment of hypertension: A meta-analysis. *Annals of Behavioral Medicine, 16,* 35–45.

Markovitz, J. H. (1998). Hostility is associated with increased platelet activation in coronary heart disease. *Psychosomatic Medicine, 60,* 586–591.

Morrill, R. G. (1978). The future of mental health in primary health care programs. *American Journal of Psychiatry, 135,* 1351–1355.

Murphy, J. K., Edwards, N. B., Downs, A. D., Ackerman, B. J., & Rosenthal, T. L. (1990). Effects of doxepin on withdrawal symptoms in smoking cessation. *American Journal of Psychiatry, 147,* 1353–1357.

Polk, D. E., Kamarck, T. W., & Shiffman, S. (2002). Hostility explains some of the discrepancy between daytime ambulatory and clinic blood pressure. *Health Psychology, 21,* 202–206.

Pratt, L. A., Ford, D. E., Crum, R. M., Armenian, H. K., Gallo, J. J., & Eaton, W. W. (1996). Depression, psychotropic medication, and risk of myocardial infarction: Prospective data from the Baltimore ECA follow-up. *Circulation, 94,* 3123–3129.

Richter, J. E. (1992). Overview of diagnostic testing for chest pain of unknown origin. *Medical Clinics of North America, 92*(Suppl. 5A), S41–S45.

Ridker, P. M., Hennekens, C. H., Buring, J. E., & Rifai, N. (2000). C-reactive protein and other markers of inflammation in the prediction of cardiovascular disease in women. *New England Journal of Medicine, 342,* 836–843.

Ross, R. (1999). Atherosclerosis: An inflammatory disease. *New England Journal of Medicine, 340,* 115–126.

Rozanski, A., Blumenthal, J. A., & Kaplan, J. (1999). Impact of psychological factors on the pathogenesis of cardiovascular disease and implications for therapy. *Circulation, 99,* 2192–2217.

Schwartz, S. M., Gramling, S. E., & Mancini, T. (1994). The influence of life stress, personality, and learning history on illness behavior. *Journal of Behavior Therapy and Experimental Psychiatry, 25,* 135–142.

Schwartz, S. M., Lipman, H., Glasburg, D., Pagano, C., Jones, D., Deaner, S. L., & Lehmann, M. H. (2002). Gender differences in symptom reporting in patients with palpitations. *Psychosomatic Medicine, 64,* 135.

Schwartz, S. M., Trask, P. C., & Ketterer, M. W. (1999). Understanding chest pain: What every psychologist should know. *Journal of Clinical Psychology in Medical Settings, 6,* 333–351.

Sears, S. F., Todaro, J. F., Lewis, T. S., Sotile, W., & Conti, J. B. (1999). Examining the psychosocial impact of implantable cardioverter defibrillators: A literature review. *Clinical Cardiology, 22,* 481–489.

Sheehan, D. V. (1983). *The anxiety disease.* New York: Scribner.

Stetson, B. A., Rahn, J. M., Dubbert, P. M., Wilner, B. I., & Mecury, M. G. (1997). Prospective evaluation of the effects of stress on exercise adherence in community-residing women. *Health Psychology, 16,* 515–520.

Trask, P. C., Schwartz, S. M., Deaner, S. L., Paterson, A. G., Johnson, T., Rubenfire, M., & Pomerleau, O. P. (2002). Behavioral medicine: The challenge of integrating psychological and behavioral approaches into primary care. *Effective Clinical Practice, 5*(2), 75–83.

CHAPTER 16

Behavioral Management of Type 2 Diabetes

AHNA L. HOFF, JANELLE L. WAGNER,
LARRY L. MULLINS, AND JOHN M. CHANEY

Type 2 diabetes (DM2) is a chronic illness characterized by a dysregulation of glucose metabolism secondary to an imbalance between insulin sensitivity and insulin secretion. An estimated 11 million people in the United States were diagnosed with diabetes in the year 2000 (Boyle et al., 2001), and approximately 90% of those individuals were diagnosed with DM2. The number of individuals diagnosed with DM2 has been rising at an alarming rate over the past several decades (Harris, 1998). It has been estimated that this figure will increase by 165% to 29 million by the year 2050, reflecting a 7.2% prevalence rate. Such an increase is hypothesized to be the result of changes in demographic composition of the population, population growth, and increasing prevalence rates (Boyle et al., 2001).

Personal and public health consequences associated with DM2 are profound. For example, individuals with diabetes experience a greater number of health complications (Harris, 1998) and are at higher risk for depression than are their medically well counterparts

(Anderson, Freeland, Clouse, & Lustman, 2001). On a more global scale, the economic impact of diabetes is staggering; in 1997, the direct and indirect costs associated with diabetes in the United States were an estimated $98 billion (Ray, Thamer, Gardner, & Chan, 1998). Thus, the increasing prevalence of diabetes in the United States represents a critical public health problem with respect to health care use and resources.

Fortunately, DM2 is medically manageable, and many of the serious medical complications that are associated with the illness are preventable through adequate control of blood glucose levels. Therefore, the primary treatment goal for individuals with DM2 is to maintain blood glucose levels within a normal range. This requires individuals with diabetes to consistently maintain a complicated, lifelong treatment regimen with few immediate tangible rewards for their efforts. For many, maintaining this complex treatment regimen is difficult, and assistance with disease management is often warranted. As such, researchers and the medical community have recognized the critical role of behavioral sciences in optimizing regimen adherence and health outcomes among patients with DM2 (Glasgow et al., 1999; Wysocki & Buckloh, 2002).

The purpose of this chapter is to review the psychosocial aspects and behavioral management of DM2. First, information regarding the nature of the illness, including etiology and complications, is reviewed. Then, psychological factors and symptomatology commonly associated with DM2 are presented. Next, the assessment and treatment of the medical and psychological aspects of DM2 are discussed, including a review of psychosocial interventions focused on improving global adjustment to diabetes. It should be noted that there are a number of studies reviewed here that used combined samples of individuals with type 1 and type 2 diabetes. Where possible, information specific to DM2 is presented and indicated as such.

BACKGROUND AND ETIOLOGY

There are two primary types of diabetes: type 1 and type 2. Type 1 diabetes (often referred to in the past as juvenile diabetes or insulin-dependent diabetes mellitus) occurs when the islet cells of the pancreas are destroyed and cannot produce insulin. Consequently, exogenous insulin is required for survival. In contrast, DM2 is characterized by chronic hyperglycemia due to impaired insulin secretion and increased insulin resistance in the body's cells. Insulin resistance refers to a defect in glucose transport and metabolism. As a result, glucose does not enter the body's cells where it can be used as fuel, and subsequently, a higher level of glucose remains in the bloodstream. Early in the course of DM2, the pancreas attempts to counteract the high levels of blood glucose by producing increased amounts of insulin. However, because of the sustained need for high amounts of insulin over long periods of time, the pancreas gradually loses its ability to produce sufficient amounts of insulin and so can no longer maintain euglycemia, that is, near-normal glucose levels (DeFronzo, Bonadonna, & Ferrannini, 1992).

Short-Term Complications

Hypoglycemia and hyperglycemia are two short-term complications that result from DM2. Hypoglycemia occurs when blood glucose declines to less than 60 milligrams per deciliter (mg/dl). Symptoms include shakiness, perspiration, rapid heartbeat, hunger, headache, mood changes, confusion, and attentional difficulties. If hypoglycemia is left untreated, seizures or loss of consciousness may eventually occur. Conversely, hyperglycemia is defined as a blood glucose level greater than 140 mg/dl. Symptoms include increased thirst, frequent urination, and glucose in the urine. The majority of long-term complications associated with DM2 are the result of recurrent hyperglycemia (American Diabetes Association [ADA], 1998).

Long-Term Complications

Long-term complications can be classified into two types: macrovascular and microvascular. Macrovascular diseases include heart disease, stroke, and other circulatory disorders. The leading cause of diabetes-related deaths is heart disease. Adults with diabetes are two to four times more likely to die from heart disease than are adults without diabetes (National Institute of Diabetes and Digestive and Kidney Diseases [NIDDK], 2000). Individuals with DM2 are also at two to four times greater risk for stroke than are their medically well counterparts. Furthermore, approximately 73% of adults with diabetes have circulatory disorders (e.g., high blood pressure), many of which require prescription medications for hypertension (NIDDK, 2000).

Microvascular complications constitute some of the most debilitating complications associated with DM2. Microvascular complications include retinopathy, nephropathy, and neuropathy. Diabetic retinopathy is caused by changes in the tiny vessels that supply the retina with blood. It is the leading cause of visual impairment among adults ages 20 to 74 years, resulting in an estimated 12,000 to 24,000 new cases of blindness in the United States each year (NIDDK, 2000). Nephropathy, another microvascular complication associated with diabetes, is the result of damage to the blood vessels of the kidneys. In severe cases, it can result in kidney failure, a condition referred to as end stage renal disease (ESRD). ESRD can be a life-threatening complication, and individuals who experience kidney failure must undergo dialysis or a kidney transplant. The relationship between diabetes and ESRD is clear; diabetes accounts for 43% of new cases of ESRD (NIDDK, 2000).

Neuropathy (neuronal disease) is a common microvascular complication affecting approximately 60% to 70% of individuals with mild to severe forms of nervous system damage (NIDDK, 2000). Characteristic symptoms include pain, numbing, burning, loss of feeling, and (in more severe cases) paralysis in the extremities. Neuropathy may also cause digestive problems, impotence, and incontinence. Severe forms of nerve damage are a major cause of lower extremity amputations.

Etiological Risk Factors

Demographic and Genetic Factors. A number of demographic and genetic factors are associated with DM2, including age, race, prior history of gestational diabetes, family history of diabetes, and obesity. In terms of age, those over age 45 years are at the highest risk for developing DM2, and approximately 20% of individuals over age 65 years have diabetes (NIDDK, 2000). Similarly, differential rates of DM2 are found among various ethnic groups. For example, African Americans, Native Americans, and Hispanic/Latino Americans have demonstrably higher prevalence rates for

DM2 than do other ethnic groups (Harris, 1998). Furthermore, women who experience gestational diabetes during one or more of their pregnancies are at greater risk for developing DM2 later in life than are women who do not (NIDDK, 2000). Finally, those with a family history of diabetes are also at heightened risk. Indeed, first-degree relatives of individuals with early-onset DM2 are 40% more likely to develop diabetes than are individuals with no family history of the disease (Owen, Ayers, Corbett, & Hattersley, 2002). Thus, there are a number of demographic factors that are associated with a heightened risk for DM2.

Obesity. The previously mentioned risk factors can be mitigated by the most critical and modifiable risk factor for DM2, that is, obesity. It is estimated that up to 75% of the risk for DM2 is directly attributable to obesity (Manson & Spelsberg, 1994). For example, Hillier and Pedula (2001) demonstrated an inverse linear relationship between the Body Mass Index (weight in kilograms divided by height in squared meters) and age at diagnosis of DM2. In other words, those who are more overweight are more likely to be diagnosed with DM2 at a younger age. Although the mechanisms responsible for the relationship between weight and DM2 are not entirely clear, recent evidence suggests that body weight is associated with insulin resistance and subsequently glycemic control (Maggio & Pi-Sunyer, 1997). Consequently, the majority of DM2 prevention and intervention programs target weight loss (for a review, see Wing et al., 2001). Such weight loss efforts have been shown to be effective in preventing the onset of DM2 (Diabetes Prevention Program Research Group [DPPRG], 2002). A primary challenge for behavioral researchers and those at risk for diabetes is to determine effective methods to maintain long-term weight loss given that it is well known that maintenance of weight loss is difficult to achieve (Wing et al., 2001). In summary, the most influential risk factor for DM2 is also potentially the most modifiable.

PSYCHOLOGICAL FACTORS AND TYPE 2 DIABETES

Individuals with DM2 constitute a population at risk for experiencing both illness-related and general distress. Many individuals experience subclinical adjustment problems directly related to living with diabetes, including distress associated with the onset of diabetes, diabetes complications, and the treatment regimen. Still others experience clinically significant levels of psychological distress, including depression and anxiety. This section reviews both diabetes-specific distress, as outlined by Rubin and Peyrot (2001), and more general distress, such as depression and anxiety.

Distress Related to Diabetes Onset

The diagnosis of diabetes represents a period of crisis for many. Unfortunately, few empirical studies have examined levels of distress immediately following diagnosis of DM2 among adults. However, increased levels of distress immediately following diagnosis is common among children diagnosed with type 1 diabetes. For most, this distress then dissipates over the first year following diagnosis (Kovacs, Brent, Steinberg, Paulauskas, & Reid, 1986). Thus, Rubin and Peyrot (1994) recommended regular monitoring of patients' distress levels following diagnosis. Individuals experiencing clinically significant distress should be referred for intervention as a means of minimizing the impact on diabetes management.

Distress Related to Medical Complications

The onset of medical complications can trigger a crisis for many individuals, and health care providers should not underestimate the potential emotional impact of new complications. However, research examining the impact of specific diabetes complications is quite limited and has primarily examined psychological correlates of sexual dysfunction and visual impairment. Sexual dysfunction is a prevalent problem among men with diabetes; approximately 50% of men with diabetes experience impotence. Although the prevalence of sexual dysfunction is not known for women, one study reported that women with DM2 reported significantly lower levels of sexual desire or orgasmic capacity, lubrication, and sexual satisfaction in their relationships than did nondiabetic control participants (Schreiner-Engel, Schiavi, Vietorisz, & Smith, 1987). To date, little research has specifically examined the treatment of impotence among those with diabetes (McCulloch, Hosking, & Tobert, 1986). As such, it has been recommended that treatment for impotence proceed in accordance with the standards established for medically well individuals (Rubin & Peyrot, 2001).

Visual impairment due to diabetic retinopathy is another complication that appears to have profound psychological consequences for the patient. Individuals diagnosed with progressive diabetic retinopathy (PDR) reported a greater number of negative life experiences and psychiatric distress during the 2 years following diagnosis with PDR (Wulsin & Jacobson, 1989; Wulsin, Jacobson, & Rand, 1987). Distress related to PDR appears to be independent of the severity of vision loss and remains elevated even after vision is restored (Wulsin & Jacobson, 1989; Wulsin et al., 1987). Moreover, individuals who experienced fluctuating levels of visual impairment experienced more distress than did those with more stable and severe visual impairment (Bernbaum, Alpert, & Duckro, 1988). Common feelings related to vision loss include failure, uncertainty, and fear. Nevertheless, few studies have examined interventions to address the emotional consequences of PDR onset (Bernbaum et al., 1988). Therefore, it is recommended that clinicians regularly assess psychological distress, especially among patients who have been diagnosed with PDR.

Little is currently known about the psychological sequelae of other diabetes-specific complications. However, it has been demonstrated that the more complications a person experiences, the more likely he or she is to manifest psychological distress (Trief, Grant, Elbert, & Weinstock, 1998). Thus, health care professionals should remain cognizant of the psychological consequences of new or accruing diabetes complications for their patients.

Psychosocial Stress

Stress, often conceptualized as the interaction between an event and an individual's response to that event, is one of the most widely studied psychosocial factors associated with DM2 (Goetsch & Wiebe, 1995). It has been hypothesized that stress affects metabolic control both directly and indirectly (Peyrot & McMurry, 1985). First, stress is believed to directly affect metabolic control through physiological mechanisms. Theoretically, stress triggers the natural physiological responses ("fight or flight" response), resulting in the release of counterregulatory hormones. The release of these hormones triggers an increase in sympathetic activity to the pancreas, thereby inhibiting insulin and stimulating the release of glucagons (Goetsch & Wiebe, 1995). Glucagon then stimulates the liver to convert glycogen to glucose and release hepatic glucose stores into the bloodstream. As a result, there can be increases in blood glucose levels independent of consistent diabetic regimen adherence. A number of animal models have supported the link between acute stressors and metabolic control (Kuhn, Cochrane, Feinglos, & Surwit, 1987; Surwit, Feinglos, Livingston, Kuhn, & McCubbin, 1984; Surwit et al., 1986). However, generalization of these results to humans has been difficult. Although some studies have reported significant associations between life stress and hemoglobin A_{1c} (HbA_{1c}) independent of regimen adherence among adults with diabetes (Demmers, Neale,

Wensloff, Gronsman, & Jaber, 1989), other studies have not (Griffith, Field, & Lustman, 1990). The equivocal findings are likely due in part to the wide variety of methodologies employed, including types of stressors targeted, durations of the stressors, measures of subjective stress, interval between the stressors and the blood glucose tests, and baseline blood glucose levels. Obviously, the relationship between stress and blood glucose is a complex one that involves multiple variables, including cognitive and physiological factors.

Indirectly, stress is thought to adversely influence metabolic control through changes in self-management behaviors. The ability to maintain the demands of a complex treatment regimen may be compromised by the demands of daily life (e.g., eating fast food instead of taking the time to prepare a proper meal, skipping regular exercise to catch up on work) (Marlatt & Gordon, 1985). Future research studies are needed to identify psychological and physiological markers of individuals who are more susceptible to stress and to shed light on appropriate interventions. Interventions that directly target stress, such as relaxation training and stress management, are discussed later in the chapter.

Depression

Empirical research indicates that depression is quite prevalent among individuals with diabetes. Meta-analytic data indicate that approximately 31% of individuals with diabetes report clinically elevated depressive symptoms. Furthermore, the accrued lifetime prevalence of major depression among individuals with diabetes is estimated to be 28.5% (Anderson et al., 2001). Similarly, Egede, Zheng, and Simpson (2002) found that individuals with diabetes (type 1 or type 2), when compared with a healthy control group, are twice as likely to be diagnosed with depression. Depressive episodes also tend to occur more frequently and last longer among individuals with DM2 than among those without DM2 (Lustman, Clouse, Alrakawi, Rubin, & Gelenberg, 1997). Finally, consistent with the general population, the prevalence of depression is greater among women with diabetes than among men with diabetes (Anderson et al., 2001).

The demonstrated association between depression and diabetes provides the most striking example of the interwoven relationship between psychological functioning and diabetes outcome. Depression is strongly associated with metabolic control among individuals with DM2 (Lustman et al., 2000). In their meta-analysis, Lustman and colleagues (2000) found that depression accounted for approximately 3% of the variance in glycated hemoglobin, a salient finding given that a 1% decrease in glycated hemoglobin results in a 33% decrease in the progression rate of retinopathy (Morisaki et al., 1994). Furthermore, treatment of depression could potentially increase the proportion of individuals in good glycemic control from 41% to 58% in the diabetic population (Lustman et al., 2000). Thus, psychological functioning has direct implications for illness outcomes.

There also appears to be a relationship between health care use and depressive symptoms among patients with diabetes. For example, individuals with depression and diabetes had higher ambulatory care use (12 vs. 7 visits) and filled more prescriptions (43 vs. 21) than did their counterparts without a diagnosis of depression. Among individuals with diabetes, total health care expenditures for individuals with depression and diabetes were four and a half times higher than those for individuals without depression ($247 million vs. $55 million) (Egede et al., 2002).

Despite the influence of depression on DM2 outcome and health care use, two of three cases of depression go undiagnosed. Undiagnosed depression is likely due to the fact that many of the symptoms for depression and diabetes overlap (e.g., fatigue [Lustman et al., 1997]). In fact, the prevalence of depressive symptoms among those with diabetes argues for the routine integration of screening for mood disorders by primary health care providers into their patients' treatment plans as a means of improving their patients' psychological and physical health.

Anxiety

As with depression, rates of anxiety are significantly higher among individuals with diabetes than among the general population. In fact, rates of clinically significant anxiety among those with diabetes may be as high as 49% (Peyrot & Rubin, 1997). Gender, age, and education were variables that predicted greater anxiety symptoms (Peyrot & Rubin, 1997). In particular, females, individuals between ages 40 and 49 years, and individuals with lower educational backgrounds were more likely to report symptoms of anxiety. Individuals who had more diabetes complications also reported more anxiety symptoms. Not surprisingly, 38% of those reporting anxiety also reported comorbid depression (Peyrot & Rubin, 1997). Thus, regular screening for anxiety among patients with diabetes is also recommended, especially among those with a greater number of diabetes-related complications.

Other Psychosocial Factors

Social Support. Social support has been associated with physical and psychological health among those with DM2. Individuals with DM2 who perceive more social support from friends and family engage in more diabetes self-care than do those who perceive less social support (Garay-Sevilla et al., 1995; Peyrot, McMurry, & Davida, 1999). In fact, social support may account for as much as 17% of the variance in self-reported diabetes self-care behaviors (Wang & Fenske, 1996). Social support has also been consistently associated with decreased psychological distress among medically well and diabetes populations (Connell, Davis, Gallant, & Sharpe, 1994). Those who report more general social support are more likely to have more diabetes-specific social support and subsequently less depressive symptomatology (Littlefield, Rodin, Murray, & Craven, 1990). As such, social support appears to serve a protective function against depressive symptoms in the context of diabetes.

Illness Intrusiveness. Illness intrusiveness, which refers to the perception of the extent to which an illness constrains and disrupts valued activities, has also been associated with depressive symptoms among individuals with diabetes (Devins, Hunsley, Mandin, Taub, & Paul, 1997). To illustrate, Talbot, Nouwen, Gingras, Belanger, and Audet (1999) examined depressive symptoms in a sample of 237 individuals with DM2 cross-sectionally and found that illness intrusiveness accounted for 61% of the variance in depressive symptoms. Such findings suggest that individuals who tend to perceive their diabetes as restricting activities in valued domains (e.g., family, relationships, spirituality) are at greater risk for depression than are those who do not. To date, relatively little research has been conducted examining cognitive factors such as intrusiveness and their relationship to depression in the context of diabetes. Further research is needed in this area to determine whether these cognitive variables mediate the relationship between diabetes and depression.

Perceived Control. Another cognitive appraisal variable, perceived control, has also been related to levels of psychological distress among individuals with diabetes. Using a measure of diabetes-specific control, Peyrot and Rubin (1994) found that the type of locus of control resulted in either positive or negative health outcomes. Their work suggests that there are two types of internal control: autonomous and self-blaming. Autonomous

internal locus of control orientation (i.e., the belief that a person can manage his or her illness) was significantly associated with fewer symptoms of depression and anxiety. Conversely, a self-blaming internal locus of control (i.e., the belief that a person is responsible for his or her negative illness outcomes such as poor metabolic control) was associated with high blood glucose levels and binge eating. In addition, participants who thought that diabetes control was a matter of chance or fate were more likely to be depressed and anxious and to have lower self-esteem (Peyrot & Rubin, 1994). Certainly, more research is needed to determine how perceived control and health outcomes are causally related. However, it appears that health-related perceptions of control are important cognitive mechanisms to assess and are potentially effective targets for treatment.

Coping Style. The inconsistent findings regarding the relationship between stress and glycemic control may be partially due to differences in how individuals cope with stress. Stress has been significantly associated with higher HbA_{1c} values among those individuals who reported "ineffective" coping styles (i.e., emotional or angry responses to stress) but not among those who reported "effective" coping styles (i.e., tendency to not respond emotionally to stress) (Peyrot & McMurry, 1992). Coping styles have also been directly related to glycemic control. For example, Peyrot and colleagues (1999) found that after controlling for regimen adherence, individuals with DM2 who reported more pragmatic and stoic coping styles showed better glycemic control. Such findings suggest that changing the manner in which individuals respond to stressors may mitigate the impact that stress has on glycemic control of those with DM2.

Quality of Life. Quality of life (QOL) is a global construct that refers to health-related physical and social functioning as well as perceived physical and mental well-being. Overall, a number of studies indicate that QOL is compromised in individuals with diabetes. More specifically, those with diabetes reported reduced role and physical functioning as well as decreased perceptions of overall health. These findings are congruent with studies indicating that the presence of two or more complications is consistently associated with decreased QOL (Rubin & Peyrot, 1999; Trief et al., 1998). As seen with depression, gender differences also exist, as women report lower QOL than do men. Accordingly, women tend to be less satisfied with their treatment regimen, miss more work, and are involved in fewer leisure activities as compared with men (Rubin & Peyrot, 1998).

Because of the required changes in lifestyle and rigid adherence to treatment regimens, it is not surprising that perceived QOL is affected. In fact, it has been demonstrated that patients controlling their diabetes solely with diet and exercise had fewer diabetes quality of life (DQOL) assessed worries than did those taking oral medications. Furthermore, those taking oral medications reported more DQOL satisfaction with treatment and less burden of illness than did those taking insulin (Jacobson, deGroot, & Samson, 1994). It appears, then, that certain components of an individual's treatment regimen affect QOL. However, findings on the relationship between glycemic control and QOL are less clear. Although some studies have found significant relationships between DQOL and HbA_{1c} (Trief et al., 1998), others have not (Peterson, Lee, Young, Newton, & Doran, 1998).

Ethnic and Cultural Considerations

As stated previously, rates of DM2 are clearly higher among some ethnic groups, including African Americans, Native Americans, and Hispanic Americans (Harris, 2001). Furthermore, the frequency and severity of microvascular complications are more common among these minority groups than among Caucasian populations (Cowie et al., 1989; Franklin, Kahn, Baxter, Marshall, & Hamman, 1990; Harris, Klein, Cowie, Rowland, & Byrd-Holt, 1998; Resnick, Valsania, & Phillips, 1999). A number of potential explanations have been posited to account for these observed differences, including decreased health care access, physiological factors, and psychological factors. As an exemplar, findings from a select number of studies with African Americans are presented here.

A number of differences have been observed in health-related beliefs, attitudes, and coping styles. For instance, Samuel-Hodge and colleagues (2000) found that African American women reported that they often feel "nervous and tired" and worry about diabetes complications. Furthermore, many African American women tend to respond to the needs of others and neglect their own care in accordance with their caretaking role within the family. Coping methods may also substantially differ given that African American women tend to rely on spirituality and their belief in God to provide the strength to cope with diabetes (Samuel-Hodge et al., 2000). The aforementioned factors are just a few examples of potential ethnic and cultural differences in psychological adjustment and coping style that may exist and so should be considered in treatment plan development.

Unfortunately only a limited number of studies have examined the effectiveness of interventions designed for specific ethnic groups. The few that have been conducted demonstrate improvements in glycemic control, blood pressure control (Agurs-Collins, Kumanyika, Ten Have, & Adams-Campbell, 1997), and weight loss (Mayer-Davis et al., 2001). Such positive outcomes underscore the importance of developing culture-specific interventions The relevance of these findings is also reflected in culturally centered diabetes outreach programs (e.g., African American, Native American, Latino) recently developed by the ADA (2002b).

In the future, research is needed to determine the culture-specific factors that contribute to diabetes adjustment and effective interventions. A complete review of the literature on culture and DM2 deserves far more consideration than can be achieved within the scope of this chapter. However, it is strongly emphasized that sociocultural factors must be considered when intervening in the context of DM2.

ASSESSMENT AND TREATMENT

Primary Prevention: Risk Reduction

The substantial role of modifiable risk factors in the etiology of DM2 makes prevention efforts a primary health care objective. The majority of prevention efforts involve lifestyle interventions, targeting factors such as obesity, overeating, and physical inactivity. For example, two recent large-scale prevention studies highlight the critical role of behavioral change in diabetes care. The first, the Diabetes Prevention Program (DPP), involved a multi-center study of individuals at risk for diabetes conducted by the National Institutes of Health (Diabetes Prevention Program Research Group [DPPRG], 1999). Participants were randomly assigned to one of three groups, including a drug intervention (metformin vs. placebo) or an intensive lifestyle intervention. Participants receiving the intensive lifestyle intervention met for at least 16 sessions with case managers trained in nutrition, exercise, and behavioral modification over the first 24 weeks of the study and monthly thereafter. The curriculum consisted of general information about diet and exercise and behavioral interventions, including self-monitoring, goal setting, stimulus control, problem solving, and relapse prevention training. Participants in the lifestyle intervention also attended group courses that focused on exercise, weight loss, and behavioral issues. Group courses lasted 4 to 6 weeks, with additional optional groups offered quarterly. Those in the

drug intervention took metformin, which is designed to promote glucose homeostasis, or were administered a placebo. Overall, results for the lifestyle intervention were promising (DPPRG, 2000). At follow-up (average 2.8 years), the lifestyle intervention group demonstrated a 58% reduction in diabetes development, and the drug intervention demonstrated a 31% reduction in diabetes development, relative to the placebo group (DPPRG, 2002).

Similar results were found in the Finnish Diabetes Prevention Study (FDPS) (Tuomilehto et al., 2001), which randomized 522 overweight individuals with impaired glucose tolerance to an intensive lifestyle intervention (targeting weight loss, food intake, and physical activity) or to a control group (brief diet and exercise counseling). As in the DPP, Finnish participants in the lifestyle intervention group showed a 58% reduction in the incidence of diabetes as compared with the control group. Clearly, both the DPP and FDPS provide evidence for the impact of influential changes in eating and exercise habits on the development of diabetes.

The robust findings of the two large-scale prevention studies just described are reflected in the ADA's 2002 position statement on the prevention or delay of DM2. The ADA's statement consists of recommendations for health care providers to (a) increase patient awareness of the benefits of modest weight loss and regular exercise, (b) conduct regular screenings on high-risk populations, and (c) provide weight loss and exercise counseling for those who are found to have impaired glucose tolerance (ADA, 2002c). Although the ADA's recommendations clearly acknowledge the importance of lifestyle interventions in the prevention of DM2, the feasibility of large-scale implementation of these interventions may be problematic within the existing health care system. For example, use of an effective lifestyle intervention program requires a large number of well-coordinated resources over an extended period of time. Often, such resources do not exist or are not accessible. Thus, future research efforts should focus on how to translate the DPP and FDPS findings into cost-effective interventions that can be feasibly implemented in real-world settings.

Medical Interventions

To prevent diabetes-related complications, individuals with DM2 must manage a complicated treatment regimen on a daily basis. Such treatment regimens are individualized according to patients' medical needs and resources. They typically consist of a nutritional regimen, an exercise program, and oral medication (NIDDK, 2000). Nutritional plans generally consist of eating prescribed proportions of protein, fat, and carbohydrates as well as fiber, cholesterol, and sodium. It is also recommended that a regular exercise plan involve aerobic and muscle-strengthening exercises. For many individuals with diabetes, changes in diet and exercise are sufficient to achieve euglycemia (near-normal glucose levels). However, if diet and exercise cannot adequately sustain euglycemia, oral medications that decrease blood glucose are incorporated into the treatment regimen. Oral medications lower blood glucose either by stimulating the pancreas to produce more insulin or by increasing the efficiency of insulin use. When oral medications are not sufficient to maintain euglycemia, exogenous insulin injections are integrated into the treatment regimen. Nearly 40% of individuals with DM2 are treated with insulin to improve metabolic control. Clearly, the responsibility for diabetes self-management rests on the individual with diabetes. Therefore, the preceding treatment regimens require a number of substantial behavioral and lifestyle changes for most individuals.

Metabolic Control. The fundamental purpose of a diabetes treatment regimen is to achieve near-normal metabolic control. Thus,

individuals with diabetes must frequently self-monitor blood glucose. For individuals with DM2, glucose levels should fall between 80 and 120 mg/dl before meals and between 100 and 140 mg/dl at bedtime (ADA, 1998). It is also recommended that physicians check HbA_{1c} regularly. HbA_{1c} is an average measure of blood glucose for the previous 3 months and is an important indicator of metabolic control. Individuals who do not have diabetes typically have an HbA_{1c} percentage of less than 6% (ADA, 1998). It is recommended that individuals with DM2 maintain an HbA_{1c} of between 7% and 8%. Diabetes-related complications are greatly reduced though good metabolic control; for every 0.9% reduction in HbA_{1c}, the risk of developing microvascular diabetic complications (eye, kidney, and nerve disease) is reduced by approximately 25% (ADA, 2002a).

Preventive Screening of Diabetes Complications. Preventive screening and practices is also a vital component of the diabetes treatment regimen, particularly as it concerns diabetes complications. As stated previously, hypertension is common among individuals with diabetes and so must be monitored regularly. Adequate blood pressure control can subsequently reduce cardiovascular disease, such as heart disease and stroke, by approximately 33% to 50% and can reduce microvascular disease by approximately 33% (NIDDK, 2000). Cholesterol and lipids must also be monitored among individuals with DM2; cardiovascular complications can be reduced by 20% to 50% through improved control of cholesterol and lipids. Medications are commonly required to control cholesterol and blood pressure among those with diabetes. In addition, preventive screenings for diabetic eye disease are important. Early detection and treatment of diabetic eye disease with laser therapy can reduce the development of severe vision loss by an estimated 50% to 60%. Similarly, early detection and treatment of diabetic kidney disease can reduce the development of kidney failure by 30% to 70%. Finally, comprehensive foot care programs can reduce amputation rates by 45% to 85% (NIDDK, 2000). Given the multisystemic nature of DM2, regular screenings for these difficulties are clearly an essential component of the treatment regimen.

Difficulties With the Medical Regimen. There are a number of diabetes-related adjustment problems that are directly associated with attempts at treatment adherence. One such frustration commonly expressed by individuals with diabetes is the sense of being food deprived (Rubin & Peyrot, 2001). Some individuals may subsequently develop poor eating habits, whereas others report that they do not monitor their glucose as often as indicated. Adhering to monitoring glucose levels is also problematic. Two commonly cited reasons for not monitoring blood glucose are the pain associated with drawing blood and the inconvenience of monitoring in certain settings. Still other individuals have negative responses to excessively low or high blood glucose readings (Rubin & Peyrot, 2001). Motivation to adhere to the monitoring portion of the treatment regimen is difficult to maintain when the feedback is often negative in nature.

An additional problem often encountered by individuals with DM2 is the frustration associated with unpredictable blood glucose levels, often leading to less active self-care. To help alleviate frustration, individuals are encouraged to develop realistic standards and expectations regarding diabetes outcomes. Finally, the fear of taking insulin can prevent optimal management of blood glucose levels. Clinicians should attempt to identify specific fears related to taking insulin, including the pain associated with the injection, interference with lifestyle, experiencing hypoglycemia, and being treated differently by others (Rubin & Peyrot, 2001). For a more thorough description of the fears related to taking insulin, see Rubin and Peyrot (2001).

It is important to recognize that diabetes self-management is a complex, multidimensional construct. Typically, individuals are adherent to certain components of their treatment regimens but not to others. Indeed, perfect adherence to every aspect of the treatment regimen is extremely rare and (for many) unrealistic (Wysocki & Buckloh, 2002). Therefore, clinicians should identify the components of the treatment regimen to which patients are adhering well and those to which they are not. It is common for individuals frustrated with one aspect of their treatment regimen to generalize and conclude that they are "bad patients" or are "nonadherent" patients. Clinicians can help such individuals by identifying small specific goals to work toward. Subsequently, the treatment regimen will appear much more manageable to individuals with DM2.

Diabetes Self-Management Education. Diabetes self-management education (DSME) equips individuals with the knowledge and skills to manage their diabetes successfully. Metabolic control is potentially optimized, and future complications are minimized, when the following information and skills are taught: nutritional information, exercise recommendations, self-monitoring of blood glucose (SMBG), insulin administration, and managing of hypoglycemic and hyperglycemic events. Given that patients perform approximately 95% of this daily care independently (Anderson, 1985), DSME is considered to be the central component of the medical treatment for those with diabetes. Despite the central nature of DSME, only 40% of individuals with diabetes receive formal diabetes management education (U.S. Department of Health and Human Services, 1998), and 50% to 80% of individuals have severe deficits in their diabetes self-care knowledge (Clement, 1995). These estimates indicate that many individuals do not receive adequate DSME and suggest that the method and delivery of DSME require improvement.

There is an extensive body of literature that evaluates various methods of delivery and outcomes related to DSME. Still, no particular intervention method has been identified as optimally efficacious. Because of the multidimensionality of diabetes treatment regimens, DSME interventions are differentially effective depending on the aspects of the regimens that are assessed (Norris, Engelgau, & Narayan, 2001). In other words, interventions are generally effective in changing certain outcomes but not others. However, a recent review article by Norris and colleagues (2001) outlined several consistent findings that have emerged from the DSME literature and are summarized here.

Specifically, short-term DSME interventions have been found to be fairly effective in yielding improvements in knowledge levels, SMBG skills, and dietary habits but not in yielding improvements in weight loss and physical activity levels (Norris et al., 2001). Group intervention formats are effective in improving knowledge and SMBG and may be more effective than individual formats for lifestyle interventions. However, it is important to note that improvements in knowledge or SMBG do not necessarily translate into improvements in glycemic control. Notably, interactive, individualized, repetitive interventions are more effective in improving lipid levels than are single-session or short-term interventions. In addition, programs that promote patient participation or take a collaborative approach to instruction appear to be more effective than didactic approaches in affecting outcomes such as glycemic control, weight loss, and lipid profiles. Finally, Norris and colleagues (2001) concluded that, by and large, self-management interventions that have consistent reinforcement over long periods of time are more effective than single-session or short-term interventions.

Norris and colleagues (2001) also pointed out limitations in the existing DSME literature. They recognized that the dearth of research examining psychological outcomes makes it quite difficult to determine specific psychological factors that influence self-management behaviors. Furthermore, very few studies have reported long-term treatment outcomes. This is noteworthy given that long-term follow-up studies are less likely to find positive outcomes regarding glycemic and behavioral outcomes than are those with short-term follow-ups (Norris et al., 2001). It may be that program interventions lead to short-term behavioral change but that the newly acquired behaviors do not necessarily persist. Consequently, "refresher" sessions over the course of the illness may be warranted. It is unlikely that one intervention that improves all self-management behaviors, and that is appropriate throughout the course of the illness, will be found. Therefore, future research needs to determine which types of interventions, or combinations of interventions, are most effective for specific outcomes. Moreover, virtually no research has examined how adherence changes over time for adults with diabetes. Thus, longitudinal studies are needed to determine whether self-management behaviors follow a developmental pattern.

Psychological Interventions for Diabetes-Specific Problems

Over the past 20 years, behavioral interventions for diabetes-specific problems have shifted from knowledge- and education-based interventions to patient-centered interventions emphasizing patient efficacy, esteem, and control (Glasgow et al., 1999). Patient-centered interventions appear to be effective in improving both physical and psychological health outcomes. Three empirically supported examples of patient-centered interventions—diabetes-specific coping skills training, empowerment, and stress management interventions—are discussed here.

Diabetes-Specific Coping Skills Training. Diabetes-specific coping skills training (DSCST) is a cognitive-behavioral, psychoeducational group intervention designed to optimize emotional functioning, diabetes self-management, and metabolic control (Rubin & Peyrot, 2001). During the intervention, individuals are encouraged to identify patterns of self-care and barriers to self-care and, subsequently, to problem solve strategies to address identified problems. A series of studies evaluating DSCST have found the program to be effective in improving psychological outcomes such as depression, anxiety, self-esteem, and diabetes self-efficacy. Moreover, improvements have been observed in diabetes self-care (e.g., diet, exercise, diabetes knowledge, SMBG) and metabolic control (Rubin, Peyrot, & Saudek, 1989, 1991, 1993; Rubin, Waller, & Ellis, 1990). Several key elements of diabetes-specific coping skills training were outlined by Rubin (2000), including individualized treatment plans, problem specificity, goal setting, reinforcement, problem solving, emotional coping skills, and family involvement (for a more detailed description, see Rubin, 2000).

Empowerment. Patient empowerment interventions also appear to be effective in addressing many of the diabetes-specific difficulties that frequently accompany DM2. Empowerment interventions are designed to enhance goal setting, problem-solving, coping, stress management, social support, and self-motivation. Anderson and colleagues (1995) evaluated an empowerment intervention that consisted of six 2-hour group sessions. At a 6-month follow-up, the treatment group demonstrated significant increases in self-efficacy (setting goals, solving problems, emotional coping, obtaining support, self-motivation, and decision making) and positive diabetes-specific attitudes as well as decreases in negative diabetes-specific attitudes. Small improvements were also observed in glycemic control. This study lends further support to the value of patient-centered care that addresses the psychological aspects of living with diabetes.

Stress Management. A number of stress management interventions have been developed based on the strong theoretical link between stress and metabolic control. A variety of techniques aimed at decreasing stress have been evaluated, including biofeedback (Surwit & Feinglos, 1988), relaxation training (Surwit et al., 2002), and cognitive-behavioral strategies (Henry, Wilson, Bruce, Chisholm, & Rawling, 1997). For instance, studies examining the efficacy of biofeedback-assisted relaxation training found significant improvements in various measures of metabolic control, including improved glucose tolerance, reduced long-term hyperglycemia (Lammers, Naliboff, & Straatmeyer, 1984; Surwit & Feinglos, 1988; Surwit, Ross, McCaskill, & Feinglos, 1989), postprandial (i.e., after eating) blood glucose levels, and plasma cortisol, as compared with control participants (Surwit & Feinglos, 1983). Overall, stress management interventions show improvements in metabolic control parameters but have not been consistent at reducing psychological distress (Henry et al., 1997; Surwit et al., 2002). Future studies need to determine whether some individuals are more susceptible to the effects of stress than are others and which types of interventions effect specific stress-related outcomes.

Technology-Based Interventions

Currently, greater attention has been directed toward developing cost-effective interventions that can be easily disseminated. To this end, Glasgow, Toobert, and Hampson (1996) evaluated a brief office-based computer intervention aimed at improving diabetes self-management. Individuals in the intervention completed a computerized assessment of self-management behaviors and then were provided feedback on self-management, participated in goal-setting exercises, and selected individualized interventions. Participants also received a one-page feedback form outlining individualized obstacles to self-management. The computer-assisted intervention was fairly successful in producing dietary improvements and serum cholesterol levels but did not yield significant improvements in glycemic control or QOL (Glasgow et al., 1996). A later study by Glasgow and Toobert (2000) examined the effects of a telephone follow-up on providing community resource information to the patient in addition to the computer-assisted intervention. Neither strategy improved the outcomes of the computer-based intervention. Given these findings, the expanding use of home computers, and the increasing need for cost-effective health care, it is likely that use of computer-based interventions will continue to increase (Gonder-Frederick, Cox, & Ritterband, 2002).

Treating Psychological Distress

As indicated previously, there is high comorbidity between diabetes and psychological distress, especially depression and anxiety. Recommended treatment approaches for depression and anxiety in the context of DM2 are reviewed here.

Depression. Despite the high prevalence of clinically significant depressive symptoms among individuals with diabetes, few treatment outcome studies have been conducted. A notable exception is Lustman and colleagues' 1998 study, which compared the efficacy of cognitive-behavioral therapy (CBT) plus self-management training with that of self-management training alone in decreasing depressive symptoms among individuals with diabetes (Lustman, Griffith, Freeland, Kissel, & Clouse, 1998). Remission of depression was observed at a 10-week follow-up; at that time, 85% of those in the CBT group had remitted as compared with 25% of those in the self-management group. Moreover, treatment effects persisted; at the 6-month follow-up, the rates of depression remission were 70% for the CBT group and 33% for the self-management group. The CBT group

also showed greater improvements in glycemic control than did the self-management group. Thus, CBT appears to be an effective treatment for depression for those with diabetes (Lustman et al., 1998).

Although CBT has been shown to be effective in treating depression, the combination of behavioral interventions with antidepressant medication may be clinically indicated in some cases. Selective serotonin reuptake inhibitors such as fluoxitine are effective in treating depressive symptoms and are associated with improvements in glycemic control (Rubin & Peyrot, 1994). Furthermore, fewer than 10% of patients with diabetes taking fluoxitine experience significant side effects (Lustman et al., 2000). Tricyclic medications have also been shown to decrease depressive symptoms (Turkinton, 1980); however, the use of tricyclic medication among those with DM2 has been associated with adverse side effects, including hyperglycemia, weight gain, orthostatic hypotension, and other cardiovascular events (Lustman, Griffith, Gavard, & Clouse, 1992).

Although the treatments for depression just described appear to be effective, the constellation of organic and psychosocial factors contributing to depression among those with diabetes may well be unique. Therefore, researchers and clinicians should not assume that the research findings in medically well populations generalize to those with diabetes. Future research should focus on how cognitive processing mechanisms interface with diabetes-specific experiences and subsequently influence psychological distress. During the interim, it is recommended that clinicians use treatments for depression that are empirically supported among medically well populations (e.g., CBT, interpersonal therapy). Such interventions might be tailored to diabetes by including the identification and modification of thoughts and beliefs related to DM2 (for a review of empirically supported treatments, see also DeRubeis & Crits-Christoph, 1998).

CASE STUDY

To illustrate the potential role of psychology in optimizing both physical and psychological outcomes, the following case study is presented. In this particular case, the individual has a number of diabetes-specific problems as well as clinically significant psychological distress.

"A. J.," a 51-year-old male, presented to a diabetes clinic with a 6-year history of DM2. Since being diagnosed with diabetes, he had closely adhered to his medication regimen but inconsistently practiced dietary and exercise recommendations. Thus, A. J. was still able to maintain an acceptable (but not optimal) level of glucose control throughout the first few years of his illness. However, during the past year, A. J. had gained 30 pounds and his HbA_{1c} value had risen to 10.5%. In addition, a recent examination by his family physician revealed an ulcer on his left foot. Concerned by the rapid decline in A. J.'s metabolic control, the physician incorporated insulin into his treatment plan and referred him to a health psychologist to facilitate his regimen adherence.

During initial therapy sessions, A. J. admitted to having difficulty in adhering to his treatment regimen, citing large Sunday dinners when traditional family recipes high in fat and carbohydrates were served. He stated that he refused to miss out on this special family time by declining to eat or eating off of a different menu. Furthermore, he admitted that it was easier to ignore the problem than to change his lifestyle. He stated that his exercise regimen consisted solely of playing with his kids on the weekends and doing yard work.

In the third session, A. J. revealed that he had been laid off from his position at a local computer company approximately 4 months earlier. He stated that after he was laid off, he did not feel like playing with his kids anymore, found it difficult to get up in the morning, and felt hopeless about the future. He also reported that his wife had been nagging him more about "everything," including his diet, completing chores around the house, and being "grouchy." Like many clients that are referred to therapy, A. J. reported both diabetes-specific problems and general psychological distress. After a thorough assessment, he was diagnosed with major depressive disorder.

Given A. J.'s presentation, the focus of therapy shifted from diabetes-specific problems to treating depression. A. J. was referred to a psychiatrist for a medication evaluation and was subsequently prescribed antidepressant medication. Psychological treatment consisted of CBT in which A. J. explored his beliefs related to himself, losing his job, and the difficulty in finding employment. When appropriate, beliefs related to having diabetes were also explored, and where indicated, A. J.'s beliefs were challenged and modified. Pleasant events scheduling was also conducted. After 3 months of CBT and medication therapy, A. J.'s symptoms of depression had decreased substantially and he reported increased motivation to improve his diabetes management. Thus, a long-term treatment plan was implemented consisting of monthly meetings with the health psychologist to discuss issues surrounding weight loss, exercise, and behavioral issues as well as ongoing stress management. Specifically, A. J. learned ways in which to identify healthier alternatives for his favorite foods and instituted a regular exercise regimen consisting of running and weightlifting. A. J. and his family also joined the local diabetes support group, where he shares with others what he has learned about coping with diabetes.

As a result of his efforts, A. J. lost 20 pounds and did not develop any additional diabetes complications. He also reported that he felt more confident in his ability to manage his diabetes successfully.

Anxiety. As mentioned previously, anxiety symptoms are also common among individuals with DM2 (Peyrot & Rubin, 1997). Remarkably, no validated randomized controlled trials have evaluated the efficacy of behavioral treatment interventions targeting anxiety among those with diabetes. A number of authors have suggested that biofeedback-assisted relaxation training (described earlier in the chapter), although not yet empirically tested to target anxiety symptoms, may be an effective treatment for anxiety among those with diabetes. At this time, it is recommended that clinicians use treatments for anxiety that have been empirically supported among medically well populations (for a review of empirically supported treatments, see DeRubeis & Crits-Christoph, 1998).

Studies examining the effectiveness of pharmacological treatments for anxiety among those with DM2 are limited. However, initial reports suggest that pharmacological treatments may be potentially effective (Lustman et al., 1995). For example, individuals treated with alprazolam (Xanax) displayed improvements in glycemic control when taking this medication regardless of a formal diagnosis of anxiety (Lustman et al., 1995). Although results are promising, further research is needed to determine the most effective treatment approach for anxiety symptoms in individuals with diabetes.

Most individuals with diabetes seeking psychological services will likely have both general distress (e.g., depression) and diabetes-specific issues. When treating clients with poor regimen adherence and high levels of psychological distress, it may be difficult to determine the initial target of intervention. In the majority of cases, it may be advisable to address general distress first (Rubin, 2000) because it is unlikely that individuals experiencing high levels of distress are going to have the organizational ability or motivation necessary to effect diabetes-specific behavioral changes. As levels of general psychological distress decrease, diabetes-specific issues can be addressed more effectively.

CONCLUSIONS

DM2 is a chronic illness characterized by a dysregulation of blood glucose levels. DM2 requires individuals to manage a complex treatment regimen so as to prevent severe medical complications. Fortunately, it is a potentially manageable disease, and many of the negative physical and psychological health sequelae are preventable. However, preventing adverse diabetes outcomes requires that individuals with diabetes make multiple behavioral and lifestyle changes, a task that overwhelms many. Because of the unpredictable and complex nature of DM2, interventions may be necessary to facilitate these behavioral changes and to promote optimal health outcomes. A number of behavioral interventions have proved to be effective in preventing DM2 as well as in improving the psychological and physical outcomes of those who have diabetes.

Although great progress has been made in understanding the behavioral aspects of DM2 during the past two decades, a number of areas are in need of further investigation. First, there are virtually no longitudinal studies examining the developmental course of self-management among adults. Furthermore, additional research should address the cultural-specific impact of DM2. Not only are certain cultural groups at high risk for DM2, but research suggests that there also are potential culture-specific patterns of illness appraisal and coping strategies. In addition, studies that will help to determine the most effective treatments for clinically significant psychological distress among individuals with diabetes, specifically depression and anxiety, are warranted.

During the coming decade, there will be an increasing need for cost-effective interventions aimed at preventing and treating obesity and DM2. An exceptional review by Wing and colleagues (2001) advocated the need for public policy and community-based interventions, citing the role of environmental factors in the development and prevention of obesity and DM2. High-fat, high-calorie foods and sedentary activities, such as watching television and using computers, pervade contemporary society and shape health-related behaviors and outcomes. Thus, studies are needed to further delineate which environmental variables influence eating and physical activity and to develop community-based interventions that promote positive health behaviors.

Importantly, the development of more cost-effective interventions will also require the role of behavioral scientists to change (Gonder-Frederick et al., 2002). Rather than providing direct care, behavioral scientists will increasingly provide training and supervision to other health care professionals who directly assess and implement behavioral interventions. As a result, behavioral scientists will also be required to further examine the role of the provider-patient relationship in influencing psychological and physical outcomes and to develop interventions targeting health care providers accordingly. In sum, the fundamental challenge for behavioral scientists will be to translate available findings into feasible, cost-effective interventions that can be widely disseminated to psychologists and health care professionals (Gonder-Frederick et al., 2002).

REFERENCES

Agurs-Collins, T. D., Kumanyika, S. K., Ten Have, T. R., & Adams-Campbell, L. L. (1997). A randomized controlled trial of weight reduction and exercise for diabetes management in older African-American subjects. *Diabetes Care, 20,* 1503–1512.

American Diabetes Association. (1998). *Medical management of type 2 diabetes* (4th ed., Clinical Education Series). Alexandria, VA: Author.

American Diabetes Association. (2002a). Implications of the United Kingdom Prospective Diabetes Study. *Diabetes Care, 25*(1), S28–S32.

American Diabetes Association. (2002b, March). *Outreach programs and public awareness campaigns.* [Online]. Retrieved on May 10, 2002, from www.diabetes.org/main/application/commercewf?origin=*jsp&event=link(D57)

American Diabetes Association. (2002c). The prevention or delay of Type 2 diabetes. *Diabetes Care, 25,* 742–749.

Anderson, R. J., Freeland, K. E., Clouse, R. E., & Lustman, P. J. (2001). The prevalence of comorbid depression in adults with diabetes: A meta-analysis. *Diabetes Care, 24,* 1069–1078.

Anderson, R. M. (1985). Is the problem of compliance all in our heads? *Diabetes Educator, 11,* 31–34.

Anderson, R. M., Funnell, M. M., Butler, P. M., Arnold, M. S., Fitzgerald, J. T., & Feste, C. C. (1995). Patient empowerment. *Diabetes Care, 18,* 943–949.

Bernbaum, M., Alpert, S. G., & Duckro, P. N. (1988). Psychosocial profiles of patients with visual impairment due to diabetic retinopathy. *Diabetes Care, 11,* 551–557.

Boyle, J. P., Honeycutt, A. A., Narayan, K. M. V., Hoerger, T. J., Geiss, L. S., Chen, H., & Thompson, T. J. (2001). Projection of diabetes burden through 2050: Impact of changing demography and disease prevalence in the U.S. *Diabetes Care, 24,* 1936–1940.

Clement, S. (1995). Diabetes self-management education. *Diabetes Care, 18,* 1204–1214.

Connell, C. M., Davis, W. K., Gallant, M. P., & Sharpe, P. A. (1994). Impact of social support, social cognitive variables, and perceived threat on depression among adults with diabetes. *Health Psychology, 13,* 263–273.

Cowie, C. C., Port, F. K., Wolfe, R. A., Savage, P. J., Moll, P. P., & Hawthorne, V. M. (1989). Disparities in incidence of diabetic end-stage renal disease by race and type of diabetes. *New England Journal of Medicine, 321,* 1074–1079.

DeFronzo, R. A., Bonadonna, R. C., & Ferrannini, E. (1992). Pathogenesis of NIDDM. *Diabetes Care, 15,* 318–368.

Demmers, R. Y., Neale, A. V., Wensloff, N. J., Gronsman, K. J., & Jaber, L. A. (1989). Glycosylated hemoglobin levels and self-reported stress in adults with diabetes. *Behavioral Medicine, 15,* 167–172.

DeRubeis, R. J., & Crits-Christoph, P. (1998). Empirically supported individual and group psychological treatments for adult mental disorders. *Journal of Consulting and Clinical Psychology, 66,* 37–52.

Devins, G. M., Hunsley, J., Mandin, H., Taub, K. J., & Paul, L. C. (1997). The marital context of end-stage renal disease: Illness intrusiveness and perceived changes in family environment. *Annals of Behavioral Medicine, 19,* 325–332.

Diabetes Prevention Program Research Group. (1999). The Diabetes Prevention Program: Design and methods for a clinical trial in the prevention of Type 2 diabetes. *Diabetes Care, 22,* 623–634.

Diabetes Prevention Program Research Group. (2000). The Diabetes Prevention Program: Baseline characteristics of the randomized cohort. *Diabetes Care, 23,* 1619–1629.

Diabetes Prevention Program Research Group. (2002). Reduction in the evidence of Type 2 diabetes with lifestyle intervention or metformin. *New England Journal of Medicine, 346,* 393–403.

Egede, L. E., Zheng, D., & Simpson, K. (2002). Comorbid depression is associated with increased health care use and expenditures in individuals with diabetes. *Diabetes Care, 25,* 464–470.

Franklin, G. M., Kahn, L. B., Baxter, J., Marshall, J. A., & Hamman, R. F. (1990). Sensory neuropathy in non-insulin-dependent diabetes mellitus: The San Luis Valley Diabetes Study. *American Journal of Epidemiology, 131,* 633–643.

Garay-Sevilla, M. E., Nava, L. E., Malacara, J. M., Huerta, R., de Leon, J. D., Mena, A., & Fajardo, M. E. (1995). Adherence to treatment and social support in patients with non-insulin-dependent diabetes mellitus. *Journal of Diabetes and Its Complications, 9,* 81–86.

Glasgow, R. E., Fisher, E. B., Anderson, B. J., LaGreca, A., Marrero, D., Johnson, S. B., Rubin, R. R., & Cox, D. J. (1999). Behavioral sciences in diabetes. *Diabetes Care, 22,* 832–843.

Glasgow, R. E., & Toobert, D. J. (2000). Brief, computer assisted diabetes dietary self-management counseling: Effects on behavior, physiologic outcomes, and quality of life. *Medical Care, 38,* 1062–1073.

Glasgow, R. E., Toobert, D. J., & Hampson, S. E. (1996). Effects of a brief office-based intervention to facilitate diabetes dietary self-management. *Diabetes Care, 19,* 835–842.

Goetsch, V. L., & Wiebe, D. J. (1995). Diabetes mellitus: Considerations of the influence of stress. In A. J. Goreczny (Ed.), *Handbook of health and rehabilitation psychology* (pp. 513–534). New York: Plenum.

Gonder-Frederick, L. A., Cox, D. J., & Ritterband, L. M. (2002). Diabetes and behavioral medicine: The second decade. *Journal of Consulting and Clinical Psychology, 70,* 611–625.

Griffith, L. S., Field, B. J., & Lustman, P. J. (1990). Life stress and social support in diabetes: Association with glycemic control. *International Journal of Psychiatry in Medicine, 20,* 365–372.

Harris, M. I. (1998). Diabetes in America: Epidemiology and scope of the problem. *Diabetes Care, 21*(Suppl. 3), C11–C14.

Harris, M. I. (2001). Racial and ethnic differences in health care access and health outcomes for adults with Type 2 diabetes. *Diabetes Care, 24,* 454–459.

Harris, M. I., Klein, R., Cowie, C. C., Rowland, M., & Byrd-Holt, D. D. (1998). Is the risk of diabetic retinopathy greater in non-Hispanic African-Americans and Mexican-Americans than in non-Hispanic Caucasians with Type 2 diabetes? A U.S. population study. *Diabetes Care, 21,* 1230–1235.

Henry, J. L., Wilson, P. H., Bruce, D. G., Chisholm, D. J., & Rawling, P. J. (1997). Cognitive-behavioral stress management for patients with non-insulin-dependent diabetes mellitus. *Psychology, Health, & Medicine, 2,* 109–118.

Hillier, T. A., & Pedula, K. L. (2001). Characteristics of an adult population with newly diagnosed Type 2 diabetes: The relation of obesity and age of onset. *Diabetes Care, 24,* 1522–1527.

Jacobson, A. M., deGroot, M., & Samson, J. A. (1994). The evaluation of two measures of quality of life in patients with Type 1 and Type 2 diabetes. *Diabetes Care, 17,* 267–274.

Kovacs, M., Brent, D., Steinberg, T. F., Paulauskas, S., & Reid, J. (1986). Children's self-reports of psychologic adjustment and coping strategies during first year of insulin-dependent diabetes mellitus. *Diabetes Care, 9,* 472–479.

Kuhn, C., Cochrane, C., Feinglos, M., & Surwit, R. (1987). Exaggerated peripheral responsivity to catecholamine contributes to stress-induced hyperglycemia in the ob/ob mouse. *Physiology, Biochemistry, and Behavior, 25,* 491–495.

Lammers, C. A., Naliboff, B. D., & Straatmeyer, A. J. (1984). The effects of progressive muscle relaxation on stress and diabetic control. *Behavior Research Therapy, 22,* 641–650.

Littlefield, C. H., Rodin, G. M., Murray, M. A., & Craven, J. L. (1990). Influence of functional impairment and social support on depressive symptoms in persons with diabetes. *Health Psychology, 9,* 737–749.

Lustman, P. J., Anderson, R. J., Freeland, K. E., De Groot, M., Carney R. M., & Clouse, R. E. (2000). Depression and poor glycemic control: A meta-analytic review of the literature. *Diabetes Care, 23,* 934–943.

Lustman, P. J., Clouse, R. E., Alrakawi, A., Rubin, E. H., & Gelenberg, A. J. (1997). Treatment of major depression in adults with diabetes: A primary care perspective. *Clinical Diabetes, 15,* 122–126.

Lustman, P. J., Griffith, L. S., Clouse, R. E., Freeland, K. E., Eisen, S. A., Rubin, E. H., Carney, R. M., & McGill, J. B. (1995). Effects of alprazolam on glucose regulation in diabetes. *Diabetes Care, 18,* 1133–1139.

Lustman, P. J., Griffith, L. S., Freeland, K. E., Kissel, S. S., & Clouse, R. E. (1998). Cognitive behavioral therapy for depression in Type 2 diabetes mellitus: A randomized, controlled trial. *Annals of Internal Medicine, 129,* 613–621.

Lustman, P. J., Griffith, L. S., Gavard, J. A., & Clouse, R. E. (1992). Depression in adults with diabetes. *Diabetes Care, 15,* 1631–1639.

Maggio, C. A., & Pi-Sunyer, F. X. (1997). The prevention and treatment of obesity: Application to Type 2 diabetes. *Diabetes Care, 20,* 1744–1766.

Manson, J., & Spelsberg, A. (1994). Primary prevention of non-insulin-dependent diabetes mellitus. *American Journal of Preventive Medicine, 10,* 172–184.

Marlatt, G. A., & Gordon, J. R. (1985). *Relapse prevention: Maintenance strategies and addictive behavior change.* New York: Guilford.

Mayer-Davis, E. J., Antonio, A. D., Martin, M., Wandersman, A., Parra-Medina, D., & Schulz, R. (2001). Pilot study of strategies for effective weight management in Type 2 diabetes: Pounds Off With Empowerment (POWER). *Family and Community Health, 24*(2), 27–35.

McCulloch, D. K., Hosking, D. J., & Tobert, A. (1986). A pragmatic approach to sexual dysfunction in diabetic men: Psychosexual counseling. *Diabetes Medicine, 3,* 485–489.

Morisaki, N., Watanabe, S., Kobayashi, J., Kanzaki, T., Takahashi, K., Yokote, K., Tezuka, M., Tashiro, J., Inadera, H., & Saito, Y. (1994). Diabetic control and progression of retinopathy in elderly patients: Five year follow-up. *Journal of the American Geriatrics Society, 41,* 142–145.

National Institute of Diabetes and Digestive and Kidney Diseases. (2000). *National diabetes statistics fact sheet: General information and national estimates on diabetes in the United States.* Bethesda, MD: National Institutes of Health.

Norris, S. L., Engelgau, M. M., & Narayan, K. M. V. (2001). Effectiveness of self-management training in Type 2 diabetes: A systematic review of randomized controlled trials. *Diabetes Care, 24,* 561–587.

Owen, K., Ayers, S., Corbett, S., & Hattersley, A. (2002). Increased risk of diabetes in first-degree relatives of young-onset Type 2 diabetic patients compared with relatives of those diagnosed later. *Diabetes Care, 25,* 636–637.

Peterson, T., Lee, P., Young, B., Newton, P., & Doran, T. (1998). Well-being and treatment satisfaction in older people with diabetes. *Diabetes Care, 21,* 930–935.

Peyrot, M., & McMurry, J. F. (1985). Psychosocial factors in diabetes control: Adjustment of insulin treated adults. *Psychosomatic Medicine, 47,* 542–547.

Peyrot, M. F., & McMurry, J. F., Jr. (1992). Stress buffering and glycemic control. *Diabetes Care, 15,* 842–846.

Peyrot, M. F., McMurry, J. F., & Davida, F. K. (1999). A biopsychosocial model of glycemic control in diabetes: Stress, coping, and regimen adherence. *Journal of Health and Social Behavior, 40,* 141–158.

Peyrot, M. F., & Rubin, R. R. (1994). Psychosocial problems in diabetes treatment: Impediments to intensive self-care. *Practical Diabetology, 13,* 8–14.

Peyrot, M. F., & Rubin, R. R. (1997). Levels and risks of depression and anxiety symptomatology among diabetic adults. *Diabetes Care, 20,* 585–590.

Ray, N. F., Thamer, M., Gardner, E., & Chan, J. K. (1998). Economic consequences of diabetes mellitus in the U.S. in 1997. *Diabetes Care, 21,* 296–306.

Resnick, H. E., Valsania, P., & Phillips, C. L. (1999). Diabetes mellitus and nontraumatic lower extremity amputation in African-American and Caucasian Americans: the National Health and Nutrition Examination Survey

Epidemiologic Follow-up Study, 1971–1992. *Archives of Internal Medicine, 159,* 2470–2475.

Rubin, R. R. (2000). Psychotherapy and counseling in diabetes mellitus. In F. J. Snoek & T. C. Skinner (Eds.), *Psychology in diabetes care* (pp. 235–263). New York: John Wiley.

Rubin, R. R., & Peyrot, M. (1994). Psychosocial problems in diabetes treatment: Impediments to intensive self-care. *Practical Diabetology, 13,* 8–14.

Rubin, R. R., & Peyrot, M. (1998). Men and diabetes: Psychosocial and behavioral issues. *Diabetes Spectrum, 11,* 81–87.

Rubin, R. R., & Peyrot, M. (1999). Quality of life and diabetes. *Diabetes Metabolism Research Reviews, 15,* 205–218.

Rubin, R. R., & Peyrot, M. (2001). Psychological issues and treatments for people with diabetes. *Journal of Clinical Psychology, 57,* 457–478.

Rubin, R. R., Peyrot, M., & Saudek, C. D. (1989). Effect of diabetes education on self-care, metabolic control, and emotional well-being. *Diabetes Care, 12,* 673–679.

Rubin, R. R., Peyrot, M., & Saudek, C. D. (1991). Differential effect of diabetes education on self-regulation and lifestyle behaviors. *Diabetes Care, 14,* 335–338.

Rubin, R. R., Peyrot, M., & Saudek, C. D. (1993). The effect of diabetes education program incorporating coping skills training on emotional well-being and diabetes self-efficacy. *Diabetes Educator, 19,* 210–214.

Rubin, R. R., Waller, S., & Ellis, A. (1990). Living with diabetes: A rational-emotive therapy perspective. *Journal of Rational-Emotive Cognitive-Behavioral Therapy, 8,* 21–39.

Samuel-Hodge, C. D., Headen, S. W., Skelly, A. H., Ingram, A. F., Keyserling, T. C., Jackson, E. J., Ammerman, A. S., & Elasy, T. A. (2000). Influences on day to day management of Type 2 diabetes among African-American women. *Diabetes Care, 23,* 928–934.

Schreiner-Engel, P., Schiavi, R. C., Vietorisz, D., & Smith, H. (1987). The differential impact of diabetes type on female sexuality. *Journal of Psychosomatic Research, 31,* 23–33.

Surwit, R. S., & Feinglos, M. N. (1983). The effects of relaxation on glucose tolerance in non-insulin-dependent diabetes mellitus. *Diabetes Care, 6,* 176–179.

Surwit, R. S., & Feinglos, M. N. (1988). Stress and autonomic nervous system in Type II diabetes: A hypothesis. *Diabetes Care, 11,* 83–85.

Surwit, R. S., Feinglos, M. N., Livingston, E. G., Kuhn, C. M., & McCubbin, J. A. (1984). Behavioral manipulation of the diabetic phenotype in ob/ob mice. *Diabetes, 33,* 616–618.

Surwit, R. S., McCubbin, J. A., Kuhn, C. M., McGee, D., Gerstenfeld, D. A., & Feinglos, M. N. (1986). Alprazolam reduces stress hyperglycemia in ob/ob mice. *Psychosomatic Medicine, 48,* 278–282.

Surwit, R. S., Ross, S. L., McCaskill, C. C., & Feinglos, M. N. (1989). Does relaxation therapy add to conventional treatment of diabetes mellitus? *Diabetes, 38*(Suppl. 1), A9.

Surwit, R. S., van Tilburg, M. A. L., Zucker, N., McCaskill, C. C., Parekh, P., Feinglos, M. N., Edwards, C. L., Williams, P., & Lane, J. D. (2002). Stress management improves long-term glycemic control in Type 2 diabetes. *Diabetes Care, 25,* 30–34.

Talbot, F., Nouwen, A., Gingras, J., Belanger, A., & Audet, J. (1999). Relations of diabetes intrusiveness and personal control to symptoms of depression among adults with diabetes. *Health Psychology, 18,* 537–542.

Trief, P. M., Grant, W., Elbert, K., & Weinstock, R. S. (1998). Family environment, glycemic control, and the psychosocial adaptation of adults with diabetes. *Diabetes Care, 21,* 241–245.

Tuomilehto, J., Lindstrom, J., Eriksson, J. G., Valle, T. T., Hamalainen, H., Ilanne-Parikka, P., Keinanen-Kiukaanniemi, S., Laakso, M., Louheranta, A., Rastas, M., Salminen, V., & Uusitupa, M. (2001). Prevention of type 2 diabetes mellitus by changes in lifestyle among subjects with impaired glucose tolerance. *New England Journal of Medicine, 344,* 1343–1350.

Turkinton, R. W. (1980). Depression masquerading as diabetic neuropathy, *Journal of the American Medical Association, 243,* 1147–1150.

U.S. Department of Health and Human Services. (1998). Diabetes: A serious public health problem. *At a Glance,* pp. 1–4. (Washington, DC: Author)

Wang, C. Y., & Fenske, M. M. (1996). Self-care of adults with non-insulin-dependent diabetes mellitus: Influence of family and friends. *The Diabetes Educator, 22,* 465–470.

Wing, R. R., Goldstein, M. G., Acton, K. J., Birch, L. L., Jakicic, J. M., Sallis, J. F., & Smith-West, D. (2001). Behavioral science research in diabetes: Lifestyle changes related to obesity, eating behavior, and physical activity. *Diabetes Care, 24,* 117–123.

Wulsin, L., & Jacobson, A. M. (1989). Visual and psychological function in PDR [abstract]. *Diabetes, 38*(Suppl. 1), A242.

Wulsin, L., Jacobson, A. M., & Rand, L. I. (1987). Psychosocial aspects of diabetes retinopathy. *Diabetes Care, 10,* 367–373.

Wysocki, T., & Buckloh, L. M. (2002). Endocrine, metabolic, nutritional, and immune disorders. In S. Bennett Johnson, N. W. Perry, Jr., & R. H. Rozensky (Eds.), *Handbook of clinical health psychology* (pp. 65–99). Washington, DC: American Psychological Association.

CHAPTER 17

Psycho-oncology

SHULAMITH KREITLER

Cancer is a commonly dreaded disease that is the second leading cause of death in the Western world. The incidence of cancer, especially of specific diagnoses (e.g., breast, melanoma, thyroid, esophagus, liver), has increased during recent years, even when improvements in diagnosis and age-related trends are considered (SEER Program, 2002). If current trends continue, cancer diagnoses are expected to double over the next 50 years (Hoyert, Kochanek, & Murphy, 1999), with more than 1.3 million new cases of cancer diagnosed annually in the United States alone (Garfinkel, 1995).

Cancer denotes a family of diagnoses that may affect different body sites, including the breasts, prostate, lungs, brain, gastrointestinal organs, skin, soft tissues, and blood. It mostly consists of a tumor in a specific site but may spread to other sites (i.e., metastases), and this is one of the reasons why it is commonly considered as a systemic disease. Based on the size of the primary lesion and the spread of the disease at diagnosis, different stages (mostly four with subdivisions) are identified, reflecting increasing severity. In distinction from staging, tumor grading indicates the similarity of the tumor cells to their normal tissue counterparts (based primarily on the degree of differentiation of the malignant cells and secondarily on an estimate of their growth rate). The major treatment modalities are surgery, radiation therapy, chemotherapy, immunomodulation, and bone marrow transplantation. Treatment may last for months and may need to be administered repeatedly. Following the initial diagnosis of the disease and its treatment, remission may set in for differential periods of time. The disease-free interval ends if the disease recurs. Recurrence usually denotes a deterioration but not necessarily death.

Cancer affects individuals of both genders and of all ages and ethnic backgrounds, albeit to different degrees, so that specific cancers may be more prevalent in individuals of a particular gender, ethnic background, geographical area, or age group. The pathogen of cancer has not been identified, although several risk factors are known, ranging from genetic background to more behavioral factors such as smoking, exposure to the sun, contact with particular carcinogens, and diets that may increase the incidence of particular cancers (Garfinkel, 1995).

Psycho-oncology is the discipline of health psychology that deals with the psychological aspects of cancer. It is often considered as one of the most comprehensively studied domains of health psychology. This is probably due to the high levels of distress bound with cancer. Cancer is an anxiety-provoking disease that readily evokes the connotations of suffering and death. For patients, cancer is often associated with considerable physical and psychological suffering (e.g., pain, fatigue, and diverse symptoms that may be debilitating either temporarily or permanently) that may affect most of the domains of their lives and last for long periods. Cancer also poses difficulties for health professionals. In particular, physicians often accompany patients for long periods of time, sometimes without being able to offer the expected and desired recovery or even the required extent of palliation to moderate the patients' pain and suffering. This state of affairs has enhanced awareness for the potential contributions of psychology in oncology and has opened many venues for clinical and research psychologists in this domain.

OVERVIEW OF SPECIAL CRISES AND PROBLEMS

It is of special importance to identify the crisis situations and problems characteristic of cancer patients. These form special foci for intervention and research.

Prevention

Despite knowledge that early diagnosis and treatment of most cancer types facilitates treatment and enhances survival rates, many individuals do not undergo the medically recommended periodical tests for the early detection of cancer and might even overlook early symptoms if these occur. This is mostly due not to lack of information on the part of patients or physicians but rather to psychological factors, such as excessive fear of cancer, that may even reach the level of the psychiatrically meaningful syndrome of cancerophobia (Ingelfinger, 1975), a false sense of physical

security grounded in characteristic attitudes and beliefs, entrenched coping styles of passivity and denial, and preexisting emotional difficulties (Green, Rimer, & Elwood, 1981). As a result, cancer is often diagnosed in a later stage than would have been possible and beneficial for the patient. The delayed diagnosis not only may result in a compromising prognosis but also may have two significant psychological sequelae: sense of guilt and loss of the sense of physical security and confidence (Kreitler, Chaitchik, & Kreitler, 1990). The former reflects thoughts such as the following: "In retrospect, I can see that if I had paid more attention to myself, I could have avoided the catastrophe." The latter reflects thoughts such as the following: "How come I did not know for so long that something is wrong with my body?" and "How could I be sure now that I am not terribly sick, although I feel nothing is wrong?"

Diagnosis

Because of the alarming connotations of cancer, the diagnosis of cancer often has a shocking effect on the patient. Even the mere initiation of a series of tests in response to the patient's complaints may evoke increased anxiety and a sense of life being set "on hold" until the tests are concluded. If the diagnosis of cancer arrives, the shock may be so great that even the risk of suicide cannot be ruled out (Campbell, 1996). This state of increased stress and panic is usually resolved partly through denial and mainly through speeded-up transfer to the stage of treatments in which both the patient and the physician are interested.

Decision Making

Following diagnosis, the patient is often called on to participate in the decisions about the kind of treatment (surgery, kind of surgery, chemotherapy, specific protocol of chemotherapy, radiation, and complementary/alternative treatment, each singly or in combination), the place of treatment (which hospital or clinic and sometimes in which country), and the agent of treatment (which doctor). The tendency to transfer to patients part of the responsibility for the decisions is in accord with the generally increased empowerment of patients. Participating in treatment decisions is often difficult for patients because they mostly do not possess enough expert knowledge in the relevant domains. The difficulty is further increased by the large amounts of information that need to be mastered, the time pressure, the awareness of the momentous importance of the consequences of the involved decisions, the nearly continuous anxiety, and the overall emotional stress. Patients who tend to withdraw from the task of deciding are often exposed to the pressure from friends and family members, who remind the patients of the importance of taking responsibility for their health and may continue to question the recommendations of their doctors and the patients' initial tentative decisions. The problems of decision making may reemerge during later stages of the disease.

Undergoing Treatments

Treatments in oncology are both difficult and mostly protracted. They often include surgery, chemotherapy, and radiation. Surgery may be undertaken for different purposes: diagnostic (i.e., biopsy), therapeutic (i.e., removal of tumor or metastases), reconstructive (e.g., esophagus, bladder, breast), or palliative (e.g., biliary or urethral diversions, pleurodesis or analgesic such as cordotomy). Surgery is often accompanied by intense anxiety, especially if it is diagnostic or results in bodily changes such as stoma, loss of an organ (e.g., breast, limb), loss of a function (e.g., talking, walking), or visible disfigurement (e.g., face, neck). Changes of this kind are often accompanied by changes in body image that reflect on the patient's sense of self-esteem and self-identity (Rapoport, Kreitler,

Chaitchik, Algor, & Weissler, 1993; Sneeuw, Aaronson, & Yarnold, 1992).

Chemotherapy may be administered as a major therapeutic agent for controlling the disease and promoting remission, as adjuvant treatment subsequent to surgery for eradicating presumptive micrometastases, or as neoadjuvant treatment for reducing the tumor prior to surgery. Chemotherapy mostly consists of a combination of drugs that are administered through infusion (or sometimes tablets), in the hospital or clinic (or sometimes at home), according to a certain regimen (e.g., once every 2 or 3 weeks) over months. Chemotherapy may adversely affect the patient's quality of life (QOL). The most salient effects are due to the toxicity of the drugs themselves. Some of these effects are neuropsychological, including dementia, delirium, lethargy, depression, and even psychosis that may be evoked by prednisone as well as delirium following the use of vincristine or cisplatin. In addition, the drugs may cause nausea and vomiting, alopecia (e.g., adriamycin), weight changes (gain or loss), insomnia, gonadal dysfunction, difficulties with concentration and short-term memory, and disorders of fertility and sexuality. The short-term effects are mostly stronger following the administration of the drugs and get weaker after a few days. The side effects together with the generalized weakness and fatigue disrupt the patient's daily routine and render it difficult for the patient to keep up work or carry out planned commitments (Clark & Fallowfield, 1986).

Radiation may be undertaken as a major therapeutic agent, as an adjunct to chemotherapy designed to minimize the chance of recurrence, or for palliative and analgesic purposes. It is often of shorter duration than chemotherapy but may also be accompanied by side effects (e.g., nausea, fatigue, or anorexia, depending on the site, dose, and volume of treatment).

Other frequent treatments include immunotherapy (e.g., interferon), with side effects similar to those of chemotherapy, and bone marrow transplantation, which involves isolation and possible medical complications often accompanied by serious psychological responses (e.g., intense anxiety, psychotic symptoms) (Andrykowski, 1994).

In the course of treatments, the patient is highly vulnerable and needs a lot of support and encouragement to overcome the difficulties. However, getting treatment makes the patient feel that there is hope for recovery, thereby contributing to improving the patient's QOL (Kovner & Kreitler, 1996).

Being a Chronic Cancer Patient in Remission

Although remission is a positive state from the medical point of view, it is not necessarily so psychologically. During the first stage of remission, patients may feel anxious because of the need to learn to function on their own and handle different bodily reactions without the continuous contact with the medical staff that characterized the phase of treatments. Furthermore, patients who have completed a protracted series of treatments start to reconsider whether their lives are satisfying and meaningful enough, especially in view of the suffering they incurred during treatment. In view of the close encounter with death that patients have undergone, they may also experience the pressure to use advantageously the time they have gained by enjoying themselves or doing things they consider relevant and important for themselves. Moreover, anxiety about the possible recurrence of the disease persists. It may be further enhanced by regular follow-up visits to their doctors and is often also maintained by continuous medical treatments (e.g., tamoxifen tablets in breast cancer patients). In addition, patients may feel the need to normalize their interpersonal relations after a period characterized by getting help and social support from relatives and friends. For this reason, as well as because of their desire to reestablish their daily routines, patients may minimize their references to the disease and put on a cheerful mask of "business as usual." This may enhance their isolation and speed up the process of patients' "burnout" (Kreitler & Chaitchik, 1993).

Disease Recurrence and Deterioration

Disease recurrence is a particularly difficult phase for patients because it represents a shattering of their hopes for complete recovery or at least ensured survival. It also indicates the necessity to undergo a series of treatments, some of which may be more difficult than those during the initial phase. The situation may be exacerbated through the appearance of different physical symptoms signaling deterioration. As a result, patients may find it difficult to avoid thinking about death as a real possibility. Hence, fear of death is a theme that occurs with increasing intensity during this phase.

Terminal Stage

Physical symptoms (e.g., pain, fatigue, motor disabilities) as well as psychological symptoms (e.g., disorientation, depression) may turn this phase into a particularly difficult one for patients and their families. One impending problem is the need to decide whether to continue medical treatments, given that their contribution to prolonging life may be small and uncertain and their effect on QOL is negative, or whether to stop treatments altogether and enjoy a certain modicum of QOL that may still be possible. Thus, during this phase, some patients may be getting curative treatments, whereas others may be getting only palliative treatments or none at all. This phase is characteristically marked by the phases of dying, that is, gradual withdrawal from different preoccupations and interests (e.g., work, profession, friends, entertainment) that may be accompanied by gradual physical weakening.

Notably, the different processes described by Kübler-Ross (1969), such as anger and despair, may occur in the course of these phases, but they tend to show up concomitantly, and often together with other processes, rather than in consecutive stages. Other themes that may show up during this stage are confronting death in a personal way, taking leave of beloved ones, and finalizing issues with which patients have dealt in the past (e.g., trying to make up with friends, finishing jobs). However, sometimes patients may be expected, or even pressured by their friends and relatives, to deal with such issues even though they might not feel any tendency to do so.

During recent years, the issues of "physician-assisted suicide" and "right to die" have been increasingly discussed in regard to the terminal stage. On the basis of questionnaire surveys, it seems that about 8% to 25% of oncology patients with advanced disease express interest in death alternatives (Chochinov et al., 1995; Emanuel, Fairclough, Daniels, & Clarridge, 1996), citing mostly reasons such as fear of becoming a burden on their families or of losing dignity, lack of social support (Back, Wallace, Starks, & Pearlman, 1996), disease status, pain, and other bothersome physical symptoms (Massie, Gagnon, & Holland, 1994). In general, the desire for hastened death is more a function of psychological and psychiatric factors, such as depression, than of pain and physical problems (Cherny, 1996).

The desire for hastened death is an issue that deserves consideration apart from the operational implication of aiding the patient to die. The desire is unstable (Chochinov, Tataryn, Clinch, & Dudgeon, 1999), it increases when the patient is lonely and depressed (Rosenfeld, 2000), it decreases after the patient gets social support and exposure to empathic listening (Severson, 1997), and it is not a function of current pain (Emanuel et al., 1996; Sullivan, Rapp, Fitzgibbon, & Chapman, 1997). It is likely that considering the option of euthanasia expresses the patient's need to gain a modicum of control in a situation marked by extreme helplessness. These observations suggest that the desire for hastened death may be a cry for help when basic psychological and physical needs are unmet. Taking care of these needs may well result in a significant decrease in the patient's interest in assisted suicide.

BRIEF OVERVIEW OF RESEARCH IN THE AREA

As noted earlier, psycho-oncology has stimulated much research. This section presents the major domains of research in psycho-oncology. Each subsection includes a brief description of issues and major findings.

Cancer Prevention and Screening

A typical assumption is that at least a third of the cases of cancer could be prevented by controlling behaviors such as smoking, drinking alcohol, prolonged exposure to the sun, and contact with carcinogens. Another assumption is that undergoing regular tests in adherence with the screening regulations for the various cancers (e.g., annual PSA test for men over age 50 years, repeated self-examination of the skin for melanoma or of the breasts for suspicious lumps) could have further reduced the lethality of the disease. Despite increased efforts at information dissemination, prevention and screening have not reached the desirable levels. For example, although the contribution of smoking to cancers of all kinds has been established and is well known, only about half of the smokers have quit smoking, and very low percentages persist in not smoking for longer durations (for 1 year, 1% to 5% of smokers after treatment or self-quitters [Cinciripini, 1995]). The same is true for screening. In regard to breast screening, only about 15% to 30% of women get screened, and even individuals at risk do not comply as required. If screening is done once, it is often not repeated. This cannot be accounted for by the difficulty of performing the screening, given that it is often made very easy, or by forgetfulness, given that health authorities often remind people of their appointments for screening (U.K. Trial of Early Detection of Breast Cancer Group, 1984). Although self-examination is still widely promoted (in regard to breast cancer or melanoma [Berwick, Begg, Fine, Roush, Roush, & Barnhill, 1996; Kreitler et al., 1990]), it is not a reliable method for early detection of cancer and may lead to dangerous delays in diagnosis (Kreitler & Chaitchik, 1995).

A great number of studies have been done to understand the causes of noncompliance and to increase compliance in these areas (e.g., Cinciripini, 1995; DiPlacido, Zauber, & Redd, 1998; Rossi, Blais, Redding, & Weinstock, 1995). Studies have shown that information about risks, benefits, and dangers of doing or avoiding certain behaviors do not suffice for motivating people to comply with the medical recommendations. The health beliefs model assumes that four components play a significant role in screening behavior: beliefs about a person's susceptibility to the disease, beliefs about the severity of the disease, beliefs about the barriers and difficulties of the behavior, and beliefs about the benefits of the behavior (Janz & Becker, 1984). However, these variables often have proved insufficient for predicting or generating the desired behavior and had to be supplemented by various circumstantial factors (e.g., Janz & Becker, 1984; Murray & McMillan, 1993). Some studies suggest that noncompliance with screening may have deeper dynamic roots. First, because higher perceived risk among women with a family history of breast cancer reduces frequency of mammography screening (Polednak, Lane, & Burg, 1991), it is likely that increased fear may deter women from undergoing tests. Accordingly, reducing the anxiety by framing the medical test in a nonthreatening setup

increased attendance (Chaitchik & Kreitler, 1991). Second, women of a specific personality type (e.g., higher on negative emotions, with a restricted self-concept) were found to be more likely than other women to undergo screening tests (Kreitler et al., 1990). Findings of this kind suggest that screening may resemble other behaviors in being controlled by motivational dispositions, for example, in line with the cognitive orientation theory (Kreitler & Kreitler, 1982). This theory assumes that behavior is guided by motivational vectors defined by four types of beliefs (about oneself, reality, norms, and goals) reflecting dynamically meaningful themes rather than by conscious, voluntary, rational decisions reflecting cost-benefit considerations. Identifying the motivationally relevant beliefs enabled the successful prediction of who would undergo screening for breast, colorectal, and cervical cancers (Kreitler, 1998). The prediction for breast cancer held in regard to different populations (e.g., urban, workplace) and different kinds of screening (e.g., induced, spontaneous, personal initiative or not, examination by self or doctor), whereby the best results were obtained with repeated, self-initiated screening by a doctor (Kreitler, Chaitchik, Kreitler, & Weissler, 1994).

Coping and Adaptation

Coping is the general concept that describes strategies for dealing with threat. Strategies of coping are triggered whenever there is a large gap between the extent of the resources appraised by an individual as necessary for handling a situation and the extent of resources appraised as available to the individual (Lazarus & Folkman, 1984). Coping is evoked when the gap in appraised resources is indeed large but less than in the case of despair, often characterized as hopelessness/helplessness, and more than in the case of mere challenge, often experienced as "I could handle it if I tried hard enough." A large variety of coping mechanisms have been identified (e.g., humor, denial, fighting spirit), differing in their contributions to reducing the gap in appraised resources (e.g., social support increases the amount of available resources, humor and denial reduce the amount of required resources). The coping mechanisms used by a cancer patient are not necessarily the same as those used previously by the individual in other situations. Multiple determinants affect the use of one or another coping mechanism, mainly personal predispositions, beliefs and values, previous personal experiences, modeling of others, and the severity of the problems that need to be handled (Rowland, 1989).

There have been numerous attempts to identify the efficacy of coping mechanisms, whereby efficacy is defined in terms of improving the patient's adjustment and QOL. Most prior research suggests that there is no one specific coping mechanism that can be considered as the best because the efficacy of a strategy depends on (a) the individual (e.g., one patient may find comfort through faith and religion, another through emotional support, and another through going back to work [e.g., Schonfield, 1972]) and (b) the stage of the disease and the problems confronting the individual. Thus, the individual changes in the use of different coping mechanisms in the course of different stages of coping with the disease (Buddeberg et al., 1996; Heim, Augustini, Schaffner, & Valach, 1993). In general, the more efficacious coping mechanisms are those focused on solving problems, confronting real-life issues, actively searching for information (Felton & Revenson, 1984; Weisman & Worden, 1976–1977), having emotional discharge (e.g., through humor, through sharing experiences [Penman, 1980]), and cultivating hope and optimism (Scheier & Carver, 2001). The least effective coping mechanisms are those focused on avoidance, passivity, pessimism, yielding, blaming, acting out, apathy, and regrets about the past (O'Malley, Koocher, Foster, & Slavin, 1979).

Concerning the often-discussed mechanism of denial, the most adequate conclusion is that it may be very helpful during specific stages of coping, especially when applied selectively (e.g., to emotions and not to reality appraisal) (Kreitler, 1999). However, it seems warranted to assume that the quantity and variety of coping mechanisms that a person has at his or her disposal constitute a better guarantee for adjustment than does a specific coping mechanism, regardless of how efficacious it may be.

Some studies have investigated the efficacy of coping mechanisms in regard to the course of disease. Efficacy can be assessed in terms of the patient's adjustment. For the most part, results show that low adjustment is significantly related to recurrence (Rogentine et al., 1979) and that better adaptation 1 year after diagnosis is significantly related to fewer recurrences after 3 years and to longer survival in 5- and 7-year follow-ups (Kreitler, Kreitler, Chaitchik, Shaked, & Shaked, 1997). Only one study found that adjustment was unrelated to recurrence (Temoshok & Fox, 1984). However, studies of specific coping mechanisms did not yield clear results about the benefit of any specific coping mechanism in regard to survival. Thus, active behavioral coping was related to survival (Fawzy, Fawzy, & Canada, 2001), but the active means of distraction and problem tacking were unrelated to survival (Buddeberg et al., 1996). Again, hopelessness/helplessness was related to recurrence (Jensen, 1987) but also was unrelated to recurrence and survival (Cassileth, Lusk, Miller, Brown, & Miller, 1985; Cody et al., 1994; Ringdall, 1995). One reason for the lack of clarity of the findings is that in some studies basic medical prognostic criteria, such as the number of affected lymph nodes, were not considered. This was the case in the famous series of the Royal Mardsen studies, which reported that fighting spirit and perhaps denial had a positive effect on survival, whereas stoic acceptance, anxious preoccupation, and hopelessness/helplessness had a negative effect (Greer, Morris, & Pettingale, 1979;

Greer, Morris, Pettingale, & Haybittle, 1990; Morris, Pettingale, & Haybittle, 1992; Pettingale, Morris, Greer, & Haybittle, 1985). The results were not obtained when medical variables were adequately controlled in a replication (Watson, Haviland, Greer, Davidson, & Bliss, 1999).

Quality of Life

Quality of life is defined as the subjective evaluation by the individual of his or her own well-being and functioning in different domains of life. The major characteristics of QOL are that it is subjective (hence, it is assessed by self-reports), based on evaluation, phenomenological (causes not considered), dynamic (changes in line with changes in situations and conditions), and multidimensional (refers to various domains such as physical functioning, eating, sleeping, sex, emotional state, cognitive functioning, family life, social relations, meaning, and coherence in life). QOL differs from functional indexes that assess mainly functioning or ability of the individual to take care of himself or herself in daily life (e.g., Karnofsky's Performance Status Rating). QOL assessments mostly fail to distinguish among groups with different clinical disease statuses or different levels of performance ratings (e.g., Aaronson, Ahmedzai, Bergman, Bullinger, & Cull, 1993; McHorney, Ware, & Raczek, 1993) but are sensitive to effects in different domains of life, for example, in the course of treatments (Ganz & Coscarelli, 1995). The assessment of QOL plays an important role in clinical trials, in decisions about treatments, and in evaluating the costs of treatments in terms of QOL as compared with their contribution to survival (de Haes et al., 2000). One important finding is that QOL tends to maintain a stable optimal level based on the appraised status in the major domains of health, work, and family or social ties. If status in any of these domains is lowered for a longer duration, attempts are made to reinstate the optimal level as much as possible by establishing the new QOL level on improvements and increases in a variety of other domains such as entertainment, dwelling conditions, and meaningfulness of occupation (Kreitler, Chaitchik, Rapoport, Kreitler, & Algor, 1993). This homeostatically grounded tendency is probably also responsible for the increases in levels of QOL (even over the predisease levels) that are sometimes observed in cancer patients who find new venues for creativity and personal growth.

Effect of Psychological Factors on Disease Incidence

The major psychological factors investigated are stressful life events, psychopathology, and personality tendencies. This subsection focuses on each in turn. Table 17.1 presents the basic research designs in this domain.

Stress. Animal models show that stress hastens the onset and further growth of most virally induced tumors and inhibits the onset and growth of nonviral ones (Justice, 1985). But the results of studies investigating the relations of stressful life events and cancer incidence in humans are equivocal. Thus, case-controlled studies have shown that cancer patients, as compared with controls, had more stressful events in their earlier lives (Courtney, Longnecker, Theorell, & Gerhardsson de Verdier, 1993; Geyer, 1991), had the same number of stressful events (Edwards et al., 1990), or had fewer stressful events (Priestman, Priestman, & Bradshaw, 1985). Large-cohort studies have yielded similar results; no relation was found between stressful events earlier in life and cancer morbidity in prisoners of war (Joffres, Reed, & Nomura, 1985; Keehn, 1980; Keehn, Goldberg, & Beebe, 1974) or between stressful events earlier in life and bereaved spouses (Helsing, Comstock, & Szklo, 1982; Kaprio, Koskenvuo, & Rita, 1987), but more cancer

Table 17.1   Basic Designs Used in Studies on the Effect of Psychological Factors on Incidence and Course of Disease in Cancer

Design	Description	Advantages	Shortcomings
Retrospective	Psychological variables are assessed after cancer diagnosis	Large samples and immediate availability of all medical information	Cancer diagnosis may affect reports of premorbid personality and events
Quasi-prospective	Psychological variables are assessed after addressing doctor but prior to diagnosis	No biases of recall of the past; medical information available in short time	Psychological assessments affected by the anxiety of waiting for diagnosis and presentiments
Retro-prospective	Psychological variables are assessed long before cancer diagnosis in a cohort studied for another reason/purpose	No biases of recall of the past; medical information available in short time	Psychological assessments may be biased or not quite relevant
Prospective	Psychological variables are assessed before cancer diagnosis; course of disease is checked in follow-ups	Reliability of baseline data; control of selection biases in sample	Difficulty with follow-ups for prolonged periods of time

SOURCE: For the designs, see Temoshok and Heller (1984).

(melanoma, lymphatic and hematopoietic malignancies) was found over 20 years in parents of accident victims and among parents who had lost sons in the Yom Kippur war in Israel (Levav et al., 2000).

Psychopathology. Earlier studies suggested that schizophrenics tended to get cancer less often than did others. Yet later analyses of the findings showed that the early studies had led to erroneous conclusions because they were based on calculating proportional mortality from cancer instead of absolute mortality rates (Fox, 1978). Studies based on absolute rates show that schizophrenics do not have a reduced rate of cancer (Gulbinat et al., 1992) and that patients diagnosed with reactive psychosis may even have a slightly increased rate of cancer as compared with the general population (Jørgensen & Mortensen, 1992).

Depression is another pathological condition that has been associated with cancer, especially on the evidence of a cohort study at an electric plant in Chicago (Persky, Kempthorne-Rawson & Shekelle, 1987; Shekelle, Raynor, Ostfeld, & Garron, 1981). Yet other cohort studies did not confirm this finding. The combined evidence supported merely a null or weak relationship between depression and risk for cancer (Fox, 1989).

Personality. It has been often claimed that a certain pattern of personality characteristics, Type C, presents a risk for cancer. Type C has been described as compliant, unassertive, submissive, and avoiding the expression of negative emotions, especially of anger (Temoshok, 1987). Studies have supported some Type C tendencies. For example, one study enabled significant identification of cervix cancer patients, as compared with controls, on the basis of high defensiveness and extraversion scores (Kreitler, Levavi, & Bornstein, 1996). Suppression of emotions is the most widely investigated of the Type C tendencies. The studies of this tendency have yielded mixed results. Fox (1998b) reported that five of the main studies supported the tendency, four did not support it, and three had mixed findings. Furthermore, the apparent nonemotionality in cancer patients may be due to their intention to suppress emotions as part of their effort to appease others rather than to an authentic alexithymia (Servaes, Vingerhoets, Vreugdenhil, Keuning, & Broekhuijsen, 1996). Moreover, comparing the repressiveness of women before and after a biopsy for breast cancer and for nonrelevant control surgery showed that before surgery all women had a comparable level of repressiveness (measured by high defensiveness and low anxiety) but that after surgery there was a significant rise in the repressiveness of only those women who were given the diagnosis of cancer (reflecting a rise in defensiveness to combat anxiety) (Kreitler, Kreitler, & Chaitchik, 1993). Hence, it is likely that suppression of emotions subserves the need to control anxiety. However, the theory of cognitive orientation that enables a more extensive approach to measuring personality tendencies relevant for cancer showed that limited expression of emotions may be one of several tendencies included in the profile characterizing specific types of cancer patients. For example, it was found to be part of the profile characterizing colon cancer patients as compared with healthy controls, whereby it is probably not a result of the disease because it does not change with disease duration (Figer, Kreitler, Michal, & Inbar, 2002).

Effect of Psychological Factors on Disease Course and Survival

The main investigated factors were stress, psychopathology, and personality (see also Table 17.1).

Stress. There is no definitive evidence that stress influences the course of cancer or survival rates. For example, no relationship was found between stressful events and breast cancer survival (Barraclough et al., 1992). However, bereavement (losing a son in a war or in a traffic accident) increased the risk of death from different types of cancer, but only if the cancer had been diagnosed before the loss (and not after it) (Levav et al., 2000).

Psychopathology. To date, the evidence concerning the effect of depression is equivocal. One early study indicated higher rates of depression and psychiatric disorders in patients with shorter survival periods (Weisman & Worden, 1975). Another study showed the reverse; long-term survivors were in greater distress, whereas short-term survivors were well adjusted (Derogatis, Abeloff, & Melisaratos, 1979). Still other studies indicated that recurrence and survival in cancer patients are not related to distress (as assessed by the Symptom Checklist-90) (Holland et al., 1986) or to anxiety, depression, and anger (Jamison, Burish, & Wallston, 1987). Indeed, the recent replication of the Royal Mardsen studies showed that depression was the only psychological variable that predicted earlier mortality from cancer, but there were too few cases to make the finding reliable (Watson et al., 1999).

Personality. Of the Type C components, defensiveness was related to shorter survival (Ratcliffe, Dawson, & Walker, 1995) as well as to a particular personality type whose major characteristics are dealing with loss by despair and retaining closeness to people with whom one's relationship has ended (Grossarth-Maticek, Kanazir, Schmidt, & Vetter, 1985). However, the latter study was severely criticized in regard to reliability (Schueler & Fox, 1991; Van der Ploeg, 1991). Concerning emotional suppression, the findings are unclear; Fox (1998b) found three studies with positive results, three with negative results, and three with mixed results. There is also evidence of no correlation of psychosocial variables to recurrence or survival (Cassileth et al., 1985).

The cognitive orientation theory has enabled identifying a set of characteristics (e.g., readiness to expose a person's weaknesses, self-confidence, low seeking of approval, low obsessiveness and compulsiveness) that differentiated significantly between patients with recurrence and those without recurrence at 3 years follow-up and survival at 5 years onward. During the initial years, psychological factors contributed less to predicting survival than did medical factors, but the former's relative and absolute impacts increased with time (Kreitler et al., 1997).

In conclusion, there are two main reasons why most of the findings examining the impact of psychological factors on survival have been unclear. One is disregard for the fact that prognosis of survival should consider conjointedly medical and psychological factors. The second is the tendency to narrow research down to a specific set of psychological variables rather than to expand the search for new psychological variables by applying new methodologies.

Social Relations and Support

It has long been surmised that the social environment in which people function affects cancer incidence and prognosis. The question of whether social ties affect cancer incidence has been studied by examining two aspects of social relations: static-descriptive aspects (i.e., marital status and number of social ties) and active-functional aspects (i.e., extent of participation and involvement in social relations). In regard to cancer incidence, various studies found that married people had a lower incidence of cancer (Reynolds & Kaplan, 1990), that they had a higher incidence of cancer (Zonderman, Costa & McCrae, 1989), and that the findings probably varied with cancer site, gender, and ethnicity (e.g., Swanson, Belle, & Satariano, 1985). No effect of marriage on

recurrence was found (Burman & Margolin, 1992). In regard to survival, studies showed a small effect of better survival for married women (Goodwin, Hunt, Key, & Samet, 1987), but only when they are young (Neale, Tilley, & Vernon, 1986) and not for older women (Cassileth, Walsh, & Lusk, 1988). However, there is also evidence of shorter survival for married women (Ell, Nishimoto, Mediansky, Mantell, & Hamovitch, 1992) and of no relation between survival and being married (e.g., Dean & Surtees, 1989). The results are inconsistent, possibly because cancer site, gender, and quality of marriage have not been considered.

In regard to size of social network, studies show no relation to incidence (Reynolds & Kaplan, 1990), recurrence (Cassileth et al., 1985), or survival (Vogt, Mullooly, Ernst, Pope, & Hollis, 1992). In contrast, active social participation and active involvement have a positive effect on reduced recurrence (Hislop, Waxler, Coldman, Elwood, & Kan, 1987) and on longer survival (Vogt et al., 1992), more so with friends than with relatives (Waxler-Morrison, Hislop, Mears, & Kan, 1991).

Cancer patients often refer to their need for emotional support, which is widely believed to positively affect the course of disease. In one study, perceived family support did not predict recurrence (Levy, Herberman, Lippman, D'Angelo, & Lee, 1991). However, shorter survival was related to feeling isolated and lonely (only in women) and to having few contacts (in men) (Reynolds & Kaplan, 1990) as well as to having a high need for emotional support (Stavraky, Donner, Kincade, & Stewart, 1988), whereas longer survival was related to perceived adequacy of family support (Stavraky et al., 1988) and to getting adequate emotional support (only in women) (Ell et al., 1992). It is likely that social participation positively affects survival and disease progression because it hastens diagnosis (Neale et al., 1986) and promotes compliance with treatment (Richardson, Shelton, Krailo, & Levine, 1990).

There are often cited studies that supposedly support the effects of social support interventions on survival. The best known is the Stanford University study that claimed an additional 18 months of life for advanced breast cancer patients who got social support as compared with controls (Spiegel et al., 1999). However, the study was criticized for methodological reasons, mainly sample choice and differences between the two groups (Fox, 1998a; Kogon, Biswas, Pearl, Carlson, & Spiegel, 1997) and failed to be replicated (Goodwin et al., 2001; Spiegel et al., 1999). Methodological criticism was also leveled against other studies in regard to the effects of social support (Gellert, Maxwell, & Siegel, 1993; Morgenstern, Gellert, Walter, Ostfeld, & Siegel, 1984). In contrast, many studies show clearly the beneficial effect of social support on patients' QOL (e.g., Bloom, 1986; Dunkel-Schetter, 1984; Spiegel et al., 1999).

Future research in social support could benefit from considering the following: (a) the differential effects of various types of social support (e.g., informational, emotional), (b) the source of support (e.g., relatives, health professionals), and (c) the dependence of the need for support on personality and availability (Dunkel-Schetter, 1984).

Family

The family is involved in psycho-oncology in different aspects. First, the family is a provider of care for the patient (e.g., providing emotional support, getting information, offering help in decision making, giving concrete help, sharing financial costs, meeting social needs and costs, maintaining routine) (Lederberg, 1998). Second, the family undergoes serious changes due to the patient's disease and the involved stresses (e.g., changes in routines, roles, attachment relationships, manner of functioning, structure, and sense of well-being) (Weihs & Reiss, 1995). Third, specific family members may be exposed to special stresses (e.g., children of sick parents, parents of sick children regardless of the children's ages, partners of patients) (Keller, Henrich, Sellschopp, & Beutel, 1995; Koch, Härter, Jakob, & Siegrist, 1995). Fourth, the family is exposed to severe stresses due to the patient's sickness and everything else it involves, including the changes in daily routine and roles, the threat of impending death, and/or conflicts with the medical staff (Jacobs, Ostroff, & Steinglass, 1998). Families vary greatly in the manner in which they cope with the difficulties and respond to the stresses. Some mobilize resources and are even strengthened, whereas others disintegrate. Some families provide support or solve problems, whereas others are hostile or withdrawn (Kissane, Block, McKenzie, McDowall, & Nitzan, 1998). The state of the family is an important factor in the patient's well-being, not least because the family is a serious provider of care to the patient. The family's coping depends on several factors such as how it interprets external reality and defines its identity (Jacobs et al., 1998) as well as the degrees of communication, emotional expressiveness, and cohesion in the family (Kissane et al., 1998). There is a growing awareness in health professional circles that family members deserve special psychological support so that they can withstand adequately the hard and prolonged stresses of cancer, provide the patient with an adequate environment, and avoid turning into "second-order patients" (Jacobs et al., 1998).

Getting Information and Truth Telling

Information about diagnosis, prognosis, and treatment is one of the most central issues for the cancer patient. Its importance has been enhanced by the tendency during past generations to keep the diagnosis secret and by the current tendency to involve the patient in decisions about treatments. Information is a theme that occurs primarily during the first phase of the disease but that continues to play an important role in the further phases of the disease, mainly whenever there is a recurrence, a need to decide about treatment options, or any change in the disease, down to the preterminal and terminal phases. The kind, amount, meaning, and disclosure of information change during the different stages of the disease. Patients often use multiple sources of information that vary in completeness and reliability such as physicians (first and second opinions), nurses, social workers, psychologists, other patients, relatives, friends, the Internet, and the media (Kreitler, Chaitchik, Rapoport, & Algor, 1995). Some patients find it difficult to understand the information and its implications, to evaluate the sources, and to integrate them, especially when there are inconsistencies. Some patients (13% during initial phases to 57% during later phases) may tend to renounce the effort to deal with the information and decide to rely instead on their primary oncologists. However, this response often calls forth pressure of family members and friends on the patient to be empowered and actively involved in getting information. Getting information may turn into a coping mechanism for patients (Watson et al., 1988) but also for caretakers who feel that they will be best able to help the patient in this way. This is probably due to the fact that dealing with information may give rise to the feeling or illusion of having control over the disease.

Studies show that patients often view the amount of information they got from their doctors as less than the amount the doctors estimate they have transmitted (Chaitchik, Kreitler, Schwartz, Shaked, & Rosin, 1992). There is also a difference in the kind of information expected and that obtained. Patients often expect to get information about whether their doctors believe the treatment will help them, what their real states are, whether they are about to die, and how long they have to live. In contrast, the information they get refers to diagnosis, stage, grade, and percentages of remission following different treatments. Hence, patients are often frustrated. Another complicating factor is the conflict that many patients experience among the kind of information they want to get (e.g., good news), the kind they think they should get (e.g., how long they have to live), and the kind they get (e.g., facts about diagnosis and prognosis). Moreover, patients may be reluctant to ask for information they want or think they are entitled to get because they believe that their doctors know best what is good for them, so that if the doctors did not provide that information, it is probably not good for the patients to have it (Chaitchik et al., 1992; Kreitler, Chaitchik, Kovner, & Kreitler, 1992).

After getting the relevant information, the major issue becomes living with the information. For example, a study with head and neck patients showed that those who had a large amount of information had improved relations with family members and friends but functioned less well at work and suffered from anxiety about their medical state, those who had a little information had tense and poorer relations with family members and friends but functioned well at work and did not suffer from undue anxiety, and those who had a medium amount of information had tense relations with others as well as problems with work and anxiety (Kreitler et al., 1995).

Another aspect of information in cancer patients concerns the communication of information by the patient to others. Patients are often concerned with issues such as how much and which information about their states of health to disclose, to whom, and when. Considerations include not wanting to bother others or to burden them emotionally, preserving patients' self-esteem, avoiding the pity of others, and maintaining patients' denial of the disease. Notably, one study showed that even spouses of cancer patients know relatively little about what cancer patients experience and know, indicating a low degree of communication (Chaitchik et al., 1992).

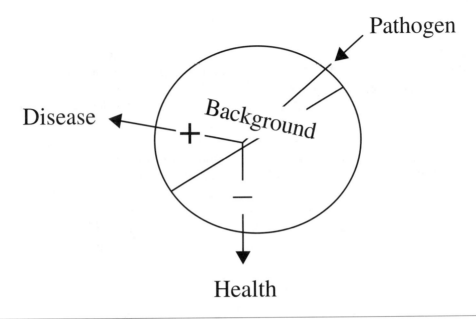

Figure 17.1   The Stimulus-Background Model of Disease

Genetic Testing and Counseling

The spectacular advances of genetic research have increased the importance of three categories of genetic determinants related to cancer: (a) cytogenetics, which concerns abnormal chromosomes; (b) single-gene traits, which concern hereditary mutations (e.g., *BRCA1*); and (c) ecogenetics, which concerns gene and environment interactions (e.g., Epstein-Barr virus causing lymphoma in individuals with specific genes). Genetic information may have serious psychological effects, including anxiety and stress in healthy and sick individuals as well as in their children. Studies have shown that individuals at risk might not undergo screening, especially if their fear is high. Furthermore, their readiness to participate in health-promoting procedures, including prophylactic treatment, depends on their anxiety, education, and beliefs about their likelihood of getting sick (Kash & Lerman, 1998).

Models of the Problem

Models in psycho-oncology about the etiology and prognosis of cancer form part of the more encompassing approach of biopsychosocial medicine, which has replaced the more limited approach of biomedical medicine and assumes that psychological factors are involved in physical disorders. Thus, in regard to disease incidence, it is assumed that each disease is caused by some pathogen (e.g., microbe, virus, material with detrimental effects for the organism such as radioactivity or carcinogens). As illustrated in Figure 17.1, the effect of the pathogen is not automatic; rather, it depends on background factors such as the organism's genetic tendencies, nutritional state, immune system, comorbidity, psychological factors, and characteristics specific to the particular disease (e.g., lipids and blood pressure in cardiological disorders). Likewise, the effect of the treatment on recovery is not automatic; rather, it depends on background factors that are of

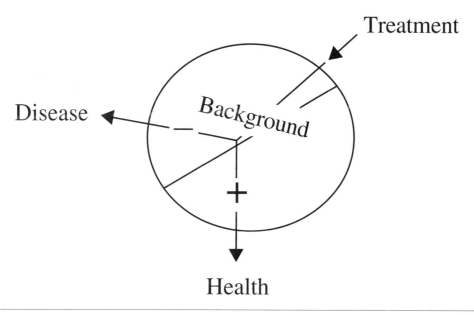

Figure 17.2 The Stimulus-Background Model of Recovery

similar categories as the factors relevant for disease occurrence (Figure 17.2). Notably, background factors always include psychological factors, but their role and extent of impact may vary in the case of different diseases and perhaps also across individuals.

Most of the etiological models in psycho-oncology are based on psychoneuroimmunology (Bovbjerg & Valdimarsdottir, 1998; Goodkin & Visser, 2000). According to this discipline, the causal matrix consists of a multiplicity of factors derived from different domains, mainly the neurological, immune, endocrinological, and psychosocial domains. However, the models differ in the interactions assumed among the factors, in the nature of the embedded causal links, in the emphasis placed on factors of different domains, and in the manner in which the different factors are structured and positioned in relation to one another. Most often, the immune system is placed in a central position and the rest of the factors are considered insofar as they affect immunological parameters (Finn, 2001;

Garssen & Goodkin, 1999). The effect of psychological factors on cancer is assumed to be through the immune system (Bovbjerg & Valdimarsdottir, 1998). However, because the overall effect of the immune system on tumor growth appears to be moderate on the whole, a variety of pathways are explored to account for the effects of psychological factors. One such pathway is infections, to which cancer patients may be particularly vulnerable and which form the major cause of cancer-related deaths (Bovbjerg & Valdimarsdottir, 1998; White, 1993). Two other likely pathways are stress, which functions through alterations in the hypothalamic–pituitary–adrenal axis and the hypothalamic–sympathetic–medullary axis (Kiecolt-Glaser & Glaser, 1999), and depression, which functions through alterations in the hypothalamic–pituitary–adrenal axis, the hypothalamic–pituitary–thyroid axis, and the hypothalamic–growth hormone axis (Musselman, McDaniel, Porter, & Nemeroff, 1998). Notably, it has been suggested that more weight should be attributed to psychological factors in psychoneuroimmunology to gain a better understanding of the immune effects on cancer and evidence of the full extent of the immunological impact on cancer incidence and progression (Bovbjerg & Valdimarsdottir, 1998).

DIAGNOSTIC AND ETIOLOGICAL ISSUES

Clinical Description

A great number of studies have examined the prevalence of mental health disorders in cancer patients. According to a review based on the findings of the first cooperative group organized for the study of these issues, 53% of cancer patients had "normal responses to cancer," whereas 47% had different psychiatric diagnoses: 32% adjustment disorders with symptoms of depression and anxiety, 6% major depression, 4% organic mental disorders (dementia or delirium), and 5% preexisting psychiatric disorders (3% personality disorders, 2% anxiety disorders) (Derogatis et al., 1983). Of all psychiatric disorders observed, 89% were related to the disease and the treatments, whereas only 11% represented prior psychiatric problems. Other studies, using various assessment instruments and criteria, reported 14% to 31% of cancer survivors with psychiatric diagnoses (for a review, see Kornblith, 1998). The estimates of the reviewed studies resemble the earlier estimate, considering that adjustment disorders are an intermediary state between normal coping under stress and pathology.

The prevalence of *adjustment disorders* is due to the special stresses of cancer: the duration and difficulties of treatments, the side effects of treatments, the fear of recurrence, the impairment of body image, and so on. Adjustment disorders are more frequent during the early phases of cancer and often subside with time or evolve into another diagnosis. In one study with adult patients, after 5 years,

71% were completely symptom free, whereas 21% had deteriorated into major depression or alcoholism (Andreasen & Hoenk, 1982).

Depressive symptoms are the most frequent kind of mental health problem in cancer patients. The estimates of their prevalence range from 1% to 53% in the various studies (DeFlorio & Massie, 1995). The reasons for the variation are differences in the tools of assessment, in the diagnoses (e.g., major depression, unipolar depression, dysthymic disorder), in the group of cancer patients in which depression is assessed (e.g., pancreatic, breast), and in the phase of the disease in which depression is assessed (e.g., preliminary, advanced). The tools of assessment vary in the ways in which they solve the problem of overlap in symptoms between depression proper and cancer (i.e., the disease and its treatments). There are four major approaches to this issue: (a) the inclusive (counts all symptoms regardless of origin), (b) the etiological (counts only symptoms due to depression proper), (c) the substitutive (replaces indeterminate symptoms such as fatigue with cognitive symptoms such as brooding), and (d) the exclusive (eliminates all symptoms due to the disease or treatment and uses other depression criteria). The narrower the definition, the lower the observed prevalence of depression. On the whole, depression is also quite frequent in other medically sick people, with its prevalence ranging from 5% to 55% (Popkin & Tucker, 1992).

Of the varieties of depression, the most prevalent in cancer patients is depressed mood coupled with a general adjustment disorder, followed by unipolar depression. Depression is higher in some cancer diagnoses than in others, for example, breast cancer survivors versus testis cancer survivors (Gritz, Wellisch, & Landsverk, 1988; Sneeuw et al., 1992). Advanced disease stage is often correlated with more depression. The factors contributing to depression in cancer patients include disabling symptoms, lower Karnovsky scores, uncontrolled pain, exhaustion/fatigue, metabolic abnormalities (e.g., anemia, hypercalcemia), endocrinological abnormalities (e.g., hyper- or hypothyroidism), different chemotherapeutic agents (e.g., vincristine, vinblastine), diverse medications (e.g., steroids, interferon, interleukin-2), and psychosocial characteristics (e.g., recent loss of spouse or friend, poor social support, previous psychopathology) (Massie & Popkin, 1998).

Although the total number of cancer patients who commit suicide is low, the risk of suicide in cancer patients is double that in the general population (Campbell, 1996). Factors correlated with the risk for suicide include gender (being male [in adults], being female [in adolescents]), site of cancer (particularly oral, pharyngeal, and lung cancers), medical state (e.g., advanced disease, poor prognosis, suffering due to pain and fatigue), and preexisting psychopathology (e.g., suicide attempts, psychosis). Suicide ideation seems to be much more frequent than suicide intent or actual suicide attempts (Breitbart, 1990). Suicidal thoughts expressed during preterminal stages also are often not steady; may subside when patients get empathy and social support. Suicidal ideation of patients may at times express primarily their desire for control, their need to test their relatives, and/or attempts to reduce their fear of death (Kreitler & Merimsky, in press).

The prevalence of *anxiety disorders* in cancer patients is probably higher than in other medical conditions but its extent is uncertain due to varying criteria, assessment instruments, and samples. Estimates vary from 15% to 28% (Carroll, Kathol, Noyes, Wald, & Clamon, 1993). There are no consistent findings about the gender, cancer site, age, and marital status correlates of anxiety. Anxiety appears to increase in the course of treatments (surgery and chemotherapy) and particularly with the advance of disease. It may be viewed as a more or less constant accompaniment of the different vicissitudes of the disease.

Anxiety may also be evoked by different metabolic states (e.g., hypocalcemia, hypoglycemia), hormone-secreting tumors, and various drugs (e.g., corticosteroids). Its manifestations include emotional lability, tension, fear, dependence, withdrawal, and an enhanced tendency to become nauseous (Noyes, Holt, & Massie, 1998).

During recent years, increasing attention has been devoted to posttraumatic stress disorder (PTSD) in cancer patients and survivors. Research was spurred particularly by the high prevalence of avoidant and intrusive symptoms in this population (Greenberg, Goorin, Gebhardt, Petersen, & Hirji, 1994). In some studies, up to 44% of patients reported PTSD-like symptoms (Cordova et al., 1995). Yet only 4% to 10% of cancer survivors actually met criteria for a diagnosis of PTSD (Alter et al., 1996), as compared with 25% to 33% of individuals exposed to traumatic events (Yehuda, Resnick, Kahana, & Giller, 1993). One important result of PTSD is that it renders recurrent exposures to medical tests and treatments more difficult emotionally for patients.

Of particular importance are *neuropsychiatric effects* due to side effects of chemotherapeutic agents or abnormal metabolic states often observed in cancer patients. For example, 5-fluorouracil may cause memory loss and confusional episodes; ifosfamide may cause hallucinations, somnolence, and mutism (Tuxen & Hansen, 1994); interferon alpha may cause agitation, emotional lability, and personality change (Quesada, Talpaz, Rios, Kurzrock, & Gutterman, 1986); and hypo- or hypercortisolism and hypo- or hypercalcemia may cause depression, delirium, and dementia (Fleishman, Lesko, & Breitbart, 1993).

Typical Etiologies

In trying to understand the psychological state or reactions of cancer patients, it is always recommended to apply a broad multidisciplinary approach and to assume interactions of factors of diverse domains. For example, the causes of anorexia, a typical symptom in cancer patients (Lesko, 1993), may be disease related (e.g., early stages of pancreatic or gastrointestinal cancer, tumor obstruction in advanced disease, uremia, anemia) or treatment related (e.g., radiation that may cause malabsorption of food, nausea, or changes in taste of nutrients; chemotherapy that may cause stomatitis of the alimentary canal or frequent diarrhea; analgesic drugs that may cause constipation and appetite loss; surgery [e.g., esophagectomy, gastrectomy] that may cause chewing and swallowing difficulties). Further contributors to anorexia are psychological factors such as depression, hopelessness/helplessness, withdrawal, anxiety, and perhaps patient burnout coupled with an unconscious desire to hasten death. Also to be considered are preexisting psychological tendencies, such as expressing noncompliance or dissatisfaction by diminished eating, certain food aversions, or phobia of obesity, that may be evoked by responses to steroids. Finally, it is not uncommon for patients to believe, on their own or following some esoteric "alternative" or dietary treatment, that they can "starve the cancer to death" by avoiding eating. Similarly complex etiologies are to be considered in regard to depression, fatigue, lethargy, anxiety, and other common symptoms in cancer patients.

ASSESSMENT AND TREATMENT

Assessment

The major assessments in psycho-oncology are focused on evaluating psychological distress, QOL, physical symptoms, and cognitive state.

Psychological Distress. Evaluating or screening for current or future psychological distress is of great importance in view of the relative paucity of professional psycho-oncologists and sometimes the reluctance of patients to admit to their psychological distress because they may regard it as a sign of weakness. The evaluations are usually based on a structured interview or self-report measures. The best known is the package referred to as Omega Screening Instruments, which is a structured interview combined with a self-report measure. It enables constructing the patient's profile on the basis of his or her responses to questions about past history (e.g., mental health, substance abuse) and social support (e.g., marriage, church), answers to the Inventory of Current Concerns, and demographic facts (Weisman, Worden & Sobel, 1980). The four measures that are commonly used and are most reliable among the self-report tools are the Brief Symptom Inventory (BSI) (Derogatis, 1993), which consists of 53 items and provides scores on 10 scales (e.g., hostility, anxiety, paranoia) and 3 global scores (Global Severity Index, Positive Symptom Distress Index, and Positive Symptom Total); the Profile of Mood States (POMS) (McNair, Lorr, & Droppelman, 1971), which consists of 65 items and provides scores on 6 scales (e.g., anger-hostility, tension-anxiety) and 1 global score (Total Mood Disturbance); the Hospital Anxiety and Depression Scale (HADS) (Johnson et al., 1995), which consists of 14 items and provides scores on 2 scales (anxiety and depression); and the Medical Outcomes Study Short Form Health Survey (MOS SF-36) (McHorney et al., 1993), which consists of 36 items and provides scores on 8 scales (e.g., physical, pain, social, vitality).

Quality of Life. Major assessment instruments of QOL include the European Organization for Research and Treatment of Cancer (EORTC), which is based largely on particular modules for different cancer diseases (Aaronson et al., 1993); the Functional Assessment of Cancer Therapy (FACT) scale (Cella et al., 1993), which is also based on specific modules for each cancer disease and requests evaluation of extent to which QOL was affected by the disease in each domain of life; and the Cancer Rehabilitation Evaluation System (CARES) (Ganz, Coscarelli Schag, Kahn, Petersen, & Hirji, 1993) and MOS 36-item short form health survey (McHorney et al., 1993), both of which include diverse scales for the assessment of specific domains in addition to the more physical one.

Physical Symptoms. The assessment of physical symptoms may be part of the assessment of QOL or independent of it. Most often, it is based on self-report symptom checklists that refer to multiple or single symptoms. Two examples of multiple symptom tools are the Memorial Symptom Assessment Scale (MSAS), which refers to 32 physical and psychological symptoms (e.g., feeling nervous, lack of energy)—each rated in terms of intensity, frequency, and distress—and provides scores on a Global Distress Index and the two physical and psychological subscales (Portenoy et al., 1994), and the Rotterdam Symptom Checklist, which refers to 30 physical and psychological symptoms, assesses their impact on physical activity and function, and provides the same scores as does the MSAS (de Haes, van Kippenberg, & Neijt, 1990).

Examples of frequently used tools that measure specific symptoms include the Brief Pain Inventory (BPI) (Daut, Cleeland, & Flanery, 1983), which assesses pain history, intensity, location, quality, and interference with overall functioning; the McGill Pain Questionnaire (MPQ) (Melzack, 1975), which evaluates through verbal descriptors the sensory, affective, and evaluative dimensions of pain; the 20-item Multidimensional Fatigue Inventory (MFI) (Smets, Garssen, Bonke, & de Haes, 1995); and the Visual Analogue Scale (VAS) for dyspnea (Borg, 1982).

Cognitive State. Some of the tools for assessing mental state focus on cognitive deficits, whereas others deal more specifically with delirium and confusional states. The Cognitive Capacity Screening Examination (CCSE) (Jacobs, 1977), which screens for organic mental syndromes, and the Mini-Mental State Exam (MMSE) (Folstein, Fetting, Lobo, Niaz, & Capozolli, 1984), which is the standard mental state instrument, are based on examining basic processes such as orientation in time and place, instantaneous recall, short-term memory, simple number calculations, and the use of language. The Neurobehavioral Cognitive Status Examination (NCSE) (Kiernan, Mueller, Langston, & Van Dyke, 1987) assesses level of consciousness, orientation, attention, and five major ability areas (language, constructions, memory, calculations, and reasoning). More specific delirium assessment tools, based on clinicians' ratings, include the Delirium Rating Scale, with 10 items based on DSM-III (*Diagnostic and Statistical Manual of Mental Disorders,* third edition [American Psychiatric Association, 1988]) criteria scanning diverse aspects such as perceptual disturbance, psychomotor behavior, hallucinations, and lability of mood (Trzepacz, Baker, & Greenhouse, 1988), and the Memorial Delirium Assessment Scale, with 10 items based on DSM-IV (American Psychiatric Association, 1994) criteria scanning disturbances in arousal and consciousness as well as in cognitive functioning and psychomotor activity (Breitbart et al., 1997).

Goals of Treatment

There are a great many psycho-oncological interventions with a diversity of goals. Most are tailored to the specific needs and benefits of the patients. The main six goals of interventions are crisis overcoming, problem solving, patient education, adjustment, medical survival, and prevention. The first five deal with treating the patients and sometimes also family members. The sixth targets primarily the population at large.

Crisis overcoming is designed to help the patient through the most difficult physical and psychological phases of the disease and treatment process. It is a kind of "psychological first aid" and consists in applying a variety of procedures geared to resolve the specific emergency situation at hand (e.g., breakdown due to disclosure of the diagnosis or finding out about disease recurrence, suicide intent, withdrawal from treatment). Stress, emotional intensity of reactions, immense fear, and a sense of being unable to go on or of having been beaten are some of the characteristics of a crisis. Resolving the crisis satisfactorily may help to prevent later stress reactions, adjustment disorders, PTSD, and further crises. When the crisis is the patient's death, the intervention may be focused on the family members and is sometimes called "grief counseling."

Problem solving is designed to help the patient solve typical disease- or treatment-related problems such as whether or how to tell others (e.g., parents, partner, children, colleagues at work) about the disease or its recurrence and whether to go on working during chemotherapy. Some of the patient's problems may have existed before the disease but were exacerbated through it (e.g., family tensions concerning partner behavior or finances).

Patient education is designed to provide the patient with information and skills to enable optimal use of medical resources and services (e.g., getting services such as psychological help, sex counseling, tax deductions, and social benefits) while minimizing harassment and different avoidable difficulties. It also includes skills at getting and evaluating medical information, assistance in clarifying misperceptions and misinformation, and suggestions for improving doctor-patient communication.

Adjustment is designed to reduce as much as possible the patient's psychological distress in the course of treatment or remission periods by controlling anxiety and depression on a long-term basis; reducing feelings of loneliness, isolation, and hopelessness; improving coping skills; raising the level of QOL; and possibly even promoting personal growth and

happiness beyond the levels attained prior to the disease. Living with cancer and living well are the goals of adjustment.

Medical survival is focused on using psychological processes to improve the patient's chances for longer survival or to extend the disease-free intervals. Sometimes, this goal is considered as strengthening the patient's immune system (Finn, 2001).

Prevention is focused on reducing the prevalence of cancer by enhancing compliance with screening guidelines in the population at large, and particularly in individuals at risk, and by modifying behaviors that increase the risk of cancer (e.g., improper diet, exposure to the sun, use of tobacco) (Cohen & Baum, 2001).

Types of Treatment

There are great variety of psychological treatments applied in the framework of psycho-oncology. Often, more than one are used conjointly or within the same setup. The major types of interventions are counseling, dynamic psychotherapy, cognitive therapy, behavioral therapy, existential therapy, psychoeducational therapy, group therapy, social support, art therapy, and guided imagery. Although the names of most of these interventions are familiar from other domains in psychology, their application in psycho-oncology is specific in several respects. First, treatments are focused on the disease with the more or less implicit assumption that the major goal is to minimize the distress occasioned by the disease and the treatments. Second, another implicit assumption is that if it were not for the cancer, the patient would not be exposed to that particular psychological intervention. Third, interactions between psychological and physiological processes constitute an integral part of the treatment, sometimes as a focal theme (e.g., in the life-extending therapies) and other times merely as a fact that is taken into consideration (e.g., in treating insomnia, the chemotherapeutic agents that the patient is getting are considered).

Two major modes of treatment are individual therapy and group therapy. Individual therapy is more costly in resources but is tailored better to the needs of the specific patient and shields him or her against the anxieties evoked by the vicissitudes in the state of other patients (i.e., downward comparisons) and against the tendency to devote himself or herself too much to helping others. For objective reasons, individual therapy may be the only option for patients with advanced disease. Group therapy is more economical, enjoys a good "reputation" in many communities, and may be less threatening for patients (Helgeson, Cohen, Schulz, & Yasco, 2001).

Each of the major kinds of treatment has been used for attaining the different goals of treatments. Thus, group therapy has been used for life extension, adjustment, and psychoeducational purposes (Fawzy & Fawzy, 1998; Spira, 1998), and art therapy has been used for adjustment and vocation of self-healing potentialities (Luzzatto & Gabriel, 1998).

The major therapeutic components or processes used in the various treatments are getting the support of others (e.g., patients, health professionals), eliminating mainly negative affect, sharing one's experiences with others, learning coping skills, facing one's fears (including fears of suffering, pain, and death), overcoming despair and strengthening hope, gaining a better understanding of oneself and one's responses, gaining a better understanding of the situation (e.g., the disease, treatments), strengthening one's sense of control, and gaining a modicum of control over one's symptoms. Some of these elements are stronger in some of the treatments; for example, getting support is often stronger in group therapy, whereas gaining a better understanding of oneself and one's responses is more salent in individual therapy.

There exist some better-known treatment protocols, mainly Spiegel's supportive-expressive therapy (Spiegel & Diamond, 2002) and Fawzy's psychoeducational intervention (Fawzy et al., 2001). Each is based on using the components mentioned previously in a more or less structured manner. Thus, Spiegel's group therapy is based on supporting other patients and receiving support from them, getting family support, getting social support, improving emotional expression, detoxifying death, reordering life priorities, facilitating communication with one's physician, and controlling symptoms (by self-hypnosis, meditation, biofeedback, etc.). Fawzy's psychoeducational intervention is based on getting health education (being informed about cancer), managing stress (identifying sources of stress, identifying one's reactions to stress, and controlling these reactions by hypnosis, relaxation, guided imagery, etc.), learning coping skills (using problem-solving techniques based on promoting the active approach and weakening avoidance coping), and getting psychological support from the staff.

There are four major therapeutic orientations used in the various treatments: the dynamic approach, the cognitive-behavioral approach, the existential approach, and the cognitive orientation approach. The dynamic approach is rooted in classical psychotherapy, so that it is based on applying transference and countertransference, exploring the patient's past, interpreting dreams and free associations, and using a specific structure of interplay between contents and process (Sourkes, Massie, & Holland, 1998). The cognitive-behavioral approach emphasizes the acquisition of skills (thoughts, beliefs, or behaviors) that enable controlling symptoms, mainly stress, pain, and anxiety. The most often used means are hypnosis, relaxation, systematic desensitization, guided imagery, and coping self-statements (Jacobsen & Hann, 1998). The existential approach is based on exploring the function, role, and meaning of the lives of humans in general and the life of the patient in particular while examining the authenticity of assumptions about oneself and the world in the framework of one's culture and society (Spira, 2000). Finally, the cognitive orientation

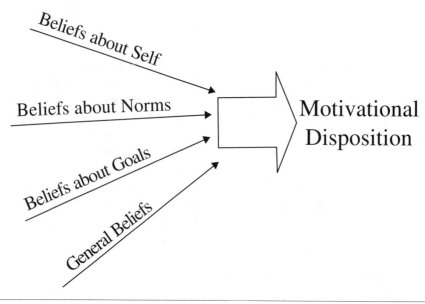

Figure 17.3 Formation of the Motivational Disposition ("behavioral intent") According to Cognitive Orientation Theory

approach is based on the assumption that any behavior—emotional, motor, cognitive, or physiological—is the product of a motivational disposition expressing the general direction of the behavior (formed as a vector based on four types of beliefs reflecting underlying meanings) and an operational program implementing the actual performance (Figure 17.3). In the case of physical disorders, the motivational disposition reflects the directionality inherent in specific themes unique for each disorder, whereas the operational program is the set of physiological processes underlying the pathological process (Kreitler & Kreitler, 1991). The treatment consists in strengthening the specific themes expressing health rather than the tendency toward the disorder.

Most treatments report effects in terms of reducing patients' distress and improving their emotional well-being (Fawzy & Fawzy, 1998; Fawzy et al., 2001; Jacobsen & Hann, 1998). The effects of the treatments on survival are less clear. Spiegel and colleagues (1999) initially reported a remarkable effect of their intervention on prolonging survival.

However, as noted earlier, their study had serious methodological shortcomings (Fox, 1998a; Kogon et al., 1997) and failed to be replicated (Goodwin et al., 2001; Spiegel et al., 1999). The replications showed that the intervention proved to affect only patients' mood (Goodwin et al., 2001; Spiegel et al., 1999) and did this for only a short duration (Edmonds, Lockwood, & Cunningham, 1999).

Fawzy and colleagues (2001) showed that their intervention had positive effects on immune system parameters 6 months after treatment, but the effects did not differ significantly between the intervention and control groups after 1 year. Furthermore, when the treatment and Breslow depth were used together as predictors, treatment did not predict recurrence of disease but instead predicted survival. The results were explained as due to better adjustment and coping in the experimental group. However, the number of participants was very small (3 were dead and 31 were alive in the experimental group, and 10 were dead and 24 were alive in the control

CASE STUDY

"S. M." was a 37-year-old woman, married with three daughters, who was diagnosed with melanoma (Stage IIb) in the cervix. She underwent surgery and was prescribed a course of chemotherapy. She kept delaying the beginning of the treatment with different excuses until she was given up in the hospital files as a case of "treatment resistance." A year later, she showed up for a regular follow-up, and it turned out that there had been disease recurrence. When the doctor raised the need for chemotherapy, S. M. again declared that she would not undergo any kind of treatment—"not now, not ever." The doctor responded by saying, "No one can be forced to undergo treatment, but I suggest that since you are already here you see the attending psycho-oncologist." S. M. said, "I will do so, but only because you are such a kind doctor who has agreed not to prescribe chemotherapy for me."

At the beginning of the meeting with the psycho-oncologist, S. M. said that she did not believe in psychology and that all that psychologists had to say was mere "literary fiction." The psychologist suggested that S. M. might want to tell the psychologist some "fictional story." S. M. readily agreed and started to tell a story about two sisters, 1 year apart in age, who were so close and inseparable that most of those who knew them thought they had a lesbian relationship, which of course was not true. When they were ages 16 and 17 years, they were invited by their uncle to spend a vacation in Canada. It is there that they went on a boat tour on the St. Lawrence River and one sister accidentally fell off the boat into the water and drowned. The other sister did not jump in to try to save her, even though she was a much better swimmer. The surviving sister went back to her own country, and because she was now the only child, she was spoiled by her parents and lived happily ever after.

The psychologist assumed the role of a "literary critic" and offered the remark that the end of the story was not convincing from a literary point of view because it seemed likely that the surviving sister suffered from a sense of guilt. S. M. rejected the criticism but agreed to explore the possibility that some readers of such a story might get the "wrong" idea that the surviving sister felt guilty. S. M. suggested that the surviving sister may have wished the other sister dead for fear that the dead sister would not have allowed her to marry and have children because "they loved too much." The psychologist then remarked, "Some people who feel guilty for actual or imaginary things they have done or felt consider undergoing chemotherapy as a kind of punishment. What do you think?" "Funny," S. M. said, "I thought chemotherapy was quite the contrary—the means for life."

S. M. did not come back to the psycho-oncologist, but she underwent the whole course of chemotherapy without any resistance. At the end of the treatment, she left the psycho-oncologist a note stating, "For me chemotherapy was a punishment, and now I have earned my right to live." Her response to the treatment was good, and after 5 years she was still in full remission.

This case illustrates the use of a brief psychological intervention for resolving noncompliance with treatment and possibly also the contribution of psychological change to medical remission.

group, at 5- to 6-year follow-up), so that the stability of the findings needs to be examined in further replications (Fawzy et al., 2001).

As discussed previously, the cognitive orientation approach has also led to significant increases of survival in the intervention group that lasted for 12 years, which is the follow-up period to date. Notably, the cognitive orientation variables predicted survival together with the medical prognostic variables, and the effect of the psychological factors became more evident the longer the time since diagnosis (Kreitler, Inbar, & Kreitler, 1999; Kreitler et al., 1997).

Furthermore, there are less conventional interventions of the mind-body sphere that mostly share several of the following components: emphasis on a holistic approach, positive attitude, mind-body unity, personal responsibility for one's health, belief in the possibility to control bodily processes, and frequent use of procedures from the Kabala, Reiki, meditation, and spiritual approaches. Results are mostly not evidence based and remain equivocal at best.

Finally, many cancer patients use psychopharmacological drugs for the control of symptoms in one or another phase of the disease. The most frequently prescribed drugs are antidepressants and antianxiety medications as well as analgesics and insomnia-controlling drugs (Massie & Lesko, 1989).

SUMMARY AND CONCLUSIONS

Psycho-oncology is one of the most active domains of health psychology and has earned for itself a relatively central role in health psychology as well as in oncology. The two main reasons for this are (a) the great need for psychological help on the part of patients and physicians alike (albeit for different reasons) and (b) the theoretical and empirical advances in gaining knowledge and understanding in oncology contributed by adding the psychological perspective to the scientific and clinical research. Psycho-oncology has become deeply interwoven in the daily practice of and research in oncology. This has made it possible to detect its contributions in the most varied domains of oncology, ranging from prevention, genetic testing, and counseling to decisions about treatment, launching of new drugs supported by QOL arguments, and euthanasia. However, if psycho-oncology is to maintain its very unique status in practice and research, three recommendations seem appropriate.

The first recommendation is increased emphasis on considering multiple background variables. This would entail assuming an inherently interactional and synergistic approach in every act of applying psycho-oncology. The second is increased emphasis on considering a variety of specifically medical variables such as histology, type of tumor, and genetic aspects. This would lead to widening the scope and generalizability of psycho-oncological findings. The third is adopting a broader and more creative approach to identifying and testing purely psychological variables. This would enable enriching the host of familiar variables, such as depression and emotional suppression, that have contributed to advancing the field up to the current level.

REFERENCES

Aaronson, N. K., Ahmedzai, S., Bergman, B., Bullinger, M., & Cull, A. (1993). The European Organization for the Research and Treatment of Cancer QLQ-C30: A quality of life instrument for use in international clinical trials in oncology. *Journal of the National Cancer Institute, 85,* 365–376.

Alter, C. L., Pelcovitz, D., Axelrod, A., Goldenberg, B., Harris, H., Meyers, B., Grobois, B., Mandel, F., Septimus, A., & Kaplan, S. (1996). Identification of PTSD in cancer survivors. *Psychosomatics, 37,* 137–143.

American Psychiatric Association. (1988). *Diagnostic and statistical manual of mental disorders* (3rd ed.). Washington, DC: Author.

American Psychiatric Association. (1994). *Diagnostic and statistical manual of mental disorders* (4th ed.). Washington, DC: Author.

Andreasen, N. C., & Hoenk, P. R. (1982). The predictive value of adjustment disorders: A follow-up study. *American Journal of Psychiatry, 139,* 584–590.

Andrykowski, M. A. (1994). Psychiatric and psychosocial aspects of bone marrow transplantation. *Psychosomatics, 35,* 13–24.

Back, A. L., Wallace, J. I., Starks, H. E., & Pearlman, R. A. (1996). Physician-assisted suicide and euthanasia in Washington State: Patient requests and physician responses. *Journal of the American Medical Association, 275,* 919–925.

Barraclough, J., Pinder, P., Crudas, M., Osmond, C., Taylor, I., & Perry, M. (1992). Life events and breast cancer prognosis. *British Medical Journal, 304,* 1078–1081.

Berwick, M., Begg, C., Fine, J. A., Roush, G. C., & Barnhill, R. L. (1996). Screening for cutaneous melanoma by skin self-examination. *Journal of the National Cancer Institute, 88,* 17–23.

Bloom, J. R. (1986). Social support and adjustment to breast cancer. In B. L. Andersen (Ed.), *Women with cancer: Psychological perspectives.* New York: Springer.

Borg, G. (1982). Psychophysical bases of perceived exertion. *Medical Science of Sports and Exercise, 14,* 377–387.

Bovbjerg, D., & Valdimarsdottir, H. B. (1998). Psychoneuroimmunology: Implications for psycho-oncology. In J. C. Holland (Ed.), *Psycho-oncology* (pp. 125–134). New York: Oxford University Press.

Breitbart, W. (1990). Cancer pain and suicide. In K. Foley, J. J. Bonica, & V. Ventrafridda (Eds.), *Advances in pain research and therapy* (Vol. 16, pp. 399–412). New York: Raven.

Breitbart, W., Rosenfeld, B., Roth, A., Smith, M., Cohen, M. D., & Passik, S. D. (1997). The Memorial Delirium Assessment Scale. *Journal of Pain and Symptom Management, 13,* 128–137.

Buddeberg, C., Sieber, M., Wolf, C., Landolt-Ritter, C., Richter, D., & Steiner, R. (1996). Are coping strategies related to disease outcome in early breast cancer? *Journal of Psychosomatic Research, 40,* 255–263.

Burman, B., & Margolin, G. (1992). Analysis of the relationship between marital relationships and health problems: An interactional perspective. *Psychological Bulletin, 112,* 39–63.

Campbell, P. C. (1996). Suicides among cancer patients. *Connecticut Health Bulletin, 80,* 207–212.

Carroll, B. T., Kathol, R. G., Noyes, R., Wald, T. G., & Clamon, G. H. (1993). Screening for depression and anxiety in cancer patients using the Hospital Anxiety and Depression Scale. *General Hospital Psychiatry, 15,* 69–74.

Cassileth, B. R., Lusk, E. J., Miller, D. S., Brown, L. L., & Miller, C. (1985). Psychosocial correlates of survival in advanced malignant disease? *New England Journal of Medicine, 312,* 1551–1555.

Cassileth, B. R., Walsh, W. P., & Lusk, E. J. (1988). Psychosocial correlates of cancer survival: A subsequent report 3 to 8 years after cancer diagnosis. *Journal of Clinical Oncology, 6,* 1753–1759.

Cella, D. F., Tulsky, D. S., Gray, G., Sarafin, B., Linn, E., Bonomi, A., Silberman, M., Yellen, S. B., Winicour, P., Brannon, J., Eckberg, K., Lloyd, S., Purl, S., Blendowski, C., Goodman, M., Barnicle, M., Stewart, I., McHale, M., Bonomi, P., Kaplan, E., Taylor, S., IV, Thomas, C. R., Jr., & Harris, J. (1993). The

Functional Assessment of Cancer Therapy (FACT) scale: Development and validation of the general version. *Journal of Clinical Oncology, 11,* 570–579.

Chaitchik, S., & Kreitler, S. (1991). Induced versus spontaneous attendance of breast screening tests by women. *Journal of Cancer Education, 6,* 43–53.

Chaitchik, S., Kreitler, S., Rapoport, Y., & Algor, R. (1992). What do cancer patients' spouses know about the patients? *Cancer Nursing, 15,* 353–362.

Chaitchik, S., Kreitler, S., Schwartz, I., Shaked, S., & Rosin, R. (1992). Doctor-patient communication in a cancer ward. *Journal of Cancer Education, 7,* 41–54.

Cherny, N. I. (1996). The problem of inadequately relieved suffering. *Journal of Social Issues, 52,* 13–30.

Chochinov, H. M., Tataryn, D., Clinch, J. J., & Dudgeon, D. (1999). Will to live in the terminally ill. *Lancet, 354,* 816–819.

Chochinov, H. M., Wilson, K. G., Enns, M., Mowchun, M., Lander, S., Levitt, M., & Clinch, J. J. (1995). Desire for death in the terminally ill. *American Journal of Psychiatry, 152,* 1185–1191.

Cinciripini, P. (1995). Current trends in smoking cessation research: Psychological therapy, nicotine replacement, and changes in smoking behavior. *Cancer Bulletin, 47,* 259–263.

Clark, A., & Fallowfield, L. J. (1986). Quality of life measurements in patients with malignant disease: A review. *Journal of Social Medicine, 79,* 165–169.

Cody, M., Nichols, S., Brennan, C., Armes, J., Wilson, P., & Slevin, M. (1994). Psychosocial factors and lung cancer prognosis. *Psycho-Oncology, 3,* 141.

Cohen, L., & Baum, A. (2001). Targets for interventions to reduce cancer morbidity. In A. Baum & B. L. Andersen (Eds.), *Psychosocial interventions for cancer* (pp. 321–340). Washington, DC: American Psychological Association.

Cordova, M. J., Andrykowski, M. A., Redd, W. H., Kenady, D. E., McGrath, P. C., & Sloan, D. A. (1995). Frequency and correlates of posttraumatic stress disorder-like symptoms after treatment for breast cancer. *Journal of Consulting and Clinical Psychology, 63,* 981–986.

Courtney, J. G., Longnecker, M. P., Theorell, T., & Gerhardsson de Verdier, M. (1993). Stressful life events and the risk of colorectal cancer. *Epidemiology, 4,* 407–414.

Daut, R. L., Cleeland, C. S., & Flanery, R. C. (1983). Development of the Wisconsin Brief Pain Questionnaire to assess pain in cancer and other diseases. *Pain, 17,* 197–210.

Dean, C., & Surtees, P. G. (1989). Do psychological factors predict survival in breast cancer? *Journal of Psychosomatic Research, 33,* 561–569.

DeFlorio, M., & Massie, M. J. (1995). Review of depression in cancer: Gender differences. *Depression, 3,* 66–80.

de Haes, J., Curran, D., Young, T., Bottomley, A., Flechtner, H., Aaronson, N., & Blazeby, J. (2000). Quality of life evaluation in oncological clinical trials: The EORTC model. *European Journal of Cancer, 36,* 821–825.

de Haes, J. C. J. M., van Kippenberg, F. C. E., & Neijt, J. P. (1990). Measuring psychological and physical distress in cancer patients: Structure and application of the Rotterdam Symptom Checklist. *British Journal of Cancer, 62,* 1034–1038.

Derogatis, J. R. (1993). *The Brief Symptom Inventory: Administration, scoring, and procedures manual.* Minneapolis, MN: National Computer Systems.

Derogatis, L., Abeloff, M., & Melisaratos, N. (1979). Psychological coping mechanism and survival time in metastatic breast cancer. *Journal of the American Medical Association, 242,* 1504–1508.

Derogatis, L. R., Morrow, G. R., Fetting, D., Penman, D., Piasetsky, S., Schmale, A. M., Henrichs, M., & Carnicke, C. L., Jr. (1983). The prevalence of psychiatric disorders among cancer patients. *Journal of the American Medical Association, 249,* 751–757.

DiPlacido, J., Zauber, A., & Redd, W. H. (1998). Psychosocial issues in cancer screening. In J. C. Holland (Ed.), *Psycho-oncology* (pp. 161–172). New York: Oxford University Press.

Dunkel-Schetter, C. (1984). Social support and cancer: Findings based on patient interviews and their implications. *Journal of Social Issues, 40,* 77–98.

Edmonds, C. V. I., Lockwood, G. A., & Cunningham, J. A. (1999). Psychological response to long term group therapy: A randomized trial with metastatic breast cancer patients. *Psycho-Oncology, 8,* 71–90.

Edwards, J. R., Cooper, C. L., Pearl, G., de Paredes, E. S., O'Leary, T., & Wilhelm, M. C. (1990). The relationship between psychosocial factors and breast cancer: Some unexpected results. *Behavioral Medicine, 16,* 5–14.

Ell, K., Nishimoto, R., Mediansky, L., Mantell, J., & Hamovitch, M. (1992). Social relations, social support, and survival among patients with cancer. *Journal of Psychosomatic Research, 36,* 531–541.

Emanuel, E. J., Fairclough, C. L., Daniels, E. R., & Clarridge, B. R. (1996). Euthanasia and physician-assisted suicide: Attitudes and experiences of oncology patients, oncologists, and the public. *Lancet, 347,* 1805–1810.

Fawzy, F. I., & Fawzy, N. W. (1998). Psychoeducational interventions. In J. C. Holland (Ed.), *Psycho-oncology* (pp. 676–693). New York: Oxford University Press.

Fawzy, F. I., Fawzy, N. W., & Canada, A. L. (2001). Psychoeducational intervention programs for patients with cancer. In A. Baum & B. L. Andersen (Eds.), *Psychosocial interventions for cancer* (pp. 235–267). Washington, DC: American Psychological Association.

Felton, B. J., & Revenson, T. A. (1984). Coping with chronic illness: A study of illness controllability and the influence of coping strategies on psychological adjustment. *Journal of Clinical Psychology, 52,* 343–353.

Figer, A., Kreitler, S., Michal, M. M., & Inbar, M. (2002). Personality dispositions of colon cancer patients. *Gastrointestinal Oncology, 4,* 81–92.

Finn, O. J. (2001). Assessing the important effector mechanisms in the immune response against cancer. In A. Baum & B. L. Andersen (Eds.), *Psychosocial interventions for cancer* (pp. 175–191). Washington, DC: American Psychological Association.

Fleishman, S. B., Lesko, L. M., & Breitbart, W. (1993). Treatment of organic mental disorders in cancer patients. In W. Breitbart & J. C. Holland (Eds.), *Psychiatric aspects of symptom management in cancer patients* (pp. 23–48). Washington, DC: American Psychiatric Association.

Folstein, M. F., Fetting, J. H., Lobo, A., Niaz, U., & Capozolli, K. (1984). Cognitive assessment of cancer patients. *Cancer, 53*(Suppl.), 2250–2255.

Fox, B. H. (1978). Cancer death risk in hospitalized mental patients. *Science, 201,* 966–968.

Fox, B. H. (1989). Depressive symptoms and risk of cancer [editorial]. *Journal of the American Medical Association, 262,* 231.

Fox, B. H. (1998a). A hypothesis about Spiegel et al.'s 1989 paper on psychosocial intervention and breast cancer survival. *Psycho-Oncology, 7,* 361–370.

Fox, B. H. (1998b). Psychosocial factors in cancer incidence and prognosis. In J. C. Holland (Ed.), *Psycho-oncology* (pp. 110–124). New York: Oxford University Press.

Ganz, P., & Coscarelli, A. (1995). Quality of life after breast cancer: A decade of research. In J. E. Dimsdale & A. Baum (Eds.), *Quality of life in behavioral medicine research* (pp. 97–113). Hillsdale, NJ: Lawrence Erlbaum.

Ganz, P., Coscarelli Schag, C. A., Kahn, B., Petersen, L., & Hirji, K. (1993). Describing the health-related quality of life impact of HIV infection: Findings of a study using the HIV Overview of Problem Evaluation Systems (HOPES). *Quality of Life, 2,* 109–119.

Garfinkel, J. (1995). Cancer statistics and trends. In G. P. Murphy, J. W. Lawrence, & R. E. Lenhard (Eds.), *American Cancer Society textbook of clinical oncology* (pp. 1–11). Washington, DC: American Cancer Society.

Garssen, B., & Goodkin, K. (1999). On the role of immunological factors as mediators between psychosocial factors and cancer progression. *Psychiatry Research, 85,* 51–61.

Gellert, G. A., Maxwell, R. M., & Siegel, B. S. (1993). Survival of breast cancer patients receiving adjunctive psychosocial support therapy: A 10-year follow-up study. *Journal of Clinical Oncology, 11,* 66–69.

Geyer, S. (1991). Life events prior to manifestation of breast cancer: A limited prospective study covering eight years before diagnosis. *Journal of Psychosomatic Research, 35,* 355–363.

Goodkin, K., & Visser, A. P. (Eds.). (2000). *Psychoneuroimmunology: Stress, mental disorders, and health.* Washington, DC: American Psychiatric Association.

Goodwin, J. S., Hunt, W. C., Key, C. R., & Samet, J. M. (1987). The effect of marital status on stage, treatment, and survival of cancer patients. *Journal of the American Medical Association, 258,* 3125–3130.

Goodwin, P. J., Leszcz, M., Ennis, M., Koopmans, J., Vincent, L., Guther, H., Drysdale, E., Hundleby, M., Chochinov, H. M., Navarro, M., Speca, M., & Hunter, J. (2001). The effect of group psychosocial support on survival in metastatic breast cancer. *New England Journal of Medicine, 345,* 1719–1726.

Green, L. W., Rimer, E. T., & Elwood, J. M. (1981). Behavioral approaches to cancer prevention and detection. In S. Weiss, A. Herd, & B. Fox (Eds.), *Perspectives on behavioral medicine* (pp. 215–234). New York: Academic Press.

Greenberg, D. B., Goorin, A., Gebhardt, M. C., Petersen, L., & Hirji, K. (1994). Quality of life in osteosarcoma survivors. *Oncology, 8,* 19–25.

Greer, S., Morris, T., & Pettingale K. W. (1979). Psychological response to breast cancer: Effect on outcome. *Lancet, 2,* 785–787.

Greer, S., Morris, T., Pettingale K. W., & Haybittle, J. L. (1990). Psychological response to breast cancer and 15 years outcome. *Lancet, 1,* 49–50.

Gritz, E. R., Wellisch, D. K., & Landsverk, J. A. (1988). Psychosocial sequelae in long-term survivors of testicular cancer. *Journal of Psychosocial Oncology, 6,* 41–63.

Grossarth-Maticek, R., Kanazir, D. T., Schmidt, P., & Vetter, H. (1985). Psychosocial and organic variables as predictors of lung cancer, cardiac infarct, and apoplexy: Some differential predictors. *Personality and Individual Differences, 6,* 313–321.

Gulbinat, W., DuPont, A., Jablensky, A., Jensen, O. M., Marsella, A., Nakane, Y., & Sartorius, N. (1992). Cancer incidence of schizophrenic patients: Results of record linkage studies in three countries. *British Journal of Psychiatry, 161*(Suppl. 18), 75–83.

Heim, E., Augustini, K. F., Schaffner, L., & Valach, L. (1993). Coping with breast cancer over time and situation. *Journal of Psychosomatic Research, 37,* 523–542.

Helgeson, V. S., Cohen, S., Schulz, R., & Yasco, J. (2001). Group support interventions for people with cancer: Benefits and hazards. In A. Baum & B. L. Andersen (Eds.), *Psychosocial interventions for cancer* (pp. 269–286). Washington, DC: American Psychological Association.

Helsing, K. J., Comstock, G. W., & Szklo, M. (1982). Causes of death in a widowed population. *American Journal of Epidemiology, 116,* 524–532.

Hislop, T. G., Waxler, N. E., Coldman, A. J., Elwood, J. M., & Kan, L. (1987). The prognostic significance of psychosocial factors in women with breast cancer. *Journal of Chronic Diseases, 40,* 729–735.

Holland, J. C., Korzun, A. H., Tross, S., Cella, D. F., Norton, L., & Wood, W. (1986). Psychosocial factors and disease-free survival in stage II breast cancer. *Proceedings of the American Society of Clinical Oncology, 5,* 237.

Hoyert, D. L., Kochanek, K. D., & Murphy, S. L. (1999). Deaths: Final data for 1997. *National Vital Statistics Reports, 47*, 1–104.

Ingelfinger, F. J. (1975). Cancer! Alarm! Cancer! [editorial]. *New England Journal of Medicine, 293*, 1319–1320.

Jacobs, J. W. (1977). Screening for organic mental syndromes in the medically ill. *Annals of Internal Medicine, 86*, 40–46.

Jacobs, J., Ostroff, J., & Steinglass, P. (1998). Family therapy: A systems approach to cancer care. In J. C. Holland (Ed.), *Psycho-oncology* (pp. 994–1003). New York: Oxford University Press.

Jacobsen, P. B., & Hann, D. M. (1998). Cognitive-behavioral interventions. In J. C. Holland (Ed.), *Psycho-oncology* (pp. 717–729). New York: Oxford University Press.

Jamison, R. N., Burish, T. G., & Wallston, K. A. (1987). Psychogenic factors in predicting survival of breast cancer patients. *Journal of Clinical Oncology, 5*, 768–772.

Janz, N. K., & Becker, M. H. (1984). The health belief model: A decade later. *Health Education Quarterly, 11*, 1–47.

Jensen, M. R. (1987). Psychobiological factors predicting the course of cancer. *Journal of Personality, 55*, 329–342.

Joffres, M., Reed, D. M., & Nomura, A. M. Y. (1985). Psychosocial processes and cancer incidence among Japanese men in Hawaii. *American Journal of Epidemiology, 121*, 488–500.

Johnson, G., Burvill, J. G., Anderson, C. S., Jamrozik, K., Stewart-Wynne, E. G., & Chakera, T. (1995). Screening instruments for depression and anxiety following stroke: Experience in the Perth Community Stroke Study. *Acta Psychiatrica Scandinavica, 91*, 252–257.

Jørgensen, P., & Mortensen, P. B. (1992). Cause of death in reactive psychosis. *Acta Psychiatrica Scandinavica, 85*, 351–353.

Justice, A. (1985). Review of the effects of stress on cancer in laboratory animals: Importance of time of stress application and type of tumor. *Psychological Bulletin, 98*, 108–138.

Kaprio, J., Koskenvuo, M., & Rita, H. (1987). Mortality after bereavement: A prospective study of 95,647 widowed persons. *American Journal of Public Health, 77*, 283–287.

Kash, K. M., & Lerman, C. (1998). Psychological, social, and ethical issues in gene testing. In J. C. Holland (Ed.), *Psycho-oncology* (pp. 196–207). New York: Oxford University Press.

Keehn, R. J. (1980). Follow-up studies of World War II and Korean conflict prisoners of war. *American Journal of Epidemiology, 111*, 194–200.

Keehn, R. J., Goldberg, I. D., & Beebe, G. W. (1974). Twenty four year mortality follow-up of army veterans with disability separation for psychoneurosis in 1944. *Psychosomatic Medicine, 36*, 27–46.

Keller, M., Henrich, G., Sellschopp, A., & Beutel, M. (1995). Between distress and support: Spouses of cancer patients. In L. Baider, C. L. Cooper, & A. Kaplan De-Nour (Eds.), *Cancer and the family* (pp. 187–224). Chichester, UK: Wiley.

Kiecolt-Glaser, J. K., & Glaser, R. (1999). Psychoneuroimmunology and immunotoxicology: Implications for carcinogenesis. *Psychosomatic Medicine, 61*, 271–272.

Kiernan, R. J., Mueller, J., Langston, J. W., & Van Dyke, C. (1987). The Neurobehavioral Cognitive Status Examination: A brief but differentiated approach to cognitive assessment. *Annals of Internal Medicine, 107*, 481–485.

Kissane, D. W., Block, S., McKenzie, M., McDowall, A. C., & Nitzan, R. (1998). Family grief therapy: A preliminary account of a new model to promote healthy family functioning during palliative care and bereavement. *Psycho-Oncology, 7*, 14–25.

Koch, U., Härter, M., Jakob, U., & Siegrist, B. (1995). Parental reactions to cancer in their children. In L. Baider, C. L. Cooper, & A. Kaplan De-Nour (Eds.), *Cancer and the family* (pp. 149–170). Chichester, UK: Wiley.

Kogon, M. M., Biswas, A., Pearl, D., Carlson, R. W., & Spiegel, D. (1997). Effects of medical and psychotherapeutic treatment on the survival of women with metastatic breast carcinoma. *Cancer, 80,* 225–230.

Kornblith, A. B. (1998). Psychosocial adaptation of cancer survivors. In J. C. Holland (Ed.), *Psycho-oncology* (pp. 223–254). New York: Oxford University Press.

Kovner, F., & Kreitler, S. (1996). Effect of palliative radiation therapy on quality of life in cancer patients. *Radiology, 201*(Suppl.), 231.

Kreitler, H., & Kreitler, S. (1982). The theory of cognitive orientation: Widening the scope of behavior prediction. In B. Maher & W. B. Maher (Eds.), *Progress in experimental personality research* (Vol. 11, pp. 101–169). New York: Academic Press.

Kreitler, S. (1998, August–September). *Undergoing tests for the early detection of cancer: The cognitive orientation approach.* Lecture delivered at the conference of the European Health Psychology Society, Vienna, Austria.

Kreitler, S. (1999). Denial in cancer patients. *Cancer Investigation, 17,* 514–534.

Kreitler, S., & Chaitchik, S. (1993). Surviving cancer: The psychological problem. *Topics on Supportive Care in Oncology, 10,* 12–14.

Kreitler, S., & Chaitchik, S. (1995). The paradox of the self-diagnosed lump in the breast. *Psycho-Oncology Letters, 6,* 39–52.

Kreitler, S., Chaitchik, S., Kovner, F., & Kreitler, H. (1992). Information in breast cancer patients: The good and the bad news [abstract]. *Journal of Cancer Education, 7*(Suppl.), 25.

Kreitler, S., Chaitchik, S., & Kreitler, H. (1990). The psychological profile of women attending breast-screening tests. *Social Science and Medicine, 31,* 1177–1185.

Kreitler, S., Chaitchik, S., Kreitler, H., & Weissler, K. (1994). Who will attend tests for the early detection of breast cancer? *Psychology and Health, 9,* 463–483.

Kreitler, S. Chaitchik, S., Rapoport, Y., & Algor, R. (1995). Psychosocial effects of information and disease severity in head-and-neck cancer patients. *Journal of Cancer Education, 10,* 144–154.

Kreitler, S., Chaitchik, S., Rapoport, Y., Kreitler, H., & Algor, R. (1993). Life satisfaction and health in cancer patients, orthopedic patients, and healthy individuals. *Social Science and Medicine, 36,* 547–556.

Kreitler, S., Inbar, M., & Kreitler, H. (1999, September). *Psychosocial factors predicting disease course in cancer patients.* Paper presented at the European Cancer Conference, Vienna, Austria.

Kreitler, S., & Kreitler, H. (1991). Cognitive orientation and physical disease or health. *European Journal of Personality, 5,* 109–129.

Kreitler, S., Kreitler, H., & Chaitchik, S. (1993). Repressiveness: Cause or result of cancer? *Psycho-Oncology, 2,* 43–54.

Kreitler, S., Kreitler, H., Chaitchik, S., Shaked, S., & Shaked, T. (1997). Psychological and medical predictors of disease course in breast cancer: A prospective study. *European Journal of Personality, 11,* 383–400.

Kreitler, S., Levavi, H., & Bornstein, G. (1996). Personality factors and cervical premalignancy. *Personality and Individual Differences, 21,* 883–890.

Kreitler, S., & Merimsky, O. (in press). Pain and suffering in cancer patients. In D. Beltrutti, S. Kreitler, A. Lamberto, & D. Niv (Eds.), *Handbook of chronic pain.* New York: Springer.

Kreitler, S., Shahar, A., & Kreitler, H. (1976). Cognitive orientation, type of smoker, and behavior therapy of smoking. *British Journal of Medical Psychology, 49,* 167–175.

Kübler-Ross, E. (1969). *On death and dying*. New York: Macmillan.

Lazarus, R. S., & Folkman, S. (1984). *Stress appraisal and coping*. New York: Springer.

Lederberg, M. (1998). The family of the cancer patient. In J. C. Holland (Ed.), *Psycho-oncology* (pp. 981–993). New York: Oxford University Press.

Lesko, L. M. (1993). Psychiatric management of eating disorders in cancer patients. In W. Breitbart & J. C. Holland (Eds.), *Psychiatric aspects of symptom management in cancer patients* (pp. 87–106). Washington, DC: American Psychiatric Association.

Levav, I., Kohn, R., Iscovich, J., Abramson, J. H., Tsai, W. Y., & Vigdorovich, D. (2000). Cancer incidence and survival following bereavement. *American Journal of Public Health, 90*, 1601–1607.

Levy, S. M., Herberman, R. B., Lippman, M., D'Angelo, T., & Lee, J. (1991). Immunological and psychosocial predictors of disease recurrence in patients with early stage breast cancer. *Behavioral Medicine, 17*, 67–75.

Luzzatto, P., & Gabriel, B. (1998). Art psychotherapy. In J. C. Holland (Ed.), *Psycho-oncology* (pp. 743–757). New York: Oxford University Press.

Massie, M., Gagnon, P., & Holland, J. (1994). Depression and suicide in patients with cancer. *Journal of Pain Symptom Management, 9*, 352–331.

Massie, M. J., & Lesko, L. M. (1989). Psychopharmacological management. In J. C. Holland & J. H. Rowland (Eds.), *Handbook of psycho-oncology: Psychological care of the patient with cancer* (pp. 470–491). New York: Oxford University Press.

Massie, J. M., & Popkin, M. K. (1998). Depressive disorders. In J. C. Holland (Ed.), *Psycho-oncology* (pp. 518–540). New York: Oxford University Press.

McHorney, C. A., Ware, J. E., & Raczek, A. E. (1993). The MOS 36 item short form health survey (SF-36): Psychometric and clinical tests of validity in measuring physical and mental health constructs. *Medical Care, 31*, 247–263.

McNair, D. M., Lorr, M., & Droppelman, L. F. (1971). *Profile of mood states*. San Diego: Educational and Industrial Testing Service.

Melzack, R. (1975). The McGill Pain Questionnaire: Major properties and scoring methods. *Pain, 1*, 277–299.

Morgenstern, H., Gellert, G. A., Walter, S. D., Ostfeld, A. M., & Siegel, B. S. (1984). The impact of a psychosocial support program on survival with breast cancer: The importance of selection bias in program evaluation. *Journal of Chronic Diseases, 37*, 273–282.

Morris, T., Pettingale, K. W., & Haybittle, J. (1992). Psychological response to cancer diagnosis and disease outcome in patients with breast cancer and lymphoma. *Psycho-Oncology, 1*, 105–114.

Murray, M., & McMillan, C. (1993). Health beliefs, locus of control, emotional control, and women's cancer screening behavior. *British Journal of Clinical Psychology, 32*, 87–100.

Musselman, D. L., McDaniel, J. S., Porter, M. R., & Nemeroff, C. B. (1998). Psychoneuroendocrinology and cancer. In J. C. Holland (Ed.), *Psycho-oncology* (pp. 135–143). New York: Oxford University Press.

Neale, A. V., Tilley, B. C., & Vernon, S. W. (1986). Marital status, delay in seeking treatment, and survival from breast cancer. *Social Science and Medicine, 23*, 305–312.

Noyes, R., Jr., Holt, C. S., & Massie, M. J. (1998). Anxiety disorders. In J. C. Holland (Ed.), *Psycho-oncology* (pp. 548–563). New York: Oxford University Press.

O'Malley, J. E., Koocher, G., Foster, D., & Slavin, L. (1979). Psychiatric sequelae of surviving childhood cancer. *American Journal of Orthopsychiatry, 49*, 608–616.

Penman, D. T. (1980). Coping strategies in adaptation to mastectomy. *Dissertation Abstracts International, 40,* B5825.

Perskey, V. W., Kempthorne-Rawson, J., & Shekelle, R. B. (1987). Personality and risk of cancer: 20-year follow-up of the Western Electric Study. *Psychosomatic Medicine, 49,* 435–449.

Pettingale, K. W., Morris, T., Greer, S., & Haybittle, J. (1985). Mental attitudes to cancer: An additional prognostic factor. *Lancet, 1,* 750.

Polednak, A. P., Lane, D. S., & Burg, M. A. (1991). Risk perception, family history, and use of breast cancer screening tests. *Cancer Detection and Prevention, 15,* 257–263.

Popkin, M. K., & Tucker, G. J. (1992). Secondary and drug-induced mood, anxiety, psychotic, catatonic, and personality disorders. *Journal of Neuropsychiatry and Clinical Neuroscience, 4,* 369–385.

Portenoy, R. K., Thaler, H. T., Kornblith A. B., Lepore, J. M., Friedlander-Klar, H., Kiyasu, E., Sobel, K., Coyle, N., Kemeny, N., & Norton, L. (1994). The Memorial Symptom Assessment Scale: An instrument for the evaluation of symptom prevalence, characteristics, and distress. *European Journal of Cancer, 30A,* 1326–1336.

Priestman, T. J., Priestman, S. G., & Bradshaw, C. (1985). Stress and breast cancer. *British Journal of Cancer, 51,* 493–498.

Quesada, J. R., Talpaz, M., Rios, A., Kurzrock, R., & Gutterman, J. (1986). Clinical toxicity of interferon in cancer patients: A review. *Journal of Clinical Oncology, 4,* 234–243.

Rapoport, Y., Kreitler, S., Chaitchik, S., Algor, R., & Weissler, K. (1993). Psychosocial problems in head-and-neck cancer patients and their change with disease duration. *Annals of Oncology, 4,* 69–73.

Ratcliffe, M. A., Dawson, A. A., & Walker, L. G. (1995). Eysenck Personality Inventory L-scores in patients with Hodgkin's disease and non-Hodgkin's lymphoma. *Psycho-Oncology, 4,* 39–45.

Reynolds, P., & Kaplan, G. A. (1990). Social connections and risk for cancer: Prospective evidence from the Alameda County Study. *Behavioral Medicine, 16,* 101–110.

Richardson, H., Shelton, D. R., Krailo, M., & Levine, A. M. (1990). The effect of compliance with treatment on survival among patients with hematologic malignancies. *Journal of Clinical Oncology, 8,* 356–364.

Ringdal, G. I. (1995). Correlates of hopelessness in cancer patients. *Journal of Psychosocial Oncology, 13,* 47–66.

Rogentine, G. N., van Kammen, D. P., Fox, B. H., Docherty, J. P., Rosenblatt, J. E., Boyd, S. C., & Bunney, W. E., Jr. (1979). Psychological factors in the prognosis of malignant melanoma: A prospective study. *Psychosomatic Medicine, 41,* 647–655.

Rosenfeld, B. (2000). Assisted suicide, depression, and the right to die. *Psychology, Public Policy, and Law, 6,* 467–488.

Rossi, J. S., Blais, L. M., Redding, C. A., & Weinstock, A. M. (1995). Preventing skin cancer through behavior change. *Dermatological Clinics, 13,* 613–622.

Rowland, J. H. (1989). Intrapersonal resources: Coping. In J. C. Holland & J. H. Rowland (Eds.), *Handbook of psycho-oncology: Psychological care of the patient with cancer* (pp. 44–57). New York: Oxford University Press.

Scheier, M. F., & Carver, C. S. (2001). Adapting to cancer: The importance of hope and purpose. In A. Baum & B. L. Andersen (Eds.), *Psychosocial interventions for cancer* (pp. 15–36). Washington, DC: American Psychological Association.

Schonfield, J. (1972). Psychological factors related to delayed return to an earlier life-style in successfully treated cancer patients. *Journal of Psychosomatic Research, 16,* 41–46.

Schueler, G., & Fox, B. H. (1991). Questions about Grossarth-Maticek's procedures and results. *Psychological Inquiry, 2,* 257–261.

SEER Program. (2002). *Cancer incidence in the U.S.* Washington, DC: National Cancer Institute. Retrieved on January 20, 2003, from http://seer.cancer.gov/publications/raterisk

Servaes, P., Vingerhoets, A., Vreugdenhil, G., Keuning, J., & Broekhuijsen, M. A. (1996). Breast cancer and nonexpression of emotions. *Psychosomatic Medicine, 58,* 67.

Severson, K. T. (1997). Dying cancer patients: Choices at the end of life. *Journal of Pain and Symptom Management, 14,* 94–98.

Shekelle, R. B., Raynor, W. J., Ostfeld, A. M., & Garron, L. A. (1981). Psychological depression and 17-year risk of death from cancer. *Psychosomatic Medicine, 43,* 117–123.

Smets, E. M. A., Garssen, B., Bonke, B., & de Haes, J. C. J. M. (1995). The Multidimensional Fatigue Inventory (MFI): Psychometric qualities of an instrument to assess fatigue. *Journal of Psychosomatic Research, 39,* 315–325.

Sneeuw, K. C. A., Aaronson, N. K., Yarnold, J. R., Broderick, M., Regan, J., Ross, G., & Goddard, A. (1992). Cosmetic and functional outcomes of breast conserving treatment for early stage breast cancer: II. Relationship with psychosocial functioning. *Radiotherapy and Oncology, 25,* 160–166.

Sourkes, B. M., Massie, M. J., & Holland, J. C. (1998). Psychotherapeutic issues. In J. C. Holland (Ed.), *Psycho-oncology* (pp. 694–700). New York: Oxford University Press.

Spiegel, D., & Diamond, S. (2002). Psychosocial interventions in cancer: Group therapy techniques. In A. Baum & B. L. Andersen (Eds.), *Psychosocial interventions for cancer* (pp. 215–233). Washington, DC: American Psychological Association.

Spiegel, D., Morrow, G. R., Classen, C., Raubertas, R., Stott, P. B., Mudaliar, N., Pierce, H. I., Flynn, P. J., Heard, L., & Riggs, G. (1999). Group psychotherapy for recently diagnosed breast cancer patients: A multicenter feasibility study. *Psycho-Oncology, 8,* 482–493.

Spira, J. L. (1998). Group therapies. In J. C. Holland (Ed.), *Psycho-oncology* (pp. 701–716). New York: Oxford University Press.

Spira, J. L. (2000). Existential psychotherapy in palliative care. In H. M. Chochinov & W. Breitbart (Eds.), *Handbook of psychiatry in palliative medicine* (pp. 197–214). New York: Oxford University Press.

Stavraky, K. M., Donner, A. P., Kincade, J. E., & Stewart, M. A. (1988). The effect of psychosocial factors on lung cancer mortality at one year. *Journal of Clinical Epidemiology, 41,* 75–82.

Sullivan, M., Rapp, S., Fitzgibbon, D., & Chapman, C. R. (1997). Pain and the choice to hasten death in patients with painful metastatic cancer. *Journal of Palliative Care, 13,* 18–28.

Swanson, G. M., Belle, S. H., & Satariano, W. A. (1985). Marital status and cancer incidence: Difference in the black and white populations. *Cancer Research, 45,* 5883–5889.

Temoshok, L. (1987). Personality coping style, emotion, and cancer: Towards an integrative model. *Cancer Surveys, 6,* 545–567.

Temoshok, L., & Fox, B. H. (1984). Coping styles and other psychosocial factors related to medical status and to prognosis in patients with cutaneous malignant melanoma as a predictor of follow-up clinical status. In B. H. Fox & B. H. Newberry (Eds.), *Impact of psychoendocrine systems in cancer and immunity* (pp. 258–287). Toronto: Hogrefe.

Temoshok, L., & Heller, W. B. (1984). On comparing apples, oranges, and fruit salad: A methodological overview of medical outcome studies in psychosocial oncology. In C. L. Cooper (Ed.), *Psychosocial stress and cancer* (pp. 231–260). Chichester, UK: Wiley.

Trzepacz, P. T., Baker, R. W., & Greenhouse, J. (1988). A symptom rating scale for delirium. *Psychiatry Research, 23,* 89–97.

Tuxen, M. K., & Hansen, S. W. ((1994). Complications of treatment: Neurotoxicity secondary to antineoplastic drugs. *Cancer Treatments Review, 20,* 191–214.

U.K. Trial of Early Detection of Breast Cancer Group. (1984). Trial of Early Detection of Breast Cancer: Description of method. *British Journal of Cancer, 44,* 618–627.

Van der Ploeg, H-M. (1991). What a wonderful world it would be: A reanalysis of some of the work of Grossarth-Maticek. *Psychological Inquiry, 2,* 280–285.

Vogt, T. M., Mullooly, J. P., Ernst, D., Pope, C. R., & Hollis, J. F. (1992). Social networks as predictors of ischemic heart disease, cancer, stroke and hypertension: Incidence, survival, and mortality. *Journal of Clinical Epidemiology, 45,* 659–666.

Watson, M., Greer, S., Young, J., Inayat, Q., Burgess, C., & Robertson, C. (1988). Development of a questionnaire measure of adjustment to cancer: The MAC scale. *British Journal of Psychiatry, 18,* 203–209.

Watson, M., Haviland, J. S., Greer, S., Davidson, J., & Bliss, J. M. (1999). Influence of psychological response on survival in breast cancer: A population-based cohort study. *Lancet, 354,* 1351–1356.

Waxler-Morrison, N., Hislop, T. G., Mears, B., & Kan, L. (1991). Effects of social relationships on survival for women with breast cancer: A prospective study. *Social Science and Medicine, 33,* 177–183.

Weihs, K., & Reiss, D. (1995). Family reorganization in response to cancer: A developmental perspective. In L. Baider, C. L. Cooper, & A. Kaplan De-Nour (Eds.), *Cancer and the family* (pp. 3–30). Chichester, UK: Wiley.

Weisman, A. D., & Worden, J. W. (1975). Psychological analysis of cancer deaths. *Omega, 6,* 61–75.

Weisman, A. D., & Worden, J. W. (1976–1977). The existential plight of cancer: Significance of the first 100 days. *International Journal of Psychiatry in Medicine, 7,* 1–15.

Weisman, A. D., Worden, J. W., & Sobel, H. J. (1980). *Psychosocial screening and intervention with cancer patients.* Research report, Harvard Medical School and Massachusetts General Hospital.

White, M. H. (1993). Prevention of infection in patients with neoplastic disease: Use of a historical model for developmental strategies. *Clinical Infectious Diseases, 17,* S355–S358.

Yehuda, R., Resnick, H., Kahana, B., & Giller, E. L. (1993). Long lasting hormonal alterations to extreme stress in humans: Normative or maladaptive? *Psychosomatic Medicine, 55,* 287–297.

Zonderman, A. B., Costa, P. T., & McCrae, R. R. (1989). Depression as a risk for cancer morbidity and mortality in a nationally representative sample. *Journal of the American Medical Association, 262,* 1191–1195.

CHAPTER 18

Sexual Dysfunctions
Etiology and Treatment

Sheila Garos

Studies indicate that problems in sexual functioning may be quite common (Spector & Carey, 1990). As early as 1970, Masters and Johnson estimated that 50% of couples in the United States suffered from a sexual dysfunction (Masters & Johnson, 1970). Other estimates suggest that up to 24% of the U.S. population will experience a sexual dysfunction at some point in their lives (Robins et al., 1984). In 1992, Laumann and colleagues conducted a study to assess the prevalence and risk of experiencing sexual dysfunction across social groups (Laumann, Gagnon, Michael, & Michaels, 1995). They found that sexual dysfunction was more prevalent in women (43%) than in men (31%) and was associated with characteristics such as age, educational attainment, poor physical and emotional health, experiences in sexual relationships, and overall well-being. Having a sexual problem or dysfunction can invoke embarrassment, fear, shame, and feelings of inadequacy. For these reasons, the number of individuals who suffer with a sexual dysfunction is often greater than what reported statistics reflect.

Table 18.1 outlines the current classification scheme of sexual disorders found in the DSM-IV (*Diagnostic and Statistical Manual of Mental Disorders,* fourth edition [American Psychiatric Association, 1994]). Sexual dysfunctions are further classified into three subtypes: pain disorders, arousal disorders, and orgasmic disorders. To understand the etiology and treatment of sexual disorders, it is necessary to have some knowledge of the psychobiology of the human sexual response.

BACKGROUND AND ETIOLOGY

The Human Sexual Response

Biomedical advances and clinical studies suggest that for most people, human sexual functioning proceeds sequentially and rudimentarily involves a biphasic response that is composed of (a) *tumescence,* or the engorgement of the genitals with blood that leads to erection in men and vaginal lubrication and swelling in women, and (b) *detumescence,* or the outflow of blood from the genitals following orgasm (Bancroft, 1995; Herbert, 1996; Schiavi & Segraves, 1995; Wincze & Carey, 1991). However, the psychobiological mechanisms

Table 18.1   DSM-IV Classifications of Sexual Dysfunctions

Pain Disorders	Desire Disorders	Arousal Disorders	Orgasm Disorders	Miscellaneous Classifications
Dyspareunia	Hypoactive sexual desire disorder	Female sexual arousal disorder	Female orgasmic disorder	Sexual dysfunction due to a medical condition
Vaginismus	Sexual aversion disorder	Male erectile disorder	Male orgasmic disorder	Substance-induced sexual dysfunction
		Premature ejaculation		Sexual dysfunction not otherwise specified

that underlie the sexual response are far more complex and warrant further investigation (Davis, 2001; Gaither & Plaud, 1997; Jupp & McCabe, 1989; Meston & Frohlich, 2000; Pfaus, 1999; Regan, 1996; Stoleru et al., 1999).

Masters and Johnson (1970) described a physiological model of the sexual response that included four physiological phases: excitement, plateau, orgasm, and resolution (Table 18.2). However, this model failed to address those patients who reported difficulty in becoming aroused or who expressed an aversion to sex (Kaplan, 1977). Subsequently, a "desire stage" was conceived that was believed to precede the "excitement" phase described by Masters and Johnson. Desire involves a patient's "cognitive and affective readiness for, and interest in, sexual activity" (Wincze & Carey, 1991, p. 4).

Etiological Factors

Given the complexity of sexual performance, sexual desire, sexual satisfaction, and meaning of sexual behavior that is constructed from dominant culture and beliefs, one must not rely exclusively on physiological models to describe or assess sexual functioning (Laqueur, 1990; Tiefer, 1991). Diagnosis and assessment must include an evaluation of organic causes as well as psychogenic factors that contribute to, or occur secondarily to, a sexual dysfunction (Pollets, Ducharme, & Pauporte, 1999) such as conflict (Metz & Epstein, 2002), guilt (Walser & Kern, 1996), depression and other affective states (Seidman & Roose, 2001), trauma (van Berlo & Ensink, 2000), and anxiety (Shires & Miller, 1998). Likewise, principles of learning and conditioning in regard to the sexual response must be considered (Lalumiere & Quinsey, 1998), as should cognitive appraisals and expectancies about sexual arousal and desire (Palace, 1995; Weisberg, Brown, Wincze, & Barlow, 2001), relationship distress (Metz & Epstein, 2002), and developmental issues such as age and a person's stage in life (Avina, O'Donohue, & Fisher, 2000; Bartlik & Goldstein, 2001; Dennerstein, Dudley, & Burger, 2001). Many patients develop sexual dysfunctions as the result of medical conditions such as spinal cord injuries (Sipski, Alexander, & Rosen, 2001), kidney disease (Malavaud, Rostaing, Rischmann, Sarramon, & Durand, 2000), diabetes (Bhugra, 2000), cancer (Merrick, Wallner, Butler, Lief, & Sutlief, 2001; Shifren et al., 2000), and other chronic illnesses (Schover, 1989). Finally, medications prescribed to treat a variety of medical and psychological conditions can often lead to reduced sexual desire or other interference with sexual performance (Gelenberg, Delgado, & Nurnberg, 2000; Waldinger et al., 2002).

Table 18.2 Sexual Response Phases and Associated Dysfunctions

Phase	Characteristics	Dysfunction
1. Desire	Characterized by subjective feelings of sexual interest, desire, urges, and fantasy; no physiological correlates	Hypoactive sexual desire disorder Sexual aversion disorder
2. Excitement	Characterized by subjective and physiological concomitants of sexual arousal such as penile erection in men and vaginal engorgement and lubrication in women	Female sexual arousal disorder Male erectile disorder
3. Orgasm	Characterized by climax or peaking of sexual tension, with rhythmic contractions of the genital musculature and intense subjective involvement	Female orgasmic disorder Male orgasmic disorder Premature ejaculation
4. Resolution	Characterized by a release of tension and a sense of pleasure or well-being	Dyspareunia Vaginismus

SOURCE: Adapted from Weiner and Davis (1999, p. 411). In T. Millon, P. H. Blaney, & R. D. Davis (Eds.), *Oxford Textbook of Psychopathology.* Copyright © 1999 by Oxford University Press, Inc. Used by permission.

ASSESSMENT AND TREATMENT

Basic Principles of Sex Therapy

Traditionally, sex therapy is a short-term therapy designed for the special treatment of sexual dysfunctions. Sex therapy is a behaviorally based, systematic protocol designed to move patients through a series of "graded experiences, from an avoided, partial, or pleasureless response to a fully pleasurable response" (Birk, 1999, p. 525). Contemporary approaches to sex therapy often address issues in the patient as well as in his or her partnership more systemically. Emotional, spiritual, cultural, affective, cognitive, and social factors are addressed and evaluated. Thus, effective treatment of psychogenic sexual dysfunctions requires knowledge of family systems and family therapy as well as extensive experience in working with couples in general.

Overall Evaluation and Assessment

During an initial evaluation the clinician will typically seek demographic information, the nature and development of the dysfunction, a psychosexual history, a description of the patient's current sex life, the partners' perception of the quality of their relationship, the degree of psychopathology of one or both partners, physical health, and the patient's motivation for and commitment to treatment (LoPiccolo & Heiman, 1978). The initial evaluation can seem quite invasive for the patient, and it is important to inform him or her why the type of information sought is necessary. Questions must be specific to ascertain the nature and degree of dysfunction and to help delineate between possible organic and psychogenic causes of the problem. Additional information that may be sought includes, but is not limited to, the patient's personality, professional life, education, sexual development, sexual values, experiences with other partners, history of masturbatory behaviors, and attitudes about pleasure, family life, and religious background.

Overall Treatment Approach

Thoughts, attitudes, and feelings play a significant role in mediating physiological responses to sex. The goal of many techniques is to "replace antisexual anxiety with sexual pleasure" (Heiman, 1978, p. 123). Thus, facilitation and maintenance of arousal and associated thoughts, feelings, and attitudes are an important component in treating sexual dysfunctions. Psychophysiological measures such as nocturnal penile tumescence and daytime arousal evaluation can be used to assess subjective and objective measures of arousal. In addition, men being evaluated for erectile dysfunction (ED) may undergo a penile blood pressure examination.

A number of psychosocial interventions are available to help with sexual difficulties. Perhaps the most common is sensate focus, which involves teaching patients and their partners to engage in intimate physical and emotional closeness in a gradual nonthreatening manner. Homework is assigned in which couples engage in various stages of the protocol. Explicit instructions are given to couples as to how to approach each stage of treatment. "Rules" of engagement are outlined, with some of these rules prohibiting genital contact during the earlier phases of the exercise. Modifications can be made to best address the needs of the patient and the type of dysfunction being treated. Inclusion of steps and the duration of each is left to clinical judgment. An outline of sensate focus is presented in Table 18.3.

Female Sexual Dysfunctions

Hypoactive Sexual Desire Disorder. According to Laumann, Gagnon, Michael, and Michaels (1994), approximately 33% of women experience a lack of sexual interest at some point in their lives. From ages 18 to 24 years, about 32.0% of women report some difficulty with sexual desire; at ages 30 to 34 years, this number decreases to 29.5%. The largest group affected is women ages 35 to 39 years (37.6%). Among women ages 40 to 54 years, the number of women reporting desire disturbances declines, only to increase once again after that.

In the DSM-IV (American Psychiatric Association, 1994), sexual desire disorders fall into two categories: hypoactive sexual desire disorder (HSDD), defined as a "deficiency or absence of sexual fantasies and desire for sexual activity" (p. 496), and sexual aversion disorder (SAD). Diagnosis of HSDD generally involves clinical judgment as well as corroborating information from the patient's partner (Rosen & Leiblum, 1989). It is important to keep in mind that often a partner with higher desire becomes the referent for the partner with lower desire, in which case it may be indicative of a desire discrepancy as opposed to a desire disorder. Clinical judgment must also take into account interpersonal determinants, frequency and chronicity of the symptom, subjective distress, effect on other areas of functioning, and the person's current life situation. Some individuals have difficulty in initiating sexual activity; others are unresponsive to sexual advances from their partners (i.e., lack of receptivity). It is important to determine whether HSDD is global, with the patient lacking interest in any or all sexual activity, or situational, with the patient's lack of desire occurring only with a specific partner or type of activity.

HSDD can occur as a secondary condition when other sexual dysfunctions are present (e.g., anorgasmia in women, ED in men). HSDD may also result from a number of physiological or psychological conditions, including other medical conditions (Phillips & Slaughter, 2000), stress, substance use, low self-esteem, anhedonia, hormonal changes, and negative self-evaluation (Heiman & Meston, 1997; Morokoff, 1985; Rosen & Leiblum, 1989). Medication side effects are another possible cause of reduced desire (Wincze & Carey, 1991). Finally, a history of sexual abuse or trauma, abuse, or assault can lead to decreased desire due to "chronic fears of vulnerability of loss of control, inability to establish intimate relationships, or a conditioned aversion to all forms of sexual contact" (Rosen & Leiblum, 1989, p. 27).

Table 18.3   Treatment Stages of Sensate Focus

Stage I: Nongenital pleasuring

At this stage, each partner will touch one another for at least 20 minutes. One partner will initiate and touch for the specified time, and then the two will switch roles and positions. The partner who is touching should be assertive by touching the other in ways and places (minus breasts, buttocks, and genitals) that are pleasing for the one doing the touching. Experimentation with touching each partner in new places and in new ways is encouraged. A partner can use his or her legs, hands, face, arms, and the like when touching the other partner. The partner being touched should concentrate on relaxing his or her whole body and the sensations that touch by the other partner is creating. If spectatoring or anxiety is a problem, the couple should stop for a few moments until relaxed and then start again. If either partner becomes aroused, it is permissible to masturbate to relieve tension so long as the person does it himself or herself. In some cases (e.g., a past history of trauma), the partners can begin this stage with their clothes on.

Stage II: Touching for One's Own and One's Partner's Pleasure

This stage is similar to Stage I. Each stage has two parts, with one partner caressing and touching the other first and then the partners switching roles. What differs is that at Stage II, each partner indicates to the other what he or she would like the other to do. A hand can be placed over that of the partner to demonstrate how one would like the touch to feel (e.g., faster, harder, softer, slower, more to the right). It is still up to the person who is doing the caressing to decide what he or she will do. Partners are encouraged to discuss their experience after each stage.

Stage III: Sensate Focus With Genital Focus

The same basic principles apply to this and the remaining stages of treatment. A ban on intercourse remains; however, genital contact with the mouth and/or hands is now permitted. A will caress B, and then B will caress A. During this stage, change in the pressure, speed, or direction of touch can profoundly affect the sensation received. Thus, communication is of utmost importance. Couples are told not to focus on genital regions exclusively and to spend as much time as before on genital kissing and touching. At this stage, lubricants, oils, and lotions are permitted to enhance pleasure of both partners. The main objective is still to concentrate on and enjoy the bodily sensations being experienced. Should one of the partners become aroused or experience orgasm, the session can continue. It is important to remember that orgasm is not the "goal" of the session.

Stage IV: Sensate Focus With Genital Contact and Simultaneous Caressing

The focus of this stage is on simultaneous caressing that enables both partners to give and receive pleasure at the same time. Partners are encouraged to communicate to each other when one is doing something that feels particularly nice. Self-assertion and self-protection are also encouraged.

Stage V: Vaginal Containment

Once the sensate focus is established with consistency, some ejaculatory control is exercised, and erections can remain reasonably firm, the couple is ready for Stage V. This stage is designed to facilitate sensory focus and enjoyment without performance anxiety. Once the partner is ready and the patient is able to maintain a reasonably firm erection, the partner will guide the patient's penis into her vagina. The most accommodating position for this is the "female superior" position, where the patient lies flat on his back with the partner kneeling above him with her knees on either side of his body, roughly at the level of his nipples. The woman will gently insert her partner's penis into her vagina. This allows the partner to have greater control. The goal of this stage is for the partners to reorient themselves with the sensation of the penis and the vagina. The woman should tighten and relax her vaginal muscles on her partner's penis. Genital caressing may resume. The patient is told to concentrate on sensations while the partner keeps control of what is happening. Couples are also to resist the desire to thrust.

(Continued)

Table 18.3   (Continued)

Stage VI: Vaginal Containment With Movement

It is important to remind the partners at this stage that they are to employ the same principles concerning physical contact that they used at the beginning of treatment. Giving and receiving pleasure, and touching each other in a way that is pleasing to both partners, remains the aim of treatment. Mutual caressing continues and involves both genital and nongenital areas. Each partner should feel aroused and receptive before vaginal entry takes place.

After vaginal containment is tried for some time, limited thrusting can be tried to assess each partner's sensations and feelings. Either partner is allowed to tell the other to stop at any time so as to set limits and boundaries without fearing that the partner will become angry. It is also important to remember that responsiveness will vary from stage to stage and from month to month. At this point, the clinician should reiterate that orgasm, particularly mutual orgasm, is not the goal that must be satisfied to meet the expectations of the patient or his partner.

Cognitive restructuring techniques, such as challenging negative attitudes and learning to reduce intrusive thoughts, are often incorporated into treatment. Communication training is often a vital element in the treatment of sexual dysfunctions because many couples lack effective communication skills in general and are particularly reluctant to communicate their sexual needs, likes, dislikes, and desires.

The use of erotic materials or "toys" is sometimes recommended to patients and should be approached as exposure to a sexual experience with attention paid to mood and setting. Of course, it is essential to assess the patient's or couple's views about the use of such materials to determine whether these approaches are viable and would not be considered offensive or objectionable. Masturbation training with fantasy should be approached with similar caution. It should not be assumed that all patients know how to masturbate or how to do so effectively. Masturbation training, when used successfully, can help to build sexual confidence and desire.

Other treatments for male sexual dysfunctions include vasoactive therapies, which involve the use of intracorporeal injections of papaverine or transurethral alprostadil suppositories. These agents act as vasodilators. Surgical approaches can be used to correct male erectile dysfunction and include the placement of an implantable penile prosthesis, penile arterial revascularization, and penile venous ligation. Vacuum devices can also be used to draw blood into the corpora cavernosa of the penis. Placing a band around the base of the penis then traps the blood. Among pharmacotherapeutic agents, the most recent, and perhaps most popular, is sildenafil (Viagra).

In the assessment of HSDD, frequency of activity should not be considered a reliable indicator of sexual desire. However, initiation is an important consideration because it serves as an indicator of female motivation to engage in sexual behavior (Wallen, 1990). Often, a patient will engage in frequent coitus or other sexual activities out of a sense of obligation, coercion, or an attempt to please or accommodate his or her partner's wishes and preferences. Likewise, one must consider that symptoms of low desire may reflect problems of relationship intimacy, power differentials, or territoriality in the relationship (Verhulst & Heiman, 1988).

Masturbatory practices vary, as do cognitive correlates of desire such as fantasy (Schreiner-Engel & Schiavi, 1986). Moreover, gender differences must be taken into account in the evaluation of cognitive descriptors of desire (Denney, Field, & Quadagno, 1984; Jones & Barlow, 1990; McCauley & Swann, 1978, 1980; Person, Terestman, Myers, Goldberg, & Salvadori, 1989).

A number of treatment strategies are available to address problems associated with sexual desire disorder (for a review, see O'Donohue, Dopke, & Swingen, 1997). These approaches include (a) psychotherapy (Kaplan,

1977; Scharff, 1988), (b) cognitive-behavioral approaches (Rosen & Leiblum, 1989), (c) cognitive restructuring (LoPiccolo & Friedman, 1988), (d) analysis of interactional and communication patterns (Schwartz & Masters, 1988), (e) "territorial interactions" (e.g., "When you touch my body, I feel like you are invading my space"), (f) "rank-order" communication (e.g., "I always feel like the underdog in sexual relationships"), and (g) "attachment interactions" (e.g., "I find it hard to trust you after my feelings have been hurt") (Verhulst & Heiman, 1979, 1988). Other strategies include the use of pharmacological agents, hormonal treatments, and the "coital alignment technique" that can help to increase effective stimulation for women during intercourse (Pierce, 2000). In some cases, the use of sex toys and other stimuli (e.g., fantasy, erotic material) and "orgasm consistency" training (Hurlbert, White, Powell, & Apt, 1993) may be helpful.

Sexual Aversion Disorder. SAD is a more severe disruption in desire. SAD is characterized by a "marked aversion to, and active avoidance of, all genital contact with a sexual partner" (American Psychiatric Association, 1994, p. 499). The aversion to genital contact "may be focused on a particular aspect of sexual experience (e.g., genital secretions, vaginal penetration) . . . [or] revulsion to all sexual stimuli, including kissing and touching" (p. 499). This disorder is often accompanied by poor body image and avoidance of nudity (Katz, Gipson, & Turner, 1992; Ponticas, 1992). Women with SAD may experience reactions such as terror, panic, and nausea. Efforts to cope with the disorder may include avoidance of sexual contact, substance use, and neglect of one's personal appearance. Although SAD and HSDD are distinct, the two conditions are often related and have similar causes such as endocrine alterations, medical conditions, psychological distress, relationship factors, prior sexual trauma, and

negative learning experiences (Halvorsen & Metz, 1992).

In treating SAD, it is important to understand the "approach-avoidance" conflict that exists in many of these patients (Ponticas, 1992). Given that most causes of SAD are not physiological, addressing psychological issues that underlie the disorder is of particular importance in treatment. In addition to psychotherapy, systematic desensitization and vicarious extinction techniques can be used to reduce or minimize the patient's anxiety and fear response (Wincze, 1971).

Female Orgasmic Disorder. Anorgasmia is regarded as the most common sexual dysfunction in women (Heiman & Grafton-Becker, 1989; Spector & Carey, 1990). Moreover, approximately 85% to 90% of women report having orgasms without difficulty; however, only one third have had an orgasm during intercourse (Seeber & Gorrell, 2001). In addition, the incidence of orgasmic difficulty tends to be higher in single women (Laumann et al., 1994).

Female orgasmic disorder is characterized by "a persistent or recurrent delay in, or absence of, orgasm following a normal sexual excitement phase" (American Psychiatric Association, 1994, p. 505). Clinical judgment is an important factor in diagnosing this condition given that a woman's orgasmic capacity must be determined to be less than would be "reasonable for her age, sexual experience, and the adequacy of sexual stimulation she receives" (p. 505). Many women express concern that something is "wrong with them" if they do not experience orgasm during intercourse or if they have multiple or simultaneous orgasms. Patients need to know that many women do not reach orgasm during coitus because penile stimulation is often not intense or direct enough to produce orgasm.

Women's orgasmic potential and type of orgasm are variable. Orgasmic capacity has been associated with sexual assertiveness

(Hurlbert, 1991), comfort with masturbation (Kelly, Strassberg, & Kircher, 1990), and relationship and psychological distress (Kaplan, 1992; McGovern, Stewart, & LoPiccolo, 1975). Most women have clitoral orgasms that result from stimulus to the clitoris and surrounding tissues. Fewer women have pelvic floor or vaginal orgasms, and for some women orgasm involves a combination of the two. It is important to discern whether the patient's orgasmic disorder is situational (i.e., the patient is able to reach orgasm via masturbation but not by manual stimulation or intercourse) or generalized (i.e., occurring across all situations and partners). Female orgasmic disorder typically does not arise from a physiological condition and is generally not correlated with vaginal size or pelvic muscle strength. However, some conditions (e.g., spinal cord injuries, vaginal excision and reconstruction) have been associated with orgasmic difficulty. Medications such as benzodiazepines, antihypertensives, neuroleptics, and antidepressants may contribute to orgasmic difficulty, as can substance use and abuse.

Often, the source of orgasmic difficulty in women is their own or their partners' lack of knowledge about the female sexual response and female genitalia. The problem is often resolved by helping clients and their partners learn to extend stimulation and lovemaking beyond genitally focused sex. Greater sensate exchange between partners, expanding women's arousal pattern, directed masturbation, and anxiety management also can be helpful.

Dyspareunia and Vulvodynia. Estimates of the prevalence of dyspareunia range from 8.0% (Osborn, Hawton, & Gath, 1988) to 33.5% (Glatt, Zinner, & McCormack, 1990). Although accurate prevalence rates are difficult to determine, studies have shown that causal attributions of pain are related to levels of adjustment. For example, women who cited psychosocial attributions indicated greater psychosocial distress, more problems with sexual function, and more frequent reports of sexual assault as well as lower levels of marital adjustment (Meana, Binik, Khalife, & Cohen, 1999).

Pain is a subjective experience. In dyspareunia, the phenomenology of pain is genital and associated with intercourse. In some cases, pain occurs before or after intercourse as well. In women, "the pain may be described as superficial during intromission or as deep during penile thrusting..., [with] symptoms rang[ing] from mild discomfort to sharp pain" (American Psychiatric Association, 1994, p. 511). Vulvodynia refers to pain located specifically in the vulva. Dyspareunia can be lifelong or acquired as well as generalized or situational. Abarbanel (1978) suggested four phenomenological categories of pain associated with dyspareunia: (a) perception of a sharp but momentary pain that varies in intensity, (b) repeated and intense discomfort, (c) aching, and (d) intermittent painful pangs or twinges. A thorough medical examination must be conducted to rule out physical factors such as pelvic tumors, hymeneal remnants, prolapsed ovaries, and scarring that occurs as a result of either an episiotomy or vaginal repair (Bancroft, 1995). Hormonal changes that result from contraceptive use or menopausal changes can lessen vaginal lubrication and subsequently cause soreness and irritation during intercourse or penetration. Once organic causes of pain are ruled out, psychological factors such as anxiety, poor body image, religiosity, anger, and distrust toward the patient's partner should be investigated.

Psychotherapy is an important element in the treatment of dyspareunia and should be approached in a multimodal framework to examine the patient's (a) behavior (e.g., deficits and shortcomings in sexual techniques), (b) affect (e.g., feelings of guilt, shame, and anger), (c) sensation (e.g., assessment of the location, type, frequency, and intensity of pain), (d) imagery (e.g., body image, negative memories), (e) cognition (e.g., negative self-statements, dysfunctional beliefs), (f) interpersonal functioning (e.g., communication, climate between partners), and (g) biological factors (e.g., improper hygiene, medications) (Leiblum & Rosen, 1989).

Vaginismus. Vaginismus is a relatively rare disorder characterized by "recurrent or persistent involuntary contraction of the perineal muscles surrounding the outer third of the vagina when vaginal penetration with penis, finger, tampon, or speculum is attempted" (American Psychiatric Association, 1994, p. 513). In some women, thoughts of penetration alone can create spasms. Contractions can be mild, creating tightening and discomfort, or severe, preventing any penetration. Sexual desire, pleasure, and orgasmic capacity can be impaired as a result of the disorder. The patient should be screened for potential organic factors that can contribute to formation of the disorder such as vaginal hysterectomies or other surgeries, atrophic vaginitis, endometriosis, painful hymenal tags, and urethral caruncle (Lamont, 1978; Tollison & Adams, 1979). Although many of these conditions are not directly responsible for vaginismus, they may be associated with the disorder indirectly through classical conditioning.

The main objective is to eliminate the "spasmodic reflexive contraction of the muscles controlling the vaginal entrance typically through a series of gradual approximations with the insertion of increasingly larger dilators" (Leiblum, Pervin, & Campbell, 1989, p. 113). Use of graduated rubber or plastic catheters helps to extinguish the conditioned spasmodic response via systematic desensitization. The patient or her partner's fingers can also do insertion. In addition, it is important that the patient feel in control of what is happening, and this extends to her guiding penile entry during coitus. Use of the female superior position during intercourse should be suggested because this can help the patient to maintain control of entry and movement. Cognitive-behavioral approaches are also used to challenge underlying thoughts and beliefs that drive the conditioned fear response. Psychotherapy can be used to explore unconscious fears and conflicts that may underlie the disorder. Therapy should include progressive relaxation techniques and fantasy exercises to help alleviate fears of gynecological exams as well as intercourse.

Male Sexual Dysfunctions

Male Erectile Disorder. An estimated 30 million men suffer from ED in the United States. ED prevalence rates increase to more than 50% in men ages 50 to 70 years, and ED occurs in approximately 40% of men with diabetes (Feldman, Goldstein, McKinlay, Hatzichristou, & Krane, 1994). In men under age 35 years, approximately 70% suffer from psychogenic ED, whereas 85% of men over age 50 years have organic ED (Weiss & Mellinger, 1990).

ED has been defined as an inability to achieve or sustain an erection of sufficient rigidity or duration to enable satisfactory sexual performance (American Psychiatric Association, 1994). Often, ED is associated with older age (Marumo, Nakashima, & Murai, 2001). There are different patterns to ED, with some patients reporting an inability to obtain an erection from the onset of sexual activity and others reporting having a satisfactory erection at the onset of sex but then losing the erection when attempting penetration or once penetration is complete. Particularly when ED is psychogenic, patients will frequently report having an erection on awakening or during self-masturbation. Subtypes include lifelong versus acquired and generalized versus situational.

To obtain a diagnosis of ED and an accurate understanding of the etiology of the disorder, assessment should include a detailed sexual and medical history, physical examination, and psychological interview. A medical history and a physical examination are particularly important because a number of physiological factors contribute to the pathophysiology of ED. These conditions include, but are not limited to, (a) cardiovascular disease and hypertension (Burchardt et al., 2001), (b) other vascular disorders and neuropathy associated with diabetes (Dey & Shepherd, 2002; Hecht, Neundorfer, Kiesewetter, & Hiltz, 2001), (c) prostate cancer or prostate cancer treatments (Incrocci, Slob, & Levendag, 2002; McCullough, 2001; Potters, Torre, Fearn, Leibel, & Kattan, 2001), (d) spinal cord lesions (Biering-Sorensen & Sonksen, 2001), and (e) hyperparathyroidism (Chou et al., 2001). Depression (Seidman & Roose, 2000), cigarette smoking (McVary, Carrier, & Wessells, 2001; Spangler, Summerson, Bell, & Konan, 2002), and medications (Gelenberg et al., 2000; Rizvi, Hampson, & Harvey, 2002) can also affect erectile function.

Other assessment techniques include measurement of voluntary contractile activity of the ischiocavernosus muscle (Kawanishi et al., 2001), penile pharmacotesting with alprostadil (Aversa et al., 2002), sexual stimulation penograms (Choi et al., 2002), and measures of nocturnal penile tumescence (Basar, Atan, & Tekdogan, 2001).

Several treatment options are available for organic causes of ED. There are pharmacological agents such as apomorphine (Altwein & Keuler, 2001; Mulhall, Bukofzer, Edmonds, & George, 2001), yohimbine (an alpha-adrenoreceptor blocker) (Tam, Worcel, & Wyllie, 2001), hormonal treatments, and (most recently) sildenafil citrate (Viagra). Sildenafil has been shown to be efficacious in treating ED in men who suffer from mild to moderate depressive illness (Muller & Benkert, 2001; Seidman, Roose, Menza, Shabsigh, & Rosen, 2001) and spinal cord injury (Sanchez et al., 2001). Sildenafil has also been shown to be a safe and effective treatment of ED in both long- and short-term treatment (Burls, Gold, & Clark, 2001; Fagelman, Fagelman, & Shabsigh, 2001; Steers et al., 2001) and has been found to improve the quality of life in those patients who use sildenafil (Giuliano,

Pena, & Mishra, 2002). Studies suggest that sildenafil is particularly effective in cases of arterial insufficiency and psychogenic causes of ED (Basar, Tekdogan, et al., 2001) and that the drug is well tolerated in men over age 65 years (Tsujimura et al., 2002). However, even when the patient is treated effectively with sildenafil, it is important to address the psychosocial factors that either preceded or developed as a result of ED (Dunn, Croft, & Hackett, 1999; McDowell, Snellgrove, & Bond, 2001), given that sexual satisfaction (Shirai, Takimoto, Ishii, & Iwamoto, 2001), quality of partnership (Muller, Ruof, Graf-Morgenstern, Porst, & Benkert, 2001; Paige, Hays, Litwin, Rajfer, & Shapiro, 2001), and attitudes toward interventions have important consequences for the planning and treatment of sexual problems and partner satisfaction.

Intracavernosal injections are another treatment option (Richter, Vardi, Ringel, Shalev, & Nissenkorn, 2001). Intracavernosal injection of alprostadil (Caverject) has resulted in reported success rates of 67% to 85% (Engelhardt, Plas, Hübner, & Pflüger, 1998). When injected directly into the corpus cavernosum, alprostadil causes the arteriolar smooth muscle cells to relax. No more than three injections per week, with a period of 24 hours between administrations, is recommended. Another option is transurethral alprostadil. Once the suppository is inserted, it will first diffuse into the corpus spongiosum and then into the corpus cavernosum, whereby the arteriolar smooth muscle relaxes, resulting in an erection (Viera, Clenney, Shenenberger, & Green, 1999).

A third option in the treatment of organic ED is a vacuum erection device. Most devices work by creating a vacuum in a cylinder placed over the penis. The vacuum draws blood into the corpora cavernosa and is trapped by placing a constricting band at the base of the penis. Another option is the penile prosthetic implant. Two types of implants exist: a semi-rigid silicone implant (Small, Carrion, &

Gordon, 1975) and a hydrolic inflatable device (Scott, Bradley, & Timm, 1973). However, factors such as poor marital adjustment and poor coping ability have been associated with poor postsurgical results (Meisler, Carey, & Krauss, 1988; Schover, 1989).

In cases of psychogenic ED, the patient should be referred for sex therapy, the goal of which is to restore the patient's potency to the best level possible. The meaning of impotence must be explored and transformed into cognitive and emotional experience because "attentional processes are highly salient in creating disruption of genital responsivity" (Beck, 1986, p. 218). Men with psychogenic impotence often express feelings of inadequacy, confusion, fear, anger, and shame. Performance anxiety becomes central in their sexual experience as they take on a "spectator" role, watching to see whether their penises will "perform" at will as expected. Once an erectile "failure" occurs, the cycle of anxiety, fear, and shame repeats itself. Self-generated distraction techniques that use cognitive interference have been used successfully to help manage anxiety in patients with ED (Beck, 1986; Beck & Barlow, 1986a, 1986b).

Partners of men with psychogenic impotence experience their own fears and frustrations. It is common for a partner to think that she is somehow responsible for the patient's difficulties. For example, the partner may think that she is no longer attractive to the patient or that the patient is having an affair. Thus, it is important to include the partner in treatment so that the relationship can be treated as well (Leiblum, 2002). Men with psychogenic ED can overcome the disorder "by understanding their responses to their dilemmas, integrating previously unacknowledged feelings, seeking new solutions to old problems, increasing communication, surmounting the barriers to intimacy, and restoring sexual confidence" (Althof, 1989, p. 239).

Various interventions can be used in the treatment of psychogenic ED. Behavioral exercises and cognitive-behavioral therapy can be used to confront performance anxiety, dispute irrational beliefs, counteract negative body image issues, and heighten sensuality. Sensate focus is a central aspect of treatment (Table 18.3). In addition to using these behavioral approaches, the couple needs to be educated about sexual function and anatomy. Therapy can also address the destructive sexual system and dysfunctional relationship dynamics that inevitably develop in these cases.

Male Orgasmic Disorder. Male orgasmic disorder is characterized by "persistent or recurrent delay in, or absence of, orgasm following a normal sexual excitement phase" (American Psychiatric Association, 1994, p. 507). Consideration of this diagnosis must take into account the patient's age and whether the amount of stimulation the patient receives is adequate in duration and intensity. Delayed ejaculation can occur during lovemaking and/or during masturbation. Most men with orgasmic disorder report feeling sufficiently aroused at the onset of sex. However, coital thrusting soon feels like a chore rather than a source of pleasure. Maintaining an erection is not a problem. Soreness and discomfort due to prolonged rubbing can aggravate matters and often makes for greater frustration for both the patient and his partner. Certain medical conditions (e.g., spinal injuries, nerve damage, diabetes), substance abuse, and medications (e.g., beta blockers, antidepressants) can cause the disorder. In fact, drug therapies are the most common cause of the dysfunction. A thorough examination by a physician is warranted. Psychological problems, such as traumatic childhood experiences, extreme anxiety or guilt, ridicule from a past partner, and feelings of anger, can also contribute to the disorder.

A distinction must be made between male orgasmic disorder and "retrograde ejaculation." Normally, ejaculation is caused by contraction of the pelvic muscles, which are behind the penis and expel semen out of the penis through the urethra. Retrograde ejaculation is a condition in which semen travels back into the bladder instead of forward through the urethra (Wolf, 2001). Although semen is absent, the sensation of orgasm is still usually pleasant.

A third type of orgasmic disorder is called anejaculation. In this condition, the patient is unable to ejaculate at all. Anejaculation can be caused by spinal injury or duct abnormalities (Cole, 2002; Goldstone, 2000) or by psychological factors. A thorough medical examination is necessary to rule out any physiological causes, at which point referral to a sex therapist or psychologist is warranted.

If an orgasmic disorder is caused by medication, symptoms should remit once the medication is discontinued or the dose is adjusted. In the case of retrograde ejaculation, oral medications are available that can help to contract bladder neck muscles. Psychotherapy can help by giving the patient "permission" to concentrate on his own pleasure as well as by examining underlying psychological factors that may be contributing to the problem.

Early or Premature Ejaculation. Despite its common occurrence, it is difficult to estimate the frequency of premature ejaculation (PE). Estimates have ranged from as low as 4% (Metz, Pryor, Abuzzahab, Nesvacil, & Koznar, 1997) to as high as 36% (Nettelbladt & Uddenberg, 1979). It is estimated that approximately 25% of men report having an unsuccessful first intercourse experience, with the most common reason being that ejaculation occurs before vaginal penetration (McCarthy, 1989). The DSM-IV (American Psychiatric Association, 1994) defines PE as the "persistent or recurrent onset of orgasm and ejaculation with minimal sexual stimulation before, on, or shortly after penetration and before the person wishes it" (p. 509). Definitions of PE vary, and this is reflected in experimental and clinical research (Rowland, Cooper, & Schneider, 2001).

When considering a diagnosis of PE, it is important to take into account the patient's age, novelty of the sexual experience or partner, and frequency of sexual activity. Relationship stress, anger at one's partner, anxiety about intimacy, and low frequency of intercourse are other possible causes of PE. Assessment of PE should include an investigation of neurological conditions, acute physical illness, physical injury, and medication side effects (Metz & Pryor, 2000). It is also important to determine whether early ejaculation occurs during masturbation and whether it is partner specific.

It is helpful to understand the physiology of the male orgasm to better understand PE. Ejaculation occurs as a result of many different physiological events. Many young men think that orgasm and ejaculation are the same when in fact the two are related but separate processes. It is possible for men to have an orgasm without ejaculating (dry orgasm), just as it is possible to experience a partial ejaculation without the sensation of orgasm.

Early in sexual development, masturbation is often practiced in a rapid, intense, and goal-oriented fashion. As a result, the "adolescent male focuses only on penis stimulation and is intent on reaching orgasm and the associated few seconds of intense pleasure" (McCarthy, 1989, p. 145), and this is counter to the process of learning ejaculatory control. Feelings of guilt, anxiety, shame, and/or fear of being caught may contribute to the problem. Eventually, a combination of high anxiety and sexual excitement can create a pattern of early ejaculation, which is often made worse by the tendency of the patient to self-monitor his orgasmic response. Thus, an important component of treatment is teaching the patient to experience masturbation and intercourse as a more sensual, pleasure-focused, and "whole body" experience.

Orgasm in males is a two-phase process consisting of the emission phase and the ejaculatory phase. Emission is the movement of semen into the urethra. Expulsion is the propulsion of semen out of the urethra at orgasm. A reflex of pelvic floor muscles that

CASE STUDY

"Reggie," age 30 years, and "Marsha," age 27 years, sought therapy with a presenting complaint of marital discord. The partners stated that their marriage of 2 years was already in trouble and that therapy was their "last resort." Both Reggie and Marsha said that they loved one another and did not want to separate or pursue a divorce. Neither was married before. The partners had no children but expressed that having children was something they would like to do in the future. Marsha was in the third year of her doctoral program in education. Reggie was currently working two part-time jobs while searching for employment as a data operations manager. Reggie had his B.S. degree but had "no desire to go back to graduate school."

The partners agreed that over the past 8 months their relationship had become more and more strained. Marsha expressed aggravation with what she termed "Reggie's lack of motivation in seeking stable employment." Marsha was feeling extremely pressured with graduate school, and although she earned a small income by teaching, the couple was having to rely on school loans as its main source of support. Reggie disagreed with Marsha's assessment of his job search efforts. He maintained that Marsha's anger was due to her desire to start a family and that she interpreted his "lack of motivation" as an indicator that his desire for children was not as great as hers. As the assessment continued, more information was gained about the partners' respective developmental histories, family lives, family compositions, and medical conditions. Neither had any past psychiatric history. Both were occasional "social" drinkers, with no history of substance abuse. Neither partner smoked.

When asked about previous relationships, Reggie stated that he had been engaged at age 22 years but that his fiancé had called off the wedding. Since that time, he dated and had sexual relationships with several women until he began dating Marsha 3 years ago. Marsha dated in high school. She had two long-term relationships; one lasting 2½ years and the other lasting 6 years. The 6-year relationship was with her "high school sweetheart" and began when Marsha was age 17 years. The other relationship took place with a man she met in college when Marsha was age 24 years. Reggie and Marsha had experience with sex prior to their marriage. Reggie claimed that he found sex pleasurable but that he recently had trouble maintaining an erection. He stated that he had less interest in sex. He denied any past erectile difficulties. In contrast, Marsha suffered pain with intercourse that worsened over time. She began having pain at age 23 years. Marsha described the pain as a "sharp stab high up inside me" that occurred after entry and during intercourse. Marsha was recently referred to a urologist, who told her that one reason for her pain was that her urethra was situated very close to her vagina, and this could create abdominal pain during intercourse, particularly during orgasm. She was given an antispasmodic medication. Marsha complained about using the medication because it had to be taken with a lot of water several hours prior to intercourse.

Marsha and Reggie were seen individually for one session. In the session with Marsha, she stated that she is able to lubricate without difficulty and can experience orgasm during oral sex and masturbation. She also reiterated her suspicion that Reggie might not want children after all. She expressed feeling angry and betrayed. Marsha also described herself as "focused and intense" and stated that Reggie tends to be much more passive in the relationship, causing Marsha to feel as though she has to be "the responsible one." Marsha reported that another source of discord was Reggie's avoidance of conflict. Marsha insisted that Reggie will "tell me what I want to hear" rather than what he really thinks.

In the session with Reggie, he disclosed that he was not ready to have children and felt great pressure from Marsha to "get his act together" so that the couple will be in a better financial position to start a family. Reggie expressed that he moved across the country and left a good-paying position so that Marsha could attend graduate school. He felt resentful that Marsha "seems to forget that." Reggie stated that since his erectile difficulties began, he has been able to maintain an erection on some occasions during masturbation. He has also awakened with an erection periodically. Reggie stated that he rarely initiates sex. When Marsha initiates sex, he tells her that he is tired or not in the mood.

Reggie and Marsha had a number of relational issues that needed to be addressed in therapy before sex therapy would become the focus of treatment. During the first month of treatment, the couple's relationship was the focus of therapy. Reggie and Marsha were asked not to engage in sexual activity during this time. They were encouraged to show affection and be close if and when they were comfortable with doing so. As the partners' relationship began to improve, they began spending more time with each other, reported enjoying each other's company more, and were expressing more affection toward one another. Working on their relationship in general helped to move them to greater nonsexual intimacy, and this is often an important step in sex therapy. Despite the request not to do so, the couple attempted intercourse twice before sex therapy began. Each time, Reggie was unable to maintain his erection. Marsha complained that she was still finding the experience painful. It is common for couples to "break the rules" during treatment and to engage in sexual intercourse or other forms of genital contact. Thus, it is important to let the couple know that unsuccessful attempts are a frequent and "normal" occurrence so as to avert further setbacks.

Reggie had expressed feeling upset with himself. Marsha admitted that she would become frustrated and angry when "sex didn't work." Reggie was experiencing interfering thoughts prior to and during sexual relations. He admitted feeling "like less of a man" since his problem began. He readily became worried about the quality and duration of his erection as well as images of Marsha's displeasure, disappointment, and anger. These thoughts would lead to greater anxiety and depression.

It was important to work with Reggie to help him restructure his thoughts and focus on thoughts that would facilitate feeling pleasure rather than those that would inhibit his sexual function. Once Reggie was better able to establish a positive sexually facilitating thought process, he was ready to proceed with sensate focus. During this time, Marsha's fear that she was somehow responsible for her husband's lack of sexual interest, and the subsequent feelings of inadequacy and frustration, were explored. This was an important component in assessing Marsha's cognitive process. Misunderstandings on the part of the partner can sabotage treatment. Educating the couple about ED helped to alleviate some of Marsha's fears and resentment. The couple also had to be educated about sensate focus and why certain restrictions were warranted during the intervention.

Prior to beginning sensate focus, couples should be told to assert and protect themselves during each session. Self-assertion involves the expression of phrases such as "I would like you to . . ." and "Why don't you . . ." Examples of self-protective phrases would include "I don't find that pleasing" and "Please touch me somewhere else." A gentle removal of a partner's hand can also serve this purpose. One reason for this is that partners need to realize that likes and dislikes can be communicated without personalizing one another's statements. A formal agreement is made between the partners to ban attempts at intercourse or other genital contact during early stages of the program. This agreement removes the pressure to "succeed" or perform. Goals of sensate focus include (a) learning to touch one's partner for *one's own* pleasure, (b) relaxing when being caressed and using a protective statement or gesture when one finds the touch unpleasant, (c) learning to recognize when one is "spectatoring," (d) recognizing how nice it is to touch and be with one's partner, (e) recognizing how nice it is to be touched, and (f) becoming more acutely aware of what one is feeling physically and emotionally during the session.

Reggie and Marsha began sensate focus treatment that, in their case, lasted approximately 3 months. Throughout the treatment process, it was necessary to monitor the partners' communication with one another regarding both sexual and nonsexual matters. It was also important to check out the couple's comfort levels during the duration of treatment and to attend to any interfering thoughts or compliance problems that surfaced during the intervention period. Reggie and Marsha also were instructed to conduct their "sessions" in an environment that was free of distractions and conducive to facilitating an erotic experience. This meant that they also needed to schedule their sessions when they had adequate time to be together. Relational issues and the general quality of the couple's relationship continued to be an integral part of therapy.

Table 18.3 outlines the progressive stages of sensate focus therapy. The couple was to spend at least 30 minutes together, three times per week. As Marsha and Reggie approached the fifth stage of sensate focus, which involved vaginal containment without thrusting, certain modifications had to be made to try to alleviate

Marsha's pain and discomfort. During this stage, the receptive partner controls activity. In this way, the amount of movement and depth of penetration can be controlled by the partner. Having Marsha assume the "top" position further enhanced her control. By doing so, she was better able to angle her pelvis in such a way that she had less discomfort. In the supine position, Marsha was encouraged to place pillows under her hips and to experiment with the height and angle that is most comfortable. During the final stage of sensate focus treatment when intercourse resumed, it was suggested that Marsha use a certain lubricant to ensure adequate lubrication and to heighten arousal. Once Reggie's ED resolved, the couple was given videotapes that demonstrated varied sexual positions and techniques. These tapes gave the couple additional information about positions that would be most comfortable for Marsha and satisfying to both partners.

Eventually, Reggie and Marsha were able to resolve their sexual difficulties. Treatment success was due in large part to the partners' commitment to the therapeutic process, their resolve to work through their marital and relational issues, and their compliance with the sensate focus intervention. They were seen approximately 6 months after the termination of therapy for a follow-up visit. No problems were noted at that time.

rhythmically contract causes ejaculation. There is a point at which men are not able to voluntarily control ejaculation. This is called the point of "ejaculatory inevitability," which is usually a few seconds before the start of ejaculation. A central intervention in the treatment of PE is to help the patient learn to identify and control the point of ejaculatory inevitability. One method used to accomplish this involves what is called the "stop-start" technique. The patient begins by instituting the "start-stop" technique during masturbation. Usually this begins without the use of lubrication. This allows the patient more privacy and control. The patient stops self-stimulation until he feels like he has regained control. At that time, he begins stimulating his penis again. This procedure is repeated over time until the patient is able to prolong his engagement in sexual stimulation while controlling his urge to ejaculate. Eventually, this procedure is transferred to stimulation with the partner. The couple can institute the technique by having the partner on top with the patient instructing the partner to stop movement when he senses he is losing control. Often, the couple can progress to simply slowing down when the patient begins to feel close to ejaculating.

A second method of intervention is the use of the "squeeze technique," which involves stimulation to the penis until the patient is close to ejaculation. Just prior to ejaculation, the patient or his partner places his or her hand just below the head of the penis and squeezes hard enough to cause partial loss of the patient's erection. This technique is meant to help the patient become aware of sensations that precede orgasm and to then control and delay orgasm on his own. This technique progresses from manual stimulation to motionless intercourse and eventually to intercourse with movement.

Drug therapy can also be effective. Low doses of antidepressant medications such as Zoloft, Anafronil, and Prozac are often used because of their sexual side effects that include the prolongation of orgasm. More recently, topical agents such as anesthetics and herbal medications have been investigated as a possible treatment option (Choi et al., 1999, 2002; Morales, 2000).

CONCLUSIONS

The field of sexual science has advanced considerably; however, the conceptual framework that guides the practice of sex therapy has traditionally been, and continues to be, rooted in biological science. A failure to broaden our understanding and integration of individual, relational, spiritual, and psychosocial factors that may contribute to the problem at hand compromises our effectiveness in helping those who struggle with issues pertaining to sex and sexuality. Treatments have continued to be more technologically or pharmacologically advanced. Granted, sex therapy can be credited for its ability to treat sexual problems quickly and effectively; however, the goal of most approaches is performance based. By shifting the traditional behavioral or cognitive-behavioral approaches "to one that moves beyond behavior and communication to personal growth in relationship, we discover new horizons in human sexual potential" (Kleinplatz, 2001, p. 190). An important factor in sex therapy is to help guide individuals in exercising greater personal agency over their relational needs as well as their erotic potential. Interventions should be geared toward treating the individual as a whole, not simply as a malfunction in biological equipment.

REFERENCES

Abarbanel, A. (1978). Diagnosis and treatment of coital discomfort. In J. LoPiccolo & L. LoPiccolo (Eds.), *Handbook of sex therapy* (pp. 241–259). New York: Plenum.

Althof, S. E. (1989). Psychogenic impotence: Treatment of men and couples. In S. R. Leiblum & R. C. Rosen (Eds.), *Principles and practice of sex therapy: Update for the 1990's* (pp. 237–265). New York: Guilford.

Altwein, J. E., & Keuler, F. U. (2001). Oral treatment of erectile dysfunction with apomorphine SL. *Urologia Internationalis, 67,* 257–263.

American Psychiatric Association. (1994). *Diagnostic and statistical manual of mental disorders* (4th ed.). Washington, DC: Author.

Aversa, A., Isidori, A. M., Caprio, M., Cerilli, M., Frajese, V., & Fabbri, A. (2002). Penile pharmacotesting in diagnosing male erectile dysfunction: Evidence for lack of accuracy and specificity. *International Journal of Andrology, 25*(1), 6–10.

Avina, C., O'Donohue, W. T., & Fisher, J. E. (2000). Sexual dysfunction in later life. In S. K. Whitbourne (Ed.), *Psychopathology in later life* (pp. 173–187). New York: John Wiley.

Bancroft, J. (1995). *Human sexuality and its problems* (2nd ed.). London: Longman.

Bartlik, B., & Goldstein, M. Z. (2001). Men's sexual health after midlife. *Psychiatric Services, 52,* 291–293.

Basar, M., Atan, A., & Tekdogan, U. Y. (2001). New concept parameters of RigiScan in differentiation of vascular erectile dysfunction: Is it a useful test? *International Journal of Urology, 8,* 686–691.

Basar, M., Tekdogan, U. Y., Yilmaz, E., Basar, H., Atan, A., & Batislam, E. (2001). The efficacy of sildenafil in different etiologies of erectile dysfunction. *International Urology and Nephrology, 32,* 403–407.

Beck, J. G. (1986). Self-generated distraction in erectile dysfunction: The role of attentional processes. *Advances in Behaviour Research & Therapy, 8,* 205–221.

Beck, J. G., & Barlow, D. H. (1986a). The effects of anxiety and attentional focus on sexual responding: I. Physiological patterns in erectile dysfunction. *Behaviour Research & Therapy, 24,* 9–17.

Beck, J. G., & Barlow, D. H. (1986b). The effects of anxiety and attentional focus on sexual responding: II. Cognitive and affective patterns in erectile dysfunction. *Behaviour Research & Therapy, 24,* 19–26.

Bhugra, D. (2000). Literature update: A critical review. *Sexual and Relationship Therapy, 15,* 421–427.

Biering-Sorensen, F., & Sonksen, J. (2001). Sexual function in spinal cord lesioned men. *Spinal Cord, 39,* 455–470.

Birk, L. (1999). Sex therapy. In A. M.. Nicholi (Ed.), *The Harvard guide to psychiatry* (pp. 525–542). Cambridge, MA: Belknap Press of Harvard University Press.

Burchardt, M., Burchardt, T., Anastasiadis, A. G., Kill, A. J., Shabsigh, A., de la Taille, A., Pawar, R. V., Baer, L., & Shabsigh, R. (2001). Erectile dysfunction is a marker for cardiovascular complications and psychological functioning in men with hypertension. *International Journal of Impotence Research, 13,* 276–281.

Burls, A., Gold, L., & Clark, W. (2001). Systematic review of randomized controlled trials of sildenafil (Viagra) in the treatment of male erectile dysfunction. *British Journal of General Practice, 51,* 1004–1012.

Choi, H. K., Choi, Y. J., Choi, Y. D., Rha, K. H., Kim, J. H., & Kim, D. K. (2002). SS-penogram: A new diagnostic test for erectile dysfunction. *Yonsei Medical Journal, 43*(1), 1–6.

Choi, H. K., Xin, Z. C., Choi, Y. D., Lee, W. H., Mah, S. Y., & Kim, D. K. (1999). Safety and efficacy study with various doses of SS-cream in patients with premature ejaculation in a double-blind, randomized, placebo controlled clinical study. *International Journal of Impotence Research, 11,* 261–264.

Chou, F. F., Lee, C. H., Shu, K., Yu, T. J., Hsu, K. T., & Sheen-Chen, S. M. (2001). Improvement of sexual function in male patients after parathyroidectomy for secondary hyperparathyroidism. *Journal of the American College of Surgeons, 193,* 486–492.

Cole, J. (2002). *Delayed ejaculation.* [Online]. Retrieved May 22, 2002, from www.bbc.co.uk/health/mens/rel_sex_delay.shtml

Davis, S. (2001). *Testosterone and sexual desire in women.* [Online]. Retrieved May 2, 2001, from www.aasect.org/jsetarticle.cfm

Dennerstein, L., Dudley, E., & Burger, H. (2001). Are changes in sexual functioning during midlife due to aging or menopause? *Fertility and Sterility, 76,* 456–460.

Denney, N. W., Field, J. K., & Quadagno, D. (1984). Sex differences in sexual needs and desires. *Archives of Sexual Behavior, 13,* 233–245.

Dey, J., & Shepherd, M. D. (2002). Evaluation and treatment of erectile dysfunction in men with diabetes mellitus. *Mayo Clinic Proceedings, 77,* 276–282.

Dunn, K. M., Croft, P. R., & Hackett, G. I. (1999). Association of sexual problems with social, psychological, and physical problems in men and women: A cross sectional population. *Journal of Epidemiology and Community Health, 53,* 144–148.

Engelhardt, P., Plas, E., Hübner, W. A., & Pflüger, H. (1998). Comparison of intraurethral liposomal and intracavernosal prostaglandin-E1 in the management of erectile dysfunction. *British Journal of Urology, 81,* 441–444.

Fagelman, E., Fagelman, A., & Shabsigh, R. (2001). Efficacy, safety, and use of sildenafil in urologic practice. *Urology, 57,* 1141–1144.

Feldman, H. A., Goldstein, I., McKinlay, J. B., Hatzichristou, D. G., & Krane, R. J. (1994). Impotence and its medical and psychosocial correlates: results of the Massachusetts male ageing study. *Journal of Urology, 151,* 54–61.

Gaither, G. A., & Plaud, J. J. (1997). The effects of secondary stimulus characteristics on men's sexual arousal. *Journal of Sex Research, 34,* 231–236.

Gelenberg, A. J., Delgado, P., & Nurnberg, H. G. (2000). The side effects of antidepressant drugs. *Current Psychiatry Reports, 2,* 223–227.

Giuliano, F., Pena, B., & Mishra, A. (2002). Efficacy results and quality-of-life measures in men receiving sildenafil citrate for the treatment of erectile dysfunction. *Quality of Life Research, 11,* 613.

Glatt, A. E., Zinner, S. H., & McCormack, W. M. (1990). The prevalence of dysparenia. *Obstetrics and Gynecology, 75,* 433–436.

Goldstone, S. E. (2000). *Retrograde ejaculation.* [Online]. Available: www.gayhealth.com/iowa-robot/common/condition.html?record=51

Halvorsen, J. G., & Metz, M. E. (1992). Sexual dysfunction: I. Classification, etiology, and pathogenesis. *Journal of the American Board of Family Practice, 5*(1), 51–61.

Hecht, M. J., Neundorfer, B., Kiesewetter, F., & Hiltz, M. J. (2001). Neuropathy is a major contributing factor to diabetic erectile dysfunction. *Neurological Research, 23,* 651–654.

Heiman, J. R. (1978). Uses of psychophysiology in the assessment and treatment of sexual dysfunction. In J. LoPiccolo & L. LoPiccolo (Eds.), *Handbook of sex therapy* (pp. 123–137). New York: Plenum.

Heiman, J. R., & Grafton-Becker, V. (1989). Orgasmic disorders in women. In S. R. Leiblum & R. C. Rosen (Eds.), *Principles and practice of sex therapy: Update for the 1990's* (pp. 51–88). New York: Guilford.

Heiman, J. R., & Meston, C. M. (1997). Evaluating sexual dysfunction in women. *Clinical Obstetrics and Gynecology, 40,* 616–629.

Herbert, J. (1996). Sexuality, stress, and the chemical architecture of the brain. *Annual Review of Sex Research, 7,* 1–43.

Hurlbert, D. F. (1991). The role of assertiveness in female sexuality. *Journal of Sex and Marital Therapy, 17,* 183–190.

Hurlbert, D. F., White, L. C., Powell, R. D., & Apt, C. (1993). Orgasm consistency training in the treatment of women reporting hypoactive sexual desire: An outcome comparison of women-only groups and couples-only groups. *Journal of Behavior Therapy and Experimental Psychiatry, 24,* 3–13.

Incrocci, L., Slob, A. K., & Levendag, P. C. (2002). Sexual (dys)function after radiotherapy for prostate cancer: A review. *International Journal of Radiation Oncology, Biology, Physics, 52,* 681–693.

Jones, J. C., & Barlow, D. H. (1990). Self-reported frequency of sexual urges, fantasies, and masturbatory fantasies in heterosexual males and females. *Archives of Sexual Behavior, 19,* 269–279.

Jupp, J. J., & McCabe, M. (1989). Sexual desire, general arousability, and sexual dysfunction. *Archives of Sexual Behavior, 18,* 509–516.

Kaplan, H. S. (1977). Hypoactive sexual desire. *Journal of Sex and Marital Therapy, 3,* 3–9.

Kaplan, H. S. (1992). Does the CAT technique enhance female orgasm? *Journal of Sex and Mental Therapy, 18,* 285–291.

Katz, R. C., Gipson, M., & Turner, S. (1992). Brief report: Recent findings on the Sexual Aversion Scale. *Journal of Sex and Marital Therapy, 18,* 141–146.

Kawanishi, Y., Kishimoto, T., Kimura, K., Yamaguchi, K., Nakatuji, H., Kojima, K., Yamamoto, A., & Numata, A. (2001). Spring balance evaluation of the ischiocavernosus muscle. *International Journal of Impotence Research, 13,* 294–297.

Kelly, M. P., Strassberg, D. S., & Kircher, J. R. (1990). Attitudinal and experiential correlates of anorgasmia. *Archives of Sexual Behavior, 19,* 165–177.

Kleinplatz, P. J. (2001). *New direction in sex therapy: Innovations and alternatives.* New York: Taylor & Francis.

Lalumiere, M. L., & Quinsey, V. L. (1998). Pavlovian conditioning of sexual interests in human males. *Archives of Sexual Behavior, 27,* 241–252.

Lamont, J. A. (1978). Vaginismus. *American Journal of Obstetrics and Gynecology, 131,* 632–636.

Laqueur, T. (1990). *Making sex: Body and gender from the Greeks to Freud.* Cambridge, MA: Harvard University Press.

Laumann, E. O., Gagnon, J. H., Michael, R. T., & Michaels, S. (1994). *The social organization of sexuality.* Chicago: University of Chicago Press.

Laumann, E. O., Gagnon, J. H., Michael, R. T., & Michaels, S. (1995). *National health and social life survey, 1992* [computer file, ICPSR version]. Ann Arbor, MI: National Opinion Research. (Chicago: University of Chicago Press)

Leiblum, S. R. (2002). After sildenafil: Bridging the gap between pharmacologic treatment and satisfying sexual relationships. *Journal of Clinical Psychiatry, 63*(5), 17–22.

Leiblum, S. R., Pervin, L. A., & Campbell, E. H. (1989). The treatment of vaginismus: Success and failure. In S. R. Leiblum & R. C. Rosen (Eds.), *Principles and practice of sex therapy: Update for the 1990's* (pp. 113–138). New York: Guilford.

Leiblum, S. R., & Rosen, R. C. (Eds.). (1989). *Principles and practice of sex therapy: Update for the 1990's.* New York: Guilford.

LoPiccolo, J., & Friedman, J. M. (1988). Broad-spectrum treatment of low sexual desire. In S. R. Leiblum & R. C. Rosen (Eds.), *Sexual desire disorders* (pp. 107–144). New York: Guilford.

LoPiccolo, J., & Heiman, J. R. (1978). Sexual assessment and history interview. In J. LoPiccolo & L. LoPiccolo (Eds.), *Handbook of sex therapy* (pp. 103–113). New York: Plenum.

Malavaud, B., Rostaing, L., Rischmann, P., Sarramon, J. P., & Durand, D. (2000). High prevalence of erectile dysfunction after renal transplantation. *Transplantation, 69,* 2121–2124.

Marumo, K., Nakashima, J., & Murai, M. (2001). Age-related prevalence of erectile dysfunction in Japan: Assessment by the International Index of Erectile Function. *International Journal of Urology, 8,* 53–59.

Masters, W. H., & Johnson, V. E. (1970). *Human sexual inadequacy.* Boston: Little, Brown.

McCarthy, B. W. (1989). Cognitive and behavioral strategies and techniques in the treatment of early ejaculation. In S. R. Leiblum & R. C. Rosen (Eds.), *Principles and practice of sex therapy: Update for the 1990's* (pp. 143–167). New York: Guilford.

McCauley, C., & Swann, C. P. (1978). Male-female differences in sexual fantasy. *Journal of Research in Personality, 12,* 76–86.

McCauley, C., & Swann, C. P. (1980). Sex differences in the frequency and functions of fantasies during sexual activity. *Journal of Research in Personality, 14,* 400–411.

McCullough, A. R. (2001). Prevention and management of erectile dysfunction following radical prostatectomy. *Urologic Clinics of North America, 28,* 613–627.

McDowell, A. J., Snellgrove, C. A., & Bond, M. J. (2001). Beyond Viagra: Psychological issues in the assessment and treatment of erectile dysfunction. *Australian Family Physician, 30,* 867–873.

McGovern, K. B., Stewart, R. C., & LoPiccolo, J. (1975). Secondary orgasmic dysfunction: I. Analysis and strategies for treatment. *Archives of Sexual Behavior, 4,* 265–275.

McVary, K. T., Carrier, S., & Wessells, H. (2001). Smoking and erectile dysfunction: Evidence based analysis. *Journal of Urology, 166,* 1624–1632.

Meana, M., Binik, Y. M., Khalife, S., & Cohen, D. (1999). Psychosocial correlates of pain attributions in women with dyspareunia. *Journal of Consultation Liaison Psychiatry, 40,* 497–502.

Meisler, A. W., Carey, M. P., & Krauss, D. J. (1988). Success and failure in penile prosthesis surgery: Two cases highlighting the importance of psychosocial factors. *Journal of Sex and Marital Therapy, 14,* 108–119.

Merrick, G. S., Wallner, K., Butler, W. M., Lief, J. H., & Sutlief, S. (2001). Short-term sexual function after prostate brachytherapy. *International Journal of Cancer, 96,* 313–319.

Meston, C. M., & Frohlich, P. F. (2000). The neurobiology of sexual function. *Archives of General Psychiatry, 57,* 1012–1030.

Metz, M. E., & Epstein, N. (2002). Assessing the role of relationship conflict in sexual dysfunction. *Journal of Sex and Marital Therapy, 28,* 139–164.

Metz, M. E., & Pryor, J. L. (2000). Premature ejaculation: A psychophysiological approach for assessment and management. *Journal of Sex and Marital Therapy, 26,* 293–320.

Metz, M. E., Pryor, J. L., Abuzzahab, F., Nesvacil, L., & Koznar, J. (1997). Premature ejaculation: A psychophysiological review. *Journal of Sex and Marital Therapy, 23,* 3–23.

Morales, A. (2000). Developmental status of topical therapies for erectile and ejaculatory dysfunction. *International Journal of Impotence Research, 12*(4), S80–S85.

Morokoff, P. J. (1985). Effects of sex guilt, repression, sexual "arousability," and sexual experience on female sexual arousal during erotica and fantasy. *Journal of Personality and Social Psychology, 49,* 177–187.

Mulhall, J. P., Bukofzer, S., Edmonds, A. L., & George, M. (2001). An open-label, uncontrolled dose-optimization study of sublingual apomorphine in erectile dysfunction. *Clinical Therapeutics, 23,* 1260–1271.

Muller, M. J., & Benkert, O. (2001). Lower self-reported depression in patients with erectile dysfunction after treatment with sildenafil. *Journal of Affective Disorders, 66,* 255–261.

Muller, M. J., Ruof, J., Graf-Morgenstern, M., Porst, H., & Benkert, O. (2001). Quality of partnership in patients with erectile dysfunction after sildenafil treatment. *Pharmacopsychiatry, 34*(3), 91–95.

Nettelbladt, P., & Uddenberg, N. (1979). Sexual dysfunction and sexual satisfaction in 58 married Swedish men. *Journal of Psychosomatic Research, 23,* 141–147.

O'Donohue, W., Dopke, C. A., & Swingen, D. N. (1997). Psychotherapy for female sexual dysfunction: A review. *Clinical Psychology Review, 17,* 537–566.

Osborn, M., Hawton, K., & Gath, D. (1988). Sexual dysfunction among middle aged women in the community. *British Medical Journal, 296,* 959–962.

Paige, N. M., Hays, R. D., Litwin, M. S., Rajfer, J., & Shapiro, M. E. (2001). Improvement in emotional well-being and relationships of users of sildenafil. *Journal of Urology, 166,* 1744–1748.

Palace, E. M. (1995). A cognitive-physiological process model of sexual arousal and response. *Clinical Psychology: Science and Practice, 3,* 370–384.

Person, E. S., Terestman, N., Myers, W. A., Goldberg, E. L., & Salvadori, C. (1989). Gender differences in sexual behaviors and fantasies in a college population. *Journal of Sex and Marital Therapy, 15,* 187–198.

Pfaus, J. G. (1999). Neurobiology of sexual behavior. *Current Opinion in Neurobiology, 9,* 751–758.

Phillips, R. L., & Slaughter, J. R. (2000). Depression and sexual desire. *American Family Physician, 62,* 782–786.

Pierce, A. P. (2000). The coital alignment technique (CAT): An overview of studies. *Journal of Sex and Marital Therapy, 26,* 257–268.

Pollets, D., Ducharme, S., & Pauporte, J. (1999). Psychological considerations in the assessment of erectile dysfunction. *Sexuality and Disability, 17*(2), 129–145.

Ponticas, Y. (1992). Sexual aversion versus hypoactive sexual desire: A diagnostic challenge. *Psychiatric Medicine, 10,* 274–281.

Potters, L., Torre, T., Fearn, P. A., Leibel, S. A., & Kattan, M. W. (2001). Potency after permanent prostate brachytherapy for localized prostate cancer. *International Journal of Radiation Oncology, Biology, Physics, 50,* 1235–1242.

Regan, P. C. (1996). Rhythms of desire: The association between menstrual cycle phases and female sexual desire. *Canadian Journal of Human Sexuality, 5*(3), 145–156.

Richter, S., Vardi, Y., Ringel, A., Shalev, M., & Nissenkorn, I. (2001). Intracavernous injections: Still the gold standard for treatment of erectile dysfunction. *International Journal of Impotence Research, 13,* 172–175.

Rizvi, K., Hampson, J. P., & Harvey, J. N. (2002). Do lipid-lowering drugs cause erectile dysfunction? A systematic review. *Family Practice, 19*(1), 95–98.

Robins, L. N., Helzer, J. E., Weissman, M. M., Orvaschel, H., Gruenberg, E., Burke, J. D., Jr., & Reiger, D. A. (1984). Lifetime prevalence of specific psychiatric disorders in three sites. *Archives of General Psychiatry, 41,* 949–958.

Rosen, E. C., & Leiblum, S. R. (1989). Assessment and treatment of desire disorders. In S. R. Leiblum & R. C. Rosen (Eds.), *Principles and practice of sex therapy: Update for the 1990's* (pp. 19–50). New York: Guilford.

Rowland, D. L., Cooper, S. E., & Schneider, M. (2001). Defining premature ejaculation for experimental and clinical investigations. *Archives of Sexual Behavior, 30,* 235–253.

Sanchez, R. A., Vidal, J., Jauregui, M. L., Barrera, M., Recio, C., Giner, M., Toribio, L., Salvador, S., Sanmartin, A., de la Fuente, M., Santos, J. F., de Juan, F. J., Moraleda, S., Mendez, J. L., Ramirez, L., & Casado, R. M. (2001). Efficacy, safety, and predictive factors of therapeutic success with sildenafil for erectile dysfunction in patients with different spinal cord injuries. *Spinal Cord, 39,* 637–643.

Scharff, D. E. (1988). An object relations approach to inhibited sexual desire. In S. R. Leiblum & R. C. Rosen (Eds.), *Sexual desire disorders* (pp. 45–74). New York: Guilford.

Schiavi, R. C., & Segraves, R. T. (1995). The biology of sexual function. *Clinical Sexuality, 18*(1), 7–23.

Schover, L. R. (1989). Sexual problems in chronic illness. In S. R. Leiblum, E. Rosen, & C. Raymond (Eds.), *Principles and practice of sex therapy* (3rd ed., pp. 398–422). New York: Guilford.

Schreiner-Engel, P., & Schiavi, R. C. (1986). Lifetime psychopathology in individuals with low sexual desire. *International Journal of Group Psychotherapy, 17,* 211–224.

Schwartz, M. F., & Masters, W. H. (1988). Inhibited sexual desire: The Masters and Johnson Institute treatment model. In S. R. Leiblum & R. C. Rosen (Eds.), *Sexual desire disorders* (pp. 229–242). New York: Guilford.

Scott, F. B., Bradley, W. E., & Timm, G. W. (1973). Treatment of urinary incontinence by implantable prosthetic sphincter. *Urology, 1,* 252–259.

Seeber, M., & Gorrell, C. (2001, November–December). The science of orgasm. *Psychology Today,* pp. 48–59.

Seidman, S. N., & Roose, S. P. (2000). The relationship between depression and erectile dysfunction. *Current Psychiatry Reports, 2,* 201–205.

Seidman, S. N., & Roose, S. P. (2001). Sexual dysfunction and depression. *Current Psychiatry Reports, 3,* 202–208.

Seidman, S. N., Roose, S. P., Menza, M. A., Shabsigh, R., & Rosen, R. C. (2001). Treatment of erectile dysfunction in men with depressive symptoms: Results of a placebo-controlled trial with sildenafil citrate. *American Journal of Psychiatry, 158,* 1623–1630.

Shifren, J. L., Braunstein, G. D., Simon, J. A., Casson, P. R., Buster, J. E., Redmond, G. P., Burki, R. E., Ginsburg, E. S., Rosen, R. C., Leiblum, S. R., Caramelli, K. E., & Mazer, N. A. (2000). Transdermal testosterone treatment in women with impaired sexual function after oophorectomy. *New England Journal of Medicine, 343,* 682–688.

Shirai, M., Takimoto, Y., Ishii, N., & Iwamoto, T. (2001). Influence of erectile dysfunction on daily life and general attitudes towards treatment. *Japanese Journal of Urology, 92,* 666–673.

Shires, A., & Miller, D. (1998). A preliminary study comparing psychological factors associated with erectile dysfunction in heterosexual and homosexual men. *Sexual and Marital Therapy, 13,* 37–49.

Sipski, M., Alexander, C. J., & Rosen, R. (2001). Sexual arousal and orgasm in women: Effects of spinal cord injury. *Annals of Neurology, 49,* 35–44.

Small, M. P., Carrion, H. M., & Gordon, J. A. (1975). Small-Carrion penile prosthesis: New implant management of impotence. *Journal of Urology, 167,* 1190.

Spangler, J. G., Summerson, J. H., Bell, R., & Konen, J. C. (2002). Cigarette smoking and erectile dysfunction. *Journal of Family Practice, 51,* 81.

Spector, I. P., & Carey, M. P. (1990).. Incidence and prevalence of the sexual dysfunctions: A critical review of the empirical literature. *Archives of Sexual Behavior, 19,* 389–401.

Steers, W., Guay, A. T., Leriche, A., Gingell, C., Hargreave, T. B., Wright, P. J., Price, D. E., & Feldman, R. A. (2001). Assessment of the efficacy and safety of Viagra (sildenafil citrate) in men with erectile dysfunction during long-term treatment. *International Journal of Impotence Research, 13,* 261–267.

Stoleru, S., Gregoire, M., Gerard, D., Decety, J., Lafarge, E., Cinotti, L., Lavenne, F., Le Bars, D., Vernet-Maury, E., Rada, H., Collet, C., Mazoyer, B., Forest, M. G., Magnin, F., Spira, A., & Comard, D. (1999). Neuroanatomical correlates of visually evoked sexual arousal in human males. *Archives of Sexual Behavior, 28,* 1–21.

Tam, S. W., Worcel, M., & Wyllie, M. (2001). Yohimbine: A clinical review. *Pharmacology and Therapeutics, 91,* 215–243.

Tiefer, L. (1991). Commentary on the status of sex research: Feminism, sexuality, and sexology. *Journal of Psychology and Human Sexuality, 4,* 5–42.

Tollison, C. D., & Adams, H. E. (1979). *Sexual disorders: Treatment, theory, and research.* New York: Gardner.

Tsujimura, A., Yamanaka, M., Takahashi, T., Mura, H., Nishmura, K., Koga, M., Iwasa, A., Takeyama, M., Matsumiya, K., Takahara, S., & Okuyama, A. (2002). The clinical studies of sildenafil for the ageing male. *International Journal of Andrology, 25*(1), 28–33.

van Berlo, W., & Ensink, B. (2000). Problems with sexuality after sexual assault. *Annual Review of Sex Research, 11,* 235–257.

Verhulst, J., & Heiman, J. R. (1979). An interactional approach to sexual dysfunction. *American Journal of Family Therapy, 7,* 19–36.

Verhulst, J., & Heiman, J. R. (1988). A systems perspective on sexual desire. In S. R. Leiblum & R. C. Rosen (Eds.), *Sexual desire disorders* (pp. 243–270). New York: Guilford.

Viera, A. J., Clenney, T. L., Shenenberger, D. W., & Green, G. F. (1999). Newer pharmacologic alternatives for erectile dysfunction. *American Family Physician, 60,* 1159–1172.

Waldinger, M. D., van De Plas, A., Pattij, T., van Oorschot, R., Coolen, L. M., Veening, J. G., & Oliver, B. (2002). The selective serotonin re-uptake inhibitors fluvoxamine and paroxetine differ in sexual inhibitory effects after chronic treatment. *Psychopharmacology, 160,* 293–289.

Wallen, K. (1990). Desire and ability: Hormones and the regulation of female sexual behavior. *Neuroscience and Biobehavioral Reviews, 14,* 233–241.

Walser, R. D., & Kern, J. M. (1996). Relationships among childhood sexual abuse, sex guilt, and sexual behavior in adult clinical samples. *Journal of Sex Research, 33,* 321–326.

Weiner, D. W., & Rosen, R. C. (1999). Sexual dysfunctions and disorders. In T. Millon, P. H. Blaney, & R. D. Davis (Eds.), *Oxford textbook of psychopathology* (pp. 410–443). New York: Oxford University Press.

Weisberg, R. B., Brown, T. A., Wincze, J. P., & Barlow, D. H. (2001). Causal attributions and male sexual arousal: The impact of attributions for a bogus erectile difficulty on sexual arousal, cognitions, and affect. *Journal of Abnormal Psychology, 100,* 234–334.

Weiss, J. N., & Mellinger, B. C. (1990). Sexual dysfunction in elderly men. *Clinical Geriatric Medicine, 6,* 185–196.

Wincze, J. P. (1971). A comparison of systematic desensitization and "vicarious extinction" in a case of frigidity. *Journal of Behavior Therapy and Experimental Psychiatry, 2,* 285–289.

Wincze, J. P., & Carey, M. P. (1991). *Sexual dysfunction: A guide for assessment and treatment.* New York: Guilford.

Wolf, S. (2001). *Retrograde ejaculation.* [Online]. Retrieved on May 28, 2002, from http://health.discovery.com/diseasesandcond/encyclopedia/2477.html

CHAPTER 19

Human Immunodeficiency Virus and Acquired Immune Deficiency Syndrome

ANDREW C. BLALOCK AND PETER E. CAMPOS

Acquired immune deficiency syndrome (AIDS) is characterized by severe immunosuppression and ensuing opportunistic infections that result from infection with human immunodeficiency virus (HIV). The disease was first recognized in 1981 with the unexplained occurrence of clusters of cases of pneumocystis carinii pneumonia and Kaposi's sarcoma among young homosexual men. As such, it was initially referred to as gay-related immune disorder. As similar cases of these and other opportunistic infections associated with unexplained immunosuppression were subsequently reported in persons with hemophilia, recipients of blood products/transfusions, and injecting drug users and their heterosexual partners, the disease entity was renamed acquired immune deficiency syndrome.

In 1996, pharmacological treatment advances introduced a new era to the epidemic and shifted HIV/AIDS from an acute, imminently terminal medical condition to a more chronic illness. By significantly slowing disease progression, highly active antiretroviral treatment (HAART) (also called combination therapy or cocktail therapy) has extended the lives of many patients living with HIV/AIDS. Called the "Lazarus syndrome," the extended survival period has brought hope and new challenges to HIV patients and their caregivers. As the number of persons living with HIV increases, psychologists whose clinical activity once focused on crisis management and bereavement counseling will be faced with a wider, more diverse spectrum of psychosocial issues, including the emotional, behavioral, cognitive, social, and vocational aspects of chronic illness coping and adjustment.

BACKGROUND AND EPIDEMIOLOGY

In 2001, the Centers for Disease Control and Prevention (CDC) estimated that 800,000 to 900,000 individuals in the United States were living with HIV, with approximately 40,000 new HIV infections occurring in the U.S. every year (CDC, 2001a). By gender, about 70% of the new infections are in men, whereas 30%

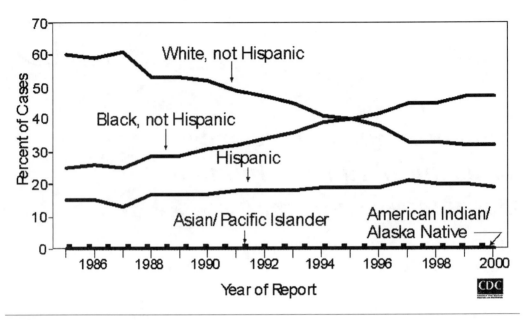

Figure 19.1   Proportion of AIDS Cases, by Race/Ethnicity and Year of Report, 1985–2000, United States

are in women. In terms of race/ethnicity, 54% of the new cases are among African Americans, 26% among Caucasians, 19% among Hispanics, and 1% among other ethnic minority groups (see Figure 19.1). In terms of the major exposure/risk factor category, approximately 42% of new HIV cases are men who have sex with men, 33% are from heterosexual contact, and 25% are from intravenous drug use (Figure 19.2). Nearly all of the pediatric AIDS cases reported (more than 90%) resulted from perinatal HIV transmission. In 1999, the annual number of AIDS cases appeared to level, while the decline in AIDS deaths slowed considerably. Although the rate of reported AIDS cases has declined gradually among Caucasian gay/bisexual male adults over age 25 years, epidemiological trends show increasing rates of infection in women (particularly women of color), African American men, and young adults under age 25 years (Figure 19.3). Moreover, despite the decline in deaths and cases, more people are living with HIV than ever before: 275,000 in

1998, 300,000 in 1999, and 323,000 in 2000. This growing population represents an increasing need for prevention and health care services (CDC, 2001c).

The HIV Disease Spectrum

Because HIV causes subtle changes in the immune system long before an infected person feels sick or develops disease symptoms, the term "HIV disease" is used to cover the entire HIV illness spectrum, from initial infection to full-blown AIDS (also called advanced HIV disease). The time that it takes for each individual person to go through disease stages varies widely. For most people, however, the process of HIV disease is fairly slow, taking several years from infection to the development of severe immunodeficiency (Cohen, 1998).

Behavioral health and health psychology issues are an important part of comprehensive health care across the entire HIV disease spectrum. Although much of behavioral health care focuses on prevention and psychosocial

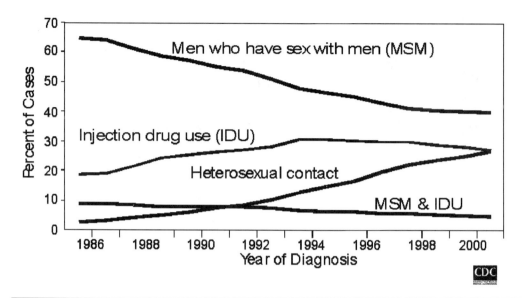

Figure 19.2 Proportion of Estimated Adult/Adolescent AIDS Cases, by Exposure Category and Year of Diagnosis, 1985–2000, United States

NOTE: Data adjusted for reporting delays and proportional redistribution of cases reported without risk.

issues of chronic illness adjustment, some psychological problems, such as mood disorders and cognitive changes, are directly related to the effect of HIV on the central nervous system. In medical and behavioral clinical care, there are two HIV-specific disease parameters (laboratory test results) that are commonly used to gauge an individual's illness status or progression. First, CD4 count is an index of immunosuppression. CD4 is a type of lymphocyte destroyed by HIV. In a noninfected individual, a CD4 count of 500 to 1,200 is considered within normal limits, whereas a CD4 count of less than 200 is considered significantly immunosuppressed and is one of the criteria for an AIDS diagnosis. Second, viral load or viral burden is an index of virus concentration in body fluids such as blood or cerebrospinal fluid. Current laboratory technology measures viral load in a range of undetectable to more than 750,000. It is crucial for patients and caregivers to remember that "undetectable" does not mean the absence of virus; rather, it means a very low concentration in the

serum at that particular time. Many HIV patients are knowledgeable about these disease parameters and frequently use them to describe their illness status. From a psychological perspective, these numbers may take on particular meaning and may be associated with a range of emotional reactions. For example, a patient may be relieved that CD4 has risen with medication or frightened that there has been no significant change in viral load after beginning a new regimen. For these reasons, psychologists who work with HIV patients and their families should be familiar with CD4 and viral load.

Transmission Risk Factors and Infection

HIV is transmitted in infectious body fluids through unprotected sexual contact, direct blood contact (including injection drug needles, blood transfusions, accidents in health care settings, and certain blood products), and mother-to-baby (prenatally/perinatally or through breast milk). Infectious body fluids

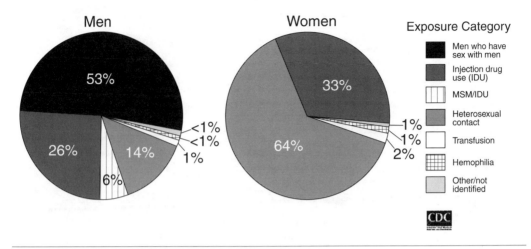

Figure 19.3   Estimated AIDS Incidence Among Adults/Adolescents Diagnosed in 2000, by Sex and Exposure Category, United States

NOTE: Data adjusted for reporting delays and estimated proportional redistribution of cases initially reported without risk. Data reported through June 2001.

include blood, semen, vaginal secretions, and breast milk, whereas noninfectious body fluids include saliva, tears, sweat, urine, and feces. Contact with the virus, called exposure, does not always lead to infection. Healthy unbroken skin is an excellent barrier to HIV infection because it does not allow viral entry. HIV can only enter through an open cut or sore or through contact with the mucous membranes. The likelihood of infection is a function of the viral concentration in the particular fluid; blood contains the highest viral concentration, followed by semen and vaginal fluids. Breast milk can contain a high concentration of the virus and so is a high-risk factor for infants because they have developing immune systems and consume a high volume of breast milk relative to body weight (American Psychiatric Association, 1998; Kalichman, 1998). People with HIV are considered to be infectious immediately after infection. Although "infectivity" is a function of viral load and may fluctuate accordingly, individuals are infectious at all times. Also, a person does not need to have

symptoms or look sick to have HIV. In fact, people may look perfectly healthy for many years despite the fact that they have HIV in their bodies. The only way in which to find out whether a person is infected is to take an HIV antibody test.

Primary (or Acute) Infection

Primary or acute HIV infection is the first stage of HIV disease, when the virus establishes itself in the body. Up to 70% of people newly infected with HIV will experience some "flu-like" symptoms that usually last no more than a few days and include fevers, chills, night sweats, and rashes (not cold-like symptoms). The remaining percentage of people either do not experience acute infection or have symptoms so mild that they might not notice them. During acute HIV infection, the virus infiltrates the lymph nodes, a process that is believed to take 3 to 5 days. Then HIV actively reproduces and releases new virus particles into the bloodstream. This burst of rapid HIV replication usually lasts about 2 months. People at this stage often have a very high HIV viral load (Cohen, 1998).

Seroconversion and Asymptomatic HIV Disease

"Seroconversion" refers to the time when the body begins producing antibodies to the virus. Approximately 95% of the people infected with HIV will develop antibodies within 3 months after infection. Nearly all of them will develop antibodies within 6 months after infection. Given these time frames, individuals who seek HIV testing should wait at least 3 months after suspected exposure for the test. If their first result is negative, they should come back for a second test 3 months later. The period of viral replication is quite variable because the virus slowly damages the immune system for years after infection. During this period, the individual will not experience or exhibit any signs of AIDS-defining illnesses because the level of immunosuppression is not critical. However, it is extremely important that people with HIV seek appropriate care even if they feel fine at the moment because the virus could already be damaging their immune systems (American Psychiatric Association, 1998; Cohen, 1998).

Symptomatic HIV Disease

Once the immune system is damaged, many people will begin to experience some mild symptoms (e.g., skin rashes, fatigue, slight weight loss, night sweats). Most will have mild symptoms such as these before developing more serious illnesses. Although a person's prognosis varies greatly depending on his or her ability to access support, services, and preventive treatment, it is generally believed that it takes the average person 5 to 7 years to experience the first mild symptom (Cohen, 1998).

AIDS

The concurrent combination of two factors, a CD4 count of less than 200 and the presence of an opportunistic infection or AIDS-defining illness, is the current criterion for an AIDS diagnosis (also called full-blown AIDS or advanced HIV disease). These illnesses are called opportunistic because they are caused by organisms that cannot induce disease in people with normal immune systems but take the "opportunity" to flourish in people with HIV. Common opportunistic infections are described in Table 19.1. Receiving an AIDS diagnosis does not necessarily mean that the person will die soon. In fact, with treatment, many individuals live for many years after their diagnosis (Cohen, 1998).

PREVENTION AND ADHERENCE

Primary Prevention: Risk Reduction

Over the years, the behavioral health care community has acquired a formidable literature base that addresses HIV prevention at both the individual and community levels. A review of this literature is well beyond the scope of this chapter; however, the CDC's (2001b) Compendium of HIV Prevention Interventions With Evidence of Effectiveness provides a summary of this research. In general, prevention strategies are based on reducing or eliminating behaviors that put an individual at risk for contracting HIV. Consistent with the two largest risk factor categories, prevention efforts are focused on changing sexual behavior and drug use behavior. Although there are numerous theories about behavior change, some of the most popular and widely used ones in HIV prevention are the harm reduction models. Unlike traditional models that emphasize abstinence from high-risk behavior, the harm reduction models assess the individual's psychological readiness to change high-risk behavior and then

Table 19.1 Common Opportunistic Infections

Opportunistic Infection	Common Name	Etiology/Symptoms
Candidiasis	Thrush	Fungal infection of the mouth, throat, or vagina
Cytomegalovirus	CMV	Viral infection that causes eye disease that can lead to blindness
Herpes simplex viruses	Oral herpes or genital herpes	Lesions or "cold sores"
Mycobacterium avium complex	MAC or MAI	Bacterial infection that can cause recurring fevers, general sick feelings, problems with digestion, and serious weight loss
Pneumocystis carinii pneumonia	PCP	Protozoal infection that causes pneumonia
Toxoplasmosis	Toxo	Protozoal infection of the brain
Kaposi's sarcoma	KS	Type of skin cancer

design/negotiate interventions that match that readiness. For sexual behavior change, prevention strategies involve education about the range of transmission risk across various sexual behaviors, negotiation/refusal skills, appropriate condom use, and the role of mood-altering substances in sexual behavior decision making. For drug use behavior, prevention strategies involve elimination of sharing injection equipment, disinfection of "works" or injection equipment, condom use, and enrollment in drug abuse treatment (American Psychiatric Association, 1998).

Even the most widely used prevention counseling models acknowledge that knowledge about HIV transmission and prevention is necessary but not sufficient for behavior change (Ajzen & Fishbein, 1980; Fisher & Fisher, 1997). More effective interventions rely on skills training and take into account individual psychosocial and cognitive strategies (Kalichman & Hospers, 1997). Effective psychological interventions help patients to perceive themselves as at risk for HIV infection, help patients to address motivation to reduce risk, and ensure that patients have the skills and resources to implement risk reduction strategies. According to the CDC's (2001b) HIV/AIDS Prevention Research Synthesis

Project, a synthesized compendium of more than 200 programs with demonstrated positive outcomes, successful prevention programs generally have several elements in common. First, they address specific goals and objectives, target specific audiences, and concentrate on specific learner priorities and behaviors to meet needs identified by the community. Second, they are developed from existing social and behavioral science theory. Third, they provide opportunities for patients to develop and practice prevention skills and for program providers to learn how to enhance those skills. Fourth, they are appropriate for and acceptable to the targeted audience culturally, developmentally, and sexually (CDC, 2001b).

Secondary Prevention: Medication Adherence

Highly active antiretroviral therapy consists of a protease inhibitor combined with at least two other drugs. HAART has been shown to suppress HIV viral load, increase CD4 count, improve clinical health, and decrease AIDS-related mortality (Carpenter et al., 1998; Catz, Kelly, Bogart, Benotsch, & McAuliffe, 2000). The success of these combination therapies is patient adherence.

Table 19.2   Nucleoside Analog Reverse Transcriptase Inhibitors

Year	Generic Name	Trade Name	Also known as
1987	Zidovudine	Retrovir	AZT, ZDV
1991	Didanosine	Videx	ddI
1992	Zalcitabine	Hivid	ddC, dideoxycytidine
1994	Stavudine	Zerit	d4T
1995	Lamivudine	Epivir	3TC
1997	Zidovudine/ Lamivudine	Combivir	Combines ZDV and 3TC
1998	Abacavir	Ziagen	1592U89
2000	Zidovudine/ Lamivudine/ Abacavir	Trizivir	Combines AZT, 3TC, Abacavir
2001	Tenofovir	Viread	bis-poc PMPA

NOTE: These were the first anti-HIV drugs. They block reverse transcription (the creation of viral DNA from RNA) by providing "decoy" building blocks that interrupt the process.

HAART regimens require that individuals take multiple daily doses of each medication in the prescribed combination. The regimens may involve as many as 20 or more pills, and each medication carries specific dose-spacing requirements. Depending on the combination, different medications may need to be taken with food, without food, with water, or in temporal sequence relative to other drugs in the combination (Catz et al., 2000). Some medications require refrigeration. Given these requirements, adherence can be a formidable challenge for even the most conscientious patient. They present even greater barriers to patients who have concurrent psychiatric illness or psychoactive substance abuse/dependence or who simply need to maintain privacy about their illness in their social and occupational environments. Because medication and adherence are such core issues for patients with HIV illness, health psychologists should become familiar with various HAART medications (Tables 19.2, 19.3, and 19.4).

Treatment success typically requires strict adherence rates (i.e., 90% to 95%), and some research has shown that even partial nonadherence to HAART greatly diminishes the benefits of treatment. For example,

adherence rates of 70% to 80%, which would be considered favorable in other medical conditions, have been associated with high rates (over 75%) of treatment failure (Montaner et al., 1998; Paterson, 1999, 2000). Successful adherence is not only related to current treatment outcome but also related to future treatment outcome. With inconsistent or poor adherence, HIV infection can become "resistant" to many current antiretrovirals, and subsequent treatment efforts often fail. Thus, patients may have a limited number of combination regimens to try. Furthermore, persons who develop drug-resistant HIV can transmit these strains to others during high-risk activities (Hecht et al., 1998; Kelly, Otto-Salaj, Sikkema, Pinkerton, & Bloom, 1998). A number of barriers to adherence have been described in the prevention literature. These barriers include (a) factors associated with the medications themselves such as adverse side effects, large numbers of pills, dosing restrictions (frequency and food/water requirements), and medication containers that are too numerous or too large to carry and (b) factors associated with stigma and confidentiality such as being reminded of one's HIV status, not wanting other people to know one's HIV status, inability to take medications privately

Table 19.3 Non-nucleoside Reverse Transcriptase Inhibitors

Year	Generic Name	Trade Name	Also known as
1996	Nevirapine	Viramune	NVP, BI-RG-587
1997	Delavirdine	Rescriptor	DLV
1998	Efavirenz	Sustiva	EFV, DMP-266

NOTE: These also interrupt reverse transcription by binding to the reverse transcriptase enzyme and restricting its activity.

Table 19.4 Protease Inhibitors

Year	Generic Name	Trade Name	Also known as
1995	Saquinavir	Invirase	SQV
1996	Ritonavir	Norvir	RTV
1996	Indinavir	Crixivan	IDV
1997	Nelfinavir	Viracept	NFV
1997	Saquinavir	Fortovase	SQV
1999	Amprenavir	Agenerase	APV, 141W94
2000	Lopinavir	Kaletra	ABT-378/r

NOTE: Protease inhibitors block the action of protease, an enzyme that cuts HIV protein chains into specific proteins needed to assemble a new copy of the virus.

while at work or in public, and integrating one's medication schedule into daily life (Catz et al., 2000). By considering these barriers, psychologists can help patients to organize and manage their medication-taking routines, plan and problem solve how they will handle medication taking in the context of their other life activities, use strategies to make complex regimens easier to recall, and consult with their health care providers when questions about regimens arise or when treatment side effects are encountered.

ASSESSMENT AND TREATMENT OF PSYCHOLOGICAL DISORDERS IN HIV ILLNESS

Depression

Introduction and Epidemiology. Depression has a significant effect on quality of life,

self-care, and illness progression. Sadness and grief are considered normal emotional responses to the multiple stressors and losses associated with HIV illness. However, when depressed mood persists for more than 2 weeks and is accompanied by social withdrawal, lack of motivation/participation in usual activities, and additional physical and cognitive symptoms, a serious depressive disorder requiring professional care may be present (Rabkin, 1997). Depression is the most common psychiatric disorder found among HIV-infected individuals (Elliot, 1997). Cross-sectional and prospective studies in both HIV+ and at-risk HIV populations estimate that the lifetime prevalence of depressive disorders ranges from 20% to 60%. Current prevalence (6 to 12 months) ranges from 0% to 18% in HIV-positive populations and from 0% to 9% in HIV-negative populations. These rates are generally higher than estimates in community samples (Rabkin, 1997; McDaniel & Blalock, 2000).

Assessment/Diagnosis. Diagnosing depression in the context of HIV disease can be complicated because some diagnostic criteria, such as loss of sexual desire, loss of appetite, insomnia, slowed movements, impaired concentration, low energy, and fatigue, are also caused by HIV-related illnesses, HIV-related pain, or the side effects of HIV medications (Elliot, 1997). This diagnostic confounding is partially addressed by making a distinction between the somatic symptoms of depression just listed and cognitive or affective symptoms such as diminished ability to concentrate and make decisions, loss of interest/pleasure, and feelings of worthlessness, guilt, hopelessness, and helplessness. These symptoms, occurring together, are more clearly indexes of depressive disorder and cannot be accounted for by the presence of medical conditions alone (Rabkin, 1997).

Psychotherapy. Psychotherapy or counseling with HIV-positive individuals has been approached from several models, including cognitive-behavioral therapy (CBT), supportive psychotherapy, and group therapy. Common themes for clients during therapy are loss of relationships and autonomy, vocational issues, physical health and appearance, spirituality, and stigma/discrimination. Supportive psychotherapy examines mood changes in response to disease-related stressors and role changes. Typically, the therapist and patient work on exploring sources of sadness/grief, building social support, and increasing self-care. In contrast, CBT focuses on reality testing and restructuring distorted, pessimistic, or unrealistic thinking patterns that perpetuate a depressive outlook or attributional style. The therapist is more directive, helping the patient with setting goals, defining target symptoms, problem solving, and investigating relationships between thoughts and emotions and their underlying assumptions. Group therapy has been used extensively with HIV-positive individuals in a variety of contexts and is highly efficient. It provides psychoeducation, confrontation regarding misperceptions about the illness, and shared experiences, all of which help to improve these individuals' mood and quality of life (Elliot, 1997).

Pharmacotherapy. The approach to pharmacotherapy for HIV-positive individuals with a major depressive disorder may be slightly different from that for the general adult population. HIV-positive individuals often respond more sensitively to medications and may need a "start low and go slow" approach. In addition, individuals with advanced HIV infection are often on multiple medications, thereby increasing the probability of drug-drug interactions. Also, side effects may occur differently, with some being helpful and some aggravating current symptoms of HIV infection itself or HIV-related illnesses (Rabkin, 1997). In general, the selective serotonin reuptake inhibitors (SSRIs) (e.g., fluoxetine, paroxetine, sertraline) are more tolerable with fewer side effects and so may lead to an increased overall effectiveness. Testosterone replacement has been shown to improve depressive symptoms in individuals with low testosterone levels, especially for those with decreased libido, sexual dysfunction, and diminished energy. In addition, stimulants have been shown to improve mood, energy, and alertness and to be effective in medically ill populations (Elliot, 1997; McDaniel & Blalock, 2000). Psychologists should be aware of the potential interaction effects of some HAART medications and some HIV medications. Ritonavir, indinavir, saquinavir, and nelfinavir all are metabolized in the same hepatic enzyme system as are many psychotropic drugs. Consequently, the simultaneous use of both classes of drugs may alter the clearance rate of one or the other. The interaction effect may alter the serum levels of either kind of drug, thereby increasing the risk of side effects or potentially decreasing the therapeutic effect (McDaniel & Blalock, 2000; Rabkin, 1997).

Anxiety

Introduction and Epidemiology. Anxiety disorders may occur at any time during the course of HIV illness, particularly at pivotal points in disease progression, and are often considered a normal psychological response to stress. In general, most patients respond adequately to the stress of living with HIV and limit the impact of disease-related anxiety on their daily functioning and quality of life. For some patients, however, the severity and duration of anxiety can cause significant, or even debilitating, impairment of daily functioning. As with other chronic medical conditions, the entire spectrum of DSM-IV (*Diagnostic and Statistical Manual of Mental Disorders,* fourth edition)-defined anxiety disorders may be seen in patients with HIV/AIDS (American Psychiatric Association, 1994; Blalock & McDaniel, in press). Prevalence rates for anxiety disorders among patients with HIV disease range from 5% to 40% (McDaniel & Blalock, 2000). But despite this wide range in prevalence estimates, a pattern of findings has emerged over the past 5 years: The prevalence of anxiety disorders in HIV-seropositive patients is not significantly different from that in HIV-seronegative patients. However, lifetime rates among patients with HIV disease are generally higher than rates found in the general population or community samples (Dew et al., 1997; Rabkin, Ferrando, Jacobsberg, & Fishman, 1997; Sewell et al., 2000).

Assessment/Diagnosis. A successful treatment plan for anxiety disorders in HIV/AIDS relies on a thorough assessment of the patient's presenting anxiety symptoms, preferred stress coping style, and repertoire of stress coping skills. Unlike mood disorders in HIV, which

may be directly caused by viral involvement in the central nervous system, the role of the AIDS virus in the etiology of anxiety disorders is unclear and remains under investigation (Sciolla, Atkinson, & Grant, 1998). In patients with HIV/AIDS, anxiety symptoms may occur in several HIV-related medical conditions and with psychoactive substance intoxication or withdrawal (American Psychiatric Association, 1998). Similarly, anxiety may also be a manifestation of side effects from HIV medication regimens, psychotropic medication, or other pharmacological agents used to treat HIV-related medical problems (American Psychiatric Association, 1998).

Psychotherapy. Psychological treatment of anxiety disorders usually involves a two-phase process: acute symptom reduction in the short term and development of more adaptive coping skills in the long term. In general, CBT is particularly useful in the treatment of anxiety disorders because it focuses on distorted cognitive schemas and maladaptive behaviors. Progressive muscle relaxation and breathing exercises are often used to treat the physiological manifestations of anxiety and prevent impending panic attacks. For specific phobias and situationally determined panic attacks, systematic desensitization is helpful and is frequently used in conjunction with the relaxation techniques. For more generalized anxiety or anxious personality styles, techniques such as rational-emotive-behavioral therapy and cognitive restructuring are designed to identify and refute irrational, pessimistic, and self-defeating thought patterns and attributional styles (McDaniel & Blalock, 2000). With all types of anxiety disorders, therapist modeling and therapist-client role-playing are concrete learning experiences that can be beneficial. Most of the cognitive-behavioral techniques can be incorporated into individual psychotherapy sessions, short-term psychoeducational groups, or ongoing interpersonal process therapy groups (Karasic & Dilley, 1998).

Pharmacotherapy. Unless contraindicated by a history of psychoactive substance dependence, benzodiazepines are frequently prescribed for short-term treatment of acute anxiety symptoms. Ideally, they are then gradually tapered as the individual learns more psychologically or behaviorally based coping strategies. Antidepressants, particularly SSRIs, may also be quite effective (Blalock & McDaniel, in press).

Cognitive Disorders

Introduction and Epidemiology. HIV penetrates the blood-brain barrier early in the course of infection and can be found in the cerebrospinal fluid in nearly half of infected individuals before the development of AIDS-defining illnesses. Early or subtle impairment may manifest as HIV-associated minor cognitive motor disorder: mild deficits of attention, information processing speed, learning and memory, and psychomotor skills. The problems may be quite mild such as loss of train of thought, word-finding difficulties, short-term memory problems, and decreased efficiency in fine motor speed and dexterity. HIV-associated minor cognitive disorder may be complicated by the presence of depression or anxiety but is not caused by psychiatric problems (American Psychiatric Association, 1998; Grant & Martin, 1994). In more advanced disease stages, neurocognitive impairment may be quite prominent with HIV-associated dementia, a progressive disorder that initially presents as apathy, inertia, cognitive slowing, memory loss, and social withdrawal. As the dementia progresses, multiple cognitive functions become increasingly impaired. The terminal phases are characterized by global cognitive impairment, mutism, and severe psychomotor retardation. Unlike minor cognitive disorder, HIV-associated dementia rarely develops prior to constitutional problems and usually does not develop prior to other AIDS-defining illnesses (Grant & Martin, 1994; Sciolla

et al., 1998). According to a national cohort study, the incidence rate of HIV-associated dementia over a 5-year period was approximately 7% for those with a CD4 count of less than 100, 3% for those with a CD4 count between 101 and 200, and 2% or less for those with a CD4 count of more than 200. Thus, HIV-associated dementia is principally a disease found in advanced HIV illness (Price, 1998).

Assessment/Diagnosis. As with any suspected cognitive impairment, a collateral interview with a caregiver or significant other is a crucial part of assessment. Cognitive problems may be episodic or subtle and may escape detection by short cognitive screening or brief interviewing techniques. Thorough neuropsychological testing can detect mild problems across the spectrum of cognitive and psychomotor functions. The neuropsychological evaluation also includes assessment of personality functioning to help identify other psychiatric disorders and to distinguish the cognitive problems associated with mood disturbance and more disease-based cognitive problems (Grant & Martin, 1994; Moore, van Gorp, Hinken, & Stern, 1997).

Psychotherapy. Depending on the extent of cognitive impairment, traditional psychotherapies may be of limited use. For mild to moderate impairment, patients often find it helpful to explore fear, anger, and sadness about loss of previous level of functioning. The degree of distress is frequently related to the real-life impact of the patient's cognitive impairment. For some individuals, the changes interfere minimally with daily functioning and are helped by simple strategies such as using written reminders and simplifying sequential tasks. For others, however, the changes may necessitate a reevaluation of vocational/leisure abilities or even daily living and self-care skills. Conjoint therapy (e.g., family, partner, caregiver) is usually indicated in patients with HIV-associated cognitive disorders because

CASE STUDY

"Rita" is a 44-year-old, bisexual Caucasian female with a 12-year history of HIV disease who was referred for a crisis evaluation by her medical provider. Three months prior to consultation, her viral load increased markedly from a previously undetectable level and her CD4 count decreased from 250 to 75, prompting a change in her antiretroviral regimen from zidovudine, didanosine, and indinavir to stavudine, lamivudine, and efavirenz. Three months later during a medical follow-up visit, Rita became acutely agitated when she learned that her CD4 and viral load had remained unchanged despite the new regimen. She considered herself a "treatment failure" and was convinced that she would die.

Rita described herself as a recovered alcoholic with 7 years of sobriety. She also reported a long-standing history of marijuana use and had continued to smoke daily over the past 2 years, finally quitting only recently because she could no longer afford to use marijuana. Once Rita was substance free, her underlying psychiatric symptoms emerged. She revealed a long history (preceding her HIV diagnosis) of obsessive worrying, restlessness/irritability, sleep disturbance, and poor stress coping that was consistent with a diagnosis of generalized anxiety disorder. She also reported a history of sub-syndromal depressive symptoms and fear of being open with others about her sexual identity. Although she was eventually able to abstain from alcohol, she continued to use marijuana as a way in which to diminish her chronic anxiety.

Rita was finally diagnosed with generalized anxiety disorder after a stable drug-free period, with her differential diagnostic picture also including major depressive episode, depression/anxiety secondary to a general medical condition, and substance/medication-induced depression/anxiety. The long-term treatment plan for her anxiety included a combination of medication and cognitive-behavioral psychotherapy. Benzodiazepines were contraindicated given her history of substance dependence. Instead, she was prescribed the antidepressant mirtazepine (15 milligrams at bedtime) to alleviate her anxious/depressive symptoms. Her weekly psychotherapy focused on preventing substance use relapse and strengthening problem-solving and stress-coping skills. During therapy, Rita made progress in several important areas that improved her overall psychological functioning, including disclosing her HIV status and sexual orientation to family members, applying for disability income benefits, and finding a suitable housemate to reduce living expenses.

Rita's case illustrates three important issues for treating anxiety disorders in HIV clinical care. First, anxiety disorders or anxious character styles may precede infection and increase vulnerability to problems with chronic illness coping. Second, psychoactive substances are frequently part of a complex history and symptom picture and require careful consideration in assessment and treatment. Third, a thorough differential diagnosis, including medical and medication-induced causes, must be considered when assessing and treating anxiety-related symptoms.

these patients may require a range of assistance from others. This becomes particularly crucial for medication adherence due to forgetfulness or confusion.

Pharmacotherapy. Pharmacological treatment strategies for cognitive disorders can be divided into four types: (a) antiretroviral therapies, (b) therapies aimed at immunological measures or inflammatory mediators, (c) therapies aimed at bolstering the response of the brain to the onslaught of the infection (e.g., neurotransmitter manipulation), and (d) nutritional therapies (American Psychiatric Association, 1998).

CONCLUSION

Although health psychologists may treat patients with HIV disease independently, health psychologists are typically part of a multidisciplinary treatment team composed of infectious disease specialists, psychiatrists, nurses, and social service workers. An integrated knowledge base helps to bridge existing gaps between medicine and mental health, and it positions health psychologists to be uniquely skilled professionals in the HIV health care arena.

REFERENCES

American Psychiatric Association. (1994). *Diagnostic and statistical manual of mental disorders* (4th ed.). Washington, DC: Author.

American Psychiatric Association. (1998). *Practice guidelines for the treatment of patients with HIV/AIDS.* Washington, DC: Author.

Ajzen, I., & Fishbein, M. (1980). *Understanding attitudes and predicting behavior.* Englewood Cliffs, NJ: Prentice Hall.

Blalock, A. C., & McDaniel, S. J. (in press). Anxiety disorders in HIV infection and AIDS. In A. Beckett, K. Citron, & M. J. Brouillette (Eds.), *HIV and psychiatry.* Cambridge, MA: Cambridge University Press.

Carpenter, C., Fischl, M., Hammer, S., Hirsch, M., Jacobsen, D., Ketzenstein, D., Montaner, J., Richman, D., Saag, M., Schooley, R., Thomson, M., Vella, S., Yeni, D., & Volberding, D. A. (1998). Antiretroviral therapy for HIV infection in 1998: Updated recommendations of the International AIDS Society, U.S. Panel. *Journal of the American Medical Association, 280,* 78–86.

Catz, S. L., Kelly, J., Bogart, L., Benotsch, E., & McAuliffe, T. (2000). Patterns, correlates, and barriers to medication adherence among persons prescribed new treatments for HIV disease. *Health Psychology, 19,* 124–133.

Centers for Disease Control and Prevention. (2001a). *A glance at the HIV epidemic* (HIV/AIDS Update). Atlanta, GA: Author.

Centers for Disease Control and Prevention. (2001b). *HIV/AIDS Prevention Research Synthesis Project: Compendium of HIV prevention interventions with evidence of effectiveness.* Atlanta, GA: Author.

Centers for Disease Control and Prevention. (2001c, February). *HIV/AIDS surveillance report midyear 2001 edition* (Vol. 13, No. 1). Atlanta, GA: Author.

Cohen, P. T. (1998). Clinical overview of HIV disease. *HIV Insite Knowledge Base Chapter.* (San Francisco: University of California, San Francisco)

Dew, M. A., Becker, J. T., Sanchez, J., Caldararo, R., Lopez, O. L., Wess, J., Dorst, S. K., & Banks, G. (1997). Prevalence and predictors of depressive, anxiety, and substance use disorders in HIV-infected and uninfected men: A longitudinal evaluation. *Psychological Medicine, 27,* 395–409.

Elliot, A. (1997, May). *Depression and HIV: Assessment and treatment.* San Francisco: Project Inform.

Fisher, J. D., & Fisher, W. A. (1997). Changing AIDS-risk behavior. *Psychological Bulletin, 111,* 455–474.

Grant, I., & Martin, A. (Eds.). (1994). *Neuropsychology of HIV infection.* New York: Oxford University Press.

Hecht, F. M., Grant, R. M., Detropolus, C. J., Dillon, B., Chesney, M. A., Tian, W., Hellman, N. S., Brandapalli, N. I., Diglio, L., Bronson, B., & Kahn, J. O. (1998). Sexual transmission of an HIV-1 variant resistant to multiple reverse-transcriptase and protease inhibitors. *New England Journal of Medicine, 339,* 307–311.

Kalichman, S. (1998). *Understanding AIDS: Advances in research and treatment* (2nd ed.). Washington, DC: American Psychological Association.

Kalichman, S. C., & Hospers, H. J. (1997). Efficacy of behavioral-skills enhancement: HIV risk-reduction interventions in community settings. *AIDS, 11*(Suppl. A), S191–S199.

Karasic, D. H., & Dilley, J. W. (1998). Anxiety and depression: Mood and HIV disease. In J. W. Dilley & R. Marks (Eds.), *The USCF AIDS Health Project guide to counseling* (pp. 227–248). San Francisco: Jossey-Bass.

Kelly, J. A., Otto-Salaj, L. L., Sikkema, K. J., Pinkerton, S. D., & Bloom, F. R. (1998). Implications of HIV treatment advances for behavioral research on AIDS: Protease inhibitors and new challenges in HIV secondary prevention. *Health Psychology, 17,* 310–319.

McDaniel, S. J., & Blalock, A. C. (2000). Diagnosis and management of HIV-related mood and anxiety disorders. In *New directions in psychiatric services* (No. 87, pp. 51–56). San Francisco: Jossey-Bass.

Montaner, J. S. G., Reiss, P., Cooper, D., Vella, S., Harris, M., Conway, B., Weinberg, M. A., Smith, D., Robinson, P., Hall, D., Myers, M., & Lange, J. M. A., for the INCAS Study Group. (1998). A randomized, double-blind trial comparing combinations of nevirapine, didanosine, and zidovudine for HIV-infected patients. *Journal of the American Medical Association, 279,* 930–937.

Moore, L., van Gorp, W., Hinken, C., & Stern, M. (1997). Subjective complaints versus actual cognitive deficits in predominantly symptomatic HIV-1 seropositive individuals. *Journal of Neuropsychiatry and Clinical Neuroscience, 9*(1), 37–44.

Paterson, D., Swindells, S., Mohr, J., Brester, M., Vergis, R., Squier, C., Wagener, M., & Singh, M. (1999, January). *How much adherence is enough? A prospective study of adherence to protease inhibitor therapy using MEMS caps.* Paper presented at the Sixth Conference on Retroviruses and Opportunistic Infections, Chicago.

Paterson, D., Swindells, S., Mohr, J., Brester, M., Vergis, R., Squier, C., Wagener, M., & Singh, M. (2000). Adherence to protease inhibitor therapy and outcomes in patients with HIV infection. *Annals of Internal Medicine, 133,* 21–30.

Price, R. (1998). AIDS dementia complex. *HIV Insite Knowledge Base Chapter.* (San Francisco: University of California, San Francisco)

Rabkin, J. (1997, October). Meeting the challenge of depression in HIV. *GMHC Treatment Issues, 11*(10). (New York: Gay Men's Health Crisis)

Rabkin, J. G., Ferrando, S. J., Jacobsberg, L. B., & Fishman, B. (1997). Prevalence of Axis I disorders in an AIDS cohort: A cross-sectional, controlled study. *Comprehensive Psychiatry, 38*(3), 146–154.

Sciolla, A., Atkinson, J., & Grant, I. (1998). Neuropsychiatric features of HIV disease. In W. G. van Gorp & S. L. Buckingham (Eds.), *Practitioner's guide to the neuropsychiatry of HIV/AIDS* (pp. 106–200). New York: Guilford.

Sewell, M. C., Goggin, K. J., Rabkin, J. G., Ferrando, S. J., McElhiney, M. C., & Evans, S. (2000). Anxiety syndromes and symptoms among men with AIDS: A longitudinal controlled study. *Psychosomatics, 41,* 294–300.

CHAPTER 20

Irritable Bowel Syndrome

Jeffrey M. Lackner

Irritable bowel syndrome (IBS) is a chronic gastrointestinal (GI) disorder characterized by a constellation of symptoms, including abdominal pain/discomfort associated with altered bowel function (e.g., diarrhea, constipation) that occurs in the absence of organic disease. Because the locus of the problem is in how the gut functions and not in abnormalities of its physical structure, IBS is considered a functional disorder. There are 25 functional GI disorders concentrated in one of five anatomic regions: esophagus, gastro-duodenal, biliary, intestines, and anorectum (Drossman, 1994). Other functional GI disorders include functional dyspepsia, functional constipation, and chronic functional abdominal pain. Of the functional GI disorders, IBS is the most prevalent, costly, and disabling.

BACKGROUND AND ETIOLOGY

Epidemiology

Epidemiological studies conducted over the past two decades indicate that 10% to 20% of individuals in the United States and Canada experience symptoms consistent with IBS (Drossman et al., 1993). In the United States, approximately 20 to 40 million individuals—1 in 6 Americans—suffer from IBS (Lynn & Friedman, 1993). These figures make IBS not only one of the most prevalent chronic pain disorders (Crombie, Croft, Linton, LeResche, & Von Korff, 1999) but also one of the most prevalent chronic illnesses in general. The prevalence rate of IBS is at least as common as, if not more common than, that of hypertension and is much more common than the prevalence rates of asthma, diabetes, and congestive heart failure (Adams & Benson, 1991). Although the great majority (80% to 90%) of IBS patients do not seek medical attention, the 10% to 20% who do consult physicians represent 28% of all visits to GI practices and 12% of all primary care visits, making IBS one of the most common disorders seen by physicians, according to Scott-Levin's *Physician Drug and Diagnosis Audit*, a commercial database derived from a monthly survey of physicians in active office-based practice in the United States. Factors that differentiate treatment-seeking individuals from

AUTHOR'S NOTE: Preparation of this chapter was supported in part by National Institutes of Health Grant DK-54211.

non-treatment-seeking individuals include the severity of abdominal pain, psychological distress, and sociocultural influences. To illustrate, IBS is more common among males in rural populations in India and Sri Lanka, where gender identity strongly influences help-seeking behavior (Jain, Gupta, Jajoo, & Sidwa, 1991). On the other hand, in the United States, where females outnumber males in medical care clinics that treat IBS, IBS is four times more common among females than among males. The financial costs on the U.S. health care system were estimated in 1995 to have been $8 billion annually (Talley, Gabriel, Harmsen, Zinsmeister, & Evans, 1995). The course of IBS varies greatly among people, but episodes can have serious debilitating effects on physical function. IBS has been identified as second only to the common cold as a cause of work absenteeism (Drossman et al., 1993). It has been reported that approximately 30% of IBS sufferers take sick leave because of the disorder, with half of these individuals being absent from work at least 2 weeks per year. IBS affects quality of life (QOL) as much as, or more than, does congestive heart failure (Whitehead, Burnett, Cook, & Taub, 1996).

Clinical Features

Although IBS is a multisymptom problem, patients characterize abdominal pain or discomfort as their most frequent and bothersome complaint (Drossman, Whitehead, & Camilleri, 1997; Hahn, Yan, & Strassels, 1999). For this reason, abdominal pain is considered the cardinal feature of IBS. Pain associated with IBS is experienced as a diffuse crampy, colicky, and aching sensation concentrated diffusely (as opposed to localized) in the abdomen that is often relieved with defecation or flatulence. Pain is sometimes associated with defecation and a change in stool frequency or form (appearance). In addition to changes in bowel habits, IBS pain can be associated with mucus found around or within the stools, a sense of urgency (a strong sensation of the immediate need to move the bowels), a feeling of incomplete evacuation, flatulence, and abdominal bloating. Although bloating is not a diagnostic feature of IBS, it is a particularly bothersome clinical feature that warrants attention (Maxton, Morris, & Whorwell, 1989). The duration of IBS symptoms is relatively short, with the longest set of symptoms—pain/discomfort and bloating—lasting for 5-day periods (Hahn et al., 1999). For purpose of treatment planning, patients are often classified on the basis of the relative predominance of their bowel symptoms (diarrhea, constipation, or pain) at the time of diagnosis. Diarrhea-prominent IBS patients experience more than three bowel movements per day, loose or watery stools, and urgency. Constipation-predominant IBS patients, on the other hand, are typically characterized by having two or more of the following symptoms: fewer than three bowel movements per week; hard, pellet-shaped, or lumpy stools; and straining during bowel movements. The predominant classification system is particularly useful for patients with one consistent predominant symptom. However, for the majority of patients, symptoms fluctuate over time, with the predominant symptom alternating among diarrhea, constipation, and normal bowel function. Thus, the predominant classification system functions best as a heuristic that helps to conceptualize patients at a single point in time rather than as an empirically grounded classification scheme that reflects the clinical realities of IBS over time.

One factor that complicates accurate diagnosis is the comorbidity with and/or temporal contiguity of organic GI disease (Isgar, Harman, Kaye, & Whorwell, 1983). There is increasing evidence that a sizable, albeit minority, group of patients develop IBS symptoms following infectious enteritis (Rodriguez & Ruigozmez, 1999). Although the hypothesis that acute bacterial infection is causally related to IBS awaits confirmation in a controlled investigation, 20% to 30% of patients develop IBS after bouts of acute bacterial infection (McKendrick, 1996; McKendrick & Read, 1994). What is particularly interesting is that individuals who develop IBS after a bout of gastroenteritis had higher levels of psychological distress at the time of infection than did individuals who did not develop IBS after bacterial infection (Gwee, 2001). A significant number of IBS patients report upper GI symptoms, including reflux, vomiting, nausea, noncardiac chest pain, and dyspepsia. Approximately 40% of individuals with IBS have reflux symptoms and 45% have dyspepsia. Patients' symptom patterns can transition between disorders such that they have symptoms of one disorder (e.g., IBS) that in turn are replaced by symptoms of another (e.g., reflux). There is a higher prevalence of IBS in patients whose Crohn's disease and ulcerative colitis—collectively known as inflammatory bowel disease (IBD)—are in remission. In comparison with controls, IBS patients report more extraintestinal somatic symptoms, including sexual dysfunction, insomnia, fibromyalgia, facial pain, chronic pelvic pain, and chronic fatigue (Whitehead, Palsson, & Jones, 2002).

Natural History

IBS is most commonly seen in patients during late adolescence and middle age. More than 50% of patients are diagnosed with IBS before age 35 years, whereas another 40% are diagnosed between ages 35 and 50 years (Dalton & Drossman, 1997). After age 65 years, the incidence and onset of IBS decreases among males and females (Maxwell, Mendall, & Kumar, 1997; Sandler, Jordan, & Shelton, 1990). For these reasons, IBS has been characterized as a "young person's illness." It is unclear whether age differences reflect developmental issues (e.g., age-related differences in gut physiology), differences in health-seeking behaviors, or an alternative factor(s). Data based on epidemiological studies suggest that the apparent age difference may at least partly reflect the diagnostic practices used to establish prevalence data (Talley, Gabriel, et al., 1995). Some researchers argue that correcting for this difference would bring the prevalence rate of IBS among the elderly in line with the prevalence rates among younger age groups (O'Keefe, Talley, Zinsmeister, & Jacobsen, 1995). What information is available indicates that more than 15% of individuals age 65 years or over report IBS-like symptoms (e.g., pain, constipation) that are classified as "painful diverticular disease" (O'Keefe et al., 1995). On the other end of the age spectrum, the occurrence of IBS in children is similar to the rate in adults (5% vs. 20%). Symptoms consistent with a diagnosis of IBS have been reported in 6% of 12- and 13-year-olds and in 14% of 15- and 16-year-olds (Hyams, Burke, Davis, Rzepski, & Andrulonis, 1996). As noted previously, there is a strong gender disparity in prevalence of IBS. Community surveys indicate that women outnumber men with IBS by a two-to-one margin. In clinical settings, the gender difference is even more dramatic (Drossman et al., 1993). Patients with higher education, high income levels, and a high severity of pain and stress are more likely to seek medical treatment for IBS. With respect to racial differences, the rate of IBS is lower in Hispanic samples than in both African American and Caucasian samples, with the latter two groups having comparable prevalence rates (e.g., Olubuyide, Olawuyi, & Fasanmade, 1995). Aggravating factors include psychological stress, dietary triggers, meal consumption, and (for some females) hormonal changes around menses. The long-term prognosis of IBS is favorable, with symptoms generally improving over time. Positive prognostic factors include gender (i.e., male), quality of physician-patient relationship (i.e., patients whose physicians maintain a positive sympathetic relationship with them, address patient concerns and expectations, set limits, and involve the patients in treatment decisions achieve better outcomes and require fewer follow-up visits), and predominant bowel habit involving constipation or painless diarrhea. There is a strong family history of IBS-like symptoms in first-degree relatives but not spousal relatives of IBS patients (Morris-Yates, Talley, Boyce, & Andrews, 1995). Although these data have been interpreted as suggestive evidence of a genetic component that contributes to the development of IBS, an alternative hypothesis that has not been ruled out is that these familial patterns are acquired through learning processes (e.g., parental modeling of sick behavior).

Diagnosis

The nonspecific nature of IBS symptoms complicates accurate diagnosis. Drossman (1994) identified 31 disorders across 13 classes of medical diseases whose symptoms are descriptively similar to IBS symptoms (Table 20.1).

GI diseases whose symptoms overlap with IBS symptoms include colorectal cancer, IBD, endocrine disorders and tumors, enteric infections, and malabsorption syndrome. Because IBS symptoms mimic these and other diseases with detectable physical pathology, proper diagnosis of IBS is a two-part process: (a) excluding possible organic, infectious, metabolic, or structural diseases that may account for symptoms and (b) assessing the presence of IBS symptoms in accord with diagnostic criteria known as the Rome II criteria (Drossman, Corazziari, Talley, Thompson, & Whitehead, 2000). Rome II criteria represent the current standard for diagnosing IBS. To meet a diagnosis for IBS, Rome II criteria require that, during the preceding 12 months, the patient must experience 12 weeks (which need not be consecutive) of abdominal pain or discomfort with two of the following three features: (a) relieved with defecation, (b) onset associated with a change in frequency of stool, and (c) onset associated with a change in form (appearance) of stool. In addition to delineating

criteria that tend to covary in patients with IBS, Rome II includes a set of symptoms with a greater than 25% occurrence that cumulatively support the diagnosis but are not essential for diagnosis. These symptoms consist of (a) abnormal stool frequency (may be defined as more than three bowel movements per day or less than three bowel movements per week), (b) abnormal stool form (lumpy/hard or loose/watery), (c) abnormal stool passage (straining, urgency, or feeling of incomplete evacuation; passage of mucus), and (d) bloating or feeling of abdominal distension.

Confirmation of an IBS diagnosis using Rome II criteria is conducted within the context of a thorough medical examination, which includes a comprehensive medical history and physical examination and the identification of the predominant symptom. There is a consensus among IBS experts that because Rome II offers a set of "positive" (i.e., symptom-based) diagnostic criteria, a strategy that relies on excessive diagnostic tests to rule out likely organic disease is not only unnecessary but also inefficient and potentially harmful. For this reason, diagnostic testing to confirm IBS may be limited to a complete blood count, determination of erythrocyte sedimentation, and a colonoscopy for patients who are age 50 years or over and report sudden onset of symptoms and/or those with a family history of colon polyps or GI cancer (Thompson, Dotevall, Drossman, Heaton, & Kruis, 1989). Because symptoms of IBS mimic those of organic disease, it is not prudent to diagnose IBS on the basis of symptoms per se without the benefit of a sufficiently thorough medical examination. Signs and symptoms that are not typically associated with IBS and may signify alternative or coexisting GI disease include visible or occult blood in stool, weight loss, fever, laboratory indicators of inflammation, frequent nocturnal symptoms, abrupt (i.e., nongradual) onset of symptoms, and onset of symptoms in patients who are age 40 years or over. Patients with these symptoms or signs may require a more

Table 20.1   Differential Diagnoses of Chronic/Recurrent Bowel Dysfunction

Physical Condition	Example
Irritable bowel syndrome	
Lactase deficiency	
Drugs	Laxative/cathartics/Mg^{2+} antacids, diuretics, cholinergic agents, prostaglandins (e.g., misoprostil)
Bacterial infection	*Salmonella* species, *Campylobacter jejuni, Yersinia enterocolitica, Clostridium difficile*
Parasitic infection	*Giardia lamblia, Entameba histoltica,* cryptosporidiosis
Inflammatory bowel disease	Crohn's disease, ulcerative colitis
Malabsorption	Chronic pancreatitis, celiac sprue, postgastrectomy syndromes
Metabolic disorders	Diabetes mellitus, thyrotoxicosis
Endocrine/ hormone-producing tumors	Gastrinoma, carcinoid, VIPoma, endometriosis
Psychiatric disorders	Depression, anxiety/panic disorders, somatization disorders
Intestinal pseudo-obstruction	Primary visceral myopathy/neuropathy (e.g., scleroderma, diabetes)
Other colonic diseases	Collagenous/lymphocytic colitis, mast-cell disease, villous adenoma
Opportunistic infections in immunocompromised hosts	

SOURCE: Adapted from Drossman (1994). Reprinted with permission.

extensive medical evaluation to rule out organic disease.

Pathophysiology

Altered Gut Motility. The biomedical approach has historically sought to explain IBS symptoms in light of underlying physiological mechanisms within the GI tract. The most prominent biomedical theory has conceptualized IBS as a disorder of colonic motility caused by alterations in the smooth muscle spasms of the GI tract. The nature of abnormal patterns of motility and peristalsis presumably determine the type of bowel disturbance, with hypermotility resulting in diarrhea and hypomotility resulting in constipation. According to the "dysmotility hypothesis," vigorous contractions of the colon aggravate pain. Findings consistent with the notion that IBS symptoms involve disruptions in colonic motility come from research showing that types of IBS patients exhibit certain disordered motor abnormalities throughout the GI tract, particularly in the small and large intestine. IBS patients whose predominant bowel habit is diarrhea may have accelerated whole gut transit times, a greater number of fast contractions, and more high-amplitude propagated contractions in the colon as compared with normal individuals (Whitehead, Engel, & Schuster, 1990). Some patients whose predominant bowel habit is constipation, on the other hand, may have delays in colonic transit and fewer high-amplitude propagated contractions than is the case in normal individuals (Bazzacchi et al., 1990). That being said, dysmotility may be more appropriate as a mechanistic explanation for specific subtypes of IBS than as a general rule for understanding the pathophysiology of IBS across patients. In general, however, clear-cut differences in colonic motor responses between IBS patients and normal controls have not been consistently replicated. Although IBS patients exhibit heightened reactivity to a variety of stimuli that stimulate colonic motility (e.g., meals, rectal distension, strong emotions, cholinergic drugs, injection of cholecystokinin [a hormone released in the duodenum]), healthy controls exhibit a similar albeit less exaggerated motility response pattern (Almy, Kern, & Tulin, 1949). In other words, IBS patients show a quantitative difference but not a qualitative difference in motor response as compared with normal individuals. The lack of clear-cut clinical differences has prompted researchers to study motor activity in the small bowel. This line of research has focused on discrete clustered contractions (DCCs), that is, abnormal bursts of motor activity in the duodenum and ileum. DCCs are seen more often in IBS patients, but they are also exhibited in both healthy controls and patients with other GI disorders (e.g., pseudo-obstruction, intestinal obstruction). In other words, DCCs are nonspecific. Perhaps most problematic is the relatively weak correspondence between DCCs and symptoms. DCCs correlate with pain in IBS patients only 25% of the time (Kellow & Phillips, 1987). Thus, abnormal motility may well enhance gut reactivity in some patients, but its role is nonspecific and has limited clinical significance and explanatory value.

Visceral Sensitivity and Perception. Because of the inconsistent association between the pain and measured colonic motility, there has been an increased focus on the phenomenon of visceral hypersensitivity, which refers to a state of heightened awareness of and sensitivity to normal intestinal activity (e.g., gas, normal intestinal contractions) that arises within the gut during digestion as well as painful distension of the colon. Visceral hypersensitivity research has been based largely on a series of balloon distension studies that involve placing a balloon catheter in the lower large intestine (colon). The balloon is connected to a computerized pump (barostat) that inflates the balloon to specific pressure levels designed to be mildly moderately uncomfortable for a short time to simulate abdominal discomfort. These studies have demonstrated that a significant proportion of IBS patients, particularly those with diarrhea-predominant IBS, experience abdominal pain at significantly lower levels of pressure and intraluminal volume than do controls when their rectums, sigmoids, or small intestines are distended by a balloon (i.e., visceral hyperalgesia). They also experience distensions at a given volume as more intense than do healthy controls (Mertz, Naliboff, Munakata, Niazi, & Mayer, 1995). IBS patients may also experience discomfort in the GI tract in response to normal gut stimuli (e.g., gas, stool) that do not typically elicit discomfort in non-IBS patients. In IBS patients, the phenomenon of visceral sensitivity appears to be specific to the GI tract and does not characterize thresholds for somatic pain stimuli (e.g., cold pressor test) that range from normal to above average as compared with controls (Cook, Van Eeeden, & Collins, 1987). Visceral hypersensitivity is neither limited to the colon nor restricted to pain sensation. Visceral hyperalgesia has been demonstrated at different sites in the GI tract (e.g., stomach, colon, small intestine, esophagus). Beyond pain, visceral hypersensitivity is reflected in IBS patients' complaints of excess gas, even though they actually show no differences in their composition or accumulation rate as compared with asymptomatic controls.

Several peripheral and central neural mechanisms have been proposed to explain visceral sensitivity. In peripheral sensitization, noxious stimulation (e.g., acute enteric infection, injury to the viscera) reduces the threshold for mechanical stimuli (e.g., pinching, cutting, stretching) in high-threshold nociceptors and may recruit "silent" nociceptors that are normally unresponsive to stimuli and become activated only in the presence of inflammation (Cervero & Laird, 1999). The sensitization of these nociceptors may in turn contribute to pain in response to normally innocuous stimuli (e.g., colon contractions) that are below the normal perceptual threshold (Cervero & Laird, 1999). An alternative—but not mutually exclusive—mechanism emphasizes increased excitability of the GI neural system (i.e., central sensitization). In central sensitization, noxious stimulation may cause structural and functional reorganization of synaptic connections in dorsal horn neurons, inducing a hypersensitive state that Carr (1996) aptly likened to a "posttraumatic stress phenomenon in the spinal cord . . . that persists long after such stimuli cease" (p. 1114). Long-term changes in the nervous system associated with central sensitization are reflected by "windup" amplification of pain (i.e., progressively increasing activity in dorsal horn cells), reduced pain threshold, expansion of reception fields of spinal cord dorsal horn neurons, and persistence of pain in the absence of input from the periphery (Coderre, Katz, Vaccarino, & Metzack, 1993). In effect, pain may persist because an ongoing barrage of pain signal imprints in the central nervous system (CNS) a "memory" of pain whose conscious perception no longer requires input from the periphery (e.g., inflammation). Neuroplastic changes may explain why IBS patients, particularly those with more severe symptoms, experience an amplification or exaggeration of pain to a stimulus that is normally painful (e.g., rectal stimulation) and also report pain from a stimulus that does not normally provoke pain (e.g., gas, stool, small meals).

CNS Modulation of Visceral Sensations. A related theory that has grown out of visceral sensitivity research suggests that hypersensitivity is due to abnormal central processing defects. This line of research comes partly from neuroimaging studies using both position emission tomography (PET) and functional magnetic resonance imaging (fMRI). Neuroimaging research has determined that areas of the limbic system function differently in IBS patients, as compared with controls, in response to visceral pain. IBS patients, in contrast to controls, fail to activate the anterior cingulate cortex (ACC) on rectal distension (Naliboff et al., 2001; Silverman et al., 1997). Data using fMRI, on the other hand, indicate that painful stimuli cause significantly greater activation of the ACC in IBS patients than in controls (Mertz et al., 2000). Notwithstanding disparate findings of PET and fMRI studies, both lines of research implicate abnormalities in ACC activity in visceral pain perception. The ACC is a site of opiate down-regulation of pain that may, when activated, inhibit sensory input that contributes to pain production. Based on PET data, IBS patients not only fail to activate the ACC in response to visceral pain but also demonstrate activation of the left prefrontal cortex, whereas no such response occurs in normal individuals. The prefrontal cortex is a brain structure associated with the emotional feelings (e.g., anxiety) directed partly toward long-term implications of having pain (e.g., "suffering") in relation to or in anticipation of pain. Taken together, PET data suggest that IBS patients may paradoxically respond to visceral pain stimuli by activating a brain area (prefrontal cortex) that amplifies pain perception rather than a brain area (ACC) with important pain modulatory properties.

Although the concept of visceral hypersensitivity addresses some of the limitations of the dysmotility hypothesis, it cannot be definitively characterized as an etiological mechanism for a variety of reasons. First, the phenomenon characterizes only a subset of IBS patients. Diarrhea-prominent IBS patients exhibit stronger rectal urgency at lower balloon volumes and exhibit greater sensitivity to rectal distension than do constipation-predominant IBS patients (Prior & Whorwell, 1990a, 1990b). Furthermore, non-treatment-seeking IBS patients do not exhibit visceral hypersensitivity. Given the more psychologically distressed profiles of their treatment-seeking counterparts (Whitehead et al., 2002), this suggests that psychological factors may contribute to visceral hyperalgesia, perhaps by aggravating nociception stimulation of visceral afferent nerves in at least a subset of IBS patients.

Psychological Factors. Like many benign chronic painful medical conditions, IBS has been historically conceptualized as a physical manifestation of a variety of psychiatric conditions, including hypochondriasis, personality disturbance, somatization, depression, and anxiety (e.g., Clouse, 1988; Hislop, 1971; Latimer, 1983). Although there is no evidence to support IBS as a psychiatric disorder, psychological factors influence onset, expression, and course, particularly in more severely affected patients. Research has pointed to three main pathways through which psychological factors influence IBS. The first key pathway is directly through physiological systems. Psychological factors (e.g., stress, negative emotional states) can normatively induce changes in gut function (Tache, 1989), and their effect is particularly pronounced in IBS patients (e.g., Welgan, Meshkinpour, & Hoehler, 1985). For example, psychological factors (e.g., negative mood states, expectation, attention) can modulate pain severity. The mechanism underlying benign abdominal pain perception is not well known. Many IBS researchers have been guided by Melzack and Wall's (1965) gate control theory of pain as an explanatory model for understanding the relationship between psychological factors and pain. According to Melzack and Wall, afferent (i.e., moving to the spinal cord) stimuli, such as nociceptive stimuli entering the spinal cord at the substantia gelatinosa, are modulated by other afferent stimuli (e.g., counterstimulation) and descending spinal pathways (e.g., higher order mental processes, emotions, thoughts, images, attentional focus) in a way that blocks or "gates" the perception of pain signals.

Psychological factors not only attenuate pain but also may produce clinical pain sensations in the absence of peripheral injury at a physiological level (Fields, 1991). According to Fields (1991), the response of an individual to damaging or potentially damaging stimuli depends on the stimulus as well as on the stimulus context. Pain perception and the behavioral response to noxious stimuli are controlled by CNS pain-modulating circuits that can be activated by environmental stimuli. This circuit is activated by opioids and controls pain transmission neurons in the spinal cord. The circuit contains several opioid and nonopioid neuropeptides, three classes of opioid receptors, and biogenic amine neurotransmitters such as norepinephrine and serotonin. Furthermore, this circuit exerts bidirectional control of pain transmission through the activity of two functional classes of brain stem neurons whose activity is correlated reciprocally with behavioral responses to painful stimulation. Neurons of one class (i.e., on cells) are activated by noxious stimuli, whereas those of the other class (i.e., off cells) are inhibited by noxious stimuli. The cells activated by noxious stimuli facilitate nociception, whereas those inhibited by noxious stimuli inhibit nociception. Fields (1991) argued that psychological processes (e.g., attention, expectancy) may contribute to pain production at a neurobiological level by "kick[ing] the responses of pain transmission neurons to non-noxious neurons into the noxious range and creat[ing] pain where there was no pain" (p. 88). If correct, this has relevance for understanding benign painful medical disorders such as IBS.

The second pathway through which psychological factors influence IBS symptoms is the adoption of illness behaviors that can exacerbate symptoms. Health behaviors are strongly influenced by an individual's psychological health. IBS patients as a group show higher levels of psychosocial distress as measured either through standardized questions or with structured psychiatric diagnostic interviews (Blanchard & Scharff, 2002). Over the past 15 years, Blanchard (2001) has conducted a series of studies that have systematically evaluated levels of psychopathology in treatment-seeking IBS patients. Whereas levels of depressive symptoms, as measured by the Beck Depression Inventory, fall consistently within "mild" diagnostic ranges, IBS patients report higher levels of anxiety, as measured by the State-Trait Anxiety Inventory. IBS patients had a mean state anxiety score of 47, which falls at the 45th percentile for psychiatric patients, the 61st percentile for general medical patients, and the 84th percentile for normal middle-age females. Trait anxiety scores averaged between 47 and 48, which falls at the 54th percentile for psychiatric patients, the 72nd percentile for general medical patients, and the 90th percentile for normal middle-age females. The notion that IBS is a psychosomatic disorder has also been fueled by research reporting high rates of comorbid psychiatric disorders among IBS patents. The results of studies using well-validated semistructured methodologies with adequate sample size indicate that between 40% and 60% of IBS patients have a diagnosable psychiatric disorder, with anxiety being the most common disorder (followed by mood and somatization disorders). Among diagnosable anxiety disorders, the most common is generalized anxiety disorder (Blanchard, Scharff, Schwarz, Suls, & Barlow, 1990). The prevalence of an Axis I psychiatric disorder not only is high in IBS patients but also exceeds the prevalence of a psychiatric disorder among patients with organic GI disorders (56 vs. 18%), whose clinical features are similar to those with IBS (e.g., IBD).

Although a select number of studies have failed to confirm high rates of psychiatric disorder (Blewett et al., 1996), there has emerged a general consensus that a sizable number of IBS patients have higher levels of distress and substantial psychiatric comorbidity in proportions that are conservatively at least twice as high as in patients with organic GI disorders and healthy counterparts. IBS patients with comorbid psychological symptoms are more likely to report more severe symptoms and

seek treatment than are their nondistressed counterparts (Drossman, 1999; Whitehead, Bosmajian, Zonderman, Costa, & Schuster, 1988). In fact, non-treatment-seeking IBS patients do not differ from healthy controls on measures of psychopathology (Whitehead et al., 1988). In other words, IBS patients with comorbid psychological symptoms are more likely to complain of symptoms and seek treatment than are their nondistressed counterparts. The precise mechanism underlying the relationship between treatment seeking and IBS symptoms has not been identified. It is possible that this relationship may exist because unpleasant mood states predispose one to making threat appraisals of stimuli (Cohen, Kessler, & Gordon, 1995), which in turn lead to heightened physiological reactivity and the acquisition of illness behaviors. Treatment-seeking behaviors may also be influenced by psychological stress. Research has found that IBS patients report more stressful events, more stress-related changes in stool patterns, and greater reactivity to stress than do controls (Bennet, Tennant, Piesse, Badcock, & Kellow, 1998). Creed, Craig, and Farmer (1988) found that major life events preceded the onset of IBS in 60% to 66% of IBS patients. In comparison, 25% of controls experienced similarly severe events at an arbitrary time. Lacking a sufficiently developed repertoire of coping skills (Drossman, Li, et al., 2000), IBS patients may respond physically to psychological stress by seeking medical attention that may in turn implicitly reinforce their disease conviction, promote a sense of invalidism, and lead to maladaptive illness behaviors.

A third pathway through which psychological factors influence IBS is by increasing the risk of developing IBS. In general, IBS researchers have focused on two types of psychosocial factors—reinforcement mechanisms and childhood abuse—that mediate the risk for IBS onset (Drossman, 1994). There is a relatively large body of literature linking a history of early (i.e., preadolescence) abuse to

IBS symptoms in a sizable number of female patients. A history of major traumatic events (i.e., physical and/or sexual abuse) is present in patients with IBS more frequently than in healthy controls. A history of severe emotional trauma, such as physical and sexual abuse (especially during childhood), also appears to be associated with an increased risk for IBS. Drossman and colleagues (1990) found that the frequency of a history of abuse among IBS patients was 30% greater than in women with an organic GI disease. Female IBS patients with a positive history of abuse report more pain, more sick days, a higher level of distress and health care use, worse behavioral functioning, and more surgeries. Although the mechanism underlying the relationship between abuse and IBS symptoms is not well defined (Drossman, Talley, Olden, Lesermann, & Barreioro, 1995), abuse likely represents an important risk factor for IBS symptoms and outcome in select patients.

Drawing from social learning theory (Bandura, 1977), Whitehead and colleagues (1988) approached early-life experiences from a reinforcement perspective. Social learning theory (SLT) is arguably the prevailing theoretical framework used in health behavior and health promotion research. In SLT, human behavior is explained in terms of a three-way, dynamic, reciprocal theory in which personal factors, environmental influences, and behavior interact continually. A basic premise of SLT is that people learn not only through their own experiences but also by observing the actions of others (i.e., modeling) and the results of those actions (consequences). Whitehead and colleagues argued that complaints of IBS symptoms are partly acquired in a family environment, where children learn through direct experience and by observing how others respond to IBS. In support of the principle of familial transmission are results of a large telephone survey (Whitehead, Winget, Fedoravicius, Wooley, & Blackwell, 1982)

that found that IBS patients were more likely than non-IBS respondents to recall that their parents both responded to pain complaints with the provision of positive reinforcement (e.g., gifts, toys) and demonstrated illness behaviors that can negatively reinforce illness behaviors.

Biopsychosocial Model

Although psychopathology, abnormal motility, visceral hypersensitivity, and CNS modulation all have been implicated in the expression of IBS, none of these processes is sufficient to explain IBS symptoms within and across all patients. For this reason, IBS is currently conceptualized from the perspective of a biopsychosocial model (Drossman, 1997). The biopsychosocial model holds that individual biology (e.g., genetic predisposition, GI physiology), behavior, and higher order cognitive processes (e.g., coping, illness beliefs, abnormal central processing of gut stimuli) influence IBS through their interaction with each other, with early-life factors (e.g., trauma, modeling), and with the individual's social and physical environments (e.g., reinforcement contingencies).

At the heart of the model is the belief that IBS involves a dysregulation in interactions among the CNS; peripheral sensory, motor, and autonomic nerves; and the enteric nervous system (ENS). This neural network is referred to as the "brain-gut axis." The ENS, the sympathetic nervous system (SNS), and the parasympathetic nervous system (PNS) comprise the three divisions of the autonomic nervous system (ANS), the part of the nervous system that regulates involuntary actions, including smooth muscle, cardiac muscle, and glands. The ANS's enteric division (i.e., ENS) is located in the sheaths of tissue lining the GI tract from the esophagus to the rectum. The ENS is composed of both local sensory neurons, which detect and relay information regarding changes in the tension of the gut walls, and its chemical environment and motor neurons, which control muscle contractions of the gut wall and secretion. The ENS plays a major role in maintaining homeostasis in the body by controlling GI blood vessel tone, motility, gastric secretion, and fluid transport. Because of its heavy concentration of neurotransmitters (e.g., serotonin, substance P, vasoactive intestinal peptide, calcitonin gene-related peptide), the fact that it is embryologically derived from the same part of the neural crest that forms the brain, and its unique ability among other parts of the peripheral nervous system to mediate reflex behavior (i.e., gut function) in the absence of input from the brain or spinal cord (Gershon, 1998), the ENS has been referred to as the "second brain."

Normal digestive functions involve communication links between the ENS and the CNS. These links take the form of parasympathetic and sympathetic fibers that either connect the CNS and ENS or connect the CNS directly with the digestive tract. Through these cross-connections, sensory inputs from the gut are relayed to and processed by higher cortical centers where they modulate affect, pain perception, and behavioral response. Because the neural transmission lines of the brain-gut axis are bidirectional and reciprocal, the CNS receives information from the digestive tract and modulates the ENS. The bidirectional relationship of the brain-gut axis means that higher order mental processes (e.g., attention, emotion, sensation, taste, thought) can influence GI function, secretion, and sensation (Drossman, 1994). Normal GI function is typically characterized by a relatively high degree of coordination of the brain-gut axis. In IBS patients, however, there is a persistent disruption in the interaction of the neuroenteric system that is manifested in abnormal motility and visceral hypersensitivity of gut stimuli whose sensation/perception is modulated by CNS regions closely linked to emotion and pain perception.

ASSESSMENT AND TREATMENT

Like other chronic illnesses, IBS does not lend itself to a "cure" or "fix." Therefore, the goals of treatment are to normalize bowel function, decrease pain/discomfort, and improve the QOL through a combination of pharmacological agents, behavioral self-change interventions, and lifestyle modification. The exact constellation of treatment strategies is not prescriptive but rather based on the nature (e.g., predominant bowel habit) and severity of symptoms (mild, moderate, or severe) of the individual patient. IBS symptom severity is a general term that, in the context of IBS, reflects not only the intensity and duration of symptoms but also the emotional unpleasantness and illness behaviors (e.g., treatment seeking) associated with IBS (Drossman, 1999; Drossman et al., 1997). The importance of symptom severity as a measure of a patient's symptom experience comes from research showing that psychological functioning is strongly associated with the severity of symptoms (Drossman, 1999).

Mild Symptoms

The majority (70%) of individuals who meet the IBS diagnosis can be classified as mild in that the symptoms occur relatively infrequently (e.g., two or three times per month), do not prompt medical care, and are not associated with impairment in physical or psychological function. First-line treatment for mildly affected patients is corrective information and education about the benign nature of IBS and dietary advice. For example, patients are encouraged to exercise, eat well-balanced regular meals, avoid fatty and gas-forming foods such as legumes, increase intake of dietary fiber, and reduce intake of caffeine, sorbitol (e.g., sugarless gum, dietetic candy), and alcohol (Drossman et al., 1997). Fiber supplementation (e.g., psyllium, bran) is often emphasized for patients with mild IBS, at least for those whose symptoms do not include bloating. Although most physicians recommend increasing fiber intake (e.g., increasing consumption of fruits, vegetables, and whole grains) for the majority of their patients, its therapeutic value has not been consistently established in quality clinical trials and is surprisingly controversial (Jailwala, Imperiale, & Kroenke, 2000). It appears that patients with constipation-predominant and mixed-type IBS are most likely to derive maximum benefit from fiber supplements because they act as bulk-forming laxatives that ease stool passage. However, fiber has no demonstrated positive effect on pain. Because bran has a normalizing effect on colonic function, it is often recommended for diarrhea-prominent patients. Pharmacotherapy is not typically recommended as a first-line treatment for mild IBS.

Moderate Symptoms

In IBS patients with moderate symptoms, the intensity and duration of symptoms (e.g., two or three times per week) typically interferes with activities of daily living and is associated with greater psychological distress than is the case in mildly affected IBS patients. Treatment for IBS patients with moderate symptoms may require the addition of pharmacotherapy directed at the gut to control symptom exacerbations, more extensive lifestyle modification, and behavioral self-management techniques that often begin with symptom self-monitoring. The goal of treatment is to increase awareness and identification of specific triggers (dietary, stress, and hormonal fluctuations) and conditions under which IBS symptoms are likely to occur, increase patients' sense of predictability, and foster self-management skills. Moderately affected patients may also be prescribed behavioral interventions, including hypnosis, stress management, and relaxation techniques, in an effort to dampen arousal and increase self-care skills. If pharmacological agents are pursued, they are structured around the most predominant symptoms. For patients with diarrhea-predominant IBS, a therapeutic trial of loperamide (Imodium), diphenoxylate (Lomotil), psyllium (Metamucil), or methylcellulose (Citrucel) or a low-dose tricyclic antidepressant (TCA) is often pursued. Patients with constipation-predominant IBS often undergo a trial of increased dietary fiber, supplemental fiber, an osmotic laxative (e.g., milk of magnesia, lactulose), and/or a stool softener if symptoms are not relieved by dietary fiber alone. Because of their anticholinergic side effects, however, TCAs can cause or exacerbate constipation and are often not recommended for constipation-predominant IBS patients (Clauw & Chrousos, 1997). Patients with pain/gas/bloating-predominant IBS may benefit from a trial of an antispasmodic agent, such as dicyclomine (Bentyl) or hyoscyamine with phenobarbital (Levsin), or a low-dose antidepressant.

Severe Symptoms

In the case of patients with severe symptoms (daily or near daily symptoms of severe intensity), a tertiary treatment center where psychotropic medications (e.g., antidepressants), psychiatric management, and psychological interventions are integrated into standard medical care is recommended.

Psychological Assessment

Consistent with the biopsychosocial conceptualization of IBS, the protocol of a psychological testing battery includes measures that reflect the range of psychosocial factors that influence IBS, including psychological distress, coping resources, negative cognitions, pain, behavioral functioning, QOL, and illness behaviors. The first step in the evaluation is assessing the nature and severity of symptoms; their natural history; the circumstances, patterns, determinants, and consequences of symptoms; and the patient's treatment history (current and lifetime). These goals can be achieved using a three-part semistructured interview, the Albany GI History, developed by Edward Blanchard's group at the State University of New York–Albany (SUNY–Albany) (Blanchard, 2001). The Albany GI History is organized in terms of a functional analysis of the clinical problem. Part 1 covers history and description of GI symptoms. Symptoms of pain, bowel disturbance, and associated symptoms (e.g., flatulence, bloating) are assessed in terms of their severity, frequency, and duration. The Albany GI History is sufficiently detailed to support (but not derive) a diagnosis using Rome II criteria once physical pathology has been ruled out medically. In addition, the interview covers situational factors that precede the onset of a symptom and consequent events. Part 2 is devoted to exploration of the family history of GI disorders in the extended family, a psychosocial history and description of psychosocial functioning, and related problem areas in the patient's life (e.g., relationship with peers, job strain, marital relations). Part 3 consists of a brief mental status examination. In addition to the Albany GI History, the Rome II Integrative Questionnaire (Talley, Drossman, Whitehead, Thompason, & Corassiari, 2000) is a comprehensive assessment tool whose items reflect Rome II criteria for functional GI disorders. Although the Rome II questionnaire does not assess psychosocial features of IBS and was designed for epidemiological research, its structure, ease of use, and comprehensiveness have advantages for clinicians and researchers looking for a well-designed survey measure of clinical symptoms of functional GI disorders.

A major part of data collection involves self-monitoring of symptoms using the GI symptom diary. IBS symptoms vary considerably over time and across dimensions of frequency, duration, and intensity. The temporal variability makes retrospective recall imprecise and of questionable validity. Daily recording and daily monitoring are important in both clinical and research settings. Although there is no established self-monitoring format, the form used at SUNY–Buffalo was developed by Blanchard and used in numerous clinical trials over 15 years. Patients make a series of daily severity ratings (beginning 2 to 4 weeks before treatment begins) for abdominal pain and tenderness, diarrhea, constipation, flatulence, belching, and bloating on a 5-point scale ranging from 0 (*not a problem*) to 4 (*debilitating*). They also record feelings of incomplete evacuation, whether pain was relieved by bowel movements, avoidance of foods and activities associated with symptoms, medication use, and (for women) the first day of their periods. There are a number of advantages with self-monitoring data, including accuracy, sensitivity to temporal variations, and objectivity (Meissner, Blanchard, & Malamood, 1997). For these reasons, many regard GI symptom diaries as the "gold standard" in IBS research. The daily symptom diaries are used to calculate Composite Primary Symptom Reduction (CPSR) scores, a previously validated measure of symptom change that describes clinically significant improvements in GI symptoms (Blanchard & Schwarz, 1988). To calculate the CPSR score, one must first calculate, for each patient and for each primary symptom, a Symptom Reduction Score (SRS). To avoid the statistical problem of multiple comparisons between groups inherent in a multisymptomatic disorder such as IBS, Blanchard developed a single metric, the CPSR score, for hypothesis testing. An SRS for each of the primary GI symptoms (abdominal pain and abdominal tenderness combined, diarrhea, and constipation) was calculated. For example, a diarrhea SRS is calculated as follows:

$$\text{Diarrhea Reduction Score} = \frac{100 \times \text{Baseline Diarrhea Ratings} - \text{Posttreatment Diarrhea Ratings}}{\text{Baseline Diarrhea Ratings}}.$$

The CPSR score was calculated by averaging the two or three symptom rating scores relevant to the individual patient:

CPSR = Pain and Tenderness Reduction Score
+ Diarrhea Reduction Score

$$+ \frac{\text{Constipation Reduction Score}}{\text{2 or 3 (depending on number of symptoms present).}}$$

Blanchard has defined a CPSR score of 0.50 or more (an average reduction of GI symptoms of 50% or more) as representing clinically significant improvement.

Pain. Because a majority of IBS patients identify pain as their most bothersome symptom, clinicians may want to supplement daily measurements of abdominal pain/discomfort with data from additional pain instruments. Whereas daily monitoring provides relatively precise data regarding the intensity and frequency of pain, it provides only limited information regarding other important aspects of the pain experience. The McGill Pain Questionnaire (MPQ) provides valuable information regarding the sensory, affective, and evaluative dimensions of the pain experience (Melzack, 1975). The MPQ contains 78 pain words grouped into 20 subclasses of 3 to 5 descriptive words. Within these subclasses, the patient ranks the 3 to 5 words according to the implied pain intensity. The 20 subclasses are grouped into four sections: sensory (e.g., cramping), affective (e.g., agonizing), evaluative (e.g., intense), and miscellaneous. In addition to the 78 pain words, the temporal pattern of pain is assessed with 9 words (e.g., constant, periodic). The location of pain is assessed with a drawing of the body with the words "external/internal" added. The MPQ also includes a 5-point pain rating scale that requires the patient to indicate his or her current level of pain by choosing a description that most closely matches his or her pain. Scores range from 0 (mild) to 4 (excruciating). Patients' intensity scores reflect the word that best describes their pain level, with higher scores indicating more intensive levels of reported pain.

An important part of pain assessment includes the evaluation of patients' behavioral and cognitive response to pain (i.e., coping).

Research has shown that patients with persistent painful medical disorders develop certain strategies to cope, tolerate, and deal with pain (Keefe et al., 1987a, 1987b). Particularly important coping responses include efforts to ignore or reinterpret pain sensations as benign, pacing activities, increasing activity level, praying or hoping, and disputing negatively skewed thinking patterns using positive self-statements about patients' ability to cope or manage. Pain coping strategies that are adopted and used over prolonged time periods may influence physical and psychological functioning significantly. In some patients, an adaptive set of coping strategies may buffer them from the adverse effects of medical illness. In others, maladaptive coping patterns may become entrenched, thereby heightening the severity of pain and the impact of pain on behavior.

One coping style linked to IBS patients is an overreliance on a negatively skewed thinking pattern (i.e., catastrophizing) (Drossman, Li, et al., 2000). The term "catastrophizing" refers to an aberrant information processing style marked by magnification, helplessness, and rumination toward painful stimuli. The pattern of these data is similar to that in research findings with osteoarthritis patients with persistent knee pain; those who rate themselves as more effective in managing pain and who report less catastrophizing cope with pain more effectively (Keefe et al., 1987b). Pain coping responses can be assessed effectively with the Pain Coping Skills Questionnaire (CSQ) (Rosenstiel & Keefe, 1983). On the CSQ, patients are asked to indicate how they cope with everyday painful experiences. The CSQ measures the frequency of use of seven pain coping strategies, six of which are cognitive (diverting attention, reinterpreting pain sensations, coping self-statements, ignoring pain sensations, praying and hoping, and catastrophizing) and one of which is behavioral (increasing behavioral activity). The CSQ also includes two ratings of coping efficacy: one rating of perceived efficacy of coping in decreasing pain and one rating of perceived efficacy of coping in controlling pain. Previous research has shown that coping strategies measured by the CSQ are predictive of pain, psychological function, activity level, and physical impairment of patients with chronic pain problems independent of disease severity. The CSQ provides a profile of the use of a range of pain coping strategies that appear to be useful in predicting adjustments to persistent medical conditions.

Psychiatric Comorbidity. As noted previously, IBS is associated with significant psychiatric comorbidity that is formally assessed using the Structured Clinical Interview for DSM-IV Axis I Disorders (SCID) (First, Spitzer, Gibbon, & Williams, 2001). The SCID is a semistructured interview for obtaining major DSM-IV (*Diagnostic and Statistical Manual of Mental Disorders,* fourth edition [American Psychiatric Association, 1994]) Axis I and Axis II diagnoses. There are other structured diagnostic interviews, including the Anxiety Disorders Interview (ADIS-R) (DiNardo & Barlow, 1988), that have been used in clinical research with IBS patients. The SCID has some advantages over the ADIS and other semistructured psychiatric interviews in that it yields a more thorough assessment of non-anxiety-related disorders that may accompany IBS. Several standardized self-report measures provide useful information regarding psychological functioning. Additional psychological self-report measures tap psychopathology. These include the Brief Symptom Inventory (Derogatis, 1993) for psychopathology, the Beck Depression Inventory (Beck, Rush, Shaw, & Emery, 1979), the State-Trait Anxiety Inventory (Spielberger, 1983), and the Penn State Worry Questionnaire (PSWQ) (Mayer & Raybould, 1990), a measure of habitual worry due to the high rate (40%) of generalized anxiety disorder comorbidity (Blanchard et al., 1990).

Quality of Life. Because IBS is a chronic condition that can compromise an patients' emotional, social, and physical well-being, patients are administered the IBS–Quality of Life Measure (IBS-QOL) (Patrick, Drossman, Frederick, DiCesare, & Puder, 1998), whose 34 items each fall into one of eight domains (dysphoria, activity interference, body image, health worry, food avoidance, social relations, sexual activity, or intimate relationships) clinically relevant to IBS. QOL measures are useful in assessing the extent to which IBS compromises patients' general sense of happiness and satisfaction in important life domains (e.g., health, recreation). In comparison with more traditional biological measures that focus on infirmity or disease status, QOL measures focus on both objective functioning and subjective well-being. These data sources are usually better for assessing the social and emotional outcomes of the treatment and disease process and for proving an overall picture of how treatments or illnesses affect patients' ability to function in life.

The IBS-QOL concentrates on the perceived well-being of the patient and not more objective measures of physical functioning (e.g., activities of daily living). Because there is general consensus that QOL involves both objective functioning and subjective well-being, the IBS-QOL is supplemented with information from the MOS 36-Item Short Form (SF-36) (Ware & Sherbourne, 1992). The SF-36 assesses eight health dimensions (Stewart & Ware, 1992) that the IBS-QOL does not assess directly: (a) limitations in physical activities due to health problems, (b) limitations in social activities due to health or emotional problems, (c) limitations in usual role activities due to health problems, (d) bodily pain, (e) general medical health (i.e., psychological distress and well-being), (f) limitations in usual role activities due to emotional problems, (g) vitality (e.g., energy and fatigue), and (h) self-evaluation of general health status. The SF-36 has been used to measure health-related QOL in IBS patients (Hahn et al., 1999).

Treatment Efficacy

Pharmacotherapy. As noted previously, a number of dietary and pharmacological agents that are currently used to treat IBS represent the first- and second-line therapies for IBS patients (Table 20.2). The most common classes of medications currently used for IBS are laxatives, antidepressants, antidiarrheals, and antispasmodics. There is no universally agreed-on medical option for IBS. No class of medications or single medication within a class currently available has been demonstrated in well-designed and well-controlled clinical trials to be consistently superior to placebo treatment for the spectrum of IBS symptoms. This conclusion is based largely on the findings of an influential 1988 systematic review of randomly controlled drug trials. Klein (1988) concluded that because of methodological flaws, "no therapy has been shown to be effective in treating IBS" (p. 232).

Since the publication of the Klein (1988) review, a slightly more positive appraisal of pharmacological agents has emerged. One recent review (Poynard, Regimbeau, & Benhamou, 2001) of 23 randomized studies with eight different agents published up to 2000 offered some of the strongest existing evidence for direct smooth muscle relaxants (e.g., calcium channel blockers, antispasmodics) when pain is the predominant symptom. These medications influence motor activity and decrease colonic responsiveness. However, none of the muscle relaxants identified as effective (cimetropium bromide, panivorous bromide, and trimebutine) is available in the United States (Poynard et al., 2001).

The efficacy of smooth muscle relaxants available in the United States has not been well established due to methodological shortcomings of the clinical trials. In relatively brief clinical trials, anticholinergics (e.g., dicyclomine, hyoscyamine) are associated with global improvement, but the extent to which they improve specific IBS symptoms (e.g., diarrhea, constipation) is not known. Patients with diarrhea are often prescribed antidiarrheals, which are designed to reduce colonic transit through direct action on the smooth muscle of the GI tract. One example is the opioid agonist loperamide, which is designed to increase stool consistency and decrease frequency by enhancing intestinal water absorption, strengthening anal sphincter tone, and reducing intestinal transit. Loperamide is preferred over other opioid agonists (e.g., diphenoxylate) due to its potency, longer duration of action, and favorable side effect profile (e.g., lower potential for physical dependence). However, loperamide does not appear to have an analgesic effect.

Bulking agents such as fiber supplements (e.g., calcium polycarbophil, methylcellulose, psyllium) are often prescribed for patients with constipation-prominent IBS because these supplements facilitate peristalsis and improve colonic and oral-anal transit. Although fiber supplements may decrease constipation in a subset of patients, their therapeutic benefit may come at the expense of aggravating some IBS symptoms (e.g., bloating, distension, cramping, flatus). Furthermore, they have no established analgesic properties. Dietary fiber supplements are of conclusive benefit only in constipation-predominant patients.

With respect to antidepressants, the tricyclic class represents the most commonly prescribed and investigated option. In a meta-analysis of the efficacy of TCAs on functional GI disorders (vs. IBS per se), Jackson and colleagues (2000) reviewed data from 11 placebo-controlled trials (2 non-ulcer dyspepsia and 9 IBS) and concluded that TCAs were effective in relieving pain. Furthermore, because most of the dosages given were lower than required to achieve psychotropic effects, Jackson and colleagues suggested that TCAs "work" via their neuromodulatory and analgesic properties (vs. psychotropic effects). The intrinsic anticholinergic effects of TCAs (e.g., constipation) may broaden the therapeutic value (e.g., decrease diarrhea) of TCAs, at least in patients with diarrhea-predominant IBS (Jailwala et al., 2000). Patients with constipation-predominant IBS appear less responsive to TCAs than do those with either pain-predominant or diarrhea-predominant IBS. The four most commonly prescribed and studied TCAs are nortriptyline (Pamelor), imipramine (Tofranil),

Table 20.2 Common Pharmacological Treatment for IBS

Agent and Examples	Predominant Symptom(s)	Possible Side Effects/Comment
Antidiarrheal Agents Diphenoxylate-atropine (Lomotil)	Diarrhea	Controlled substance, nervousness, drowsiness, dizziness, constipation, headache, urinary retention
Loperamide (Immodium)		Preferred over diphenoxylate/atropine due to more favorable side effect profile and no abuse potential; adverse side effects include sedation, drowsiness, fatigue, dizziness, cramping, nausea, rash, and constipation; may improve diarrhea, urgency, borborygmi,[a] frequency of bowel movement, and stool consistency but not abdominal pain or distention
Bulk-Forming Laxatives Methylcellulose (Citrucel)	Constipation	May worsen abdominal distension, bloating, and flatulence
Psyllium (Metamucil)		
Antispasmodic Agents Dicyclomine (Bentyl)	Abdominal pain, diarrhea	Anticholinergic side effects (urinary retention, decreased sweating, headache, dizziness, congestion, blurred vision, dry mouth, tachycardia, rash)
Hyoscyamine (Levsin)		
Tricyclic Antidepressants Amitriptyline (Elavil)	Abdominal pain, nausea, nonspecific symptoms	May cause or worsen constipation; may stimulate appetite, cause urinary retention, cause blurred vision, and worsen constipation; may be useful for diarrhea-predominant IBS
Desipramine (Norpramin)		
Selective Serotonin Reuptake Inhibitors Citalopram (Celexa) Fluoxetine (Prozac) Fluvoxamine (Luvox) Paroxetine (Paxil) Sertraline (Zoloft)	Comorbid anxiety, depression	May worsen diarrhea
5-HT3 Serotonin Receptor Antagonist Alosetron (Lotronex)	Non-constipation-predominant IBS in females	May worsen constipation and headache
5-HT4 Serotonin Receptor Agonist Tegaserod (Zelnorm/Zelmac)	Constipation-predominant IBS in females	May worsen diarrhea, abdominal pain, nausea, flatulence, and headache

NOTE: IBS = irritable bowel syndrome.

a. Borborygmi is noisy rumbling of air moving through the intestine.

amitriptyline (Elavil), and desipramine (Pertofrane). Because of their fewer side effects, desipramine and nortriptyline are often preferred over amitriptyline and imipramine. Selective serotonin reuptake inhibitors have no established therapeutic effect on IBS symptoms but are frequently used to manage the psychiatric comorbidity (e.g., anxiety, depression).

Some of the newer pharmacotherapies, known as serotonin modulators, are directed at specific serotonin receptor sites in the gut, which contains 95% of the body's serotonin. Serotonin receptors are heavily concentrated in the ENS and play an important role in mediating gut response and sensation. These medications include alosetron (Lotronex), a serotonergic type 3 antagonist agent, and tegaserod (Zelnorm), a type 4 agonist. Alosetron is marketed for non-constipated females, whereas tegaserod is designed for constipated females. Both medications are unique among pharmacological agents in their ability to target multiple symptoms. Alosetron has been effective in reducing pain and diarrhea, ostensibly by slowing colonic transit time. Tegaserod has been found to be effective in reducing pain, constipation, and bloating, perhaps by stimulating peristalsis and chloride secretion, accelerating colonic transit time, and blocking pain signals from the gut. Neither medication has established itself as any more effective than placebo for male IBS patients.

The manufacturer of Lotronex voluntarily withdrew it after serious GI events, specifically ischemic colitis and complications of constipation, were reported in association with its use. Lotronex has subsequently been reintroduced to the marketplace with Food and Drug Administration approval under restricted conditions of use. In sum, the most positive, evidence-based appraisal of the efficacy of pharmacological agents can be described thusly: Specific agents can be effective for some patients with discrete symptoms and/or specific types of IBS.

Psychological Treatment. Whereas the overall track record for pharmacological agents is generally modest to disappointing (with a few exceptions), the track record for psychological interventions can be described as controversial depending on the "eye of the beholder." Doubts about the track record of psychological treatments were perhaps expressed most clearly by Talley, Fett, and Zinsmeister (1995), whose influential systematic review concluded that the efficacy of psychological treatments had not been established due to methodological flaws of clinical trials. Talley and colleagues' study was not so much a systematic review as an analysis of the methodological quality of then available clinical trials. The review itself suffered from a number of methodological problems that compromise the interpretability of its conclusions (Lackner, Morley, Dowzer, Mesmer, & Hamilton, 2003). Notwithstanding its limitations, Talley and colleagues' study was a landmark one in that it was the first to evaluate systematically methodological quality of psychologically oriented clinical trials across multiple a priori quality criteria. On the other side of the fence are those researchers who point to a series of quality smaller scale studies over the past 20 years as evidence of the clinical effectiveness of psychotherapy. A comprehensive review of the outcome research is beyond the scope of this chapter but can be found in a recent article (Blanchard & Scharff, 2002).

Four different classes of psychological treatments—brief psychodynamic psychotherapy with relaxation, hypnotherapy, cognitive-behavioral therapy, and cognitive therapy—have been shown to be superior to symptom monitoring or routine medical care in reducing IBS symptoms (Blanchard, 2001). Treatments featuring cognitive therapy and hypnotherapy have been replicated and found to be superior to attention placebo control conditions. According to Blanchard and Sharff's (2002) narrative review, hypnotherapy has the strongest empirical support (Whorwell, Prior, & Faragher, 1984) in that its therapeutic benefit has been replicated independently by two other research groups (Galovski & Blanchard, 1998; Harvey, Hinton, Gunary, & Barry, 1989) and is maintained over time (Whorwell, Prior, & Colgan, 1987).

The psychological treatment with the second most consistently positive track record is cognitive therapy. Cognitive therapy for IBS is designed to reduce excessive emotional or physiological reactions associated with GI symptoms by modifying or eliminating negatively skewed thinking patterns (e.g., jumping to conclusions) and belief systems (e.g., perfectionism) that underlie these reactions. A related goal of cognitive therapy is to provide patients with a general set of problem-solving or coping skills to manage a wide range of situations associated with IBS. Quality data based on a series of smaller scale clinical trials indicate that 60% to 80% of IBS patients who undergo cognitive therapy achieve at posttreatment (up to 3 months) a clinically significant (50% or more) reduction in IBS symptoms and maintain these gains at 3-month follow-up. Treatment gains associated with cognitive therapy are not limited to a reduction in GI symptoms alone. A significant proportion of patients also show substantial reductions in comorbid psychological distress (e.g., anxiety) at posttreatment.

One of the most interesting aspects of the psychological treatment literature is the inconsistent support for multicomponent cognitive-behavioral protocol used effectively with other painful medical conditions (e.g., arthritis, low back pain, fibromyalgia). Although cognitive-behavioral therapy has been found to be more effective than symptom monitoring, it appears to be no more effective than a credible attention placebo condition (Blanchard et al., 1992; Toner et al., 1998). Drossman and colleagues (1999) conducted a narrative review of 15 psychologically oriented clinical trials and derived conclusions similar to those of Blanchard and Scharff (2002). There was, according to Drossman and colleagues (1999), sufficient evidence in 10 of 13 studies for the efficacy of psychological treatments in reducing bowel symptoms at posttreatment (2 studies were dropped from the review because the participation rate dropped below 40%).

Complications

Successfully treating IBS is a rewarding but challenging endeavor. For change to be achieved and maintained, patients require motivation and a willingness to invest the requisite effort, time, and commitment in self-care skills. This can be particularly difficult among those patients who are not psychologically minded, have a strong disease conviction, or see psychological treatments as reserved for mental illness. Therefore, it should be emphasized to patients that their treatment is really no different from other, more widely accepted behavioral treatments used for physical health problems. Just as a cardiologist may attempt to alter cardiac disease by prescribing behavioral changes (e.g., increase physical activity, decrease stress, change diet) for a heart patient, so too do the cognitive or behavioral interventions, which form the basis of treatment, attempt to alter gut function by changing behaviors. By drawing a parallel between the treatment options of IBS and those of other, seemingly more legitimate medical conditions, therapists attempt to mobilize patients' change resources in the direction of a self-management approach. This is not to say that change will necessarily ensue. Patients are reminded about the importance of regular practice and patience.

There are at least two groups of patients who seem resistant to treatment. The first group is patients with strong disease conviction and ongoing investment in pursuing a medical cure for symptom relief. Although these patients may attend treatment regularly, they seem to merely "go through the motions" of treatment. Their disease conviction limits the effort, commitment, and motivation required to complete a treatment successfully, which places a premium on behavioral self-change. One approach to these patients is to encourage them to obtain whatever medical care has been found to be effective and to reinforce the value of *simultaneously* learning self-management skills for managing a chronic illness that currently defies a medical solution.

CASE STUDY

"Rachel" is a 35-year-old, married Caucasian female with 16 years of education who was referred by her gastroenterologist to the SUNY–Buffalo Medical School Behavioral Medicine Clinic for evaluation and treatment of a 9-year history of IBS. Her assessment was conducted during two sessions as part of the pretreatment phase of a National Institutes of Health-funded clinical trial of a group-based cognitive therapy for IBS. Rachel's primary complaints were abdominal pain associated with constipation, bloating, and gas. On the MPQ, she described abdominal pain as a cramping sensation associated with a sharp, stabbing, shooting feeling in the rectum. She characterized the affective dimension of pain as exhausting and cruel. Rachel rated the typical abdominal pain intensity as being of moderate intensity. During the clinical interview, she characterized current pain as "discomforting" and within moderate intensity on the MPQ. That being said, pain occasionally reached severe levels. Pain was relieved when she either had a soft, loosely formed bowel movement or exercised. Pain tended to ease on its own after approximately 60 minutes. In addition to pain, she experienced periods of constipation, bloating, nausea, and gas. She characterized constipation as having no bowel movement for 3 or more days. Several times a week, she experienced a sense after a bowel movement that she had been unable to pass all of the fecal matter (i.e., incomplete evacuation).

Prior to presentation, Rachel had consulted her family physician, obstetrician/gynecologist, gastroenterologist, and proctologist. Her gastroenterologist had diagnosed her with IBS after her family physician expressed uncertainty about whether her symptoms were symptomatic of colitis. She had undergone a variety of diagnostic tests to detect an underlying organic basis of her symptoms. These included an upper GI series, gallbladder series, sigmoidoscopy, colonoscopy, and stool tests for ova, parasites, and blood. At the time of the examination, she was prescribed Librax. She was also taking a number of over-the-counter agents, including Citrucel, Colace, Triphasil, and Rosewater. Both prescription and over-the-counter agents provided limited relief of pain and bowel disturbance. With the exception of IBS, Rachel was in generally good physical health. She was not being treated for any extraintestinal health problems. Her only prior operation was a tonsillectomy in 1980. There was no family history of colon polyps, IBD, colon cancer, or liver disease.

Although Rachel had never been treated for a psychiatric condition, the clinical picture that emerged from testing was a nervous, tense, shy individual with strong perfectionistic inclinations. She described herself as a "longtime worrier" prone to high levels of general anxiety. Much of her worries focused on interpersonal and evaluative stressors whose resolution necessitated self-assertion, conflict negotiation, and direct communication (e.g. refusing requests). On the PSWQ, she acknowledged that her worries took on excessive ("Many situations make me worry") and uncontrollable

("I know I shouldn't worry about things, but I just can't help it") qualities. She was particularly prone to worrying when she felt increased work pressure in her job as a social worker. Although she had no history of a psychiatric condition, she reported a positive history of sexual abuse that was perpetrated by an older neighborhood boy when she was approximately 9 years old.

Rachel participated in a 10-session group-based treatment program that was offered as part of a current outcome trial. She was randomly assigned to a cognitive therapy condition. The cognitive-based treatment for IBS, described more fully in Blanchard (2001), is designed to teach the patient to learn to identify and correct maladaptive beliefs and information processing errors with the goal of reducing GI symptoms and related distress. Within this treatment, cognitive interventions consist of four overlapping phases: (a) educating the patient about IBS and the processes that maintain the disorder, with a focus on its situational, cognitive, and emotional triggers; (b) training the patient in the identification and modification of his or her cognitive appraisals and interpretations of situations, thoughts, and behaviors; (c) changing underlying or "core" beliefs supporting negative cognitions; and (d) receiving formal training in problem solving to strengthen the ability to cope more effectively with realistic stressors associated with IBS. Rachel met with four other IBS patients for 10 sessions (90 minutes long) in a small group setting with a single therapist over the course of 10 weeks. The provision of education about the nature and pathophysiology of IBS (e.g., role of visceral sensitivity, abnormal gut motility) and corrective information concerning the myths associated with IBS (e.g., "not real," "all in your head") was the first objective of treatment. Rachel and her group members learned that IBS was a benign medical condition whose symptoms are due neither to a detectable organic problem nor to psychopathology. Instead, IBS was presented as a legitimate illness due to a lack of coordination in the interaction between the brain and the gut. It was explained that psychological factors (e.g., expectancies, stress, strong emotions) are capable of disrupting how the brain and the gut function with each other in a way that aggravates symptoms in both IBS patients and nonclinical individuals. This effect is exaggerated in IBS patients. In Rachel's case, cognitive factors associated with IBS included her tendency to think the worst in the face of uncertainty (i.e., overestimate the probability of negative events), underestimate her ability to cope with adversity, and focus on the emotional distress of a stressor rather than on her ability to manage it effectively regardless of the accompanying distress. To increase awareness of the link between cognitive processes and symptoms, Rachel monitored IBS-related symptoms, their situational antecedents, her accompanying thoughts, and her responses (e.g., emotional, physical) using "dysfunctional thought records." On monitoring sheets, she detailed the content of her worries, their estimated "heat of the moment" probability, and evidence to support them. To the extent that worries could not be substantiated, she was instructed to revise her estimation of the probability of worrisome negative events based on realistic appraisals of the evidence if any existed. A major goal of this technique is to encourage patients to treat automatic thoughts not necessarily as facts but rather as hypotheses ("dressed up as facts") whose factual basis could be determined both by using evidence-based logic and by generating alternative explanations for negatively skewed appraisals. For realistic stressors, Rachel was taught a set of "decatastrophizing" techniques that emphasized acceptance/resignation over unmodifiable events, the importance of both adopting a "so-what approach" and attending to the immediate environment, and the limited value of responding physically to psychological stressors. The goals of decatastrophizing techniques were to strengthen both Rachel's confidence that she had sufficient coping resources to endure adversity and her understanding of the limited utility of worrying about negative life circumstances over which she had limited, if any, control. Through problem-solving techniques, Rachel learned a more flexible and varied set of coping strategies for resolving realistic stressors that aggravated symptoms. Once basic cognitive restructuring skills were developed, cognitive therapy shifted toward challenging and disputing underlying core beliefs that in Rachel's case included a strong sense of perfectionism, that is, the belief that she needed to be perfect in all endeavors and that falling short of this standard is unacceptable. As her self-management skills improved, her GI symptoms decreased. After about the fourth week, the intensity, frequency, and duration of both pain and diarrhea decreased in comparison with pretreatment levels. Interestingly, she experienced no appreciable change in bloating.

When Rachel returned for her 2-week posttreatment follow-up, she reported that GI symptoms had decreased by approximately 75% and that pain had decreased by approximately 50% to 60% since pretreatment baseline. Consistent with her global reports of improvement were data obtained from daily GI symptom diaries. Whereas symptoms occurred four or five times weekly at moderate to severe levels at pretreatment and were associated with significant distress and diminished function (e.g., role limitations, reduced QOL), she now described once-weekly episodes of abdominal pain whose intensity she rated as mild and nondisabling at posttreatment. In addition to improvement in GI symptoms, she completed treatment with an improved QOL. A board-certified gastroenterologist who was blind to her treatment independently evaluated her symptoms as "markedly improved." Beyond improvements in IBS symptoms, she demonstrated improvement in broader health status. Postsession evaluation for Axis I indicated that she no longer met full DSM-IV criteria for generalized anxiety disorder. Rachel was seen two additional times at 3- and 12-month follow-up to gauge her maintenance of treatment gains. She experienced no significant exacerbation of GI symptoms, mood disturbance, or functional limitations. Table 20.3 illustrates the course of Rachel's symptom severity across the treatment period.

Table 20.3 Symptom Severity at Pretreatment, Posttreatment, and Follow-Up Assessments

Outcome Measure	Pretreatment	Posttreatment	3-Month Follow-Up	12-Month Follow-Up
Gastrointestinal symptoms	1.27	0.74	0.54	0.57
Monitoring index				
State Anxiety[a]	49	30	35	24
Trait Anxiety[a]	50	30	37	34
Depression[b]	11	3	5	4
Quality of Life[c]	35	17	15	14
Role limitations				
Emotional[d]	45	45	45	45
Pain[d]	61	51	46	51
Social functioning[d]	70	44	44	44
Mental health[d]	56	56	51	44

a. State-Trait Anxiety Inventory (summed scores).
b. Beck Depression Inventory (summed score).
c. Irritable Bowel Syndrome–Quality of Life Inventory.
d. SF-36 (T-scores).

In other words, patients are encouraged to treat their IBS in much the same way that they, their friends, or their family members would approach any other chronic medical illness such as diabetes, asthma, or heart disease.

The second group of treatment-resistant patients is patients who are unable to link fluctuations in IBS symptoms to stress or other psychological triggers. These patients are not necessarily defensive or inclined to "fake good." It is quite possible that their IBS symptoms are subject to limited psychological meditation (e.g., dietary or hormonal fluctuations). Therefore, there does not seem to be much value in attempting to force the patients to recognize a relationship between stress and IBS that might not exist. For these patients, one approach is to encourage them to use their symptoms as situational triggers of potentially maladaptive responses that may subsequently aggravate symptoms.

To illustrate, one patient who was unable to identify situational triggers discovered that she responded fearfully and with catastrophic thoughts to symptoms that seemed to come "out of the blue." Although she was unable to reduce the frequency of symptoms, she used

cognitive-behavioral techniques and learned to respond more constructively in a way that decreased symptom intensity and duration. Another potential complication involves compliance with homework assignments. As a behavioral self-management treatment, cognitive therapy necessitates active commitment to attend treatment and complete between-session homework assignments so as to learn more adaptive skills (and to unlearn maladaptive ones). This can be a difficult task, particularly with patients who are inclined to overschedule their lives. It is emphasized that the degree of relief that patients invest in treatment corresponds with their investment in behavioral assignments. No apologies are made for the behavioral tasks assigned in treatment. If patients cannot complete time- and effort-intensive assignments, it is suggested that a behavioral treatment program might not be a good match for them, and they are encouraged to seek alternative treatment. Patients seem more likely to carry out assignments if they have developed a positive expectancy regarding treatment efficacy, which is reinforced by discussing the track record of behaviorally based treatments for IBS. Finally, patients who are undergoing a high level of objective chronic stress (e.g., transportation difficulties, financial pressures) seem to have difficulty in carrying out behavioral assignments, although this observation has not been formally evaluated.

CONCLUSIONS

IBS is a chronic, potentially disabling, painful medical disorder that exacts a heavy toll on society, employers, and its sufferers. IBS is not explainable by structural or biochemical mechanisms. Symptoms are best explained from a biopsychosocial perspective that emphasizes a number of factors, including abnormal motility, visceral hypersensitivity, abnormal cerebral processing of bowel stimuli, and psychological processes. Currently, there are no empirically validated medical options that target the full spectrum of symptoms associated with IBS. That being said, a number of well-defined, short-term psychological treatments have been developed that offer hope and symptom relief for the 35 million individuals with IBS. This chapter has attempted to illustrate the application of a cognitive therapy approach that emphasizes patient education, cognitive restructuring, and problem-solving training in relieving abdominal pain, bowel dysfunction, and related distress.

REFERENCES

Adams, P. F., & Benson, V. (1991). Current estimates from the National Health Interview Survey. In *Vital Health Statistics* 10 (Volume 83, pp. 92–1590). Hyattsville, MD: U.S. Department of Health and Human Services.

Almy, T. P., Kern, F. J., & Tulin, M. (1949). Alternation in colonic function in man under stress: Experimental production of sigmoid spasm in healthy persons. *Gastroenterology, 12,* 425–436.

American Psychiatric Association. (1994). *Diagnostic and statistical manual of mental disorders* (4th ed.). Washington, DC: Author.

Bandura, A. (1977). Self-efficacy: Toward a unifying theory of behavioral change. *Psychological Review, 84,* 191–215.

Bazzacchi, G., Ellis, J., Villanueava-Meyer, J., Jing, J., Reddy, S. N., Mena, I., & Snape, W. J., Jr. (1990). Postprandial colonic transit and motor activity in chronic constipation. *Gastroenterology, 98,* 686–693.

Beck, A. T., Rush, A., Shaw, B., & Emery, G. (1979). *Cognitive therapy of depression.* New York: Guilford.

Bennet, E. J., Tennant, C. C., Piesse, C., Badcock, C. A., & Kellow, J. E. (1998). Level of chronic life stress predicts clinical outcome in irritable bowel syndrome. *Gut, 42,* 256–261.

Blanchard, E. B. (2001). *Irritable bowel syndrome: Psychosocial assessment and treatment.* Washington, DC: American Psychological Association.

Blanchard, E. B., & Scharff, L. (2002). Psychosocial aspects of assessment and treatment of irritable bowel syndrome in adults and recurrent abdominal pain in children. *Journal of Consulting and Clinical Psychology, 70,* 725–738.

Blanchard, E. B., Scharff, L., Schwarz, S. P., Suls, J. M., & Barlow, D. H. (1990). The role of anxiety and depression in the irritable bowel syndrome. *Behavior Research and Therapy, 28,* 401–405.

Blanchard, E. B., & Schwarz, S. P. (1988). Clinically significant changes in behavioral medicine. *Behavioral Assessment, 10,* 171–188.

Blanchard, E. B., Schwarz, S. P., Suls, J. M., Gerardi, M. A., Scharff, L., Greene, B., Taylor, A. E., Berreman, C., & Malamood, H. S. (1992). Two controlled evaluations of multicomponent psychological treatment of irritable bowel syndrome. *Behavior Research and Therapy, 30,* 175–189.

Blewett, A., Allison, M., Calcraft, B., Moore, R., Jenkins, P., & Sullivan, G. (1996). Psychiatric disorder and outcome in irritable bowel syndrome. *Psychosomatics, 37,* 155–160.

Carr, D. B. (1996). Preempting the memory of pain. *Journal of the American Medical Association, 279,* 1114–1115.

Cervero, F., & Laird, J. M. (1999). Visceral pain. *Lancet, 353,* 2145.

Clauw, D. J., & Chrousos, G. P. (1997). Chronic pain and fatigue syndromes: Overlapping clinical and neuroendocrine features and potential pathogenic mechanisms. *NeuroImmunoModulation, 4,* 134–153.

Clouse, R. (1988). Anxiety and gastrointestinal illness. *Psychiatric Clinics of North America, 11,* 399–417.

Coderre, T. J., Katz, J., Vaccarino, A. L., & Metzack, R. (1993). Contribution of central neuroplasticity to pathological pain: Review of clinical and experimental evidence. *Pain, 52,* 259–285.

Cohen, S., Kessler, R. C., & Gordon, L. K. (1995). *Measuring stress.* New York: Oxford University Press.

Cook, U., Van Eeeden, A., & Collins, S. M. (1987). Patients with irritable bowel syndrome have greater pain tolerance than normal subjects. *Gastroenterology, 93,* 727–733.

Creed, F., Craig, T., & Farmer, R. (1988). Functional abdominal pain, psychiatric illness, and life events. *Gut, 29,* 235–242.

Crombie, I. K., Croft, P. R., Linton, S. J., LeResche, L., & Von Korff, M. (1999). *Epidemiology of pain.* Washington, DC: IASP Press.

Dalton, C., & Drossman, D. A. (1997). Diagnosis and treatment of irritable bowel syndrome. *American Family Physician, 55,* 883–885.

Derogatis, L. R. (1993). *Brief Symptom Inventory.* Minneapolis, MN: National Computer Systems.

DiNardo, P. A., & Barlow, D. H. (1988). *Anxiety Disorders Interview Schedule— Revised (ADIS-R).* Boston: Center for Anxiety and Related Disorders.

Drossman, D. A. (1994). Irritable bowel syndrome. *The Gastroenterologist, 2,* 315–326.

Drossman, D. A. (1997). Presidential address: Gastrointestinal illness and the biopsychosocial model. *Psychosomatic Medicine, 60,* 258–267.

Drossman, D. A. (1999). Do psychosocial factors define symptom severity and patient status in irritable bowel syndrome? *American Journal of Medicine, 107*(5A), S41–S50.

Drossman, D. A., Corazziari, E., Talley, N. J., Thompson, W. G., & Whitehead, W. E. (Eds.). (2000). *Rome II: The functional gastrointestinal disorders: Diagnosis, pathophysiology, and treatment—A multinational consensus* (2nd ed.). McLean, VA: Degnon Associates.

Drossman, D. A., Creed, F. H., Olden, K. W., Svedlund, J., Toner, B. B., & Whitehead, W. E. (1999). Psychosocial aspects of the functional gastrointestinal disorders. *Gut, 45,* 1125–1130.

Drossman, D. A., Li, Z., Leserman, J., Keefe, F. J., Hu, Y. J., & Toomey, T. C. (2000). Effects of coping on health outcome among female patients with gastrointestinal disorders. *Psychosomatic Medicine, 62,* 309–317.

Drossman, D. A., Talley, N. J., Olden, K. W., Lesermann, J., & Barreioro, M. A. (1995). Sexual and physical abuse and gastrointestinal illness: Review and recommendations. *Annals of Internal Medicine, 123,* 782–794.

Drossman, D. A., Thompson, W. G., Talley, N. J., Funch-Jensen, P., Janssens, J., & Whitehead, W. E. (1990). Identification of subgroups of functional bowel disorders. *Gastroenterology, 3,* 159–172.

Drossman, D. A., Whitehead, W. E., & Camilleri, M. (1997). Irritable bowel syndrome: A technical review for practice guideline development. *Gastroenterology, 112,* 2120–2137.

Drossman, D. A., Zhiming, L., Andruzzi, E., Temple, M. D., Talley, K. W., & Thompson, D. A. (1993). U.S. householders' survey of functional gastrointestinal disorders: Prevalence, sociodemography, and health impact. *Digestive Diseases and Science, 38,* 1569.

Fields, H. (1991). Depression and pain: A neurobiological model. *Neuropsychiatry, Neuropsychology, and Behavioral Neurology, 4*(1), 83–92.

First, M. B., Spitzer, R. L., Gibbon, M., & Williams, J. (2001). *Structured Clinical Interview for DSM-IV-TR Axis I Disorders, research version, non-patient edition (SCID-I/NP).* New York: New York State Psychiatric Institute.

Galovski, T. E., & Blanchard, E. B. (1998). The treatment of irritable bowel syndrome with hypnotherapy. *Applied Psychophysiology and Biofeedback, 23,* 219–232.

Gershon, M. (1998). *The second brain.* New York: HarperCollins.

Gwee, K. A. (2001). Postinfectious irritable bowel syndrome. *Gut, 4,* 287–291.

Hahn, B. A., Yan, S., & Strassels, S. (1999). Impact of irritable bowel syndrome on quality of life and resource use in the United States and United Kingdom. *Digestion, 60,* 77–81.

Harvey, R. F., Hinton, R. A., Gunary, R. M., & Barry, R. E. (1989). Individual and group hypnotherapy in treatment of refractory irritable bowel syndrome. *Lancet, 1,* 424–425.

Hislop, I. G. (1971). Psychological significance of the irritable colon syndrome. *Gut, 12,* 452–457.

Hyams, J. S., Burke, G., Davis, P. M., Rzepski, B., & Andrulonis, P. A. (1996). Abdominal pain and irritable bowel syndrome in adolescents: A community-based study. *Journal of Pediatrics, 129,* 220–226.

Isgar, B., Harman, M., Kaye, M. D., & Whorwell, P. J. (1983). Symptoms of irritable bowel syndrome in ulcerative colitis in remission. *Gut, 24,* 190–192.

Jackson, J., O'Malley, P. G., Tomkins, G., Balden, E., Santoro, J., & Kroenke, K. (2000). Treatment of functional gastrointestinal disorders with antidepressant medications: A meta-analysis. *American Journal of Medicine, 108,* 65–72.

Jailwala, J., Imperiale, T., & Kroenke, K. (2000). Pharmacologic treatment of the irritable bowel syndrome: A systematic review of randomized, controlled trials. *Annals of Internal Medicine, 133,* 136–147.

Jain, A. P., Gupta, O. P., Jajoo, U. N., & Sidwa, H. K. (1991). Clinical profile of irritable bowel syndrome at a rural based teaching hospital in central India. *Journal of Associated Physicians India, 39,* 385–386.

Keefe, F. J., Caldwell, D. S., Queen, K., Gil, K. M., Martinez, S., Crisson, J. E., Ogden, W., & Nunley, J. (1987a). Osteoarthritic knee pain: A behavioral analysis. *Pain, 28,* 309–321.

Keefe, F. J., Caldwell, D. S., Queen, K. T., Gil, K. M., Martinez, S., Crisson, J. E., Ogden, W., & Nunley, J. (1987b). Pain coping strategies in osteoarthritis patients. *Journal of Consulting and Clinical Psychology, 55,* 208–212.

Kellow, J. E., & Phillips, S. F. (1987). Altered small bowel motility in irritable bowel syndrome is correlated with symptoms. *Gastroenterology, 92,* 1885–1893.

Klein, K. (1988). Controlled treatment trials in the irritable bowel syndrome: A critique. *Gastroenterology, 95,* 232–241.

Lackner, J. M., Morley, S. M., Dowzer, C., Mesmer, C., & Hamilton, S. (2003). *Systematic review and meta-analysis of randomized controlled trials of psychological treatments for irritable bowel syndrome.* Unpublished manuscript, State University of New York, Buffalo, Medical School.

Latimer, P. R. (1983). *Functional gastrointestinal disorders: A behavioral medicine approach.* New York: Springer.

Lynn, R. B., & Friedman, L. S. (1993). Irritable bowel syndrome. *New England Journal of Medicine, 329,* 1940–1945.

Maxton, D. G., Morris, J. A., & Whorwell, P. J. (1989). Ranking of symptoms by patients with the irritable bowel syndrome. *British Medical Journal, 299,* 1138.

Maxwell, P. R., Mendall, M. A., & Kumar, D. (1997). Irritable bowel syndrome. *Lancet, 350,* 1691–1695.

Mayer, E. A., & Raybould, H. E. (1990). Role of visceral afferent mechanisms in functional bowel disorders. *Gastroenterology, 99,* 1688–1704.

McKendrick, M. W. (1996). Post salmonella irritable bowel syndrome: 5 year review. *Journal of Infection, 32,* 170–171.

McKendrick, M. W., & Read, N. W. (1994). Irritable bowel syndrome: Post salmonella infection. *Journal of Infection, 29,* 1–3.

Meissner, J. S., Blanchard, E., & Malamood, H. S. (1997). Comparison of treatment outcome measures for irritable bowel syndrome. *Applied Psychophysiology and Biofeedback, 22*(1), 55–62.

Melzack, R. (1975). The McGill Pain Questionnaire: Major properties and scoring methods. *Pain, 1,* 277–299.

Melzack, R., & Wall, P. D. (1965). Pain mechanisms: A new theory. *Science, 150,* 971–979.

Mertz, H., Morgan, V., Tanner, G., Pickens, D., Price, R., Shyr, Y., & Kessler, R. (2000). Regional cerebral activation in irritable bowel syndrome and control subjects with painful and non-painful rectal distention. *Gastroenterology, 118,* 842–848.

Mertz, H., Naliboff, B., Munakata, J., Niazi, N., & Mayer, E. A. (1995). Altered rectal perception is a biological marker of patients with irritable bowel syndrome. *Gastroenterology, 109,* 40–52.

Morris-Yates, A. D., Talley, N. J., Boyce, P., & Andrews, G. (1995). Evidence of a genetic contribution to self-reported symptoms of irritable syndrome [abstract]. *Gastroenterology, 108,* A652.

Naliboff, B. D., Derbyshire, S. W., Munakata, J., Berman, S., Mandelkern, M., Chang, L., et al. (2001). Cerebral activation in patients with irritable bowel syndrome and control subjects during rectosigmoid stimulation. *Psychosomatic Medicine, 63,* 365–375.

O'Keefe, E. A., Talley, N. J., Zinsmeister, A. R., & Jacobsen, S. J. (1995). Bowel disorders impair functional status and quality of life in the elderly: A population-based study. *Journal of Gerontology, 50*(4), M184–M189.

Olubuyide, I. O., Olawuyi, F., & Fasanmade, A. A. (1995). A study of irritable bowel syndrome diagnosed by Manning criteria in an African population. *Digestive Diseases and Science, 40,* 983–985.

Patrick, D. L., Drossman, D. A., Frederick, I. O., DiCesare, J., & Puder, K. L. (1998). Quality of life in persons with irritable bowel syndrome: Development of a new measure. *Digestive Diseases and Science, 43,* 400–411.

Poynard, T., Regimbeau, C., & Benhamou, Y. (2001). Metaanalysis of smooth muscle relaxants in the treatment of irritable bowel syndrome. *Alimentary Pharmacology and Therapeutics, 15,* 355–361.

Prior, A. M. D., & Whorwell, P. J. (1990a). Anorectal manometry in irritable bowel syndrome: Differences between diarrhea and constipation predominant subjects. *Gut, 31,* 458–462.

Prior, A. C. S., & Whorwell, P. J. (1990b). Changes in rectal sensitivity after hypnotherapy in patients with irritable bowel syndrome. *Gut, 31,* 896.

Rodriguez, L. A. G., & Ruigozmez, A. (1999). Increased risk of irritable bowel syndrome after bacterial gastroenteritis: A cohort study. *British Medical Journal, 318,* 656–666.

Rosenstiel, A. K., & Keefe, F. J. (1983). The use of coping strategies in chronic low back pain patients: Relationship to patient characteristics and current adjustment. *Pain, 17,* 33–44.

Sandler, R. S., Jordan, M. C., & Shelton, B. J. (1990). Demographic and dietary determinants of constipation in the U.S. population. *American Journal of Public Health, 80,* 185–189.

Silverman, D. H., Munakate, J. A., Ennes, H., Mandelkern, M. A., Hoh, C. K., Phelps, M. E., & Mayer, E. A. (1997). Regional cerebral activity in normal and pathological perception of visceral pain. *Gastroenterology, 112,* 64–72.

Spielberger, C. D. (1983). *Manual for the State-Trait Anxiety Inventory (STAI).* Palo Alto, CA: Consulting Psychologists Press.

Stewart, A. L., & Ware, J. E. (1992). *Measuring functioning and well-being: The medical outcomes study approach.* Durham, NC: Duke University Press.

Tache, Y. (1989). Central control of gastrointestinal transit and motility by brain-gut peptides. In W. J. Snape, Jr. (Ed.), *Pathogenesis of functional bowel disease* (pp. 55–78). New York: Plenum.

Talley, N., Drossman, D. A., Whitehead, W. E., Thompson, W. G., & Corassiari, E. (2000). Rome II Integrative Questionnaire. In D. A. Drossman, E. Corazziari, N. J. Talley, W. G. Thompson, & W. E. Whitehead (Eds.), *Rome II: The functional gastrointestinal disorders: Diagnosis, pathophysiology, and treatment—A multinational consensus* (2nd ed., pp. 690–714). McLean, VA: Degnon Associates.

Talley, N. J., Fett, S. L., & Zinsmeister, A. R. (1995). Self-reported abuse and gastrointestinal disease in outpatients: Association with irritable bowel-type symptoms. *American Journal of Gastroenterology, 90,* 366–371.

Talley, N. J., Gabriel, S. E., Harmsen, W. S., Zinsmeister, A. R., & Evans, R. W. (1995). Medical costs in community subjects with irritable bowel syndrome. *Gastroenterology, 109,* 1736–1741.

Thompson, W. G., Dotevall, G., Drossman, D. A., Heaton, K. W., & Kruis, W. (1989). Irritable bowel syndrome: Guidelines for the diagnosis. *Gastroenterology International, 2,* 92–95.

Toner, B. B., Segal, Z. V., Emmott, S., Myran, D., Ali, A., DiGasbarro, I., & Stuckless, N. (1998). Cognitive behavioral group therapy for patients with irritable bowel syndrome. *International Journal of Group Psychotherapy, 48,* 215–243.

Ware, J. E., & Sherbourne, C. D. (1992). The MOS 36-Item Short Form Health Survey (SF-36). *Medical Care, 30,* 473–483.

Welgan, P., Meshkinpour, H., & Hoehler, F. (1985). The effect of stress on colon motor and electrical activity in irritable bowel syndrome. *Psychosomatic Medicine, 47,* 139–149.

Whitehead, W. E., Bosmajian, L., Zonderman, A.B., Costa, P.T., & Schuster, M. M. (1988). Symptoms of psychologic distress associated with irritable bowel syndrome: Comparison of community and medical clinical samples. *Gastroenterology, 95,* 709–714.

Whitehead, W. E., Burnett, C. K., Cook, E. W., & Taub, E. (1996). Impact of irritable bowel syndrome on quality of life. *Digestive Diseases and Science, 41,* 2248–2253.

Whitehead, W. E., Engel, B. T., & Schuster, M. M. (1990). Perception of rectal distention is necessary to prevent fecal incontinence. *Advanced Physiological Science, 17,* 203–209.

Whitehead, W. E., Palsson, O., & Jones, K. R. (2002). Systematic review of the comorbidity of irritable bowel syndrome with other disorders: What are the causes and implications? *Gastroenterology, 122,* 1140–1156.

Whitehead, W. E., Winget, C., Fedoravicius, A. S., Wooley, S., & Blackwell, B. (1982). Learned illness behavior in patients with irritable bowel syndrome and peptic ulcer. *Digestive Diseases and Science, 27,* 202–209.

Whorwell, P. J., Prior, A., & Colgan, S. M. (1987). Hypnotherapy in severe irritable bowel syndrome: Further experience. *Gut, 28,* 423–425.

Whorwell, P. J., Prior, A., & Faragher, E. B. (1984). Controlled trial of hypnotherapy in the treatment of severe refractory irritable bowel syndrome. *Lancet,* 1232–1234.

CHAPTER 21

Insomnia and the Sleep Disorders

VALERIE A. WOLFE AND SHERI D. PRUITT

Insomnia and the sleep disorders present a variety of problems. Some are primarily behavioral, whereas others have a dominant biological component. Regardless of etiology, sleep problems are remarkably common. Approximately 65 million Americans suffer each year from transient sleep difficulties, and about 30 million more Americans have chronic insomnia (Hauri & Linde, 1996). Moreover, approximately 35% of adults report some type of sleep disturbance each year, with half of these individuals describing their sleep problems as "serious" (Gallup Organization, 1995; Mellinger, Balter, & Uhlenhuth, 1985).

The cost of sleep disorders is exorbitant. In 1990, the National Commission on Sleep Disorders Research, a commission created by Congress to investigate sleep disorders and their effects on the population, reported the annual cost of sleep problems to be in the tens of billions of dollars (Dement & Vaughan, 1999). In addition, estimates indicate that 24,000 people die each year from accidents related to falling asleep while driving (Dement & Vaughan, 1999). The report generated by the commission advocated extensive training for primary care doctors, a national awareness campaign on insomnia, and increased awareness of the behavioral and medical treatments available for the treatment of sleep disorders.

Despite recommendations from the National Commission on Sleep Disorders Research, physicians rarely receive training in the assessment and treatment of sleep problems. Medical students obtain between 0 and 2 hours of training specific to sleep disorders (Dement & Vaughan, 1999), and this lack of training is reflected in clinical practice. For example, many physicians do not ask about insomnia during office visits (Dement & Vaughan, 1999). Moreover, when insomnia is recognized, physicians defer to medication treatment rather than very efficacious behavioral treatments. In fact, practice guidelines from the American Medical Association, the Canadian Medical Association, and many health maintenance organizations indicate that behavioral interventions should be the treatment of choice for insomnia.

BACKGROUND AND ETIOLOGY

The Basics of Sleep, Sleep Architecture, and Sleep Cycles

Sleep is an exceedingly important activity. Although scientists are not certain how sleep helps daytime functioning, it is fairly easy to assess the difficulties associated with sleep deprivation. Without enough sleep, individuals find themselves edgy and irritable. In addition, their concentration and ability to learn new information begin to decline. One of the first symptoms of sleep deprivation is depression. After a few days of no sleep, some people will perform as if they are intoxicated. When people have been denied sleep for about a week, they can experience visual and auditory hallucinations. Sleep deprivation impairs function in nearly everyone. However, the amount of sleep deprivation a single person can tolerate without ill effects varies.

Fatigue also contributes to a host of psychiatric and medical diagnoses. Both anxiety and depression have a strong sleep component. Among patients with depression, 85% report insomnia and 10% to 15% complain of hypersomnia (Ford & Kamerow, 1989). Patients with bipolar disorder frequently function energetically for days or weeks on a few hours of sleep and then have periods of hypersomnia associated with major depressive episodes. Changes in sleep can predict a major depressive episode (Perlis, Giles, Buyesse, Tu, & Kupfer, 1997), and denying sleep to someone who has bipolar disorder can trigger a manic episode (Ford & Kamerow, 1989). Patients with posttraumatic stress disorder also report sleep disturbance, including nightmares and insomnia (American Psychiatric Association, 1994).

Insomnia is also associated with chronic obstructive pulmonary disease, osteoarthritis, asthma, fibromyalgia, headaches, and chronic pain. Between 50% and 70% of patients with a pain diagnosis suffer from a sleep disturbance (Moffitt, Kalucy, Kalucy, Baum, & Cooke, 1991; Pilowsky, Crettenden, & Townley, 1985). Patients with fibromyalgia, rheumatoid arthritis, back pain, and/or headaches have been found to have alpha wave intrusions into their delta sleep, indicating that their deep sleep is interrupted by

wakefulness (Gupta, Gupta, & Haberman, 1986; Moldofsky, 1989).

Sleep deprivation can also cause pain. When individuals have their deep delta sleep interrupted, they complain of musculoskeletal tenderness, which resolves after 2 nights of noninterrupted sleep (Hauri & Hawkins, 1973). Sleep is also essential for normal functioning of the body's immune system and for healthy cell growth. This explains why sleep-deprived individuals are more likely to get sick and tend to heal less rapidly as compared with well-rested individuals (Hauri & Linde, 1996).

The amount of sleep that humans need to function maximally varies both by individual and by age. Whereas newborns need about 16 hours of sleep per day, 2-year-olds need about 13 hours. Teenagers require about 9 hours of sleep per night, and adults need 7 to 8 hours on average. Interestingly, the amount of sleep an individual may require varies from about 5 hours to 11 hours. Therefore, 7 or 8 hours per night reflects an average. Adults over age 65 years need as much sleep as do younger adults, but their sleep tends to be less deep and they tend to wake more during the night. Researchers are not sure why this is the case, but they believe that it may be a natural outcome of aging or that it may be related to decreased activity, medications, and/or having a variable schedule. Approximately half of adults over age 65 years have a chronic sleep disorder.

Sleep Cycles

There are five stages of sleep that occur in cycles during the night. These are referred to as Stages 1 to 4 and REM (rapid eye movement) sleep. Each stage is defined by depth of sleep, brain wave activity, eye movements, and muscle tone. Stage 1 sleep is a light sleep and is characterized by short fast brain waves (called theta waves) and slow eye movements. This type of sleep occurs at the beginning of the night or during the day with boredom or fatigue. People are easily aroused from a Stage 1 sleep and on wakening can perform cognitive and physical tasks without grogginess. Variable brain wave lengths (called sleep spindles and K complexes) characterize Stage 2 sleep. Eye movements stop and brain activity slows down. Stage 3 sleep is a deeper stage of sleep and is characterized by slower delta waves interspersed with small quick waves. Stage 4 sleep is a very deep sleep and is identified by delta wave activity that is not interspersed with shorter waves. Although it is easy to arouse someone from Stage 1 or 2 sleep, it is much more difficult to wake from Stage 3 or 4 sleep. It is during this deep delta sleep (Stage 4) that bed-wetting and sleepwalking occur.

REM sleep is distinct from the other stages of sleep. Humans are very active physiologically during REM. For example, during REM, the muscles of the body stiffen, eyes move rapidly, and heart rate, blood pressure, oxygen use, and respiration become more rapid and variable. In addition, during REM, reflexes, kidney function, and hormonal patterns change. The body's temperature regulation is affected such that people will not sweat or shiver. During REM sleep, both genders experience engorgement of the genital region—causing erections in males and clitoral engorgement in females. It is during REM sleep that humans dream.

A typical sleep cycle lasts about 90 minutes, and healthy sleepers complete four to six cycles per night on average. After a few minutes in Stage 1 sleep, Stages 2, 3, and 4 occur. Stage 2 sleep repeats, followed by REM sleep, before the next 90-minute cycle begins. During the early part of the night, a greater amount of time is spent in deep Stages 3 and 4 sleep. Closer to morning, REM sleep is lengthier. During the night, normal adults spend about 5% of the night in Stage 1 sleep, 50% in Stage 2 sleep, 5% in Stage 3 sleep, 10% to 15% in Stage 4 sleep, and 20% to 25% in REM sleep. Most people can function well if they are able to complete four to six sleep cycles during a night (thereby sleeping about 6 to 9 hours).

Insomnia

Insomnia is the most common sleep problem. It is characterized by an inability to fall asleep quickly (generally within 30 minutes), waking during the night with difficulty in returning to sleep, waking too early in the morning, and/or having nonrestorative sleep. In addition, sleep disruption must occur at least 3 nights per week.

Insomnia is typically categorized in terms of chronicity. Transient insomnia typically lasts a few nights to a few weeks. Most people will experience transient insomnia sometime during a year. Transient insomnia can be triggered by a variety of factors, including stress, life changes, illness, a poor sleep environment, shift work, medication changes, jet lag, and poor sleep habits. Transient insomnia can become chronic due to classical conditioning. For example, one patient described insomnia that started after a divorce. He described waking during the night because of stress and sadness; after smoking a cigarette, he was able to fall back asleep. This patient reported that the divorce was finalized 3 years ago. He felt like he had moved on emotionally, but he still awakened during the night and could not fall asleep until he smoked a cigarette. Unfortunately, the attempts made to try to improve sleep often worsen the problem. Chronic insomnia can last from a month to many decades, causing both functional (e.g., decreased concentration, depression) and medical (e.g., headaches, hypertension) complications.

Restless Leg Syndrome and Periodic Limb Movement Disorder

Restless leg syndrome (RLS) is defined as an urge to move or shake the lower extremities because of an uncomfortable sensation. Most often, this affects the legs, but it also is experienced in the arms or in muscles in other parts of the body. The feeling typically is more exaggerated in the evening and often can prevent a person from relaxing enough to fall asleep. Moving the legs relieves the discomfort or aching. Diabetes, anemia, chronic renal failure, and certain medications can cause RLS, but often the root cause is not apparent. RLS may worsen with age.

Periodic leg movement disorder (PLMD) is an insomnia disorder that is accompanied by repetitive episodes of muscle contractions (0.5 to 5.0 seconds in duration) separated by intervals of 20 to 30 seconds. Awakenings may be associated with these movements. Most patients with RLS have PLMD.

The prevalence of RLS and PLMD in the general population is between 9% and 15% (Hening et al., 1999). The number of cases increases as people age and the symptoms can become more intrusive with time. Approximately 43% of people with RLS describe the onset of the disorder before age 20 years (Hening et al., 1999). Prevalence rates for PLMD in people age 60 years or over range from 20% to 58% (Dickel & Mosko, 1990).

Sleep Apnea

The definition of a sleep apnea episode is the cessation of airflow through the nose or mouth that lasts 10 seconds or longer. Sleep apnea can be caused by a variety of conditions and can be exacerbated by alcohol use or allergies. There are three types of sleep apnea: central, obstructive, and mixed. Central sleep apnea is the cessation of breathing due to lack of respiratory effort. Obstructive sleep apnea is characterized by sufficient respiratory effort from the lungs but blockage (obstruction) of the airway. The mixed category refers to apnea in which the obstructive phase follows a central phase, thereby combining both central and obstructive sleep apnea. People of any age can have sleep apnea, although it is more common in older adults and in those who are obese.

Patients should be evaluated for sleep apnea if they are experiencing excessive daytime sleepiness. This manifests in falling asleep at inopportune times, for example, while driving or during meetings. Sleep apnea sufferers also tend to snore loudly. The consequences of sleep apnea can be severe because patients not only will lack sufficient oxygen in the blood but also will have excess carbon dioxide. They frequently have comorbidities, including cardiac arrhythmia, headache, malaise, fatigue, weight gain, and night sweats. In addition, sleep apnea sufferers are frequently awakened through the night as they try to clear their airways; they rarely complete 90-minute sleep cycles. To clear their airway, sufferers may gasp or describe a feeling of drowning. They tend to be the most fatigued patients referred to sleep clinics for evaluation.

Narcolepsy

Narcolepsy is a disorder distinguished by the rapid onset of a sleep cycle, typically triggered by periods of excitement. People often have their first episode of narcolepsy between ages 10 and 30 years (Hauri & Linde, 1996). Reports indicate that there are 100,000 to 600,000 narcoleptics in the United States (Hauri & Linde, 1996).

Narcolepsy is characterized by cataplexy (i.e., lack of muscle tone), hypnagogic hallucinations (i.e., dreamlike hallucinations), and sleep paralysis. During a narcoleptic episode, the patient immediately will go into REM sleep. Patients with narcolepsy often report vivid dreams or hallucinations. Obviously, this disorder is an extremely dangerous condition given that people can fall asleep without warning while driving or operating heavy machinery.

The cause of narcolepsy appears to be genetic, and treatment is usually medication. Both stimulants and antidepressants have been prescribed, and some patients find relief by taking naps during the day. More recently, modafinil has improved wakefulness in patients with this problem. Although untreated narcoleptic patients fall asleep rapidly and without warning during the day, they often report difficulty in falling asleep at night.

Dreams, Nightmares, Sleep Terrors, and Sleepwalking

People dream during REM sleep; therefore, dreams typically occur at the end of the night when REM sleep is longer. People dream for about 2 hours every night and recall dreams if awakened quickly from REM sleep. Dreams can also be remembered through specific training strategies designed to enhance recall.

Throughout history, people have looked to their dreams for meaning and prophecy. There are varying theories as to the importance of dreams; some psychologists (e.g., Carl Jung) have spent much of their careers investigating the role of dreams as a window to the unconscious. Other professionals believe that dreams are simply people's interpretations of the physiological arousal that occurs with REM sleep (Walsleben & Baron-Faust, 2000). Regardless, many laypeople believe that dreams are meaningful and are disturbed when they have anxiety-producing dreams or nightmares.

Sleep terrors typically occur in children. Unlike nightmares, sleep terrors occur earlier in the evening during the deep delta sleep (Stages 3 and 4). Nightmares tend to occur toward the end of the night when REM sleep is longer. Because children have more delta sleep than do adults, children are more prone to night terrors.

ASSESSMENT AND TREATMENT

Evaluation/Assessment Phases

Because the etiologies of sleep disorders are multifaceted, a thorough evaluation is imperative to ensure appropriate treatment planning. An initial interview should include questions regarding sleep onset, number of awakenings, total hours of sleep achieved, sleep habits, snoring, and level of fatigue during the day. Diet, caffeine, alcohol, tobacco, medications, herbs, medical conditions, and exercise should also be evaluated. It is important to note that patients will frequently underestimate the amount of sleep they achieve. Therefore, it can be useful to interview a spouse to corroborate the information given. Another method of evaluating sleep patterns is to have the patient complete a sleep journal. Unfortunately, patients often have difficulty in complying with this recommendation, or they report inaccurate information.

When self-report techniques are insufficient for diagnosis and treatment planning for a sleep disorder, a patient may benefit from a polysomnogram test. A polysomnogram involves using electroencephalography (EEG) to monitor brain and muscle activity, heart rate, and respiration. By interpreting brain waves and muscle activity, a specialist can identify the type of sleep disorder.

If a patient complains of loud snoring and reports periods of no breathing followed by gasps for air, an evaluation for possible sleep apnea should be arranged. A test for blood oxygen levels, called oximetry, is often used to evaluate for sleep apnea.

Treatment of Insomnia

Treatment of insomnia integrates sleep hygiene (i.e., good sleep habits), stimulus control, relaxation training, and sleep restriction components. These behavioral strategies are effective for 70% to 80% of patients with primary insomnia (Morin et al., 1999). In a review of the literature on the use of nonpharmacological treatments for insomnia, Morin and colleagues (1999) found that patients treated with behavioral interventions were "better off" (i.e., they fell asleep faster after treatment) than approximately 80% of untreated controls. In addition, patients taught cognitive-behavioral skills slept longer, awakened less frequently and for shorter time periods, and reported higher sleep quality after treatment than did 50% to 70% of untreated controls (Morin et al., 1999).

Improvements in sleep were maintained on follow-up. After 3 and 6 months, patients given cognitive-behavioral intervention maintained gains realized in sleep onset and number of awakenings (Morin et al., 1999). In fact, some studies show that patients actually sleep longer at night 6 months following treatment than during the initial posttreatment assessment (Morin et al., 1999). This may be because patients need a few months to fully integrate behavioral strategies into their lives. Additional long-term benefits of cognitive-behavioral training for insomnia include a reduction in medication use and increased independence from medical intervention (Morin et al., 1999).

Reflecting the breadth of literature supporting the use of behavioral treatments for insomnia and the side effect profiles of most hypnotics, current best practice guidelines from the American Medical Association and the Canadian Medical Association indicate that behavioral treatment should be the frontline treatment for insomnia. However, because of inadequate provider training and an over-reliance on the "quick fix" (i.e., medication), physicians rarely use structured behavioral treatments to treat insomnia. Instead, most people who suffer from insomnia use over-the-counter medications or prescription sleep aids.

Core Components of Cognitive-Behavioral Treatment for Insomnia

Stimulus Control Therapy. Stimulus control therapy teaches patients to use environmental cues to augment, rather than inhibit, sleep. The premise of the therapy is that individuals will be reconditioned to sleep efficiently when sleep-incompatible activities are reduced and sleep-associated activities are increased. Patients receive the following basic rules pertaining to the bedroom environment.

First, they are to use their beds for sex and sleep only; they are not to read, watch television, or do business or other work in bed; and they are not to stay in bed if awake for longer than 20 minutes at a time. Second, they are to go to bed only when sleepy. Third, they are to maintain a regular wake-up time. Fourth, they are to avoid napping during the day.

Sleep Restriction. The goal of sleep restriction is to train patients to sleep more efficiently by limiting the amount of time spent in bed. This strategy capitalizes on fatigue so as to train their bodies to fall asleep quickly and to sleep through the night. Patients are first instructed to compute their sleep efficiency by dividing their time spent sleeping by their time spent in bed. They estimate the average amount of time they spend sleeping at night. Next, they choose a wake-up time that they will adhere to every day of the week. Additional recommendations are to avoid napping and to get out of bed if still awake after 20 minutes (e.g., from stimulus control training). After the assessment and setup phase, patients select one of the following techniques.

Significantly delay going to bed. This strategy is the most difficult because it requires the patient to go to bed much later than usual while keeping his or her wake-up time constant. First, the patient determines a wake-up time that can be adhered to strictly. The initial bedtime is established using the average number of hours of sleep a patient achieves. For example, if a woman typically spends 9 hours in bed but only sleeps 6 hours because of waking, the recommendation is to spend only 6 hours in bed. If her wake-up time is 6:00 a.m., she would go to bed at midnight the first night. She would follow the stimulus control strategy and get up if she is not asleep within 20 minutes. She would also get out of bed if she wakes for longer than 20 minutes during the night. The patient then would continue to go to bed at midnight until she achieves

90% sleep efficiency. When this marker is reached, she would go to bed 15 minutes earlier, stopping at the hour at which she can maintain a sleep efficiency of 85% or better and wake feeling rested and refreshed. The first night of this program is the most difficult because patients who are already fatigued have a difficult time staying up later than usual. Napping during the day or falling asleep briefly before bedtime will usually sabotage this strategy.

Delay bedtime by 15 minutes. This strategy advises the patient to go to bed 15 minutes later than usual every night until he or she is able to fall asleep quickly and sleep through the night. Therefore, the previously mentioned patient would still have a consistent wake-up time of 6:00 a.m. and would still follow the 20-minute rule, but instead of going to bed at 9:00 p.m., she would go to bed at 9:15 p.m. If she cannot achieve 85% sleep efficiency after a few nights, she would go to bed at 9:30 p.m. Eventually, this patient may find that if she goes to bed at 10:45 p.m., she is able to fall asleep quickly and sleep through the night.

Use an intermediate delay in going to bed. The third strategy is an intermediate one between the first two strategies. The patient first sets a consistent wake-up time, avoids napping, and follows the 20-minute rule. The patient is then instructed to go to bed as late as possible. This intermediate strategy works well for many patients because they cannot stay up late enough to use the first strategy. Also, this third strategy tends to work more quickly than the second strategy. The previously mentioned patient would continue to stay up late until she achieves above 85% sleep efficiency. Then, she would go to bed 15 minutes earlier until she found the time when she could maintain good sleep efficiency and feel rested during the day.

These sleep restriction techniques capitalize on patients' fatigue to help them learn, adopt, and maintain good sleep habits. Many insomniacs actually cause their own insomnia by going to bed too early and by failing to maintain a consistent sleep schedule. Typically, patients will have one or two bad nights of sleep because of a transient event and will adjust their bedtime to be earlier because they feel fatigued. This is problematic because the body is not accustomed to spending additional time in bed, and in an attempt to accommodate the change in bedtime, sleep cycles are altered and sleep becomes less efficient.

When informed of this pattern, patients often identify that their sleep difficulties began when they initiated a change in their bedtime by going to bed earlier due to a partner's schedule, an illness, or a stressful period. With appropriate information, patients learn after a few nights of poor sleep to go to bed a little later. They understand that attempts to address a few nights of poor sleep by going to bed earlier is not effective, even though going to bed earlier makes intuitive sense if a person is fatigued.

Sleep Hygiene (i.e., good sleep habits). Sleep hygiene refers to health practices (e.g., diet, exercise, substance use) and environmental factors (e.g., noise, light, a comfortable bed, ambient temperature) that may be inhibiting sleep. In terms of health practices, patients are instructed to reduce caffeine use to less than five cups of coffee or tea a day and to avoid using any caffeine after 2:00 p.m. Caffeine has a half-life of 4 hours; therefore, half of the caffeine consumed at 4:00 p.m. will still be in the body at 8:00 p.m., and a quarter of the initial cup of coffee or tea consumed at 4:00 p.m. will be in the body at midnight.

Patients should also limit nicotine intake and never smoke if they wake during the night. This suggestion will help to eliminate waking to smoke. Frequently, smokers classically condition themselves to wake at the end of each 90-minute sleep cycle for a cigarette. Finally, patients are told to refrain from using alcohol as a sleep-inducing aid. Although alcohol can make people feel sleepy, it inhibits good sleep cycles and can cause nighttime waking.

In terms of sleep hygiene, patients are also educated about the benefits of daily exercise for sleep but are cautioned to avoid vigorous exercise too close to bedtime. Exercising intensely before going to bed can cause problems with falling asleep because people may find themselves too energized (due to the release of the endorphins) or too hot to sleep. The body naturally cools as it prepares to sleep. Therefore, if people are too hot due to exercise or hot summer temperatures, they often have a hard time sleeping.

In addition, individuals need to make sure that their rooms are dark and quiet and that their beds are comfortable. Because light helps to reset the biological clock, it is essential to avoid bright lights in the evening and to expose the body to bright light in the morning. Shift workers can have a difficult time falling asleep after the "graveyard shift," particularly if they drive home in the morning light without sunglasses.

Patients sometimes state that their partners snore or that there is intermittent noise coming from the street that keeps them awake at night. Unfortunately, intermittent noise is the worst type of noise for sleep. The body can acclimate to consistent noise (e.g., the sound of crickets or of a nearby freeway) or to total quiet, but intermittent noise can cause waking. Suggestions for managing this include using white noise (e.g., turning on a fan or a fish tank) and using earplugs. It is not uncommon for couples to sleep apart if one snores loudly or has PLMD.

Most often, sleep hygiene rules are integrated into a treatment program. A few studies have evaluated the effectiveness of using sleep hygiene education alone and have found a modest effect (Morin et al., 1999). One study found that approximately 27% of patients improved when given sleep hygiene education (Schoicket, Bertelson, & Lacks, 1988), but other studies have found a more

modest response to this intervention (Morin et al., 1999). In general, sleep hygiene is considered a necessary part of an intervention but insufficient as a stand-alone treatment.

Relaxation-Based Interventions. Relaxation techniques have also proved to be useful in insomnia treatment. Studies have shown that progressive muscle relaxation, biofeedback, imagery training, and thought stopping all can reduce autonomic arousal and facilitate sleep (Morin et al., 1999). Biofeedback and progressive muscle relaxation help individuals to relax the muscles of the body and activate the parasympathetic nervous system or relaxation response. Imagery training and thought stopping help to retrain the mind to focus on calming thoughts, thereby reducing the sympathetic nervous system response and hopefully activating the parasympathetic nervous system. Although other relaxation-based interventions have been advocated for insomnia (e.g., diaphragmatic breathing, meditation, hypnosis), these have not been adequately evaluated (Morin et al., 1999).

Relaxation-based interventions are important in facilitating sleep. Many insomniacs become so anxious about falling asleep that they activate the sympathetic nervous system, thereby releasing endorphins, tensing the muscles, and increasing heartbeat and respiration rate. As one might expect, this response is incompatible with falling asleep. Through classical conditioning (i.e., anxiety regarding falling asleep that is then paired with one's bed), a transient sleep problem can become chronic. Insomniacs who have developed a strong association between anxiety and their beds often say that they can fall asleep easily in a hotel room or in the guest room but can never fall asleep quickly in their own beds. The primary goal of the relaxation therapies is to reassociate the bed with a restful state and help reduce the anxiety or autonomic arousal associated with sleep.

Paradoxical Intention. Paradoxical intention is a cognitive technique in which the patient is requested to stay awake. If the patient is instructed to stay awake, falling asleep is no longer the anxiety-producing goal. Thus, by prescribing the patient's worst fear—staying awake—the patient paradoxically responds by falling asleep more quickly. In essence, this intervention helps to reduce the performance anxiety associated with sleeping.

Developing a Cognitive-Behavioral Sleep Improvement Program

Most of the treatment programs in use today include multiple sessions and integrate stimulus control, sleep hygiene, relaxation training, and sleep restriction components. These programs are often six to eight sessions in length and may require additional sessions for screening and paperwork. Evaluations of these programs are often dependent on patient self-report through sleep diaries, although a few studies use polysomnogram tests to measure outcome.

At Kaiser Permanente in Sacramento, California, a single-session treatment program was developed and evaluated using individual ($n = 20$) and group ($n = 72$) formats (Wolfe & Helge, 2002). Primary care physicians referred patients to a health psychologist, who administered an insomnia treatment protocol. Individual sessions were 25 minutes, and the group sessions were 90 minutes. Before treatment, each patient completed a brief questionnaire that included queries about sleep onset, awakenings, daytime fatigue, and sleep habits. In addition, there were questions regarding substance use, diet, and exercise. Approximately 75% of referred patients attended the program (Wolfe & Helge, 2002).

The first section of the intervention was informational, including information about sleep cycles, sleep architecture, individual variations in sleep, and sleep changes over the life cycle. The second section of the intervention included information regarding stimulus control, sleep restriction, and thought stopping. The final section included a review of sleep hygiene, exercise, sleeping pills, herbs, and melatonin. The information regarding sleep cycles and sleep architecture was designed to provide the supporting rationale for implementation of sleep restriction, stimulus control, and sleep hygiene. Patients created a personalized sleep plan during the group and individual appointments (Wolfe & Helge, 2002).

One month after treatment, patients' progress was assessed by telephone follow-up. Results indicated that 90% of the patients who had individual appointments and 74% of the patients who attended group appointments improved the amount of time spent sleeping at night (Wolfe & Helge, 2002). Individuals gained an average of 1.78 hours of sleep per night, and group members gained an average of 1.90 hours of sleep per night (Wolfe & Helge, 2002). A second cohort of patients ($n = 35$) who participated in the same treatment protocol, but with a different health psychologist, had results slightly better than participants in the initial cohort (Wolfe, Helge, & Jacobs, 2002). One month after treatment, 87% of these patients reported improved sleep by an average of 2.38 hours per night (Wolfe et al., 2002). All participants were to be reassessed 1 year following treatment to determine whether treatment gains were maintained.

Anecdotal comments from participants were interesting. A common theme was skepticism about the techniques. For example, a typical remark was "I thought what you suggested was silly, but I decided to try it anyway." Another typical patient comment was "I did not think it would work, but I was amazed at the results." Finally, some patients noted benefits from the information about insomnia: "I thought I had depression, but now I realize I was just sleep deprived."

This intervention was developed with the purpose of efficiently and effectively treating primary care patients with insomnia. The groups were not limited to specific populations; any patients complaining of sleep problems were considered appropriate. However, if a physician believed that a patient would not do well in a group setting, or if a patient could not attend because of scheduling conflicts, the patient was seen individually. The findings of this uncontrolled clinical trial indicate that a single-session brief intervention that integrates evidence-based interventions can be extremely effective for primary care patients experiencing insomnia. However, because this study is limited from a methodological perspective, further research regarding the utility of brief, behaviorally based interventions in primary care is essential.

Medications Used to Treat Insomnia

In today's "quick fix" society, patients and providers alike have a penchant for medications as the frontline treatment for insomnia. Even before office visits, patients have often tried over-the-counter medications such as diphenhydramine and Tylenol PM (a combination of diphenhydramine and Tylenol) for sleep. If these medications were as effective as advertised, it is unlikely that patients would continue to seek assistance from their primary care providers.

Benzodiazepines are commonly prescribed for sleep. These agents replaced barbiturates and barbiturate-like substances that were associated with addiction, respiratory problems, and occasional deaths. A benefit of benzodiazepines and other hypnotics used for insomnia is that they work quickly. However, hypnotics can cause daytime sedation, tolerance, and rebound insomnia.

Current guidelines from the National Institutes of Health (1984, 1991) suggest that short-term use of hypnotic medications may be indicated for acute insomnia, but these medications should be used with caution. If prescribed for sleep, hypnotics should not be taken for more than 2 weeks. At the time of prescribing, a tapering strategy should be in place to minimize risk for potential problems. One strategy to avoid tolerance is to have the patient use the medication only 3 or 4 nights a week and to use the lowest effective dose. A patient who has an abuse history or who has to perform tasks that require alertness and quick reaction times (e.g., driving) on awakening should be cautioned when prescribed sleep aids. Finally, hypnotics prescribed to elder adults require extra care.

Trazadone is an antidepressant frequently prescribed for people who have insomnia and a depressive disorder. However, the Food and Drug Administration has not approved the use of trazadone for people with insomnia. Trazadone should be used with caution because it can cause daytime sedation, priapism, and hypotension.

Melatonin is a hormone often used for insomnia. It is released by the pineal gland into the bloodstream and is produced from tryptophan. Tryptophan is converted to 5-hydroxytryptophan, then to serotonin, then to N-acetylserotonin, and finally to melatonin. Melatonin regulates the body's sleep cycle, circadian rhythm, and endocrine production and is essential for sexual maturation, growth control, pain control, balance, and regulation of sexual activity (Natural Medicines Comprehensive Database, 2002). People produce more melatonin when it is dark, thereby stimulating the onset of sleep. It may be an effective agent to help some adults with sleep onset. Moreover, melatonin may be useful for symptoms of jet lag, for shift workers, and for insomniacs with blindness. However, data demonstrating the efficacy of melatonin are inconclusive.

Although most consider melatonin relatively safe, it is not for use in children because it may affect their maturation. There also is concern that taking melatonin may increase daytime somnolence. In addition, melatonin may interfere with the effectiveness of cardiac medication and medications used to reduce immune system response (e.g., steroids, other cortisone drugs). There is some indication that melatonin can help depression, particularly when the depression comes with insomnia, but other studies indicate that melatonin can make depressive symptoms worse (Natural Medicines Comprehensive Database, 2002). Interestingly, it has been documented that patients with depression and patients diagnosed with fibromyalgia can have low levels of melatonin (Natural Medicines Comprehensive Database, 2002).

Treatment of RLS and PLMD

Behavioral strategies for treating RLS and PLMD include moderate amounts of exercise in the evening, hot baths, and distraction. Walking before bedtime has been helpful for some patients. However, intense exercise appears to exacerbate the symptoms for many sufferers. Hot baths are effective for some patients, and distraction exercises (i.e., tasks that require intense concentration) have support for symptom reduction. In addition, some patients find relief from massage or vibrating stimulation before sleep, and there is some evidence that reducing caffeine and improving sleep habits are useful. Most of the published literature has focused on medication treatment for RLS and PLMD, but there is some evidence to support integrating behavioral strategies with pharmacological regimens.

Unfortunately, many of the medications used in treating RLS and PLMD have limited effectiveness and can cause tolerance and rebound symptoms. There are five classes of medications typically prescribed: dopaminergic medications, opioids, benzodiazepines, adrenergic medications, and anticonvulsant medications. A review of the costs and benefits of these agents is beyond the scope of this chapter, but Hening and colleagues (1999) provided an excellent review of the treatments for RLS and PLMD.

Folic acid and iron supplements have proved to be effective for patients with RLS and PLMD who are deficient in these minerals. Some

reports suggest that the selective serotonin reuptake inhibitor (SSRI) or tricyclic medications reduce symptoms of RLS, whereas other reports indicate that these medications can aggravate the disorder (Hening et al., 1999).

Treatment of Sleep Apnea

Treatment of sleep apnea is dependent on the etiology. For example, in children, a common cause of sleep apnea is enlarged tonsils. With tonsil removal, the apnea can be relieved. Other surgical techniques, lauded as permanent cures for obstructive sleep apnea, have not been as effective as originally expected. With patients who are obese, the best treatment is weight reduction because this serves to open adequate space for airflow. One of the most successful treatments for other patients with obstructive sleep apnea is the continuous positive airway pressure machine (CPAP).

The CPAP provides continuous positive airway pressure through the nostrils to force the airway clear, enabling the patient to breathe. This treatment is effective for many people, but a major complaint is discomfort in wearing the apparatus. In fact, many of the patients given a CPAP do not adhere to recommendations to use it. It is critical that the facemask fits properly and that the patient acclimates to the machine. This is often done by training the patient in relaxation techniques and having him or her use the machine while awake but during sedentary activities such as watching television. Having a machine force air through one's nose can be extremely uncomfortable, especially while trying to initiate sleep onset. Therefore, adequate training and problem solving are essential given that the consequences of living with untreated sleep apnea are unfortunate and avoidable.

Light Therapy

Light therapy has been investigated as a treatment for patients with a variety of problems, including seasonal affective disorder, shift work sleep, delayed sleep phase syndrome, and advanced sleep phase syndrome. Light therapy also has been evaluated as a potential solution for sleep complaints in the elderly (Chesson et al., 1999).

In general, light therapy is effective in treating delayed sleep phase syndrome and advanced sleep phase syndrome (Chesson et al., 1999). With delayed sleep phase syndrome, the individual has difficulty in initiating sleep at the appropriate time and awakens too late. With advanced sleep phase syndrome, the patient falls asleep too early at night and awakens too early in the morning. With both sleep phase disorders, the release of hormones and the level of body temperature indicate that the person's sleep phase is not oriented correctly. Having individuals expose themselves to bright light in the morning and wear darkened glasses at night appears to be effective in resetting the circadian rhythm and resuming a regular sleep schedule (Chesson et al., 1999). In addition, light therapy appears to be useful with seasonal affective disorder (Chesson et al., 1999). Light therapy is described as a safe intervention when used according to American Academy of Sleep Medicine guidelines. It may be useful for shift work problems, jet lag, and non-24-hour sleep/wake syndrome in some blind patients (Chesson et al., 1999).

Napping and Sleep Deprivation

Approximately a quarter of all Americans are sleep deprived (National Sleep Foundation, 2002). This translates into billions of dollars in lost productivity and accidents. In response to this pervasive sleep debt, many businesses have created special environments for napping, and there have been articles in the popular press describing the benefit of quick "power naps."

Sleep "debt" can be "repaid" with a brief nap during waking hours; however, there is an optimal strategy for napping. Ideally, a nap should last between 15 and 40 minutes or be 2 hours in length. A brief nap can be very restorative. The most favorable time to take a nap is early afternoon. This is when people's natural biological clock indicates that it may be time for a sleep cycle. Some patients successfully time their naps halfway between the time they awaken in the morning and the time they go to bed, finding a 15- or 20-minute nap to be adequate to renew their concentration and energy. However, insomniacs should be wary of napping. Napping late in the afternoon can negatively influence nighttime sleep. If an insomniac has rested during the day, he or she might not be fatigued enough to fall asleep quickly at night.

Treatment of Nightmares and Night Terrors

Nightmares tend to be more common when patients are under stress. There are two main treatments to help patients cope with undesirable dreams. The first involves reassurance that intense dreams are common and that dreaming about something is not an indication that one would act in a similar manner in real life. Often, patients present with sexual or violent dreams and express concern that these dreams are indicative of underlying desires. Through reassurance and normalization, their distress can be reduced. Recommendations to avoid the daily news, violent movies, and other negative images before bedtime also are helpful. In addition, patients can learn to dream about pleasant scenes by rehearsing these images before bed.

For recurrent nightmares (e.g., being chased or pummeled by a foe), patients are instructed to return to the dream and change the ending. This is particularly helpful with children who are taught to imagine themselves as their favorite superhero and then turning on the foe and winning the battle. For this strategy to be effective, the patient should create the image that makes the most sense to him or her to be

---

CASE STUDY

"John Doe," a 39-year-old male, presented to his primary care physician with symptoms of anxiety, irritability, decreased concentration, headaches, and insomnia. He stated that his problems began about 5 years ago when he relocated, married, and changed his job. He reported feeling happy with his current situation and satisfied with his marital relationship and his job, but he revealed that he felt "run down."

When queried about sleep habits, John denied having difficulty in falling asleep but stated that he awakened frequently during the night. He said that he went to bed at 9:30 p.m. because he was "too tired to stay up any later," but then he awakened at 3:30 a.m. and drifted in and out of sleep until it was time to get ready for work at 6:30. He was concerned that he may be depressed because he felt "worn out and sad" even though his life was good.

John noted that his sleep habits changed following his marriage. When single, he would go to bed at midnight and get up at 6:30 a.m. He reported that with this schedule, he felt rested and refreshed. However, when he married, he began to go to bed at 10:00 p.m. because this was his wife's bedtime. During the past year, he altered his bedtime to 9:30 p.m. in an effort to combat his ever-present fatigue. He was concerned that his lack of energy was beginning to affect his work and relationships.

A physical examination determined that John was in good health. Laboratory results were within normal limits. The patient was instructed to use sleep restriction to retrain his body to sleep well. Specifically, he was to go to bed later in the evening until he could fall asleep quickly and sleep through the night. He was reminded that he felt rested after 6.5 hours of sleep and that his previous sleep schedule of going to bed at midnight and waking at 6:30 a.m. was effective for him.

After 1 week, John reported feeling much better. He stated that going to bed later was very difficult at first because he was so tired, but after 3 nights his sleep had improved and he began to feel better. In addition, he started walking daily at lunch and found that his energy level and mood had improved. During a follow-up visit, his progress was reviewed and recidivism was discussed. John was quite pleased with his improvements because he felt more like himself again. In addition, he reported that his mood and concentration were better and that his headaches had decreased. One year later, he denied any ongoing problems with sleep. He noted that during periods of transient insomnia, he continued to use sleep restriction strategies that provide him with rapid improvement.

---

victorious. Nightmares can also be reduced through psychotherapy that addresses underlying anxiety.

Night terrors can be particularly alarming to parents. They often involve brief periods of screaming; children may open their eyes, begin perspiring, and appear to be experiencing a state of panic. After a few minutes, a calm state of sleep returns. Usually, an individual experiencing a night terror will not awaken and will not remember the incident in the morning. Night terrors are more frequent during periods of stress. They cause no harm to the individual, so an optimal coping strategy is reassurance for the parents. Parents are instructed to either gently comfort the child or ignore the disruption altogether.

Three additional strategies can be helpful in reducing night terrors. First, psychotherapy for stress reduction is useful. Second, advising the patient to sleep for a longer period, thereby reducing the amount of deep delta sleep, can help. Third, physicians may prescribe a benzodiazepine, such as diazepam, for a few days to reduce the delta sleep associated with night terrors. This last strategy may be helpful if a child is sleeping away from home and is concerned about arousing others. However, benzodiazepines should always be used with caution.

Sleepwalking is also associated with delta sleep and is more common with children than with adults. It is also more frequent when people are under stress or sleep deprived, and it can be a result of certain medications. Sleepwalking can be quite dangerous. Treatments include reducing stress, getting adequate sleep, ensuring a safe sleeping environment, and taking medication.

CONCLUSIONS

Each year, sleep disorders affect millions of people and cost billions of dollars in lost productivity, health care, and accidents. For the majority of sleep problems, including insomnia and nightmares, cognitive-behavioral intervention is the treatment of choice. For other sleep disorders, such as sleep apnea, RLS, and PLMD, behavioral interventions play a significant role. However, it is far from routine practice for patients with sleep problems to receive these interventions or learn about them during visits to primary care clinics.

Enhanced training during medical school has been recommended as one strategy to improve assessment and intervention for patients with sleep problems (Dement & Vaughan, 1999). Unfortunately, physician training continues to be limited in this regard, and this deficiency is reflected in clinical practice; medications continue as the first line of intervention for sleep problems that would be better treated with behavioral interventions. This observation is not too surprising. Physicians generally report difficulties in identifying behavioral problems in their patients and frustration with implementing behavioral change strategies (Alto, 1995).

A realistic practice solution is access to behavioral experts who can provide effective cognitive-behavioral interventions in primary care. This strategy is practical because many patients with a sleep disorder will also present with medical and psychiatric complaints. A behavioral-medical approach, the integration of medical and behavioral sciences, appears to be an excellent solution for the sizable population of those suffering with sleep disorders.

REFERENCES

Alto, W.A. (1995). Prevention in practice. *Primary Care, 22,* 543–554.

American Psychiatric Association. (1994). *Diagnostic and Statistical Manual of Mental Disorders* (4th ed.). Washington, DC: Author.

Chesson, A. L., Littner, M., Davila, D., Anderson, M., Grigg-Damberger, M., Hartse, K., Johnson, S., & Wise, M. (1999). Practice parameters for the use of light therapy in the treatment of sleep disorders. *Sleep, 22,* 641–660.

Dement, W. C., & Vaughan, C. (1999). *The promise of sleep.* New York: Delacorte.

Dickel, M. J., & Mosko, S. S. (1990). Morbidity cut-offs for sleep apnea and periodic leg movements in predicting subjective complaints in seniors. *Sleep, 13,* 155–166.

Ford, D. E., & Kamerow, D. B. (1989). Epidemiologic study of sleep disturbance and psychiatric disorders: An opportunity for prevention? *Journal of the American Medical Association, 262,* 1479–1484.

Gallup Organization. (1995). *Sleep in America.* Princeton, NJ: Author. (Poll conducted for the National Sleep Foundation)

Gupta, M. A., Gupta, A. K., & Haberman, H. F. (1986). Psychotropic drugs in dermatology: A review and guidelines for use. *Journal of the American Academy of Dermatology, 14,* 633–645.

Hauri, P., & Hawkins, D. R. (1973). Alpha-delta sleep. *Electroencephalography and Clinical Neurophysiology, 34,* 233–237.

Hauri, P., & Linde, S. (1996). *No more sleepless nights.* New York: John Wiley.

Hening, W., Allen, R., Earley, C. E., Kushida, C., Picchietti, D., & Silber, M. (1999). The treatment of restless leg syndrome and periodic limb movement disorder. *Sleep, 22,* 970–999.

Mellinger, G. D., Balter, M. B., & Uhlenhuth, E. H. (1985). Insomnia and its treatment. *Archives of General Psychiatry, 42,* 225–232.

Moffitt, P. F., Kalucy, E. C., Kalucy, R. S., Baum, F. E., & Cooke, R. D. (1991). Sleep difficulties, pain, and other correlates. *Journal of Internal Medicine, 230,* 245–249.

Moldofsky, H. (1989). Sleep and fibrositis syndrome. *Rheumatic Disease Clinics of North America, 15*(1), 91–103.

Morin, C. M., Hauri, P. J., Espie, C. A., Spielman, A. J., Buyesse, D. J., & Bootzin, R. R. (1999). Nonpharmacologic treatment of chronic insomnia. *Sleep, 22,* 1134–1155.

National Institutes of Health. (1984). Drugs and insomnia: The use of medication to promote sleep. *Journal of the American Medical Association, 18,* 2410–2414.

National Institutes of Health. (1991). Consensus Development Conference statement: The treatment of sleep disorders of older people. *Sleep, 14,* 169–177.

National Sleep Foundation. (2002). *Sleep in America poll.* [Online]. Retrieved January 20, 2003, from www.sleepfoundation.org

Natural Medicines Comprehensive Database. (2002). *Melatonin* [monograph]. [Online]. Retrieved January 20, 2003, from www.naturaldatabase.com/monograph.asp?mono_id=940&hilite=1

Perlis, M. L., Giles, D. E., Buyesse, D. J., Tu, X., & Kupfer, D. J. (1997). Self-reported sleep disturbance as a prodromal symptom in recurrent depression. *Journal of Affective Disorders, 42,* 209–212.

Pilowsky, I., Crettenden, I., & Townley, M. (1985). Sleep disturbance in pain clinic patients. *Pain, 23,* 27–33.

Schoicket, S. L., Bertelson, A. D., & Lacks, P. (1988). Is sleep hygiene a sufficient treatment for sleep maintenance insomnia? *Behavior Therapy, 19,* 183–190.

Walsleben, J. A., & Baron-Faust, R. (2000). *A woman's guide to sleep.* New York: Crown.

Wolfe, V. A., & Helge, T. D. (2002, April). *Utilizing a brief, behaviorally based intervention to treat insomnia in primary care.* Paper presented at the meeting of the Society of Behavioral Medicine, Washington, DC.

Wolfe, V. A., Helge, T. D., & Jacobs, J. R. (2002, November). *Effectiveness of a single session group appointment to treat insomnia in primary care.* Poster presented at the meeting of the Association for Advancement of Behavior Therapy, Reno, NV.

Part IV

SPECIAL ISSUES

Introduction to Part IV

The final seven chapters of this handbook focus on topics that are critical for effective practice of clinical health psychology; however, the issues are more crosscutting than those in the chapters in Parts II and III, which focused on specific health behaviors and disease. As in any applied discipline, clinical health psychologists must be sensitive to ethical issues, cultural and individual diversity, and the challenges that are unique to this multidisciplinary field. The editors identified seven important topics and recruited authors to provide an overview of the issues that are critical to clinical health psychology. Although not exhaustive of the issues that will challenge the practitioner, the resulting chapters provide a solid foundation for the practice of clinical health psychology.

In Chapter 22, Siegfried and Porter provide an overview of the "Ethical Principles of Psychologists and Code of Conduct" adopted by the American Psychological Association and illustrate, through case vignettes, aspects of the code that are of particular importance to the practice of clinical health psychology. For each of the principles of the ethical code, practical advice is given and cases are used to illustrate the issues. It is only through the maintenance of the highest standards that clinical health psychology will have its largest influence.

In Chapter 23, Myers and Hwang review the literature on ethnocultural issues in clinical health psychology. The chapter begins with a review of the health disparity issues as they relate to various ethnic minority groups in the United States. These disparities are then discussed in terms of a biopsychosocial model that appears to be useful for understanding the role of ethnic differences in functional health status. The authors also provide an overview of various treatment efforts that are tailored to minority communities. In addition, the chapter provides specific recommendations that should enhance the practice of clinical health psychology.

In Chapter 24, Csoboth reviews special issues relevant to women's health. The author provides a model that emphasizes the different life course events that women experience and discusses how women's health is differentially related to the unique physiological and social changes during these life stages. Psychosocial factors such as stress, social support, role identity, and socioeconomic factors appear to differentially influence women and men. These differences are reviewed. The author also briefly reviews selected health problems that occur at greater rates in women, with an emphasis on the importance of developing interventions specifically for women.

In Chapter 25, Edelstein and his colleague provide an in-depth review of issues that are unique to working with geriatric populations. This is clearly an area where there is great demand for services and great need for specialized training. The authors begin with an in-depth discussion of age-related changes, with a focus on those changes that are unique to older adults. Perhaps one of the more critical sections of this chapter is the discussion of psychological manifestations and correlates of physical disease. Effective practice of clinical health psychology requires an understanding of how many physical disease states in the elderly have natural symptoms that are consistent with psychiatric disorders. Recognition of the cause of the psychiatric symptoms is critical for working with this population. The authors review adverse medication effects and other problem areas that are unique to older adults. Finally, the chapter provides a thoughtful review of end-of-life issues, with a discussion of how such decisions are made.

In Chapter 26, Tucker, Klapow, and Simpson focus their contribution on the public health approach to the treatment and prevention of disease. They challenge the notion that psychological practice needs to be focused on the individual, and they encourage clinical health psychologists to consider the role that they can and should play in public health efforts that are more population focused. The training program at the University of Alabama at Birmingham is presented as one model for such training, wherein students are provided with in-depth public health experiences while pursuing training in clinical health psychology.

In Chapter 27, Palm and her colleagues focus on the unique challenges and skills that are necessary to conduct psychological research in medical settings. Using their own research as an illustrative model, the authors cover the basic questions of the development of a research question, design of the study, recruitment of participants, and recruitment of support from administrators and staff. Problems that are unique to medical institutions are openly discussed, and practical solutions are offered. The chapter concludes with a discussion of ethical issues and conflict of interest issues.

Finally, in Chapter 28, Borrego and Follette address program evaluation in medical settings. The authors provide a step-by-step outline for program evaluation that focuses on the development of the question(s) to be addressed and proceeds to selection of populations and assessment methods. A great deal of attention is given to why program evaluation is needed and to how to conduct such evaluations. The authors make the case that the practice of clinical health psychology is greatly enhanced when practitioners actively evaluate the services they provide and modify services where needed.

CHAPTER 22

Ethical Issues for Clinicians in Behavioral Medicine Settings

NICOLE J. SIEGFRIED AND CHEBON A. PORTER

The continued expansion and integration of health psychology into medical settings raises complex practical, ethical, and professional issues. Much has been written on the logistics of integrating psychology into medicine with ethical issues often overlooked. The "Ethical Principles of Psychologists and Code of Conduct" (American Psychological Association [APA], 1992) is applicable to all psychologists, including those in medical and health settings. It is expected that psychologists guide their practice based on the principles of competence (Principle A), integrity (Principle B), professional and scientific responsibility (Principle C), respect for people's rights and dignity (Principle D), concern for others' welfare (Principle E), and social responsibility (Principle F) (for a complete description of these principles, see APA [1992] guidelines). This chapter outlines the ethical responsibilities of health psychologists based on these principles, with a focus on issues related to health and medical settings. Common scenarios with ethical implications are presented in an attempt to clarify the psychologist's role.

PRINCIPLE A: COMPETENCE

Psychologists strive to maintain high standards of competence in their work. They recognize the boundaries of their particular competencies and the limitations of their expertise. They provide only those services and use only those techniques for which they are qualified by education, training, and experience. Psychologists are cognizant of the fact that the competencies required in serving, teaching, and/or studying groups of people vary with the distinctive characteristics of those groups. In those areas where recognized professional standards do not yet exist, psychologists exercise careful judgment and take appropriate precautions to protect the welfare of those with whom they work. They maintain knowledge of relevant scientific and professional information related to the services they render, and they recognize the need for ongoing education. Psychologists make appropriate use of scientific, professional, technical, and administrative resources (APA, 1992).

APA (1992) guidelines clearly emphasize the importance of pursuing and maintaining competence for psychologists. Several issues related to competence are relevant to health psychology, including achieving and recognizing boundaries of competence, conducting appropriate assessment batteries, and identifying appropriate roles in a medical setting.

Achieving Boundaries of Competence

The initial challenge of achieving and recognizing boundaries of competence requires a professional commitment from health psychologists. Minimum levels of competence for psychologists have been defined (APA, 1981). Although these recommendations are guidelines and not requirements, they can be useful in defining limits of expertise. Criteria for competence in specialization areas of psychology are more ambiguous. General guidelines for adequate training in health psychology have been presented and include graduate coursework in health psychology and supervised clinical experience in health/medical settings (Stone, 1983). In the absence of specific guidelines, conservative estimates of competence are recommended. It is considered the responsibility of the psychologist to recognize and practice within his or her areas of competence as well as to evaluate the appropriateness of additional training. Consultation with senior colleagues can be helpful in evaluating the appropriateness of training endeavors. In addition, it is recommended that further training be sought via forums with appropriate accreditation. Someone who has not achieved adequate training in health psychology cannot ethically promote himself or herself as a health psychologist. Consider the following scenario.

Case 1. "Dr. Jones," originally trained as a psychoanalyst, completed a weekend seminar on motivational therapy with cardiac patients. After the seminar, she felt capable of generalizing this therapy to many patients in health settings. She called the yellow pages and had her advertisement changed to read "clinical health psychologist specializing in motivational treatment for health problems."

Dr. Jones failed to act ethically in this example. Although recommendations for training in health psychology are not specific (e.g., Belar, 1980; Stone, 1983), a weekend seminar is not sufficient to achieve competence. Although it may be within Dr. Jones's boundaries of competence to treat individuals with comorbid medical/health issues (so long as she seeks consultation in areas where she is not well trained), she cannot ethically promote herself as a "clinical health psychologist."

Case 2. "Dr. Brooke," a clinical health psychologist trained in women's health disorders, is treating "Ms. Jacobs," who suffers from depression. As therapy progresses, it becomes clear that Ms. Jacobs's sleep problems are beyond those expected for depressive symptomatology and beyond Dr. Brooke's areas of expertise. Dr. Brooke continues to see Ms. Jacobs for her depression but refers her to a sleep disorders specialist for further evaluation of her sleep difficulties.

Dr. Brooke acted ethically in this example. Her evaluation of her training stands in stark contrast to Dr. Jones's lack of regard to her limits of expertise in the previous example. Dr. Brooke found Ms. Jacobs's sleep disturbance to exceed a typical depressive reaction and was therefore attending to the "distinctive characteristics" (APA, 1992) of Ms. Jacobs's clinical presentation. Furthermore, although Dr. Brooke was trained in health psychology, she realized the limits of her competence and sought outside guidance when appropriate.

Another instance in which health psychologists may inappropriately cross the boundaries of competence is providing medical interventions for which they are not appropriately trained (Belar & Deardorff, 1999). Because psychologists in medical settings become very familiar with medical diagnoses and medications for these illnesses, they may become comfortable making unethical recommendations for medical treatment. Consider the following example.

Case 3. "Dr. Logan" trained "Mr. Collins" in relaxation training and biofeedback to help control the patient's blood pressure. As Mr. Collins became more skilled with his relaxation training, Dr. Logan encouraged him to cut back slowly on his blood pressure medication so that the patient could achieve his goal of behaviorally managing his hypertension.

Dr. Logan behaved unethically in this example. Medication management is not part of his role as a clinical health psychologist. A more appropriate course of action would have been for either Dr. Logan or Mr. Collins to discuss the issue with Mr. Collins's physician. Although health psychologists are trained for medical settings, they must remember that their role is to provide psychological interventions. Medical diagnosis and intervention require medical training, just as psychological interventions require psychological training. Providing medical interventions as a health psychologist is practicing medicine without a license.

Conducting Psychological Assessments

Psychological assessment plays an integral role in the practice of health psychology. According to Belar and Deardorff (1999), "Assessment . . . is inextricably intertwined with the consultation activity" of health psychologists (p. 39). Multiple ethical issues surround competence and psychological assessment in health/medical settings. First, the battery of instruments to which a health psychologist has access should be generally sufficiently broad and sensitive to the unique consultative needs and patient variables serviced. In this context, norm groups that are used must be appropriate to the patient. Many norm groups for personality, behavioral, and cognitive tests are comprised of psychiatric

patients, and it may be inaccurate or even inappropriate to compare a patient presenting in a medical context with psychiatric patients (APA, 1992, Standard 2.04). It has been recommended (Belar & Deardorff, 1999) that, whenever possible, psychological test results of medical patients should be compared with both medical and psychiatric populations, and a discussion of the differences should be included in the assessment report. When comparable norm groups are not available, the clinician must consider the lack of appropriate norms in the interpretation of the test data. In addition, it is the responsibility of the clinician to maintain expertise with the instruments used. This includes maintaining knowledge of current literature and published research on the instruments.

Second, assessment results must be communicated to the patient in plain language. In fact, it has been recommended that the assessment report also be written in clear simple language given that many reports are read by the patient (Keith-Spiegel & Koocher, 1998). The psychologist is required to explain to the patient not only the purpose of testing but also the results of testing, avoiding psychological jargon that is difficult to interpret (APA, 1992, Standard 2.09).

Finally, although a health psychologist is often consulted to provide a report to a team of medical professionals, he or she is primarily accountable to the patient. It is recommended that the psychologist's allegiance to the patient be clarified routinely at the outset of the consultation with the patient and medical team.

The following scenario contains several ethical issues related to psychological assessment in a medical setting.

Case 4. "Dr. Stephens" was consulted by the medical team at a chronic pain clinic to provide a psychological evaluation for "Mr. Thomas," who presented with lower leg pain with no apparent organic etiology. Mr. Thomas was a first-generation immigrant with

6 years of formal education who did not speak English as his primary language. Dr. Stephens conducted an evaluation that consisted of projective and objective personality measures as well as a number of other symptom checklists. After examining the results, Dr. Stephens concluded that Mr. Thomas demonstrated personality tendencies consistent with the production of physical symptoms for attention. Dr. Stephens concluded the consultation by reporting his findings to the medical team, which promptly referred Mr. Thomas for psychotherapy targeted at his personality issues.

Dr. Stephens demonstrated several ethical violations in this example. First, he should have compared his patient's test results with those of the appropriate norm group or made adjustments to his interpretations based on differences between his patient and the comparison group. Dr. Stephens should have also been more careful not to pathologize physical symptoms. Health psychologists should make it clear in their written and oral reports that the presence of psychological symptoms does not necessarily negate the presence of physical symptoms. Results from psychological evaluations are expected to augment—not replace—physical exams. Persuasive language loosely based on test data can be dangerous, not only because it may be inaccurate but also because it may convince medical professionals to ignore valid physical symptoms in their search for a diagnosis. Second, Dr. Stephens should have shared his findings directly with the patient. Although the ethical standards do not mandate that results be delivered directly by the psychologist, the psychologist must ensure that the patient receives a clear and accurate explanation of the evaluation findings. The attending physician may have related findings to the patient. However, most medical personnel are not trained in interpreting and conceptualizing psychological assessments. Therefore, it is recommended that, whenever possible, the psychologist who conducted the evaluation provide the feedback to the patient.

PRINCIPLE B: INTEGRITY

Psychologists seek to promote integrity in the science, teaching, and practice of psychology. In these activities, psychologists are honest, fair, and respectful of others. In describing or reporting their qualifications, services, products, fees, research, or teaching, they do not make statements that are false, misleading, or deceptive. Psychologists strive to be aware of their own belief systems, values, needs, and limitations and the effect of these on their work. To the extent feasible, they attempt to clarify for relevant parties the roles they are performing and to function appropriately in accordance with those roles. Psychologists avoid improper and potentially harmful dual relationships. (APA, 1992)

Psychologists are expected to behave ethically and honestly in their profession. They present themselves genuinely and with integrity. They conduct their services without bias and avoid situations that may impair their objectivity in their relationships with their patients. Although all points in the principle of integrity are applicable to health psychologists, perhaps the most relevant is the issue of relationships with patients and colleagues.

Relationships With Patients

Dual role relationships with patients is one of the most common ethical dilemmas reported by psychologists (Pope & Vetter, 1992). Although health psychologists might not be any more vulnerable to potential dual relationship violations, relationship boundaries in medical settings may be more blurred than in other settings. Psychologists who work as part of a medical team interact with other medical professionals with differing sets of ethical guidelines. For example, the American Medical Association (AMA) guidelines for sexual relationships with former patients are quite different from the APA ethical guidelines, which clearly discourage sexual relationships with former patients and mandate a 2-year period before a sexual relationship can be initiated with a former patient (for a complete description of sexual misconduct in medical practice, see AMA, 1991). Furthermore, non-sexual social relationships with patients are not addressed by the AMA. Health psychologists need to be aware that although the behavior of other professionals may be considered ethical based on guidelines for their respective fields, this behavior might not be ethical based on psychological standards.

Relationships With Colleagues

Relationships with colleagues also raise ethical dilemmas for psychologists who work in medical settings. Many medical professionals are not well educated as to the role of psychology in a medical setting and/or the influence of psychological issues in medical diagnoses. For instance, an attending physician might unknowingly request inappropriate use of assessment results or recommend an unsubstantiated psychological-behavioral intervention. Although this situation may be uncomfortable for the health psychologist, he or she must educate the physician and the treatment team as to his or her role in the medical setting and on the appropriate use of psychiatric instruments for assessment in medical populations.

The following case demonstrates ethical dilemmas related to relationships with both patients and colleagues.

Case 6. "Dr. Goode" recently provided a psychological evaluation for "Dr. Smith," a physician in a nearby town and a current patient in a drug rehabilitation program. "Dr. Pressling," the attending physician for the treatment team, coordinated a golf outing for the treatment team and some area physicians, including Dr. Smith. Although Dr. Smith is still in outpatient treatment at the drug rehabilitation center, Dr. Goode has completed his portion of the assessment. With encouragement

from Dr. Pressling, Dr. Goode decides to attend the golf outing.

Although the APA ethical guidelines for nonsexual dual relationships are not as specific as those for sexual relationships, the guidelines clearly state that

> a psychologist refrains from entering into or promising another personal, scientific, professional, financial, or other relationship with [patients] if it appears likely that such a relationship reasonably might impair the psychologist's objectivity or otherwise interfere with the psychologist's effectively performing his or her functions as a psychologist, or might harm or exploit the other party. (APA, 1992, Standard 1.17)

Although the ethics of Dr. Goode's behavior are debatable, his golf outing with the patient does raise several potential ethical violations. First, although Dr. Goode received pressure from his employer to attend the golf outing, the dual relationship with the patient was avoidable. Dr. Smith was still a patient in the program, and Dr. Goode may be called on to give interpretations/assessments of Dr. Smith's progress that might be biased by his relationship with him as a golf partner. Second, based on the power differential between Dr. Goode and Dr. Pressling, Dr. Goode entered a professional dual relationship with Dr. Pressling when he accepted the invitation to play golf. Although it can be argued that Dr. Goode may suffer the potentially negative repercussions of this dual relationship, there is also a potential of harm to future patients in that such a dual relationship may interfere with Dr. Goode's judgment in future consultations. This scenario serves as a nice example in that the potential for harm to the patient is debatable. In addition to the responsibility to "avoid improper and potentially harmful dual relationships," Dr. Goode is required to "promote integrity" in his behavior (APA, 1992). When the potential harmfulness of a dual relationship is debatable, the promotion of integrity in science and clinical practice may prove to be a clearer guideline. This seems particularly applicable when health psychologists are forced to interface with colleagues who operate under different ethical guidelines.

PRINCIPLE C: PROFESSIONAL AND SCIENTIFIC RESPONSIBILITY

Psychologists uphold professional standards of conduct, clarify their professional roles and obligations, accept appropriate responsibility for their behavior, and adapt their methods to the needs of different populations. Psychologists consult with, refer to, or cooperate with other professionals and institutions to the extent needed to serve the best interests of their patients, clients, or other recipients of their services. Psychologists' moral standards and conduct are personal matters to the same degree as is true for any other person except as psychologists' conduct may compromise their professional responsibilities or reduce the public's trust in psychology and psychologists. Psychologists are concerned about the ethical compliance of their colleagues' scientific and professional conduct. When appropriate, they consult with colleagues to prevent or avoid unethical conduct. (APA, 1992)

Psychologists define their role for patients and colleagues, and they strive to perform this role appropriately. Role clarification is particularly important for health psychologists who typically work as part of a multidisciplinary team. In addition, health psychologists are expected to promote the field of psychology by consulting with colleagues, behaving responsibly, and participating in scientific and professional endeavors.

Clarifying Professional Roles

Health psychologists typically maneuver in a work environment of a variety of health care providers, including physicians, rehabilitation therapists, nurses, and social workers. In this context, it is important that health psychologists remain cognizant of their role and inform patients and colleagues of this role. Some patients, who often have several appointments throughout the course of the day, may be unclear as to the role of each of their providers. Consider for a moment a patient who has been visited by a speech therapist, a physical therapist, and a physician during the first 3 hours of the morning, only to have a fourth individual, a health psychologist, enter her room with a variety of questions and assessment instruments. From the patient's perspective, the role of the health psychologist may be understandably confused with the services of other providers. The health psychologist is directed to explain his or her role and the purpose of the interventions to the patient at the outset of the session and must ensure that the patient has a clear understanding of the role that the health psychologist is expected to play.

In addition to patients, members of the treatment team may be unclear as to the health psychologist's role, training, and expertise. An interdisciplinary team consists of several independent agendas that are coordinated to reach a collective goal. Amid the agendas, a full appreciation and understanding of the role of fellow providers can become even more ambiguous. Therefore, it is of utmost importance that the health psychologist define his or her purpose to team members as well as to clarify his or her professional responsibilities.

Ensuring High Standards of Professional Conduct

Ensuring high standards of professional conduct and scientific responsibility is an active process. Health psychologists are encouraged to routinely consult with colleagues as a means of reinforcement, education, and professional accountability. In addition, health psychologists are encouraged to maintain a presence at patient staffings (as opposed to sending psychological technicians, interns, or graduate students) as another means of illustrating their role and taking responsibility for assessment and treatment of their patients. Also, health psychologists are encouraged to make grand rounds presentations, provide in-service training sessions, and remain active in professional societies to facilitate both public and institutional awareness.

PRINCIPLE D: RESPECT FOR PEOPLE'S RIGHTS AND DIGNITY

> Psychologists accord appropriate respect to the fundamental rights, dignity, and worth of all people. They respect the rights of individuals to privacy, confidentiality, self-determination, and autonomy, always being mindful that legal and other obligations may lead to inconsistency and conflict with the exercise of these rights. Psychologists are aware of cultural, individual, and role differences, including those due to age, gender, race, ethnicity, national origin, religion, sexual orientation, disability, language, and socioeconomic status. Psychologists try to eliminate the effect on their work of biases based on those factors, and they do not knowingly participate in or condone unfair discriminatory practices. (APA, 1992)

Multiple issues are pertinent to a discussion of respect of others for health psychologists in a medical setting, including patient rights to privacy, confidentiality, and respect for diversity. Health psychologists are also sensitive to individual differences of their patient populations and consider these differences in interactions with patients as well as with the treatment team.

Confidentiality

APA (1992) guidelines clearly describe the psychologist's commitment to confidentiality: "Psychologists have a primary obligation and take reasonable precautions to respect the confidentiality rights of those with whom they work or consult, recognizing that confidentiality may be established by law, institutional rules, or profession" (APA, 1992, Standard 5.02). The commitment to confidentiality and the limits of this commitment are discussed with the patient/potential patient at the outset of therapy/intervention. These limits include (a) harm to self, (b) harm to others, (c) child/elderly abuse or neglect, and (d) court order. Ethical dilemmas related to confidentiality are common and can become more complex in medical settings.

Maintaining Confidentiality

Various ethical dilemmas related to the maintenance of confidentiality are inherent in the medical setting. The health psychologist has a primary responsibility to the patient. The intricacies of such a responsibility can at times be easily overlooked amid the shuffle of multiple interventions applied by the medical team. Therefore, it is essential that all limitations and exceptions to confidentiality be openly discussed with the patient at the outset of assessment and/or treatment regardless of the estimated length of contact. The health psychologist is also required to inform the patient as to who will have access to assessment results/reports and records of the psychologist-patient interactions. Although not ethically mandated, written documentation of the clinician's explanation and the patient's understanding of confidentiality is recommended from a legal and practical perspective.

The health psychologist not only must thoroughly explain confidentiality to the patient but also must ensure that confidentiality is protected. In medical settings, chart information is typically widely accessed by hospital staff. Therefore, it is recommended that, whenever possible, detailed notes be kept separately within the psychologist's therapy records and only cryptic general notes be included as part of the medical chart (Belar & Deardorff, 1999). This practice protects patient data from possible misinterpretation by nonpsychiatric staff and maintains confidentiality of potentially sensitive, yet irrelevant, patient information.

Another issue pertinent to maintaining confidentiality is privacy for psychological consultations. It is often difficult to secure privacy for a clinical interview given that families and/or other patients might be present in the hospital room and the patient might not be ambulatory for the purpose of moving to a testing/interview office. When possible, it is recommended that the health psychologist pre-schedule individual time in the patient's room. Coordinating in advance with other members of the treatment team can often facilitate making such arrangements. Also, in cases where multiple patients share a room, a less than ideal but simple alternative is to close the divider curtains around the patient's bed.

Finally, the issue of confidentiality in medical settings can often be obscured by the numerous interventions and assessments conducted on a particular patient. Although the patient may have consented for some data (e.g., medical data) to be shared with family members or with other health professionals, psychological data are considered separate and the patient must consent for this information to be shared with others. It is also important that the health psychologist remain cognizant of what the patient consented to in the original consultation. In a hurried, sometimes chaotic medical setting, the precise limits of the patient's original consent can be overlooked or misunderstood, even with the best of intentions.

Exceptions to Confidentiality

Although the limits of confidentiality are clearly stated in the ethical guidelines, these boundaries can be somewhat ambiguous in medical settings. Confidentiality may need to be breached in situations where the patient is a threat to himself or herself. It is important from both a legal and an ethical standpoint that the health psychologist thoroughly evaluate the suicidal patient and carefully consider

the consequences of breaching/not breaching confidentiality. Several issues may complicate a thorough evaluation of suicidality in a medical setting. Assessments of potentially suicidal patients in a medical setting, particularly in the emergency room, may be rushed. Furthermore, the clinician does not have the advantage of a well-established relationship with the patient to facilitate a thorough appraisal of suicidality.

If the patient is deemed to be a threat to himself or herself, the health psychologist must exhaust non-confidentiality-breaching solutions prior to breaking confidentiality. When a breach is required, it is recommended that, whenever possible, the provider inform the patient of the pending breach and reasons for such action. Obviously, the importance of the initial discussion of the limits of confidentiality becomes glaringly apparent. To appropriately protect the patient and preserve the therapeutic relationship, the health psychologist must be thoroughly familiar with guidelines related to confidentiality. When a solution to a dilemma related to breaching confidentiality is unclear, the psychologist should consult with other colleagues to ensure an appropriate resolution.

Another exception to confidentiality occurs when the patient is assessed as a potential harm to others. The psychologist's duty to warn was well established in the case of *Tarasoff v. Board of Regents of the University of California* (1976), in which the California Supreme Court ruled that it is the psychologist's responsibility to assess the threat of harm in patients and to take measures to protect potential victims. The *Tarasoff* case has generated confusion for psychologists as to when it is necessary to preserve or break confidentiality with potentially dangerous patients. Moreover, much of the controversy surrounds the degree of intent to commit a violent act suggested by patients' statements and overt behavior. Obviously, this dilemma may become even more ambiguous in a medical setting where threat of harm may relate not only to physical violence but also to the intentional and unintentional spread of contagious diseases.

For instance, based on the duty to warn, are psychologists under ethical obligation to inform sexual or needle-sharing partners of HIV-positive patients? As with all "duty to warn" scenarios, careful consideration of each case and its particular issues is imperative. Thorough documentation, consultation, and review of specific state regulations concerning HIV reporting are necessary before making the decision to breach or preserve confidentiality. States have differing guidelines regarding the duty to warn in infectious disease cases. The health psychologist needs to be familiar with state laws in determining whether confidentiality should be breached for a specific case. When state laws permit or mandate notification of third parties about risk of HIV infection, it is recommended that confidentiality be maintained except in circumstances where patients are unwilling to reduce the risk of spreading infection to partners (APA, 1991). When confidentiality is breached in these unusual cases, the practitioner must maintain detailed records providing a rationale for breaking confidentiality, inform the patient that the third party will be contacted, and attempt to conceal patient-identifying information in the contact (APA, 1991). Consider the following scenario.

Case 6. "Dr. Rey Actte" is treating "Ms. Bowen." Ms. Bowen reports to Dr. Actte that she is HIV-positive. She has been dating her partner for about 3 months. Although she has not informed her partner that she is HIV-positive, she has been very cautious in their sexual relationship, using appropriate protection to prevent the exchange of bodily fluids. She states that she will tell her partner at some point but that the time has not been right. As Ms. Bowen continues to describe her partner, it becomes apparent that he is an acquaintance of Dr. Actte. After the session concludes, Dr. Actte determines that, based on the guidelines for his state (which allow a breach of confidentiality to

inform others of HIV risk), it is his duty to inform the partner. Dr. Actte calls the partner and lets him know that Ms. Bowen is HIV-positive and that he is at risk.

Dr. Actte committed several ethical violations in this example. First, Ms. Bowen was protecting her partner from her infection, so the risk of harm was negligible. This case can be contrasted to cases in which the patient maliciously spreads the virus with the intent to infect others or neglectfully engages in risky virus-spreading behaviors. As mentioned previously, the APA states that when the patient takes precautions to protect his or her partner, the clinician is not mandated to warn the partner of HIV risk. Second, even if Dr. Actte determined that Ms. Bowen was placing her partner at risk and that he had a duty to intervene, he could have handled the situation more responsibly. He and Ms. Bowen could have discussed the risks to her partner and the consequences of not informing him of her status. Then, Dr. Actte could have encouraged Ms. Bowen to tell her partner rather than breaking confidentiality to inform the partner. Finally, if Ms. Bowen refused to tell her partner after this discussion and Dr. Actte found it necessary to warn the partner, he should have first informed Ms. Bowen of his intentions and preserved her privacy as much as possible in his report to the partner.

Recognizing the Influence of Multicultural Issues

In addition to maintaining confidentiality, health psychologists must respect the rights of others by recognizing and understanding diversity. Although all psychologists need to be cognizant of cultural influences (APA, 1992, Standard 1.08), patient populations continue to grow more culturally diverse, suggesting the ever-increasing need for greater cultural awareness (Iwamasa, 1997). Clearly, health psychologists should avoid prejudice and discrimination in the process of evaluation and treatment. Understanding, appreciating, and implementing cultural sensitivity reaches far beyond political correctness.

Multiple factors contribute to cultural diversity, including ethnicity, gender, socioeconomic status, geographic region, and religion. The Western medical model adhered to in hospitals may represent viewpoints and expectations for behavior that stand in stark contrast to those of cultures with which many patients identify. For example, cultural belief systems vary as to perceptions of illness behavior, use of medication, etiological understanding of illness, and family participation. The health psychologist is encouraged to be cognizant of his or her own ethnocentrism and to take steps to appropriately acknowledge and incorporate the patient's cultural belief system whenever possible. Even the most politically correct health psychologist can provide inaccurate interpretations and contraindicated treatments by missing the influence of culture. Consider the following example.

Case 7. "Dr. Hayden" is treating "Ms. Layten," who has type 2 diabetes. She had not been taking her medication, and she was referred for psychological and behavioral interventions. Ms. Layten had been described by the referring physician as "difficult and noncompliant with recommended treatments." The referring physician reported trying several medications to no avail, and he is concerned that she may need insulin; however, he is afraid that she would refuse to take it, just like she had the other medications. After Dr. Hayden met with Ms. Layten for several sessions, she shared with him that medical interventions were against her spiritual beliefs. Although she had tried to share this with the referring physician, he had told her that many diabetics do not like the thought of medications and that she would get used to it if she just tried it for a while. Dr. Hayden discussed with Ms. Layten alternatives to medication, as well as the perceived consequences of not taking medications, to assist her in her treatment decision.

Dr. Hayden has so far acted ethically in this example. Although medication is recommended for non-diet-controlled type 2 diabetics, it is Ms. Layten's decision as to whether she wants to take the medication. The referring physician made pejorative assumptions about Ms. Layten's motivation because he ignored her cultural belief system. These assumptions not only pathologized Ms. Layten's belief system but also potentially exacerbated her "noncompliance." Ms. Layten's case is a good example of multicultural influences. Similar to the general population, health care professionals are at risk for unintentionally stigmatizing patients based on cultural ignorance and their own ethnocentrism. Health psychologists are encouraged to remain aware that multicultural issues are present in nearly every patient-therapist relationship and that cultural diversity surpasses race to include factors such as nationality, disability, socioeconomic status, gender, geographic location, and religion.

PRINCIPLE E: CONCERN FOR OTHERS' WELFARE

> Psychologists seek to contribute to the welfare of those with whom they interact professionally. In their professional actions, psychologists weigh the welfare and rights of their patients or clients, students, supervisees, human research participants, and other affected persons as well as the welfare of animal subjects of research. When conflicts occur among their obligations or concerns, psychologists attempt to resolve these conflicts and to perform their roles in a responsible fashion that avoids or minimizes harm. Psychologists are sensitive to real and ascribed differences in power between themselves and others, and they do not exploit or mislead other people during or after professional relationships. (APA, 1992)

APA (1992) guidelines define the psychologist's role in providing informed consent as follows:

(a) Psychologists obtain appropriate informed consent to therapy or related procedures, using language that is reasonably understandable to participants. The content of informed consent will vary depending on many circumstances; however, informed-consent generally implies that the person (1) has the capacity to consent, (2) has been informed of significant information concerning the procedure, [and] (3) has freely and without undue influence expressed consent and [that] (4) consent has been appropriately documented. (Standard 4.02a)

The health psychologist must be committed to explaining the therapy process and to ensuring that the patient is consenting without pressure or force. Although not mandated by ethical codes, it has been recommended that informed consent be provided in both oral and written form (Keith-Spiegel & Koocher, 1998). Providing both written and oral explanations of therapy decreases confusion for the patient and provides documentation for the health psychologist. The consent form should be thorough yet simple and may address the following: expectations for therapy, potential risks and benefits of treatment, commitment to and limits of confidentiality, and an agreed-on fee.

Logistics of informed consent become more complex for the psychologist in a medical setting. In a consultation environment, the psychologist is often asked to provide a brief intervention or assessment. In these situations, informed consent is often inappropriately overlooked. Although failing to provide informed consent in itself is an ethical violation, this ethical infraction can lead to additional ethical dilemmas. Consider the following scenario.

Case 8. "Bob" is currently in outpatient cardiac rehabilitation. He reports symptoms of anhedonia and insomnia. "Dr. Johnson," a clinical health psychologist, is consulted to provide an assessment of Bob. Dr. Johnson is finishing with a staffing when she gets the consult and figures that she does not have time to see Bob before his next appointment. Thus, she orders a small battery of paper-and-pencil assessment instruments to be added to Bob's agenda for the day. On one of the instruments, it is later discovered that Bob endorses suicide intent. After ordering the additional tests, Dr. Johnson makes a note to see Bob the following day.

Dr. Johnson failed to act ethically in this example. First, she did not obtain Bob's consent. Measures were simply left with him, and he complied with the request to complete them. Second, she did not describe the purpose of the additional assessment procedures to Bob. The patient has the choice as to whether to complete these measures, and his options were not explained to him. Third, she did not describe confidentiality and its limits. Because Dr. Johnson is ethically required to protect Bob from harm to himself, which may include breaching confidentiality, she is now in a precarious situation. Not only has she potentially breached the trust in a patient-psychologist relationship, but she has essentially conducted an assessment on a patient without any permission from the patient. This is clearly a breach of ethics and a generally poor standard of practice.

Another situation related to informed consent that can be difficult for health psychologists in medical settings is ensuring consent for medical procedures. Psychologists often work with medical patients in exploring their perceptions and their options for medical treatment. Psychologists in health settings can facilitate informed consent for medical procedures by helping patients to understand the medical procedures, encouraging patients to ask for explanations and options from their physicians, persuading physicians and medical personnel to provide concise and understandable explanations of treatment to patients, and assisting patients in planning for and adjusting to the medical procedures (Belar & Deardorff, 1999).

PRINCIPLE F: SOCIAL RESPONSIBILITY

Psychologists are aware of their professional and scientific responsibilities to the community and the society in which they work and live. They apply and make public their knowledge of psychology so as to contribute to human welfare. Psychologists are concerned about and work to mitigate the causes of human suffering. When undertaking research, they strive to advance human welfare and the science of psychology. Psychologists try to avoid misuse of their work. They comply with the law and encourage the development of law and social policy that serve the interests of their patients and clients as well as the public. They are encouraged to contribute a portion of their professional time for little or no personal advantage. (APA, 1992)

The principle of social responsibility stands as a nucleus for any professional endeavor made by a psychologist and is particularly applicable to the health psychologist. More than other clinical specialties, health psychologists routinely interact with patients who are experiencing physical suffering that may include pain, deterioration of motor ability, or even impending death. It is not uncommon for patients to be concerned about the emotional and financial welfare of their family members. Likewise, family members are often concerned about the level of suffering and emotional welfare of patients. When appropriate, it is recommended that health psychologists maintain knowledge of local resources such as low-income hospice care, psychological and psychiatric treatment, charitable organizations, churches, and other services that may be necessary. Such information might not be a part of the consultation question and is typically viewed as a social worker's domain. However, health psychologists should be prepared to at least have reasonable referral information when confronted with inquiring patients and their families. Health psychologists must also be sensitive to the emotional needs of friends and family members of their patients. Health psychologists are obviously encouraged to maintain appropriate boundaries. However, sound professional boundaries do not necessarily exclude a few minutes of supportive contact for patients and their families.

CONCLUSIONS

This chapter has provided an overview of ethical guidelines specific to health psychologists. Although the APA guidelines may appear to be straightforward, these recommendations are often distorted by ambiguous situations. It is suggested that the health psychology student not only become familiar with the APA guidelines but also review situations that raise ethical dilemmas. This chapter introduced some of these difficult situations, but further study is required to become a health psychologist who behaves with integrity to protect patients and promote the field of health psychology.

REFERENCES

American Medical Association. (1991). Sexual misconduct in the practice of medicine. *Journal of the American Medical Association, 266,* 2741–2745.
American Psychological Association. (1981). Specialty guidelines for the delivery of services. *American Psychologist, 36,* 640–681.

American Psychological Association. (1991, August). Legal liability related to confidentiality and the prevention of HIV transmission. *American Psychological Association AIDS-Related Policy Statements.* (Washington, DC: Author)

American Psychological Association. (1992). Ethical principles of psychologists and code of conduct. *American Psychologist, 47,* 1597–1611.

Belar, C. D. (1980). Training the clinical psychology student in behavioral medicine. *Professional Psychology, 11,* 620–627.

Belar, C. D., & Deardorff, W. W. (1999). *Clinical health psychology in medical settings: A practitioner's guidebook.* Washington, DC: American Psychological Association.

Iwamasa, G. Y. (1997). Behavior therapy and a culturally diverse society: Forging an alliance. *Behavior Therapy, 28,* 347–358.

Keith-Spiegel, P., & Koocher, G. P. (1998). *Ethics in psychology: Professional standards and cases.* New York: McGraw-Hill.

Pope, K. S., & Vetter, V. A. (1992). Ethical dilemmas encountered by members of the American Psychological Association. *American Psychologist, 47,* 397–411.

Stone, G. C. (Ed.). (1983). National Working Conference on Education and Training in Health Psychology. *Health Psychology, 2*(Suppl. 5), 1–153.

Tarasoff v. Board of Regents of the University of California, 551 P. 2d 334 (Cal. Sup. Ct. 1976).

CHAPTER 23

Ethnocultural Issues in Behavioral Medicine

HECTOR F. MYERS AND WEI-CHIN HWANG

There are substantial and persistent racial/ethnic disparities in health. Compared with Caucasian Americans, ethnic minorities have poorer health (Keppel, Pearcy, & Wagener, 2002; Williams, 2000), receive poorer quality health care, and have poorer prognoses and treatment outcomes (Smedley, Stith, & Nelson, 2002; U.S. Department of Health and Human Services, 1999). Moreover, these health disparities remain even after adjusting for socioeconomic status, severity of illness, and discrepancies in access to care. The continued failure to close these persistent racial/ethnic disparities in health status, combined with the rapid increase in the ethnic and cultural diversity in the United States, has serious public health consequences and results in increased demand on an already challenged health care system. If left unattended, racial/ethnic disparities in health will eventually lead to a decline in quality of life for all Americans (Smedley et al., 2002).

This chapter is organized into four main sections. First, a brief review of ethnic disparities in cardiovascular disease (CVD), diabetes, cancer, and pain, conditions of special relevance to behavioral medicine, is presented. Second, some of the salient factors that contribute to the disparities are discussed. Third, examples of behavioral interventions with these disorders in minorities are presented. Fourth, a series of recommendations distilled from the most successful interventions is provided.

ETHNIC DISPARITIES IN HEALTH AND HEALTH CARE

Current evidence indicates that, compared with Caucasian Americans, African Americans and Native Americans evidence a significant health disadvantage, Hispanic Americans have equal or slightly poorer health, and Asian Americans evidence significant health advantages for some disorders (National Center for Health Statistics, 2000). For example, African Americans and other minorities are more likely to report poorer subjective health and well-being (Hughes & Thomas, 1998), poorer functional status, and greater disability than are Caucasians, but minorities are more likely to report comparable or better rates of other indicators of mental health (Kington & Nickens, 2000; Williams & Harris-Reid, 1999).

It is also well known that African Americans have the highest rate of essential hypertension, develop the disease at an earlier age, develop a more severe form of the disease earlier, and suffer from more severe complications and death from the disease than does any other ethnic group in the United States (National Heart, Lung, and Blood Institute, 1996). A similar pattern is observed in the prevalence and rates of mortality from CVD and cancer, which are the two leading causes of death in the United States. These rates are significantly higher in African Americans and Caucasian Americans and are lower in Asian Americans, Hispanic Americans, and Native Americans (American Cancer Society, 2002; Cooper et al., 2000). However, recent reports offer some good news, with significant reductions in heart disease reported in all ethnic groups.

Unfortunately, these positive trends are not observed in all health problems, nor are the trends equally positive for all ethnic groups. For example, the rates of non-insulin dependent diabetes mellitus (NIDDM) are increasing and affect minority groups disproportionately. African Americans, Hispanic Americans, Native Americans, and some Asian American subgroups suffer from NIDDM at higher rates than do Caucasian Americans and are also more likely to suffer from complications secondary to the disease such as blindness, end-stage renal disease, amputations, and mortality (Carter, Pugh, & Monterrosa, 1996).

Also, although there has been a significant reduction in mortality rates from lung and breast cancer in the U.S. population overall, Native Americans evidenced increased mortality rates and Asian Americans evidenced little reduction in mortality from these diseases (National Center for Health Statistics, 2000). Miller and colleagues (1996) also reported that Vietnamese Americans, Korean Americans, and Chinese Americans have liver cancer incidence and mortality rates several times higher than that of the U.S. population and that African Americans and Hispanic Americans

evidence rates approximately twice as high as that of Caucasian Americans. They also found higher incidence rates of stomach cancer in Korean Americans, Vietnamese Americans, Japanese Americans, Alaskan Natives, and Native Hawaiians.

Not only are there ethnic differences in chronic illnesses, but several clinical and experimental studies have also reported ethnic differences in the perception, sensitivity, and tolerance of pain as well as in pain-related avoidance of activity and physical and psychosocial disability (Bates & Edwards, 1992; Edwards, Doleys, Fillingim, & Lowery, 2001; McCracken, Matthews, Tang, & Cuba, 2001). In their study of ethnic differences in pain perception in chronic pain patients, Bates and Edwards (1992) found that Hispanic patients reported significantly greater intensity of pain than did the Caucasian subgroups and that these ethnic differences were moderated by locus of control; Anglo-Americans and Polish Americans with high internal locus of control reported experiencing more intense pain, whereas high internal locus of control respondents from the other ethnic groups reported lower pain ratings.

McCracken and colleagues (2001) compared pain experiences in treatment-seeking African American and Caucasian American chronic pain patients and found that although the groups did not differ on the chronicity of pain, medical diagnosis, work status, or previous surgeries, African American patients reported higher pain severity, more avoidance of activity, more fearful thinking, more physical symptoms, and greater physical and psychological disability than did Caucasian American patients. These results were also confirmed by Faucett, Gordon, and Levine (1994) in their study of ethnic differences in acute postoperative dental pain in four ethnic groups. They found that European Americans reported less severe pain, whereas African American and Hispanic American patients reported more severe pain. The basis for these ethnic differences in pain are unclear, but Bates (1987) argued for a biosocial model of pain, suggesting that the observed differences in pain are not due to physiological differences but rather are likely due to differences in cultural experiences, attitudes, and meanings of pain. These, in turn, influence the neurophysiological processes that govern pain perception and tolerance as well as the psychological and behavioral responses to pain.

Two factors that are implicated in the persistence of many of these ethnic health disparities are ethnic differences in help seeking and quality of health care received. Many studies indicate that ethnic minorities typically delay seeking professional health care for both physical and mental health needs, and they attribute this delay to a greater reliance on informal sources of help than is the case with Caucasian Americans (Zhang, Snowden, & Sue, 1998). Other more apparent reasons include financial and other barriers to access such as health insurance, language barriers, and stigma against mental health services (Takeuchi, Leaf, & Kuo, 1988; Thomas & Snowden, 2001). However, results from some studies on help seeking suggest that pathways to care are more complex than thought previously. For example, Snowden (1998) found that African Americans tend to rely more on both formal and informal sources of help for their health needs than do Caucasian Americans. In addition, whereas Asian Americans as a whole tend to seek help at the lowest rates relative to their representation in the general population (Matsuoka, Breaux, & Ryujin, 1997; Ying & Hu, 1994), Southeast Asians evidence higher rates of use (Ying & Hu, 1994).

Data from inpatient and outpatient mental health services confirm this complexity. For example, Snowden and Cheung (1990) reported higher use of inpatient services by African Americans and Native Americans/Alaskan Natives, whereas Hispanic Americans and Asian Americans/Pacific Islanders underuse these services, as compared with Caucasian Americans. In contrast, Padgett, Patrick, Burns, and Schlesinger (1994) found that African Americans and Hispanic Americans used outpatient mental health services less than did Caucasian Americans, even after controlling for a number of demographic variables.

Although the results from studies of help seeking among different ethnic groups are somewhat inconsistent, there is strong evidence that ethnic groups differ in the quality of care received once they enter the health care system. In a recent review on racial and ethnic differences in health care, Smedley and colleagues (2002) found that ethnic minorities are less likely to receive appropriate diagnostic tests, treatment, and follow-up care for diseases such as cancer, diabetes, CVD, and human immunodeficiency virus (HIV). These differences were evident even after controlling for factors such as delayed help seeking, health insurance coverage, income, severity of disease, and differences in use of services, all of which might affect access to care.

Smedley and colleagues (2002) also noted that a variety of patient, provider, and health care system variables contribute to these differences in health care. Ethnic minorities, especially the poor, are more likely to delay seeking care, adhere poorly to treatment regimens, and often refuse recommended services. Several studies also indicate that physicians tend to stereotype minority clients as less intelligent and educated, prefer patients of certain ethnicities, and provide different treatment to patients through the type of procedures suggested, the amount and type of medication prescribed, and/or the frequency of contact. In addition, a number of health care system variables, such as geographic distribution of health care facilities, health insurance coverage, availability of translation and interpretation services, and effectiveness of outreach services, also contribute to the disparities in health care.

In summary, there is substantial evidence indicating that ethnic differences in health status do exist and that there also appear to be ethnic differences in perceived overall health, in functional status, and in the availability and quality of health care provided. Moreover, the magnitude of these group differences may be underestimated because of the failure to appreciate the considerable sociocultural and historical heterogeneity among the various racial/ethnic groups. In addition, ethnic minority overrepresentation in lower socioeconomic status levels and the risks associated with low socioeconomic status (e.g., environmental and occupational hazards, possible differences in social and behavioral risks) contribute to the persistence of the disparities in health and functional status and to the disproportionate burden of morbidity and mortality among ethnic minorities and the poor.

FACTORS THAT CONTRIBUTE TO THE HEALTH DISPARITIES

Health outcomes, whether they are chronic conditions such as CVD and NIDDM or associated pain, are clearly the by-product of the complex interaction of many factors. These include individual differences such as biological predispositions, behavioral lifestyle, psychological characteristics, and environmental and psychosocial factors.

In a recent review, Myers and Hwang (2002) proposed an integrative biopsychosocial model of how psychosocial stress and related factors might account for ethnic differences in functional health status. The proposed model makes explicit that sociostructural factors (e.g., race/ethnicity, social class), environmental factors, and biological factors (e.g., genetic vulnerabilities, family medical and psychiatric histories) interact over time to increase the burden of psychosocial adversities experienced over the life course. These adversities are hypothesized to be the primary predictors of risk and include chronic life stresses, major life change events, ethnicity-related stresses, age-related

stresses, and personality characteristics (e.g., anger/hostility, neuroticism, pessimism) that serve as psychological vulnerabilities. The negative effects of these adversities, in turn, are magnified by health-endangering behaviors (e.g., smoking, alcohol and drug abuse, sedentary lifestyle, overeating) (Contrada et al., 2000; Myers, Kagawa-Singer, Kumanyika, Lex, & Markides, 1995; Myers, Lewis, & Parker-Dominguez, 2002).

The model also hypothesizes that these lifetime adversities exert their effects on health through biobehavioral pathways, including the chronic triggering of physiological response mechanisms, constitutional predispositions or vulnerabilities, and overtaxed allostatic load (i.e., wear-and-tear on the system) (Geronimus, 1992; McEwen & Seeman, 1999). In turn, this allostatic load is hypothesized to contribute over time to cumulative vulnerability and ultimately to functional outcomes, including physical and psychological distress and dysfunction (Seeman, Singer, Rowe, Horwitz, & McEwen, 1997).

However, the model also acknowledges that a number of psychosocial and behavioral factors serve as psychosocial assets or advantages that can moderate risk. These include psychological characteristics such as dispositional optimism and perceived control (Eizenman, Nesselroade, Featherman, & Rowe, 1997), healthy lifestyles (Myers et al., 1995), flexible stress appraisal and coping strategies (Wong & Ujimoto, 1998), and the availability and use of adequate social support resources (Seeman, Lusignolo, Albert, & Berkman, 2001). Therefore, it is hypothesized that it is the balance between cumulative adversities and cumulative advantages over the life course that ultimately contributes to differences in functional status and health trajectories (Singer & Ryff, 1999), and it is the lifetime imbalance between cumulative adversities relative to assets that is hypothesized as contributing to the persistence of health disparities. This model has not been formally tested, but it offers a series of testable hypotheses to guide future research on ethnic health disparities.

BEHAVIORAL HEALTH INTERVENTIONS

Behavioral scientists have made a number of significant contributions toward closing the health disparities gap by designing and testing theoretically driven, culturally appropriate interventions for a variety of medical conditions, such as CVD, as well as risk behavior change, such as weight reduction, smoking cessation, and increased participation in cancer and diabetes screening.

CVD Risk Reduction Interventions

Behavioral scientists have made some of their most significant contributions to addressing ethnic issues in behavioral medicine through the design and implementation of interventions to reduce CVD risks in minority populations. Most of this work has been conducted on African Americans and Hispanic Americans, with a few studies targeting Asian Americans and Native Americans. These interventions have focused attention on a variety of risk factors, including blood pressure control, weight loss, smoking, and increased physical exercise. They have also targeted different age groups (e.g., children, adolescents, adults, the elderly), focused on community and clinic-based patient populations, and been introduced in a variety of settings such as schools, churches, hospitals, community health centers, and social service agencies (Magnus, 1991). These studies have used a variety of both quantitative and qualitative methodologies. However, few of these studies have used well-controlled, large-scale clinical trial methodologies to test and validate theoretically driven interventions, and this limits the utility and generalizability of their results.

Nevertheless, there are a number of successful approaches that have been implemented to improve cardiovascular health in minority populations. Many CVD risk reduction programs for African Americans have focused on blood pressure reduction and control, smoking cessation, dietary changes, weight loss, and physical exercise. Many of these programs are faith based, thereby taking advantage of the historical role of the African American church as a credible community institution central to African American community life (Magnus, 1991). Reviews of programs such as Project Joy (Yanek, Becker, Moy, Gittelsohn, & Koffman, 2001), Lighten Up (Oexmann, Ascanio, & Egan, 2001), Wisewoman (Rosamond et al., 2000), and the Heart Smart Program (Johnson et al., 1991), as well as weight reduction programs (Kumanyika, Obarzanek, Stevens, Hebert, & Whelton, 1991), all indicate that cultural sensitivity, in conjunction with a focus on specific risk behaviors that test behavioral principles, yields the best results. However, because many of these community-based interventions are not rigorously evaluated, it is difficult to identify the specific mechanisms and intervention components that account for their overall success.

Similar conclusions are drawn in reviews of CVD risk reduction programs for Hispanic Americans such as the Language for Health program for low-literate Latinos reviewed by Elder and colleagues (2000). The same is true for programs designed specifically for Asians such as the Vietnamese Community Health Promotion Project, the Chinese Community Cardiac Council, and the Heart Health for Southeast Asians reviewed by Chen (1993). A number of similar programs have been designed for Native Americans such as the Checkerboard Cardiovascular Curriculum for American Indian and Hispanic American children, and the Acoma-Cañoncito-Laguna Adolescent Health Program reviewed by LeMaster and Connell (1994). All of these CVD risk reduction programs were conducted in community settings by members of the specific ethnic groups who understand the cultural norms of the groups and who are familiar with the groups' specific needs (e.g., speak the native language, know the cultural customs, use culturally congruent and effective modes of communication and caregiving). The curricula are also designed specifically to address the cultural beliefs, behavioral norms, and language requirements of each group. However, as noted previously, many of these ethnic-specific programs are not rigorously evaluated, nor do they use rigorous research methodologies to test their efficacy, and this tends to reduce confidence in their results. Also, until their results are replicated, it cannot be determined whether their findings will generalize to other ethnic communities.

Interventions to Increase Participation in Cancer and Diabetes Screening

Another focus of attention of behavioral scientists working with ethnic minority populations is increasing participation in early screening programs for diseases such as cancer and diabetes. Both of these diseases are very prevalent and are associated with significant ethnic disparities in disability and mortality. Although early detection and treatment reduces both disability and mortality risk, ethnic minorities are significantly less likely to participate in early screening programs. Therefore, a number of intervention programs have been designed to address this obstacle to effective treatment, especially in diabetes and breast and cervical cancer.

Current evidence indicates that minority women, especially Chinese Americans (Taylor et al., 2002), Vietnamese Americans (McPhee et al., 1997), and Native Hawaiians (Gotay et al., 2000), have some of the lowest rates of Pap smears and breast and cervical cancer testing of all ethnic groups. Deficits in knowledge, lack of familiarity, embarrassment, and the inability to afford services pose barriers to

testing and early identification of problems. As a result, several studies have been designed to address this problem, and many have shown measurable improvement in screening behavior in these populations. For example, Gotay and colleagues (2000) reported the results of a controlled trial of a culturally tailored breast and cervical cancer screening intervention for Native Hawaiian women. They used lay educator-led groups, or *Kokua* groups, to deliver culturally tailored education and support for screening. This group-led intervention produced significant improvements in both knowledge and screening behaviors in the Native Hawaiian women participants, and they in turn shared what they learned in the program with other women in the community, thereby extending the program's impact to the community-at-large.

Similar results were obtained by Taylor and colleagues (2002) in their randomized trial to increase cervical cancer screening in Chinese American women in Seattle, Washington, and Vancouver, British Columbia. They tested the impact of a Chinese-language education-entertainment video, a motivational pamphlet, and a fact sheet on Pap smear testing on women who were randomly assigned to an intensive outreach intervention versus direct mail versus usual care. They found both higher participation and significant increases in Pap smear testing in women in the more intensive intervention.

Similar programs have also been developed for urban and rural African American women (Earp et al., 2002; Paskett et al., 1999), for low-income Latinas (Hiatt et al., 2001; Valdez, Banerjee, Ackerson, & Fernandez, 2002), for Cambodian women (Jackson et al., 2000), for Alaska Native women (Lanier, Kelly, & Holck, 1999), and for Native American women (Hodge, Fredericks, & Rodriguez, 1996). In addition, similar programs to test for prostate cancer in men have been developed (Myers et al., 1999).

In one of the most comprehensive reviews of the effectiveness of interventions to promote mammography among women who underuse these services, Legler and colleagues (2002) found that the most effective interventions used access-enhancing (e.g., aggressive outreach, removal of barriers to access) and individual-directed (e.g., tailored interventions to change high-risk behaviors) strategies, which resulted in an estimated 27% increase in mammography use. The combination of access-enhancing and system-directed interventions—for example, interventions that improve the cultural competence of health care providers, working to establish satellite facilities in ethnic communities that provide ethnic-specific services—also yielded an impressive 20% increase in screening. Legler and colleagues concluded that access-enhancing strategies are an important complement to individual- and system-directed interventions for women with low screening rates.

IMPLICATIONS AND RECOMMENDATIONS FOR BEHAVIORAL MEDICINE

There are a number of ways in which behavioral health care providers can help to reduce the large and persistent racial/ethnic disparities in health. At the systems level, these include expanding and improving current risk reduction interventions, reducing systematic barriers that limit health care use and efficacy, and providing training that increases the cultural sensitivity and competency of service providers. At the individual and group levels, more attention needs to be given to basic research about behavioral and psychosocial factors that enhance risk or serve as buffers or protective factors to illness in racial/ethnic minority populations. Both comparison and ethnic-specific studies are needed. Knowledge about these risk and protective factors, and about possible mediators or moderators of risk and protection, is

integral to the design and execution of effective interventions with minority populations. These include addressing issues of acculturation and acculturative stress, providing indigenous support resources, identifying and sensitively addressing group norms and beliefs that might undermine treatment efficacy, and focusing on cultural strengths such as family support, religiosity, and respect for traditional values and practices.

In addition, behavioral health care systems need to learn the lessons of the more effective public health agencies and work to establish meaningful working relationships with the ethnic communities they intend to serve. This can be accomplished by establishing relationships with community centers and groups, with educational and vocational settings, and with faith-based organizations in the community. In addition, meaningful relationships should be established with community leaders and gatekeepers who have community credibility, who can act as cultural consultants, and who are able to evaluate and make culturally congruent suggestions for modifying the design, content, and implementation of the planned interventions. Special effort should be made to ensure that relationships formed with the community are truly collaborative and long-lasting and are not exploitative.

To increase the efficacy and use of behavioral services, interventions should be delivered by indigenous providers and in the communities where the participants reside, and every effort should be made to remove or reduce barriers to participation (e.g., stigma, language, financial, child care, transportation). These barriers can be removed by using community settings that participants are likely to be familiar and comfortable with as well as by expanding outreach by advertising information and referrals for services of which patients might be unaware. Treatment participation, adherence, and retention may also be improved by subtle but important changes in treatment settings (e.g., decorating the setting with cultural symbols) and by providing linkages that facilitate patient access to other community resources as needed such as vocational, welfare, child care, and other ancillary services.

The efficacy of behavioral health interventions is also likely to be improved by increased understanding of how informal and natural support networks enhance or interfere with professional health service seeking and use. Currently, very little is known about how networks and mechanisms in indigenous cultures identify persons in need of services or about how they facilitate access and use of services. Understanding and using indigenous services and culturally sanctioned pathways of care often improves the feasibility and enhances the effectiveness of more traditional behavioral interventions, for example, using Latina *Consejeras,* African American lay counselors, American Indian talking circles, and Native Hawaiian *Kokua* groups.

In addition, health education and community outreach services not only are integral to increasing knowledge about health care issues but also provide information about how to obtain those services. Once clients come in for services, special effort should be made to provide proper education on the importance of treatment adherence. Obviously, all information must be provided in the clients' primary language, with trained translators being used when native speakers are not available. This is more desirable than using children in the clients' families as translators or cultural brokers. This resource is especially important for recent immigrants and refugees, who may be unfamiliar with the U.S. health care system or who may be mistrustful or too embarrassed to seek services.

At the provider level, increasing the cultural competency of behavioral health care providers should be a top priority. This can be accomplished by having health care providers take cultural competency workshops and seminars and by hiring consultants and cultural competency experts to teach about their communities and suggest feedback on the modification of intervention services. In so doing, special care should be taken to develop effective provider-patient communication, to establish and maintain patient comfort and trust, and to establish provider credibility. Assumptions should not be made that ethnic minority providers are interchangeable such that members of one minority group are culturally competent in working with members of other ethnic minority groups. Cultural competence, like any other skill, must be mastered and not assumed by accident of a person's birth. In addition, attention should be given to understanding possible cultural differences in the expression and reporting of symptoms and illnesses as well as to identifying provider biases that may influence perceptions and possible differences in treatments given to patients from different ethnic backgrounds.

SUMMARY AND CONCLUSIONS

Ethnic minorities, as compared with Caucasian Americans, carry a disproportionate burden of morbidity and mortality, receive poorer quality health care, and have poorer prognoses and treatment outcomes. Although all of the reasons for the racial/ethnic health disparities and the disproportionate burden of disease remain to be identified, the extant literature suggests that biological predispositions, behavioral lifestyle, psychological characteristics, environmental and psychosocial factors, and health care system factors all contribute to these disparities. The chapter authors (Myers & Hwang, 2002) have offered a conceptual framework that provides testable hypotheses about how these disparate factors might operate to produce these health outcomes, and they hypothesize that it is the balance between cumulative adversities and cumulative advantages over the life course that ultimately contributes to differences in functional status and health trajectories. In addition, the literature suggests that the systematic removal of a number of barriers to help seeking (e.g., financial, insurance, language, stigma against mental health services) and a greater understanding and integration of indigenous and informal but culturally congruent services may facilitate access and use of professional services and reduce delayed help seeking and poor treatment adherence. Moreover, health care providers can also reduce ethnic disparities in health by improving and expanding on culturally sensitive interventions, increasing health education and outreach efforts, and examining their own biases when providing services to culturally different clients.

REFERENCES

American Cancer Society. (2002). *Cancer facts and figures* (surveillance research report). Atlanta, GA: Author.

Bates, M. S. (1987). Ethnicity and pain: A biocultural model. *Social Science and Medicine, 24*(1), 47–50.

Bates, M. S., & Edwards, W. T. (1992). Ethnic variations in the chronic pain experience. *Ethnicity & Disease, 2*(1), 63–83.

Carter, J. S., Pugh, J. A., & Monterrosa, A. (1996). Non-insulin dependent diabetes mellitus in minorities in the United States. *Annals of Internal Medicine, 125,* 221–232.

Chen, M. S. (1993). Cardiovascular health among Asian Americans/Pacific Islanders: An examination of health status and intervention approaches. *American Journal of Health Promotion, 7,* 199–207.

Contrada, R. J., Ashmore, R. D., Gary, M. L., Coups, E., Egeth, J. D., Sewell, A., Ewell, K., Goyal, T. M., & Chasse, V. (2000). Ethnicity-related sources of stress and their effects on well-being. *Current Directions in Psychological Science, 9*(4), 136–139.

Cooper, R., Cutler, J., Desvigne-Nickens, P., Fortmann, S. P., Friedman, L., Havlik, R., Hogelin, G., Marler, J., McGovern, P., Morosco, G., Mosca, L., Pearson, T., Stamler, J., Stryer, D., & Thom, T. (2000). Trends and disparities in coronary heart disease, stroke, and other cardiovascular diseases in the United States: Findings of the National Conference on Cardiovascular Disease Prevention. *Circulation, 102,* 3137–3147.

Earp, J. A., Eng, E., O'Malley, M. S., Altpeter, M., Rauscher, G., Mayne, L., Mathews, H. F., Lynch, K. S., & Qaqish, B. (2002). Increasing use of mammography among older, rural African American women: Results from a community trial. *American Journal of Public Health, 92,* 646–654.

Edwards, R. R., Doleys, D. M., Fillingim, R. B., & Lowery, D. (2001). Ethnic differences in pain tolerance: Clinical implications in a chronic pain population. *Psychosomatic Medicine, 63,* 316–323.

Eizenman, D. R., Nesselroade, J. R., Featherman, D. L., & Rowe, J. W. (1997). Intraindividual variability in perceived control in an older sample: The MacArthur successful aging studies. *Psychology & Aging, 12,* 489–502.

Elder, J. P., Candelaria, J. I., Woodruff, S. I., Criqui, M. H., Talavera, G. A., & Ruff, J. W. (2000). Results of language for health: Cardiovascular disease nutrition education for Latino English-as-a-second-language students. *Health Education & Behavior, 27*(1), 50–63.

Faucett, J., Gordon, N., & Levine, J. (1994). Differences in postoperative pain severity among four ethnic groups. *Journal of Pain & Symptom Management, 9,* 383–389.

Geronimus, A. T. (1992). The weathering hypothesis and the health of African-American women and infants: Evidence and speculations. *Ethnicity & Disease, 2,* 207–221.

Gotay, C. C., Banner, R. O., Matsunaga, D. S., Hedlund, N., Enos, R., Issell, B. F., & DeCambra, H. (2000). Impact of a culturally appropriate intervention on breast and cervical screening among Native Hawaiian women. *Preventive Medicine, 31,* 529–537.

Hiatt, R. A., Pasick, R. J., Stewart, S., Bloom, J., Davis, P., Gardiner, P., Johnston, M., Luce, J., Schorr, K., Brunner, W., & Stroud, F. (2001). Community-based cancer screening for underserved women: Design and baseline findings from the Breast and Cervical Cancer Intervention Study. *Preventive Medicine, 33,* 190–203.

Hodge, F. S., Fredericks, L., & Rodriguez, B. (1996). American Indian women's talking circle: A cervical cancer screening and prevention project. *Cancer, 78,* 1592–1597.

Hughes, M., & Thomas, M. E. (1998). The continuing significance of race revisited: A study of race, class, and quality of life in America, 1972–1996. *American Sociological Review, 63,* 785–795.

Jackson, J. C., Taylor, V. M., Chitnarong, K., Mahloch, J., Fisher, M., Sam, R., & Seng, R. (2000). Development of a cervical cancer control intervention program for Cambodian American women. *Journal of Community Health, 25,* 359–375.

Johnson, C. C., Nicklas, T. A., Arbeit, M. L., Harsha, D. W., Mott, D. S., Hunter, S. M., Wattigney, W., & Berenson, G. S. (1991). Cardiovascular intervention for high-risk families: The Heart Smart Program. *Southern Medical Journal, 84,* 1305–1312.

Keppel, K. G., Pearcy, J. N., & Wagener, D. K. (2002, January). Trends in racial- and ethnic-specific rates for the health status indicators: United States, 1990–1998. *Statistical Notes,* No. 23. (Atlanta, GA: Centers for Disease Control and Prevention)

Kington, R. S., & Nickens, H. W. (2000). Racial and ethnic differences in health: Recent trends, current patterns, future directions. In N. Smelser, W. Wilson, & F. Mitchell (Eds.), *America becoming: Racial trends and their consequences* (Vol. 2, pp. 253–310). Washington, DC: National Academy Press.

Kumanyika, S. K., Obarzanek, E., Stevens, V. J., Hebert, P. R., & Whelton, P. K. (1991). Weight-loss experience of black and white participants in NHLBI-sponsored clinical trials. *American Journal of Clinical Nutrition, 53*(Suppl.), S1631–S1638.

Lanier, A. P., Kelly, J. J., & Holck, P. (1999). Pap prevalence and cervical cancer prevention among Alaska Native women. *Health Care Women International, 20,* 471–486.

Legler, J., Meissner, H. I., Coyne, C., Breen, N., Chollette, V., & Rimer, B. K. (2002). The effectiveness of interventions to promote mammography among women with historically lower rates of screening. *Cancer Epidemiology, Biomarkers, & Prevention, 11*(1), 59–71.

LeMaster, P. L., & Connell, C. M. (1994). Health education interventions among Native Americans: A review and analysis. *Health Education Quarterly, 21,* 521–538.

Magnus, M. H. (1991). Cardiovascular health among African-Americans: A review of the health status, risk reduction, and intervention strategies. *American Journal of Health Promotion, 5,* 282–290.

Matsuoka, J. K., Breaux, C., & Ryujin, D. H. (1997). National utilization of mental health services by Asian Americans/Pacific Islanders. *Journal of Community Psychology, 25,* 141–145.

McCracken, L. M., Matthews, A. K., Tang, T. S., & Cuba, S. L. (2001). A comparison of blacks and whites seeking treatment for chronic pain. *Clinical Journal of Pain, 17,* 249–255.

McEwen, B. S., & Seeman, T. (1999). Protective and damaging effects of mediators of stress: Elaborating and testing the concepts of allostasis and allostatic load. In N. E. Adler, M. Marmot, B. S. McEwen, & J. Stewart (Eds.), *Socioeconomic status and health in industrial nations: Social psychological, and biological pathways* (pp. 30–47). New York: New York Academy of Sciences.

McPhee, S. J., Stewart, S., Brock, K. C., Bird, J. A., Jenkins, C. N. H., & Pham, G. Q. (1997). Factors associated with breast and cervical cancer screening practices among Vietnamese American women. *Cancer Detection & Prevention, 21,* 510–521.

Miller, B. A., Kolonel, L. N., Bernstein, L., Young, J. L., Jr., Swanson, G. M., West, D., Key, C. R., Liff, J. M., Glover, C. S., & Alexander, G. A. (Eds.). (1996). *Racial/Ethnic patterns of cancer in the United States 1988–1992* (NIH Pub. No. 96-4104). Bethesda, MD: National Institutes of Health.

Myers, H. F., & Hwang, W. C. (2002, March). *Cumulative psychosocial risks and resilience: A conceptual perspective on ethnic health disparities in late life.* Paper presented at the National Research Council panel on "Ethnic Disparities in Aging Health," Washington, DC.

Myers, H. F., Kagawa-Singer, M., Kumanyika, S. K., Lex, B. W., & Markides, K. S. (1995). Panel III: Behavioral risk factors related to chronic diseases in ethnic populations. *Health Psychology, 14,* 613–621.

Myers, H. F., Lewis, T. T., & Parker-Dominguez, T. (2002). Stress, coping, and minority health: Biopsychosocial perspective on ethnic health disparities. In G. Bernal, J. Trimble, K. Burlew, & F. Leong (Eds.), *Handbook of racial and ethnic minority psychology* (pp. 377–400). Thousand Oaks, CA: Sage.

Myers, R. E., Chodak, G. W., Wolf, T. A., Burgh, D. Y., McGrory, G. T., Marcus, S., Diehl, J. A., & Williams, M. (1999). Adherence by African American men to prostate cancer education and early detection. *Cancer, 86,* 88–104.

National Center for Health Statistics. (2000). *Health, United States, 2000: Adolescent health chartbook.* Hyattsville, MD: Author.

National Heart, Lung, and Blood Institute. (1996). *Chartbook of cardiovascular, lung, and blood diseases: Morbidity and mortality.* Washington, DC: National Institutes of Health.

Oexmann, M. J., Ascanio, R., & Egan, B. M. (2001). Efficacy of a church-based intervention on cardiovascular risk reduction. *Ethnicity Disease, 11,* 817–822.

Padgett, D. K., Patrick, C., Burns, B. J., & Schlesinger, H. J. (1994). Women and outpatient mental health services: Use by black, Hispanic, and white women in a national insured population. *Journal of Mental Health Administration, 21,* 347–360.

Paskett, E. D., Tatum, C. M., D'Agostino, R., Rushing, J., Velez, R., Michielutte, R., & Dignan, M. (1999). Community-based interventions to improve breast and cervical cancer screening: Results of the Forsyth County Cancer Screening (FoCas) Project. *Cancer Epidemiology, Biomarkers, & Prevention, 8,* 453–459.

Rosamond, W. D., Ammerman, A. S., Holliday, J. L., Tawney, K. W., Hunt, K. J., Keyserling, T. C., Will, J. C., & Mokdad, A. H. (2000). Cardiovascular disease risk factor intervention in low-income women: The North Carolina WISEWOMAN project. *Preventive Medicine, 31,* 370–379.

Seeman, T. E., Lusignolo, T. M., Albert, M., & Berkman, L. (2001). Social relationships, social support, and patterns of cognitive aging in healthy, high functioning older adults: MacArthur studies of successful aging. *Health Psychology, 20,* 243–255.

Seeman, T. E., Singer, B. H., Rowe, J. W., Horwitz, R. I., & McEwen, B. S. (1997). Price of adaptation-allostatic load and its health consequences: MacArthur studies of successful aging. *Archives of Internal Medicine, 157,* 2259–2268.

Singer, B., & Ryff, C. D. (1999). Hierarchies of life histories and associated health risks. In N. E. Adler, M. Marmot, B. S. McEwen, & J. Stewart (Eds.), *Socioeconomic status and health in industrial nations: Social, psychological, and biological pathways* (pp. 96–115). New York: New York Academy of Sciences.

Smedley, B. D., Stith, A. Y., & Nelson, A. R. (2002). *Unequal treatment: Confronting racial and ethnic disparities in health care.* Washington, DC: National Academy Press.

Snowden, L. R. (1998). Racial differences in informal help seeking for mental health problems. *Journal of Community Psychology, 26,* 429–438.

Snowden, L. R., & Cheung, F. K. (1990). Use of inpatient mental health services by members of ethnic minority groups. *American Psychologist, 45,* 347–355.

Takeuchi, D. T., Leaf, P. J., & Kuo, H-S. (1988). Ethnic differences in the perception of barriers to help-seeking. *Social Psychiatry & Psychiatric Epidemiology, 23,* 273–280.

Taylor, V. M., Hislop, T. G., Jackson, J. C., Tu, S. P., Yasui, Y., Schwartz, S. M., The, C., Kuniyuki, A., Acorda, E., Marchand, A., & Thompson, B. (2002). A randomized controlled trial of interventions to promote cervical cancer screening among Chinese women in North America. *Journal of the National Cancer Institute, 94,* 670–677.

Thomas, K. C., & Snowden, L. R. (2001). Minority response to health insurance coverage for mental health services. *Journal of Mental Health Policy and Economics, 4*(1), 35–41.

U.S. Department of Health and Human Services. (1999). *Mental health: A report of the surgeon general.* Rockville, MD: U.S. Department of Health and Human Services, Substance Abuse and Mental Health Services Administration, Center for Mental Health Services.

Valdez, A., Banerjee, K., Ackerson , L., & Fernandez, M. (2002). A multimedia breast cancer education intervention for low-income Latinas. *Journal of Community Health, 27,* 33–51.

Williams, D. R. (2000). Racial variations in adult health status: Patterns, paradoxes, and prospects. In N. Smelser, W. Wilson, & F. Mitchell (Eds.), *America becoming: Racial trends and their consequences* (Vol. 2, pp. 371–410). Washington, DC: National Academy Press.

Williams, D., & Harris-Reid, M. (1999). Race and mental health: Emerging patterns and promising approaches. In A. Horwitz & T. Scheid (Eds.), *A handbook for the study of mental health: Social contexts, theories, and systems* (pp. 295–314). New York: Cambridge University Press.

Wong, P. T. P., & Ujimoto, V. K. (1998). The elderly: The stress, coping, and mental health. In L. C. Lee & N. W. S. Zane (Eds.), *Handbook of Asian American psychology* (pp. 165–209). Thousand Oaks, CA: Sage.

Yanek, L. R., Becker, D. M., Moy, T. F., Gittelsohn, J., & Koffman, D. M. (2001). Project Joy: Faith based cardiovascular health promotion for African American women. *Public Health Report, 116*(Suppl. 1), 68–81.

Ying, Y., & Hu, L. (1994). Public outpatient mental health services: Use and outcome among Asian Americans. *American Journal of Orthopsychiatry, 64,* 448–455.

Zhang, A. Y., Snowden, L. R., & Sue, S. (1998). Differences between Asian and white Americans' help seeking and utilization patterns in the Los Angeles area. *Journal of Community Psychology, 26,* 317–326.

CHAPTER 24

Women's Health Issues

Csilla T. Csoboth

In the developed world, women today have a longer life expectancy and lower mortality rates than do men at all ages, but epidemiological studies show that women report more chronic disease and disability (Khoury & Weisman, 2002). During the past two decades, the science of behavioral medicine has recognized the importance of women's health in research and in patient care. Knowledge about the biological, psychological, and social factors influencing women's health has grown considerably, and efforts to change the thinking of the scientific community and the general public have led to a better understanding of women's health. The enhancement of research in this field resulted in more sensitive health care and the construction of specific preventive interventions that serve to improve the health status of women worldwide.

LIFE COURSE PERSPECTIVES

Although it is impossible to examine the issue of women's health in full detail in this chapter, an overview of special issues to be considered during everyday clinical work with women is provided. Specifically, women's physical and mental health is influenced substantially by physiological and social role changes during the life stages. Viewed from this life course perspective, gender influences life experience, psychological development and functioning, and the nature of psychopathology (Zanardi, 1990) and so can result in different psychological developmental patterns. Three important stages are discussed in this section: adolescence, pregnancy and childbirth, and menopause.

Adolescence

The period of adolescence is well known for the biological, social, and cognitive changes in both genders. The transition into adulthood is usually a positive experience for young women, but in some the biological and psychosocial changes increase the risk for certain psychopathologies, for example, the development of depression or eating disorders. Young women are at great risk for harmful health behaviors that influence their psychological and physical well-being, including smoking, binge drinking, illicit drug use, negative consequences of sexual behavior, and victimization. Gender differences in psychosocial factors of health-damaging behavior are already seen during adolescence; for example, alcohol abuse has a stronger connection to depression in girls than in boys (Clark et al., 1997).

There is evidence that emotional functional disorders and symptoms are significantly more frequent among young females than among young males. In one study, female university students were more likely to see their futures as hopeless and reported frequent use of emotionally oriented coping strategies, namely eating, drinking, and/or taking drugs in difficult life situations. Likewise, a close relationship between different self-destructive behavioral forms was found among women. Smoking was closely correlated with other harmful health behaviors, namely alcohol consumption, sedentary lifestyle, consumption of high-cholesterol foods, and little sleep. Women who exercised regularly had a reduced risk for suicide attempts and using emotional coping strategies and also had more goals in life. In contrast, the correlation between self-destructive behavior and psychological symptoms was not significant among young men (Kopp & Skrabski, 1995).

Adolescence is one of the most vulnerable periods of development. It is also a phase of constant change, and young women are more sensitive to conflict or change in the family environment. Studies have shown that the timing of pubertal development is influenced by family conflict and family structure. Maturation of young women has been found to be closely correlated with the home atmosphere, with earlier maturation being predicted by conflict and lack of approval in families with both parents living at home (Graber & Brooks-Gunn, 1998). Earlier onset of menarche has been reported in young women who live in households where there is parental conflict or where the mother is the only parent (Moffitt, Caspi, Belsky, & Silva, 1992).

Protective health factors of adolescence include tight social network, high social support, development of positive coping strategies, resiliency, and hardiness. The prevention of the harm caused by psychological distress, which might result in psychiatric disorders, is an important task of mental health professionals and can be achieved by developing or enhancing health protective factors at an early age. Young women need to be taught how to cope with different stressors, for example, functioning in multiple roles and learning to resist peer or social pressure inducing them to participate in harmful health habits that they most likely will experience later on in life.

Pregnancy and Childbirth

The transition to parenting for women and men is usually a normal biological task, but women frequently spend a great deal of time involved in caregiving and so experience many biological and psychosocial changes during this period of time. A woman's experience of pregnancy and childbirth will most likely affect her role as a mother, her perceptions of the child and herself, and her relationship with her partner (Shearer, 1983). A correlation between the discrepancy of a person's actual self-concept and his or her ideal self-concept and the amount of post-birth distress has been reported (Alexander & Higgins, 1993). For example, parents with a large discrepancy between how they saw themselves and what they perceived as an ideal self suffered increases in post-birth distress relative to those parents with a small discrepancy between actual and ideal (Alexander & Higgins, 1993).

Studies have shown that more negative psychosocial outcomes appear to be associated with cesarean section births than with vaginal deliveries (DiMatteo et al., 1996). Cesarean section not only decreases the positive experience of giving birth to a child but also may have certain negative psychological outcomes. The postponed encounter between mother and child may be a consequence of breast-feeding or bonding and may result in less positive maternal reactions to the newborn (Cranley, Hedahl, & Pegg, 1983). Women who experience cesarean section or other interventions need to be given additional psychological support to cope with difficulties arising after childbirth.

Substance use during pregnancy presents unique problems for women. Substance-dependent women experience feelings of low self-esteem, lower expectations for themselves, and higher levels of anxiety than do men (Jarvis & Schnoll, 1995). Pregnant, substance-abusing women commonly present with poly-substance abuse (Fischer, Bitschnau, Peternell, Eder, & Topitz, 1999). They experience specific health problems, such as sexually transmitted diseases, malnutrition, and vitamin and mineral deficiencies, but fail to acquire treatment for their problems, and many do not present to medical facilities for prenatal care. Psychiatric comorbidities, mainly depression and chronic anxiety, and social problems, chaotic familial backgrounds, and abusive relationships are frequently reported by drug-abusing women. Women who are convinced to attend prenatal care in multidisciplinary collaboration with psychiatrists, gynecologists, obstetricians, social workers, and psychotherapists can reduce substance intake and improve the health situation of the fetus (Boer, Smit, VanHuis, & Hogerzeil, 1994).

Menopause

In the developed countries, menopause generally is viewed by women as a negative phase of life when symptoms and loss of well-being and function are bound to occur (Hvas, 2001). Menopause involves biological and psychological changes and can be an important developmental phase that is influenced by specific sociocultural factors (Dennerstein, 1996). Evidence shows that women at age 50 years are generally in good health and experience emotional stability as well as positive personal development (Fodor & Franks, 1990). Studies during past decades have shown that the duration, severity, and impact of symptoms vary by individuals as well as by populations. Preconceived attitudes concerning menopause

are influenced by personality, coping styles, mood history, and exposure to a greater or lesser degree of life stressors (Polit & LaRocco, 1980; Greene & Cooke, 1980). Positive or negative expectations of menopause are correlated with the number of symptoms experienced; negative expectations were associated with more symptoms, whereas positive expectations were associated with fewer symptoms (Matthews, 1992). Perception of menopause is ethnically and culturally related; for example, Japanese women are far less likely to experience hot flashes than are women living in the Western world (Lock, 1993). Research has also shown that the menopausal experience may be influenced, either directly or indirectly, by socioeconomic status. Lower educational level, lack of employment outside of the home, and lower socioeconomic status are associated with increased severity or longer duration of menopausal symptoms (Avis, Crawford, & McKinlay, 1997). Occurrence of mood and sleep disturbances and somatic symptoms has also been found to be predicted by social class and employment status.

Up to 100 symptoms have been attributed to menopause; depression, anxiety, joint pain, headaches, insomnia, loss of sexual interest, hot flashes, and vaginal atrophy have been perceived as the "menopausal syndrome" (Derry, Gallant, & Woods, 1997). Research has suggested that the prevalence of depression in women is substantially higher during menopause than during other phases of life, possibly due to the changing hormone levels (Kaufert, Gilbert, & Tate, 1992). Estrogen is capable of modulating serotonergic function in the central nervous system, and this interaction may explain the increased vulnerability to affective disorders in women during menopause (Joffe & Cohen, 1998). Population-based studies, however, have failed to find a co-occurrence of symptoms. Most symptoms, other than hot flashes, night sweats, vaginal atrophy, and insomnia, do not increase in frequency during the menopausal years (Ballinger, 1990). Recent studies have shown that the reductions in estrogen during menopause do not influence mental well-being (Slaven & Lee, 1998); therefore, the occurrence of depression cannot be attributed to hormonal deficiency. Epidemiological studies have shown mainly that psychosocial stressors were more likely to predict depression. Such stressors may include existent health problems, responsibility for the care of relatives, negative attitudes toward aging, and history of previous depression (Woods & Mitchell, 1996).

In summary, menopause can be regarded as a natural process with symptoms that may vary individually. Unfortunately, it is often viewed as a medical problem, labeling experiences as symptoms and illness instead of underlining the positive aspects such as the possibility for inner growth and the strengthening of inner wisdom and power (Hvas, 2001). Midlife distress occurring at the time of menopause can be attributed to personal, familial, or social events that occur more frequently around the time of menopause. Counseling women is important. Counseling must not only address medical risks and physical symptoms but also help women to overcome life event stressors, through which women's inner resources are strengthened, so as to avoid medicalization and disempowerment (Hollnagel & Malterud, 1995).

PSYCHOSOCIAL FACTORS INFLUENCING WOMEN'S HEALTH

Stress and Coping

Stress is an everyday phenomenon that influences the lives of women and men and affects each person differently. Learning to cope adaptively with everyday stressors is important for mental health in both genders. The amount of stress that one can withstand, and the length of time that a person experiences a stressor, is an important factor to take into consideration

with stress-related disorders. Personality, modeling, learned coping strategies, and severity of the stressor have an interlocking effect on health.

Research has shown that, in general, women report higher distress and lower quality of life than do men (Gamma & Angst, 2001). Women may also experience different types of stressors than do men. Women are more vulnerable to specific life events causing distress such as physical and sexual abuse, sexual discrimination, distorted body image, and living with multiple roles in life. Men, on the other hand, experience stress from high-responsibility jobs or hazardous occupations (O'Leary & Helgeson, 1997). Historically, women have suffered more from relationship stressors and have been more vulnerable to partnership or marital dissatisfaction. Parent role stress and the quality of the parent-child relationship seem to cause greater distress for women than for men, probably because women generally are more socialized to feel responsible for their families (Simon, 1992).

In women, marital stress has been shown to have a significant effect on cardiovascular health. Women admitted to the hospital with an acute coronary event and who reported marital stress at baseline had a worse prognosis than did those who did not report marital stress. Moreover, women with severe marital stress had a threefold greater risk for a new coronary event than did those not experiencing marital stress (Orth-Gomér et al., 2000). In contrast to men, work stress did not have an effect on the recurrence of a new coronary episode among women. The experience of stress and the impact it has on health are shown to be gender specific; therefore, interventions designed to train women to cope with stress must take these differences into account.

Ways of coping with specific stressors are divided into problem-focused coping (i.e., changing the actual stressful situation) and emotion-focused coping (i.e., attempting to palliate the reaction to stress) (Lazarus & Folkman, 1984).

Adaptive or maladaptive coping mechanisms are incorporated into a person's lifestyle during youth through learning and modeling from parents and peers. Strategies for coping with stressful life events depend on personal character, relationship characteristics, and the nature of the stressor. Coping style, whether positive or negative, influences health as well as the outcome of an illness. Women have been found to use more expressive ways of coping (e.g., expressing feelings, turning to their social support network), whereas men use more rational ways of coping with stress (e.g., exercising). Coping with stress through the use of social support seems to be more important in women (Thoits, 1991). Ruminating over stressful events also seems to be a more common coping mechanism in women than in men; men usually distract themselves from the stressful situation (Nolen-Hoeksema, 1987). One can conclude that there are some specific differences in coping strategies between the genders and that prevention of mental disorders, mainly depression, can be targeted by developing more adaptive ways of coping among women.

Social Support

Both the quality and quantity of a person's social network define perceived social support. Two types of social support measures are usually distinguished, namely *structural*, characterized by the quantity and structure of the social network, and *functional*, reflecting emotional, instrumental, and informational support and social companionship (Wills, 1998). Social support has been recognized as a major protective factor for physical illness (e.g., cardiovascular disease) as well as for mental disorders.

Women are extremely vulnerable to psychological distress if their social support system is inadequate. Perceived high emotional support is directly associated with better physical and psychological health, and it usually decreases health-damaging effects of negative life events and chronic strain (Kessler & McLeod, 1985). Women more frequently perceive their spouses as less supportive, and this can lead to strain in relationships. A Swedish prospective study showed that men usually perceive their spouses as the primary providers of social support, whereas women typically name close female relatives as the persons giving them support (Karasek, Baker, Marxer, Ahlbom, & Theorell, 1981). Given women's critical need for emotional functional support, the development of community social support systems for women could lead to the prevention of psychological distress.

Multiple Roles

During the past decade, numerous studies have shown the positive effects of multiple-role involvements on women's physical and mental well-being (Barnett & Baruch, 1985). The more roles a woman fulfills, the better physical health, higher life satisfaction, and less depression she may experience. Multiple roles are beneficial, but the quality and combination of roles can sometimes have a negative influence on a woman's life. Many roles drain energy, and this may result in conflict and have a negative influence on well-being (Barnett, 1993). Family roles are regarded as women's core roles, and success in the roles of wife and mother has been considered fundamental for psychological well-being and thought to be less stressful than the worker role. Wife roles can often be in conflict with mother roles, and this can lead to distress. In today's modern society, declaring the distribution of roles between both genders, but not depriving either from its natural or assumed roles, may actually assist women and men in participating in both family and work lives without experiencing a great degree of role stress.

Studies show that women sometimes use psychoactive substances to ameliorate anxieties, depression, and feelings of worthlessness resulting from gender role expectations that are difficult for them to meet (Bollerud, 1990; Root, 1989). Results of several studies have found inconsistencies regarding family roles. Some studies have found that there are advantages for married women (e.g., Verbrugge, 1982), whereas others have shown that life satisfaction and well-being are just as high or higher among single and employed women (Nadelson & Notman, 1981). Multiple roles clearly improve self-esteem, satisfaction with life, and well-being if the roles complement each other, that is, if the roles result in the feeling of being successful both personally and financially.

Two hypotheses have been constructed to explain the ways in which social mechanisms influence health differently between the genders. The *differential exposure hypothesis* posits that women have higher levels of demands and obligations in their social roles and have fewer coping resources to help them solve arising problems and that this leads them to complain more about ill health than do men. The *differential vulnerability hypothesis* posits that women have stronger reactions to life events or stressors that men also experience and that this increased reactivity and low levels of coping resources lead to ill health (Walters, McDonough, & Strohschein, 2002). Although the mechanisms of gender differences in ill health remain unresolved to this day, it is obvious that social support (from both family and society) and the development of adaptive coping mechanisms should help women to overcome distress arising from multiple roles and that this, in turn, should lead to better health status of women.

Socioeconomic Factors

It is well known that socioeconomic status significantly influences physical and mental health. Women around the world live in greater poverty and have lower education and employment status than do men; therefore, the impact of socioeconomic factors is greater among women. Socioeconomic inequalities result in disparities in health and determinant factors of income inequality; for example, an increase in the number of female-headed households and an increase in the number of women in the job market can intensify this effect on women's health. Psychosocial health determinants, such as job characteristics, job strain, low level of control at work, high demands, limited personal resources, frustration, and discrimination in the workplace (Moss, 2002), all can lead to distress, and this can be deleterious to health when experienced chronically.

Women commonly work in jobs that involve high psychological demands and offer low levels of control (Karasek & Theorell, 1990), and this low level of control can lead to cardiovascular disease, sickness, absence from work, and psychological distress (Walters et al., 2002). Nevertheless, women working in paid jobs generally have better health status than do full-time homemakers (Khlat, Sermet, & Le Pape, 2000). Women working full-time outside their homes are usually responsible for domestic labor, sometimes leading to role strain. In studying the influence of family, work, and material circumstances on health, it was found that ill health among women was subject not only to employment status, occupational class, and housing tenure (as found among men) but also to marital and parental status (Arber, 1991). Recently, a study found that the most important predictors of good health among women were being in the highest income category, working full-time, caring for a family, and having high levels of social support (Denton & Walters, 1999).

Health is determined by the coexistence of biologic, genetic, psychological, and social factors. Social relations, such as discrimination, exclusion, and exploitation, have an indirect influence on the health of women, especially those who are part of a minority ethnic group, through economic and social well-being. In studying ethnic groups, it was found that health differences between the genders were accentuated, but after controlling for educational level and employment status, members of minority groups were in equally good health as those not belonging to ethnic minority groups (Cooper, 2002).

Self-ratings of health and diseases are reliable predictors of morbidity. A recent study showed that personal income inequalities were connected with differences in self-rated morbidity in women but not as significantly as in men. Men were more susceptible to income inequality or to the loss of hierarchy status, which coexists with lower socioeconomic status. Nevertheless, depression was a more important predictor of self-rated morbidity than were socioeconomic deprivation factors. This indicates that socioeconomic deprivation predicts morbidity much more significantly if it is associated with depressive symptomatology (Kopp, Skrabski, & Szedmák, 2000).

It can be concluded that socioeconomic factors play an important role in women's health but that women are at greater risk for these effects if they are suffering from depressive symptoms. Prevention programs should include specific target groups, generally minority women and women who are at risk for, or suffering from, depressive symptoms.

WOMEN'S MENTAL HEALTH

There is a growing awareness of the increasing burden of disability associated with mental illness (U.S. Department of Health and Human Services, 1999), resulting in decreased functioning and well-being. Depressive symptoms and anxiety disorder are among the most common health problems. Depression and anxiety are important women's health issues because these disorders occur nearly twice as often in women than in men. The early onset, chronic, and recurrent nature of depression and anxiety impede the lives of women, who are unable to function as whole humans due to their disorders. Secondary and tertiary prevention of debilitating disability in life is crucial so as to allow women to lead fulfilling lives.

Depression

Depression is the second most common disease worldwide, with a lifetime prevalence of 15% and perhaps as high as 25% for women (Kaplan & Sadock, 1998). Women experience longer episodes of depression, symptoms can be more severe, and recurrence is more common. The occurrence of depression during childhood in both genders is similar, but the onset of depression is found to be earlier in women, and depression is already found twice as frequently in adolescent girls as in adolescent boys (Angold & Worthman, 1993). The gap in the prevalence of depression starts to widen during adolescence; young women in their teens already experience depressive symptoms more frequently than do their male counterparts. Depressive symptoms are more common among women with low socioeconomic status, women living in poverty, and women experiencing role strain, marital discord, and physical or psychological abuse. Research studying the relationship between health-damaging behavior and depression in women has shown that binge drinking is closely correlated with depression (Dunne, Galatopoulos, & Schipperheijn, 1993) and that daily or weekend drinking is associated with low self-esteem (Turnbull & Gomberg, 1988).

Women are often vulnerable to depressive symptoms at certain periods of the reproductive cycle. Depressive symptoms can be experienced by women before the onset of menstruation, after giving birth to a child, or at the time of menopause. The changes in hormonal levels alone do not explain the true cause of the depressive symptoms. Most likely, psychosocial and biological factors both contribute to the whole clinical picture.

Premenstrual syndrome (PMS) is a condition that presents during the luteal phase of the menstrual cycle, a few days before menstruation. Investigations of PMS have not been able to find conclusive evidence of hormonal differences (i.e., in estrogen and progesterone) or changes in the neurotransmitter system's response to gonadal hormones. Cultural and psychological factors resulting in PMS must also be taken in account when studying the etiology of the disorder. According to cognitive theory, distress can be induced by the physical symptoms themselves and by the meaning given to these symptoms by women. Many times, the symptoms mean a lack of control of a woman's own body and may result in depression and anxiety. A controlled trial of cognitive-behavioral therapy (Blake, Salkovskis, Gath, Day, & Garrod, 1998) for premenstrual syndrome was associated with significant improvement of symptoms, depression, and associated impairments.

Postpartum blues and postpartum depression are also part of the mood disturbances spectrum connected with hormonal changes. Postpartum blues usually presents 3 to 5 days after delivery and lasts for several days or a few weeks. Symptoms include dysphoria, crying spells, clinging dependence, irritability, and emotional lability and occur in 20% to 40% of women who give birth. Postpartum blues can be explained by either sudden hormonal withdrawal occurring after delivery or by the activation of oxytocin, which is needed for the development of mother-infant attachment (Miller, 2002). When mothers are supported by the environment and experience low levels of stress after childbirth, the neurophysiological changes promote attachment, but depression can result when mothers experience low levels of support and high levels of stress (Miller & Rukstailis, 1999). Postpartum blues can lead to postpartum depression, which occurs in 10% to 20% of women in the United States within 6 months of delivery. A history of major depression, a history of PMS, the presence of a psychosocial stressor, and low levels of social support all can act as predisposing factors for postpartum depression (O'Hara, Schlechte, Lewis, & Varner, 1991).

The prevention and treatment of depression warrants the charting of biological and psychosocial factors for women. Women are predisposed to unique stressors that can develop into depression, and these factors need to be addressed by screening for individuals at risk. School, community, and workplace mental health programs designed specifically to prevent depressive symptoms and enhance protective factors can reduce suffering from major depression and improve the quality of life of women predisposed to this debilitating disorder.

Anxiety Disorders

The prevalence of anxiety disorders is nearly three times higher in women than in men. Anxiety disorders often are undiagnosed for years, and women suffer in all functions of their lives. The symptoms of anxiety affect women's families and close relationships, resulting in overdependency, conflict in relationships, substance abuse, and/or domestic violence. Women with anxiety disorders are sometimes blamed for their symptoms and regarded as not being strong enough to control the symptoms, and the reduction of self-esteem worsens the symptoms of anxiety.

Sensitivity to anxiety is thought to influence perception of health. Women with high anxiety sensitivity reported more severe menstrual symptoms, more preoccupation with body sensations, and more negative attitudes toward illness (Sigmon, Dorhofer, Rohan, & Boulard, 2000). These women, after performing a rumination task, also showed greater skin conductance response magnitude than did those with low anxiety sensitivity. Women suffering from panic disorder also reported more severe menstrual symptoms, higher anxiety sensitivity, state and trait anxiety, fear of body sensations, and illness-related concerns than did controls (Sigmon et al., 2000).

Women suffering from anxiety disorders are at a greater risk for alcohol or other substance abuse. Agoraphobia and social phobia have been found to frequently precede alcohol use disorders (Vogeltanz & Wilsnack, 1997), implying that alcohol or other substances are used as self-medication to alleviate the symptoms of anxiety and to restore function to a certain extent. Consequences of anxiety disorders in women highlight the importance of identifying women suffering from anxiety early and offering them effective treatment to prevent further functional and health impairment.

SPECIAL ISSUES

Dysmenorrhea

Dysmenorrhea, or painful menstruation, is the most common gynecologic disorder among young women, with a prevalence of 60% to 93% (Banikarim, Chacko, & Kelder, 2000). A variety of symptoms, such as vomiting, fatigue, back pain, and headaches, occur during the experience of pain. Dysmenorrhea shows a strong correlation with premenstrual symptoms but is not associated with emotional distress in adolescents (Freeman, Rickels, & Sondheimer, 1993). Studies measuring pain threshold have shown that women with dysmenorrhea show enhanced pain perception (e.g., Granot, 2001).

Research studying the psychosocial background factors of dysmenorrhea has found that dysmenorrheic women report less social support, characterized by inadequate and geographically distant relationships (Whittle, Slade, & Ronalds, 1987). A disrupted social support system moderates the relationship between distress and menstrual pain, and these women complained of more symptoms than did those whose social network was intact (Alonso & Coe, 2001). Depression and anxiety were also found to be strongly associated with menstrual pain. In addition, self-esteem was found to be lower in young (15-year-old) women suffering from severe primary dysmenorrhea, but this loss of self-esteem is compensated at about age 25 years by the development of more achievement-oriented and aggressive attitudes (Holmlund, 1990).

These results imply that social support systems of women seeking treatment for dysmenorrhea should be evaluated and also should be screened for depression and anxiety when disrupted social support systems are found. Treatment interventions include relaxation alone or with imagery, effectively reducing resting time in spasmodic dysmenorrhea (Amodei, Nelson, Jarrett, & Sigmon, 1987).

Chronic Pelvic Pain

The relationship of primary chronic pain and psychological factors has been studied during the past two decades, but inconclusive data do not clear the picture. The prevalence rates of chronic pain range from as low as 5% to as high as 87% (Réthelyi, Berghammer, & Kopp, 2001), and depression has been shown to be more prevalent among chronic pain patients. Chronic pelvic pain, or pain experienced in the area of the pelvis for more than 6 months, is the cause of 10% of all gynecological outpatient visits, 40% of all laparoscopies, and 10% to 15% of all hysterectomies (Gelbaya & El-Halwagy, 2001) and is an important women's health issue.

The etiology of chronic pelvic pain, even after laparoscopy, remains unknown in a significant proportion of patients. Some connection has been found between high scores on measures of neuroticism, but other studies have found no connection between chronic pelvic pain and anxiety or depression (Wilkie & Schmidt, 1998). Childhood traumatic events are also hypothesized to be closely associated with chronic pain, and high incidences of sexual abuse (Toomey, Hernandez, Gittelman, & Hulka, 1994) and physical abuse (Rapkin, Kames, Darke, Stampler, &

Naliboff, 1990) were found in chronic pelvic pain patients.

Chronic pelvic pain has a tremendous impact on the lives of women who suffer from this disorder. Uncertainty and anxiety concerned with the pain plays an important role in functional impairment. Many times, women are confronted with a lack of concern and understanding or disbelief expressed by health care professionals (Savidge, Slade, Stewart, & Li, 1998). Verbal reassurance by health care workers that the cause for the pain cannot be found does not alleviate the distress experienced by women with this disorder.

Psychological treatment of chronic pelvic pain of unknown cause should, after careful medical examination, include behavioral therapy techniques, such as operant conditioning, to decrease the frequency of illness behavior and to strengthen health-promoting behaviors. Relaxation techniques are also recommended to decrease muscle tension in the pelvic area. Cognitive therapy, by treating depressive symptoms and anxiety accompanying chronic pain, is also an effective method of treatment (Wilkie & Schmidt, 1998).

Infertility

About 10% of infertility cannot be attributed to either partner (Guidice, 1998). Researchers hypothesize that infertility has psychological causes (known as the *psychogenic hypothesis*) or that infertility has psychological consequences (known as the *psychological consequences hypothesis*). Numerous studies have provided evidence that infertility does not have significant psychological causes (Greil, 1997).

The experience of infertility differs between the genders. Infertility is a more stressful experience for women than it is for men, and there are specific psychological measures that are more common among women, namely lower self-esteem, more depressive symptoms, lower life satisfaction, and more self-blame (Greil, 1997). In one study, nearly half of the women reported that infertility was the worst experience in their lives (Freeman, Boxer, Rickels, Tureck, & Mastroianni, 1985). Women are also known to seek treatment for infertility more often than are men; therefore, women also experience the distress of medicalization of their problems. Psychological distress is usually caused by undiagnosed (or idiopathic) infertility; otherwise, the diagnosis seems to be unrelated to psychological distress (Shatford, Hearn, Yuzpe, Brown, & Casper, 1988). Pregnancy has been found to decrease the level of psychological distress in infertile women (Benazon, Wright, & Sabourin, 1992).

It can be concluded that infertile women are clearly affected by their feelings of inadequacy to fulfill a parental role and that mental health professionals often need to identify and treat the distress in these women. Evidence shows, however, that the level of distress experienced by infertile women is not higher than that experienced by fertile women.

Victimization of Women

A large percentage of women all over the world are victims of sexual, physical, and/or psychological abuse. Abuse can be perpetrated by parents, close relatives, intimate partners, employers, or coworkers. Both physical abuse and sexual abuse have serious effects on physical and mental health, with domestic violence and rape significantly causing morbidity and mortality among women ages 15 to 44 years worldwide, accounting for 6% of the total disability-adjusted life years of healthy life lost and 90% of the morbidity associated with disability from injury (World Bank, 1993). Unfortunately, abused women rarely seek health care for their health complaints, and when they do seek such help, they are secretive about the causes of their symptoms.

Violence against women causes significant psychological distress, which most frequently is a direct consequence of their experience of abuse. Across all cultures, battered women who are abused by their partners are characterized by low self-esteem, increased insomnia, hypervigilance, an augmented startle response, a sense of disorder, and unhappiness (Fishbach & Herbert, 1997). Research has shown that battering may subsequently result in longlasting psychiatric morbidity (Mullen, Romans-Clarkson, Walton, & Herbison, 1988) and that abuse is considered to be a significant predictor of the development of lifelong mental health problems (Kilpatrick, Best, Veronen, Villeponteaux, & Ruff, 1985). Psychiatric morbidity, in association with sexual or physical abuse, includes depression (Goldberg, 1994), posttraumatic stress disorder (Roth, Newman, Pelcovitz, Van Der Kolk, & Mandel, 1997), substance use disorders (Schafer, Schnack, & Soyka, 2000), dissociative symptomatology (Brunner, Parzer, Schuld, & Resch, 2000), and dissociative identity disorder (Hocke & Schmidtke, 1998).

A major task for medical professionals is to identify and give proper treatment to abused women. Health care providers need to be educated on how to include questions on battering and sexual abuse while taking patients' histories, how to react to an emerging problem, and how to determine the type of treatment to which women should be referred. Battered women are in great need of psychological interventions, social support, and support from culture and society. Society also has to be informed about the problems arising from battering and needs to adopt an attitude of not tolerating violence in the culture.

SUMMARY AND CONCLUSIONS

Health issues concerning women highlighted in this chapter underline the necessity of health promotion and disease prevention interventions designed specifically for women. Interventions should take into account health problems arising in minority groups, in the lower socioeconomic strata, among women with lower education, and among women who are victims of violence.

Especially important is the primary prevention of mental health disorders, targeting young women and teaching them skills of adaptive ways of coping, hardiness, and resiliency. Such protective factors are important to enable young women to withstand peer pressure for health-damaging behavior, to prevent the disabling effect of chronic distress, and to take responsibility for their own health. Special attention needs to be given to women who are at high risk for developing certain mental disorders, for example, women living in homes with parental conflict, women experiencing sexual or physical abuse, and women who drop out of school early.

Improving social support systems for women seems to be a crucial issue in preventing psychological distress and disorder as well as illnesses resulting from chronic stress. Hotlines readily available for women in crisis and counseling services in schools, communities, and workplaces are important ways of giving support to women in need. But most important of all is raising awareness in the community and among health professionals about not only the physical but also the psychosocial aspects of physical and mental illness. Raising such awareness may eventually result in better health among women.

REFERENCES

Alexander, M. J., & Higgins, E. T. (1993). Emotional trade-offs of becoming a parent: How social roles influence self-discrepancy effects. *Journal of Personality and Social Psychology, 65,* 1259–1269.

Alonso, C., & Coe, C. L. (2001). Disruptions of social relationships accentuate the association between emotional distress and menstrual pain in young women. *Health Psychology, 20,* 411–416.

Amodei, N., Nelson, R. O., Jarrett, R. B., & Sigmon, S. (1987). Psychological treatments of dysmenorrhea: Differential effectiveness for spasmodics and congestives. *Journal of Behavior Therapy and Experimental Psychiatry, 18,* 95–103.

Angold, A., & Worthman, C. W. (1993). Puberty onset of gender differences in rates of depression: A developmental, epidemiologic, and neuroendocrine perspective. *Journal of Affective Disorders, 29,* 145–158.

Arber, S. (1991). Comparing inequalities in women's and men's health: Britain in the 1990s. *Social Science & Medicine, 44,* 773–787.

Avis, N. E., Crawford, S. L., & McKinlay, S. M. (1997). Psychosocial, behavioral, and health factors related to menopause symptomatology. *Women's Health, 3,* 103–120.

Ballinger, C. (1990). Psychiatric aspects of the menopause. *British Journal of Psychiatry, 156,* 773–787.

Banikarim, C., Chacko, M. R., & Kelder, S. H. (2000). Prevalence and impact of dysmenorrhea on Hispanic female adolescents. *Archives of Pediatrica and Adolescent Medicine, 154,* 1226–1229.

Barnett, R. C. (1993). Multiple roles, gender, and psychological distress. In L. Goldberger & S. Breznitz (Eds.), *Handbook of stress.* New York: Free Press.

Barnett, R. C., & Baruch, G. K. (1985). Women's involvement in multiple roles and psychological distress. *Journal of Personality and Social Psychology, 49,* 135–145.

Benazon, N., Wright, J., & Sabourin, S. (1992). Stress, sexual satisfaction, and marital adjustment in infertile couples. *Journal of Sex and Marital Therapy, 18,* 273–284.

Blake, F., Salkovskis, P., Gath, D., Day, A., & Garrod, A. (1998). Cognitive therapy for premenstrual syndrome: A controlled trial. *Journal of Psychosomatic Research, 45,* 307–318.

Boer, K., Smit, B. J., VanHuis, A. M., & Hogerzeil, H. V. (1994). Substance use in pregnancy: Do we care? *Acta Paediatrica, 404*(Suppl.), 65–71.

Bollerud, K. (1990). A model for the treatment of trauma related syndromes among chemically dependent inpatient women. *Journal of Substance Abuse Treatment, 7,* 83–87.

Brunner, R., Parzer, P., Schuld, V., & Resch, F. (2000). Dissociative symptomatology and traumatogenic factors in adolescent psychiatric patients. *Journal of Nervous and Mental Disease, 188,* 71–77.

Clark, D. B., Pollock, N., Bukstein, O. G., Mezzich, A. C., Bromberger, J. T., & Donovan, J. E. (1997). Gender and comorbid psychopathology in adolescents with alcohol dependence. *Journal of the American Academy of Child and Adolescent Psychiatry, 36,* 1195–1203.

Cooper, H. (2002). Investigating socio-economic explanations for gender and ethnic inequalities in health. *Social Science & Medicine, 54,* 693–706.

Cranley, M. S., Hedahl, K. J., & Pegg, S. H. (1983). Women's perceptions of vaginal and cesarean deliveries. *Nursing Research, 32,* 10–15.

Dennerstein, L. (1996). Well-being, symptoms, and the menopausal transition. *Maturitas, 23,* 147–157.

Denton, M., & Walters, V. (1999). Gender differences in structural and behavioural determinants of health: An analysis of the social production of health. *Social Science & Medicine, 48,* 1221–1235.

Derry, P. S., Gallant, S. J., & Woods, N. F. (1997). Premenstrual syndrome and menopause. In S. J. Gallant, G. P. Keita, & R. Royak-Schaler (Eds.), *Health care for women.* Washington, DC: American Psychological Association.

DiMatteo, M. R., Morton, S., Lepper, H. S., Damush, T., Carney, M., Pearson, M., & Kahn, K. L. (1996). Cesarean childbirth and psychosocial outcomes: A meta-analysis. *Health Psychology, 15,* 230–241.

Dunne, F. J., Galatopoulos, C., & Schipperheijn, J. M. (1993). Gender differences in psychiatric morbidity among alcohol misusers. *Comprehensive Psychiatry, 34*, 95–101.

Fischer, G., Bitschnau, M., Peternell, A., Eder, H., & Topitz, A. (1999). Pregnancy and substance abuse. *Archives of Women's Mental Health, 2*, 57–65.

Fishbach, R. L., & Herbert, B. (1997). Domestic violence and mental health: Correlates and conundrums within and across cultures. *Social Science & Medicine, 45*, 1161–1176.

Fodor, I. G., & Franks, V. (1990). Women in midlife and beyond: The new prime of life? *Psychology of Women Quarterly, 14*, 445–449.

Freeman, E. W., Boxer, A. W., Rickels, K., Tureck, R., & Mastroianni, L. (1985). Psychological evaluation and support in a program of in vitro fertilization and embryo transfer. *Fertility and Sterility, 4*, 48–53.

Freeman, E. W., Rickels, K., & Sondheimer, S. J. (1993). Premenstrual symptoms and dysmenorrhea in relation to emotional distress factors in adolescents. *Journal of Psychosomatic Obstetrics and Gynaecology, 14*, 41–50.

Gamma, A., & Angst, J. (2001). Concurrent psychiatric comorbidity and multi-morbidity in a community study: Gender differences and quality of life. *European Archives of Psychiatry and Clinical Neuroscience, 251*(Suppl. 2), 43–46.

Gelbaya, T. A., & El-Halwagy, H. E. (2001). Focus on primary care: Chronic pelvic pain in women. *Obstetrical & Gynecological Survey, 12*, 757–764.

Goldberg, R. T. (1994). Childhood abuse, depression, and chronic pain. *Clinical Journal of Pain, 10*, 277–281.

Graber, J. A., & Brooks-Gunn, J. (1998). Puberty in behavioral medicine and women. In E. A. Blechman & K. D. Brownell (Eds.), *Behavioral medicine and women: A comprehensive handbook* (pp. 51–58). New York: Guilford.

Granot, M. (2001). Pain perception in women with dysmenorrhea. *Obstetrics & Gynecology, 98*, 407–411.

Greene, J. G., & Cooke, D. J. (1980). Life stress and symptoms at the climacterium. *British Journal of Psychiatry, 136*, 486–491.

Greil, A. L. (1997). Infertility and psychological distress: A critical review of the literature. *Social Science & Medicine, 45*, 1679–1704.

Guidice, L. (1998). Reproductive technologies. In E. A Blechman & K. D. Brownell (Eds.), *Behavioral medicine and women* (pp. 515–519). New York: Guilford.

Hocke, V., & Schmidtke, A. (1998). *Zeitschrift fur Kinder- und Jugendpsychiatrie und Psychotherapie, 26*, 273–284.

Hollnagel, H., & Malterud, K. (1995). Shifting attention from objective risk factors to patients self-assessed health resources: A clinical model for general practice. *Family Practice, 12*, 423–429.

Holmlund, U. (1990). The experience of dysmenorrhea and its relationship to personality variables. *Acta Psychiatrica Scandinavica, 82*, 182–187.

Hvas, L. (2001). Positive aspects of menopause: A qualitative study. *Maturitas, 39*, 11–17.

Jarvis, M. A. E., & Schnoll, S. H. (1995). Methadone use during pregnancy. *NIDA Research Monographs, 149*, 58–77.

Joffe, H., & Cohen, L. S. (1998). Estrogen, serotonin, and mood disturbance: Where is the therapeutic bridge? *Biological Psychiatry, 44*, 798–811.

Kaplan, H. I., & Sadock, B. J. (1998). *Kaplan and Sadock's synopsis of psychiatry: Behavioral sciences/clinical psychiatry* (8th ed.). Baltimore, MD: Williams & Wilkins.

Karasek, R., Baker, D., Marxer, F., Ahlbom, A., & Theorell, T. (1981). Job decision latitude, job demands, and CVD: A prospective study of Swedish men. *American Journal of Public Health, 71*, 694–705.

Karasek, R., & Theorell, T. (1990). *Healthy work: Stress, productivity, and reconstruction of working life.* New York: Basic Books.

Kaufert, P. A., Gilbert, P., & Tate, R. (1992). The Manitoba Project: A re-examination of the link between menopause and depression. *Maturitas, 14,* 143–155.

Kessler, R., & McLeod, J. (1985). Social support and mental health in community samples. In S. Cohen & S. L. Syme (Eds.), *Social support and health.* New York: Academic Press.

Khlat, R., Sermet, C., & Le Pape, A. (2000). Women's health in relation with their family and work roles: France in the early 1990s. *Social Science & Medicine, 50,* 1807–1825.

Khoury, A. J., & Weisman, C. S., (2002). Thinking about women's health: The case for gender sensitivity. *Women's Health Issues, 12,* 61–65.

Kilpatrick, D. G., Best, C. L., Veronen, L. J., Villeponteaux, L. A., & Ruff, G. A. (1985). Mental health correlates of criminal victimization: A random community survey. *Journal of Consulting and Clinical Psychology, 53,* 866–873.

Kopp, M., & Skrabski, A. (1995). *Behavioural sciences applied to a changing society.* Budapest, Hungary: Bibliotheca Septem Artium Liberalium.

Kopp, M. S., Skrabski, A., & Szedmák, S. (2000). Psychosocial risk factors, inequality, and self-rated morbidity in a changing society. *Social Science & Medicine, 51,* 1351–1361.

Lazarus, R. S., & Folkman, S. (1984). *Stress, appraisal, and coping.* New York: Springer.

Lock, M. (1993). *Encounters with aging: Mythologies of menopause in Japan and North America.* Berkeley: University of California Press.

Matthews, K. (1992). Myths and realities of the menopause. *Psychosomatic Medicine, 54,* 1–9.

Miller, L. J. (2002). Postpartum depression. *Journal of the American Medical Association, 287,* 762–765.

Miller, L. J., & Rukstailis, M. (1999). Beyond the "blues" hypotheses about postpartum reactivity. In L. J. Miller (Ed.), *Postpartum mood disorders* (pp. 3–19). Washington, DC: American Psychiatric Press.

Moffitt, T. E., Caspi, A., Belsky, J., & Silva, P. A. (1992). Childhood experience and the onset of menarche: A test of a sociobiological model. *Child Development, 63,* 47–58.

Moss, N. E. (2002). Gender equity and socioeconomic inequality: A framework for the patterning of women's health. *Social Science & Medicine, 54,* 649–661.

Mullen, P. E., Romans-Clarkson, S. E., Walton, V. A., & Herbison, G. P. (1988). Impact of sexual and physical abuse on women's mental health. *Lancet, 1,* 841–845.

Nadelson, C. C., & Notman, M. T. (1981). To marry or not to marry: A choice. *American Journal of Psychiatry, 138,* 1352–1356.

Nolen-Hoeksema, S. (1987). Sex difference in unipolar depression: Evidence and theory. *Psychological Bulletin, 101,* 259–282.

O'Hara, M. W., Schlechte, J. A., Lewis, D. A., & Varner, M. W. (1991). Controlled prospective study of postpartum mood disorders: Psychological, environmental, and hormonal variables. *Journal of Abnormal Psychology, 100,* 63–73.

O'Leary, A., & Helgeson, V. S. (1997). Psychosocial factors and Women's health: Integrating mind, heart, and body. In S. J. Gallant, G. P. Keita, & R. Royak-Schaler (Eds.), *Health care for women: Psychological, social, and behavioral influences* (pp. 25–40). Washington, DC: American Psychological Association.

Orth-Gomér, K., Wamala, S. P., Horsten, M., Schenck-Gustafsson, K., Schneiderman, W., & Mittleman, M. A. (2000). Marital stress worsens prognosis in women with coronary heart disease. *Journal of the American Medical Association, 284,* 3008–3014.

Polit, D. F., & LaRocco, S. A. (1980). Social and psychological correlates of menopausal symptoms. *Psychosomatic Medicine, 42,* 335–345.

Rapkin, A. J., Kames, L. D., Darke, L. L., Stampler, F. M., & Naliboff, B. D. (1990). History of physical and sexual abuse in women with chronic pelvic pain. *Obstetrics & Gynecology, 76,* 92–96.

Réthelyi, J. M., Berghammer, R., & Kopp, M. S. (2001). Comorbidity of pain-associated disability and depressive symptoms in connection with socio-demographic variables: Results from a cross-sectional epidemiological survey in Hungary. *Pain, 93,* 115–121.

Root, M. P. P. (1989). Treatment failures: The role of sexual victimization in women's addictive behavior. *American Journal of Orthopsychiatry, 59,* 542–549.

Roth, S., Newman, E., Pelcovitz, D., Van Der Kolk, B., & Mandel, F. S. (1997). Complex PTSD in victims exposed to sexual and physical abuse: Results from the DSM-IV field trial for postraumatic stress disorder. *Journal of Traumatic Stress, 10,* 539–555.

Savidge, C. J., Slade, P., Stewart, P., & Li, T. C. (1998). Women's perspectives on their experiences of chronic pelvic pain and medical care. *Journal of Health Psychology, 3,* 103–116.

Schafer, M., Schnack, B., & Soyka, M. (2000). Sexual and physical abuse during early childhood or adolescence and later drug addiction. *Psychotherapy, Psychosomatic Medicine, Medical Psychology, 50,* 38–50.

Shatford, L. A., Hearn, M. T., Yuzpe, A. A., Brown, S. E., & Casper, R. F. (1988). Psychological correlates of differential infertility diagnosis in an in vitro fertilization program. *American Journal of Obstetrics and Gynecology, 158,* 1099–1107.

Shearer, E. C. (1983). How do parents really feel after cesarean birth? *Birth, 10,* 91–92.

Sigmon, S. T., Dorhofer, D. M., Rohan, K. J., & Boulard, N. E. (2000). The impact of anxiety sensitivity, bodily expectations, and cultural beliefs on menstrual symptom reporting: A test of the menstrual reactivity hypothesis. *Journal of Anxiety Disorders, 14,* 615–633.

Sigmon, S. T., Dorhofer, D. M., Rohan, K. J., Hotovy, L. A., Boulard, N. E., & Fink, C. M. (2000). Psychophysiological, somatic, and affective changes across the menstrual cycle in women with panic disorder. *Journal of Consulting and Clinical Psychology, 68,* 425–431.

Simon, R. (1992). Parental role strains, salience of parental identity, and gender differences in psychological distress. *Journal of Health and Social Behavior, 33,* 25–35.

Slaven, L., & Lee, C. (1998). A cross-sectional survey of menopausal status, symptoms, and psychological distress in a community sample of Australian women. *Journal of Health Psychology, 3,* 117–123.

Thoits, P. A. (1991). Gender differences in coping with emotional distress. In J. Eckenrole (Ed.), *The social context of coping* (pp. 107–138). New York: Plenum.

Toomey, T. C., Hernandez, J. T., Gittelman, D. F., & Hulka, J. F. (1994). Relationship of sexual and physical abuse to pain and psychological assessment variables in chronic pelvic pain patients. *Pain, 56,* 105–109.

Turnbull, J. E., & Gomberg, E. S. (1988). Impact of depressive symptomatology on alcohol problems in women. *Alcoholism, Clinical, and Experimental Research, 12,* 374–381.

U.S. Department of Health and Human Services. (1999). *Mental health: A report of the surgeon general.* Rockville, MD: U.S. Department of Health and Human Services, Substance Abuse and Mental Health Services Administration, Center for Mental Health Services.

Verbrugge, L. M. (1982). Women's social roles and health. In P. Berman & E. Ramey (Eds.), *Women: A developmental perspective* (Publication No. 82-2298). Washington, DC: Government Printing Office.

Vogeltanz, N. D., & Wilsnack, S. C. (1997). Alcohol problems in women: Risk factors, consequences, and treatment strategies. In S. J. Gallant, G. P. Keita, & R. Royak-Schaler (Eds.), *Health care for women* (pp. 75–96). Washington, DC: American Psychological Association.

Walters, V., McDonough, P., & Strohschein, L. (2002). The influence of work, household structure, and social, personal, and material resources on gender differences in health: An analysis of the 1994 Canadian National Population Health Survey. *Social Science & Medicine, 54,* 677–692.

Whittle, G. C., Slade, P., & Ronalds, C. M. (1987). Social support in women reporting dysmenorrhea. *Journal of Psychosomatic Research, 31,* 79–84.

Wilkie, A., & Schmidt, U. (1998). Gynecological pain. In E. A. Blechman & K. D. Brownell (Eds.), *Behavioral medicine and women* (pp. 463–469). New York: Guilford.

Wills, T. A. (1998). Social support. In E. A. Blechman & K. D. Brownell (Eds.), *Behavior medicine and women* (pp. 118–123). New York: Guilford.

Woods, N., & Mitchell, E. (1996). Patterns of depressed mood among midlife women: Observations from the Seattle Midlife Women's Study. *Research in Nursing and Health, 19,* 111–123.

World Bank. (1993). *World Development Report 1993: Investing in health.* New York: Oxford University Press.

Zanardi, C. (1990). *Essential papers on the psychology of women.* New York: New York University Press.

CHAPTER *25*

Issues With Geriatric Populations

BARRY A. EDELSTEIN, ANDREA K. SHREVE-NEIGER,
ADAM P. SPIRA, AND LESLEY P. KOVEN

The U.S. older adult population is growing at a remarkable rate. There were 35 million individuals age 65 years or over in the United States in 2000 (Hetzel & Smith, 2001). This represents 12.4% of the U.S. population and a 12% increase from 1990. In 2000, there were 18.4 million individuals who were between ages 65 and 74 years, and there were 12.4 million individuals between ages 75 and 84 years. Those individuals age 85 years or over (i.e., the oldest old) numbered 4.2 million and represented the most rapid growth of the older adult population (Hetzel & Smith, 2001). The number of oldest old increased 38% during the 1990s. By 2030, there will be approximately 70 million individuals age 65 years or over, twice the number reported in 2000 (Administration on Aging, 2001).

Although many adults age successfully (cf. Rowe & Kahn, 1998), most older adults have at least one chronic health problem, and many have several. In 1999, 26.1% of older adults rated their health as fair or poor as compared with only 9.2% of all individuals who did so (Administration on Aging, 2001). The most frequently occurring chronic health problems among older adults are arthritis (49% of older adults), hypertension (36%), hearing impairments (30%), heart disease (27%), cataracts (17%), orthopedic impairments (18%), sinusitis (12%), and diabetes (10%) (Administration on Aging, 2001). In 1999, older adults were hospitalized four times as many days as were those under age 65 years (1.6 vs. 0.4 days) and remained hospitalized longer (6.0 vs. 4.1 days). Moreover, community-dwelling older adults had more contact with their physicians than did younger individuals (6.8% vs. 3.5%) (Administration on Aging, 2001).

The mental health problems of older adults also invite attention, with estimates of approximately 25% of older adults meeting criteria for a mental disorder (Gatz, Kasl-Godly, & Karel, 1996). In addition, comorbid health and mental health problems are common among older adults, particularly among those seen in medical clinics (Lichtenberg, 2000) and in long-term care settings. The combination of health and mental health problems, coupled with multiple medications and potential adverse effects and interactions, yields a challenging array of diagnostic and treatment issues for the clinician.

This chapter provides a brief review of age-related sensory and cognitive changes to help underscore potential limitations associated with normal aging. This is followed by a discussion of various psychological correlates of physical disease that are particularly important in light of age-related increases in probability of debilitating diseases and conditions. This is followed by a related discussion of adverse effects of medications that are more likely in older adults. The subsequent section discusses some common problem areas that, for the most part, do not fall within the realm of diseases but nevertheless constitute significant problems with psychological implications. Age-related diagnostic issues are then addressed, with particular attention given to differences in the presentation of various disorders. Finally, a brief discussion of patient decision making and end-of-life issues is provided.

AGE-RELATED CHANGES

Aging begins at birth. An exhaustive discussion of age-related changes in the body and their psychological and behavioral concomitants is beyond the scope of this chapter. Some of the age-related sensory and cognitive changes are briefly reviewed here (for more thorough discussions of theses changes, see Edelstein, Martin, & Goodie [2000] and Whitbourne [1996]).

Many older adults have sensory deficits that can influence the assessment and treatment process and may be associated with a variety of psychological problems (e.g., social isolation, paranoia). Sight, hearing, touch, smell, and taste all suffer loss to some degree over time. Although all of these declines are common in older adults, this chapter focuses on sight and hearing. Thickness of the lens of the eye increases with age, causing increased light absorption, light scattering within the lens, increased susceptibility to glare, and difficulty in adjusting to abrupt changes in light intensity. The increased lens density reduces the amount of light reaching the retina, as

does pigmentation of the vitreous humor, reduction in the number of photoreceptors (rods and cones), and size of the pupil. The lens capsule loses elasticity with age, resulting in losses in accommodation and visual acuity (usually realized as presbyopia). Finally, numerous diseases can affect the visual system (e.g., diabetes mellitus, cataracts, glaucoma, macular degeneration, myotonic dystrophy, hypoparathyroidism, Wilson's disease).

Approximately 30% of adults over age 60 years suffer from significant hearing impairment (Zarit & Zarit, 1987). These impairments are due not only to aging but also to drugs used by older adults (e.g., certain antibiotics, certain diuretics) and various diseases and organic disorders (e.g., acoustic neuromas, syphilis, multiple sclerosis, cerebrovascular accidents, circulatory disorders) (Vernon, 1989). As with visual impairment, hearing impairment can have psychological consequences (e.g., paranoia, reduction of leisure activities, suspiciousness, hostility, depression). The ability to understand conversational speech decreases with age, due primarily to diminished ability to detect high-frequency tones. Thus, older adults may experience difficulty in understanding the speech of women and children in particular. Finally, the ability to understand speech in the presence of background noise can be impaired in older adults.

Older adults may also experience age-related declines in memory and cognition, although such declines are not inevitable. Difficulties with working memory may be experienced, as may difficulty with inhibiting thoughts or external stimuli, when attempting to learn or recall information. Inhibitory control tends to be worse for older adults in the afternoon and evening due to age-related changes in circadian rhythms (Edelstein, Martin, & Koven, 2003). Age-related changes in cognitive skills include diminished information processing speed, attention, mental flexibility, abstraction, calculation, and capacity for inductive reasoning (Park, 2000). Overall, it is important to appreciate that many older adults never experience many of the deficits discussed and that many important cognitive abilities are maintained.

PSYCHOLOGICAL MANIFESTATIONS AND CORRELATES OF PHYSICAL DISEASE

As discussed previously, a number of changes occur as part of the normal aging process. An unfortunate factor associated with aging is the increased prevalence of chronic physical diseases (Frazer, Leicht, & Baker, 1996). In this section, the psychological and behavioral manifestations and correlates of chronic diseases that commonly occur in older adults are discussed.

Parkinson's Disease

Parkinson's disease (PD) is a chronic progressive disorder of the central nervous system involving a deficiency of dopamine in the basal ganglia (Thompson, 2000). This leads to a range of symptoms, including muscular rigidity, difficulty in initiating movement, shuffling gait, resting tremor, and a flat unchanging facial expression. In addition to physical symptoms, PD is associated with elevated rates of psychiatric symptoms, including anxiety, depression, and psychosis. In a review of anxiety disorders in PD, Marsh (2000) cited prevalence rates as high as 24% for panic disorder and from 12% to 38% for generalized anxiety disorder. Based on observations that anxiety symptoms commonly occur before motor symptoms of PD, elevated rates have been attributed to the neuropathological processes underlying PD (Menza, 2002).

Elevated rates of depression have also been observed among individuals with PD. Estimates suggest that approximately 40% of individuals with PD report depressive symptoms (Cummings, 1992). However, the diagnosis of a true depressive disorder is complicated by the overlap between symptoms observed in PD and symptoms of depression (e.g., reduced appetite, sleep disturbances, apathy, motor retardation) (Kremer & Starkstein, 2000). This point was illustrated by Hoogendijk, Sommer, Tissingh, Deeg, and Wolters (1998), who conducted a study in which PD patients were assessed for major depressive disorder (MDD) using both the American Psychiatric Association's (1987) DSM-III-R criteria (*Diagnostic and Statistical Manual of Mental Disorders,* third edition, revised) and a clinician-administered depression rating scale. After controlling for the presence of MDD symptoms that could be accounted for by PD, a reduction in diagnoses of nearly 50% was observed. Hoogendijk and colleagues recommended that "depressed mood" should be considered mandatory for a diagnosis of MDD for individuals with PD and that depressive symptoms that covary with PD symptoms should be diagnosed as "mood disorder due to a general medical condition." Others have determined that most symptoms of MDD (i.e., those other than motor retardation, anergia, and early-morning awakening) that occur in individuals with PD tend to be legitimate instances of depression rather than symptoms of PD (Kremer & Starkstein, 2000).

Psychotic symptoms are also quite common in individuals with PD, although it is not always clear whether these symptoms are due to pathophysiological changes related to PD, delirium, medications, or other psychological disorders (Holroyd, Currie, & Wooten, 2001). In a recent study, 16% of patients with PD experienced hallucinations and delusions (Aarsland, Larsen, Cummings, & Laake, 1999). Rates were higher among individuals residing in institutions. Holroyd and colleagues (2001) found a prevalence of visual hallucinations of 26.5% in outpatients. This rate was negatively associated with visual acuity and cognitive ability and was positively associated with depression level and disease severity.

Chronic Obstructive Pulmonary Disease

Chronic obstructive pulmonary disease (COPD) refers to a group of pathological processes affecting the airways (e.g., bronchial tubes, lungs), including emphysema and chronic bronchitis. COPD is characterized by dyspnea (perceived shortness of breath), sputum production, and cough (Frazer et al., 1996). Depression and anxiety are common psychological correlates of COPD. A recent meta-analysis found that depression and anxiety symptoms occur in approximately 40% and 36% of older adults with COPD, respectively (Yohannes, Baldwin, & Connolly, 2000). Karajgi, Rifkin, Doddi, and Kolli (1990) reported that 16% of a sample of outpatients with COPD had an anxiety disorder and that 8% of the sample had panic disorder. Results from another study indicated that 34% of a sample of respiratory unit patients had an anxiety disorder (Yellowlees, Alpers, Bowden, Bryant, & Ruffin, 1987). In addition, significant relations have been shown to exist between the degree of depression and anxiety and the extent of functional impairment, even after controlling for disease severity (Kim et al., 2000). Cognitive impairment, or delirium attributed to anoxia, has also been observed in individuals with COPD (Morrison, 1997).

Diabetes Mellitus

Diabetes mellitus is a disease of the endocrine system that appears in two forms: type 1 (insulin dependent) and type 2 (non-insulin dependent). The symptoms of diabetes are attributable to pancreatic dysfunction and a resultant deficiency in insulin excretion. This deficiency impairs the affected individual's ability to process glucose, and this in turn produces an accumulation of blood glucose, known as hyperglycemia. In one study, Lustman, Griffith, Clouse, and Cryer (1986) reported that 71% of the individuals with diabetes had experienced at least one psychiatric disorder and that the degree of psychiatric disturbance exhibited by these individuals was inversely related to the degree of metabolic control that they obtained. Common psychiatric correlates of diabetes include depression and anxiety. Lustman and colleagues reported lifetime prevalences of major depressive episode and generalized anxiety disorder in diabetic patients to be 33% and 41%, respectively. In addition, panic-like symptoms (e.g., dizziness, rapid pulse, sweating) have been reported to occur when blood glucose drops excessively (Morrison, 1997). Agoraphobia appears to occur more frequently among individuals with type 2 diabetes than among those with type 1 diabetes (Lustman et al., 1986). Based on the observation of higher levels of functioning in psychogeriatric inpatients with uncontrolled diabetes than in inpatients with hypoglycemia, Hontela and Muller (1975) suggested that the elevated levels of blood glucose might actually maintain higher levels of functioning than those observed in older adults with hypoglycemia.

Thyroid Disturbances

Thyroid disturbances comprise another set of endocrine diseases that are relatively common in older adults. The thyroid gland's primary role is the regulation of metabolic rate. Thus, thyroid dysfunction can have a significant impact on metabolic processes. Decreased thyroid function can lead to a pathological condition known as hypothyroidism, which includes symptoms of depressed mood, weight gain, low energy, and loss of appetite. These symptoms closely resemble, and can easily be mistaken for, symptoms of depressive disorders. Krahn (1987) reported that even minor degrees of thyroid deficiency can be associated with significant depressive symptoms, particularly in the elderly. In addition, hypothyroidism has been associated with cognitive impairment, even at subclinical levels of thyroid deficiency

(Ganguli, Burmeister, Seaberg, Belle, & DeKosky, 1996).

Hyperthyroidism refers to thyroid overactivity that produces excessive amounts of thyroid hormone (thyrotoxicosis) and the subsequent "speeding up" of metabolic processes. In younger adults, behavioral symptoms of hyperthyroidism can resemble symptoms of mania and include restlessness and irritability. In older adults, however, this is far less likely. According to Gregerman (as cited in Frazer et al., 1996), less than 50% of older individuals with hyperthyroidism report these symptoms; older adults tend to report heart palpitations and a subjective sense of "racing." When depression is observed in the context of hyperthyroidism, it is referred to as *apathetic hyperthyroidism* (Morrison, 1997; Thomas, Mazzaferri, & Skillman, 1970). In addition, generalized anxiety symptoms (e.g., nervousness, tremor, tension) have been reported in 40% of patients with hyperthyroidism (Hall, 1983).

Cerebrovascular Accident

A cerebrovascular accident, or stroke, refers to brain trauma resulting from vascular pathology. A cerebrovascular accident may occur due to anoxia caused by atherosclerosis, thrombosis, embolism, or cardiac dysfunction. In addition, hemorrhage due to a ruptured aneurysm can cause lesions. Although the location in the brain of the stroke can largely determine its specific behavioral impact (e.g., strokes resulting in lesions in the right hemisphere have been associated with increased levels of depression more than have those resulting in lesions in the left hemisphere [Dam, Pedersen, & Ahlgren, 1989]), depression is widely observed following strokes. It has been reported to occur in 30% of cases within the year following a cerebrovascular accident (Wade, Legh-Smith, & Hewer, 1987). Other symptoms that have been observed during the year following stroke include

agoraphobia, irritability, and "pathological emotionalism" (House et al., 1991). The psychiatric symptoms of these community-dwelling patients in this study diminished over the course of the year following stroke.

Cancer

Cancer is associated with a range of psychiatric conditions, including anxiety, depression, and delirium (Gagnon, Allard, & Masse, 2000). The overlap between symptoms of psychiatric disorders and symptoms secondary to cancer or its treatment has been known to complicate the study of these correlates of cancer (Pasacreta, 1997). Panic attacks were reported in approximately one fifth of inpatients with cancer referred for psychosomatic consultations (Slaughter et al., 2000). A number of studies have documented the occurrence of depression in the context of cancer. Greenberg (1989) reported that information regarding the type, course, and treatment of a tumor is important in the diagnosis of depression in individuals with cancer. In one study, 30% of patients referred to an outpatient oncology department were assessed as having a "probable" psychiatric disorder (Ford, Lewis, & Fallowfield, 1995); this dropped to 22% at a 6-month follow-up. Using another measure, Ford and colleagues (1995) found that 26% of patients had significant anxiety problems and that 7% had significant depressive symptoms; anxiety symptoms decreased significantly 6 months later. The treatment of breast cancer in postmenopausal women often requires the cessation of estrogen replacement therapy to suppress cancer cell growth (Duffy, Greenberg, Younger, & Ferraro, 1999). Clinicians working with such patients should be aware that the withdrawal of estrogen replacement therapy in this population results in a rapid decrease in estrogen and has been known to produce depressive symptoms (Duffy et al., 1999). Pasacreta (1997) found that depressive symptoms occurred in 24% of a sample of women who had been diagnosed and treated surgically for breast cancer 3 to 7 months prior to assessment; MDD occurred in 9% of the sample. Within this study, 35% of the variance in functional status was accounted for by physical distress and depressive symptoms.

ADVERSE MEDICATION EFFECTS

Most older adults have at least one chronic health problem that often requires medication (e.g., arthritis, hypertension, heart disease, diabetes, sinusitis, esophagitis, constipation) (Administration on Aging, 2001; Knight, Santos, Teri, & Lawton, 1995). Older adults take an average of five prescription drugs each day (Golden et al., 1999) and use 40% of all nonprescription drugs (Conry, 2000). Stoehr, Ganguli, Seaberg, Echement, and Belle (1997) found that 87% of older adults report using at least one over-the-counter medication. Each of these drugs has the potential for adverse effects, and the potential interactions among multiple drugs can compound this number. Col, Fanale, and Kronholm (1990) found that 28% of 89 older adult hospital admissions were due to medication-related problems, and 60% of these were attributed to adverse drug reactions.

Older adults are at greater risk for such adverse effects than are younger adults due to age-related physiological changes (Rho & Wong, 1998). Increases in the likelihood of adverse anticholinergic effects can result from age-related reduced parasympathetic nervous system activity. Reductions in gastric acidity and gastrointestinal motility can slow drug absorption and the drug action. The elimination of drugs is slowed by reduced activity of hepatic enzyme systems and decreased renal functions. The slowed elimination of drugs can also increase the risk for drug interactions.

What appear to be symptoms of psychological disorders can be the result of medications taken by older adults given that older adults are more sensitive to some of the side effects of medications. For example, prednisone, a corticosteroid used to treat chronic obstructive pulmonary disease, can cause anxiety, euphoria, depression, and psychosis (Frazer et al., 1996). Beta blockers such as propranolol, taken for chronic heart failure, can cause confusion, depression, delusions, paranoia, disorientation, agitation, and fatigue (Salzman, 1998). Medications used to treat Parkinson's disease (e.g., levodopa, carbidopa) can lead to confusion, hallucinations, and nightmares (Smith & Reynard, 1992). Finally, diphenhydramine, taken for allergies, can cause cognitive impairment in healthy older adults (Morrison & Katz, 1989; Oslin, 2000). Thus, clinicians are well advised to examine thoroughly each client's medical record with an eye to current and past prescription and over-the-counter medications and their potential adverse effects.

COMMON PROBLEM AREAS

Falls

Falls are a common experience among older adults. Approximately one third of community-dwelling older adults (Studenski et al., 1994), 20% of older adults in acute care facilities (Kay & Tideiksaar, 1990), and half of older adults in long-term care facilities (Tinetti et al., 1994) fall each year. Within a year, half of these fallers will have fallen again (Wolinsky, Johnson, & Fitzgerald, 1992).

Falls can result in a variety of physical consequences, ranging from minor injuries (e.g., abrasions, contusions, sprains, lacerations) to serious injuries (e.g., head trauma, spinal cord injuries, fractures, internal injuries). Nearly one third (31%) of falls result in minor injury, and another 6% result in serious injury (Morse, Tylko, & Dixon, 1987). Most deaths and long-term disability after falls are related to complications of fall-related fractures, especially hip fractures (Melton & Riggs, 1985).

Psychological consequences of falls are common. Depression (Luukinen, Koski, Laippala, & Kivela, 1995) and fear of falling (Drozdick & Edelstein, 2001) are often experienced following a fall. Fear of falling is associated with higher dependency, greater physical symptomatology, greater drug consumption (Downton & Andrews, 1990), higher reported depression and anxiety (Arfken, Lach, Birge, & Miller, 1994), restriction of movement and activities (Howland, Peterson, Levin, & Fried, 1993), and increased morbidity.

Risk factors for falls can be categorized as either intrinsic or extrinsic. Intrinsic risk factors include physical impairment (e.g., muscle weakness, hearing loss, visual acuity loss), the results of various physical impairments (e.g., ambulation, gait, and balance problems), medical disorders (e.g., Parkinson's disease, cardiovascular disease), psychological factors (e.g., denial of limitations, cognitive status), and number, types, and amount of medications (e.g., antidepressants, sedatives) (Edelstein & Drozdick, 1998). Extrinsic risk factors include environmental hazards, restraints, improper footwear, improper use of a walking aid, the winter season, and difficulty with stairs (Edelstein & Drozdick, 1998).

Sleep

Complaints of disturbed sleep may be categorized as sleep onset problems (trouble getting to sleep), sleep maintenance problems (trouble staying asleep), or early morning awakening (Morgan, 2000). These symptoms may occur alone or in combination and may be transient or long term. Disturbed sleep may also present, not as a complaint of sleeplessness but rather as a report of excessive daytime sleepiness (Morgan, 2000). The prevalence of disturbed sleep increases with age; insomnia has been estimated to affect approximately 5% of those ages 18 to 30 years versus 30% of those age 65 years or over (Newman, Enright, Manolio, Haponik, & Wahl, 1997).

Dissatisfaction with sleep is more common among elderly women than among elderly men (Newman et al., 1997) and is higher among individuals with lower income and education levels (Ohayon, 1996).

Increasing age is associated with changes in the nature and duration of sleep complaints. Problems in getting to sleep tend to be most common in younger insomniacs, whereas problems staying asleep become increasingly common in later life (Maggi et al., 1998). Symptoms of disturbed sleep are more likely to become chronic in older age groups (Hohagen et al., 1994).

Continuity of sleep, duration of sleep, and depth of sleep also show differences with age. Relative to younger adults' sleep, older adults' sleep is characterized by more frequent "shifts" from one sleep stage to another and more frequent intrasleep arousals (Boselli, Parrino, Smerieri, & Terzano, 1998). Both events result in sleep that is more broken and more likely to be rated as poor in quality (Oswald, 1980). Similarly, sleep efficiency (time spent asleep divided by time spent in bed) also tends to decrease with age (Bliwise, 1993). Older adults tend to be "lighter" sleepers (Morgan, 2000) and to wake more easily with lower levels of noise than do younger adults (Busby, Mercier, & Pivik, 1994).

In addition to changes in the structure of nighttime sleep, the circadian rhythm itself has been found to show age-related decay, with sleep becoming desynchronized and more likely to occur during the day (Morgan, 2000). Controlled-release melatonin replacement therapy has been found to correct some circadian rhythm desynchrony, leading to improvements in both sleep efficiency and sleep onset (Haimov et al., 1995).

Appetite

Approximately 40% to 70% of elderly patients who are hospitalized or institutionalized are malnourished (Brocker, Vellas,

Albarede, & Poynard, 1994). Although social and financial factors play important causative roles in malnutrition, decreased appetite associated with aging may also contribute to weight loss and malnutrition. Common physical causes of decreased appetite in older adults include dental conditions, gastrointestinal disorders, side effects of medications, loss of taste and smell, and particular vitamin or mineral deficiencies. Furthermore, cholecystokinin, a hormone known to suppress appetite, has been found in greater levels in older adults than in younger adults (Baez-Franceshi & Morley, 1999).

Psychological causes of decreased appetite include depression, anxiety, loneliness, and grief (American Psychiatric Association, 1994). Psychologists may play important roles in treating decreased appetite in older adults; however, physiological causes should be considered before treating low appetite as a psychological problem.

Dementia

The dementias refer to a broad range of disorders characterized by memory problems and at least one other cognitive disturbance, such as aphasia (language disturbance), apraxia (motor disturbance), agnosia (inability to recognize objects), or a disturbance in executive functioning (American Psychiatric Association, 1994). Although many dementias are progressive, some are nondegenerative. However, all are characterized by irreversible declines in cognitive functioning and impairment in social and occupational functioning.

Dementia has many different etiologies, each with its own range of symptoms and progression. But despite the etiologic heterogeneity of dementias, two basic types of dementia exist. *Cortical* dementias, such as Alzheimer's disease, involve pathological alterations in the cerebral cortical areas of the brain, although some alterations in subcortical regions are also present (Kaufer & Cummings, 2000).

Subcortical dementias include disorders such as Parkinson's disease, Huntington's disease, subcortical vascular disease, white matter disease, and hydrocephalus (Kaufer & Cummings, 2000). Cortical dementias are characterized by deficits in elementary intellectual skills, such as language, visuospatial functions, and mathematical abilities, whereas simple sensory and motor functioning is typically preserved. Subcortical dementias, in contrast, are characterized by slowing and wasting of executive functions, affective and personality changes, forgetfulness, and movement disorders (Cummings & Benson, 1982).

The underlying organic pathology associated with various forms of dementia can produce a variety of behavior problems, including physical aggression, screaming, and wandering. Many of these behaviors fall within the category of "agitation." Agitation has been defined as "inappropriate verbal, vocal, or motor activity that is not explained by needs or confusion per se" (Cohen-Mansfield & Billig, 1986, p. 712) and includes behavior that is abusive or aggressive, occurs at an inappropriate frequency, or is socially inappropriate (Cohen-Mansfield, Werner, Watson, & Pasis, 1995). Agitation is problematic for the agitated individual, caregivers, and others in the agitated individual's immediate environment. Such behavior puts individuals at physical risk and increases caregiver stress (Bourgeois, Schulz, & Burgio, 1996).

Pain

Pain is one of the most common concerns of older adults and is associated with nearly all illnesses and diseases (Grange & Morrison, 2002; Wallace, 2001). Pain is reported by 25% to 50% of community-dwelling older adults (Ferrell, 1991) and by as many as 80% of nursing home residents (Ferrell, Ferrell, & Osterweil, 1990). In general, older adults are more likely to experience pain, and are less likely to report pain, have pain recognized, and be treated for the pain, than are younger adults (Murray & Seely, 2002). This is even more likely to be the case among cognitively impaired older adults (Feldt, Ryden, & Miles, 1998; Gibson & Helme, 1999). Moreover, a study by Chakour, Gibson, Bradbeer, and Helme (1996) suggested that older adults may experience some forms of pain differently than do younger adults.

Pain assessment in older adults can be complicated by severe cognitive impairment where traditional self-reports of pain become unobtainable due to loss of verbal abilities and sensory declines. An alternative to self-reported pain is reliance on direct observation of nonverbal pain indicators (e.g., moaning, facial grimacing, bracing, restlessness, rubbing) (Feldt, 2000). The psychological (e.g., depression, diminished cognitive functioning) and behavioral (e.g., agitation, screaming, irritability) consequences of pain can pose considerable challenges in the assessment of older adults. In light of the decreased likelihood of pain reports by older adults and the tremendous impact of pain on quality of life, the presence of pain should always be assessed when observing changes in behavior, particularly among cognitively impaired older adults who might have trouble reporting pain. Pain should always be suspected when changes in behavior, particularly among cognitively impaired older adults, are observed.

DIAGNOSTIC ISSUES

The diagnosis of mental disorders in older adults can be quite challenging. The prevalence, and even the phenomenology (e.g., Blazer, George, & Landerman, 1986) and presentation, of mental disorders can change with age. In the latter case, for example, depressed older adults are more likely to present somatic symptoms (e.g., decreased energy, chronic pain, changes in appetite, changes in sleep patterns, gastrointestinal complaints), psychomotor

agitation, and increased irritability (Blazer et al., 1986; Fiske, Kasl-Godley, & Gatz, 1998), and are less likely to report depressed mood (Fiske et al., 1998), than are younger adults. Patterns of depression have also reflected what has been termed "depletion," characterized by symptoms of loneliness, guilt, and sleep disturbance (Newmann, Engel, & Jensen, 1990).

Older adults may differ from younger adults with regard to both the prevalence and the content of fears and worries. For example, Kirkpatrick (1984), Kogan and Edelstein (1997), and Liddell, Locker, and Burman (1991) all found that the number of fears decreases with age. Although the number decreases, Kogan and Edelstein (1997) found that even low levels of fears interfered with the daily lives of older adults. Finally, Kogan and Edelstein (in press) found that the nature of fears also changes with age and appears to reflect developmentally appropriate themes.

There is mounting evidence that subclinical or subsyndromal levels of anxiety (e.g., DeBeurs et al., 1999; Himmelfarb & Murrell, 1984; Palmer, Jeste, & Sheikh, 1997) and depression (e.g., Lewinsohn, Solomon, Seeley, & Zeiss, 2000) are both common and clinically significant among older adults. This research suggests that anxiety and depression among older adults might be best conceptualized along continua rather than in the context of diagnostic thresholds. In addition, these findings should alert clinicians to subthreshold levels of anxiety and depression among older adults that could require intervention.

DECISION MAKING AND END-OF-LIFE ISSUES

Competency and Capacity for Decision Making

A number of older adults who use behavioral health services experience various degrees of dementia or may exhibit central nervous system damage as a result of cardiovascular accident, coronary artery disease, or other chronic health problems that often result in cognitive impairment. Consequently, these older adults' capacity to make decisions and overall competency may be called into question and may need to be assessed. *Competency* is a legal term referring to an individual's decision-making abilities for a specific criminal or civil matter and so is generally declared in a court of law (Moye, 1999). *Capacity* refers to an individual's specific abilities in a number of areas and is frequently assessed by a clinician.

Capacity is defined as the ability to comprehend information relevant to the decision, the ability to deliberate about the choices in accordance with personal values and goals, and the ability to communicate with caregivers (Hastings Center, 1987). Clinicians are frequently asked to assess decision-making capacity of older adults for a number of areas, including financial and medical decision making and independent living skills (Moye, 1999).

Although few measures of capacity with established psychometrics exist, a few that have recently been developed show promise, including the Hopemont Capacity Assessment Interview (Edelstein, Nygren, Northrop, Staats, & Pool, 1993) and the Clinical Competency Test Interview (Marson, Cody, Ingram, & Harrell, 1995). The Hopemont Capacity Assessment Interview presents scenarios to the client. Some scenarios involve medical decisions, and others involve financial or money management decisions. Following scenario presentations, a number of questions are asked to assess information comprehension, understanding of the risks and benefits involved, and how the decision or choice is made. The same format is followed with the Clinical Competency Test Interview, but in this case the scenarios involve medical decision making only.

It should be remembered that all adults are considered competent unless determined otherwise by a court of law. A capacity evaluation is one method for assessing an aspect of competency, but it should not be used as the sole determinant for surrogate or legal guardian assignment. An older adult suffering from dementia may have the capacity for one type of decision making but lack capacity in another area.

Decision-making capacity is frequently assessed when issues related to death and dying are at stake. The next subsection addresses aspects of death and dying that the behavioral health care provider should be aware of when treating an older adult, especially if the adult in question is terminally ill.

Death, Dying, and Related Issues

Death is one aspect of life that is as natural as birth. As a result of modern scientific advances, many medical or health-related professionals do all they can to prevent death, even at the expense of the patient's wishes. Medical professionals are trained to save lives, and society has made great advances in medical technology that allow people to live longer than ever before, but there are people for whom death remains imminent nonetheless. In these cases, health care professionals can have a positive impact on the dying process by making it a more comfortable and dignified experience.

Fordyce (2001) listed the health care practitioner's most important contributions to the dying client as being (a) amelioration of any unpleasant physical or mental symptoms the client is experiencing; (b) meeting the client's emotional needs as much as possible; (c) educating, reassuring, and comforting the client; and (d) preventing futile interventions and investigations that may result in discomfort for the client. Aiding a client in the dying process by nurturing mind, body, and spirit is one of the most effective ways in which a health care professional can make the process easier. In addition to addressing spiritual or religious issues, the dying older adult may have a desire to reminisce or write the story of his or her life in a journal, especially for loved ones (Tobin & Lindsey, 1999). Providing favorite music, games, or hobbies for the dying client is also a way to make the final days or months of his or her life meaningful and ultimately more enjoyable.

Tobin and Lindsey (1999) referred to death as a natural part of living that requires preparation and the expenditure of considerable effort. Health care providers should stress to their older adult clients that preparation is an important part of dying, and as such, these clients should be considering key decisions that may need to be made. These decisions may involve life support, resuscitation, whether they wish to die at home or in a hospital, and which family and friends they would like involved in the process. In addition, older adults should feel free and be encouraged to discuss their living wills, who they have chosen as proxies, and whether they have documented their wishes in writing. These all are considerations to be made in advance of the terminal stages of illness or death. In addition to legal and medical considerations, other issues such as religiosity and spirituality may emerge as older adults prepare for death.

Recent surveys indicate that 94% of Americans believe in God, 90% pray, 75% report that religious involvement is a positive and enriching experience, and 88% believe that religion is either very important or fairly important in their lives (Gallup, 1994). Religious practice is especially common among older adults, with a large number reporting active participation in religious activities and prayer (Koenig, Larson, & Matthews, 1999). Imminent death brings with it a period of spiritual reflection for many people. Questions such as "What is the meaning of life" and "What have I done with my life?" are frequently asked (Tobin & Lindsey, 1999). Questioning one's existence and its relation to a bigger picture or an afterlife is a normal concomitant of contemplating death

and should not be discouraged; rather, it should be encouraged by health care professionals. It is not necessary to have answers for dying people, but health care professionals should let them voice their fears, concerns, and/or beliefs and should try to offer some kind of reassurance. It is important not to challenge a terminally ill older adult's religious or spiritual beliefs but rather to respect them (Hastings Center, 1987) and be open to listening to the patient discuss aspects of faith or religion that are especially important or even troubling to him or her.

When death is imminent, it is also important for the health care professional to recognize the normal physical changes associated with death; the health care professional should not try to prevent or stop them but rather should make the client as comfortable as possible. The client normally does not experience discomfort or pain during these changes. Loss of appetite, mottling of the skin, poor circulation, and loss of thirst are typical prior to death (Fordyce, 2001). In addition, marked weight loss and loss of body functions occur in close proximity to death. The client should be kept clean, and adult diapers should be changed frequently to aid in comfort. None of these changes is cause for alarm; rather, they all are part of the normal dying process (Tobin & Lindsey, 1999). Although further elaboration on end-of-life issues is beyond the scope of this chapter, the interested reader is referred to Benner (2001), Coppola and Trotman (2002), and Corr, Nabe, and Corr (2000).

End-of-life issues involving death and decision making are complex in today's health care setting, as technology allows for life to be sustained in circumstances where in the past it would have ceased. Although every human eventually must face his or her mortality, the process of death and dying is unique to each individual, and it is the health care professional who can grant the older adult a sense of control and help to make the process of dying the individual's own experience.

SUMMARY AND CONCLUSIONS

This chapter has briefly presented information that a clinician likely would find helpful when providing psychological services to older adults in health care settings. Much of the information pertains to age-related issues ranging from sensory processes to the presentation of depression. It is particularly important that the reader appreciate the ways in which adults can change as they age and how these changes can affect their experiences and presentations of problems and disorders. These changes, the presence of multiple chronic diseases, the psychological correlates of these diseases, and the adverse responses to drugs used to treat them can present an enigmatic collection of behaviors that may complicate assessment and intervention.

Older adults are, by definition, closer to death than are younger adults due to age and increased risk of life-threatening diseases. Thus, the health care professional must educate himself or herself regarding the major medical and financial decisions commonly faced by older adults and how to participate in the determination of capacity to make these decisions. Finally, because death is experienced more often by older adults than by younger adults, it is important that the health care professional obtain knowledge regarding end-of-life issues and how to contribute to the care of dying patients. As has been said before, "We will not get out of this life alive." However, the health care professional can assist others in making that transition as physically and psychologically comfortable as possible.

REFERENCES

Aarsland, D., Larsen, J. P., Cummings, J. L., & Laake, K. (1999). Prevalence and clinical correlates of psychotic symptoms in Parkinson's disease. *Archives of Neurology, 56,* 595–600.

Administration on Aging. (2001). *A profile of older adults: 2001* [Online]. Retrieved January 20, 2003, from www.aoa.gov/aoa/stats/profile/2001

American Psychiatric Association. (1987). *Diagnostic and statistical manual of mental disorders* (3rd ed.). Washington, DC: Author.

American Psychiatric Association. (1994). *Diagnostic and statistical manual of mental disorders* (4th ed.). Washington, DC: Author.

Arfken, C. L., Lach, H. W., Birge, S. J., & Miller, J. P. (1994). The prevalence and correlates of fear of falling in elderly persons living in the community. *American Journal of Public Health, 84,* 565–570.

Baez-Franceshi, D., & Morley, J. E. (1999). *Causes of malnutrition in the elderly* [Online]. Retrieved January 20, 2003, from www.healthandage.com/html/min/basel/content/publi02.htm

Benner, P. (2001). Death as a human passage: Compassionate care for persons dying in critical care units. *American Journal of Critical Care, 10,* 355–359.

Blazer, D., George, L. K., & Landerman, R. (1986). The phenomenology of late-life depression. In P. E. Bebbington & R. Jacoby (Eds.), *Psychiatric disorder in the elderly* (pp. 143–151). London: Springer.

Bliwise, D. (1993). Sleep in normal aging and dementia. *Sleep, 16,* 40–81.

Boselli, M., Parrino, L., Smerieri, A., & Terzano, M. G. (1998). Effects of age on EEG arousals in normal sleep. *Sleep, 21,* 351–357.

Bourgeois, M. S., Schulz, R., & Burgio, L. (1996). Interventions for caregivers of patients with Alzheimer's disease: A review and analysis of content, process, and outcomes. *International Journal of Aging and Human Development, 43,* 35–92.

Brocker, P., Vellas, B., Albarede, A. L., & Poynard, T. (1994). A two-centre, randomized double-blind trial of ornithine oxoglutarate in 194 elderly, ambulatory, convalescent subjects. *Age and Aging, 23,* 303–306.

Busby, K. A., Mercier, L., & Pivik, R. T. (1994). Ontogenic variations in auditory arousal threshold during sleep. *Psychophysiology, 31,* 182–188.

Chakour, M. C., Gibson, S. J., Bradbeer, M., & Helme, R. D. (1996). The effect of age on A delta- and C-fibre thermal pain perception. *Pain, 64,* 143–152.

Cohen-Mansfield, J., & Billig, N. (1986). Agitated behaviors in the elderly: I. A conceptual review. *Journal of the American Geriatrics Society, 34,* 711–721.

Cohen-Mansfield, J., Werner, P., Watson, V., & Pasis, S. (1995). Agitation among elderly persons at adult day-care centers: The experiences of relatives and staff members. *International Psychogeriatrics, 7,* 447–458.

Col, N., Fanale, J. E., & Kronholm, P. (1990). The role of medication noncompliance and adverse drug reactions in hospitalizations of the elderly. *Archives of Internal Medicine, 150,* 841–845.

Conry, M. (2000). Polypharmacy: Pandora's medicine chest. *Geriatric Times, 1,* 1–6.

Coppola, K., & Trotman, F. (2002). *Dying and death: Decisions at the end of life.* New York: Springer.

Corr, C., Nabe, C., & Corr, D. (2000). *Death and dying, life and living* (3rd ed.). Washington, DC: American Psychological Association.

Cummings, J. L. (1992). Depression and Parkinson's disease. *American Journal of Psychiatry, 149,* 443–454.

Cummings, J. L., & Benson, D. F. (1982). Subcortical dementia. *Archives of Neurology, 39,* 616–620.

Dam, H., Pedersen, H. E., & Ahlgren, P. (1989). Depression among patients with stroke. *Acta Psychiatrica Scandinavica, 80,* 118–124.

DeBeurs, E., Beekman, A., van Balkom, A., Deeg, D., van Dyck, R., & van Tilburg, W. (1999). Consequences of anxiety in older persons: Its effect on disability, well-being, and use of health services. *Psychological Medicine, 29,* 583–593.

Downton, J. H., & Andrews, K. (1990). Postural disturbance and psychological symptoms amongst elderly people living at home. *International Journal of Geriatric Psychiatry, 5,* 93–98.

Drozdick, L. W., & Edelstein, B. A. (2001). Correlates of fear of falling in older adults who have experienced a fall. *Journal of Clinical Geropsychology, 7,* 1–13.

Duffy, L. S., Greenberg, D. B., Younger, J., & Ferraro, M. G. (1999). Iatrogenic acute estrogen deficiency and psychiatric syndromes in breast cancer patients. *Psychosomatics, 40,* 304–308.

Edelstein, B. A., & Drozdick, L. W. (1998). Falls among older adults. In B. Edelstein (Ed.), *Comprehensive clinical psychology,* Vol. 7: *Clinical geropsychology* (pp. 349–370). New York: Pergamon.

Edelstein, B., Martin, R., & Goodie, J. (2000). Considerations for older adults. In M. Hersen & M. Biaggio (Eds.), *Effective brief therapies: A clinician's guide* (pp. 433–448). San Diego: Academic Press.

Edelstein, B., Martin, R., & Koven, L. (2003). Assessment in geriatric settings. In J. R. Graham & J. A. Naglieri (Eds.), *Comprehensive handbook of psychology,* Vol. 10: *Assessment psychology* (pp. 389–414). New York: John Wiley.

Edelstein, B., Nygren, M., Northrop, L., Staats, N., & Pool, D. (1993, August). *Assessment of capacity to make financial and medical decisions.* Paper presented at the meeting of the American Psychological Association, Toronto.

Feldt, K. S. (2000). The checklist of nonverbal pain indicators. *Pain Management Nursing, 1,* 13–21.

Feldt, K. S., Ryden, M. B., & Miles, S. (1998). Treatment of pain in cognitively impaired compared with cognitively intact older patients with hip-fracture. *Journal of the American Geriatrics Society, 46,* 1079–1085.

Ferrell, B. A. (1991). Pain management in elderly people. *Journal of the American Geriatrics Society, 29,* 64–73.

Ferrell, B. A., Ferrell, B. R., & Osterweil, D. (1990). Pain in the nursing home. *Journal of the American Geriatrics Society, 38,* 409–414.

Fiske, A., Kasl-Godley, J. E., & Gatz, M. (1998). Mood disorders in late life. In B. Edelstein (Ed.), *Comprehensive clinical psychology,* Vol. 7: *Clinical geropsychology* (pp. 193–229). New York: Pergamon.

Ford, S., Lewis, S., & Fallowfield, L. (1995). Psychological morbidity in newly referred patients with cancer. *Journal of Psychosomatic Research, 39,* 193–202.

Fordyce, M. (2001). At the end of life. *Annals of Long-Term Care, 9,* 80–84.

Frazer, D. W., Leicht, M. L., & Baker, M. D. (1996). Psychological manifestations of physical disease in the elderly. In L. Carstensen, B. A. Edelstein, & L. Dornbrand (Eds.), *The practical handbook of clinical gerontology* (pp. 217–235). Thousand Oaks, CA: Sage.

Gagnon, P., Allard, P., & Masse, B. (2000). Delirium in terminal cancer: A prospective study using daily screening, early diagnosis, and continuous monitoring. *Journal of Pain and Symptom Management, 19,* 412–426.

Gallup, G., Jr. (1994). *The Gallup Poll: Public opinion 1993.* Wilmington, DE: Scholarly Resources.

Ganguli, M., Burmeister, L. A., Seaberg, E. C., Belle, S., & DeKosky, S. T. (1996). Association between dementia and elevated TSH: A community-based study. *Biological Psychiatry, 40,* 714–725.

Gatz, M., Kasl-Godley, J. E., & Karel, M. J. (1996). Aging and mental disorders. In J. Birren & K. W. Schaie (Eds.), *Handbook of the psychology of aging* (4th ed., pp. 365–382). San Diego: Academic Press.

Gibson, S., & Helme, R. (1999). Cognitive factors and the experience of pain and suffering in older persons. *Pain, 85,* 375–383.

Golden, A. G., Preston, R. A., Barnett, S. D., Llorente, M., Hamdan, K., & Silverman, M. A. (1999). Inappropriate medication prescribing in homebound older adults. *Journal of the American Geriatrics Society, 47,* 948–953.

Grange, T., & Morrison, A. (2002). The relationship between medical and psychological problems in residential care. In R. D. Hill, B. L. Thorn, J. Bowling, & A. Morrison (Eds.), *Geriatric residential care* (pp. 77–98). Mahwah, NJ: Lawrence Erlbaum.

Greenberg, D. B. (1989). Depression and cancer. In R. G. Robinson & P. V. Rabins (Eds.), *Depression and coexisting disease* (pp. 103–115). New York: Igaku-Shoin.

Haimov, I., Lavie, P., Laudon, M., Herer, P., Vigder, C., & Zisapel, N. (1995). Melatonin replacement therapy of elderly insomniacs. *Sleep, 18,* 598–603.

Hall, R. C. W. (1983). Psychiatric effects of thyroid hormone disturbances. *Psychosomatics, 24,* 7–18.

Hastings Center. (1987). *Guidelines on the termination of life sustaining treatment and the care of the dying.* Bloomington: Indiana University Press.

Hetzel, L., & Smith, A. (2001). *The 65 years and over population: 2000.* Washington, DC: U.S. Bureau of the Census. Retrieved May 20, 2002, from www.census.gov/prod/2001pubs/c2kbr01-10.pdf

Himmelfarb, S., & Murrell, S. A. (1984). The prevalence and correlates of anxiety symptoms in older adults. *Journal of Psychology, 116,* 159–167.

Hohagen, F., Kappler, C., Schramm, E., Rink, K., Weyerer, S., Riemann, D., & Berger, M. (1994). Prevalence of insomnia in general practice attenders and the current treatment modalities. *Acta Psychiatrica Scandinavica, 90,* 102–108.

Holroyd, S., Currie, L., & Wooten, G. F. (2001). Prospective study of hallucinations and delusions in Parkinson's disease. *Journal of Neurology, Neurosurgery, and Psychiatry, 70,* 734–738.

Hontela, S., & Muller, H. F. (1975). Uncontrolled diabetes in psychogeriatric subjects. *Journal of the American Geriatrics Society, 23,* 58–62.

Hoogendijk, W. J. G., Sommer, I. E. C., Tissingh, G., Deeg, D. J. H., & Wolters, E. C. (1998). Depression in Parkinson's disease: The impact of symptom overlap on prevalence. *Psychosomatics, 39,* 416–421.

House, A., Dennis, M., Mogridge, L., Warlow, C., Hawton, K., & Jones, L. (1991). Mood disorders in the year after first stroke. *British Journal of Psychiatry, 158,* 83–92.

Howland, J., Peterson, E. W., Levin, W. C., & Fried. L. (1993). Fear of falling among the community dwelling elderly. *Journal of Aging and Health, 5,* 229–243.

Karajgi, B., Rifkin, A., Doddi, S., & Kolli, R. (1990). The prevalence of anxiety disorders in patients with chronic obstructive pulmonary disease. *American Journal of Psychiatry, 147,* 200–201.

Kaufer, D. I., & Cummings, J. L. (2000). Dementia: An overview. In M. J. Farah & T. E. Feinberg (Eds.), *Patient-based approaches to cognitive neuroscience* (pp. 355–368). Cambridge, MA: MIT Press.

Kay, A. D., & Tideiksaar, R. (1990). Falls and gait disorders. In W. B. Abrams & R. Berkow (Eds.), *Merck manual of geriatrics* (pp. 52–68). Rahway, NJ: Merck.

Kim, H. F. S., Kunik, M. E., Molinari, V. A., Hillman, S. L., Lalani, S., Ornego, C. A., Petersen, N. J., Nahas, Z., & Goodnight-White, S. (2000). Functional impairment in COPD patients: The impact of anxiety and depression. *Psychosomatics, 41,* 465–471.

Kirkpatrick, D. R. (1984). Age, gender, and patterns of common intense fears among adults. *Behaviour Research and Therapy, 22,* 141–150.

Knight, B. G., Santos, J., Teri, L., & Lawton, M. P. (1995). The development of training in clinical geropsychology. In B. G. Knight, L. Teri, P. Wohlford, & J. Santos (Eds.), *Mental health services for older adults: Implications for training and practice in geropsychology* (pp. 1–8). Washington, DC: American Psychological Association.

Koenig, H. G., Larson, D. B., & Matthews, D. A. (1999). Religion and psychotherapy with older adults. *Journal of Geriatric Psychiatry, 29,* 155–184.

Kogan, J. N., & Edelstein, B. A. (1997). *Fears of middle-aged and older adults: Relations to daily functioning and life satisfaction.* Unpublished manuscript, West Virginia University.

Kogan, J. N., & Edelstein, B. A. (in press). Modification and psychometric examination of self-report measure of fear in older adults. *Journal of Anxiety Disorders.*

Krahn, D. D. (1987). Affective disorder associated with subclinical hypothyroidism. *Psychosomatics, 28,* 440–441.

Kremer, J., & Starkstein, S. E. (2000). Affective disorders in Parkinson's disease. *International Review of Psychiatry, 12,* 290–297.

Lewinsohn, P. W., Solomon, A., Seeley, J. R., & Zeiss, A. (2000). Clinical implications of subthreshold depression symptoms. *Journal of Abnormal Psychology, 109,* 345–351.

Lichtenberg, P. A. (2000). Asssessment of older adults in medical settings. *Clinical Geropsychology News, 7,* 5.

Liddell, A., Locker, D., & Burman, D. (1991). Self-reported fears (FSS-II) of subjects aged 50 years and over. *Behaviour Research and Therapy, 29,* 105–112.

Lustman, P. J., Griffith, L. S., Clouse, R. E., & Cryer, P. E. (1986). Psychiatric illness in diabetes mellitus: Relationship to symptoms and glucose control. *Journal of Nervous and Mental Disease, 174,* 736–742.

Luukinen, H., Koski, K., Laippala, P., & Kivela, S. L. (1995). Risk factors for recurrent falls in the elderly in long-term institutional care. *Public Health, 109,* 57–65.

Maggi, S., Langlois, J. A., Minicuci, N., Grigoletto, F., Pavan, M., Foley, D. J., & Enzi, G. (1998). Sleep complaints in community-dwelling older persons: Prevalence, associated factors, and reported causes. *Journal of the American Geriatrics Society, 46,* 161–168.

Marsh, L. (2000). Anxiety disorders in Parkinson's disease. *International Review of Psychiatry, 12,* 307–308.

Marson, D. C., Cody, H. A., Ingram, K. K., & Harrell, L. E. (1995). Neuropsychologic predictors of competency in Alzheimer's disease using a rational reasons legal standard. *Archives of Neurology, 52,* 955–959.

Melton, L. J., & Riggs, B. L. (1985). Risk factors for injury after a fall. *Clinics in Geriatric Medicine, 1,* 525–539.

Menza, M. A. (2002). Psychiatric aspects of Parkinson's disease. *Psychiatric Annals, 32,* 99–104.

Morgan, K. (2000). Sleep and aging: An overview. In K. L. Lichstein & C. M. Morin (Eds.), *Treatment of late life insomnia* (pp. 3–36). New York: Russell Sage.

Morrison, J. R. (1997). *When psychological problems mask medical disorders: A guide for psychotherapists.* New York: Guilford.

Morrison, R. L., & Katz, I. R. (1989). Drug-related cognitive impairment: Current progress and recurrent problems. *Annual Review of Gerontology and Geriatrics, 9,* 232–279.

Morse, J. M., Tylko, S. J., & Dixon, H. A. (1987). Characteristics of the fall-prone patient. *The Gerontologist, 27,* 516–522.

Moye, J. (1999). Assessment of competency and decision making capacity. In P. Lichtenberg (Ed.), *Handbook of assessment in clinical gerontology* (pp. 488–528). New York: John Wiley.

Murray, M. A., & Seely, J. F. (2002). Strategies to improve cancer pain control in long-term care. *Annals of Long-Term Care, 10,* 55–60.

Newman, A. B., Enright, P. L., Manolio, T. A., Haponik, E. F., & Wahl, P. W. (1997). Sleep disturbance, psychosocial correlates, and cardiovascular disease in 5,201 older adults: The Cardiovascular Health Study. *Journal of the American Geriatrics Society, 45,* 1–7.

Newmann, J. P., Engel, R. J., & Jensen, J. (1990). Depressive symptom patterns among older women. *Psychology and Aging, 5,* 101–118.

Ohayon, M. (1996). Epidemiologic study on insomnia in the general population. *Sleep, 19*(Suppl.), S7–S15.

Oslin, D. W. (2000). Prescription and over-the-counter drug misuse among the elderly. *Geriatric Times, 1,* 1–5.

Oswald, I. (1980). Sleep studies in clinical pharmacology. *British Journal of Clinical Pharmacology, 10,* 317–326.

Palmer, B., Jeste, D., & Sheikh, J. (1997). Anxiety disorders in the elderly: DSM-IV and other barriers to diagnosis and treatment. *Journal of the Affective Disorders, 46,* 183–190.

Park, D. (2000). The basic mechanisms accounting for age-related decline in cognitive function. In D. C. Park & N. Schwarz (Eds.), *Cognitive aging: A primer* (pp. 1–22). New York: Psychology Press.

Pasacreta, J. V. (1997). Depressive phenomena, physical symptom distress, and functional status among women with breast cancer. *Nursing Research, 46,* 214–221.

Rho, J. P., Wong, F. S. (1998). Principles of prescribing medications. In T. T. Yoshikawa, E. L. Cobbs, & K. Brummel-Smith (Eds.), *Practical ambulatory geriatrics* (2nd ed., pp. 19–25). St. Louis, MO: C. V. Mosby.

Rowe, J. W., & Kahn, R. L. (1998). *Successful aging.* New York: Pantheon Books

Salzman, C. (1998). *Clinical geriatric psychopharmacology* (2nd ed.). Baltimore, MD: Williams & Wilkins.

Slaughter, J. R., Jain, A., Holmes, S., Reid, J. C., Bobo, W., & Sherrod, N. B. (2000). Panic disorder in hospitalized cancer patients. *Psycho-Oncology, 9,* 253–258.

Smith, C. M., & Reynard, A. M. (1992). *Textbook of pharmacology.* Philadelphia: W. B. Saunders.

Stoehr, G. P., Ganguli, M., Seaberg, E. C., Echement, D. A., & Belle, S. (1997). Over-the counter medication use in an older rural community: The Movies Project. *Journal of the American Geriatrics Society, 45,* 158–165.

Studenski, S., Duncan, P. W., Chandler, J., Samsa, G., Prescott, B., Hogue, C., & Bearon, L. B. (1994). Predicting falls: The role of mobility and nonphysical factors. *Journal of the American Geriatrics Society, 42,* 297–302.

Thomas, F. B., Mazzaferri, E. L., & Skillman, T. G. (1970). Apathetic thyrotoxicosis: A distinctive clinical and laboratory entity. *Annals of Internal Medicine, 72,* 679–685.

Thompson, R. F. (2000). *The brain: A neuroscience primer* (3rd ed.). New York: Worth.

Tinetti, M. E., Baker, D. I., McAvay, G., Claus, E. B., Garrett, P., Gottschalk, M., Koch, M. L., Trainor, K., & Horwitz, R. I. (1994). A multifactorial intervention to reduce the risk of falling among elderly people living in the community. *New England Journal of Medicine, 331,* 821–827.

Tobin, D. R., & Lindsey, K. (1999). *Peaceful dying.* Cambridge, MA: Perseus Books.

Vernon, M. (1989). Assessment of persons with hearing disabilities. In T. Hunt & C. J. Lindley (Eds.), *Testing older adults: A reference guide for geropsychological assessments* (pp. 150–162). Austin, TX: Pro-Ed.

Wade, D. T., Legh-Smith, J., & Hewer, R. A. (1987). Depressed mood after stroke. *British Journal of Psychiatry, 151,* 200–205.

Wallace, M. (2001). Pain in older adults. *Annals of Long-Term Care, 9,* 50–58.

Whitbourne, S. (1996). *The aging individual: Physical and psychological perspectives.* New York: Springer.

Wolinsky, F. D., Johnson, R. J., & Fitzgerald, J. F. (1992). Falling, health status, and the use of health services by older adults: A prospective study. *Medical Care, 30,* 587–597.

Yellowlees, P. M., Alpers, J. H., Bowden, J. J., Bryant, G. D., & Ruffin, R. E. (1987). Psychiatric morbidity in patients with chronic airflow obstruction. *Medical Journal of Australia, 146,* 305–307.

Yohannes, A. M., Baldwin, R. C., & Connolly, M. J. (2000). Mood disorders in elderly patients with chronic pulmonary disease. *Reviews in Clinical Gerontology, 10,* 193–202.

Zarit, J. M., & Zarit, S. H. (1987). Molar aging: The physiology and psychology of normal aging. In L. Carstensen & B. Edelstein (Eds.), *Handbook of clinical gerontology* (pp. 18–32). New York: Pergamon.

CHAPTER 26

Public Health Approaches
Finding the Interface With Health Psychology

JALIE A. TUCKER, JOSHUA C. KLAPOW,
AND CATHY A. SIMPSON

After decades of delivering psychological services primarily in the form of psychotherapy, the settings and scope of psychological practice have expanded into health care, work site, organizational, and community settings (Tucker, 1999). Health psychology research and practice have been vital to this trend, and many of the innovations have been concerned with understanding and modifying relations among health, disease, and behavior. Services that support health behavior change now span interventions that vary in scope, intensity, cost-effectiveness, target audience, and population impact. Services range from individual clinical services to focused interventions for select risk groups to brief, low-intensity interventions for communities or populations.

In other words, clinical care is increasingly being supplemented by interventions that are more in line with a public health approach (Curry & Kim, 1999; Pronk, Boucher, Gehling, Boyle, & Jeffery, 2002). In clinical care, persons who have developed problems seek help from professionals and receive treatments that are relatively intensive and effective but costly. Treatment seekers, however, tend to be a small minority of the larger population with problems, and they tend to have more serious problems. In public health practice, populations or at-risk groups are actively targeted with brief interventions that typically are more preventive than therapeutic in focus. Compared with clinical care, public health interventions do not involve as much personal contact, can be delivered by trained nonprofessionals, and are more accessible; for example, they may involve written or videotaped materials and can be delivered by telephone, television, or via the Internet. Although public health interventions typically are less efficacious than clinical interventions, they are less costly per person and can reach

AUTHORS' NOTE: Manuscript preparation was supported in part by National Institute on Alcohol Abuse and Aging Grant K02 AA000209 to Jalie Tucker and by National Institute on Aging Grant K23 AG00932 to Joshua Klapow.

many more people. Thus, in the aggregate, the overall impact on the health status of communities or populations may be considerably greater from public health interventions than from clinical care.

In combination, the two approaches can contribute to the development of systems of care that span the conventional end points of public health and clinical practice and that include both preventive and therapeutic services. The need for such coordinated systems of care is widely recognized (e.g., Galea et al., 2001; U.S. Department of Health and Human Services, 1999), but implementation is challenging and uncommon (e.g., Humphreys & Tucker, 2002). Psychologists have much to contribute to such initiatives. But to participate effectively, they would benefit from greater public health knowledge and skills, which are not routinely covered in graduate education in psychology. Although not exhaustive, relevant content areas include (a) population distributions and dynamics of health and behavioral health problems as well as the nature of relations between them; (b) organization and economics of health care systems, patterns of and influences on service utilization, and cost-utility analysis; (c) research methods suitable for studying populations and organizations rather than individuals; (d) intervention marketing and dissemination to groups, communities, and organizations; and (e) health outcomes assessment and health policy research, including mental health policy.

Psychologists, in turn, can offer unique knowledge and skills that are fundamental to an effective merger of clinical and public health approaches to health promotion and disease prevention and management. In addition to their strong research skills, psychologists have comprehensive knowledge and skills concerning mental health disorders, behavior change, theory and measurement of behavior, and the role of behavior in health and disease. By merging the disciplinary strengths of psychology

with those of public health, synergies should emerge that enhance the population impact of behavioral interventions to promote health and to prevent and manage disease.

This chapter provides an overview of the public health field for psychologists. Concepts, methods, and findings from epidemiology, behavioral epidemiology, and health outcomes assessment are emphasized because they are likely points of intersection with health psychology. The chapter summarizes the history and key concepts in these areas, discusses educational opportunities in public health generally, and then selectively illustrates education and training in the field of health outcomes assessment, which is a natural connection for psychologists. The chapter ends with consideration of differences in the "worldviews" of psychology and public health, discussed in the context of mental health research and practice. These differences must be understood and respected if the disciplines are to collaborate effectively.

HISTORICAL ISSUES AND KEY CONCEPTS

The beginnings of contemporary public health research and practice lie in the field of *epidemiology,* which is the study of the determinants of disease in populations. The origins of epidemiology can be traced to observational studies of infectious disease transmission patterns during the mid-1800s such as John Snow's classic analysis of how cholera was transmitted by contaminated drinking water in London (Turnock, 1997). Snow collected data on the frequency and distribution of cholera deaths in London as a function of the decedents' source of water. From these data, he was able to identify contaminated water sources, thereby preventing further exposure and cholera deaths.

As Snow's research exemplifies, epidemiology typically uses nonexperimental correlational methods to assess the strength of association in large samples between possible causes of disease and patterns of disease onset, transmission, morbidity, and mortality (Hennekens & Buring, 1987). Key measures of association are *incidence* and *prevalence*. Incidence is a measure of the rate of disease onset and represents the number of new cases in a population over a given period of time. Prevalence reflects the total number of cases in a population either at a single point in time (i.e., "point" prevalence) or over a given time period (e.g., annual or lifetime prevalence). Incidence and prevalence are interrelated because prevalence is a function of both the rate of new cases (i.e., incidence) and the duration of disease.

Other central concepts in epidemiology are *risk* and *risk factors* for disease (Fletcher, Fletcher, & Wagner, 1996). Risk is the likelihood that persons who are exposed to a particular factor or who have a given characteristic will develop the disease of interest. Risk factors are the characteristics, circumstances, or behaviors that are associated with an increased risk of disease occurrence. Because relations between exposure to risk factors and disease are evaluated at the population level, the observed relations do not necessarily hold for individuals (Kaplan, 1984). Many persons who have a negative health outcome have no known risk factors, even when a robust relationship between risk factors and disease has been established at the population level. Moreover, empirical support for risk factors typically comes from nonexperimental research methods (e.g., case control studies) that fall short of the standards for causal inference as defined and investigated in experimental psychology.

A recent development of relevance to health psychologists is the emergence of the subspecialty of *behavioral epidemiology*, which involves the application of concepts and methods from epidemiology to investigate the role of behavior and psychological variables in health and disease at a population level (Sexton, 1979; Tucker, Phillips, Murphy, & Raczynski, in press). Behavioral epidemiology and health psychology share common goals of understanding and modifying behavior and psychological factors involved in health and disease but differ in the scope of application and methods of study. Research in behavioral epidemiology has been instrumental in identifying modifiable risk factors for disease that involve behavior and that are appropriate targets for intervention. For example, diet, smoking, and inactivity have been established as risk factors for coronary heart disease (National Heart, Lung, and Blood Institute, 1994). In addition, increased risk of coronary heart disease has been associated with specific components of "Type A" behavior patterns such as hostility, reactivity, and time pressure (e.g., Houston, Chesney, Black, Cates, & Hecker, 1992; Krantz, 1988) and with the presence of depressive symptoms in conjunction with Type A behavior patterns (Frasure-Smith, Lesperance, Juneau, Talajic, & Bourassa, 1999). As another example, several modifiable risk factors for human immunodeficiency virus (HIV) infection have been identified, including drug of choice, injection practices, and sexual practices (Peterson, Dimeff, Tapert, Stern, & Gorman, 1998).

Another relevant subspecialty is *health outcomes research* (Clancy & Eisenberg, 1998), including health outcomes assessment (Klapow, Kaplan, & Doctor, in press). Historically, the primary outcome measures in epidemiology were mortality and morbidity as represented by biological indicators of disease. This focus, however, does not represent many important functional domains that contribute to health and disease status. This limitation led to the development of the "quality-adjusted life year" (QALY) as an alternative measure (e.g., Weinstein & Stason, 1977). QALYs reflect in a single measure the benefits of reduced morbidity and mortality, and it was an important advance in the assessment of health outcomes.

The scope of health outcomes assessment has continued to expand to include a range of monetary cost measures and measures of patient functioning and satisfaction. Economic analyses (e.g., cost-effectiveness, cost-benefit analysis) are becoming a standard part of evaluation research on health outcomes (Drummond, O'Brien, Stoddart, & Torrence, 1997). This work has shown, for example, that including mental health benefits in comprehensive health plans tends to reduce the use and cost of medical services (Cummings, O'Donohue, & Ferguson, 2002). This medical "cost offset" effect provides strong support for the economic utility of insuring mental health services.

Expansion into the assessment of patient functioning poses measurement challenges not present in pure economic evaluations. Health status and health-related quality of life are functional constructs that encompass symptoms, behavior, and psychological and social functioning. Operationalizing these constructs and evaluating them are well within the expertise of health psychologists. Skills in psychometrics, behavioral assessment, and instrument development and validation are a cornerstone of their training. Given that definitions of health are shifting from a biomedical process model (e.g., physiological markers of health) to a patient-focused outcomes model (e.g., symptoms, distress, functioning), so too must the measurement of health shift from a biomedical process to outcomes assessment. The process of defining and operationalizing a construct (e.g., health, anger, pain, hostility), quantifying it through instrument development, validating the instrument to ensure reliability and accuracy of measurement, and interpreting data obtained from such an instrument are common practices in health psychology (Klapow et al., in press).

In summary, public health and health psychology share many common goals, but they have approached the study of health, disease, and the role of the environment and behavior in different yet potentially complementary ways. Public health brings a broad population perspective to bear on the issues and offers a level of generality that is unattainable in psychology. In comparison, psychology offers a more intensive individual level of analysis that often is better grounded in theory and sound measurement practices. To promote interdisciplinary synergies, researchers and practitioners in each discipline should acquire a working knowledge of the other's field. Basic training and skills in public health for psychologists are described next.

SPECIALIZED TRAINING AND SKILLS NEEDED

This section provides an overview of graduate education in public health and pathways for acquiring specialized training and skills in public health for psychologists. This material is followed by a more detailed discussion of opportunities and educational requirements in the area of health outcomes assessment, which exemplifies opportunities for psychologists in health services research. The section ends with a description of the joint clinical psychology–public health program at the University of Alabama at Birmingham (UAB), which shows how education and training in the two fields can be integrated effectively at the predoctoral level.

Public Health Education Programs

Probably the most direct way for psychologists to gain knowledge about public health is to enroll in courses or degree programs in graduate programs in public health. This subsection describes graduate education in public health, including core content areas required for program accreditation by the Council on Education for Public Health (CEPH).

Much like the American Psychological Association's Committee on Accreditation periodically reviews doctoral programs in psychology, the CEPH serves this function for schools of public health and related academic programs, including community health/preventive medicine programs and community health education programs. As of June 2002, CEPH-accredited programs included 32 schools of public health, 36 community health/preventive medicine programs, and 14 community health education programs. The current list may be obtained from the CEPH Web site (www.ceph.org). In addition to serving a general quality assurance function, CEPH accreditation allows programs to be eligible for certain federal funds such as research awards from the Centers for Disease Control and Prevention (CDC). Linkages between public health programs and the CDC are a unique feature not enjoyed by conventional doctoral psychology programs.

All CEPH-accredited programs offer educational experiences leading to the master of public health (M.P.H.) degree, which is a professional degree recognizing broad knowledge of content and method relevant to the practice of public health. Additional generalist and specialist degrees may be offered, for example, the academically oriented M.S.P.H. degree and doctoral degrees that are professional (Dr.P.H.) or academic (Ph.D., Sci.D.) in nature. Five core areas of knowledge are required in M.P.H. programs: biostatistics, epidemiology, environmental health sciences, health services administration, and social and behavioral sciences. These core areas often serve as the defining basis of departments in schools of public health, although this arrangement is not a CEPH requirement per se.

Educational Opportunities in Health Services Research and Practice

The delivery of health care services is a complex and dynamic process. As discussed in a report of the World Health Organization (WHO, 2002) titled *Innovative Care for Chronic Conditions: Building Blocks for Action,* health care systems can be divided into three levels: *micro, meso,* and *macro.* The micro level of health care consists of services

that involve direct patient interaction. This is the foundation of training for health psychologists. The meso level consists of the organizational entities that deliver health care services and their associations with community resources. The macro level consists of policies that create the parameters within which health care organizations, communities, and providers function. As noted in the WHO report, lines of demarcation between the levels are not always clear. Nevertheless, when health care policies, organizations, communities, and interventions align, the quality of health care services is likely to improve (cf. Humphreys & Tucker, 2002).

As discussed in Frank, Farmer, and Klapow (in press), as a profession of behavioral scientists, health psychologists are potentially capable of functioning at any of these levels. Health psychologists receive rigorous graduate education in the scientific method, research methodology, statistics, psychometric theory, personality theory, learning theory, and behavior change interventions. To date, however, the application of this knowledge base has been limited primarily to the micro level of the health care system. By offering educational opportunities that convey the necessary expertise at the meso and macro levels, health psychologists will be prepared to contribute across the multiple levels of the system of care.

Doing so, however, will require changes in psychology doctoral programs. Graduate programs understandably hesitate to require more coursework and expand the curriculum (Elliott & Klapow, 1997), but failure to do so will continue to limit the contributions of health psychologists to the micro level of health care systems. A training model that blends core skills in health psychology with a working knowledge of the levels of the health care system will enable future psychologists to apply their skills in the dynamic health care system and to deal effectively with future economic and organizational changes (Elliott & Klapow, 1997).

Although the possibilities for content are virtually endless when considering the study of health care systems, several core areas are essential for a basic level of expertise: health economics, health insurance, health policy, quality improvement, program evaluation, patient-based outcomes evaluation, cost-effectiveness analysis, and design and evaluation of clinical trials. It is important to note that these content areas are in addition to the foundation of training that health psychologists now receive. Thus, it is assumed that health psychologists who explore these content areas have requisite skills in statistics, psychometric theory, instrument development and validation, and research methods. With a health psychology foundation and these additional content areas, health psychologists can pursue opportunities across the spectrum of health care. Without such knowledge, they are limited in their ability to work within the meso (health care organization) and macro (health policy) levels.

Although it is necessary for health psychologists to have an understanding of the health care system from the micro level to the macro level, the method of education can take several forms. Integration of coursework and areas of concentration into doctoral programs, continuing education opportunities, and additional postgraduate degrees all are possible, depending on the depth of understanding desired. If comprehensive health services and outcomes training programs are not available or feasible, psychologists can gain some understanding in the core content areas through individual courses, independent reading, and continuing education classes.

Psychologists also can acquire knowledge of health policy and the political environment through fellowship programs. The Robert Wood Johnson Foundation sponsors a health policy fellowship that supports the participation of psychologists and other health professionals in the formulation of national health policy in the U.S. Congress. Similar programs are offered by the American Psychological Association and the U.S. Public Health Service (De Leon, Hagglund, Ragusea, & Sammons, in press). For example, some psychologists (including the first two chapter authors) have obtained knowledge and skills in public health through receipt of competitive Public Health Service career development awards (i.e., "K-awards").

Health Outcomes Assessment

Measurement is a cornerstone of psychology. The field of health psychology has made significant progress in transitioning the principles of psychometric theory into a variety of assessment applications in the field of medicine. For the most part, however, measurement in health psychology has focused on (a) identifying psychological processes associated with health and illness, (b) evaluating psychological and social contextual variables and their relationship to biological markers of health, and (c) assessing psychological distress as a primary outcome (Klapow et al., in press; Pennebaker, Kiecolt-Glaser, & Glaser, 1988). Although these are important contributions, the somewhat narrow focus has limited health psychology's role in health outcomes assessment.

As discussed in Frank and colleagues (in press), because chronic conditions are increasing as the U.S. population ages, effective medical management of chronic conditions is growing in importance. Heretofore, biological markers have been used as primary end points for disease assessment, but such measures are only modestly correlated with health outcomes. Low correlations between biological measures of disease process and patient outcomes have been observed in many areas of medicine (Feinstein, 1994). For example, rheumatologists often measure disease activity by sedimentation rates or the number of swollen joints, but these measures are poorly correlated with patient disability and capacity to function. Thus, biological measures serve only a limited role in predicting patient outcomes. Functional disability and capacity to function (i.e., ability to carry out activities of daily living) also are relevant measures, and measures of psychosocial and behavioral variables (e.g., stress levels, coping responses, health behaviors, social networks) further contribute to the prediction of health outcomes (Kurki, 2002; Tucker et al., in press). These nonbiological variable classes fall within the domain of psychology and are important lines of research for health psychologists to pursue.

In general, definitions of health are shifting from a *biomedical process model* that is based on physiological markers of health and disease to a *patient-focused outcomes model* that encompasses symptoms, functioning, and distress (Kaplan & Anderson, 1996; Kaplan, Anderson, & Ganiats, 1993). Medicine is increasingly faced with evaluating interventions for chronic conditions, rationing health care based on improvements in health and quality of life, and viewing patients as consumers of care. These changes are propelling the shift in models and measurement of health outcomes, and they pose challenges for the medical community, which is not well versed in the assessment of nonbiological outcomes. Thus, psychologists have an opportunity to apply their expertise in measurement across the health care field in ways that should contribute to better conceptual and operational definitions of health and to sound assessment practices. The process of defining and operationalizing a construct (e.g., health, anger, pain, hostility), quantifying it through instrument development, validating the instrument to ensure reliability and accuracy, and collecting and interpreting data using the instrument are common practices in health psychology. The requisite skills in psychometrics, behavioral assessment, and instrument development and validation are cornerstones of training in psychology. Thus, health psychologists are poised to become leaders in the evaluation of health outcomes.

Joint Training Programs in Psychology and Public Health: The UAB Example

Growing opportunities for psychologists to work in select areas of public health are nurturing educational initiatives aimed at providing them with the requisite knowledge and skills as part of their graduate education. One such program exists at UAB, a large urban university that offers undergraduate, graduate, and professional degrees and is recognized for its excellence in health-related research. Three schools at UAB (Social and Behavioral Sciences, Public Health, and Medicine) are collaborating to offer educational opportunities for psychologists to gain expertise in health services and outcomes research at the predoctoral, postdoctoral, and professional levels of training.

The joint Ph.D./M.S.P.H. (master of science in public health) program in Medical Clinical Psychology and Health Outcomes and Policy Research is the most comprehensive program. The program provides psychology doctoral students with coursework and research experiences in outcomes and policy research that complement their existing training in clinical health psychology. Students enrolled in the program complete basic coursework in clinical health psychology and then are permitted to enroll in the Outcomes and Policy Research M.S.P.H. program in the School of Public Health. The curriculum for the program is presented in Table 26.1. Students complete the core content areas and two elective courses. The electives enable students to concentrate their efforts in health policy, advanced analytics, or clinical outcomes evaluation. Because of their foundation of skills in statistics and research design, the biostatistics requirements are waived. On completion of the coursework, each student conducts an independent research project under the mentorship of a School of Public Health faculty member. The program typically can be completed in 1 year and so adds an additional year to students' doctoral training in psychology. Graduates of the joint degree program gain knowledge and skills necessary to investigate the effects of medical and public health interventions on survival, quality of life, and resource utilization. They are prepared for careers in public health, health care

Table 26.1   Required Courses for the Coordinated Master of Science of Public Health (M.S.P.H.)
and Doctor of Philosophy (Ph.D.) in Medical Psychology at the University of
Alabama at Birmingham

M.S.P.H. core

  Biostatistics I (3 hours)
  Biostatistics II (3 hours)
  Principles of epidemiologic research (4 hours)
  Principles of epidemiologic research lab

Outcomes research

  Design of clinical trials
  Health economics
  Patient-based outcomes measurement
  Social and ethical issues in public health
  Health insurance and managed care
  Cost-effectiveness analysis for public health and medicine
  Decision analysis for public health and medicine

Approved electives

  Regression analysis
  Health program evaluation
  Applied logistic regression
  Clinical trials and survival analysis
  Survey research methods
  Public health policy
  Public health law
  Improving health care quality outcomes
  Aging policy
  Policy analysis: Modeling and simulation
  Special problems in policy analysis

Research experience

  Master's-level research project

NOTE: These requirements are in addition to the requirements of the Ph.D. program in psychology.

settings, and health services research such as program evaluation, health outcomes assessment, and pharmacoeconomics.

For those who have already completed a Ph.D., the UAB Center for Outcomes and Effectiveness Research and Education (COERE) offers a 1- to 2-year postdoctoral fellowship that provides research experiences in outcomes and health services research. During the fellowship, psychologists are exposed to a variety of outcomes and health services research projects, the content of which varies from year to year depending on faculty

research programs. All projects address core outcomes and health services research topics such as quality improvement, cost-effectiveness analyses, patient-centered outcomes evaluation, program evaluation, and clinical trials. Fellows attend weekly research discussion groups and journal clubs, attend health services methods workshops, and can enroll in the courses offered in the previously described M.S.P.H. program. The COERE fellowship provides opportunities to collaborate with other fellows from diverse disciplines, including medicine, health economics, and health administration. Psychology fellows are jointly supervised by the center directors and by a clinical psychologist (this chapter's second author), who serves as a division director in the COERE.

CONCLUDING COMMENTS: DISCIPLINARY DIFFERENCES IN PERSPECTIVE AND VALUES

As the preceding discussion suggests, a fundamental feature of public health that is new to many psychologists is its interdisciplinary and collaborative nature. In conventional psychology settings, psychologists often labor alone or in small teams with graduate students. This is uncommon in public health because the scale of problems that are the subject of research and practice often cannot be addressed unless multiple areas of expertise are involved.

For example, in 1999, the surgeon general released a report on mental health (U.S. Department of Health and Human Services, 1999) that highlighted the need to expand approaches to mental health research and practice beyond dominant clinical approaches to include population-based public health approaches. The historical, but diminishing, dominance of psychiatry in the mental health field had promoted a long-standing clinical approach to the neglect of a public health approach. Soon thereafter (in November 2000), the National Institute on Mental Health held a meeting in Rockville, Maryland, titled "Research on Mental Disorders: Overcoming Barriers to Collaborations Between Basic Behavioral Scientists and Public Health Scientists" that was attended by this chapter's first author. The following disciplines were represented at the meeting and exemplify the breadth of relevant expertise common in public health research: biostatistics; clinical, experimental, health, and social psychology; community health sciences; epidemiology; health communications; health economics;

health services research; health education; psychiatry; public health; and medicine.

An overarching goal of the meeting was to explore barriers to collaboration between clinical and public health scientists. The following points emerged during the meeting:

- Basic and public health scientists place different values on many research activities and products, including individual investigator versus collaborative research, hypothesis testing versus applied research, research on interactions that support mediation/moderation of theoretically meaningful effects versus strong main effects with intervention implications, small versus large samples, and internal versus external validity and generalizability.

- Because of these value differences, the criteria for tenure and promotion, publications, grants, and other career advancement opportunities often differ.

- Training opportunities in the "two worlds" of basic behavioral science and public health science are lacking. Several psychologists in attendance had acquired knowledge about public health through mid-career development K-awards. Creating educational opportunities at earlier (e.g., predoctoral) levels of training is essential to advancing the disciplinary interface.

- Even among informed professionals, key terms often convey important and subtle differences in meaning in different disciplines. For example, scientists from disciplines other than epidemiology often do not recognize that *incidence* is a technical term that refers to a measure of rate with time in the denominator. Similarly, *attitude* is a well-researched construct in psychology, but this body of work often is unfamiliar to nonpsychologists, who use the term in the vernacular.

- Considerable comorbidity exists between health problems and mental health problems. However, the issue is underresearched, and the extent of comorbidity is underdiagnosed and undertreated in practice settings, in part because of historical lines drawn among the pertinent disciplines.

These points are instructive about the challenges involved in moving across the disciplinary boundaries of psychology and public health. But many opportunities exist as well. As noted earlier, psychologists have research skills that would enhance the quality of evaluation research on public health behavioral interventions. They also are knowledgeable about etiology and conceptual issues in abnormal behavior and human change processes. In this regard, helping the public health field to move beyond its reliance on the health belief and transtheoretical models was noted as a conceptual issue that would benefit from input by psychologists.

In the arena of practice and applied research, promoting adherence to health-related programs was identified as a critical issue that must be tied more closely to technological and pharmaceutical innovations in care. In addition, because primary health care professionals are overburdened, calling on them to do more in the behavioral health arena was viewed as unrealistic. Helping to refine their focus and increasing the efficiency of what they do, making greater use of "physician extenders," and increasing direct patient access to assessment and intervention options were recommended as alternatives. It was further recommended that, in nonspecialized health care settings, mental health services should be "bundled" with other behavioral health services to increase efficiency and to decrease the stigma of mental illness. The timing of delivery of such services to optimize access, utilization, and outcomes remains poorly understood and underresearched.

Psychologists have much to contribute in these areas of application, but relatively few have acquired the "hybridized" skills and knowledge needed to work effectively in an interdisciplinary health care or research environment. As discussed in this chapter, there are a number of paths to acquiring essential knowledge and skills, and joint psychology–public health programs are likely to become more common in response to the need for behavioral scientists with the necessary breadth of knowledge and skills. Interdisciplinary approaches are essential to finding satisfactory solutions to many contemporary health-related challenges, including expanding prevention programs, improving health care access and effectiveness, reducing health disparities, and containing costs without reducing the quality of care.

Psychologists have been underrepresented in these endeavors, probably due in part to their historical efforts to practice independently without medical supervision and to the corresponding applied research agenda that emphasized comparative outcome evaluations of different types of psychotherapy. These initiatives were successful, but the struggle for professional independence may have inadvertently deterred the participation of psychologists in interdisciplinary teams that are the hallmark of public health research and practice. The expertise of psychologists is needed, and they will almost certainly find the collegiality and respectfulness that are characteristic of public health collaborations to be more productive and satisfying than the medical hierarchy model that dominated the early years of psychology's professional development.

REFERENCES

Clancy, C. M., & Eisenberg, J. M. (1998). Outcomes research: Measuring the end of health care. *Science, 282,* 245–246.

Cummings, N. A., O'Donohue, W. T., & Ferguson, K. E. (2002). *The impact of medical cost offset on practice and research: Making it work for you* (Foundation for Behavioral Health, Healthcare Utilization and Cost Series, Vol. 5). Reno, NV: Context Press.

Curry, S. J., & Kim, E. L. (1999). Public health perspective on addictive behavior change interventions: Conceptual frameworks and guiding principles. In J. A. Tucker, D. M. Donovan, & G. A. Marlatt (Eds.), *Changing addictive behavior: Bridging clinical and public health strategies* (pp. 221–250). New York: Guilford.

De Leon, P. H., Hagglund, K. J., Ragusea, S. A., & Sammons, M. (in press). Expanding roles for psychologists: The 21st century. In G. Stricker & T. A. Widiger (Eds.), *Clinical psychology: Handbook of psychology* (Vol. 8). New York: John Wiley.

Drummond, M. F., O'Brien, B., Stoddart, G. L., & Torrence, G. W. (1997). *Methods for the economic evaluation of health care programmes* (2nd ed.). Oxford, UK: Oxford University Press.

Elliott, T. E., & Klapow, J. C. (1997). Training psychologists for a future in evolving health care delivery systems: Building a better Boulder model. *Journal of Clinical Psychology in Medical Settings, 4,* 255–269.

Feinstein, A. R. (1994). Art, science, and the doctor-patient relationship. *Annals of the New York Academy of Sciences, 729,* 19–21.

Fletcher, R. H., Fletcher, S. W., & Wagner, E. H. (1996). *Clinical epidemiology: The essentials.* Baltimore, MD: Williams & Wilkins.

Frank, R. G., Farmer, J. E., & Klapow, J. C. (in press). The relevance of health policy to the future of health psychology. In R. G. Frank, A. Baum, & J. Wallander (Eds.), *Handbook of clinical health psychology,* Vol. 1: *Models and perspectives in healthcare psychology.* Washington, DC: American Psychological Association.

Frasure-Smith, N., Lesperance, F., Juneau, M., Talajic, M., & Bourassa, M. G. (1999). Gender, depression, and one-year prognosis after myocardial infarction. *Psychosomatic Medicine, 61,* 26–37.

Galea, S., Factor, S. H., Bonner, S., Foley, M., Freudenberg, N., Latka, M., Palermo, A. G., & Vlahov, D. (2001). Collaboration among community members, local health service providers, and researchers in an urban research center in Harlem, New York. *Public Health Reports, 116,* 530–539.

Hennekens, C. H., & Buring, J. E. (1987). *Epidemiology in medicine.* Boston: Little, Brown.

Houston, B. K., Chesney, M. A., Black, G. W., Cates, D. S., & Hecker, M. H. (1992). Behavioral clusters and coronary heart disease risks. *Psychosomatic Medicine, 54,* 447–461.

Humphreys, K., & Tucker, J. A. (2002). Toward more responsive and effective intervention systems for alcohol-related problems. *Addiction, 97,* 126–132.

Kaplan, R. M. (1984). The connection between clinical health promotion and health status: A critical overview. *American Psychologist, 39,* 755–765.

Kaplan, R. M., & Anderson, J. P. (1996). The general health policy model: An integrated approach. In B. Spilker (Ed.), *Quality of life and pharmacoeconomics in clinical trials* (pp. 309–322). Philapdelphia: Lippincott-Raven.

Kaplan, R. M., Anderson, J. P., & Ganiats, T. G. (1993). The Quality of Well-Being Scale: Rationale for a single quality of life index. In S. R. Walker & R. M. Rosser (Eds.), *Quality of life assessment: Key issues in the 1990s* (pp. 65–94). London: Kluwer Academic.

Klapow, J., Kaplan, R., & Doctor, J. (in press). Outcomes measurement: The role of health psychology. In T. Boll (Ed.), *Health and behavior handbook.* Washington, DC: American Psychological Association.

Krantz, D. S. (1988). Environmental stress and biobehavioral antecedents of coronary heart disease. *Journal of Consulting and Clinical Psychology, 56,* 333–341.

Kurki, T. S. (2002). Prediction of outcome in cardiac surgery. *Mount Sinai Journal of Medicine, 69,* 68–72.

National Heart, Lung, and Blood Institute. (1994). *Report of the Task Force on Research in Epidemiology and Prevention of Cardiovascular Diseases.* Washington, DC: U.S. Department of Health and Human Services.

Pennebaker, J. W., Kiecolt-Glaser, J., & Glaser, R. (1988). Disclosure of traumas and immune function: Health implications for psychotherapy. *Journal of Consulting and Clinical Psychology, 56,* 239–245.

Peterson, P. L., Dimeff, L. A., Tapert, S. F., Stern, M., & Gorman, M. (1998). Harm reduction and HIV/AIDS prevention. In G. A. Marlatt (Ed.), *Harm reduction: Pragmatic strategies for managing high-risk behaviors* (pp. 218–297). New York: Guilford.

Pronk, N. P., Boucher, J. L., Gehling, E., Boyle, R. G., & Jeffery, R. W. (2002). A platform for population-based weight management: Description of a health plan-based integrated systems approach. *American Journal of Managed Care, 8,* 847–857.

Sexton, M. M. (1979). Behavioral epidemiology. In O. F. Pomerleau & J. P. Brady (Eds.), *Behavior medicine: Theory and practice* (pp. 3–21). Baltimore, MD: Williams & Wilkins.

Tucker, J. A. (1999). Changing addictive behavior: Historical and contemporary perspectives. In J. A. Tucker, D. M. Donovan, & G. A. Marlatt (Eds.), *Changing addictive behavior: Bridging clinical and public health strategies* (pp. 3–44). New York: Guilford.

Tucker, J. A., Phillips, M. M., Murphy, J. G., & Raczynski, J. M. (in press). Behavioral epidemiology and health psychology. In R. G. Frank, A. Baum, & J. Wallander (Eds.), *Handbook of clinical health psychology,* Vol. 1: *Models and perspectives in healthcare psychology.* Washington, DC: American Psychological Association.

Turnock, B. J. (1997). *Public health: What it is and how it works.* Gaithersburg, MD: Aspen.

U.S. Department of Health and Human Services. (1999). *Mental health: A report of the surgeon general.* Rockville, MD: U.S. Department of Health and Human Services, Substance Abuse and Mental Health Services Administration, Center for Mental Health Services.

Weinstein, M., & Stason, W. (1977). Foundations of cost-effectiveness analysis for health and medical practices. *New England Journal of Medicine, 296,* 716–721.

World Health Organization. (2002). *Innovative care for chronic conditions: Building blocks for action* (WHO annual report). Geneva, Switzerland: Author.

CHAPTER 27

Practical Research in a Medical Setting Is Good Medicine

KATHLEEN M. PALM, JACK L.-M. MUTNICK, DAVID O. ANTONUCCIO, AND ELIZABETH V. GIFFORD

Conducting clinical research in medical settings is becoming increasingly important in the behavioral health care field. In the wake of managed care, the role of the behavioral health care provider is shifting. Some experts speculate that the 50-minute therapy session will eventually become extinct (Cummings, 2000; Hayes, Barlow, & Nelson-Gray, 1999). Behavioral health care specialists will increasingly need to function within different contexts.

As the practice of behavioral care specialists shifts, so must the focus of research. There is a growing need to assess the effectiveness of psychological treatments outside of controlled laboratory settings. Controlled studies assess the efficacy of treatments by testing whether interventions work under ideal circumstances. Typical medical settings, however, include numerous factors that cannot be controlled and are hardly ideal. Because this is where many interventions will be delivered, this is where the research needs to be conducted.

There are many advantages to doing research in medical clinics. For example, researchers can contact more patients, observe a greater range of complaints, and interact with multidisciplinary teams. Perhaps most important, researchers can study treatment and treatment outcomes as they occur in "real-world" treatment settings. Before beginning a research program in these settings, however, there are special issues to consider. This chapter describes a brief history of research in medical settings and then details institutional and research considerations. Common roadblocks are discussed, and practical advice is provided. A case study illustrates how different issues and roadblocks can be addressed.

CASE STUDY

Throughout this chapter, the authors draw on a specific real-world example of clinical

AUTHORS' NOTE: This research was supported by National Institute on Drug Abuse Grant 1R01DA013106-03.

research in a medical setting. The investigators of this study sought to examine the impact on smoking cessation of bupropion sustained release (SR) versus bupropion SR plus behavior therapy. Approximately 300 patients participated and were treated at the local Veterans Affairs (VA) hospital, a family medicine clinic, or the psychiatry clinic at the University of Nevada School of Medicine. All patients received a 10-week course of bupropion SR and were given the standard instructions for taking the medication. Participants were randomly assigned to one of three groups: medication only, medication plus assessment, or medication plus assessment plus behavior therapy. Behavior therapy involved 10 weeks of individual and group treatment. Assessment was conducted at intake, Week 3, Week 7, posttreatment, 6-month follow-up, and 12-month follow-up. Although the research design and outcomes from this study were enlightening, the locations in which this study took place perhaps presented more information and challenging questions than did the initial research hypotheses. As different parts of this chapter are highlighted, brief examples from this study are provided to illustrate how the investigators addressed the challenges of working within these medical clinics.

HISTORICAL AND ETHICAL ISSUES

Before commencing a program of research within a medical setting, it is useful to consider the historical context. Two important historical angles are the history of research in medical practice and the history of the integration of psychological interventions with traditional medical practice. Investigators are also encouraged to become familiar with the tradition of research within the specific clinics in which they will be working.

One historical issue to consider is the treatment of research participants in medical research. There is a history in medical research where the focus was more on advancing science for the sake of knowing rather than for the sake of healing human suffering. Examples from the 19th and early 20th centuries illustrate how the burden of serving as research participants fell largely on poor ward patients, whereas the luxury of improved medical care went primarily to private and wealthier patients. One example of maltreatment of research participants is the exploitation of unwilling prisoners as participants in Nazi concentration camps (Shuster, 1997). In the United States during the 1940s, the Tuskegee Syphilis Study used disadvantaged, rural, African American men to study the untreated course of a disease that was by no means confined solely to that population (Fairchild & Bayer, 1999). To avoid interruptions in the study, these individuals were deprived of demonstrably effective treatment long after such treatment became available to the general public (Fairchild & Bayer, 1999).

It is against this historical background that the concepts of justice and ethical practice being relevant to research involving human participants (Francis, 2001) is painfully clear. And it is for these reasons that the selection of research participants needs to be scrutinized to ensure that particular groups of people are not being selected simply because of availability, compromised position, or manipulability. Rather, participants should be selected for reasons related to the problems being studied. Ultimately, when research supported by public funds leads to the development of new therapies and procedures, ethical guidelines demand that these treatments not provide advantages only to those who can afford them and that such research should not unduly involve persons from groups unlikely to be among the beneficiaries of subsequent applications of that research.

Three basic ethical principles are particularly relevant to the ethics of research involving human participants: "respect of persons," "beneficence," and "justice" (U.S. National Commission for the Protection of Human

Subjects of Biomedical and Behavioral Research, 1979). Respect for persons incorporates at least two ethical convictions, namely, that (a) individuals should be treated as autonomous agents and (b) persons with diminished autonomy are entitled to protection. Beneficence requires that participants be treated in an ethical manner not only by respecting their decisions and protecting them from harm but also by making efforts to secure their well-being. Two general rules have been devised as corresponding expressions of beneficent actions, namely, to (a) do no harm and (b) maximize possible benefits and minimize possible harms (Reitsma & Moreno, 2002). The final basic ethical principle widely accepted in research is that of justice. In delving into this expansive topic, one needs to consider the question of who should receive the benefits of research and who should bear its burdens. This is a question of justice in the sense of "fairness in distribution" or "what is deserved."

A very important topic that may be underemphasized is "informed consent." Informed consent is a process, not just a form to be signed. It is necessary for the researcher to present all of the pertinent information to the participants to enable these individuals to voluntarily decide whether or not to participate. It is fundamental to ensure respect for persons through provision of thoughtful consent for a voluntary act (Casari & Massimo, 2002). The procedures used in obtaining informed consent should be designed to educate the participants in terms that they can comprehend. Therefore, the language and documentation must be written in terms that are understandable to the people being asked to participate.

The essential components that should be included when attempting to obtain informed consent from research participants are as follows: (a) a description of the overall experience that participants can expect; (b) a description of the benefits that participants may reasonably expect; (c) reasonable alternatives to the proposed intervention; (d) an account of the relevant risks, benefits, and uncertainties related to each alternative; and (e) reassurance that personally identifiable private information will be held in strict confidence (Ashford, Scollay, & Harrington, 2002). One must remember that informed consent originates from the research participants' legal and ethical right to direct what happens to their bodies and from the ethical duty of the research team to involve the participants in the decision-making process.

In the medical industry, there often seems to be a distinction made between research and practice. *Research* is thought to focus on data, whereas the term *practice* connotes a focus on healing. One of the biggest distinguishing factors of research conducted within medical settings is the need to interact effectively with an existing system that typically prioritizes clinical practice above research demands. Many medical clinics have not experienced the effective integration of research and practice. This chapter outlines how to develop a research program that will work within these settings.

DEFINING A RESEARCH QUESTION

When working within a fast-paced setting with limited time and staff resources, it is important to pose a question in the most efficient way possible. In other words, consider posing the question in a way such that the findings add the most information to the current state of knowledge in the field. For example, investigating the question "Does Treatment X work?" may be interesting, but one can gather more informative data if the question is posed in such a way that health care providers can determine *which* treatment is best for *which* people under *which* conditions (Paul, 1967). Therefore, studying multiple factors that may influence the effects of treatment will provide more information than simply inquiring whether or not treatment works. Furthermore, investigating the mechanism of change in addition to outcomes might better inform treatment development (Follette, 1995). Researchers can also maximize efficiency by exploring alternative explanations to the investigated problem. For instance, in the described case study, the investigators hypothesized that treating emotional avoidance would function to reduce cigarette smoking. They also investigated alternative mechanisms of change for smoking cessation, including social support, stage of readiness, and the taste of cigarettes after taking the medication. By assessing various possible mediating variables, the investigators could identify which mechanisms accounted for the largest degree of change in outcomes.

SELLING THE RESEARCH IDEA

Despite the most exciting research ideas, one of the main obstacles to confront is selling the ideas to staff at the medical facility. Depending on the size of the medical setting and the size of the project, it will be more or less feasible to pitch research ideas to the administration and staff. Research may be an integral part of some medical settings, whereas other facilities have never participated in research projects. Before pitching the research idea, it would be helpful to assess how supportive the clinic or hospital is of research. If it has supported research in the past, it would be ideal to talk to investigators working in that setting so as to anticipate possible institutional barriers that might arise. For example, one practical consideration to anticipate may be related to the increased security measures that have developed in hospitals and clinics during recent years. It may be important to show the staff and administration that the researchers share their concerns about security and will make every effort to work within their regulations.

There are several steps researchers can take to facilitate the adoption of new ideas in medical settings (Strosahl, 2001). First, researchers should attain the support of the administration (e.g., chief executive officers, directors of units). They should ask these people whether they would be willing to help pitch the idea to the rest of the clinic. Second, if possible, researchers should try to attend staff and/or residents meetings. Getting to know the people within the clinic can be helpful in trying to advance project implementation. Having others' support will help to facilitate assessment and treatment and may also increase the likelihood of obtaining more referrals. A related strategy involves enlisting an employee of the institution as a collaborator or consultant on the study. In the case study, physicians from the various clinic sites were invited to be consultants on the study. The investigators also attended residency meetings to educate the residents about bupropion SR, describe the research goals, and enlist the support of the medical staff.

Third, researchers should find out whether there is specific information of interest to clinic staff. Some information can be easily collected along with other data. Being open to gathering information relevant to the practice setting increases the chance that the clinic will accept the research idea. Also, when presenting the idea, researchers should try to have as much detail formulated as possible while maintaining a degree of openness to change. Providing a clearly explicated project will bolster confidence in the competence of the investigators. At the same time, maintaining a degree of flexibility will also increase the likelihood of success in these settings.

In addition to information, the medical clinic or clinic staff may be in need of services that the researchers can provide. For instance, the investigators in the case study provided instruction on using the Internet to clinic nurses at one site and permitted use of the assessment computers when these computers were not being used by research participants. In exchange for the use of these resources, the clinic provided the researchers with office space and referrals to the smoking cessation program.

Researchers should try, to the extent possible, to incorporate data collection into the normal routine of treatment. In the case study, the investigators simply set up an adjunctive smoking cessation clinic in the VA Mental Health Clinic at another site. Participation by veterans in these adjunctive clinics was counted as use of VA services.

INSTITUTIONAL CONSIDERATIONS

Medical settings use written and unwritten policies that include, but are not limited to, institutional review board regulations, particular guidelines and protocols of the medical setting, and other research review procedures. It is important to investigate and address these institutional policies to facilitate cooperation within the clinic. There are two policy matters to which researchers must attend (a) the ethics of the proposed research study and (b) practical concerns related to the logistics of conducting the study.

Researchers should be aware of the ethical guidelines followed by the medical facility. Although most adhere to standard guidelines, some facilities may incorporate additional considerations. For example, investigators should become familiar with the institutional protocol for adverse events. If none is specified, procedures should be created indicating who should be contacted in an emergency, what reports need to be written in such a case, who should receive copies of the reports, and what needs to be done in response to specific adverse events. In addition, some medical settings may have special policies related to patients' response, or lack of response, to treatment. Patients should always be adequately informed of potential risks, including iatrogenic effects and nonresponse to treatment. In fact, some medical facilities may insist on additional exclusion criteria based on institutional concerns about appropriate candidates for treatment. Researchers should work collaboratively with the medical setting staff to develop the safest, most efficient, and strongest research design possible given the requirements of the setting.

In addition to ethical issues, investigators often will need to negotiate more practical concerns. The issue of office space is frequently a dilemma. Researchers may have limited space, if any at all, within which to work. Although having an office for the investigators may be ideal, researchers might not have any office space available and will have to work quickly in the hallways between seeing patients. For this reason, it is important to have organized assessments that are easily accessible and include clear instructions. Practical issues regarding the everyday operation of a research study might seem inconsequential at first. However, these problems can potentially interfere with the flow of research and possibly the eventual completion of the project. Therefore, it is important to carefully plan how treatment and assessments will be conducted. In addition to space concerns, researchers should clearly outline the format of assessments (e.g., paper and pencil, computer), where patients will complete assessments, where data will be stored, who will have access to the data, and which personnel will be collecting the data.

RESEARCH DESIGN

There are a variety of design options to use when conducting research in a medical setting. These designs range from single-case methodology to large randomized control trials. Although a review of research designs is beyond the scope of this chapter, the reader is referred to Barlow and Hersen (1984) for single-case methodology and to

Kazdin (1998a, 1998b) for group design methodology.

The context of the medical setting introduces special issues that might not apply in other settings. For example, hospitals may differ in their views of what types of control conditions are acceptable. Although ethical guidelines provide a framework from which to work, some hospitals or clinics may have more stringent policies. Again, researchers need to become knowledgeable about local policies and how to best structure research projects in ways that work within these systems. It is important to find the best balance between workability within the hospital system and strength of the conclusions that can be drawn from the study. Ideally, researchers should identify extraneous variables and implement procedures that will best control for them. In the case study, the investigators speculated that contact with assessment staff during the course of treatment might affect the outcome. Consequently, an additional condition was added in which participants continued to receive medication but had limited contact with assessment staff during the treatment phase of the study.

In many medical clinics, multiple health care providers see one patient. Within one clinic, it is not uncommon for a patient to be involved in an anger management group, individual therapy for posttraumatic stress disorder, and treatment for diabetes. It is possible that treatments other than the one under investigation might influence outcomes. In other words, outcomes may be due to changes that are occurring in another treatment domain. It is also plausible that an intervention targeted at another problem is dampening the impact that the treatment under investigation may have. Tracking a patient's participation across health services can help to identify the impact of other treatments on patient outcome. Some other questions to ask include the following: Has the patient already participated in identical or similar treatments such that little improvement can be expected? Does the patient population

have large enough variability in symptom severity to detect differences? Are the assessments sensitive enough to detect changes over the duration of the study?

Another issue that should be addressed is attrition. Some patients might leave the study before they have completed their participation. Although these patients might not have received the full treatment, information about these individuals can be very useful. Collecting information about why the patients quit treatment can inform providers about which patients are more likely to adhere to the treatment in the future. If participants do not agree to complete the assessment portion of the study, using a brief telephone follow-up questionnaire or mailing a brief assessment packet can be invaluable. In the case study, the investigators decided to use a brief, 5-minute telephone follow-up format to collect information about smoking status, participation in other treatments, hypothesized mediating variables (e.g., avoidance, social support), and why patients were choosing to quit the study at that time. This procedure allowed the researchers to gather minimal outcome data and preliminary data about which individuals were not as likely to benefit from the intervention.

It is also important to track and report information regarding participants who were excluded from the study. Often, there are treatment options that are proscribed given certain conditions. For example, in the smoking cessation study, the investigators found that bupropion SR was contraindicated for people who, among other things, were taking selective serotonin reuptake inhibitors or had a history of seizures. Given these precautions, many veterans were unable to participate in the study due to medical exclusions (Kohlenberg, Antonuccio, Hayes, Gifford, & Piasecki, 2002). These data provided useful information regarding the effectiveness of using this treatment option within the VA clinic. Identifying populations for whom treatments are not suitable is as important as identifying those for whom treatments are effective.

RECRUITMENT

Before recruiting participants for a study, it is important to define what the inclusion and exclusion criteria will be. As described previously, patients may have medical or psychiatric conditions that would preclude their participation. It is useful to have a script and a standardized screening assessment for staff so that all participants receive the same information during the initial phone screen. The script should include a thorough discussion of the expectations of study participants. Although patients will be presented with informed consent documents when they enter the study, in the chapter authors' experience, patients seem to participate more fully in the program when informed consent and commitment-enhancing procedures are implemented during the first contact with the patients.

ASSESSMENT

There are several issues that should be considered before assessment systems are put into place. First, investigators should identify whether or not reactivity to assessments might be a concern. For example, researchers have found that people can change behavior and their physiology when they have access to physiological measures (Abueg, Colletti, & Kopel, 1985; McDowell et al., 1999; Scharff, Marcus, & Masek, 2002). In the case study, researchers were measuring carbon monoxide readings from smoking patients and decided to ensure that patients did not see their ratings until after the study was completed. Providing an attractive graph of the patients' readings only at the end of the study reduced the possible effects of reactivity to this measure and gave patients something additional to take away from their participation in the study.

In conducting good assessment, it is important to collect meaningful and efficient measures. Documentation and referrals should be easy (Hollis et al., 2000), especially if clinic personnel are collecting data as part of the research program. It is imperative to consider the time demands of busy practice environments. In addition, investigators should carefully research the most persuasive data. For example, is self-report of cigarettes smoked better than carbon monoxide reading? In addition, researchers should consider the length of time for which data are being collected and whether it is possible to see a change in these data during that amount of time.

Finally, it is important for investigators to constantly attend to the morale of the people involved in the project as well as to the relationship between research assistants and the medical facility staff. The number of obstacles that can be encountered during a research study can be demoralizing. Barriers may range from dealing with institutional politics to trying to get patients to adhere to treatment and complete assessments. Within this context, treatment and assessment staff may become less committed to the project, drift in their delivery of services, and not be as attentive to maintaining respectful and effective relationships with coworkers. Investigators can plan ongoing training opportunities, hold regular meetings, and provide a great deal of encouragement to everyone involved in the study to maintain healthy relationships and morale. As the investigators found in the case study, food nearly always works.

TREATMENT

Before interventions are implemented, there are a few steps that researchers can take to assist in the flow of the project. To begin, researchers should design protocols that explicate the roles of the staff that are involved in the study. Research and medical staff should be trained on what *is* and is *not* expected of each. These protocols should also outline who should be contacted for psychiatric and/or medical emergencies. Additional items that should be addressed in the protocols might include the training of treatment providers and the monitoring of treatment adherence.

Also, staff roles should fit efficiently into office flow (Hollis et al., 2000). It is important to have a steady flow and good communication between health providers and research assistants. For example, in the smoking cessation study, research assistants conducted the screening and initial assessments and then provided physicians with a summary of this information so as to work more efficiently with the doctor. To avoid losing possible participants, investigators should also plan on minimizing the time between obtaining a referral, conducting the phone screen, and starting treatment.

Training of treatment providers will vary depending on who will be delivering treatment. If the research team is providing the clinicians, investigators often have the luxury of time and resources to spend on training. However, if the clinicians are current staff from within the medical setting, researchers will need to develop a quick and efficient training program for the clinicians. Providing manuals, videotapes, CD-ROMs, one-time training meetings, or some combination of these options may be the best approach to training. To monitor any drift in treatment delivery and to ensure that treatment is being provided as it should be, researchers should periodically monitor adherence to treatment protocols while the treatment phase is in progress (Elkin, 1999). For example, adherence can be assessed through coding tapes of clinicians who are providing the intervention. Periodic monitoring of treatment delivery during the treatment phase of the study can provide opportunities to give feedback to treatment providers.

Investigators should also define what they consider to be a treatment "completer." To conclude whether or not treatment was effective, researchers must be able to show that patients actually received the treatment in totality. For example, if patients were taking an antidepressant, did they take the indicated number of pills per day? Or, if they were using a nicotine patch, did they use the patch as indicated? To measure their adherence, patients could record whether or not they receive treatment each day of the week. The problem with this procedure, however, is that self-monitoring has been found to be an effective treatment in and of itself (Abueg et al., 1985; Gillmore et al., 2001). Therefore, it would be difficult to tease apart the effects of the self-monitoring versus the treatment being studied. An alternative way of assessing adherence to treatment might be to use a version of the time line follow-back procedure (Sobell, Brown, Leo, & Sobell, 1996). In this procedure, the research assistant reviews a calendar with the patients, who indicate the days on which they complied with the treatment protocol. Researchers should always consider how the delivery and monitoring of treatment affects outcomes.

In the smoking cessation study, the researchers specified how many therapy sessions a patient had to attend to be considered someone who completed the treatment. Likewise, they needed to specify the definition of adherence to the study medication. These decisions should be made before treatment begins.

CONFLICT OF INTEREST ISSUES

Conducting research within medical settings is influenced by factors that lie inside and outside of the actual clinics. It is not uncommon for these factors to interfere with appropriate research and clinical practice. However, researchers have a moral and ethical obligation to address these difficult issues and to make sure that important information is disseminated. Some of these dilemmas include financial conflicts of interests and publication biases. These factors are especially complicated to address when medications are included in the study. For example, it is difficult to think of any arena involving information about medications that does not have significant industry financial or marketing influences. Industry financial influences extend to federal regulatory agencies, professional organizations and their journals, continuing medical education, scientific researchers, media experts, and consumer advocacy organizations (Antonuccio, Burns, & Danton, 2002). Respected psychiatric researchers such as Marks (Marks et al., 1993) and Fava (1998) have warned that such widespread corporate interests may result in self-selecting academic oligarchies influencing clinical and scientific information. In fact, those who produce data contrary to industry interests may find themselves vulnerable to legal, professional, or even personal attack, either directly or indirectly financed by the industry (Antonuccio et al., 2002).

Furthermore, there are widely acknowledged publication biases, often related to conflicts of interest, that favor pharmaceutical industry products (Antonuccio et al., 2002). In fact, these biases have so eroded the credibility of the medical literature (Quick, 2001) that new proposals call for stringent accountability guidelines (e.g., Davidoff et al., 2001; Moses & Martin, 2001) aimed at ensuring researcher independence in study design, access to data, and right to publish. It remains to be seen whether these new guidelines will have the desired effect of improving the quality and credibility of the literature. The bottom line is that researchers in a medical setting have a moral and ethical obligation to their human participants to independently design, implement, analyze, and publish the results of their studies, no matter whose ox is gored. The integrity of medical research is at stake and is worth fighting for.

CONCLUSIONS

Conducting research in medical settings presents challenges that are typically not encountered in more traditional behavioral research environments. Investigators often must study politics and persuasion nearly as much as they study their research question. Although these added pressures can be daunting, the rewards of doing this work far surpass the costs. Within 15 months, the researchers in the case study helped approximately 300 patients to quit smoking. Many of these patients would not have had the opportunity to join this program if it had been located outside of their medical clinics. Although it took time and patience to conduct this project, preliminary analyses indicate that 27% of those patients who could be contacted for assessment 6 months after treatment remained smoke free.

The ultimate goal in health care is to develop and provide the best treatments possible for those individuals who need them. Implementing research programs within medical settings helps to accomplish this goal in several ways. First, this practice can foster the dissemination of effective treatments. Second, it can force researchers to develop treatments that are more acceptable within these environments. Most important, by moving into medical clinics, patients who need care will have access to a greater number of opportunities to decrease their suffering.

REFERENCES

Abueg, F. R., Colletti, G., & Kopel, S. A. (1985). A study of reactivity: The effects of increased relevance and saliency of self-monitored smoking through enhanced carbon monoxide feedback. *Cognitive Therapy & Research, 9,* 321–333.

Antonuccio, D. O., Burns, D. D., & Danton, W. G. (2002). Antidepressants: A triumph of marketing over science? *Prevention and Treatment, 5,* Article 25. [Online]. Retrieved January 20, 2003, from http://journals.apa.org/prevention/volume5/pre0050025c.html

Ashford, R. U., Scollay, J., & Harrington, P. (2002). Obtaining informed consent. *Hospital Medicine, 63,* 374.

Barlow, D. H., & Hersen, M. (1984). *Single case experimental designs: Strategies for studying behavior change.* New York: Pergamon.

Casari, E. F., & Massimo, L. M. (2002). From informed to shared: The developing process of consent. *Minerva Pediatrica, 54,* 211–216.

Cummings, N. A. (2000). A psychologist's proactive guide to managed care: New roles and opportunities. In A. J. Kent & M. Hersen (Eds.), *A psychologist's proactive guide to managed mental health care* (pp. 141–161). Mahwah, NJ: Lawrence Erlbaum.

Davidoff, F., DeAngerlis, C. D., Drazen, J. M., Nicholls, M. G., Hoey, J., Hoigaard, L., Horton, R., Kotzin, S., Nicholls, M. G., Nylenna, M., Overbeke, A. J. P. M., Sox, H. C., Van der Weyden, M. B., & Wilkes, M. S. (2001). Sponsorship, authorship, and accountability. *New England Journal of Medicine, 345,* 825–827.

Elkin, I. (1999). A major dilemma in psychotherapy outcome research: Disentangling therapists from therapies. *Clinical Psychology: Science & Practice, 6,* 10–32.

Fairchild, A. L., & Bayer, R. (1999). Uses and abuses of Tuskegee. *Science, 284,* 919–921.

Fava, G. A. (1998). All our dreams are sold. *Psychotherapy and Psychosomatics, 67,* 191–193.

Follette, W. C. (1995). Correcting methodological weaknesses in the knowledge base used to derive practice standards. In S. C. Hayes, V. M. Follette, R. M. Dawes, & K. E. Grady (Eds.), *Scientific standards of psychological practice: Issues and recommendations* (pp. 229–247). Reno, NV: Context Press.

Francis, C. K. (2001). The medical ethos and social responsibility in clinical medicine. *Journal of the National Medical Association, 93,* 57–69.

Gillmore, M. R., Gaylord, J., Hartway, J., Hoppe, M. J., Morrison, D. M., Leigh, B. C., & Rainey, D. T. (2001). Daily data collection of sexual and other health-related behaviors. *Journal of Sex Research, 38,* 35–42.

Hayes, S. C., Barlow, D. H., & Nelson-Gray, R. O. (1999). *The scientist practitioner: Research and accountability in the age of managed care* (2nd ed.). Needham Heights, MA: Allyn & Bacon.

Hollis, J. F., Bills, R., Whitlock, E., Stevens, J. J., Mullooly, J., & Lichtenstein, E. (2000). Implementing tobacco interventions in the real world of managed care. *Tobacco Control, 9,* 18–21.

Kazdin, A. E. (1998a). *Methodological issues and strategies in clinical research* (2nd ed.). Washington, DC: American Psychological Association.

Kazdin, A. E. (1998b). *Research design in clinical psychology* (3rd ed.). Needham Heights, MA: Allyn & Bacon.

Kohlenberg, B. S., Antonuccio, D. O., Hayes, S. C., Gifford, E. V., & Piasecki, M. P. (2002). *Bupropion SR for nicotine dependent smokers: Limited applicability?* Unpublished manuscript, University of Nevada School of Medicine.

Marks, I. M., Swinson, R. P., Basoglu, M., Kuch, K., Noshirvani, H., O'Sullivan, G., Lelliott, P. T., Kirby, M., McNamee, G., Sengun, S., & Wickwire, K. (1993). Alprazolam and exposure alone and combined in panic disorder with agoraphobia: A controlled study in London and Toronto. *British Journal of Psychiatry, 162,* 776–787.

McDowell, B. J., Engberg, S., Sereika, S., Donovan, N., Jubeck, M. E., Weber, E., & Engberg, R. (1999). Effectiveness of behavioral therapy to treat incontinence in homebound older adults. *Journal of the American Geriatrics Society, 47,* 309–318.

Moses, H., & Martin, J. B. (2001). Academic relationships with industry: A new model for biomedical research. *Journal of the American Medical Association, 285,* 933–935.

Paul, G. (1967). Strategy of outcome research in psychotherapy. *Journal of Consulting and Clinical Psychology, 31,* 109–118.

Quick, J. (2001). Maintaining the integrity of the clinical evidence base. *Bulletin of the World Health Organization, 79,* 1093.

Reitsma, A. M., & Moreno, J. D. (2002). Ethical regulations for innovative surgery: The last frontier. *Journal of the American College of Surgery, 184,* 792–801.

Scharff, L., Marcus, D. A., & Masek, B. J. (2002). A controlled study of minimal-contact thermal biofeedback treatment in children with migraine. *Journal of Pediatric Psychology, 27,* 109–119.

Shuster, E. (1997). Fifty years later: The significance of the Nuremberg Code. *New England Journal of Medicine, 337,* 1436–1440.

Sobell, L. C., Brown, J., Leo, G. I., & Sobell, M. B. (1996). The reliability of the Alcohol Timeline Followback when administered by telephone and by computer. *Drug & Alcohol Dependence, 42,* 49–54.

Strosahl, K. (2001). The integration of primary care and behavioral health: Type II changes in the era of managed care. In N. A. Cummings, W. O'Donohue, S. C. Hayes, & V. M. Follette (Eds.), *Integrated behavioral healthcare: Positioning mental health practice with medical/surgical practice* (pp. 45–69). San Diego: Academic Press.

U.S. National Commission for the Protection of Human Subjects of Biomedical and Behavioral Research. (1979). *The Belmont Report: Ethical principles and guidelines for the protection of human subjects of research.* [Online]. Retrieved July 15, 2002, from http://ohsr.od.nih.gov/mpa/belmont.php3

CHAPTER 28

Evaluating Outcomes in Health Care Settings

JOAQUIN BORREGO, JR., AND
WILLIAM C. FOLLETTE

During this era of managed care and increased consumer awareness, there is an ever-increasing demand from different entities (e.g., federal agencies, third-party reimbursements, consumer advocate groups) to ask for evidence of professional service effectiveness. This demand is amplified by the dramatic cost increases in providing quality health care (Relman, 1988). In turn, public and private organizations are beginning to incorporate evaluation components into different service delivery programs (Brown & Reed, 2002). This change is especially evident in health care settings that serve a wide range of populations with different health problems (Fink, 1993).

One way of directly addressing professional accountability is through the systematic evaluation of the services delivered. This systematic evaluation of different service components is called *program evaluation*. The goal of program evaluation is the collection, analysis, and interpretation of data pertaining to intervention efforts (Rossi & Freeman, 1993). With program evaluation, a multitude of service delivery practices can be evaluated, ranging from

examining the effectiveness of a specific treatment for diabetes for a particular individual to assessing for client satisfaction with the services received at a community outpatient clinic. Along with measuring intervention effectiveness, there is also an increasing focus on evaluating prevention efforts in health-related problems such as substance abuse (Hansen, 2002). Evaluation of existing programs can focus on both process and overall program effectiveness (Kelley, Van Horn, & De Maso, 2001). This flexibility allows professionals to answer a multitude of questions in different practice settings (Posavac & Carey, 1997).

Program evaluation is defined as a systematic methodology that allows professionals to (a) document whether the treatment was implemented as intended, (b) choose appropriate measures that are sensitive to behavior change, (c) demonstrate treatment effectiveness, and (d) demonstrate how a particular intervention produces change (if desired). The ideas set forth in this chapter are meant to be broad enough so that the concepts covered can be implemented in multiple settings (e.g., private practice, medical centers) targeting different services (e.g., individual vs. group treatment, case management, consultation).

Program evaluation can be applied to address a host of physical (e.g., obesity, diabetes) and psychological (e.g., depression, anxiety) problems encountered in health care settings. Questions addressed by program evaluation strategies can range from simple objective questions (e.g., "Does Intervention X work with Population Y?") to more complex and subjective questions (e.g., "Are clients satisfied with the services that are offered in a community clinic and why?").

Although it is beyond the scope of the chapter to outline the technical details of all aspects of program evaluation, there is one distinction to keep in mind: the distinction is between a cost-benefit analysis and a cost-effectiveness analysis. Cost-benefit analyses are procedures used to measure programs and outcomes on the same metric, namely dollars. Program costs are determined (e.g., costs per employee in an employee assistance program) and benefits are measured in terms of dollars saved in medical services use or dollars saved in employee replacement costs. Often, companies or policymakers contracting for or funding services are interested in these kinds of program evaluations.

Individual providers and clients are frequently more interested in cost-effectiveness data. In this type of analysis, costs are still generally computed in dollars, whereas outcomes are measured in terms of specific effects. For example, it might cost $400 to add an additional harm reduction treatment module to a substance abuse intervention to produce a specific effect such as a demonstrable increase in employer satisfaction. Details of the differences between these two strategies and technical details of how to conduct each can be found elsewhere (e.g., Yates, 1996). Instead, this chapter provides the reader with an overview of issues to consider when developing and implementing a program evaluation component into one's practice setting.

STEPS IN PROGRAM EVALUATION

There are several steps involved in conducting a thorough program evaluation. The first step in program evaluation is defining the specific targets or questions that the clinician is interested in addressing in the evaluation. As an example, a clinician in private practice might be interested in evaluating the effectiveness of cognitive-behavioral group treatment with an obese population. In contrast, a clinician in a rural community setting might be interested in conducting a systemwide program evaluation and so would prefer to assess treatment accessibility, treatment acceptability, and treatment satisfaction within a particular community catchment area.

Once the question (or set of questions) and hypotheses have been identified, the next step is to identify the population to be involved in the program evaluation. The target population can range from being broad in nature (e.g., assessing for satisfaction in services received in a multipurpose clinic) to addressing clinically related questions with a specific population (e.g., asking whether Treatment Z would work with diabetes patients). With the former question, clinicians are accessing all clients who use services that are offered in the clinic, whereas the latter question might focus on only a subset of the clinic population (e.g., diabetic patients).

Once the target population has been identified, the next step involves identifying the independent and dependent variables that are going to be used in the program evaluation. The independent variables that are going to be identified are related to the treatment the clinician is interested in evaluating. The key to this process is selecting variables that are specific. Instead of asking "Does my antidepression treatment program work with depressed clients?," one can develop a more precise question such as "How does each component of an antidepressant treatment program contribute to the outcome?" or "Does the level of training in a particular therapy modality affect the outcome in this clinic?" On the outcome or dependent variable side of the evaluation, it is again useful to identify maximally useful measures. Although one might be interested in the question "Are clients satisfied with treatment?," it may be much more informative to ask "Does a particular antidepression program lead to a decrease in Beck Depression Inventory scores and an improvement in life satisfaction, and does that lead to increased client satisfaction with services, session attendance, and even fee remittance?" This latter version of the specification of the dependent variable gives a glimpse of the potential power of program evaluation in that processes that serve the program and the clients alike can be highlighted.

Identifying and Defining Behaviors of Interest

Before a treatment is implemented and evaluated, the clinician should define what behaviors he or she is interested in changing given the target population (e.g., decreasing smoking in smokers if abstinence is the goal vs. decreasing the number of cigarettes smoked if harm reduction is the goal). This selection process involves identifying *target behaviors* and should occur early in the assessment process (Hawkins, 1986). Three criteria for identifying, defining, and choosing target behaviors are that they must be observable, specific, and measurable. Although private events (e.g., cognitions) can be measured, it is easier for clinicians and clients to measure observable events. As an example, although the clinician can assign a homework assignment to monitor the number of times a person "thinks" about having a cigarette, it might be more beneficial to have the patient monitor the number of times he or she smokes during a specified time period (e.g., each day, each week).

The second criterion involves choosing a behavior or a set of behaviors that is specific rather than vague. As an example, instructing a client to "eat better" can be improved by specifying the actual behaviors that the clinician is interested in modifying: eating two or three servings of vegetables per day, decreasing fatty food intake by 30 fat grams per day, drinking 64 ounces of water per day, and so on. As another example, a direction to "exercise more" can be improved by making specific recommendations: stretching for 10 minutes per day, walking for 20 minutes per day/four times per week, and so on.

Meeting the criteria for choosing observable and specific target behaviors makes it easier for clinicians to measure outcomes. It is much easier to measure behaviors that are observable and specific (e.g., monitoring the frequency with which a person smokes per day) than to measure events that are unobservable and vague (e.g., "thinking patterns" that may or may not be highly correlated with the actual treatment goals). Appealing to hypothetical constructs (e.g., the mind, the subconscious) makes it difficult to monitor and document the behaviors, and so they are not as amenable to change through standard clinical practices. In contrast, measuring behavior change involving observable and specific behaviors makes it easier for clients to follow directions and increases the likelihood of compliance. It may be helpful to make use of simple instrumentation in some cases. Walking can be monitored using a pedometer. Medication can be monitored with pill counts or with more expensive devices that can record when and how often a pill bottle is opened.

Other Types of Assessment Methods

Several assessment methods are available to the clinician in documenting and demonstrating behavior change. Some of these methods include interviews, self-report measures (e.g., rating scales), and direct observation in analog (i.e., clinic) and natural settings. Although interviews are considered to be qualitative in nature, they are nonetheless important because they provide the clinician with information from the client's perspective about his or her history and current environmental situation. Methods such as time line follow-back (Sobell & Sobell, 1996) can be reliable and useful ways in which to gather baseline data. Self-report measures are also important in helping to choose target behaviors to change. When available, staff trained to a high level of reliability should be used to conduct behavioral observations of specific client behaviors using instruments validated in the literature. A highly structured environment (e.g., medical center setting) can facilitate the process of making systematic observations but might lack ecological validity. Natural environments can pose problems of their own, although time sampling using audiotapes may provide useful data if the clinician is evaluating communication training in a family therapy intervention. Institutional settings provide unique data-gathering opportunities of their own (for a particularly creative reference to program evaluation in institutional settings, see Paul & Menditto, 1992).

Choosing Appropriate and Sensitive Measures

Choosing appropriate measures will also assist clinicians in determining what and when to measure. As stated previously, clinicians should choose variables of interest that are clinically meaningful (Biskupiak, 2001). Given the question that is asked and the independent and dependent variables that are chosen, measures should be chosen that are suitable for the project. In program evaluation, it is important to choose a measure or a set of measures that is appropriate and sensitive enough to detect changes for the evaluation of targeted behaviors. When appropriate, clinicians should choose instruments that are suitable for measuring the behavior change being monitored (e.g., changes in distress as a result of decreasing food intake).

Given the target behavior in question, some instruments will be more applicable than others. Choosing instruments that are sensitive to change is important because not all instruments display the same level of sensitivity. As with the previous example, some measures might be more applicable in measuring changes in global distress patterns over a longer period of time (e.g., 4 months), whereas other instruments might be more suitable for detecting subtle changes in client behavior on a shorter time basis (e.g., daily, weekly). If clinicians are interested in tracking subtle changes but choose an instrument that is designed to detect global changes, actual changes in client behavior will not be detected.

Other Issues Related to the Selection of Assessment Strategies

Program evaluation can have a variety of goals and occurs in many types of settings. One goal may be to assess for the presence or absence of a diagnostic label before and after an intervention. Such assessments will have certain characteristics (Silva, 1993a, 1993b). If a program assumes a unitary cause for a particular problem, or if the program is designed to deliver a structured, standardized, comprehensive treatment for a problem, reliable standardized assessments of client problem changes and treatment integrity may be sufficient (cf. Follette, Naugle, & Linnerooth, 2000; Haynes, 1992; Haynes, Leisen, & Blaine, 1997).

However, some programs and many practices allow treatment staff to vary treatment depending on client characteristics. In this case, the service providers in a program ought to attend to the selection of assessment procedures that demonstrate *treatment utility* (Hayes, Nelson, & Jarrett, 1987; Silva, 1993b). Treatment utility of assessment is the degree to which information derived from an assessment procedure would lead a therapist to alter an intervention in a way that would affect outcome. For example, an assessment of a client's activity level might lead a therapist to include a behavioral activation component to treatment for depression. If decisions based on such an assessment lead to improved outcomes, the assessment procedure has treatment utility. However, not all programs allow such flexibility.

Levels of Analysis Affecting Design Considerations

Program evaluation can occur at many levels, including the individual client level (i.e., the efficacy of a type of intervention for a type of client), the clinic level, or even the institutional level. For simplicity, the following discussion is limited to the first two cases.

Single-Case Designs. For single-case designs, multiple baseline data points can be collected before starting treatment. Gathering multiple data points during baseline helps to guard against reactivity to measures, lack of reliability of a single measurement point, and regression to the mean artifacts. Multiple data points also help in determining the trend and level of the problem being assessed. A single-case design allows for the use of repeated measurement of changing client behaviors, allowing clinicians (or other evaluators) to track behavior on an individual basis and to tailor the measurement to fit their clinical needs (e.g., daily monitoring, weekly therapy session change, within-session change).

For individual cases, a strategy that offers clinical utility is that of graphing data for clients (Figure 28.1). Graphing data creates a visual analysis for clinicians that can be shared directly with clients. In turn, the graphed data can lead to therapeutic gains (Hawkins, Mathews, & Hamdan, 1999). More important, if a reliable coding system is in place for the coding of different behaviors, the graphed data can serve as an objective measure of client progress during the intervention (Hawkins et al., 1999). This is important information for both clinicians and clients. For clinicians, it

allows for the systematic examination of progress (or lack thereof) when dealing with individual clients (Hawkins & Mathews, 1999). Although statistical analytic procedures are available for analyzing single-case designs, visual analysis is frequently appropriate when working with individuals. As recommended by Franklin, Allison, and Gorman (1996), comparison of the dependent measure across treatment conditions can provide objective data from which to infer clinical significance.

Group Designs. An often-neglected step involved in program evaluation is checking to see whether the treatment was implemented as intended. The process of evaluating the degree to which the treatment was delivered as intended is called *treatment integrity* (Kazdin, 1992). Checking for treatment integrity allows clinicians to check whether the independent variable (i.e., the delivered treatment) was successfully manipulated (Follette & Compton, 1999). Figure 28.2 highlights the four possible outcomes involved in conducting a manipulation check. In Quadrant I, the independent variable has been successfully implemented, and there was an observed change in the dependent variable. Clinically, this is the best possible outcome because there is a level of certainty that the observed change in targeted behavior is due to the introduction of treatment. In Quadrant II, the treatment was successfully implemented, but there was no observed change in behavior (i.e., no change in the dependent variable). If group design research is being conducted, one possible explanation is that the treatment did not work in accomplishing the clinically relevant goals (assuming that there was sufficient statistical power). In Quadrant III, the treatment was not successfully implemented, but there was still an observed change in the desired outcome (e.g., decrease in smoking frequency). Unfortunately, the change in the dependent variable cannot be attributed to the implemented treatment. The observed change might

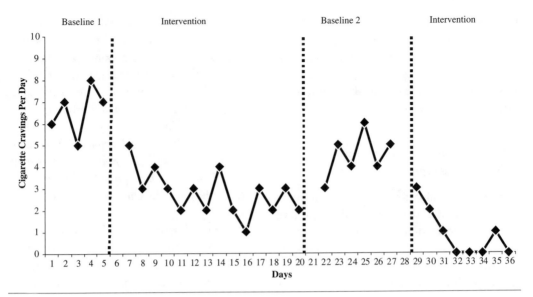

Figure 28.1   Individual Monitoring of Behavior Change

be due to non-treatment-related events (e.g., new medical information received from a physician during the course of treatment) or to threats to internal validity (e.g., changes due to history and maturation) (Follette & Compton, 1999; Kazdin, 1992). In Quadrant IV, the treatment was not successfully implemented, and there was no observed change in the targeted behavior. From a program evaluation perspective, this result would highlight the need to implement better therapy training or to identify another therapy that might be easier to deliver for the population being evaluated.

In summary, the best clinical condition to have is that in Quadrant I, where clinicians have a level of certainty that a change in a client's behavior (e.g., decrease in weight) is due to the treatment delivered (e.g., targeting weight loss). For clinicians who use treatment manuals as a means of delivering treatment, treatment protocol checklists are available in many of the treatment manuals. If treatment manuals are not available, it is possible to develop treatment integrity

checklists that are specific to the treatment of interest (for a detailed discussion on treatment integrity checklists, see Waltz, Addis, Koerner, & Jacobson, 1993).

ANALYSIS OF OUTCOME EVALUATION

If clinicians are interested in evaluating outcomes for groups of individuals, there are a variety of analytic techniques that are available. Using conventional inferential statistical analyses targeting groups, clinicians can compare (a) one treatment condition with another or (b) a specific treatment with a placebo or "wait list" group or some "treatment as usual" condition (i.e., control group) (Figure 28.3).

There is a growing literature that provides an alternative to traditional null hypothesis testing in the form of model fitting (Bakeman & Gottman, 1997). Model-fitting strategies test a priori models of processes that might explain change. The notion in model fitting is

Changes in Dependent Variable (DV)

		Yes	No
Manipulation of Independent Variable (IV)	Yes	Change in IV (+) Change in DV (+) **I**	Change in IV (+) No Change in DV (-) **II**
	No	No Change in IV (-) Change in DV (+) **III**	No Change in IV (-) No Change in DV (-) **IV**

Figure 28.2   Treatment Integrity Quadrant

NOTE: IV = independent variable; DV = dependent variable.

that clinicians can posit those factors that account for change and then test the goodness of fit of the proposed model to the actual data. Clinicians can identify sources of change that are not modeled to refine their understanding of the change process. These techniques are somewhat more demanding in terms of software and numbers of subjects required for analysis, but they can produce data that guide theory and treatment development in ways that conventional statistics cannot.

Methods of Describing Change

Although most conventional group statistical approaches to summarizing outcomes make use of reporting the mean change averaged across all participants, many researchers looking for ways in which to better describe the meaningfulness of change have proposed alternatives to merely reporting mean changes between treatment or program conditions. Three strategies deserve some mention here (see also Follette & Callaghan, 2001).

First, clinicians can summarize program effects in terms of Cohen's effect size statistics (Cohen, 1988) that are often used in meta-analyses (Rosenthal & DiMatteo, 2001). Rather than showing only that a program produces a change larger than zero, effect size statistics suggest how large a program change is compared with similar programs if such summary data exist. Regardless of the availability of comparison data, effect sizes and confidence intervals give some indication of the magnitude of change a program produces.

A second approach gaining acceptance is that of normative comparisons (Kendall, Marrs-Garcia, Nath, & Sheldrick, 1999; Rogers, Howard, & Vessey, 1993). In this strategy, if normative data on nonclinical samples exist, the posttreatment means are tested to see whether those treated for a problem are improved to a degree that is equivalent to a nonclinical normative sample. For example, if a program is designed to address problems of child externalizing behavior (i.e., acting out), two analytic steps would occur. First, the

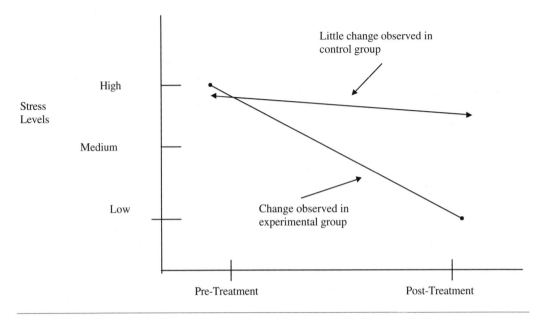

Figure 28.3   Traditional Monitoring of Behavior Change

change from pretreatment to posttreatment would be assessed statistically. If the change was significant, the posttest level of externalizing behavior would be compared with the norms for a nonclinical sample to see whether the program returned participants to a normal level of functioning. These kinds of data are useful in providing consumers and program designers with information about the practical magnitude of change an intervention produces.

Although equivalence or normative testing is useful, it assesses average changes at the level of the group. The third alternative for summarizing data is done at the level of the individual. In an approach similar to equivalence testing, each individual's result is tested to see whether the program both produced a reliable change and returned the client to a normal level of functioning (Jacobson, Follette, & Revenstorf, 1984; Jacobson & Truax, 1991). Like equivalence testing, this approach requires the existence of good normative data on nonclinical participants for dependent measures. The advantage of this approach over others is that

it allows evaluators to categorize program results in terms of what proportion of individual clients actually significantly improved to become indistinguishable from normal controls, what proportion improved but still differed from controls, what proportion did not improve, and what proportion deteriorated as a result of treatment.

These three methods of describing change produced by a program are clinically relevant to clients and providers alike, whereas cost-benefit analyses and even cost-effectiveness analyses may be more meaningful to policymakers or those who contract for services.

Assessment of Social Validity

An often-neglected aspect of program evaluation is assessing what clients find to be acceptable treatment and their satisfaction with the treatment process and outcome. Assessing for these two components involves assessment of social validity. Wolf (1978) addressed the important issue of assessing for social validity in the context of services offered with respect to three criteria. The first criterion for social validity is assessing for the social significance of the identified target behaviors and treatment goals. If clinicians were to identify treatment goals, would clients find the target behaviors and treatment goals to be acceptable? It is very important for clients to have input on the target behaviors given that not agreeing on the same target behaviors can interfere with and impede treatment progress. As an example, if a clinician is working with a Mexican American woman with diabetes, the target goal of decreasing her intake of fat and sugar and increasing her intake of steamed vegetables (e.g., broccoli) would probably fail given that the client has a history of eating different kinds of food that are prepared and cooked differently (i.e., Mexican diet). The second criterion to address is the social appropriateness of the treatment procedures. It is important to assess whether clients find a specific treatment to be acceptable. The assumption is that clients who find a treatment more acceptable are more likely to participate in treatment than are those who do not find the treatment to be acceptable. Finally, the third criterion to address is the social importance of the treatment effects. This is the "consumer satisfaction" component of social validity in that it informs clinicians as to whether clients were satisfied with the services offered. Assessing for consumer satisfaction can be tailored to fit the clinician's or agency's needs. As an example, consumer satisfaction can vary from assessing a client's satisfaction with the actual treatment to assessing his or her satisfaction with administrative services and the like.

Unfortunately, social validity as an assessment component has historically been neglected, as is apparent by the low percentage of published material that assesses for social validity (Carr, Austin, Britton, Kellum, & Bailey, 1999). Neglect in the assessment for social validity might be due to the "subjectivity" involved. Social validity is considered to be subjective in the sense that clinicians are asking clients what they thought of or how they perceived the treatment process and whether they were satisfied with the intervention. Because of the subjective nature of clients' responses, assessing for treatment satisfaction is often omitted in the scientific evaluation of treatment programs. Although there is a subjective component to assessing for social validity, it is nonetheless an important variable to assess for because it can provide valuable clinical information. Information that assesses for client acceptability of the treatment process and client satisfaction with the treatment should be considered as important as objective indexes of behavior change (e.g., reported change on a psychometrically sound rating scale). The likelihood of sustained change observed in treatment may be affected by clients' acceptability of the treatment and their satisfaction with the treatment and services offered.

CONCLUSIONS

This chapter has attempted to make an argument for the systematic method of conducting program evaluations that can be adapted for different types of practice settings. Different contingencies (e.g., third-party reimbursements) have placed an even greater emphasis on professionals becoming active participants in the continuous evaluation of their services. Implementing a program evaluation component forces professionals to focus on the question of "What should be measured and why?" This measurement question can range from evaluating patients' quality of life to gauging their satisfaction with clinical services. Without outcome measurements, clinicians cannot determine the impact of the intervention, nor can they optimize care (Toscani & Pizzi, 2001).

In spite of noted methodological weaknesses and challenges (e.g., el-Guebaly, Hodgins, Armstrong, & Addington, 2002; Ellingstad, Sobell, Sobell, & Planthara, 2002; Follette, 1995), professionals can incorporate into their practice a program evaluation component that would enhance the quality of services offered. Program evaluation is a relatively easy process, with the numerous benefits including maintaining high ethical and practice standards, monitoring program efficiency and effectiveness, and providing important financial information (Cone, 2000). Although program evaluation seems like a daunting task for clinicians, it is hoped that the recommendations offered in this chapter make clinicians appreciate the benefits of conducting program evaluations whether in private practice or in a medical center. The data gathered should lead clinicians to ask further questions regarding what they practice and the way in which they practice. The data obtained from program evaluations can lead to future needs assessments and the development, refinement, and implementation of practice standards. The results from a well-planned program evaluation can place a practitioner or an agency at a competitive advantage when asked to justify costs, resources, and growth of services.

Program evaluation is flexible enough in its methodology that different services, ranging from individual or group therapy to case management, can be monitored for their efficiency and effectiveness. What may be more challenging for clinicians is choosing treatments that are conceptually coherent and that specify the mechanisms of behavior change. Theoretically, the chosen intervention should include a strong rationale for why specific treatment components are included and what they are intended to change.

Continuous evaluation of one's practice should be as much part of a professional's repertoire as is being ethically responsible. Program evaluation data should also lead to the dissemination of more effective standards of practice. In turn, better developed standards of practice can lead to more effective ways in which clinicians actually practice (Dawes, 1995). As managed care continues to change the landscape and manner in which clinicians practice, it is becoming increasingly important to demonstrate the effectiveness of their interventions. As the commitment to the systematic evaluation of programs continues to grow, treatment efficiency and effectiveness will also continue to improve.

REFERENCES

Bakeman, R., & Gottman, J. M. (1997). *Observing interactions: An introduction to sequential analysis.* London: Cambridge University Press.

Biskupiak, J. E. (2001). Selecting variables and constructs to measure. In R. Patterson (Ed.), *Changing patient behavior: Improving outcomes in health and disease management* (pp. 201–222). San Francisco: Jossey-Bass.

Brown, R. E., & Reed, C. S. (2002). An integral approach to evaluating outcome evaluation training. *American Journal of Evaluation, 23,* 1–17.

Carr, J. E., Austin, J. L., Britton, L. N., Kellum, K. K., & Bailey, J. S. (1999). An assessment of social validity trends in applied behavior analysis. *Behavioral Interventions, 14,* 223–231.

Cohen, J. (1988). *Statistical power analysis for the behavioral sciences* (2nd ed.). Hillsdale, NJ: Lawrence Erlbaum.

Cone, J. D. (2000). *Evaluating outcomes: Empirical tools for effective practice.* Washington, DC: American Psychological Association.

Dawes, R. M. (1995). Standards of practice. In S. C. Hayes, V. M. Follette, R. M. Dawes, & K. E. Grady (Eds.), *Scientific standards of psychological practice* (pp. 31–43). Reno, NV: Context Press.

el-Guebaly, N., Hodgins, D. C., Armstrong, S., & Addington, J. (2002). Methodological and clinical challenges in evaluating treatment outcome of substance-related disorders and comorbidity. *Canadian Journal of Psychiatry, 44,* 264–270.

Ellingstad, T. P., Sobell, L. C., Sobell, M. B., & Planthara, P. (2002). Drug treatment outcome methodology (1993–1997): Strengths, weaknesses, and a comparison to the alcohol field. *Addictive Behaviors, 27,* 319–330.

Fink, A. (1993). *Evaluation fundamentals: Guiding health programs, research, and policy.* Newbury Park, CA: Sage.

Follette, W. C. (1995). Correcting methodological weaknesses in the knowledge base used to derive practice standards. In S. C. Hayes, V. M. Follette, R. M. Dawes, & K. E. Grady (Eds.), *Scientific standards of psychological practice* (pp. 229–247). Reno, NV: Context Press.

Follette, W. C., & Callaghan, G. M. (2001). The evolution of clinical significance. *Clinical Psychology: Science and Practice, 8,* 431–435.

Follette, W. C. & Compton, S. (1999). *Correcting methodological weaknesses in traditional psychotherapy outcome research.* Unpublished manuscript, University of Nevada, Reno.

Follette, W. C., Naugle, A. E., & Linnerooth, P. J. (2000). Functional alternatives to traditional assessment and diagnosis. In M. J. Dougher (Ed.), *Clinical behavior analysis* (pp. 99–125). Reno, NV: Context Press.

Franklin, R. D., Allison, D., & Gorman, B. S. (1996). *Design and analysis of single-case research.* Mahwah, NJ: Lawrence Erlbaum.

Hansen, W. B. (2002). Program evaluation strategies for substance abuse prevention. *Journal of Primary Prevention, 22,* 409–436.

Hawkins, R. P. (1986). Selection of target behaviors. In R. O. Nelson & S. C. Hayes (Eds.), *Conceptual foundations of behavioral assessment* (pp. 331–386). New York: Guilford.

Hawkins, R. P., & Mathews, J. R. (1999). Frequent monitoring of clinical outcomes: Research and accountability for clinical practice. *Education & Treatment of Children, 22,* 117–135.

Hawkins, R. P., Mathews, J. R., & Hamdan, L. (1999). *Measuring behavioral health outcome: A practical guide.* Dordrecht, Netherlands: Kluwer Academic.

Hayes, S. C., Nelson, R. O., & Jarrett, R. B. (1987). The treatment utility of assessment: A functional approach to evaluating assessment quality. *American Psychologist, 42,* 963–974.

Haynes, S. N. (1992). *Models of causality in psychopathology: Toward synthetic, dynamic, and nonlinear models of causality in psychopathology.* Needham Heights, MA: Allyn & Bacon.

Haynes, S. N., Leisen, M. B., & Blaine, D. D. (1997). Design of individualized behavioral treatment programs using functional analytic clinical case models. *Psychological Assessment, 9,* 334–348.

Jacobson, N. S., Follette, W. C., & Revenstorf, D. (1984). Psychotherapy outcome research: Methods for reporting variability and evaluating clinical significance. *Behavior Therapy, 15,* 336–352.

Jacobson, N. S., & Truax, P. (1991). Clinical significance: A statistical approach to defining meaningful change in psychotherapy research. *Journal of Consulting and Clinical Psychology, 59,* 12–19.

Kazdin, A. E. (1992). *Research design in clinical psychology* (2nd ed.). New York: Macmillan.

Kelley, S. D., Van Horn, M., & De Maso, D. R. (2001). Using process evaluation to describe a hospital-based clinic for children coping with medical stressors. *Journal of Pediatric Psychology, 26,* 407–415.

Kendall, P. C., Marrs-Garcia, A., Nath, S. R., & Sheldrick, R. C. (1999). Normative comparisons for the evaluation of clinical significance. *Journal of Consulting and Clinical Psychology, 67,* 285–299.

Paul, G. L., & Menditto, A. A. (1992). Effectiveness of inpatient treatment programs for mentally ill adults in public psychiatric facilities. *Applied & Preventive Psychology, 1,* 41–63.

Posavac, E. J., & Carey, R. G. (1997). *Program evaluation: Methods and case studies* (5th ed.). Upper Saddle River, NJ: Prentice Hall.

Relman, A. S. (1988). Assessment and accountability: The third revolution in medical care. *New England Journal of Medicine, 319,* 1220–1222.

Rogers, L. K., Howard, K. I., & Vessey, J. T. (1993). Using significance tests to evaluate equivalence between two experimental groups. *Psychological Bulletin, 113,* 553–565.

Rosenthal, R., & DiMatteo, M. R. (2001). Meta-analysis: Recent developments in quantitative methods for literature reviews. *Annual Review of Psychology, 52,* 59–82.

Rossi, P. H., & Freeman, H. E. (1993). *Evaluation: A systematic approach.* Newbury Park, CA: Sage.

Silva, F. (1993a). *Psychometric foundations and behavioral assessment.* Newbury Park, CA: Sage.

Silva, F. (1993b). Treatment utility: A reappraisal. *European Journal of Psychological Assessment, 9,* 222–226.

Sobell, L. C., & Sobell, M. B. (1996). *Alcohol timeline follow-back (TLFB) users' manual.* Toronto: Addiction Research Foundation.

Toscani, M. R., & Pizzi, L. T. (2001). Measuring and improving the intervention. In R. Patterson (Ed.), *Changing patient behavior: Improving outcomes in health and disease management* (pp. 177–200). San Francisco: Jossey-Bass.

Waltz, J., Addis, M. E., Koerner, K., & Jacobson, N. S. (1993). Testing the integrity of a psychotherapy protocol: Assessment of adherence and competence. *Journal of Consulting and Clinical Psychology, 61,* 620–630.

Wolf, M. (1978). Social validity: The case for subjective measurement or how applied behavior analysis is finding its heart. *Journal of Applied Behavior Analysis, 11,* 203–214.

Yates, B. T. (1996). *Analyzing costs, procedures, processes, and outcomes in human services.* London: Sage.

Name Index

Subject Index

About the Editors

Lee M. Cohen, Ph.D., is Assistant Professor in the Clinical Division of the Department of Psychology at Texas Tech University and Assistant Adjunct Professor in the Department of Neuropsychiatry and Behavioral Sciences at the Texas Tech University Health Sciences Center. He completed his predoctoral clinical internship and a postdoctoral fellowship funded by the National Institute on Drug Abuse at the University of California, San Diego, specializing in behavioral medicine. He completed his graduate training in clinical psychology at Oklahoma State University. His research interests involve systematically exploring the behavioral and physiological mechanisms that contribute to nicotine use and dependence.

Dennis E. McChargue, Ph.D., is Research Assistant Professor in the Clinical Division of the Department of Psychology at the University of Illinois at Chicago and Health Research Scientist in Research Services at Edward Hines, Jr., Veterans Affairs Hospital. He is currently funded by the National Institute on Drug Abuse on a Mentored Clinical Scientist Development Award. He completed his predoctoral clinical internship at Boston University/Boston Veterans Affairs Medical Center Consortium and completed his postdoctoral training at the University of Illinois at Chicago. He completed his graduate training in clinical psychology at Oklahoma State University. His research interest revolves around testing biobehavioral mechanisms that contribute to the development, maintenance, and eventual treatment of tobacco use disorders, especially among those individuals vulnerable to psychopathology.

Frank L. Collins, Jr., Ph.D., is Professor and Director of Clinical Training in the Department of Psychology at Oklahoma State University and Adjunct Professor in the Department of Psychiatry at the University of Oklahoma Health Sciences Center, where he serves on the executive committee for the Oklahoma Center for Alcohol and Drug-Related Studies. He received his doctorate from Auburn University and completed his clinical psychology internship at the University of Mississippi Medical Center. Prior to coming to Oklahoma State University, he was on the faculty at West Virginia University and Rush-Presbyterian-St. Luke's Medical Center in Chicago. His research focuses on biobehavioral models of nicotine dependence.

About the Contributors

Mustafa al'Absi, Ph.D., is Associate Professor of Behavioral Medicine at the University of Minnesota School of Medicine. He directs a research program focusing on stress, risk for hypertension, and tobacco addiction. His research has been funded by grants from the National Cancer Institute, National Institute on Drug Abuse, and National Health, Lung, and Blood Institute. He completed his biological and clinical psychology training at the University of Oklahoma and Oklahoma State University. He completed his clinical psychology residency, specializing in behavioral medicine, at the University of Mississippi Medical Center. He has led several collaborative research initiatives focusing on biobehavioral mechanisms of hypertension and tobacco addictions.

David O. Antonuccio, Ph.D., is Professor of Psychiatry and Behavioral Sciences at the University of Nevada School of Medicine and Director of the Stop Smoking Program at the Reno Veterans Affairs Medical Center. He received his doctorate in clinical psychology from the University of Oregon in 1980. He served on the Nevada State Board of Psychological Examiners from 1990 to 1998. He holds a diplomate in clinical psychology from the American Board of Professional Psychology and is a fellow of the American Psychological Association. His clinical and research interests include the behavioral treatment of depression, anxiety, and smoking.

Krista A. Barbour, Ph.D., is a Postdoctoral Fellow in Behavioral Medicine in the Department of Psychiatry and Behavioral Sciences at the Duke University Medical Center. She completed her predoctoral clinical internship at the University of Mississippi Medical Center/Jackson Veterans Affairs Medical Center Consortium, specializing in health psychology. She received her doctorate in clinical psychology at the University of Southern California. Her research interests involve examination of physical activity in the treatment of depression and chronic disease and the relationship between emotional expression and health.

Cynthia D. Belar, Ph.D., A.B.P.P., is Executive Director of the American Psychological Association Education Directorate and Professor in the Department of Clinical and Health Psychology at the University of Florida Health Science Center. She received her doctorate from Ohio University in 1974 after completing an internship at the Duke University Medical Center. Since then, she has been engaged in education, training, research, practice, and administration in clinical and health psychology.

Nicole E. Berlant, Ph.D., is a Behavioral Medicine Consultant in the Departments of Neurology and Adult Medicine for the Permanente Medical Group in Sacramento, California. She received her doctorate in clinical health psychology from the University of Florida in 2002. She received her undergraduate degree from the University of California, San Diego, and completed a clinical internship at the Veterans Affairs Medical Center in Long Beach, California. She has authored or coauthored more than 10 professional articles, abstracts, and book chapters in the area of behavioral medicine.

Andrew C. Blalock, Ph.D., is a Coordinating Center Liaison for the Mental Health HIV Services Collaborative Program, a 5-year Substance Abuse and Mental Health Services Administration-funded service project. He completed his doctoral training at Georgia State University and completed his predoctoral internship in the Department of Psychiatry at the University of Chicago. He was awarded a National Institute of Mental Health HIV/AIDS clinical research postdoctoral fellowship through the Department of Psychiatry and Behavioral Sciences at Emory University before joining the Department of Behavioral Sciences and Health Education in the Rollins School of Public Health. His clinical and research interests include employment and return-to-work issues for persons with HIV/AIDS and neuropsychological aspects of HIV disease progression.

Lindsey Bloor, M.S., is a graduate student in the Clinical Health Psychology Program of the Department of Psychology at the University of Utah. Her research interests involve exploring the influence of psychosocial factors, particularly social support, on physical and mental health outcomes. Her clinical interests include facilitating support groups for people living with cancer.

Jennifer L. Boothby, Ph.D., is Assistant Professor in the Department of Psychology at Indiana State University. She completed her graduate training in clinical psychology at the University of Alabama in Tuscaloosa and completed her predoctoral clinical internship at the University of North Carolina School of Medicine. Her research interests involve the application of forensic issues to health psychology and chronic pain such as pain and malingering, personal injury assessment, and health issues affecting prisoners.

Joaquin Borrego, Jr., Ph.D., is Assistant Professor in the Clinical Division of the Department of Psychology at Texas Tech University and Clinical Professor in the Communication Disorders Department in the School of Allied Health at the Texas Tech University Health Sciences Center. He received his master's and doctorate in clinical psychology from the University of Nevada, Reno. He completed his predoctoral clinical internship at the University of California, San Diego. His research interests include the assessment and treatment of child physical abuse, behavioral observations of physically abusive parent-child relationships, assessment of different cultural parenting and discipline practices in the context of child maltreatment, community interventions with ethnic minority populations, and the development, implementation, and evaluation of psychosocial treatments with Spanish-speaking populations.

Peter E. Campos, Ph.D., is Director of PRN Data, a private health research consulting business. He currently serves as coordinator of the clinical core of the Substance Abuse and Mental Health Services Administration-funded Mental Health HIV Services Collaborative Program through the Rollins School of Public Health at Emory University. He received his doctorate in clinical/community psychology at the University of Hawaii and completed his predoctoral internship at the University of Mississippi Medical Center. He was previously a faculty member in psychiatry and behavioral sciences at Emory University's School of Medicine, where he was clinical director of mental health services at the Grady Infectious Disease Program. His interests in HIV work include culturally competent mental health services, psychosocial and psychiatric sequelae of living with HIV, and the intersection of Eastern philosophy and cognitive-behavioral therapy.

John M. Chaney, Ph.D., is Professor of Clinical Psychology at Oklahoma State University and Clinical Associate Professor of Psychiatry at the University of Oklahoma Health Sciences Center. He completed his internship in pediatric psychology at the Oklahoma University Health Sciences Center and received his doctorate from the University of Missouri–Columbia in 1991. He is the current president of the National Society of Indian Psychologists and serves on the American Psychological Association's Committee on Ethnic Minority Affairs. His research interests focus on children's adjustment to chronic medical illness and on implicit racism affecting academic achievement among Native Americans.

Anna Chur-Hansen, Ph.D., is Senior Lecturer in the Department of Psychiatry at the University of Adelaide in South Australia. She is a member of the Australian Psychological Society's College of Health Psychologists and was the recipient of the Australian and New Zealand Association for Medical Education Award for Research in 2000. She has taught medical undergraduate students in the behavioral sciences since 1987. Her research focuses on evaluations of teaching initiatives and their assessment for medical and health sciences students, particularly the disciplines of psychology, anthropology, and psychiatry.

Matthew M. Clark, Ph.D., A.B.P.P., is Associate Professor of Psychology and Co-Section Head of Outpatient Medical Psychiatry and Psychology, as well as Director of the Medical Psychology Fellowship Program, in the Department of Psychiatry and Psychology at the Mayo Clinic in Rochester, Minnesota. He received his doctorate in clinical psychology from Fordham University, was a predoctoral clinical psychology intern at the Syracuse Veterans Affairs Medical Center, completed a postdoctoral fellowship in behavioral medicine at the Brown University School of Medicine, and is a board-certified clinical health psychologist. His research focuses on behavioral interventions for weight management, nicotine dependence, and coping with cancer. Currently, his research is funded by the National Cancer Institute.

Monica Cortez-Garland, B.A., is a doctoral student in the Clinical Division of the Department of Psychology at Texas Tech University. Her research interests fall within addictive disorders. Her current research endeavors include the investigation of personality characteristics and their relation to smoking behavior.

Csilla T. Csoboth, M.D., is Assistant Professor in the Institute of Behavioral Sciences at Semmelweis University in Budapest, Hungary. She received her medical diploma at Semmelweis University and specializes in psychiatry. She is currently completing her doctorate on the psychosocial risk factors affecting women's mental health. Her other research interests include health-damaging behavior (e.g., obesity, nicotine and alcohol abuse), violence against women, and methods of prevention among women.

Patricia M. Dubbert, Ph.D., is Associate Chief of Mental Health and Director of Psychology at the G. V. (Sonny) Montgomery Veterans Affairs Medical Center and Professor of Psychiatry, Preventive Medicine, and Medicine at the University of Mississippi School of Medicine. She received her bachelor's degree in nursing in 1968 from the University of Missouri–Columbia, her master's in mental health nursing in 1972 from New York University, and her doctorate in psychology in 1982 from Rutgers University.

Mitch Earleywine, Ph.D., is Associate Professor of Clinical Sciences in the Department of Psychology at the University of Southern California. He received his doctorate from Indiana University and completed internship at the University of Mississippi Medical School Consortium. He has more than 40 publications in the addictions literature, including the book *Understanding Marijuana*.

Barry A. Edelstein, Ph.D., is Professor of Psychology in the Clinical Psychology Program at West Virginia University. His current research interests include decision-making processes, assessment of decision-making competence, anxiety, and suicidality among older adults.

Sadie Emery, B.S., is a doctoral student in the Clinical Division of the Department of Psychology at Texas Tech University. Her current research interests include investigating whether cortisol is a marker for nicotine withdrawal and investigating the effect of emotional expressive writing on nicotine withdrawal.

Joel Erblich, Ph.D., is Assistant Professor of Biobehavioral Medicine in the Cancer Prevention and Control Program of the Ruttenberg Cancer Center at the Mount Sinai School of Medicine in New York City. He completed his predoctoral clinical internship at the University of California, Los Angeles, and completed a postdoctoral fellowship funded by the National Cancer Institute at the Memorial Sloan Kettering Cancer Center, specializing in behavioral medicine. He completed his graduate training in clinical psychology at the University of Southern California. His research interests involve understanding the cognitive, behavioral, and genetic influences on risk for addiction.

Myles S. Faith, Ph.D., is Associate Research Scientist at the New York Obesity Research Center (NYORC) and Assistant Professor of Psychology in Psychiatry at the Columbia University College of Physicians and Surgeons. He received his doctorate in clinical/school psychology from Hofstra University in 1995, after which he completed a 3-year postdoctoral fellowship at the NYORC. During this fellowship, he received training in behavioral-genetic methods for studying human obesity and focused on determinants of childhood obesity. He is funded to study genetic and environmental influences on caloric regulation and body fat in young children and has conducted behavioral interventions for childhood obesity.

William C. Follette, Ph.D., is Associate Professor in the Clinical Program of the Department of Psychology, as well as Research Associate Professor in Family and Community Medicine, at the University of Nevada, Reno. He received his doctorate in clinical psychology from the University of Washington. He has served on a number of review panels for the National Institutes of Health and the National Institute on Drug Abuse. In addition to interests in applied clinical behavior analysis and psychotherapy research design and methodology, he studies psychotherapy treatment development.

Michael D. Franzen, Ph.D., is Associate Professor of Psychiatry in the Hahnemann School of Medicine at Drexel University and Chief Psychologist at Allegheny General Hospital in Pittsburgh, Pennsylvania. He completed his doctorate in clinical psychology at Southern Illinois University at Carbondale. He completed an internship and a postdoctoral fellowship in neuropsychology at the University of Nebraska School of Medicine. He is a fellow of Division 40 of the American Psychological Association and a fellow of the National Academy of Neuropsychology. He has published extensively in the area of neuropsychological assessment, test construction, dementia, and head injury.

Sheila Garos, Ph.D., is Assistant Professor in the Department of Psychology at Texas Tech University and Assistant Adjunct Professor in Neuropsychiatry in the Division of Urology at the Texas Tech University Health Sciences Center. She has more than 18 years of experience in mental health. Her areas of clinical expertise include the assessment and treatment of sexual disorders and dysfunctions, marital therapy, addiction, and adult psychopathology. Her research interests include sexual attraction, compulsive sexual behaviors, women's sexuality, and psychometrics.

Elizabeth V. Gifford, B.A., is a doctoral candidate at the University of Nevada, Reno, and an intern at the Veterans Affairs (VA) Palo Alto Health Care System. She is currently working with the Center for Health Care Evaluation at Stanford University, the VA Palo Alto Health Care System, and the VA Task Force on Violence Prevention. She is the recipient of a Career Development Award from the National Cancer Institute. Her interests include addiction treatment, tobacco control, social context and coping, and social and health policy.

Suzy Bird Gulliver, Ph.D., is Staff Psychologist and Director of Health Psychology at the Veterans Affairs Boston Healthcare System Outpatient Clinic as well as Assistant Professor in the Boston University School of Medicine's Department of Psychiatry and Assistant Clinical Professor in the Department of Psychology at Boston University. She completed her doctoral training in clinical psychology at the University of Vermont. Her predoctoral internship was conducted at the West

Haven Veterans Affairs Medical Center, followed by a National Institute on Alcohol Abuse and Alcoholism postdoctoral fellowship in alcohol treatment outcome at Brown University. Her research interests are in cross-addictions, comorbid psychopathology, and the role of affect (dys)regulation.

Kimberly R. Haala, B.S., is a graduate student in clinical psychology at Oklahoma State University. She received her bachelor's degree at Minnesota State University, Mankato. Her research interests include investigating behavioral and physiological correlates of nicotine use.

Ahna L. Hoff, M.S., is a pediatric psychology intern in the Department of Psychology at Columbus Children's Hospital in Columbus, Ohio. She completed her graduate training in clinical child psychology at Oklahoma State University. Her research interests include the development of behavioral and cognitive interventions designed to mitigate psychological distress in the context of chronic illness.

Richard G. Hoffman, Ph.D., is Associate Professor of Behavioral Sciences and Associate Dean for Medical Education and Curriculum at the University of Minnesota School of Medicine in Duluth. He completed his predoctoral clinical internship in clinical and pediatric psychology and his postdoctoral fellowship in clinical neuropsychology at the University of Oklahoma Health Sciences Center. He completed his graduate training in clinical psychology in the Brooklyn Center at Long Island University. His research interests include brain-behavior relationships in closed head injury and the effects of stress on neuropsychological functioning.

Timothy T. Houle, Ph.D., is a postdoctoral fellow in behavioral medicine in the Center for Pain Studies at the Rehabilitation Institute of Chicago/Northwestern Medical School. He completed his predoctoral clinical internship at the University of Mississippi Medical Center/Jackson Veterans Affairs Medical Center Consortium, specializing in health psychology. He completed his graduate training in clinical psychology at the Illinois Institute of Technology. His research interests involve the use of time-series analysis in the clinical management of chronic pain.

Wei-Chin Hwang, C.Phil., is a graduate student in clinical psychology at the University of California, Los Angeles. He is currently completing his predoctoral clinical internship at the Richmond Area Multi-Services' National Asian American Psychology Training Center. His research interests include cultural influences on the prevalence, etiology, diagnosis, and expression of mental illness as well as ethnocultural differences in help seeking and treatment progress.

Mark W. Ketterer, Ph.D., is a member of the Senior Bioscientific Staff at Henry Ford Hospital and Adjunct Associate Professor of Psychology at Wayne State University. He received his doctorate from the University of Maryland, completed his internship at the Johns Hopkins University School of Medicine, and completed a postdoctoral fellowship at the Uniformed Services University of the Health Sciences. His research interests include behavioral risk factors in coronary heart disease, circumventing denial/minimization of emotional distress in coronary heart disease patients, treatment of anginal chest pain with cognitive-behavioral therapy and selective serotonin reuptake inhibitors, clinical trials, and health care reform.

Joshua C. Klapow, Ph.D., is Associate Professor in the Departments of Psychology and Health Care Organization and Policy at the University of Alabama at Birmingham. He received his doctorate in clinical psychology from the University of California, San Diego, where he also completed a postdoctoral fellowship in geriatric health services research. His research focuses on the evaluation of health status and quality of life in chronic illness, including the use of multivariate statistical modeling to evaluate change in health status.

Lesley P. Koven, M. A., is a doctoral student in the Clinical Psychology Program at West Virginia University. She earned her bachelor's degree at the University of Manitoba and earned her master's in clinical psychology at West Virginia University. Her research interests include geropsychology and behavioral medicine. Her most current project involves the examination of etiological variables related to the "sundown syndrome" in nursing home residents with dementia.

Shulamith Kreitler, Ph.D., is Professor of Psychology in the Department of Psychology at Tel-Aviv University and Head of the Psycho-Oncology Unit at Tel-Aviv Medical Center. She completed her doctorate in psychology and psychopathology at Bern University in Switzerland. She also was a postdoctoral fellow at Yale University and a research fellow at the Educational Testing Service in Princeton, New Jersey. Her research interests involve exploring the psychological correlates of disease occurrence and different kinds of disease course, especially in cancer.

Melissa C. Kuhajda, Ph.D., is Assistant Professor in the Department of Community and Rural Medicine and the Department of Psychiatry and Behavioral Medicine in the College of Community Health Sciences at the University of Alabama in Tuscaloosa. She is also Assistant Director for Research in the University of Alabama Institute for Rural Health Research and is Adjunct Assistant Professor in the Department of Psychology. She completed her doctorate in clinical psychology at the University of Alabama and completed her predoctoral internship at the Memphis Veterans Affairs Hospital. Her research interests involve the study of treatments for chronic pain management and rural health issues.

Jeffrey M. Lackner, Psy.D., is Assistant Professor in the Department of Medicine, as well as Research Assistant Professor in the Departments of Neurosurgery and Anesthesiology, at the State University of New York, Buffalo, Medical School. He completed his predoctoral clinical internship at the University of Texas Medical School in Houston before receiving a National Institutes of Health-funded postdoctoral fellowship in behavioral medicine/pain at the University of Rochester Medical School. He completed his graduate training in social psychology at the London School of Economics, in experimental psychology at the College of William and Mary, and in clinical psychology at Rutgers University. His primary research interests include outcome research and cognitive processes underlying painful medical disorders as well as their relationship to physiological mechanisms of health and illness.

Thad R. Leffingwell, Ph.D., is Clinical Psychologist and Assistant Professor in the Department of Psychology at Oklahoma State University. He completed his graduate training at the University of Washington and his predoctoral internship at the Puget Sound Veterans Affairs Healthcare System–Seattle. His research interests include brief motivational interventions for health behavior change and motivational predictors of self-directed and assisted behavior change. He has worked on five different federal, state, and privately funded intervention projects that investigated adaptations of motivational interviewing.

William R. Lovallo, Ph.D., is Professor of Psychiatry and Behavioral Sciences at the University of Oklahoma Health Sciences Center and Director of the Behavioral Sciences Laboratories at the Oklahoma City Veterans Affairs Medical Center. His doctorate in biological psychology is from the University of Oklahoma. He was associate director of the MacArthur Foundation's Research Network on Mind-Body Interactions and is the author of *Stress and Health: Biological and Psychological Interactions*. He has received funding from the Veterans Administration and the National Institutes of Health to study stress mechanisms and risk for disease.

Alexander Michas, B.A., is currently pursuing his graduate education in California. He completed his undergraduate education in psychology with honors at the University of California, Santa Cruz. After working as a mentor and counselor in California, he joined the Health Psychology Clinic at the Veterans Affairs Boston Healthcare System Outpatient Clinic as a senior research assistant.

Brian I. Miller, B.S., is a doctoral student in clinical psychology at Oklahoma State University. He completed his bachelor's degree at the State University of New York at Binghamton, majoring in psychobiology. His research interests include exploring the role of the acoustic startle response and emotion-modulated startle in deprived and nondeprived smokers.

Larry L. Mullins, Ph.D., is Professor of Clinical Psychology and Associate Director of Clinical Training at Oklahoma State University as well as Clinical Professor of Psychiatry at the University of Oklahoma Health Sciences Center. He completed his internship in pediatric psychology at the Oklahoma University Health Sciences Center and received his doctorate from the University of Missouri–Columbia in 1983. His research interests focus on the relationship of cognitive appraisal mechanisms and children's adjustment to various chronic illnesses.

Jack L.-M. Mutnick, B.S., is a medical student at the University of Nevada School of Medicine and will be completing his M.D. in May 2004. He earned his bachelor's degree in biology at the University of Nevada, Reno.

Hector F. Myers, Ph.D., is Professor of Psychology at the University of California, Los Angeles (UCLA), and Director of the Research Center on Ethnicity, Health, and Behavior at the Charles R. Drew University of Medicine and Science. He received his doctorate in clinical psychology from UCLA and is actively involved in research on psychosocial stress and behavioral contributors to ethnic health disparities in hypertension and cerebrovascular disease, HIV/AIDS, and mood disorders. He has more than 100 publications and has received several awards for his research and student mentoring.

Kathleen M. Palm, M.A., is a graduate student in clinical psychology at the University of Nevada, Reno. She received her master's in clinical psychology from Minnesota State University, Mankato, in 1998. Her research and clinical interests involve issues related to trauma and behavioral medicine.

Chebon A. Porter, Ph.D., is Staff Psychologist at the Birmingham Veterans Affairs Medical Center's (BVAMC) Southeastern Blind Rehabilitation Center. He is also Assistant Professor in the Department of Psychology at the University of Alabama at Birmingham (UAB) School of Medicine and Assistant Adjunct Professor in the Department of Psychology at Samford University. He completed his postdoctoral fellowship in the UAB Department of Psychiatry and Behavioral Neurobiology, completed his predoctoral clinical internship at the UAB/BVAMC Clinical Psychology Training Consortium, and completed his graduate training in clinical psychology at Oklahoma State University. His research interests include mental health issues in American Indians and Alaska Natives.

Eric H. Prensky, M.A., is a doctoral student in the American Psychological Association-accredited Clinical Psychology Program at Texas Tech University. His research interests involve smokeless tobacco and personality variables.

Sheri D. Pruitt, Ph.D., is Director of Behavioral Medicine for the Permanente Medical Group in Sacramento, California. She received her doctorate in clinical psychology from the University of New Mexico in 1990. She has 20 years of health care experience in both the private and public sectors and has been a faculty member at the University of California, San Diego, School of Medicine and in the Department of Psychology at San Diego State University. She has worked as a scientist for the World Health Organization (WHO), was the principal writer for the recently published WHO global report on innovative care for chronic conditions, and continues to be an ongoing consultant to the WHO's Department of Noncommunicable Diseases. She has authored more than 50 professional articles, abstracts, and book chapters in the area of behavioral medicine.

Steven M. Schwartz, Ph.D., is Director of Research for Oakwood Healthcare System and Clinical Assistant Professor in the Behavioral Medicine Program of the Department of Psychiatry at the University of Michigan. He received his doctorate in clinical psychology from Virginia Commonwealth University with a behavioral medicine specialty and completed his predoctoral internship at Henry Ford Hospital in Detroit, specializing in medical psychology. He went on to a postdoctoral fellowship in the Behavioral Medicine Program at the University of Michigan, where he subsequently served as the faculty coordinator of behavioral medicine services for University of Michigan Hospital until taking over as director of research for Oakwood. His research interests include behavioral cardiology, self-management of chronic illness, and effectiveness research.

Richard J. Seime, Ph.D., A.B.P.P., is Associate Professor of Psychology, Co-Head of the Section of Integrated Evaluation and Treatment, and Coordinator of the Adult Behavioral Therapy–Clinical Health Psychology Track in the Medical Psychology Fellowship Program of the Department of Psychiatry and Psychology at the Mayo Clinic in Rochester, Minnesota. He received his doctorate at the University of Minnesota, completed his internship at the Minneapolis Veterans Affairs Medical Center, and is board certified in clinical psychology. He previously served as professor and chief in the Section of Psychology of the Department of Behavioral Medicine and Psychiatry at the West Virginia University School of Medicine. His current research and clinical focus is the identification and treatment of depression.

Andrea K. Shreve-Neiger, M.A., is a doctoral student in the Clinical Psychology Program at West Virginia University. She earned her bachelor's degree at the College of Wooster and earned her master's in clinical psychology at West Virginia University. Her primary research and clinical interests lie in geropsychology, with a special interest in spiritual and religious issues.

Nicole J. Siegfried, Ph.D., is Assistant Professor in the Department of Psychology at Samford University. She is also Project Manager in the Department of Medicine of the Division of Preventive Medicine at the University of Alabama at Birmingham (UAB) School of Medicine, where she also completed her postdoctoral fellowship. She completed her predoctoral clinical internship at the UAB/Birmingham Veterans Affairs Medical Center Clinical Psychology Training Consortium. Her graduate training was completed at Oklahoma State University. Her research interests focus on prevention and treatment of women's health disorders.

Cathy A. Simpson, Ph.D., is Assistant Professor of Psychology at Jacksonville State University. She completed her predoctoral clinical internship at the University of Mississippi Medical Center/G. V. (Sonny) Montgomery Veterans Affairs Consortium and completed postdoctoral fellowships at the University of Kentucky and the University of Alabama at Birmingham, specializing in addictive behaviors. She completed her graduate training in clinical psychology at Auburn University. Her research interests involve behavioral economic models and analyses of substance use and abuse.

Timothy W. Smith, Ph.D., is Professor in the Department of Psychology at the University of Utah. He completed his graduate training in clinical psychology at the University of Kansas. He completed his predoctoral clinical internship and a postdoctoral fellowship at Brown University, specializing in behavioral medicine. He is a past president of the Division of Health Psychology of the American Psychological Association and is a member of the Academy of Behavioral Medicine Research. His research interests focus on personality and social risk factors for cardiovascular disease, particularly in the context of close personal relationships such as marriage.

Kristen H. Sorocco, Ph.D., is a National Institute on Alcohol Abuse and Alcoholism postdoctoral fellow in the Behavioral Sciences Labs of the Department of Psychiatry and Behavioral Sciences at the University of Oklahoma Health Sciences Center. She completed her graduate training in clinical psychology at Oklahoma State University, where she is now a visiting assistant professor. She completed her predoctoral clinical internship at the Veterans Affairs Palo Alto Health Care System, specializing in geropsychology. Her research interests involve examining the relationship between psychological stress and physiological processes among dementia caregivers.

Adam P. Spira, M.A., is a doctoral student in the Clinical Psychology Program at West Virginia University. He earned his bachelor's degree at the State University of New York at Stony Brook and earned his master's in clinical psychology at West Virginia University. His research interests include operant conditioning with older adults with dementia and functional neuroimaging.

J. Kevin Thompson, Ph.D., has been affiliated with the Department of Psychology at the University of South Florida since 1985. He received his doctoral degree in clinical psychology from the University of Georgia in 1982. He has authored, coauthored, edited, or coedited four books in the area of eating disorders, body image, and obesity. His current research interests involve the identification of risk factors for the development of eating disorders, body image disturbance, and obesity. He has been on the editorial board of the *International Journal of Eating Disorders* since 1990 and is also on the editorial boards of four other journals.

Beverly E. Thorn, Ph.D., is Professor and Director of Clinical Training in the Department of Psychology at the University of Alabama. She completed her graduate training in clinical psychology at Southern Illinois University and completed her predoctoral clinical internship at the University of Alabama at Birmingham. Her research interests involve the assessment and treatment of chronic pain and illness. She is particularly interested in component analyses of cognitive-behavioral treatments for chronic pain.

Jalie A. Tucker, Ph.D., M.P.H., is Professor in the Department of Health Behavior of the School of Public Health at the University of Alabama at Birmingham (UAB). Her research, funded by the National Institute on Alcohol Abuse and Alcoholism, investigates help seeking for drinking problems and how change occurs through different pathways, including natural resolutions. Because of the relevance of public health approaches, in 1998 she earned a master of public health degree in health care organization and policy from UAB.

Janelle L. Wagner, M.S., is a graduate student in clinical psychology at Oklahoma State University. Her research interests focus on psychosocial adjustment in children with chronic illnesses, specifically the juvenile rheumatic diseases, and their families.

Stephen P. Whiteside, Ph.D., is a postdoctoral fellow in the Department of Psychiatry and Psychology at the Mayo Clinic in Rochester, Minnesota. He completed his predoctoral clinical internship at Geisinger Medical Center in Danville, Pennsylvania, specializing in pediatric psychology. He completed his graduate training in clinical psychology at the University of Kentucky. His research interests involve investigating the effectiveness of psychological interventions, including the effects of cognitive-behavioral therapy on the cognitive misattributions and neural activity in obsessive-compulsive disorder.

Deborah J. Wiebe, M.P.H., Ph.D., is Associate Professor in the Department of Psychology at the University of Utah, where she is Director of Clinical Training.

She also holds an adjunct faculty appointment in the Department of Family and Preventive Medicine at the University of Utah Health Sciences Center. She completed her graduate training in clinical psychology at the University of Alabama at Birmingham, specializing in medical psychology and public health. She completed her predoctoral clinical internship in behavioral medicine at the West Virginia University Health Sciences Center. Her research interests involve personality, self-regulation, health, and the interpersonal and developmental aspects of coping with chronic illness.

Helen R. Winefield, Ph.D., is Associate Professor in the Faculty of Health Sciences at the University of Adelaide in South Australia, where she has joint appointments in the Departments of Psychology and Psychiatry. She is also a fellow of the Australian Psychological Society; a member of its Colleges of Clinical, Organizational, and Health Psychologists; and a registered psychologist. The author of an early textbook in behavioral science for medical students, she currently directs the university of Adelaide's Clinical Psychology Program and holds a research grant from the Better Outcomes in Mental Health Care initiative in Australia.

Valerie A. Wolfe, Ph.D., is Behavioral Medicine Consultant at Kaiser Permanente in Northern California. She received her doctorate in counseling and health psychology from Stanford University. She was a teaching fellow at Stanford, an adjunct faculty member at Santa Clara University, and a researcher/clinician at the Palo Alto, Menlo Park, and Albuquerque Veterans Affairs hospitals. Before starting at Kaiser, she was the director of a 30-bed residential treatment center. She has trained hundreds of physicians in the use of cognitive-behavioral strategies to treat insomnia and has presented at national meetings regarding the treatment and evaluation of insomnia.

Barbara A. Wolfsdorf, Ph.D., is Staff Psychologist and Associate Director of Health Psychology at the Veterans Affairs (VA) Boston Healthcare System Outpatient Clinic and Assistant Professor of Psychiatry at the Boston University School of Medicine. She completed her doctoral training in clinical psychology at the University of Miami. She subsequently completed a predoctoral internship at the Boston VA Internship Consortium and a National Institutes of Health postdoctoral fellowship in combined treatment outcome research at the Brown University School of Medicine. The focus of her research is the process of emotion regulation as it applies to psychopathology (e.g., depression, posttraumatic stress disorder) and addictions (e.g., alcohol, nicotine) as well as the treatment of these difficulties.